DIRECTORY OF
EUROPEAN POLITICAL SCIENTISTS

DIRECTORY OF EUROPEAN POLITICAL SCIENTISTS

Third fully revised edition

Compiled and edited by

JEAN BLONDEL and CAROL WALKER

European Consortium for Political Research, University of Essex

HOLMES & MEIER PUBLISHERS, INC. • NEW YORK

First published in the United States of America 1979 by

HOLMES & MEIER PUBLISHERS, INC.
30 Irving Place, New York, N.Y. 10003

Library of Congress Cataloging in Publication Data

European Consortium for Political Research.
    Directory of European political scientists
    3rd fully revised ed.

    Includes index.
    1. Political scientists — Europe — Directories
I. Blondel, Jean, 1929-   II. Walker, Carol.
III. Title.
JA84.E9E89 1979   320'.025'4   79-10686

ISBN 0-8419-0498-7

PRINTED IN GREAT BRITAIN

CONTENTS

Foreword to the third edition

The publication of a third edition of this directory of the political science profession across Europe by the European Consortium for Political Research is evidence of the full recognition of a large, fast-growing and well-established profession and, hopefully, will give impetus for further developments. In the late 1940s, perhaps two hundred scholars could be described as political scientists, teaching mainly general social science in economics, law or history faculties or institutes. They may have been political scientists at heart but they were not recognised as such. They had to tailor their courses to the needs of other disciplines and often their research had to meet the requirements of these. In the last thirty years, the profession has not only grown five-fold or more but has gained recognition in the majority of universities: political science courses have been established and research has mushroomed. The importance of the discipline is recognised by other academics, by governments and official bodies and, increasingly, by the public at large. To make this point is not to underrate the value of inter-disciplinary studies, nor the major contributions which lawyers, historians, sociologists and economists have made and continue to make to political science. Without their contribution, the size of this directory would be considerably reduced, but in order to prosper, a subject-matter as important as politics needs well-defined institutional centres from which other disciplines will benefit, as witnessed by the efforts made by scholars from these other disciplines to build political science centres.

Yet in stressing the magnitude of the intellectual and institutional achievement of European political science in the last thirty years, we must not underrate the efforts required for the future. This, too, is one of the aims of this directory, as well as of the ECPR: to enable political scientists across Europe to become part of one profession. This is not to say that the discipline must have only one body of theory, or one body of methodology. Differences among political scientists are not merely a fact, but one of which to be proud in a discipline which is alive and dynamic. They are indeed a fact which needs to be fostered, but at the same time this directory seeks to enable those who have the same interests to recognise each other, to work together better and thus contribute more effectively to the dissemination of their views and approaches to the subject. As long as the profession is composed of scholars who do not know each other, and do not know each other's work, there can be no real profession. Cleavages are due, not to differences in ideological or scientific standpoints, but to parochial geographical boundaries, either co-extensive with national boundaries or connected to linguistic boundaries, often limited to the narrow confines of an institution or a small group of institutions. These need to be broken down if the profession is to be intellectually alive and challenging. This directory should be used as a working reference and should help to suggest the names of others who are interested in research and approaches similar to one's own.

Consciously or not, this collaborative aim has already been recognised by many in the profession. Between 1971 and 1978, the ECPR grew from a small body of eight institutions to a much more representative organization of over 90 departments or institutes from all Western European countries. But the response has been magnificent not just to the ECPR itself. The individual response of scholars to the questionnaire which was sent shows that both within and outside the ECPR the need for better contacts, for better knowledge of research and developments is very widely felt. Replies would not have come so readily if the need had not been felt. While wishing to thank formally each and every one who thus helped to make the *Directory* truly representative, and, we hope, close to being comprehensive, it seems only fair to note that, in doing so, all were contributing to the overall co-operative task of creating a common profession. We trust that this edition of the *Directory* will be, even more than the previous editions, a useful guide and thus contribute significantly to the goal of European collaboration in political science.

Jean Blondel

Colchester, Essex, England
November, 1978

INTRODUCTION

The third, fully revised and expanded edition of this directory provides a who's who of political scientists currently resident in Europe. The second edition of the directory was published by the European Consortium for Political Research in 1973 and included some 1,400 entries. The third edition is more comprehensive both in the overall number of scholars it lists, and in the number of institutions and European nations covered. It contains a total of 2,153 entries. Entries are based on replies to a postal survey mailed in late 1977 and during the course of 1978. Some 2,900 political scientists, together with an additional number drawn from membership lists of several political science associations, were asked to complete and return the questionnaire. Heads of departments of the major political science departments in Western Europe were also asked to assist to ensure accurate and up-to-date coverage of their departments.

Because the European Consortium for Political Research has closer contacts with its member institutions (see page xvi) than with other establishments of higher education and research in Europe, it is inevitable that the representation of these institutions in the *Directory* is higher. However, every effort has been made — particularly through the co-operation of national political science associations — to ensure as wide coverage as possible of non-ECPR affiliated institutions, and it is hoped that representation of the latter, (especially in Eastern Europe, where coverage is virtually non-existent), will improve in future editions.

Questionnaire response

The total response to an initial and one follow-up mailing of questionnaires — was some 68%, or a total of 1,950 scholars. A small percentage (2.6%) of replies do not however appear in the *Directory*, as they did not meet the criteria for entry. All scholars who appeared in the 1973 edition were sent a clipping of their previous entry and were asked to indicate any changes, or whether they wished to be deleted from the new edition. About 300 did not respond, despite follow-up reminders, and information for these entries has therefore been simply repeated from the previous edition, with the addition of an asterisk * sign. It must follow that all unverified entries with an asterisk may be necessarily incomplete, or not entirely accurate and up-to-date. A number of entries came in unsolicited from individuals or departments, making the total number of entries in the *Directory* 2,153. A good number of questionnaires came in hand-written, and a few unfortunately in near illegible form. Although we have aimed to copy the information as accurately as possible, we apologise in advance for any minor errors or inaccuracies that may have crept into a number of entries as a result of difficulties of transcription and would be grateful if these could be pointed out to us, to be corrected in future editions.

Criteria for inclusion/scope

The *Directory* covers academics working on a permanent or semi-permanent basis in Europe, including scholars who are not European citizens. European scholars whose permanent residence is outside Europe have not been included. Whilst the majority of those who appear in the *Directory* are formally attached to political science departments, academics from other disciplines are included also if they have indicated a long-term interest and involvement in this discipline.

Information included

Each entry gives, as far as possible, the following information: (1) Date of birth and nationality, (2) full name and address, (3) degrees awarded with awarding institution and year of award, (4) title of doctoral thesis, (5) details of past appointments, (6) current affiliation and position, (7) major publications, (8) fields of particular academic interest/research areas.

All information included is based on the completed, or partially completed, questionnaires returned to us, and we have endeavoured, within the confines of the information provided, to make entries as consistent as possible. However, a considerable disparity in length of many entries may be apparent, as the extent of the information provided varied considerably from case to case. We have aimed to list details as uniformly as possible, but, again, with so many submissions made in numerous different languages, some inconsistencies in style and presentation may still be apparent in some entries.

The nature of the information provided for each entry is as follows:

(1) Date of birth:
A few entries lack this information, in cases where it was not indicated on the questionnaires.

(2) Address:
In most cases this is the private address of each scholar of their nominated postal address. Full official postal codes are listed, if given on the questionnaires.

(3) Degrees awarded:
In the majority of cases this cites the actual degree awarded in each scholar's country of origin, together with details of the awarding institutions (except first degrees) and the dates of award. In a few cases, however, the only information that we were given indicated "Degree", and is therefore listed in this form only.

(4) Title of doctoral thesis:
This is normally included only if the thesis has been presented. However, in

some cases it was not clear from the replies whether the thesis had been completed or not. For most non-English language entries a translation is provided in parentheses (if it was provided by the respondent), or listed in English with an annotation, e.g. ("in Dutch") etc. In a number of instances two doctoral theses were given, particularly for German entries, but we have listed the main doctoral thesis only.

(5/6) Previous and current appointments/position:
This information is provided in chronological order, precise dates being included if they were indicated by the respondent. It should be noted that some academics have appointments which have, or are, running concurrently, and in these instances it proved difficult to list appointments in strict chronological order. The last appointment or position given is each scholar's current post, although the appropriate commencement date, e.g. "1971-" was not always available. Where a scholar held more than one post at the same institution, these are linked by a comma, rather than a semi-colon.

(7) Publications:
The information provided can only serve as a *guide* to the total publishing output of some scholars. Space limitations have compelled us to include up to a maximum of eight publications only, with an emphasis on published books and monographs rather than periodical articles. Where more than this was provided on the returned questionnaires (some scholars simply forwarded a copy of their complete CV), we have not attempted to arbitrarily assess major publications, but have included: first, books, and contributions to books or collections, followed by the most recently published articles, or, alternatively, have listed the eight most recently published books, omitting any periodical literature. In some cases replies did not provide adequate references or guidelines to enable us to ascertain whether publications were books or periodical articles or reports. In a few cases, therefore, some publications may have been elevated erroneously to the status of books. Again due to limitations of space we have omitted the name of the publisher and place of publication, but have given the year of publication if included in the questionnaire data. Where more than one edition has been published, the year of publication of the *latest* edition only is listed. For multi-volume works, years of publication are listed, as, e.g. "1969/70", etc. English translations of foreign language material have been omitted. However, some literature references, although not published in English, appear to have been translated literally by the scholars submitting the information and include them in this form. Frequently the exact titles or articles in periodicals have not been given, but, instead, information was stated simply as certain articles *on* specific subjects or regional topics, or as various articles *in*, for example, *Acta Politica, European Journal of Political Research*, etc. In cases where respondents merely cited "various articles" this general reference has been omitted altogether.

(8) Fields of interest:
This consists largely of information pertaining to areas of specialization and regional interests of each political scientist included. Most of this information provided has been copied verbatim (in some cases in translated form) the questionnaires.

A number of abbreviations have been used throughout the *Directory*, and a key to these appears on page xv.

Index

An index by broad subject fields and area focus is provided on page 453, and enables users of the *Directory* to identify individuals interested in either a particular subject or a regional area of political science. The indexing is based on the "Fields of interest" data given by each respondent. It should be noted, however, that several scholars' names appear under more than one index heading. The numbers listed in the index refer to entry, *not* page numbers.

Future editions

A small proportion of the data provided may inevitably be slightly out-of-date by the time this directory is published. However, it is now hoped to produce new editions of the *Directory of European Political Scientists* every two or three years. Whilst we are indebted to all those political scientists who completed and returned the questionnaires, the successful continuation of this project needs the co-operation of academic scholars in the political science arena in all parts of Europe, ensure more up-to-date, more accurate, and more comprehensive coverage in future editions.

C. W.

Sheffield
November, 1978

Key to abbreviations used:
(other than actual degrees)

Admin	Administration/administrative
APSR	*American Political Science Review*
ASSP	*Annuaire Suisse de Science Politique*
BASS	Belgian Archives for the Social Sciences
BJPS	*British Journal of Political Science*
CERI	Centre d'études des relations internationales
Cert	Certificate
CNRS	Centre National de la Recherche Scientifique
co-ed	co-editor
Coll	College
DES	Diploma d'éstudes supérieurs
Dept	Department/Département etc
Dipl	Diploma
Dr	Doctor/Docteur/Dottore/Doctorate/etc.
Drs	Doctorandus
Econ	Economics/Economique
Ed/Eds	Editor/Editors
EEC	European Economic Community
EJPR	*European Journal of Political Research*
Em	Emeritus
FNSP	Foundation Nationale des Sciences Politiques
Govt	Government/Gouvernement
FR	Federal Republic (of Germany)
hc	*honoris causa*
Hon	Honorary/Honorarius
IEP	Institute d'études politiques
INLOGOV	Institute of Local Government
Inst	Institute/Institut
Int	International
Lic	License/Licentiate
LSE	London School of Economics and Political Science
Mass	Massachusetts
Min	Ministry/Ministère/etc.
OECD/OCDE	Organization for Economic Cooperation and Development
Ord	Ordinary/Ordinarius
Oxon	of Oxford University
PEP	Political and Economic Planning
Pol	Political/Politique/Politieke/Politische
Publs	Publications
RFSP	*Revue Francaise de Sciences Politiques*
RJP	*Revue Juridique Francais*
Sci	Science(s)
SOAS	School of Oriental and African Studies
Soc	Sociology/Social
Soton	Southampton
tr	translator
U	University/Université/Universität/etc.
UC	University College
UNDP	United Nations Development Programme
UNESCO	United Nations Educational Scientific and Cultural Organization
vol	volume
Wiss	Wissenschaftlicher

European Consortium for Political Research

Affiliated member institutions:
● indicates official ECPR representative

BELGIUM

Departement Politieke en Sociale
  Wetenschappen
Universiteit Antwerpen
Universiteitsplein 1
2610 Wilrijk
● Mr B Pijnenburg

Institute of Sociology
Brussels Free University
44 Avenue Jeanne
Brussels 5
' Professor S Bernard

Centre for Political Studies
Catholic University of Leuven
E Van Evenstraat 2B
3000 Leuven
● Professor W Dewachter

Institut des Sciences Politiques
  et Sociales
3H2-Bâtiment Jacques Leclerq
1 Place Montesquieu
1348 Louvain la Neuve
● Mr Joseph Bonmariage

Faculté de Droit
Université de Liège
2 rue Charles Magnette
Liège
● Professor P Ch Goossens

DENMARK

Institute of Political Science
University of Aarhus
8000 Aarhus C
● Professor E Damgaard

Institute of Political Science
University of Copenhagen
Rosenborggade 15
1130 Copenhagen K
● Professor Gunnar Sjöblom

Institute of History and Social
  Sciences
University of Odense
Niels Bohrs Alle
Dk-5000 Odense
● Professor Peter Hansen

Institute of Organization and Social
  Change
Copenhagen School of Economics
  and Social Science
60 Howitzvej
2000 Copenhagen F
● Professor Egil Fivelsdal

EIRE

Department of Politics
University College
Belfield
Dublin 4
● Dr Thomas Garvin

Department of Political Science
Trinity College
Dublin 2
● Professor F B Chubb

FINLAND

Institute of Political Science
University of Helsinki
Virikatu 3A
00100 Helsinki
● Mr Erkki Berndtson

Institute of Political Science
University of Turku
20500 Turku 50
● Professor Esko Antola

Institute of Political Science
University of Tampere
Lapinti 4
Tampere
● Mr Harto Hakovirta

FRANCE

Institut d'Etudes Politiques
Université de Bordeaux I
Domaine Universitaire
Boîte Postale 101
33-405 Talence
● Professor C Emeri

Institut d'Etudes Politiques
Université des Sciences Sociales de
  Grenoble
Domaine Universitaire
BP No 34
38401 St Martin d'Heres
Grenoble
● M Claude Domenach

Département de Science Politique
Université de Paris IX-Dauphine
Place du Maréchal-de-Lattre-de
  Tassigny
Paris XVIème
● Professor L Sfez

Département de Science Politique
Université de Paris-I
17 rue de la Sorbonne
75 231 Paris Cedex 05
● Professor P Birnbaum

Faculté de Droit
Université de Nice
Avenue Robert Schuman
Nice
● M Jacques Basso

Foundation Nationale des Sciences
  Politiques
27 rue Saint-Guillaume
75 341 Paris Cédex 07
● M Serge Hurtig

UER de Science Politique
Université de Paris II
83 bis rue Notre Dame des Champs
F-75 Paris 6ème
● M Jacques Cadart

Institut d'Etudes Politiques
Université de Strasbourg
9 Place de l'Université
Strasbourg
● Professor F Dreyfus

Faculté des Sciences Juridiques
   Politiques et Sociales
Université de Lille II
Rue de Lille
Sac Postale No 19
59650 Villeneuve D'Ascq
● Mme J Bécquart-Leclercq

Faculté de Droit et des Sciences
   Economiques de Rouen
Boulevard Siegfried
76 Mont-Saint-Aignan
Roven
● M Michel Troper

Faculté de Droit
Université de Clermont
BP 54
41 Boulevard Georgovia
63002 Clermont — Ferrand Cédex
● Professor Pierre Favre

FEDERAL REPUBLIC OF GERMANY

Zentralinstitut für Sozialwissen-
   schaftliche Forschung
Freie Universität Berlin
1 Berlin 31
Babelsberger Strasse 14-16
● Professor D Herzog

Zentralarchiv für Empirische
   Sozialforschung
Universität zu Köln
5 Köln-Lindenthal
Bachemer Strasse 40
● Professor F Boltken

Fachbereich Politische Wissenschaft
Universität Konstanz
775 Konstanz
Postfach 733
● Dr Manfred Schmidt

Fachbereich für Politische
   Wissenschaft
Freie Universität Berlin
1 Berlin 33 (Dahlem)
Ihnestrasse 21
● Mr Carsten Frerk

Forschungsinstitut für Politische
   Wissenschaft
Universität zu Köln
5 Köln 41
Gottfried-Keller Strasse 6
● Dr Rüdiger Zülch

Lehrstuhl für Politische Wissenschaft
Universität Mannheim
6800 Mannheim
A5
● Dr Franz Lehner

Geschwister-Scholl-Institut
Universität München
8 München 22
Ludwigstrasse 10
● Professor Dr Kurt Sontheimer

Seminar für Wissenschaft und
   Geschichte der Politik
Christian-Albrechts-Universität
2300 Kiel
Olshausenstrasse 40
Haus 38
● Professor Werner Kaltefleiter

Institute of Political Science
Faculty of Law and Economics
The Saar University
66 Saarbrücken
● Professor Jürgen Domes

Institut für Politische Wissenschaft
Universität Heidelberg
69 Heidelberg 1
Hauptstrasse 52
● Professor K von Beyme

Institut für Politikwissenschaft
Universität Tübingen
7400 Tübingen
Brunnenstrasse 30
● Dr Rudolf Hrbek

Wissenschaftszentrum Berlin
1 Berlin 33
Griegstrasse 5-7
● Professor Fritz Scharpf

Arnold Bergstraesser Institut
78 Freiburg 1 Br,
Erbprinzenstrasse 11
● Professor Dr T Hanf

ICELAND

Department of Social Sciences
University of Iceland
Reykjavik
● Professor Olafur Ragnar
   Grimsson

ITALY

Department of Sociology and
   Political Science
University of Calabria
Via Severini 30
Cozenza
● Miss A Cavazzani

Department of Sociology
University of Catania
Palazzo ESE
Via Beato Bernardo 5
Catania
● Professor Alberto Marradi

Centro Studi di Scienza Politica
10124 Torino
Via S Ottavio 20
● Professor P Farneti

Centro Studi di Scienza Politica
50121 Firenze
48 Via Laura
● Professor Umberto Gori

Istituto Politico-Amministrativo
Facoltà de Science Politiche
University of Bologna
Bologna 40126
via Giuseppe Petroni 33
● Professor Giorgio Freddi

European University Institute
Badia Fiesolana
5 via dei Roccettini
50016 San Domenico di Fiesole
Firenze
● Professor Hans Daalder

Universita Commerciale 'L Boccini'
via Sarfatti 25
20136 Milano
● Professor Givliano Urbani

THE NETHERLANDS

Institute of Political Science
University of Amsterdam
Herengracht 528-530
Amsterdam
● Dr Otto Schmidt

Department of Political Science
Free University of Amsterdam
Koningslaan 31-33
Amsterdam
● Drs R Hoppe

Department of Political Science
University of Leiden
Hugo de Grootstr 27
Leiden
● Mr G Irwin

Institute of Social Science
Catholic University of Nijmegen
Van Schaeck Mathonsingel 4
Nijmegen
● Professor K Letterie

Institute for Social Research
Catholic School of Economics
Hogeschoollaan 225
Tilburg
● Dr Felix J Heunks

Erasmus University
Postbus 1738
Rotterdam
● Dr Valentine Herman

Steinmetzarchief
Klein-Gartmanplantsoen 10
Amsterdam C
● Mr Cees P Middendorp

Technische Hogeschool Twente
Postbus 217
Enschede
● Professor Jaques Thomassen

Sociologisch Instituut
Rijksuniversiteit
Groningen
Oude Boteringestraat 23
● Professor Dr P Valkenburgh

NORWAY

Institute of Sociology
University of Bergen
Christiesgatan 19
N-5014 Bergen U
● Dr Derek Urwin

Hedmark/Oppland
Distriktshøgskole
Box 193
2601 Lillehammer
● Mr Rolf Rønning

Institute of Political Science
University of Oslo
Box 1097 Blindern
Oslo 3
● Professor Fr Kjellberg

Institute of Social Sciences
University of Tromsø
Box 1040
9001 Tromsø
● Mr Tom Christensen

SPAIN

Institut Catolica d'Estudis Socials
  de Barcelona
Enric Grandos 2
Barcelona 7
● Professor Carles Viver

Facultad de Ciencias
Politicas y Sociologia
Universidad Complutense
Madrid

Facultat de Dret
Universitat Autonoma de Barcelona
Bellaterra
Barcelona
● Dr Joseph M Valles

SWEDEN

Institute of Political Science
University of Gothenborg
Molndalsvagen 85
S-412 85 Göteborg
● Professor J Westerstahl

Department of Political Science
University of Stockholm
Fack
104 Stockholm 50
● Professor Olof Ruin

Department of Political Science
University of Umeå
901 87 Umeå
● Dr Sten Berglund

Department of Political Science
University of Lund
220 05 Lund 5
● Professor Nils Stjernquist

Department of Government
University of Uppsala
Skytteanum
751 20 Uppsala 1
● Professor Leif Lewin

SWITZERLAND

Départment de Science Politique
Université de Genève
Promenade des Bastions
1211 Genève 4
● Professor Dusan Sidjanski

Institut Universitaire de Hautes
   Etudes Internationales
132 rue de Lausanne
1200 Genève
● Mlle Lucia Scherrer

Institut de Science Politique
Université de Lausanne
rue St Martin 24
1003 Lausanne
● Professor F Masnata

Psychologisches Institut
Universität Zürich
Nägelistrasse 7
8044 Zürich
● Professor Dr G Schmidtchen

UNITED KINGDOM

Department of Government
University of Essex
Wivenhoe Park
Colchester CO4 3SQ
● Dr Martin Slater

Institute of Local Government
   Studies
University of Birmingham
PO Box 363
Birmingham B15 2TT
● Dr M Kolinsky

Faculty of Social Sciences
(Politics and Government)
The University
Canterbury
Kent
● Professor M J C Vile

School of Economics and Politics
Kingston Polytechnic
Penrhyn Road
Kingston-upon-Thames
Surrey
● Mr Ian Gordon

Department of Political Theory
   and Institutions
The University of Liverpool
Social Studies Building
PO Box 147
Liverpool L69 3BX
● Dr M Laver

London School of Economics
   and Political Science
Houghton Street
London WC2A 2AE
● Professor P J O Self

Faculty of Letters and Social
   Sciences
University of Reading
Whiteknights Park
Reading RG6 2AA
● Mr A Shlaim

Department of Politics
The University
Newcastle-upon-Tyne NE1 7RU
● Professor H B Berrington

Nuffield College
Oxford OX1 1NF
● Sir Norman Chester CBE

Nuffield College
University of Oxford
Oxford OX1 1NF
● Mr N Johnson

Department of Politics
University of Keele
Keele
Staffordshire ST5 5BG
● Dr Jeremey Richardson

Department of Politics
University of Southampton
Southampton SO9 5NH
● Mr Peter Calvert

Department of Government
University of Manchester
Manchester M13 9PL

University of Manchester Institute
    of Science and Technology
    (UMIST)
PO Box 88
Sackville Street
Manchester M60 1QD
● Dr G Roberts

Centre for the Study of
    Public Policy
University of Strathclyde
McCance Building
16 Richmond Street
Glasgow G1 1XQ
● Professor Richard Rose

Department of Politics
University of Lancaster
Fylde College
Bailrigg
Lancaster LA1 4YT
● Dr David Denver

Department of Political Science
The Queen's University
Belfast BT7 1NN
Northern Ireland
● Dr John Whyte

Department of Politics
The University
Adam Smith Building
Glasgow G12 8RT
Scotland
● Dr J G Kellas

Department of Politics
University of Warwick
Coventry CV4 7AL
Warwickshire
● Professor J F Lively

City University
St John Street
London EC1V 4PB
● Mr Keith Webb

Department of Politics
University College
PO Box 78
Cardiff
● Mr Paul Wilkinson
● Professor A P Coxon
    Sociological Research Unit

The Open University
Walton Hall
Milton Keynes MK7 6AA
● Dr Francis Castles

xxiv

Department of Politics
The University
Hull HU6 7RX
● Ms Juliet Lodge

Department of Political Science
The University
Dundee
● Professor Kenneth Newton

School of Behavioural and
    Social Science
Plymouth Polytechnic
Drake Circus
Plymouth PL4 8AA
Devon
● Mr Colin Rallings

ECPR Secretariat:
European Consortium for Political
    Research
University of Essex
Wivenhoe Park
Colchester CO4 3SQ
England

Telephone: (0206) 862286 — extension 2118

A

[1]
AAREBROT Frank
19 January 1947, Norwegian. Institute of Sociology, University of Bergen, Christiesgatgate 19, N-5000 Bergen, Norway. Degrees: Chad polit, 1976. Programmer, Inst of Sociology; Member of the Organizing Staff of the IVth European Seminar for Training in Data-processing in Soc Sci Research, responsible for the Computing Staff; part-time Research Associate, ECPR Data Information Service; Research Associate, Historical-ecological Data Archives, U of Bergen; Assistant Teacher responsible for Introductory Course in Statistics, Inst of Sociology, U of Bergen; Research Associate, Comparative Politics, Lecturer, Comparative Politics and Sociology, Inst of Soc and Pol Studies, U of Bergen. Publs: The Norwegian Archive of Historical-ecological Data in *Social Science Information* (with S Rokkan), 1969; "Nation-building, Democratization and Mass Mobilization", paper at IPSA World Congress, Munich, 1970 (with S Rokkan); *Historisk-økologske Dataarhirer*, one report in *Historical-Ecological Data-Archive*, 1st report, 1969; *Political Mobilization in Norway, 1868-1903*, 1976. Fields: Nationbuilding; political mobilization; time-series analysis; cross level analysis; populism as a political phenomenon; political elites.

[2]
AARESKJOLD Helen Vivian*
13 October 1938, American. Institute of Sociology, University of Bergen, Christiesgatgate 19, N-5000 Bergen. Degrees: BA; M Soc Sci (Stockholm), 1965. 1965 Assistant, Inst of Pol Sci, Stockholm; 1965-67 Research Assistant, Chairman, Michelsens Inst, Bergen, Norway; 1968- Research Assistant, Inst of Soc, U of Bergen. Publs: *Norge og Sverige i FN*, 1965. Fields: Comparative politics (Nordic area); West Africa; political development; foreign policy; regionalism.

[3]
ABENDROTH Wolfgang
2 May 1906, German. Neuhausstrasse 5, 6 Frankfurt am Main, FR Germany. Degrees: Dr Law (Berne), 1935; PhD (Halle), 1947. Doctoral thesis: "Die völkerrechtliche Stellung der B- und C- Mandate". 1947 Dozent, U of Halle; 1948 Professor, U of Leipzig and Jena; 1949 Professor, Hochschule für Sozialwissenschaften, Wilhelmshaven; 1950- Professor of Pol Sci, U of Marburg. Publs: *Die völkerrechtliche Stellung der B-und C-Mandate*, 1936; *Die deutschen Gewerkschaften*, 1954; *Bürokratischer Verwaltungsstaat und soziale Demokratie*, 1955; *Wirtschaft Gesellschaft und Demokratie in der Bundesrepublik Deutschland*, 1965; *Das Grundgesetz der Bundesrepublik Deutschlands*, 1972; *Antagonistische Gesellschaft und politische Demokratie*, 1972; *Einführung in die politische Wissenschaft*, 1968; *Aufstieg und Krise der deutschen Sozialdemokratie*, 1970; *Sozialgeschichte der europaïschen Arbeiterbewegung*, 1971; *A Short History of the European Working class,* 1972; *Arbeiterklasse, Demokratie und Verfassung*, 1975; *Ein Leben in der deutschen Arbeiterbewegung*, 1976. Fields: History of the anti-fascist movement in Germany; history of the working-class movement in Germany and internationally; political sociology and constitutional law in both German states; international law in international relations.

[4]
ABMA Karel Hendrik Johannes
25 July 1944, Dutch. Leidsgracht 112, 1016 CT Amsterdam, The Netherlands. Degrees: Dr Pol Sci; Drs Dutch Law. Doctoral thesis: "Territoriale decentralisatie in Nederland" (Territorial Decentralization in The Netherlands). Policy Analyst, Ministry of Finance, The Hague. Fields: Policy analysis; public decision making; planning; public organization.

[5]
ABROMEIT Heidrun
23 May 1943, German. Remscheiderstrasse 220, 5600 Wuppertal 21, FR Germany. Degrees: Dr phil; Dipl Politologe. Doctoral thesis: "Das Politische in der Werbung-Wahlwerbung und Wirtschaftswerbung in der Bundesrepublik". Assistant, Inst of Soc Sci, U of Mannheim; Akademischer Rat, Dept of Econ, U of Wuppertal. Publs: *Das Politische in der Werbung*, 1972; "Zur Identität von politischer und wirtschaftlicher Werbung-Verbandswerbung in der Bundesrepublik", in *Aus Politik und Zeitgeschichte*, 1972; "Die Wählerinitiativen in Wahlkampf 1972" (with K Burkhardt), in *Aus Politik und Zeitgeschichte*, 1973; "Der missverstandene Liberalismus", in *Liberal*, 1975; "Zum Verhältnis von Staat und Wirtschaft im gegenwärtigen Kapitalismus", *Politische Vierteljahresschrift*, 1976; "Interessen-durchsetzung in der Krise", in *Aus Politik und Zeitgeschichte*, 1977. Fields: Theory of the state; political economy; political theory; interest organizations; the role of business in politics.

[6]
ACHTERBERG Norbert*
29 May 1932, German. Universitätsstrasse 54, D-335 Marburg/Lahn, FR Germany. 1961 Assessor, Juristisches Landesprüfungsamt Hessen; 1962 Wiss Assistent (Landesregierung Nordrhein-Westfalen); 1968 Dozent; 1971 Dozent, U of Marburg. Publs: *Probleme der Funktionenlehre* 1971; *Grundzüge des Parlamentsrechts*, 1971. Fields: Parliament; international law.

[7]
ADOMEIT Hannes
9 November 1942, German. Institute of Soviet and East European Studies, University of Glasgow, Glasgow G12 8LQ, Scotland. Degrees: Dipl Pol (Berlin), 1968; MA and Russian Inst Certificate (Columbia), 1971; PhD, 1977. Doctoral thesis: "Soviet Risk Taking and Crisis Behaviour: A Theoretical and Empirical Analysis". 1972-73 Research Associate, IISS, London; 1977-78 Research Associate, Centre for International Relations, Queen's U, Kingston, Ontario; Lecturer in Soviet Foreign Policy, Inst of Soviet and East European Studies, U of Glasgow, and Reviews Editor, *Soviet Studies*. Publs: *Soviet Risk-taking and Crisis Behaviour: From Confrontation to Co-existence?*, 1973. Fields: Soviet foreign policy; Soviet military affairs; international relations.

[8]
ADRIAN Wolfgang Günter
11 October 1942, German. 5300 Bonn 2, Nietzschestrasse 44, FR Germany. Degrees: Dr phil. Doctoral thesis: "Demokratie als Partizipation — Versuch einer systematischen Wert-und empirischen Einstellungsanalyse". Assistent, U of Mannheim; Persönlicher Referent der stellvertretenden Fraktionsvorsitzenden der Sozialdemokratischen Bundestagsfraktion; Lehrauftrag, U of Mannheim. Fields: European integration.

[9]
AGNOLI Johannes
22 February 1925, German. Sybelstrasse 29, 1000 Berlin 12, FR Germany. Degrees: Dr phil habil. Doctoral thesis: "Gian Battista Vicos — Philosophie des Rechts". 1962-Assistant Professor; 1972- Professor, Otto Suhr Inst, Free U of Berlin. Publs: *Die Transformation der Demokratie*, 1967; *Die Schnelligkeit des realen Prozesses*, 1969; *Zur Faschismusdiskussion*, 1973; *Classe e Stato in Germania*, 1973; *Von der Pax Romana zur Pax Christiana*, 1975; *Überlegungen zum bürgerlichen Staat*, 1975; *Wahlkampf und sozialer Konflict*, 1977; *Lo Stato del Capitale*, 1978.

[10]
AGO Roberto*
1907, Italian. c/o Società Italiana per la Organizzazione Internazionale, Via S Marco 3, 00186 Rome, Italy. Degrees: PhD (Naples), 1929. 1930-34 Lecturer, U of Cagliari, then Messina; 1934-35 Professor, U of Catania; 1935-38 Professor, U of Genoa; 1938-56 Professor, U of Milan; 1956- Professor, U of Rome; Former Vice-President, Inst of International Law; Member, International Law Commission; Former Chairman, Governing Body of ILO; *Ad hoc* judge, International Court of Justice. Publs: *Studi di diritto internazionale privato*, 1932; *Teoria del diritto internazionale privato*, 1934; *Il requisito dell'effettività dell'occupazione in diritto internazionale*, 1934; *Lezioni di diritto internazionale privato*, 1939; *Scienza giuridica e diritto internazionale*, 1950; *Le organizzazioni internazionali e le loro funzioni nel campo dell'attività interna degli Stati*, 1956. Fields: International law; international organizations.

[11]
AGUET Jean-Pierre
18 February 1925, Swiss. 73 Avenue de France, 1004 Lausanne, Switzerland. Degrees: Licencié ès Lettres (Lausanne), 1947; Lic ès Sci Pol (Lausanne), 1950; Dr ès Lettres (Lausanne), 1954. Doctoral thesis: "Contribution à l'étude du mouvement ouvrier français: les grèves sous la Monarchie de Juillet (1830-48)". 1952-55 Rédacteur de politique étrangère à la *Gazette de Lausanne*; 1955-65 Professeur de l'enseignement secondaire; 1963-65 Chargé de cours, U of Lausanne; 1965-69 Professeur extraordinaire, U of Lausanne, enseignement de l'histoire des doctrines politiques; 1966-68 Président de l'Ecole des sciences sociales et politiques, U of Lausanne; 1969- Professor ordinaire, U of Lausanne, enseignement de l'histoire des doctrines politiques; 1969-74 Vice-président de l'Ecole des sciences sociales et politiques, U of Lausanne. Publs: *Contribution à l'étude du mouvement ouvrier français: les grèves sous la Monarchie de Juillet (1830-48)*, 1954; *Institutions politiques. La Suisse et le monde*, 1961; "La feuille d'avis de Lausanne et l'information étrangère 1872-1914", in *Deux cents ans de vie et d'histoire vaudoise, La feuille d'avis (1762-1962)*, 1962. Fields: Political theory and political ideas; history of the press; French history, 19th-20th centuries.

[12]
AHLERS Ingolf Hermann Kurt
20 July 1942, German. Seminar für Wissenschaft von der Politik der Technischen Universität Hannover, Schneiderberg 50, 3 Hannover 1, FR Germany. Degrees: Dipl (Berlin), 1971; Dr phil, 1974; Doctoral candidate, Friedrich-Ebert-Foundation. Doctoral thesis: "Colonialism and Merchant Capital". Wiss Assistent, Technische U Hannover. Publs: *The Pre-Capitalist Modes of Production*, 1973; *The Pre-Colonial Structures in West-Africa*, 1973; *Ivory Coast*, 1974; *Colonialism, Imperialism, Underdevelopment*, 1976. Fields: The political economy of early Western European colonialism, effects on the development of the metropolitan countries and their colonies; problems of under-development; the concept of Western development aid, with special reference to the relation between the Common Market and the African countries; Portuguese colonialism in Africa; new philosophies in France.

[13]
AIGNER Manfred
21 November 1943, Austrian. Hörschingergutstrasse 28, A 4020 Linz, Austria. Degrees: Dr phil. Doctoral thesis: "Definitions of Democracy and Political Education of the Youth of the Proletariat in Austro-Marxism" (in German). Professor, Teachers' Training College. Publs: *Electoral Systems in Western Constitutions*, 1976; *Democracy and Elections*, 1977; *Definitions of Politics and Democracy*, 1978; *Political Science for Teachers*, 1978. Fields: Comparative government; political education; politics and social life; psychology of politics; international politics and foreign policy.

[14]
AJA Eliseo
4 May 1946, Spanish. Maria Auxiliadora 9, Barcelona 17, Spain. Degrees: Dr Law.
Doctoral thesis: "Democracia y socialismo en el siglo XIX español pensamiento politico
de Ferdinando Garrido". Professor, Faculty of Law, U of Barcelona. Publs:.
Democracia y socialismo en el siglo XIX español, 1975; *Constituciones y poder con-
stituyente en español (1808-1936)* (with J S Tura), 1977; "La supremacia de los Cortes",
in *La izqvierva y la constitucion*, 1978; "Los partidos politicos y la democracia", in *Los
partidos politicos, arma de la democracia*, 1976; "Propuesta para la constitucionaliza-
cion de los partidos politicos", in *Teoria y practica de los partidos* (de Vega (ed)), 1977.
Fields: Constitutional aspects of modern states, especially the relation of executive and
legislative powers; the role of political parties and the structure of the state.

[15]
ALAPURO Risto Sakari
28 April 1944, Finnish. Laivanvarustajankatu 4 F 66, 00140 Helsinki 14, Finland.
1968-73 Research Assistant in Sociology, U of Helsinki; 1974- Docent in Sociology, U
of Helsinki; 1976- Senior Research Fellow in Sociology, Academy of Finland. Publs:
Akateeminen Karjala-Seura, 1973; "Students and National Politics: A Comparative
Study of the Finnish Student Movement in the Interwar Period", *Scandinavian
Political Studies*, 1973; "On the Political Mobilization of the Agrarian Population in
Finland: Problems and Hypotheses", *Scandinavian Political Studies*, 1976; "Statemak-
ing and Political Ecology in Finland", in *The Social Ecology of Change* (Z Milnar & H
Teune (eds)), 1978. Fields: Statemaking: political mass mobilization; political
movements among the intellectuals.

[16]
ALBERT Pierre
1930, French. 17 rue Foys, 94160 Saint Mandé, France. Degrees: Agrégé; Dr ès Lettres.
Doctoral thesis: "Histoire de la presse politique nationale des débuts de la IIIème
République (1871-1879)". Maître assistant; Maître de conférences, U de Droit, d'Econ
et de Sci Soc de Paris II; Directeur des études de l'Institut français de Presse. Publs:
Histoire générale de la presse française (1870-1940), 1972; *La presse en France*, 1978;
Histoire de la presse, 1970; *Tables du journal le Temps (1861-1894)*. Fields: Press; mass
media.

[17]
ALBERTINI Pierre
22 November 1944, French. 6 rue de Torigny, 76130 Mont-St-Aignan, France. Degrees:
Dr d'Etat; Admissible à l'Agrégation. Doctoral thesis: "Le droit de dissolution et les
systèmes constitutionnels français". Maître-assistant. Publs: *Le droit de dissolution et
les systèmes constitutionnels français*, 1977. Fields: Town planning and local administration; analysis of constitutional systems.

[18]
ALBRECHT Funk
31 March 1948, German. Landhausstasse 9, 1 Berlin 31, FR Germany. Degrees: MA; Dr
rer pol. Doctoral thesis: "Vergesellschafteter Raum und staatliche Politik — Die
Umstrukturierung des ländliches Raumes und die Form bürokratischer Bearbeitung".
Research Assistant, U of Berlin; Researcher, Berghof-Stiftung für Konfliktforschung.
Publs: *Abschied von der Provinz*? Fields: Public administration; European police
systems; politics of internal security.

[19]
ALBRECHT Ulrich
30 January 1941, German. Free University, Kiebitzweg 3, 1000 Berlin 33, FR Germany.
Degrees: Dipl Ing (Stuttgart), 1967; Dr phil (Stuttgart), 1970. Doctoral thesis: "Der
Handel mit Waffen" (The Arms Trade). Research Associate, Forschungstelle d VDW,
Hamburg; Research Associate, International Inst for Strategic Studies, London. Pro-
fessor of Pol Sci (Peace Research), Free U of Berlin. Publs: *Der Handel mit Waffen*,
1971; *Deutsche Waffen für die Dritte Welt-Militärhilfe und Entwicklungspolitik* (with B
A Summer), 1972; *Politik und Waffengeschäfte-Rüstungsexporte in der BRD*, 1972;
Der Staat und die Steuerung der Wissenschaft (co-author), 1976; *Rüstung und
Unterentwicklung*, 1976. Fields: International integration; military-industrial complex
hypothesis; East-West cooperation.

[20]
ALCOCK Antony Evelyn
12 September 1936, British. White Lodge, Roselick, Portstewart, Co Londonderry,
Northern Ireland. BA; MA (Stanford), 1962; PhD (Graduate Inst of International
Studies, Geneva). Doctoral thesis: "The History of the South Tyrol Question". 1970-71
International Labour Organization, Geneva; 1971-72 United Nations, Inst for Training
and Research, New York; 1972-74 EEC, Brussels; 1974- Senior Lecturer and Head of
Dept of West European Studies, New U of Ulster. Publs: *History of the South Tyrol
Question*, 1970; *History of the International Labour Organization*, 1971; *Protection of
Minorities, Three Case Studies: South Tyrol, Cyprus, Quebec*, 1975; *The De Gasperi-
Gruber Agreement in the Light of Recent Developments in the Theory of Minority Protection*, 1976; "A New Look at Protection of Minorities and the Principle of Equality
of Human Rights", *Community Development Journal*, 1977; *The Future of Cultural
Minorities* (co-ed), 1978; "A Reappraisal of Existing Theory and Practice in the Protection of Minorities", in *Minorities in History* (C A Hepburn (ed)), 1978. Fields: Nationalism; protection of cultural and ethnic minorities; regional government and
devolution; process of European integration.

[21]
ALDERMAN Geoffrey
10 February 1944, British. 172 Colindeep Lane, London NW9 6EA, England. Degrees:
MA; Dr phil (Oxon). Doctoral thesis: "The Railway Interest 1873-1913". 1968-69
Research Assistant, Dept of History, U Coll, London; 1969-70 Temporary Lecturer,
Dept of Pol Theory and Government, U Coll of Swansea; 1970-72 Postdoctoral
Research Fellow, U of Reading; 1972- Lecturer in Pol, Royal Holloway Coll, U of Lon-
don. Publs: *The Railway Interest*, 1973; *British Elections: Myth and Reality*, 1978;
"Not Quite British: The Political Attitudes of Anglo-Jewry", in *British Political
Sociology Yearbook* (I Crewe (ed)), 1975; "The National Free Labour Association: A
Case Study of Organized Strike-Breaking in the Late Nineteenth and Early Twentieth
Centuries", *International Review of Social History*, 1976. Fields: Political socialization
and integration in Britain since 1830; the politics and political activities of ethnic
minorities in modern British politics; how British Jews vote.

[22]
ALDERMAN Robin Keith
25 April 1938, British. 8 Greenfield Park Drive, Stockton Lane, York Y03 0JB,
England. Degrees: BSc; PhD (London), 1971. Doctoral thesis: "Discipline in the
Parliamentary Labour Party from the Formation of the Labour Representation Com-
mittee in 1900 to 1964". 1964-77 Lecturer, Senior Lecturer in Pol, U of York. Publs:
The Tactics of Resignation (with J A Cross), 1967; *Management Training Survey* (with
A Dunshire), 1967. Fields: Discipline in the parliamentary labour party; prime
ministerial power; minister-civil servant relationships.

[23]
ALEXANDER Alan
13 December 1943, British. 21 Proctors Road, Wokingham RG11 1RP, Berkshire, England. Degrees: MA (Glasgow), 1965. 1965-66 Research and Education Officer (Scotland), General and Municipal Workers Union; 1966-70 Lecturer and Assistant Professor, Lakehead U; 1970-71 Visiting Fellow in Politics, U of Reading; 1971 Lecturer in Politics, U of Reading. Fields: Canadian politics; British politics; land and community politics.

[24]
ALEXANDRE Pierre
1922, French. 59 rue des Mathurins, 75005 Paris, France. Degrees: Lic en Droit (Paris); Dr en Droit (Paris); Acad Dipl Soc Admin (London). 1943-58 Administrator, French Colonial Service; 1958- Professor of Bantu languages; 1960- Lecturer, EPHE; 1955-59 Editor of *L'Afrique et l'Asie*; 1960- *Cahiers d'Etudes Africaines*; 1964-72 Head of African section, ENSP, CERI: Professor, INALCO, U of Paris III. Publs: *Systèmes verbal et prédicatif du Bula*, 1967; *Langues et langages en Afrique Noire*, 1967; *Organisation politique et administrative des territoires d'Outre-Mer*, 1957. Fields: Anthropology, especially political and religious; problems of social change; decolonization and political regimes in Africa; sociolinguistics, especially political aspects of nation building; race relations; international power conflicts in Africa; African ideologies.

[25]
ALLARDT Erik Anders
9 August 1925, Finnish. Unionsgatan 45 B 40, Helsinki 17, Finland. Degrees: MA (Helsinki), 1947; PhD (Helsinki), 1952. 1958-70 Professor of Sociology, U of Helsinki; Visiting Professor of Sociology, U of California at Berkeley, 1962-63, U of Illinois (Urbana), 1966-67, U of Wisconsin (Madison), 1970-71; 1971- Research Professor of Sociology, U of Helsinki; Research Group of Comparative Sociology. Publs: *Social Structur och Politisk Aktivitet*, 1956; *Drinking Norms and Drinking Habits*, 1957; *Sociologi* (with Y. Littunen), 1970; *Yhteiskunnan Rakenne ja Sosiaalinen Paine*, 1964; *Cleavages, Ideologies and Party Systems* (with Y. Littunen (ed)), 1964; *Mass Politics* (with S Rokkan (ed)), 1970; *Att ha, att älska, att vara. Om Välfärd i Norden*, 1975. Fields: Comparative research on social structure and political behaviour; ethnicity and linguistic identity.

[26]
ALLEN Hubert John Brooke
26 December 1931, British. 97 Aronskelkweg, The Hague, NL-2555 GD The Netherlands. Degrees: BA; MA (Oxon), 1958; M Soc Sci (Birmingham), 1970; Dip Ed (Wales), 1966. 1955-62 H M Overseas Civil Service (Uganda); 1962-65 Overseas Service Coll, Surrey; 1967-70 Inst of Administration, Ahmadu Bello U, Nigeria; 1966-71 Lecturer, INLOGOV, U of Birmingham; 1971-72 UNDP Adviser on Training Methods (Public Administration), Dominican Republic; 1973- Director of Training, International Union of Local Authorities, The Hague. Publs: *Work Overseas: A Guide to Opportunities in the Developing Countries*, 1964; *Under New Management: The Evolution of the English Model of Local Government in Ireland*, 1969; Reports in *IULA* "Decentralization for Development" series: *Local Government Finance*, 1974; *The Role of Local Authorities in Planning and Plan Implementation*, 1975; *Practicas y Ejercicios Administrativos* (co-author), 1974. Fields: Comparative local government; ethics in the public service; the ecological setting of local administration and its impact on the structure of local government; training methods relevant to administration in developing countries; urbanization in the Third World.

[27]
ALLEN Kevin John
25 November 1941, British. 38 Mitre Road, Glasgow G14, Scotland. Degrees: BA. 1964-75 Lecturer in Applied Economics, U of Glasgow; 1975-77 Fellow International Inst of Management, Berlin. Associate Director, Centre for the Study of Public Policy, U of Strathclyde. Publs: *Nationalized Industries* (with G L Reid), 1970; *Regional Problems and Politics in Italy and France* (with M C MacLennan), 1971; *Nationalized Industries: The Fuel Sector* (with G L Reid and D J Haims), 1973; *An Introduction to the Italian Economy* (with A Stevenson), 1974; *Small Area Employment Forecasting: Data and Problems* (with D Yuill), 1977. Fields: Regional policy; state industry; labour markets and employment; public policy generally; Italian economy.

[28]
ALLERBECK Klaus R
18 November 1944, German. Poststrasse 5, D-4837 Verl 1, FR Germany. Degrees: Dr phil (Köln), 1971. Doctoral thesis: "Soziale Bedingungen für studentischen Radikalismus". 1970-72 Research Associate, Zentralarchiv für empirische Sozialforschung, Köln; 1972-76 Lecturer of Soc Relations, Assistant Professor of Sociology, U of Harvard; 1976 Associate Professor, Dept of Sociology, U of Bielefeld. Publs: *Aufstand der Jugend? Neue Aspekte der Jugendsoziologie* (with L Rosenmayr (ed)); *Datenverarbeitung in der empirischen Sozialforschung*, 1972; *Soziologie der radikalen Studenten-bewegungen*, 1973; *Einführung in die Jugendsoziologie* (with L Rosenmayr), 1976; *Demokratisierung und sozialer Wandel*, 1976; *Datenanalyse*, 1978. Fields: Social movements and collective behaviour; methods, data analysis; political socialization; sociological theory and comparative research.

[29]
ALLISON Lincoln Richard Petre
5 October 1946, British. 5 Beauchamp Hill, Royal Leamington Spa, England. Degrees: BA; MA (Oxon), 1973. 1975-76 Visiting Professor, Harkness Fellow, Stanford. Lecturer in Pol, U of Warwick. Publs: *Environmental Planning*, 1975; plus articles in *European Journal of Political Research*, *British Journal of Political Science*, *Stanford Journal of International Studies*, *Public Administration*, *Town Planning Review*, *Regional Studies*. Fields: Political aspects of environmental planning; political concepts and philosophy.

[30]
ALT James
16 August 1946, American. Department of Government, University of Essex, Wivenhoe Park, Colchester CO4 3SQ, Essex, England. Degrees: BA; MA (Essex), 1969; MSc (LSE), 1970. 1971- Lecturer, U of Essex. Publs: *Cabinet Studies* (co-ed), 1975; *Empirical Political Economy*, 1978. Fields: Comparative government; policy studies; political economy.

[31]
ALTENSTETTER Christa
19 January 1937, German. Dickhardt Strasse 6, 1000 Berlin 41, FR Germany. Degrees: MA; Dr phil. Doctoral thesis: "Der Federalismus in Österreich 1946-1968". 1972-76 Research Consultant, Health Policy Project, U of Yale; 1974 Visiting Professor, U of Kiel; 1972-73 Assistant Professor, U of Syracuse; 1969-72 Research Staff, The Urban Inst, Washington; 1968-69 J. F. Kennedy Memorial Fellow (post-doctoral), J. F. Kennedy School of Government, U of Harvard; 1967-68 Assistant Professor of Pol Sci, U of Heidelberg; 1977 Research Fellow, International Inst of Management, Berlin; 1973-78 Associate Professor of Pol Sci, City U of New York, The Graduate School and Queens College; 1976-77 Visiting Associate Professor, American U; 1975-76 Visiting Research Professor, Fogarty Int Center, National Inst of Health Bethesda, Maryland; Research Fellow, International Inst for Management, Berlin, and Associate Professor of Pol Sci, City U of New York, Graduate School and Queens College. Publs: *Federal State Health Policies and Impacts: The Policies of Implementation*, 1978; "The Impact of Organizational Arrangements Policy Performance", in *National-Subnational Relations in Health: Opportunities and Constraints* (ed); *The Role of the Länder in Hospital Planning — The Case of the Federal Republic of Germany* (ed); "Policy, Politics and Child Health: Four Decades of Federal Initiative and State Response", *Journal of Health Politics, Policy and Law*, 1978; "The Impact of Federal Child Health Programs", in *The Rediscovery of Federal Public Policy Making in a Federal System*, 1976; "Arbeitsplätze, Wohnunterkünfte und Schulen für Ethnische Minderheiten in Verdichtungsräumen: Ein Deutsch-Amerikanischer Vergleich", in *Minoritäten in Ballungsräumen, Ein Deutsch-Amerikanischer Vergleich* (M G Eisenstadt and W Kaltefleiter (eds)), 1975; "Intergovernmental Profiles in the Federal Systems of Austria and West Germany: A Comparative Perspective", *The Journal of Federalism*, 1975; "Medical Interests and the Public Interest: A Comparison between West Germany and the United States", *International Journal of Health Services*, 1974. Fields: Political science; public administration; intergovernmental relations; policy analysis.

[32]
ALTING VON GEUSAU Frans Alphons Marie
26 June 1933, Dutch. c/o John F Kennedy Institute, Hogeschoollaan 225, Tilburg, The Netherlands. Degrees: Phil (Collège d'Europe); Dr of Law (Leiden), 1962. 1959-60 Research Assistant, U of California at Berkeley; 1960-61 Teaching Assistant, U of Tilburg; 1961-65 Lecturer, U of Tilburg; 1965- Professor of the Law of International Organizations, U of Tilburg; 1966- Director, John F Kennedy Inst, Centre for International Studies, Tilburg; 1971-72 Visiting Professor, Massachusetts Inst of Technology and Visiting Research Scholar, Center for International Affairs, U of Harvard; Chairman, Advisory Commission on Disarmament, International Security and Peace to the Netherlands Government; Chairman, Programme Commission of the European Cultural Foundation. Publs: *European Organizations and Foreign Relations of States. A Comparative Analysis of Decision-Making*, 1962; *Beyond the European Community*, 1969; *The Future of the International Monetary System* (co-ed), 1970; *NATO and Security in the Seventies* (ed), 1971; *Denken over Wereldvrede*, 1972; *The External Relations of the European Community* (ed), 1975; *European Perspectives on World Order*, 1975; *The Lomé Convention and A New International Economic Order*, 1977; *Uncertain Détente* (ed), 1978. Fields: East-west relations; the European communities; the Middle East; international economic co-operation; arms-control and disarmament; international cultural relations.

[33]
AMANN Ronald
21 August 1943, British. 4 Naunton Close, Selly Oak, Birmingham B29 4DX, England. Degrees: B Soc Sci; M Soc Sci (Birmingham), 1967; PhD (Birmingham), 1976. Doctoral thesis: "The Soviet Research and Development System: Its Operation and Performance". 1966-68 OECD Consultant and Research Associate; 1968-69 Assistant Lecturer, CREES, U of Birmingham; 1969- Lecturer in Soviet Politics and Science Policy, CREES, U of Birmingham; 1977-78 Acting Director of the Centre. Publs: *Science Policy in the USSR* (with M J Berry and R W Davies); *The Technological Level of Soviet Industry* (with J M Cooper and R W Davies), 1977. Fields: Political economy of the USSR; international science policy.

[34]
AMAR André*
10 February 1908, French. Rue de Seine 6, Paris VIème, France. Degrees: Ancien élève de l'Ecole Normale Supérieure, 1929; Lic en philosophie, 1931. Professeur d'histoire des idées, Institut d'Etudes Politiques de Paris et Grenoble. Publs: *L'Europe a fait le monde*, 1966. Fields: History of political ideas.

[35]
AMBROSETTI Giovanni
13 January 1915, Italian. I-37100 Verona, Avesa Villa Ambrosetti, Italy. Degrees: Dr in Giurisprudenza; Accademia Nazionale di Modena; Pontificia Accademia Romana di S Tommaso d'Aquino; Associacion Internacional Francisco de Victora, Madrid. Doctoral thesis: "La società coniugale nel Rosmini". Ordinario di Filosofia del diritto a Incaricato di Storia delle Dottrine Politiche, U di Modena. Publs: *Il diritto naturale della Riforma Cattolica*, 1951; *Razionalità e storicità del diritto*, 1953; *I presupposti teologici e speculativi delle concezioni giuridiche di Grozio*, 1955; *Contributi ad una filosofia del costume*, 1959; *Diritto Naturale Cristiano*, 1970; *L'essenza dello Stato*, 1973. Fields: Philosophy of law; philosophy of politics; history of political doctrine.

[36]
AMBROSOLI Mauro Liberato*
20 June 1943, Italian. Corso G Pascoli Il, 10134 Torino, Italy. Degrees: D Litt (Turin), 1968. Doctoral thesis: "Economic and Social History of a Piedmontese Noble Family, Ferrero Fieschi di Masserano, 1685-1789". Centre for Advanced Studies on Italian Society; Bursar, U of Reading; COSPOS Research Fellow, U of Turin. Publs: "Agricoltura e sviluppo economico in Inghilterra fra 1700 e 1800", *Rivista Storica Italiana*, 1970; "Fertilità naturale e fortuna familiare: il caso des Ferrero Fieschi de Masserano nel secolo XVIII", *Bulletino Deputazione Subalphina de Storia Patria*, 1971.

[37]
AMIOT Michel*
28 April 1933, French. Carlton Carabacel, Avenue Emile-Bieckert, 06000 Nice, France. Degrees: Agrégation de philosophie, 1960. Chargé de Recherche (Sociologie), CNRS. Publs: *La consultation dans l'administration contemporaine* (contributor), 1972. Fields: State and local administration in France; cultural policy; urban politics.

[38]
AMSTRUP Niels
7 June 1928, Danish. Libravej 19, DK-8270 Højbjerg, Denmark. Degrees: Cand Mag (Copenhagen). Inst of History, U of Aarhus. Publs: *Dansk udenrigspolitik*, 1975; *The Perennial Problem of Small States: A Survey of Research Efforts. Cooperation and Conflict*, 1976. Fields: Foreign policy of small states; economics and politics in international relations since Bretton Woods; the negotiation process in international politics.

[39]
ANCHIERI Ettore
4 July 1896, Italian. Padova, Via S Pio X 5, Italy. Degrees: Dr phil. Doctoral thesis: "Il Pragmatismo di William James". Chargé de cours, Faculty of Pol Sci, U of Pavia; Professor, History of International Relations, U of Padua. Publs: *Il Canale di Suez*, 1940; *Storia della Politica Inglese nel Sudan*, 1939; *La Questione Palistinea (1915-39)*, 1940; *Constantinopoli e Gli Stretti nella Politica Russa*, 1948; *I Trattati di 1914-15*, 1950; *La Diplomazia Contemporanea*, 1959; *I Documenti Diplomatici Italiani*, V Serie (1914-1918), 1973; *Il Sistema Diplomatico Europeo*, 1977.

[40]
ANDERSON Malcolm
13 May 1934, British. 6 Binswood Avenue, Leamington Spa, Warwickshire CV4 7AL, England. Degrees: MA (Oxon); Dr phil (Oxon), 1961. Doctoral thesis: "The Parliamentary Right in France 1905-19". 1960-64 Assistant Lecturer, Lecturer in Government, U of Manchester; 1964-65 Rockefeller Research Fellow, Inst National des Sci Pol, Paris; Senior Lecturer, Professor of Pol, U of Warwick. Publs: *Government in France: an Introduction to the Executive Power*, 1970; *Introduction to the Social Sciences* (tr from M. Duverger), 1963; *Conservative Politics in France*, 1974. Fields: Regionalism; scope and method of political science; economic policy.

[41]
ANDERSON Matthew Smith
23 May 1922, British. London School of Economics and Political Science. Houghton Street, Aldwych, London WC2, England. Degrees: MA (Edinburgh), 1947; PhD (Edinburgh), 1952. Doctoral thesis: "British Diplomatic Relations with the Mediterranean, 1763-78". 1947-49 Assistant in History, U of Edinburgh; 1949-53 Assistant Lecturer in Pol Sci, LSE; 1953-61 Lecturer, 1961-72 Reader, 1972- Professor of International History, LSE. Publs: *Britain's Discovery of Russia, 1553-1815*, 1958; *Europe in the Eighteenth Century 1713-89*, 1961; *Eighteenth Century Europe 1713-89*, 1966; *The Eastern Question 1774-1923*, 1966; *The Ascendancy of Europe 1815-1914*, 1972. Fields: Historiography of the 18th century; the reign of Peter the Great in Russia; the development of diplomatic services and foreign offices; the development of ideas about international organizations and the balance of power.

[42]
ANDERSSON Hans Georg
21 August 1936, Swedish. Bygärdesvägen 22, 16357 Spånga, Sweden. Degrees: Fil lic (Stockholm), 1969. 1968-69 Assistant Secretary, Commission on Constitutional Reform; 1969- Lecturer in Pol Sci, U of Stockholm. Publs: *Vad Gör Partierna i Riksdagen*, 1969; *Riksdagsgrupperna; Statens Offentliga Utredningar*, 1970; *Riksdagens Funktioner och Arbetssätt*, 1972; *Demokratins Grundläggande Värden*, 1974. Fields: Political parties; legislative behaviour; democratic theory.

[43]
ANDEWEG Rudy B
28 February 1952, Dutch. Diamantplein 48, Leiden, The Netherlands. Degrees: Kandidaats (Leiden), 1972; Drs (Leiden), 1975; MA (Michigan), 1976. 1971-75 Research Assistant, U of Leiden; 1976- Assistant Professor of Pol Sci, Dept of Pol Sci, U of Leiden. Publs: "Waarheen, waarvoor, voor wie? Contacten van de burger met de locale overheid" (with G A Irwin and W Braak), *Bestuurswetenschappen*, 1974; "Privacy: een oud verschijnsel, probleem" (with Th van der Tak), *Ars Aequui*, 1975; "Aan de deur geen politiek? een verkennend onderzoek naar de effecten van een huisbezoekcampagne en de houdingen daartegenover" (with K Dittrich and M van Haeften), *Acta Politica*, 1975; "Om de kleur van de burgemeester; politieke aspecten van burgemeestersbenoemingen", *Acta Politica*, 1975; "Van Verstarring naar Verwarring", *Wie heeft er nog een Boodschap aan?*, 1977; "Factoren die het stemgedrag mede bepalen", in *De Nederlandse Keizer 1977* (G A Irwin (ed)), 1977; *Kabinetsformatie 1977* (with K Dittrich and Th van der Tak), 1978. Fields: Voting behaviour; political psychology; comparative politics; cohort analysis.

[44]
ANDREN Nils
12 May 1918, Swedish. Västbovägen 10, 182 35 Danderyd, Sweden. Degrees: PhD, 1947. Doctoral thesis: *Den Klassika Parlamentarismens Genombrott i England* (The Breakthrough of Parliamentary Government in England). 1947-50 Docent, U of Göteborg; 1951-62 Director, Inst for English-speaking Students, U of Stockholm; 1962-66 Chairman, Dept of Pol Sci, U of Stockholm; 1967-69 Professor of Pol Sci, U of Copenhagen; 1970- Research Associate, Research Inst of National Defence, Stockholm. Publs: *Modern Swedish Government*, 1968; *Government and Politics of the Nordic Countries*, 1964; *Power-Balance and Non-Alignment*, 1967; *The Future of the Nordic Balance*, 1977. Fields: Political integration; national security problems.

[45]
ANDRESEN Anton Fredrik
10 May 1936, Norwegian. Gregers Grams Vei 20, Oslo 3, Norway. Degrees: Lic ès sci pol (Inst de Hautes Etudes Internationales, Geneva), 1960; Magister i Statsvitenskap (Oslo), 1968. 1962-64 ed, *Rundbrev fra Norsk Selskap for Sovjetstudier*, Oslo; 1971-73 Research Fellow, Inst of Pol Sci, U of Oslo; 1974- ed, *Perspektivprosjektet*, Oslo. Publs: *Borgerand og Politisk Engasjement*, Vol 1: *Fra Montesquieu til Benjamin Constant*, 1969. Fields: Political theory, especially problems of democracy and pluralism.

[46]
ANDRESKI Stanislav Leonard
18 May 1919, British. 2 Barbaras Meadow, Long Lane, Tilehurst, Reading, England. Degrees: BSc; MSc (London); PhD (London). Doctoral thesis: "Military Organization and Social Structure". 1947-53 Lecturer in Soc, Rhodes U, South Africa; 1954-56 Senior Research Fellow, U of Manchester; 1956-57 Lecturer in Economics, Acton Technical Coll; 1957-60 Lecturer in Management Studies, Brunel Coll of Technology, London; 1960-61 Professor of Soc, School of Soc Sci, Santiago, Chile; 1962-64 Senior Research Fellow, Nigerian Inst of Soc and Econ Research, Ibadan; 1968-69 Visiting Professor of Soc and Anthropology, City U, New York; 1964- Professor, U of Reading. Publs: *Military Organization and Society*, 1970; *Parasitism and Subversion: The Case of Latin America; The African Predicament: A Study in Pathology of Modernization; Social Sciences as Sorcery; The Prospects of a Revolution in the USA; Herbert Spencer: Principles of Sociology* (ed), 1968; *Herbert Spencer: Structure, Function and Evolution* (ed), 1975; *The Essential Comte* (ed), 1974; *Reflections on Inequality* (ed), 1975. Fields: Comparative analysis.

[47]
ANDREY Georges
24 May 1938, Swiss. Route de Moncor 15, CH-1752 Villars sur Glâne, Switzerland.
Degrees: Dr phil. Doctoral thesis: 'Spécialiste de Sociologie électorale Suisse''.
Collaborateur Scientifique, Fonds national Suisse de la Recherche Scientifique; Collaborateur Scientifique, Dept Politique Fédéral, Berne. Publs: *Les électeurs au conseil National (1848-1918)*, 1978; "La discipline électorale en Suisse", *Annuaire Suisse de Science Politique*, 1973; "La conscience politique romande. Petite contribution à l'étude du fédéralisme Suisse (1848-1975)", *ASSP*, 1976; "Personnalité politique et carrière parlementaire (1848-1918)", *Geschichte und politische Wissenschaft*, 1975. Fields: Votes and elections in Switzerland; economic and political relations in Switzerland; sociological and historical elections in Switzerland; the Swiss minority; parties and parliament on democratic and cantonal level.

[48]
ANGELL Alan Edward
14 May 1939, British. St Anthony's College, Oxford, England. Degrees: BSc, 1960. Lecturer in Pol, U of Keele; Senior Research Fellow, St Anthony's Coll, Oxford and Royal Inst of International Affairs; Lecturer in Latin American Pol, St Anthony's Coll, Oxford. Publs: *Politics and the Labour Movement in Chile*, 1973. Fields: Latin American politics; politics of Labour movements; social class and political behaviour.

[49]
ANGELS Sander
4 June 1949, Danish. Karparken 20, Vamp, DK-8900 Randers, Denmark. Degrees: Cand phil. Adjunkt, Inst of Pol Sci, U of Aarhus. Fields: Political socialization; civic education.

[50]
ANGLADE Christian
29 January 1937, French. 30 Albany Road, West Bergholt, Colchester, Essex, England. Degrees: Lic és Lettres, sci pol; DES droit (Toulouse). Lecturer, U of Essex. Publs: "A Study of Political Finance in Latin America", in *Comparative Political Finance* (A Heidenheimer (ed)), 1970; various articles on political parties, the relationships between political systems and economic models, and on Brazil. Fields: Relationship between specific models of economic development and the political structures of several countries of Latin America.

[51]
ANSPRENGER Franz
18 January 1927, German. 49 Lupsteiner Weg, D I Berlin, FR Germany. Degrees: Dr phil (Berlin), 1952. Doctoral thesis: "Untersuchungen zum adoptianischen Streit im Achten Jahrhundert". 1958-67 Lecturer in History and Pol Sci, Free U of Berlin; 1967-Professor of Pol Sci, Head of African Politics Research Unit, Free U of Berlin. Publs: *Politik im schwarzen Afrika*, 1961; *Afrika, eine politische Länderkunde*, 1972; *Versuch der Freiheit, Afrika nach der Unabhängigkeit*, 1972; *Die Befreiungspolitik der OAU 1963-75*, 1975; *Auflösung der Kolonialreiche*, 1977. Fields: African history since 1880; political development; international relations; peace research.

[52]
ANTOINE Jacques Jean-Marie
19 August 1928, French. 125 Boulevard de la Reine, 78000 Versailles, France. Degrees: Polytechnique; Dipl ENSAE. 1953-58 Administrateur, INSEE; 1958-73 Directeur d'etudes écon, Soc d'Econ et Mathématiques Appliquées; Directeur général, Président, Société Française d'Enquêtes par Sondages; Professeur, Conservatoire National des Arts et Métiers; Directeur, Centre d'Etudes Socio-Economiques; Président, Comité de rédaction, *Revue française de marketing*. Publs: *L'opinion. Techniques d'enquêtes par sondage*, 1969; *Le pouvoir et l'opinion*, 1972. Fields: Public opinion; quantification in "new" qualitative fields such as: quality of life and life-styles, culture, environment; mass media and communication; social marketing; Third-World and new international order.

[53]
ANTOLA Esko Mikael
18 January 1947, Finnish. Virnakuja 6 as 5, 21200 Raisio, Finland. Degrees: Lic. Lecturer, Dept of Pol Sci, U of Turku. Fields: International relations; development studies; European studies.

[54]
ANTONIOLLI Walter*
30 December 1907, Austrian. 2344 Maria Enzersdorf, Südstadt, Ottenseinstrasse 35, Austria. Degrees: PhD (Vienna). Em Professor, U of Vienna; President of Constitutional Court. Fields: Administrative law.

[55]
APUNEN Osmo
5 October 1938, Finnish. Pähkinämäenkatu 6 D 27, 33840 Tampere 84, Finland. Degrees: Lic Pol Sci (Helsinki), 1967; Dr Pol Sci (Helsinki), 1968. Doctoral thesis: "Suomi Keisarillisen Saksan Politiikassa 1914-1915" (Finland in the Policy of the German Empire 1914-1915). 1967-71 Assistant, Inst of History, U of Helsinki; 1971-72 Acting Professor of International Pol, U of Tampere; 1972-73 Assistant Director for Pol Affairs, Ministry for Foreign Affairs; 1973- Professor of International Pol, U of Tampere. Publs: *Suomi Keisarillisen Saksan Politiikassa*, 1968; *Paasikiven-Kekkosen Linja*, 1977. Fields: Finnish foreign policy; European security disarmament.

[56]
AQUINA Herman J
9 July 1942, Dutch. Patrijslaan 106, Beuningen, The Netherlands. Degrees: Drs (Amsterdam), 1969; Dr (Nijmegen), 1974. Doctoral thesis: "Beleidswetenschap en Wetenschapsbeleid" (Policy Science and Science Policy). 1969-70 Research worker, Central Bureau of Statistics, The Hague; 1970- Senior Fellow, Inst of Pol Sci, Catholic U of Nijmegen. Fields: Policy analysis in political science; learning processes in policy-making.

[57]
ARCHER Thomas Clive
8 May 1947, British. 45 University Road, Aberdeen, Scotland. Degrees: BSc; PhD (Aberdeen), 1974. Doctoral thesis: "The Politics of the UK-Scandinavian Trade Relationship within the Context of EFTA". 1968-71 Research Student, Dept of Pol, U of Aberdeen; 1971- Lecturer in International Relations, Dept of Pol, U of Aberdeen; 1976-Secretary, Centre for Nordic Studies, U of Aberdeen. Publs: *Scandinavia and European Integration* (ed), 1971; *Report of Conference on Scandinavia and European Integration* (ed), 1973; *Security in Northern Europe: Report on a Conference* (ed), 1976. Fields: Scandinavian politics; security relations and integration politics; North Sea politics; European integration.

[58]
ARDANT Philippe
21 July 1929, French. 11 rue Vaneau, 75006 Paris, France. Degrees: Agrégé des Facultés de Droit (Paris), 1956. 1956-59 Professeur, Faculté de Droit, Rabat; 1959-60 Professeur de Droit, Faculté de Beyrouth; 1960-65 Professeur, Faculté de Poitiers; 1965-67 Conseiller culturel de l'ambassade de France en Chine; 1969-71 Professeur, Faculté de Droit, Nanterre; Conseiller culturel, Ambassade de France, Rabat; Professor, U de Droit, Econ and Soc Sci, Paris. Publs: *La responsabilité de l'Etat du fait de la fonction juridictionnelle*, 1956; *L'administration chinoise*, 1969. Fields: Developing countries; China.

[59]
ARLETTAZ Gerald
28 May 1948, Swiss. Chemin de la Forêt, 1700 Fribourg, Switzerland. Degrees: Lic ès lettres; Dr phil designatus. Doctoral thesis: "Liberalisme et Société dans le Canton de Vaud (1814-1845)". Archiviste aux Archives Fédérales (Confédération Suisse). Publs: *Les tendances libérales en Valais (1825-1839)*, 1971; "La presse libérale et la naissance de l'information politique en Suisse Française", in *Société et culture du Valais contemporain*, 1974; "Les transformations économiques et le développement du Valais", in *Développement et mutations du Valais contemporain*, 1978; "L'émigration des émigrants Suisses aux Etats Unis", *Relations internationales*, 1977; "Les finances de L'Etat fédéral de 1848 à 1939", *Etudes et Sources*, 1977. Fields: Emigration; development economics; ideologies and society; the press.

[60]
ARMANSKI Gerhard
11 May 1942, German. Eyerskansen 29, 3221 Landwehr, FR Germany. Degrees: Dipl in Pol Sci; PhD. Doctoral thesis: "The Genesis of Scientific Socialism". Assistant Professor, Research Fellow, Free U of Berlin. Publs: Various articles on the public sector; the military service; the USA and tourism. Fields: Public sector, military service; USA; tourism.

[61]
ARNDT Hans Joachim
15 January 1923, German. Inst für Politische Wissenschaft, Universität Heidelberg, 69 Heidelberg 11, Hauptstrasse 52, FR Germany. Degrees: MA (Washington), 1951; Dr phil (Heidelberg), 1952. Doctoral thesis: "Über die Ursachen der Geschichtsfremdheit der amerikanischen Soziologie". Public Relations Consultant, Esso, Hamburg; Head, Econ Dept, Liberal Party, Bonn; Consultant, German Top Management Training, Köln; Professor of Pol Sci, U of Heidelberg. Publs: *Über die Ursachen der Geschichtsfremdheit der amerikanischen Soziologie*, 1952; *Politik und Sachverstand im Kreditwahrungswesen. Die verfassungsstaatlichen Gewalten und die Funktion von Zen-*

tralbanken, 1963; *Unternehmungsführung als Fachberuf. Zur Kritik der Management-Ausbildung*, 1966; *West-Germany: Politics of Non-planning*, 1966; *Weiterbildung an der Universitätwirtschaftlicher Führungskrafte* (with S Fassbender and H Hellwig), 1968. Fields: Monetary, financial and central bank policy; governmental planning; political geography; political conservatism; organization of information input for governments.

[62]
ARON Raymond
14 March 1905, French. 87 Boulevard St Michel, 75005 Paris, France. Degrees: Agrégé de phil, 1928; Dr ès lettres, 1938. 1930-31 Lecturer, U of Cologne; 1931-33 Pensionnaire, Maison académique, Berlin; 1933-34 Professeur, Lycée du Havre; 1935-39 Secrétaire, Centre de Documentation Sociale, ENS; Professeur, ENS St Cloud; 1939 Maître de conférences, Faculté de Lettres, U de Toulouse; 1945-55 Cours à l'IEP et ENA; 1955-68 Professeur, Faculté de Lettres et Sci Humaines, U de Paris; 1960 Directeur d'Etudes, Ecole Pratique des Hautes Etudes; Professeur, Collège de France. Publs: *D'une sainte famille à l'autre*, 1969; *Les désillusions du progrès*, 1969; *Etudes politiques*, 1972; *République impériale*, 1973; *Histoire et dialectique de la violence*, 1973; *Penser la guerre; Clausewitz: l'âge européen*, 1976; *L'âge planétaire*, 1976; *Plaidoyer pour l'Europe décadente*, 1977.

[63]
ARRIGHI Giovanni
7 July 1937, Italian. Dipartimento di Sociologia e Scienza Politica, Universita della Calabria, 87030 Arcavacata di Rende, Italy. Degrees: Dr Economia (Bocconi). Doctoral thesis: "La Determinazione dei Rendimenti in una Industria Meccanica". Lecturer, UCRN, Salisbury, Rhodesia; Lecturer, UC, Dar Es Salaam, Tanzania; Professore Incaricato, Trento; Professore Incaricato di Analisi delle Classi e dei Gruppi Sociali, Dip di Sociologia e di Sci Pol, U della Calabria. Publs: *The Political Economy of Rhodesia*, 1967; *Essays on the Political Economy of Africa* (with S S Saul); *The Geometry of Imperialism*, 1968. Fields: Economic development and social structures.

[64]
ARTS Wilhelmus Antonius
6 June 1946, Dutch. Turfmarkt 55-57, Gouda, The Netherlands. Degrees: BA; MA. Sociology Dept, Erasmus U, Rotterdam; Economics Dept, Erasmus U, Rotterdam. Publs: *Inleiding tot het Sociologisch Onderzoek* (with P Hermkens and D Kruijt), 1972; *Gedrag en Struktuur* (S Lindenberg and R Wippler (co-eds)), 1976; several articles on economic policy, economic sociology and theoretical sociology. Fields: Political philosophy; economic theories of politics; economic policy.

[65]
ATKINSON Geoffrey Cyril
7 January 1931, British. 27 Hastings Avenue, Durham, England. Degrees: BA; MA (Manchester), 1952. 1956-57 Temporary Lecturer, U of Newcastle; Lecturer in Pol, U of Durham. Publs: Chapter on Durham, in *Voting in Cities*, 1967. Fields: Police studies; local government divisions city and country.

[66]
ATTEMA Tijmen
10 February 1942, Dutch. Pr Margrietplantsoen 73, Bussum, The Netherlands. Degrees: Drs. Wetenschappelijk Medewerker, Free U of Amsterdam. Publs: *Bestuursonderzoek Oost-Nederland*, 1973; *Diskussienota over de gewestelijke indeling van Haarlemmerliede en Spaarnwoude*, 1975; *Management in de Rijksdienst*, 1977. Fields: Decentralization; reorganization and management in public administration.

[67]
ATTINA Fulvio
31 May 1947, Italian. Lung C Colombo 26/A, Florence, Italy. Degrees: Laurea in Pol Sci. Researcher in International Relations, U of Florence; Associate Professor of Diplomacy, U of Catania. Publs: *I Conflitti Internazionali*, 1976; *Relazioni Internazionali* (co-ed), 1973. Fields: Foreign policy-making; diplomacy; Italian foreign policy; conflict analysis.

[68]
AUBERT Jean Francois*
11 May 1931, Swiss. 15 Avenue Soguel, 2035 Corcelles, Switzerland. Degrees: Lic en droit (Neuchâtel), 1952; Dr en droit (Neuchâtel), 1955. 1956-62 Professeur Extraordinaire, Faculté de Droit, U de Neuchâtel; 1962- Professeur ordinaire, U de Neuchâtel. Publs: *Traité de droit constitutionnel Suisse*, 1967. Fields: Constitutional law; constitutional history; foreign constitutional law; theory of state.

[69]
AUBY Jean-Marie Eugene*
15 August 1922, French. 43 avenue Léon Blum, 33 Le Bouscat, France. Degrees: Dr en droit; Lic en philosophie. Doctoral thesis: "L'inexistence des actes administratifs". Doyen de la Faculté en Droit de Bordeaux; Président de l'U de Bordeaux. Publs: *Traité de contentieux administratif*, 1962. Fields: Administrative science.

[70]
AUKEN Svend*
24 May 1943, Danish. Institute of Political Science, University of Aarhus, 8000 Aarhus C, Denmark. Degrees: Cand Sci Pol (Aarhus), 1969. Lecturer, Inst of Pol Sci, U of Aarhus. Publs: "Sikkerhed uden vaernepligt — mod et nyt forsvarsmønster i Europa", in *Forsvaret til Debat* (ed K Olesen), 1970. Fields: Regional development programmes and policies; Danish labour movement; Danish foreign policy.

[71]
AUTY Phyllis*
British. 24 Greys Hill, Henley-on-Thames, England. Degrees: BA; MA (Oxon); B Litt (Oxon). Doctoral thesis: "The Foundation Charters of the Cistercian Abbey of Byland and the Mowbray Fee". 1943-45 PID, London and AFHQ Intelligence; Visiting Professor in History, Simon Fraser U, Vancouver, Canada; 1965-66 U of Stanford 1969- Reader in History of the South Slavs, School of Slavonic and European Studies, U of London. Publs: *Yugoslavia*, 1965; *Yugoslavia's International Relations*, 1969; *Tito: A Biography*, 1970. Fields: History of the Yugoslav Communist Party; history of the kingdom of Serbia; contemporary political history of Yugoslavia.

[72]
AVINERI Shlomo
20 August 1933, Israeli. 50 Harlap Street, Jerusalem, Israel. Degrees: BA; MA, 1961; PhD, 1964. Doctoral thesis: "The Concept of Revolution in Marx's Thought". Visiting Professor at Yale, Cornell, Wesleyan U and Australian National U; 1976-77 Director-General, Israeli Ministry of Foreign Affairs; Herbert Samuel Professor of Pol Sci, Hebrew U of Jerusalem. Publs: *The Social and Political Thought of Karl Marx*, 1968; *Israel and the Palestinians*, 1971; *Hegel's Theory of the Modern State*, 1973; *Varieties of Marxism*, 1977. Fields: Political theory; Marx, Hegel; communism; Middle Eastern politics, nationalism.

[73]
AVRIL Pierre
18 November 1930, French. 48 rue Gay Lussac, 75005 Paris, France. Degrees: Agrégé de droit public et sci pol (Paris), 1972; Dr en droit; Dipl (Paris). Doctoral thesis: "Le régime politique de la Vème République". Professor, U of Poitiers, U of Paris X-Nanterre. Publs: *Le régime politique de la Vème République*, 1975; *Un président, pour quoi faire?*, 1965; *Politics in France*, 1969; *L'arrondissement devant la réforme administrative*, 1970; *UDR et gaullistes*, 1971; *Les Français et leur parlement*, 1972. Fields: Party politics; modernization and territorial structures; relations of local and national systems.

[74]
AYBERK Ahmet Ural
1935, Turkish. 25 rue de l'Athénée, 1206 Geneva, Switzerland. Degrees: Lic sci pol (Ankara), 1959; Dipl (Paris); Dr (Inst U de Hautes Etudes Internationales). Doctoral thesis: "Le mécanisme de l'élaboration des décisions communautaires en matière de relations internationales". 1962 Stagiaire, Cabinet du Premier Ministre; 1963 Directeur, Cabinet du Ministre d'Etat, Ankara; 1966-67 Boursier; 1970- Assistant, Maître assistant, Dept de Sci Pol, U de Genève. Publs: *La publicité des actes du Conseil et de la Commission de la CEE*, 1967; "Bilan des groupes et du procéssus de décision dans la CE des Six (with D Sidjanski), *Res Publica*, 1974; "La négociation CEE-Suisse dans le *Kennedy Round*", *1974;* "*La réponse del l'internationale des métaux aux compagnies* multinationales" (with J N Rey), *Il Politico*, 1978; *Le mécanisme de l'élaboration des décisions communautaires en matière de relations internationales.* Fields: Interest groups; political power at regional and international level; decision-making in the EEC; political theory.

B

[75]
BACHY Jean Paul
30 March 1947, French. 23 rue de l'Exposition, 75001 Paris, France. Degrees: Lic ès Lettres; Dipl (Paris). Attaché, Centre de Recherche en Sci Soc du Travail; Maître Assistant au Conservatoire National des Arts et Métiers, Paris. Publs: *Les étudiants et la politique*, 1973; *Représentation et information*, 1974; *Les jeunes et la civilization industrielle*, 1977. Fields: Sociology of labour; industrial relations.

[76]
BÄCK Henry
21 February 1947, Swedish. Dragonvägen 24, S-194 00, Upplands, Väsby, Sweden. Degrees: Fil pol mag. Assistantship and lecturer, Dept of Pol Sci, U of Stockholm and Dept of Soc Sci, U of Linköping; Forskningsassistant, Dept of Pol Sci, U of Stockholm. Fields: Unconventional political behaviour; local government; public administration.

[77]
BACK Pär-Erik
20 September 1920, Swedish. Dept of Pol Sci, U of Umeå, S-901 76 Umeå, Sweden. Degrees: PhD (Lund), 1956. 1956-63 Assistant Professor of Pol Sci, U of Lund; 1964 Associate Professor of Pol Sci, U of Lund; 1965- Professor of Pol Sci, U of Umeå. Publs: *Herzog und Landschaft*, 1955; *En Klass i Uppbrott*, 1961; *Sammanslutningaras roll i Politiken 1870-1910,* 1967; *Det Svenska Partiväsendet,* 1967. Fields: The political system and its boundaries; comparative studies of local governments; cross-country research in general; elite composition; outputs.

[78]
BACKHAUS Jürgen
5 August 1950, German. Postfach 5406, D-7750 Konstanz 12, FR Germany. Degrees: Dipl Volkswirt; Lic jur; Dr rer Soc. Doctoral thesis: "Wirtschaftsrecht der öffentlichen Unternehmung" (Law of Public Enterprise); "Politisch-Ökonomische Theorie der öffentlichen Unternehmung" (Politico-Economic Theory of Public Enterprise). 1974-76 Research Officer, U of Konstanz; 1977-78 Post-Doctoral Fellow, Center for Study of Public Choice, Virginia Polytechnic Inst and State U; 1978- Research Officer, U of Konstanz. Publs: "Ökonomik der Sozialisierung" in *Sozialisierung von Unternehmen* (Winter (ed)), 1976; *Wirtschaftsrecht der öffentlichen Unternehmung*, 1977; *Ökonomik der Partizipativen Unternehmung*, 1978; "Politische Ökonomie als Theorie der Begründung", *Zeitschrift für allgemeine Wissenschaftstheorie*, 1977; "Pareto on Public Choice", *Public Choice*, 1978; "Constitutional Guarantees and the Distribution of Power and Wealth", *Public Choice*, 1978; "Homogeneous Social Groups", *Zeitschrift für Wirtschafts- und Sozialwissenschaften*, 1978; "Politikwissenschaftliche Analyse interpretatorischer Veränderungen von Verfassungsnormen", *Politische Vierteljahresschrift*, 1976. Fields: Public choice; participatory enterprise; history of thought.

[79]
BADER Erwin
10 October 1943, Austrian. A-1120 Wien, Rennbahnweg 27, Austria. Degrees: Dr phil. Doctoral thesis: "Der Staatsbegriff von Karl Marx. Eine Überprüfung der ihm zugeschriebenen Theorie vom Absterben des Staates". Lecturer, U of Salzburg; Scientific Contributor, Science Ministry, Vienna; Teacher, High Schools, Vienna and U Extension. Fields: Theory of State; working class movement; peace research; Marxism and Christianity.

[80]
BADIE Bertrand
14 May 1950, French. 4 rue Louis Godet, 75007 Paris, France. Degrees: Dr sci pol. Doctoral thesis: "Le parti communiste et la grève: essai d'analyse fonctionnelle du 'parti de la classe ouvrière' ". Maître-assistant, Dept de Sci Pol de Paris I. Publs: *Stratégie de la grève- pour une approche fonctionnaliste du PCF*, 1976; *Le développement politique*, 1978; various articles in *Revue Française de Science Politique* and *Le Mouvement Social*. Fields: Political theory; political development; political change; sociology of the State; power; political parties.

[81]
BADY Jean-Pierre
25 June 1939, French. 14 rue de Remusat, 75016 Paris, France. Degrees: Agrégé de lettres; Dipl (Paris). Auditeur, Conseiller Réfendaire à la Cour des Comptes; 1969-Rapporteur à la Commission de l'Education Nationale du VIème Plan; 1972- Rapporteur du Comité français pour l'année internationale du livre; 1972-74 Conseiller technique au cabinet de J Fontanet (Minister of Education); 1974-76 Chargé de mission au cabinet de J Chirac (Prime Minister); 1976-77 Chargé de mission au cabinet de M Barre (Prime Minister); 1975- Conseiller Référendaire à la Cour des Comptes; Directeur de la Caisse nationale des Monuments Historiques et des Sites; 1970- Maître de conférences, IEP Paris. Publs: *Péguy et Jaurès, portrait d'une amitié*, 1962. Fields: Contemporary French politics.

[82]
BAECHLER Jean
28 March 1937, French. 4 Avenue de Rocroi, 91380 Chilly-Mazarin, France. Degrees: Agrégé, 1962; Dr ès lettres, 1975. Doctoral thesis: "Les Suicides". 1962-66 Professeur, Lycée du Mans; 1966- Maître de Recherche, CNRS; 1975- Chargé de conférence, Ecole des Hautes Etudes en Sci Soc; CNRS. Pubs: *Politique de Trotsky*, 1978; *Les phénomènes revolutionnaires*, 1970; *Les origines du capitalisme*, 1971; *Les suicides*, 1975; *Qu'est ce que l'idéologie?*, 1976. Fields: Comparative political systems; theory of power.

[83]
BAEHR, Peter René
1 January 1935, Dutch. Jacob van Ruisdaellaan 25, Heemstede, The Netherlands. Degrees: Drs (Amsterdam), 1960; PhD (Washington), 1964. Doctoral thesis: "Dilemmas in United States Foreign Policy in the United Nations with Regard to Problems of National Self-Determination, 1945-59". 1961-66 Staff Member, Inst for Pol Sci, U of Amsterdam; 1966-69 Lecturer in International Relations, U of Amsterdam; 1969-76 Professor of International Relations, U of Amsterdam; 1976- Executive Secretary, Scientific Council for Government Policy, The Hague. Pubs: *The Role of a National Delegation in the General Assembly*, 1970; *De Verenigde Naties*, 1976; *Power and Influence in International Politics*, 1977. Fields: Theory of foreign policy; foreign policy of the Netherlands; public opinion and foreign policy; theory of international relations; United Nations.

[84]
BAERTSCHI Wolfgang
18 July 1944, German. Wilmsstrasse 22, 1000 Berlin 61, FR Germany. Degrees: Dipl-Volkswirt; Dr rer Pol. Doctoral thesis: "Ausbeutung und Einkommensumverteilung in den internationalen Wirtschaftsbeziehungen" (Exploitation and Income Redistribution in International Economic Relations.) Assistant, German Inst for Economic Research; Assistant, Inst for International Economic Relations, Free U of Berlin; Researcher, International Institute for Comparative Social Research, Science Center, Berlin. Pubs: *Kritische Einführung in die Aussenhandelstheorie* (with H D Jacobsen), 1976; *Ausbeutung und Einkommensumverteilung in den internationalen Wirtschaftsbeziehungen*, 1976. Fields: International political economics; international political and economic interdependencies; "new" international economic order; global modelling; strategies of economic development.

[85]
BAEYENS Raymond Clément Louis*
10 August 1922, Belgian. B-1070 Bruxelles, Ave du Roi-Soldat, Belgium. Degrees: Dr en droit, 1945; Lic en criminologie, 1946; Lic en sci pol et administratives, 1952; Lic en sci pol et diplomatiques (Free U of Brussels), 1933. 1948-71 Premier auditeur, Conseil d'Etat; 1956-59 Juge, Tribunal International, Union de l'Europe Occidentale en Sarre; Professor, Vlaamse Economischer Hogerschool, Brussels; Conseiller principal, Service juridique, Commission des Communautés Européennes; Directeur des études, Centre International d'Etudes et de Recherches Européennes, Luxembourg. Fields: Comparative public law; international relations; European integration.

[86]
BAGOLINI Luigi
4 January 1913, Italian. Via Fossolo 14, 40138 Bologna, Italy. Degrees: Dr in Law
(Rome), 1936; Dr of Law (São Paulo), 1953. Doctoral thesis: "The Theory of Slavery in
Aristotle". 1948-50 Professor of Legal Philosophy and Jurisprudence, U of Siena;
1950-68 Professor of Legal Philosophy and Jurisprudence, U of Genoa; 1950-55 Professor of Jurisprudence, U of the State of São Paulo; Professor of Pol Philosophy and
Theory of the State, U of Bologna. Publs: *Esperienza Giuridica e Politica nel Pensiero
di David Hume*, 1967; "Definitions of Law and Vistas of Justice", *Archiv für Rechts-
und Sozialphilosophie*, 1966; *Visioni della Giustizia e Senso Comune*, 1978; *Filosofia
del Lavoro*, 1977; "The Topicality of Adam Smith's Notion of Sympathy and Judicial
Evaluation", in *Essays on Adam Smith*, 1975; *La Simpatia nella Morale e nel Diritto —
Aspetti del Pensiero di Adam Smith e Orientamenti Attuali*, 1976. Fields: Problems in
the relationship between politics, law and religion.

[87]
BAILEY Paul J
10 November 1947, Canadian. Kammerlweg 11, D-8021 Icking/Isartal, FR Germany.
Degrees: BA; MA (McMaster), 1971. 1969-70 Teaching Assistant, McMaster U; 1970-72
Teacher; 1977 Consultant (part-time), Press and Information Office of the European
Communities, Geneva; 1977- Freelance Researcher and Consultant. Publs: "All-
European Co-operation: the CSCE's Basket Two and the ECE" (with I Bailey-
Wiebecke), *International Journal*, 1977; "ECE and the Belgrade Follow-up Con-
ference" (with I Bailey-Wiebecke), *Aussenpolitik*, 1977. Fields: CSCE; Multinational
corporations; UN/ECE and the representation of the EC at international organizations.

[88]
BAILEY-WIEBECKE Ilka
28 April 1943, German. Kammerlweg II, D-8021 Icking/Isartal, FR Germany. Degrees:
MA (Minnesota), 1969. 1968-69 Teaching Assistant, U of Minnesota; 1970-71 Research
Assistant, PEP; 1971-72 Research Assistant, U of Sussex; 1975-77 International Civil
Servant, United Nations; 1977- Research Associate, Stiftung Wissenschaft und Politik.
Publs: *Changing American Images of the Soviet Union and Germany from 1939 to
1949; A Computerized Content Analysis*, 1969; *The Power of the Purse in the European
Communities* (with D Coombes), 1972; "All-European Co-operation: the CSCE's
Basket Two and the ECE" (with P J Bailey), *International Journal*, 1977;
"Folgewirkungen der KSZE im multilateralen Bereich: die Wirtschaftskommission der
Vereinten Nationen für Europa" (with E M Chossudovsky), in *Grünbuch zu den
Folgewirkungen der KSZE* (J Delbruck *et al* (eds)), 1977; "ECE und die KSZE-
Folgekonferenz in Belgrad" (with P J Bailey), *Aussenpolitik*, 1977; "ECE and the
Belgrade Follow-up Conference" (with P J Bailey), *Aussenpolitik*, 1977. Fields:
EC/CMEA relations; CSCE; UN Economic Commission for Europe (ECE); budgetary
powers of the European Parliament.

[89]
BAKER John Montague
25 September 1950, American. MA (Oxon); MA (Toronto); B Phil (Oxon). U of Bradford; Assistant Lecturer, U Coll, Dublin. Publs: *Utilitarianism and 'Secondary Principles'*, 1971. Fields: Utilitarianism/contractualism; liberalism/socialism; foundations
of political theory; philosophy of social sciences.

[90]
BAKER Robert Hawthorne
11 October 1943, British. Department of Politics, University of Lancaster, Bailrigg, Lancaster, England. Degrees: BA; MA (Wales), 1972. Lecturer, U of Lancaster. Publs: "Origins of Soviet Military Doctrine", *RUSIJ*, 1975; "Understanding Soviet Foreign Policy", *RUSIJ*, 1978. Fields: Concepts of totalitarianism; Soviet defence policy.

[91]
BAKKE Marit
25 January 1942, Norwegian. Katrinebjergvej, 71 4th, 8200 Aarhus N, Denmark. Degrees: Cand. Research Fellow, Inst for Mass Communications Research, U of Oslo; Associate Professor, U of Aarhus. Publs: "Some Theoretical Considerations on Leisure Time Activities", 1976. Fields: Mass media organizations; mass media consumption and leisure time activities.

[92]
BALD Detlef
1 May 1941, German. Lazarettstrasse 9, D-8000 München 19, FR Germany, Degrees: Dr phil. Doctoral thesis: "Deutsch-Ostafrika 1900-1914. Verwaltung, Interessengruppen und wirtschaftliche Erschliessung" (German East-Africa 1900-1914. Administration, Interest Groups and Economy of the Colony). Scientific Director, Federal Armed Forces Inst for Social Research, Munich. Publs: *Deutsch-Ostafrika 1900-1905*; *Wirtschaft und Wissenschaft in der deutschen Kolonialpolitik*, 1971; "Afrikanischer Kampf gegen koloniale Herrschaft. Der Maji-maji Aufstand" , *Militargeschichtliche Mitteilungen*, 1976; *Der deutsche Generalstab 1859-1939*, 1977; *Sozialgeschichte der Rekrutierung des deutschen Offizierkorps*, 1977. Fields: Social history of modern military; defence policy; colonialism in Africa.

[93]
BALJÉ Christiaan Laurens
9 October 1939, Dutch. Lijsterstraat 8, 9363 GL Marum (Gr), The Netherlands. Degrees: Cand Lett; Drs. 1965-1969 Assistant, U of Utrecht; 1969-1972 Official, European Affairs, Dutch Ministry of Foreign Affairs; 1965- Senior Lecturer in Contemporary History, State U of Groningen. Fields: History of European co-operation and unification; East-West relations.

[94]
BALLE Francis
15 June 1939, French. 13 Boulevard des Invalides, 75007 Paris, France. Degrees: Dr. Doctoral thesis: "Journaux et journalistes — évolution d'un marché et d'une profession". Professeur de phil, Maître Assistant, Sorbonne; Maître de conférences, U de Paris 11; Directeur de l'Institut français de Presse. Publs: *Guide de l'étudiant en sociologie* (with J Cazeneuve and A Akoun), 1971; *Profit d'une oeuvre: pour comprendre les médias, MacLuhan*, 1972; *Sociologie de l'information de Textes fondamentaux* (with J G Padioleau), 1973; *Institutions et publics des moyens d'information*, 1973. Fields: Social communication; methods of communication; the media.

[95]
BALLMANN Rolf Alexander Alfred
11 November 1928, German. 6204 Taunusstein 2, Feldbergstr. 7, FR Germany.
Degrees: Dr, 1959. Doctoral thesis: "Die gesellschaftlichen Grenzen einer einmaligen Vermögensabgabe — ein Beitrag zur Problematik des deutschen Lastenausgleiches". 1955-58 Dramaturgist, Theater in Frankfurt; 1958-60 Official in Charge of Press, Parliament of Hessen, Wiesbaden; 1960-73 Author, Director and Editor of documentaries, ZDF; 1974- Manager of Dept of Documentary Drama, ZDF. Publs: *Würzeln der Freiheit*; *Mensch und Maschine*; *homo musicus*; *Zwischen Tradition und Fortschritt*; *Die Sozialwissenschaften* (ed); *Die Geisteswissenschaften* (ed).

[96]
BALSER Frolinde*
6 September 1924, German. 6 Frankfrut am Main 1, Unterlindan 20, FR Germany. Degrees: Dipl (Stuttgart), 1949; Dr phil (Heidelberg), 1957. Doctoral thesis: "Die Anfänge der Erwachsenenbildung in Deutschland in der ersten Hälfte des 19. Jahrhunderts". 1949-53 Librarian; 1957-61 Research, Inst für Sozialgeschichte, U of Heidelberg; 1961-69 Hessischer Landesverband für Erwachsenenbilfung, Pädogogische Arbeitsstelle, Frankfurt am Main; Development of Adult Education Institutions in Hessen; 1964- Member of City Council, Frankfurt am Main. Publs: *Die Anfänge der Erwachsenenbildung in Deutschland in der ersten Hälfte des 19 Jahrhunderts*, 1959; *Aufbruch zur Freiheit. 1863-1963. Wege zu Mitverantwortung und sozialer Sicherheit*, 1963; *Sozial-Demokratie 1848/49-63. Die erste deutsche Arbeiterorganisation 'Allgemeine deutsche Arbeiterverbrüderung' nach der Revolution*, 1965. Fields: Party politics; regional planning and development.

[97]
BALSOM Elizabeth Mary*
11 February 1945, British. London School of Economics and Political Science, Houghton Street, Aldwych, London WC2, England. Degrees: BA; B Litt (Oxon), 1968. 1969-70 Tutorial Assistant, Department of Government, U of Manchester; Research Officer, Centre for International Studies, LSE. Publs: "Jugoslavia's Ways", *Government and Opposition*, 1971. Fields: Eastern Europe; Jugoslav political and social system; British political affairs.

[98]
BANK Jan Theodoor Maria
10 May 1940, Dutch. Maarten Lutherweg 252, 1185 AW Amstelveen, The Netherlands. Degrees: Drs. Assistant, Dept of Modern History, State U of Utrecht. Publs: *History of the Dutch Popular Movement (1945-1951)*. Fields: Decolonization; church and state.

[99]
BANKS David W
2 May 1934, British. Middle Ollerbrook, Edale, Nr Sheffield, S Yorks, England. Degrees: BA. Research Associate, U of Manchester; Executive Officer, Ministry of Agriculture and Fisheries; Head, School of Pol, Manchester Polytechnic. Fields: Land-use planning and politics; environmental politics; British administration.

[100]
BANKS Michael Henry
20 March 1936, British. London School of Economics and Political Science, Houghton Street, Aldwych, London WC2, England. Degrees: BSc; MA (U of Lehigh Bethlehem, Pennsylvania), 1959. 1961-67 Lecturer in International Relations, LSE; 1967-69 Research Associate, Centre for the Analysis of Conflict, U Coll, London; 1970- Lecturer in International Relations, LSE. Publs: articles and papers on peace research, international theory, systems analysis and US foreign policy. Fields: Theoretical aspects of international relations; conflict analysis and peace research.

[101]
BARA Judith Linda
20 March 1946, British. 16 Park Crescent, Elstree, Hertfordshire WD6 3PU, England. Degrees: BSc; MA (Essex), 1968; PhD (London), 1975. Doctoral thesis: "An Ecological Investigation of Electoral Behaviour in Four Commonwealth States". 1968-71 IBM Research Fellow, Inst of Commonwealth Studies, U of London; Senior Lecturer in Pol, Ealing Coll of Higher Education. Publs: "An Ecological Analysis of Party Support in West Malaysia", *Asian Survey*, 1971; "Ethnic Integration in Israel", *Millenium*, 1971; various review articles particularly in *Journal of Comparative and Commonwealth Studies*. Fields: The politics of the social gap in Israel; politics of development.

[102]
BARBANO Farneti Paolo*
15 December 1922, Italian. Corso M D'Azeglio 76, 10126 Torino, Italy. Degrees: Laureato in Giurisprudenza (Turin), 1947; Libero Docente in Sociologia, 1956. 1957-Professore incaricato di Sociologia, U of Turin; 1968- Professore ordinario di Sociologia, Faculty of Pol Sci, U of Turin. Publs: *Teoria e Ricerca nella Sociologia Contemporania,* 1955; *Partiti e Pubblica opinione nella Campagna elettorale,* 1961; *Sociologia della politica,* 1961; "Transformaciones y Tipos de la Teoria Sociologica contemporanea", in *Questiones de Sociologia* (ed Herner), 1971. Fields: Political theory.

[103]
BARBER James Peden
6 November 1931, British. 16 St Andrews Road, Bedford, England. Degrees: MA; PhD (Cambridge). Doctoral thesis: "Relations Between the British and the Pastoral Tribes of North East Uganda". Lecturer, U New South Wales; Lecturer, U of Exeter. Professor of Pol Sci, U of London. Publs: *Rhodesia, the Road to Rebellion,* 1967; *Imperial Frontier,* 1968; *South Africa's Foreign Policy 1945-1970,* 1973; *European Community: Vision and Reality* (ed), 1973; *The Nature of Foreign Policy* (ed), 1974; *Who Makes British Foreign Policy?,* 1976. Fields: International politics; British government; government and politics in South Africa.

[104]
BARBER John Douglas
8 October 1944, British. 90 Bournbrook Road, Birmingham B29 7BU, England. Degrees: BA: PhD (Cambridge), 1972. Doctoral thesis: "The Bolshevization of Soviet Historiography 1928-32". 1967-72 Research Fellow, Jesus Coll, Cambridge; 1972-76 Assistant Lecturer in Russian History, U of Cambridge; 1974-76 Fellow and Director of Studies in History, King's Coll, Cambridge; Research Fellow in Russian Soc History, Centre for Russian and East European Studies, U of Birmingham. Publs: "Stalin's Letter to the Editors of *Proletarskaya Revolyutuiza*", *Soviet Studies,* 1976. Fields: The Soviet working class; the Soviet intelligentsia.

[105]
BARBROOK Alexander Thomas
20 August 1927, British. 2 Leycroft Close, Canterbury, Kent, England. Degrees: BA; PhD (Loughborough), 1969. Doctoral thesis: "Voting Trends and Voting Patterns in the State of Massachusetts". 1954-61 Lecturer in Adult Education, U of Nottingham; 1961-66 Lecturer in Pol, U of Loughborough; Senior Lecturer in Pol and Government, U of Kent; 1975- Director of School of Continuing Education, U of Kent. Publs: *God Save the Commonwealth: An Electoral History of Massachusetts*, 1972; *Patterns of Political Behaviour*, 1975. Fields: American politics, federal and state; political behaviour; pressure groups.

[106]
BARING Arnulf Martin*
8 May 1932, German. Berlin 38, Ahrenshooper Zeile 64, FR Germany. Degrees: Dr jur (Free U Berlin), 1958; MA (Columbia), 1957. Doctoral thesis: "Der Vertreter des offentlichen Interesses". 1962-64 Political Ed, *Westdeutscher Rundfunk*, Cologne; 1964-65 Research Associate, Deutsche Gessellschaft für Auswärtige Politik, Bonn; 1966-68 Lecturer, Free U of Berlin; 1968-69 Research Fellow, Center for International Affairs, Harvard U, Cambridge, Mass; Professor of Pol Sci, John F Kennedy-Institut für Amerika-Studien, Free U of Berlin; Otto-Suhr-Institut, Free U of Berlin. Publs: *Charles de Gaulle, Grösse und Grenzen*, 1963; *Der 17. Juni 1953*, 1966; *Aussen-politik in Adenauers Kanzlerdemokratie*, 1969. Fields: German foreign policy since 1949; decision-making process in foreign policy; interrelationship of domestic and foreign policies; elite studies; American foreign policy since 1945; the French political system.

[107]
BARKER Anthony Philip
19 July 1938, British. Department of Government, University of Essex, Wivenhoe Park, Colchester CO4 3SQ, Essex, England. Degrees: BA; MA (Nottingham), 1961. 1961-62 Post-graduate studies, U of California at Stanford and Berkeley; 1962-65 Assistant Lecturer in Pol, U of Bristol; 1965-67 Lecturer in Pol, U of Bristol; 1967- Lecturer, Senior Lecturer, Reader in Government, U of Essex. Publs: *The Member of Parliament and his Information* (with M Rush), 1970; *Strategy and Style in Local Community Relations*, 1975; *Public Policy and Private Interests* (with D C Hague and W J M Mackenzie (eds)), 1975; *The Local Amenity Movement* (with Civic Trust), 1976. Fields: British politics; UK-US urban politics; public participation; environmental policy implementation; quasi-government studies.

[108]
BARKER Rodney Steven
24 April 1942, British. London School of Economics, Houghton Street, London WC2A 2AE, England. Degrees: BA; MA (Cambridge), 1968; PhD (LSE), 1968. Lecturer, Dept of Pol Theory and Government, U Coll, Swansea; 1967- Lecturer in Government, LSE. Publs: *Studies in Opposition* (ed and contributor), 1971; *Education and Politics, 1900-51: A Study of the Labour Party*, 1972. Fields: British politics; political ideas.

[109]
BARKER William Raymond*
26 April 1932, British. 10 South Close, Tranmere Park, Guiseley, Nr Leeds, Yorkshire, England. Degrees: BA. 1956-65 Senior Talks Producer, BBC; 1965- Lecturer in Pol, U of Bradford. Publs: *War and the United States*. Fields: Soviet-American relations, 1917-present.

[110]
BARNES Anthony John Lane*
9 April 1937, British. 139 Punch Croft, New Ash Green, Dartford, Kent, England. Degrees: BA; MA (Cambridge). 1961-64 Drosier Fellowship for Research in History, Gonville and Caius Coll, Cambridge; 1964- Assistant Lecturer, Lecturer in Pol Sci, LSE. Publs: *Baldwin. A Biography* (with R K Middlemas), 1969; "Teaching and Research in Contemporary British History", in *Contemporary History in Europe* (D C Watt (ed)). Fields: Papers of David 1st Earl Beatty; biographies of Beatty and Harold Macmillan; local politics in Greater London; party organization in Britain; inter-war political history of Britain; effects of the welfare state.

[111]
BARRAL Pierre
16 October 1926, French. 6 rue de Manège, 54 Nancy, France. Degrees: Dr ès lettres (Sorbonne), 1959. 1949-60 Professeur, Lycée de Grenoble; 1960- Professeur, U de Nancy 11. Publs: *Le Département de l'Isère sous la IIIème République*, 1962; *Les Périer dans l'Isère au XIXème siecle*, 1964; *Les agrariens français, de Méline à Pisani*, 1968; *Les fondateurs de la IIIème République*, 1968. Fields: Historical electoral sociology; regional political life in France under the Third Republic; history of agriculture and agricultural policies; comparative politics.

[112]
BARREA Jean
27 October 1939, Belgian. 25 rue de l'Angélique, 1348 Louvain-la-Neuve, Belgium. Degrees: Dr en droit (Louvain), 1964; Lic en sci pol (Louvain), 1965; Dr en sci pol (Louvain), 1969. Doctoral thesis: "L'intégration politique externe". Aspirant au Fonds National (Belge) de la Recherche Scientifique; Assistant Professor, U de Louvain. Publs: *L'intégration politique externe*, 1969. Fields: International relations; theory of international relations.

[113]
BARRILLON Raymond Pierre Emile
7 December 1921, French. 13 rue Ernest Cresson, 75014 Paris, France. Degrees: Lic ès lettres. Chef du service politique, *Le Monde*; Chroniqueur politique, *Le Midi Libre*. Publs: *Le cas Paris-Soir*, 1959; *La vie politique en France, guide d'instruction civique*, 1962; *La gauche française en mouvement*, 1967; *Servan-Schreiber pour quoi faire?*, 1971; *Dictionnaire de la Constitution* (co-author), 1976.

[114]
BARTELOUS Jean*
1 April 1914, Belgian. 155 rue Berkentral, 1060 Brussels, Belgium. Degrees: Lic en sci pol et diplomatiques (Louvain), 1943; Dr en droit. Avocat; Senateur; 1er Echevin de la commune de Forest; Conseiller communal à Forest. Publs: "Trente ans de legislation scolaire, 1884-1914; Aux origines de la question scolaire en France", *La Revue Nouvelle*, 1952.

[115]
BARTELS Willem Jan Bruno*
1 June 1937, Dutch. Van Haapstraat 60, Nijmegen, The Netherlands. Degrees: Dipl Sociology (U of Munster), 1964; Dip International Relations (Inst of Social Studies, The Hague), 1965; Drs (U of Nijmegen), 1967. Assistant, Inst of Pol Sci, and Assistant, Peace Research Centre, U of Nijmegen. Publs: "Church and Atomic Weapons", in *Keur uit de Kerkeliike pers*, 1964; "Politics and Power", in *Massamedia en Politiek*, 1969; "Peace throughout the United Nations?", *Cahiers voor Vredesvraagsrukken*, 1970; "Deterrence and Peace", in *25 Jaar Verenigde Naties*, 1971. Fields: International integration versus conflict; the role of the United Nations in integration and security the Middle-East conflict.

[116]
BARTHOL Joseph*
12 June 1944, Belgian. 109 the Grand, 6790 Athus, Belgium. Degrees: Agrégé de sci pol et sociales (Brussels), 1971. Doctoral thesis: "Les relations des communautés européennes avec les organisations internationales". 1971 Maître de conférence, Ecole normale à Virton; 1972- Attaché à la direction, Fondation Universitaire Luxembourgeoise, Arlon. Fields: Belgian elections; regionalism in Belgium; cultural history of Walloon regions; theory of power.

[117]
BARTOLINI Stefano
22 January 1953, Italian. Via Barbieri 5, Florence, Italy. Degrees: Laurea in Pol Sci (Florence), 1976. 1976- Researcher, Dept of Pol and Soc Sci, European U, Florence. Publs: "Interpretazioni Politiche del Gaullismo", *Il Mulino*, 1975; "Per una Analisi dei Rapporti tra Partiti Comunisti e Socialisti in Italia e Francia", *Rivista Italiana di Scienza Politica*, 1976; "Tensioni nei Partiti e nelle Alleanze: i Rapporti tra Comunisti e Socialisti in Francia (1972-1977)", *Il Mulino*, 1977. Fields: European political parties; European socialism and communism; French political system.

[118]
BASSAND Michel
16 February 1938, Swiss. 41 Rue de Loëx, 1213 Onex, Switzerland. Degrees: Dr. Doctoral thesis: "Urbanisation et pouvoir politique. Le cas de la Suisse". Professeur, Dept de Sociologie, U de Genève; Professeur de Sociologie, l'Ecole Polytechnique fédérale de Lausanne. Publs: *Les Ambiguïtés de la Démocratie locale* (with J P Fragnière), 1976; *Jeunesse et société* (with J Kellerhals *et al*), 1971; *Urbanisation et pouvoir politique*, 1974; *Développement urbain et logement*, 1974; *Familles urbaines et fécondité* (with J Kellerhals), 1975; "Un Essai de Démocratie Urbaine" (with C Lalive and P Thoma), 1976. Fields: Urban and rural sociology; political sociology.

[119]
BASSO Jacques Antoine*
4 July 1933, French. Villa Grande Vue, 23 Boulevard de Cambrai, 06 Nice, France. Degrees: Dr en droit (Nice); Lic ès lettres (Aix en Provence). Collaborateur technique de l'enseignement supérieur; Assistant du Doyen Trotabas; Chargé de cours, Faculté de Lettres et de Sci Humaines; Maître Assistant, Faculté de Droit et des Sci Econ, U de Nice. Publs: *Les elections législatives dans le départment des Alpes-Maritimes de 1860-1939 (Elements de sociologie électorale)*, 1968; *La Co-opération internationale culturelle, scientifique et technique* (Bulletin de documentation et d'information). Fields: Elites; pressure groups; electoral behaviour; specialized institutions in international cooperation.

[120]
BASTIDA Francisco Jose
20 January 1951, Spanish. Arda Madrid 159 7° – 1°, Barcelona 28, Spain. Degrees: Dr in Law. Doctoral thesis: "Analysis of the Political Ideology of the Supreme Court of Spain 1964-74". Assistant Professor of Constitutional Law, Dept of Pol Sci, U of Barcelona. Publs: *The Political Ideology of the Supreme Court of Spain (Study of its Jurisprudence 1964-74)*. Fields: Constitutional law; political science.

[121]
BATTISTA Anna Maria*
21 April 1934, Italian. Via Arno 88, Rome, Italy. Degrees: Libero Docente di Storia delle Dottrine Politiche (Rome). Assistente di ruolo di Storia delle Dottrine Politiche, U of Rome; Incaricato di Storia delle Dottrine Politiche, Facoltà di Lettere, U of Rome. Publs: *Alle Origini del Pensiero Politico Libertino. Montaigne e Charron*, 1966. Fields: French absolutism considered in connection with the rise of scepticism, epicureism, stoicism in the 17th century, and with the rise of the influence of Aristotle; the logical structure of the 'Democracy in America' of Tocqueville.

[122]
BAUER Rudolph
28 April 1939, German. Vor dem Steintor 57, D-2800 Bremen 1, FR Germany. Degrees: Dr phil. Doctoral thesis: "Bundestag und Kulturpolitik". Substitute Professor, U of Giessen; Assistant Professor, U of Bremen. Publs: *Wohlfahrtsverbände in der Bundesrepublik Deutschland*, 1978. Fields. Social work; social politics, institutions of social welfare and of welfare administration in industrial and undeveloped countries, especially in China; theories of deviance.

[123]
BAUM Hans Josef
9 September 1950, German. Eupener Weg 5, 4400 Münster, FR Germany. Degrees: Dipl. Verwaltungswissenschaftler, Zentralinstitut für Raumplanung, U of Münster. Fields: Public administration; problems of federalism; local government politics; theories of state (post capitalistic state or post industrial state?); implementation and evaluation of political programmes.

[124]
BAUMANN Elisabeth
29 May 1951, Swiss. 66 Boulevard St. Georges, Genève, Switzerland. Degrees: Lic ès science politique. Assistant, U of Genova; Assistant, U of California; Assistant, U of Genova. Fields: Socialization; public administration; quantitative methods.

[125]
BAXTER Robert James*
9 July 1945, British. Department of Political Science, The Queen's University, Belfast 7, N Ireland. Degrees: BA; MA (Oxon); D Phil (Oxon). Doctoral thesis: "The Liverpool Labour Party, 1918-63". Lecturer in Pol Sci, The Queen's U, Belfast. Fields: Party politics in large UK cities; voting behaviour.

[126]
BAY Aase*
9 April 1942, Danish. Institut for Historie og Samfundsvidenskab, Odense Universitet, Niels Bohrs Allé, DK-5000 Odense, Denmark. Degrees: Cand mag (Aarhus), 1969; 1968-70 Assistant, U of Aarhus; 1969 Assistant Professor in History of Antiquity, U of Odense; 1970-71 Danish Academy in Rome; 1971- Assistant Professor, U of Odense. Publs: *Det romerske kejserdømme*, 1970; *Problemvurdering og prioritering i historie* (with S Mørch), 1970. Fields: The administration of the early Roman Empire.

[127]
BAYLIS John Bruford
27 March 1946, British. 1 Glanstewi Penrhyncoch, Aberystwyth, Dyfed, Wales. Degrees: BA; MSc. Lecturer in International Pol, Inst of Extension Studies, U of Liverpool; Lecturer in International Pol, U of Wales, Aberystwyth. Publs: *Contemporary Strategy Theories and Policies* (with K Booth, J Garnett and P Williams), 1975; *British Defence Policy in a Changing World*, 1977. Fields: British defence policy; Anglo-American defence relations; strategic studies; Soviet foreign and domestic politics.

[128]
BEALEY Frank William
31 August 1922, British. Department of Politics, Kings College, University of Aberdeen, AB9 2UB, Scotland. Degrees: BSc. 1950-51 Research Assistant, Passfield Trust, LSE; 1951-52 Extra-Mural Lecturer, U of Manchester; 1952-64 Lecturer in Pol, U of Keele; 1964- Professor of Pol, U of Aberdeen. Publs: *Labour and Politics* (with H Pelling), 1958; *Constituency Politics* (with J Blondel and W P McCann), 1965; *Social and Political Thought of the British Labour Party*, 1970; *The Post Office Engineering Union*, 1976. Fields: Community politics; values underlying political opinion and political behaviour.

[129]
BEATTIE Alan James
13 June 1938, British. London School of Economics and Political Science, Houghton Street, Aldwych, London WC2, England. Degrees: BSc. Lecturer, Senior Lecturer in Pol Sci, LSE. Publs: *English Party Politics 1860-1906*; *English Party Politics 1906-70*, 1970; "Neville Chamberlain", in *British Prime Ministers of the Twentieth Century*, 1972; "Coalitions", in *Adversary Politics* (S E Finer (ed)), 1975. Fields: English constitutional theory since the 17th century, with special reference to political parties; the history of British politics since the 1880s, with particular emphasis on the working of political institutions.

[130]
BEAUFAYS Jean
30 July 1940, Belgian, 2 rue Ch Magnette, B-4000 Liège, Belgium. Degrees: Dr en sci pol et diplomatiques. Doctoral thesis: "Les partis catholiques en Belgique et aux Pays-Bas. 1918-1958". Aspirant Fonds National de la Recherche Scientifique; Chargé de recherche au Centre Interuniversitaire de Droit Public; Chargé de cours associé, U de Liège; Chargé de cours, Hautes Etudes Commerciales, Liège. Publs: *Les partis politiques en Belgique et aux Pays-Bas, 1918-1958*. Fields: Federalism; regionalism; elections; political parties.

[131]
BEAUTE Jean
10 May 1927, French. 118 Avenue de Paris, 94300 Vincennes, France. Degrees: Lic en droit, 1951; DES, 1953; DES, 1954; DES sci pol, 1957; Dr en droit, 1959; Dr en sci pol, 1970. Doctoral thesis: "Le droit de pétition dans les territoires sous tutelle"; "Les grands juristes anglais: Sir Edward Coke (1552-1634), ses idées politiques et constitutionnelles aux origines de la démocratie occidentale moderne", 1978. 1959-65 Chargé de cours, Faculté de Droit de Poitiers; 1965-67 Chef de la Revue juridique française sur l'Afghanistan; Maître-assistant, U de Droit, Econ et Sci Soc de Paris 11. Publs: *La République populaire de Chine et le droit international*, 1964; "Liberté de la presse et sécurité nationale aux Etats-Unis à propos de l'arrêt de la cour Suprême relatif aux documents du Pentagone du 30 Juin 1971", *RJP*, 1974. Fields: Parliamentary and constitutional problems and practice in the US, Britain and France; judicial power and the protection of liberties in the US, Britain and France; international law.

[132]
BECARUD Jean
1 April 1925, French. 77 rue Bonaparte, 75006 Paris, France. Degrees: Dipl (IEP); Dr. Doctoral thesis: "Géographie électorale du Parti communiste français (1920-39)". Directeur de la bibliothèque de Sénat; Chargé de cours, U de Paris IV. Publs: *La 2ème République Espagnole*; *Anarchistes d'Espagne* (with G Lapouge); *Noblesse et représentation parlementaire: les députés nobles de 1871 à 1966*. Fields: History of political life in Spain; electoral sociology and parliamentary history.

[133]
BECK Antony Richard
21 September 1940, British. 7 Grove Park, Liverpool L8 OT2, England. Degrees: BA. 1965- Lecturer, Dept of Pol Theory and Inst, U of Liverpool. Fields: Politics and literature; political philosophy.

[134]
BECKER Frans
28 May 1948, Dutch. Ouddiemerlaan 541, Diemen, The Netherlands. Degrees: Drs (Amsterdam). Inst of Pol Sci, U of Amsterdam. Publs: *Bedrijven in eigen Beheer*. *Kolonies and Produktieve Associaties in Nederland 1901-1958* (with J Frieswijk), 1976. Fields: Social history; political sociology; state theory; political philosophy.

[135]
BECKERS Frans G J M
27 March 1941, Dutch. Narcisstraat 30, 2841 AW Moordrecht, The Netherlands. Degrees: Drs. Municipality of Rotterdam. Publs: *Lokaal Bestuur in Limburg*; *Het Democratisch Centrum Nederland — Documentatie van een streven naar Partijvernieuwing*; various articles on Dutch politics and local government. Fields: Local politics and local government; public administration.

[136]
BECKMAN Björn Olaf
6 February 1944, Swedish. Sunnanväg 2B, S-222 26 Lund, Sweden. Degrees: PhD (Lund). Doctoral thesis: "Regional Administration and Regional Planning". Research Assistant, U of Lund. Publs: *Regional Administration and Regional Planning*. Fields: Regional planning; decentralization, local government and urban studies; the politics of France; the politics of Japan.

[137]
BECQUART-LECLERCQ Jeannette
22 March 1934, French. 279 Avenue de Lattre de Tassigny, St André-les-Lille 59350, France. Degrees: PhD (Sorbonne). Doctoral thesis: "Le problème du pouvoir local". Dept of Soc and Urban Affairs, U of Wisconsin; Maître Assistant, Lille. Publs: *Paradoxes du pouvoir local*, 1976; "Legitimité et pouvoir local", *Revue Française de Science Politique*, 1977; *Power, Paradigms and Community Research* (contributor) (Libert (ed)), 1977; *The Organization and its Environment* (contributor) (Karpik (ed)), 1978. Fields: Comparative research on local power.

[138]
BEDARIDA Francois
14 March 1926. French. 13 rue Jacob, 75005 Paris, France. Degrees: Agrégé d'histoire, 1949; MA (Oxon). Attaché de recherches, CNRS; 1961-66 Assistant, Sorbonne; 1966-70 Directeur, Maison Française d'Oxford; 1971- Visiting Fellow, All Souls Coll, Oxford; 1971- Professor, IEP, Paris. Fields: British social and political history; 19th and 20th century.

[139]
BEITH Alan James*
1943, British. Department of Politics, The University, Newcastle-upon-Tyne NE1 7RU, England. Degrees: MA (Oxford); B Litt (Oxford). Lecturer in Politics, U of Newcastle-upon-Tyne. Publs: "The Press", in *British General Election, 1964* (by D E Butler and A King), 1965; "The Council and the Press", *New Society*, 1965. Fields: Public administration; local government; Scandinavian studies.

[140]
BELL Coral Mary*
30 March 1923, British. London School of Economics and Political Science, Houghton Street, Aldwych, London WC2, England. Degrees: BA; MSc (London), 1954; PhD (London), 1962. 1945-51 Australian Diplomatic Service; 1952-56 Royal Institute of International Affairs, 1956-61 U of Manchester; 1961-64 U of Sydney; 1965- Reader in International Relations, U of London. Publs: *Survey of International Affairs for 1954*, 1957; *Negotiations from Strength: A Study in the Policy of Power*, 1965; *Europe Without Britain* (ed), 1963; *The Debatable Alliance: An Essay in Anglo-American Relations*, 1964; *The Balance of Power in Asia*, 1968; *The Conventions of Crisis*, 1971. Fields: Crisis management; Asian and Pacific politics; British and American foreign policy.

[141]
BELLANY Ian
21 February 1941, British. Newsham House, Barton Road, Lancaster, England. Degrees: BA; Dr phil (Oxon), 1966. 1965-68 Assistant Principal, Foreign Office, London; 1968-70 Research Fellow in International Relations, Australian National U; 1970-Lecturer, Senior Lecturer in Pol, U of Lancaster. Publs: *Australia in the Nuclear Age: National Defence and National Development*, 1972. Fields: Mathematical approaches to strategic problems and disarmament; strategic thought and its evolution; arms control and disarmament issues; defence procurement.

[142]
BELOFF Max
2 July 1913, British. University College of Buckingham, Buckinghamshire, England. Degrees: MA (Oxon), 1939; D Litt (Oxon), 1974. 1939-47 Assistant Lecturer in Modern History, U of Manchester; 1946-56 Reader in the Comparative Study of Inst, U of Oxford; 1956-57 Fellow in European Studies, Nuffield Coll, Oxford; 1957- Gladstone Professor of Government and Public Administration, U of Oxford, and Fellow, All Soul's Coll, Oxford. Publs: *The Age of Absolution 1660-1815*, 1954; *The Great Powers*, 1959; *American Federal Government*, 1959; *On the Track of Tyranny* (ed), 1960; *L'Europe du XIX et XX Siecles* (joint ed), 1961 and 1968; *New Dimensions in Foreign Policy*, 1961; *The United States and the Unity of Europe*, 1963; *The Balance of Power*, 1968; *The Future of British Foreign Policy*, 1969; *Imperial Sunset*, 1969; *The Intellectual in Politics*, 1970. Fields: The relationship of Britain's overseas and European interests since 1921 and their impact upon British society and government.

[143]
BENETON Philippe-Renaud
12 August 1946, French. 20 rue du Moulin Vert, 75014 Paris, France. Degrees: Dr. Doctoral thesis: "Histoire de mots, culture et civilisation". Assistant de sci pol, IEP Paris; Maître de conférences, U de Rennes I. Publs: *Culture, contribution à l'histoire d'un mot*, 1973; "Jacques Maritain et l'Action Française", *Revue française de Science Politique*, 1973; "Discours sur la genèse des inégalites dans les sociétés occidentales contemporaines", *RFSP*, 1975; *Histoire de mots, cultures et civilisations*, 1975; *Quelques considérations sur la mobilité sociale en France*, 1975; "Niveaux d'instruction et comportements politiques", *Information sur les sciences sociales*, 1977; "Biens collectifs, désertion, protestation et effets pervers", *Analyses de la SEDEIS*, 1978; "Les frustrations de l'égalité" *Archives européennes de sociologie*, 1978. Fields: Sociology of inequality; history of political ideas.

[144]
BENEWICK Robert Julian
23 August 1932, American. 27 Guildford Street, Brighton, East Sussex BN1 3LS, England. Degrees: BS; MA (Ohio), 1958; PhD (Manchester), 1963. Doctoral thesis: "The British Fascist Movement". 1961-62 Research Fellow, Inst of Soc and Econ Research, U of the West Indies; 1966-67 Visiting Lecturer, Smith Coll, Northampton, Mass, USA; Lecturer, Dept of Pol Studies, U of Hull. Reader in Pol, U of Sussex. Publs: *Readings on British Government and Politics* (with R E Dowse (eds)), 1968; *Political Violence and Public Order*, 1969; *Direct Action and Democratic Representation* (ed), 1971; *The British Fascist Movement*, 1972; *Knowledge and Belief in Politics* (with R N\Berki and B Parekh (eds)), 1973; plus various articles in *The Politics of Civil Liberties*, *The National Council for Civil Liberties*. Fields: Pluralism and pressure group theory; the political uses of violence; democratic theory; pressure groups; civil liberties; Chinese politics.

[145]
BENNETT Anthea
28 July 1932, British. Basement Flat, 33 Gloucester Crescent, London NW1, England. Degrees: BA. Assistant Principal and Principal, HM Treasury; Research Officer, Higher Education Research Unit, LSE; Lecturer in Government, LSE. Publs: "Royal Historical Society: Annual Bibliography of British and Irish History: Publications of 1975" (ed). Fields: Cabinet Committees 1919-39; history of British politics, 1660-1922; the Cabinet in the 20th century.

[146]
BENOIT Francis Paul
13 September 1921, French. 25 rue Lauriston, 75016 Paris, France. Degrees: Dr en droit. Doctoral thesis: "Les contrats passés au nom des sociétés anonymes en formation"; "La responsabilité de la puissance publique du fait de la police administrative". 1947-48 Professeur, Faculté française de Droit, Beyrouth; 1948-72 Professeur, Faculté de Droit, Rennes; 1972- Professeur, U de Droit, Econ et Sci Soc, Paris 11. Publs: "La responsabilité de la puissance publique", *Jurisclasseur administratif*, 1952-60; *Le droit administratif français*, 1968; "Collectivités locales", *Encyclopédia*, 1971. Fields: Political ideologies, especially liberalism (economic and political); study of critical survey on liberalism.

[147]
BENTHEM VAN DEN BERGH Godfried*
27 January 1933, Dutch. Institute of Social Studies, Molenstraat 27, The Hague, The Netherlands. Degrees: Drs (Leiden), 1958. 1960-64, 1966-67 Research Associate, Europa Inst, U of Leiden; 1964-65 Visiting Scholar, Center for International Affairs, U of Harvard; 1965-66 Research Associate, Inst of Social Studies, U of California at Berkeley; 1966- Senior Lecturer, Inst of Social Studies, The Hague. Publs: *De Associatie van Afrikaanse Staten met de Europese Economische Gemeenschap*, 1962; *Vietnam en het Westen*. 1967; *De Ideologie van het Westen*, 1969. Fields: International political dimensions of the development of societies.

[148]
BERG Elias Fridtjuv
10 February 1923, Swedish. Barrstigen 11, 161 35 Bromma, Sweden. Degrees: Fil lic (Uppsala), 1959; Fil dr (Göteborg), 1965. Doctoral thesis: "Democracy and the Majority Principle: A Study in Twelve Contemporary Political Theories". Part-time teaching, U of Uppsala and U of Göteborg; Lecturer and Docent in Pol Sci, U of Stockholm. Publs: *The Historical Thinking of Charles A. Beard*, 1957; *Democracy and the Majority Principle*, 1965. Fields: Political theory, primarily normative and historical, some empirical.

[149]
BERG Ole Trond
3 February 1944, Norwegian. Gellinesvei 31, Oslo 6, Norway. Degrees: MA (Oslo), 1968. 1970-74 University Fellow of Pol Sci; 1974- Assistant Professor in Pol Sci, U of Oslo. Publs: *Stat og Samfunn*, 1975. Fields: Health policy and politics; comparative public policy; comparative political systems.

[150]
BERGESEN Helge Ole
29 September 1949, Norwegian. Lindvedparken 62, 5260 Odense S, Denmark. Degrees: Cand Mag (Oslo); MA (Oslo). Lecturer, U of Odense. Publs: *When Interdependence Doesn't Work. A Study of World Food Politics*, 1977. Fields: North-South relations in general; transfer of technology to developing countries; international resource regimes, in particular ocean management.

[151]
BERGHAHN Volker
15 February 1938, German. 24 Binswood Avenue, Leamington Spa, England. Degrees: MA (North Carolina); PhD (London); Habilitation (Mannheim). Doctoral thesis: "Stahlhelm BDF, 1918-1935". Fellow, DFG; Lecturer, Researcher, U of East Anglia; Professor of History, U of Warwick. Publs: *Stahlhelm BDF, 1918-35*, 1966; *Der Tirpitz Plan*, 1971; *Rüstung und Machtpolitik*, 1973; *Germany and the Approach of War in 1914*, 1973; *Militarismus*, 1975. Fields: Pre-war German history; pressure groups in post-1945 Germany and Britain.

[152]
BERGLUND Sten Erik Artur
10 August 1947, Swedish. Terrängägen 36, 902 35 Umeå 4, Sweden. Degrees: Dr, 1973. Doctoral thesis: "The Mass Party as a Communications System. A Step towards Empirical Analysis" (in Swedish). Assistant, Research Assistant, Docent and Universitetslektor, Dept of Pol Sci, U of Umeå. Publs: *The Scandinavian Party Systems. A Comparative Study* (with Lindströn), 1977; *Det Svenska Partiäsendet*, 1978. Fields: Political parties; party systems; electoral behaviour; organizational theory and public policy.

[153]
BERGQUIST Mats Fingal Thorwald
5 September 1938, Swedish. Utrikesdepartementet, Box 16121, 103 23 Stockholm 16, Sweden. Degrees: Fil mag (Lund), 1960; Fil lic (Lund), 1964; Fil dr (Lund), 1970. Doctoral thesis: "Sweden and the EEC. A Study of Four Schools of Thought and their Views on Swedish Common Market Policy, 1961-62" (in Swedish). 1970- Assistant Professor of Pol Sci, U of Lund; 1964- Ministry for Foreign Affairs; 1976- Counsellor (Pol Affairs), Swedish Embassy, Washington DC. Publs: *Sverige och EEC. En Statsvetenskaplig Studie av fyra Åsiktsriktningars syn på Svensk Marknadspolitik 1961-62*, 1970; *Säkerhetspolitiska Framtidsalternativ* (co-author), 1974; *Krig och Surrogatkrig*, 1976. Fields: American post-war foreign policy; foreign policy and defence planning; methodology; East-West relations.

[154]
BERG-SCHOLOSSER Dirk
10 December 1943, German. Auinger Strasse 13, 8031 Steinebach/Woerthsee, FR Germany. Degrees: Dipl Volkswirtschaft (Munich), 1968; Dr Oec Publ (Munich), 1971. 1969-70 Research Assistant, U of California at Berkeley; 1970-71 Research Associate, Inst for Econ Research, Munich; 1971-73 Assistant Professor, Pädagogische Hochschule Rheinland, Aachen; 1975 Assistant Professor, U of Augsburg. Publs: *Politische Kultur*, 1972; *Die politischen Probleme der Dritten Welt* (ed), 1972; *Einführung in die Politikwissenschaft* (with H Maier and T Stammen), 1974. Fields: Comparative politics; political behaviour; African studies.

[155]
BERLIA Georges*
18 December 1911, French. 15 rue de Saint Simon, Paris VIIème, France. Degrees: Dr (Paris). Doctoral thesis: "Droit International Public". Professeur, Faculté de Droit and Sci Econ de Paris; Professeur, U de Paris-Droit, Econ et Sci Soc. Publs: *Droit international public*, 1938.

[156]
BERLIN Isaiah*
4 June 1909, British. Headington House, Old Headington, Oxford, England. Degrees:
MA (Oxon). Fields: Political theory; history of social and political ideas.

[157]
BERMBACH Udo
28 March 1938, German. Schwarzpappelweg 7, 2000 Hamburg 65, FR Germany.
Degrees: Dr phil (Heidelberg). Doctoral thesis: "Vorformen parlamentarischer
Kabinettsbildung in Deutschland". 1966-68 Assistant, U of Heidelberg; 1969-71 Wiss
Oberrat, U of Hamburg; 1971- Professor of Pol Sci, U of Hamburg; Publs: *Vorformen
parlamentarischer Kabinettsbildung in Deutschland*, 1967; *Sozialistischer Pluralismus*
(with F Nusdecher), 1973; *Theorie und Praxis direkter Demokratie*, 1973. Fields:
History of political ideas; modern political philosophy and theory; history of German
parliamentariansm.

[158]
BERNARD Francois Didier
21 December 1933, French. 11 rue Cernuschi, 75017 Paris, France. Degrees: Dipl
(Paris). Doctoral thesis: "The Administrative Structures of the 'National Coal
Board, ,,. Direction Générale du Affaires Culturelles au Ministre des Affaires
Etrangères; Rapporteur au Conseil Constitutionnel; Cabinet du Ministère de la Santé
Publique; Conseil d'Etat, Paris. Publs: *Structures administratives du National Coal
Board*; *Eléments d'une politique d'exportation du Cognac; Recents développements du
droit Français en matière de populations nomades; Le Conseil d'Etat et les changements
de nom*. Fields: Constitutional law; public liberties.

[159]
BERNARD Jean Pierre
11 June 1940, French. Tour Mt Blanc 19A, 15 Boulevard Maréchal Leclerc, 38000
Grenoble, France. Degrees: Dipl (IEP); Lic; Dr. Doctoral thesis: "Communisme et
littérature - Le parti communiste français et les problèmes littéraires 1921-1930". Publs:
Le parti communiste français et la question littéraire 1921-1939, 1972. Fields: Theory of
ideologies; literature and politics; French communism.

[160]
BERNARD Stéphan
31 August 1916, Belgian. 49 rue Langeveld, 1180 Brussels, Belgium. Degrees: Dr Law
(Free U of Brussels), 1940. 1956-59 Directeur d'enquête de la Dotation Carnegie pour la
Paix Internationale; 1971, 1973 Summer Seminar, U of Ottawa; Professeur, U Libre de
Bruxelles; Directeur de recherche, Inst de Sociologie, U de Bruxelles; Directeur du Centre de Sociologie Politique, Inst de Sociologie. Publs: *Le Conflit Franco-Marocain*,
1963; *The Franco-Moroccan Conflict*, 1968; *Les attitudes politiques en Démocratie —
Esquisse d'une Typologie*, 1968. Fields: Democratic regimes; influence and negotiation;
decision-making; political control; pollution; traffic accidents; university problems;
sociological aspects of the world crisis; European integration; arms races and disarmament; the political factor in models of world economy; European security.

[161]
BERNDTSON Erkki Ralf
30 November 1947, Finnish. Meritullinkatu 13 C 83, 00170 Helsinki 17, Finland. Degrees: Cand Soc Sci (Helsinki), 1970. 1969-71 Co-ed, *Politiikka*; Assistant, Inst of Pol Sci, U of Helsinki. Publs: "Emansipatorisesta Tiedonintressistä ja sen Suhteesta Politiikan Tutkimukseen", *Politiikka*, 1971; "Political Science in the Era of Post-Behaviouralism: The Need for Self-reflection", *Scandinavian Political Studies*, 1975. Fields: Theory of the state; history of political science; Japan.

[162]
BERNOUX Philippe
25 September 1927, French. 12 Montée du Belvédère, 69300 Caluire, France. Degrees: Dr. Doctoral thesis: "Une organisation patronale: le Centre des Jeunes Dirigeants d'Entreprise". Responsable de recherches, Centre Economie et Humanisme; Maître-Assistant en sociologie des organisations, Inst National des Sciences Appliquées, Lyon. Publs: *Trois ateliers d'O S*, 1973; *Les nouveaux patrons*, 1974; *Silence on ferme: Les Licenciements vus par la base* (co-author), 1976. Fields: Sociology of organizations; sociology of employers' associations and workers' associations; new forms of work organizations, enrichment of tasks; autonomous production groups.

[163]
BERRINGTON Hugh Bayard
12 December 1928, British. 4 Fenwick Terrace, Newcastle, England. Degrees: BSc. 1949-54 Local Government Officer; 1956-65 Lecturer, U of Keele; 1965- Reader in Pol, Professor of Pol, U of Newcastle-upon-Tyne. Publs: *Backbench Opinion in the House of Commons, 1955-59* (with S E Finer and D J Bartholomew), 1961; *How Nations are Governed*, 1964; *Backbench Opinion in the House of Commons, 1945-55*, 1973. Fields: Development of party cohesion in parliament in the late 19th and early 20th centuries; political behaviour; psychology of politics.

[164]
BERRY Christopher Jon
19 June 1946, British. 100 Cleveland Road, Glasgow G12 0JT, Scotland. Degrees: BA; PhD (London). Doctoral thesis: "James Dunbar 1742-98: A Study of his Thought and Place in and Contributions to the Scottish Enlightenment". Lecturer, Dept of Pol, U of Glasgow. Publs: *Adam Smith's 'Considerations' on Language*, 1974; "Eighteenth-century Approaches to Origin of Metaphor", *Neuphilo Mitt*, 1973; "Dunbar and Ideas of Sociality in Eighteenth-century Scotland", in *Il Pens Politico*, 1973; "Climate in Eighteenth-century", *TSLL*, 1974; "From Hume to Hegel: The Case of the Social Contract", *JHI*, 1977. Fields: The concept of human nature; Hegel; Hume and Scottish enlightenment; history of ideas.

[165]
BERTELING Jan
12 January 1945, Dutch. Carpentierstraat 95, 2595 HE The Hague, The Netherlands. Degrees: Drs. Doctoral thesis: "The Legal Position of Pledging Conferences within the United Nations System". Student Assistant, International Public Law, U of Amsterdam; Head of Section for Co-ordination and Specialized Agencies, International Organization Dept, Ministry of Foreign Affairs. Publs: "De intrede van de Volksrepubliek China in de gespecialiseerde organisaties van de Verenigde Naties", *Internationale Spectator*, 1962; "Inter-Secretariat Co-ordination in the United Nations System", *Netherlands International Law Review, Essays on International Law and Relations in honour of A J P Tammes*, 1977. Fields: International organizations; development cooperation; international public law; sports and politics.

[166]
BERTRAND Ton
11 September 1940, Dutch. Tolhuis 7105, 6537 RK Nijmegen, The Netherlands. Degrees: MA. Research Assistant and Teacher in Research Methods, Dept of Pol Sci, Catholic U of Nijmegen. Publs: *Burgers kijken naar hun Gemeente* (co-author), 1970; "Vervreemding", *Paradogma*, 1971; *De Nederlandse Kiezer 1972* (co-author), 1973; "Political Opinion and Class Identification in The Netherlands" (co-author), *Sociologien Neerlandica*, 1974. Fields: Crossnational research; future studies; methodology.

[167]
BESANÇON Alain
25 April 1932, French. 27 rue de Bourgogne, 75007 Paris, France. Degrees: Dr en histoire (Sorbonne); Dr ès lettres. Doctoral thesis: "La symbolique de la loi dans la culture russe". 1961 Research Associate, Moscow; 1964 Research Associate, U of Columbia, New York; 1968 Visiting Professor, U of Rochester; 1969- Directeur d'études, Ecole des Hautes Etudes, Paris. Publs: *Le tsarévisme immolé*, 1967; *Histoire et expérience du Moi*, 1972; *Education et société en Russie*, 1974; *Etre russe au XIXème siècle*, 1974; *Court traité de soviétologie à l'usage des autorités civiles et militaires et religieuses*; *Les origines intellectuelles du léninisme*, 1977. Fields: Russian history.

[168]
BETZ Joachim Michael
24 May 1946, German. Paul Löfflerweg 10, D-7400 Tübingen, FR Germany. Degrees: Dr. Doctoral thesis: "The Internationalization of Development Aid". Wiss Angestellter, Inst für Pol, U of Tübingen. Publs: "Die Multilateralisierung der Entwicklungshilfe", *Politische Vierteljahresschrift*, 1976; *Die Internationalisierung der Entwicklungshilfe*, 1978. Fields: International politics; development problems; development co-operation; new international economic order; peace research.

[169]
BEUKEL Erik Johannes
20 August 1945, Danish. Klaus Berntsensvej 119, 5793 Højby, Denmark. Degrees: Cand sci pol. Associate Professor, Inst of Soc Sci, U of Odense. Publs: *Norway's Base Policy: The Interplay Between International Security Policy and Domestic Political Needs*, 1977. Fields: International relations; security policy; European integration.

[170]
BEUVE-MERY Hubert*
5 January 1902, French. 107 Boulevard Raspail, 75 Paris VI. France. Degrees: Lic en droit (Paris); Lic ès Lettres (Paris), 1925; Dr en droit (Paris), 1928. 1944 Founder, *Le Monde*; 1944-69 Directeur, *Le Monde*; President, Centre de Formation et de Perfectionnement des Journalistes; Membre, Conseil d'Administration de l'Inst Français de Presse; Membre, Conseil d'Administration de l'Agence France-Presse; Membre, Conseil d'Administration del'hebdomadaire *La Vie Catholique*. Publs: *Théorie des pouvoirs publics, d'après Francois de Vitoria et ses rapports avec le droit public contemporain*, 1928; *Vers la plus grande Allemagne*, 1939; *Réflexions politiques*, 1952; *Suicide de la IV République*, 1958. Fields: Political, social, religious questions in France and the world.

[171]
BEYER Kurt G
12 May 1931, German. Am Luenik 55, 4300 Essen 16, FR Germany. Degrees: Dipl Pol (Free U Berlin). Lecturer, Professor of Pol Sci, U of Essen. Fields: Political economics; political sociology.

[172]
BIANCONI André Paul Henri
21 February 1932, French. 19 rue de la Chaîne, 31 Toulouse, France. Degrees: Lic Histoire; Dr sci pol (Sorbonne). Doctoral thesis: "Le syndicat national des instituteurs (1920-39)". Attaché, CNRS, FNSP; Maître-assistant, U de Sci Soc de Toulouse. Publs: "Les instituteurs, Le Syndicat des secrétaires de mairie-instituteurs", *Revue Française de Science Politique; Le syndicat national des instituteurs, de ses origines à aujourd' hui; Idéologies et stratégies dans la vie politique à travers la presse toulousaine (1902-06)*, 1918. Fields: Ideologies and their transmission through education and mass media; parties and unions.

[173]
BIAREZ Sylvie
French. 30 rue Fessart, 92100 Boulogne, France. Degrees: Dr. Doctoral thesis: "Les zones à urbaniser en priorité- essai d'interprétation par le système administratif". Attachée de recherche, FNSP, Grenoble. Publs: *Une politique d'urbanisme*, 1972; *Institution communale et pouvoir politique-le cas de Roanne* (with C Boucher *et al*), 1973; *Institutions et groupes sociaux*, 1976; *Conurbation et nouveaux types de gestion, la métropole Lille-Roubaix-Tourcoing*, 1978. Fields: Local power; state; social groups; institutional and political domination; ideology.

[174]
BICK Wolfgang
10 July 1946, German. Kasparstrasse 21, 5032 Huerth-Efferen, FR Germany. Degrees: Dipl Mathematiker; Dr rer Pol. Doctoral thesis: "Qualitative and Quantitative Aspects of Biases in Electoral Systems". Assistant, Forschungsinstitut für Pol Wissenschaften und Europäische Fragen, U of Köln. Publs: *Mehrheitsbildende Wahlsysteme und Wahlkreiseinteilung*, 1975; *Quantitative history* (with P J Müller and H Reinke), 1977; *An Inventory of the QUANTUM-Survey*, 1977; "Die Buchführung der Verwaltung als sozialwissenschaftliche Datenbasis", in *Die Analyse prozessproduzierter Daten* (P J Müller (ed)), 1977; "The Structure of Administrative Bookkeeping — Towards a Quantitative Source Criticism" (co-author), in *Quantification and Methods* (J Clubb, E K Scheuch (eds)), 1978. Fields: Interorganizational relations; social networks; information behaviour.

[175]
BIELFELDT Carola
13 July 1946, German. Hessische Stiftung für Friedens-und Konfliktforschung Leimenrode 29, 6000 Frankfurt 1, FR Germany. Degrees: Dipl Volkswirt; Dr rer Pol. Doctoral thesis: "Rüstungsausgaben und Staatsinterventionismus. Das Beispiel der Bundesrepublik Deutschland 1950-1971". Wiss Mitarbeiter in des HSFK. Publs: *Rüstungsausgaben und Staatsinterventionismus. Das Beispiel der Bundesrepublik Deutschland 1950-71*. Fields: Peace and conflict research; armament policy; economics of defence; disarmament.

[176]
BIENAYME Alain Mazin André
22 May 1934, French. 5 rue d'Estrees, 75007 Paris, France. Degrees: Dr; DES; Agrégé de sci econ (1964). Doctoral thesis: "Les oleagineux en Afrique Noire". Professor of Econ, U of Rennes; 1966-78 Economic Advisor to President Faure; Professor of Econ and Pol, Dauphine U. Publs: *L'entreprise et le pouvoir économique*, 1969; *La croissance des enterprises*, 1971-73. Fields: Economic planning; industrial economics and policy; management of higher education systems.

[177]
BILLE Lars
6 November 1943, Danish. Juelsmindevej 65, 2610 Rødovre, Denmark. Degrees: Cand phil (Copenhagen), 1969. 1969- Amanuensis in Modern Danish Political History, Inst of Contemporary History and Pol Sci, U of Copenhagen; Inst of Pol Studies, U of Copenhagen. Publs: *Samling af Nogle Danske Partiprogrammer*, 1970; *Danske Partiprogrammer 1945-1970*, 1972; *S-SF Kilder til Belysning af Forholdet mellem Socialdemokratiet og Socialistisk Folkeparti*, 1974; *Danmark 1966-1975. En Historisk Økonomish Oversigt, 1975: Det Parlipolitiske Samarlejdsmønster i Danmark 1964-1965*. Fields: Modern Danish political history; international politics, especially the problems in relation to the study of the small powers in international politics; the relationship between the United States and the Latin American states; political parties.

[178]
BILLERBECK Rudolf
4 April 1934, Parkstrasse 23, 2800 Bremen 1, FR Germany. Degrees: Dr rer Pol. Doctoral thesis: "The Members of the First German State Legislatures (1946-1951) and National Socialism". Professor of Pol Soc, U of Bremen. Publs: *Die Abgeordneten der ersten Landtage (1946-1951) und der Nationalsozialismus*, 1971. Fields: Political sociology; urban and regional planning.

[179]
BILLON-GRAND Francoise*
17 July 1937, French. 21 Boulevard Gaumbetta, 38000 Grenoble, France. Degrees: Dr, 1960. Faculté de Droit, Grenoble; Assistant, Maître Assistant, UER Sci juridique, Grenoble. Fields: Socialization and the political system.

[180]
BINSWANGER Hans Christoph
19 June 1929, Swiss. Guisanstrasse 15, St Gallen, Switzerland. Degrees: Dr Oec. Doctoral thesis: "Markt und internationale Währungsordnung". Professor, Hochschule St Gallen für Wirtschafts- und Sozialwissenschaften. Publs: *Die Neutralen in der Europäischen Integration* (with H Mayrzedt), 1970; *Handbuch der Schweizerischen Aussenpolitik* (co-ed and co-author), 1976; *Wege aus der Wohlstandsfalle — Strategien gegen Arbeitslosigkeit und Umweltgestörung* (co-ed and co-author), 1978; *Eigentum und Eigentumspolitik*, 1978. Fields: European integration; monetary order; environment; economic theory.

[181]
BIRCH Anthony Harold*
17 February 1924, British. Department of Politics, University of Exeter, Streatham Court, Rennes Drive, Exeter EX4 4PU, England. Degrees: BSc; PhD (London), 1951. Doctoral thesis: "Problems of Federal Finance and Social Legislation in Canada, Australia and the US". 1947-61 Lecturer, Senior Lecturer in Government, U of Manchester; 1961-70 Professor of Pol Studies, U of Hull; 1970- Professor of Pol Sci, U of Exeter. Publs: *Federalism, Finance and Social Legislation*, 1955; *Small-town Politics*, 1959; *Representative and Responsible Government*, 1964; *The British System of Government*, 1967. Fields: Theories of representation.

[182]
BIRCH Julian*
28 January 1945, British. Department of Political Theory and Institutions, University of Sheffield, Arts Tower, Western Bank, Sheffield S10 2TN, England. Degrees: B Soc Sci. 1966-67 Temporary Lecturer, U of Aston; 1968- Lecturer, U of Sheffield. Publs: *The Ukrainian Nationalist Movement in the USSR since 1956*, 1971. Fields: Soviet politics; local and national pressure group politics in the USSR; Albanian politics.

[183]
BIRGERSSON Bengt Owe
30 September 1941, Swedish. Ingeborgsvägen 6, 19400 Upplands Väsby, Sweden. Degrees: PhD (Stockholm), 1975. Doctoral thesis: "The Commune as a Producer of Services. Local Government Services and Service Attitudes in 36 Swedish Communes" (in Swedish). 1966-69 Research Assistant, Swedish local government group; 1969-72 Assistant Professor, U of Stockholm; 1973- Deputy Secretary in the Standing Committee of the Constitution, Swedish Parliament; 1975- Associate Professor, U of Stockholm. Publs: *Det Kommunala Informationssystemet*, 1969; *Kommunen som Service Producent*, 1975; *Medborgarna Informeras* (co-author), 1970. Fields: Local government; parliaments and the political system.

[184]
BIRNBAUM Pierre
19 July 1940, French. 12 rue de l'Epée du Bois, 75005 Paris, France. Degrees: Dr ès lettres; Dr en sociologie (Sorbonne), 1966. Doctoral thesis: "La structuration du pouvoir aux Etats-Unis". Maître assistant, U de Bordeaux; Maître assistant, U de Paris V; Maître de conférence, U de Paris 1; Professeur, IEP Paris; Professeur, U de Paris 1. Publs: *Sociologie de Tocqueville*, 1970; *La structure de pouvoir aux Etats-Unis*, 1971; *Sociologie politique* (with F Chazel), 1971; *La fin du politique*, 1975; *Le pouvoir politique*, 1975; *Les sommets de l'Etat*, 1977; *La classe dirigeante française* (co-author), 1978. Fields: Political theory; sociological theory; analysis of power and the elite.

[185]
BISCARETTI DI RUFFIA Paolo
8 January 1912, Italian. Via Alberto da Giussano 26, 20145 Milan, Italy. Degrees: Dr in Law (Rome), 1933. 1939 Ord Professor of Constitutional Law, U of Catania; 1949-63 Ord Professor of Constitutional Law, U of Pavia; 1963- Ord Professor of Constitutional Law, U of Milan. Publs: *Contributo alla Teoria Giuridica della Formazione degli Stati*, 1936; *Le Norme della Correttezza Costitutzionale*, 1939; *Lineamenti Generali dell' Ordinamento Costituzionale Sovietico*, 1956; *Diritto Costituzionale*, 1977; *Introduzione al Diritto Costituzionale Comparato*, 1974; *La Repubblica Popolare Cinese (Un 'modello' nuovo di Ordinamento Statale Socialista)*, 1977. Fields: Italian and comparative constitutional law.

[186]
BJØL Erling
11 December 1918, Danish. Arnakuaenge 13, 8270 Højbjerg, Denmark. Degrees: Dr. Doctoral thesis: "La France devant l'Europe". Professor of International Relations. Publs: *Sol og Sult*, 1960; *International Politik*, 1967; *Verdenshistorien efter 1945*, 1972-73; *Udenrigspolitik*, 1973; *Vor tids Kulturhistorie*, 1978.

[187]
BJÖRKLAND Stefan
18 January 1932, Swedish. Murklevägen 19, 752 46 Uppsala, Sweden. Degrees: Fil dr (Uppsala), 1964. Universitetslektor, Dept of Pol Sci, U of Uppsala. Publs: *Oppositionen vid 1823 års riksdag*, 1964; *Politisk teori*, 1971; *Den uppenbara lösningen*, 1977. Fields: Political belief systems; political philosophy.

[188]
BJURULF Bo
Swedish. Liggaugränden 2, 522 250 Lund, Sweden. Degrees: Fil mag; Fil lic; PhD; Docent. Doctoral thesis: "An Analysis of Some Aspects of the Voting Process". Research Assistant, Research Associate, Associate Professor, Swedish Council for Soc Sci Research. Publs: "A Probabilistic Analysis of Voting Blocs and the Occurrence of the Paradox of Voting", in *Probability Models of Collective Decision Making* (R G Niemi and H F Weisberg (eds)), 1972; "A Simulation Analysis of Selected Voting Procedures", *Statsvetarskoplig tichkrift*, 1973; *A Dynamic Analysis of Scandinavian Roll-Call Behaviour. A Test of a Prediction Model on Ten Minority Situations in Three Countries*, 1974.

[189]
BLACK Antony John
23 November 1936, British. 4 Station Crescent, Invergowrie, Dundee, Scotland. Degrees: BA; PhD (Cambridge), 1967. Doctoral thesis: "Pope, Council and Secular Powers 1431-49: Diplomacy and Doctrine". Lecturer in Pol Sci, U of Dundee. Publs: *Monarchy and Community: Political Ideas in the Later Conciliar Controversy 1430-50*, 1970. Fields: The self-governing commune as a political idea in medieval and early modern Europe; Rousseau; John of Segovia and Heimericus de Campo as social philosophers; theory of voluntary associations; late medieval and early-modern political thought.

[190]
BLAKE Robert Norman William (Baron)
23 December 1916, British. The Provost's Lodgings, The Queen's College, Oxford, England. Degrees: MA; D Litt (Glasgow), 1972. 1947-68 Student and Tutor in Pol, Christ Church Coll, Oxford; 1969- Emeritus Student; 1950-55 Censor; 1959-60 Senior Proctor; 1967-68 Ford's Lecturer in English History; 1959- Member Hebdomadal Council, U of Oxford; 1968- Provost of the Queen's Coll, Oxford. Publs: *The Private Papers of Douglas Haig*, 1952; *The Unknown Prime Minister* (Life of Andrew Bonar Law), 1955; *Disraeli*, 1966; *The Conservative Party from Peel to Churchill*, 1970; *The Office of Prime Minister*, 1975; *The Conservative Opportunity*, (with J Patten (eds)), 1976; *A History of Rhodesia*, 1977. Fields: History; broadcasting.

[191]
BLANCHARD Francoise
3 January 1939, French. 3 Avenue Franklin Roosevelt, 92330 Sceaux, France. Degrees: Lic; Dipl (IEP Paris); Dipl (Ecole des Langues Orientales), Paris. Attachée de recherche, Centre d'Etudes et Recherche Internationales, FNSP. Publs: "Une partie de l'Indonésie" in *L'Asie du sud est*, 1970; *Le parti communiste indonésien*, 1973; various articles in *Archipel, Rev Française de Science Politique, Revue de Défense Nationale*. Fields: International relations in South East Asia; Indonesian political systems.

[192]
BLANKART Franz A
27 November 1936, Swiss. Nydeggasse 15, 3011 Berne, Switzerland. Degrees: Dr phil. Doctoral thesis: "Zweiheit, Bezug und Vermittlung". First Secretary, Swiss Mission to the European Communities; Head, Swiss Office for European Integration. Publs: *Zweiheit, Bezug und Vermittlung*, 1966; *Der Neutralitätsbegriff aus logischer Sicht*, 1968; various articles on Swiss-EEC relationships. Fields: International economic cooperation.

[193]
BLANKE Bernhard
8 March 1941, German. Friedenstrasse 10, 3000 Hannover 1, FR Germany. Degrees: Dipl Politologe; Dr rer Pol; Habilitation. Doctoral thesis: "Legitimationsproblem und Staatsbegriff". Wiss Assistent, Dept of Pol, Free U of Berlin; Akademischer Rat; Privat Dozent, Seminar für Wissenschaft von der Politik; Technische U of Hannover. Publs: *Kritik der Politischen Wissenschaft* (co-author), 1973; *Systemwandel und Demokratisierung* (ed), 1975; *Die Linke im Rechtstaat* (co-ed), 1976. Fields: Legal systems; economic policy; German history; political theory, especially systems theory.

[194]
BLANKENBURG Erhard
20 October 1938, German. Meinekestrasse 6, 1000 Berlin 15, FR Germany. Degrees: MA: Dr phil; Habilitation. Doctoral thesis: "Kirchliche Bildung und Wahlverhalten". U of Freiburg; Quickborn Team, Hamburg; Prognos AG Basel, Max-Planck-Inst für Strafrecht, Freiburg; Wissenschaftszentrum Berlin. Publs: *Kirchliche Bindung und Wahlverhalten — Die sozialen Faktoren bei der Wahlentscheidung — Nordrhein-Westfalen 1961-1966*, 1967; *Auswirkungen lokaler Pressekonzentration* (with R Theis and U Kneer), 1970; *Profis, Polizisten und Prozesse* (with J Feest), 1972; *Definitionsmacht der Polizei* (with J Feest), 1972; *Strukturmodell der Zivilgerichtsbarkeit* (with H Wolff and H Morasch), 1974; *Empirische Rechtssoziologie*, 1975; *Die Staatsanwaltschaft im Prozess sozialer Kontrolle* (with K Sessar and W Steffen), 1977; *Jahrbuch für Rechtstheorie und Rechtssoziologie* (with W Kaupen (ed)), 1978. Fields: Political sociology; sociology of law; public administration.

[195]
BLASCHKE Jochen
German. 1 Berlin 30, Fuggerstrasse 26, FR Germany. Degrees: Dipl Politologe. Doctoral thesis: "Theories of the Scientific-Technical Revolution". Wiss Assistent, Free U of Berlin. Publs: Various articles on social science theories, Great Britain and Ireland. Fields: Comparative social research; industrial societies minorities and regionalism; Great Britain/Ireland.

[196]
BLIT Lucjan Eliazar
26 November 1908, British. 57 Collingwood Avenue, London N10 3EE, England.
Degrees: MA (Warsaw). Lecturer, School of Slavonic and East European Studies, LSE.
Publs: *The Eastern Pretender*; *Gomulka's Poland*; *The Origins of Polish Socialism*.
Fields: Eastern European history and politics, especially Poland.

[197]
BLOM Hans Willem
25 April 1947, Dutch. Borgesiuslaan 39, Amersfoort 3818 JV, The Netherlands.
Degrees: Drs (Amsterdam), 1977. Lecturer in Epistemology and Philosophy of Soc Sci,
Erasmus U of Rotterdam. Publs: "Filosofie en Sociale Wetenschappen", *Acta Politica*,
1974; "Waarschijnlijkheid", *Acta Politica*, 1975; "Een Legaliteitsschaal", *Beleid en
Maatschappij*, 1975; "Sir William Petty — een 17e eeuwse empirist", *Acta Politica*,
1976; "Hard onderzoek kan ook anders", *Transactie*, 1976; "Methode en Beoordeling
in de Economie", *Kennis en Methode*, 1977. Fields: Philosophy and methodology of
the social sciences; political philosophy and its history; the history of empirically orien-
tated political science since 1600.

[198]
BLONDEL Jean Fernand Pierre
26 October 1929, French. Department of Government, University of Essex, Wivenhoe
Park, Colchester, England. Degrees: Dipl (IEP Paris), 1953; Lic en droit (Paris), 1954;
B Litt (Oxon), 1955. 1958-63 Assistant Lecturer, Lecturer, U of Keele; 1963-64 Visiting
Fellow (ACLS), U of Yale, USA; 1969-70 Visiting Professor, U of Carleton, Ottawa;
1964- Professor of Government, U of Essex; Director, European Consortium for
Political Research; Part-time Visiting Professor, IEP, Paris. Publs: *Public Administra-
tion in France* (with F Ridley), 1964; *The Government of France* (with E Godfrey),
1968; *Introduction to Comparative Government*, 1969; *Reader in Comparative
Government* (ed), 1969; *Workbook for Comparative Government* (with V Herman),
1972; *Voters, Parties and Leaders*, 1972; *Comparing Political Systems*, 1972; *Thinking
Politically*, 1976; *Political Parties*, 1978. Fields: Comparative politics; general theory of
politics; formal political analysis; legislative behaviour; executives.

[199]
BLUMLER Jay George
18 February 1924, American. 31 Blackwood Rise, Leeds LS16 7BG, England. Degrees:
BA; Dr phil (Oxon), 1962. Doctoral thesis: "The Effects of Long-Term Residential
Adult Education in Britain (with particular reference to Ruskin College, Oxford)".
1949-63 Lecturer in Soc and Pol Theory, Ruskin Coll, Oxford; 1963-69 Granada Televi-
sion Research Fellow, U of Leeds; Reader in Mass Communications and Research
Director, Centre for Television Research, U of Leeds. Publs: *Television in Politics: Its
Uses and Influence*, 1968; *The Uses of Mass Communication*, 1974; *The Challenge of
Election Broadcasting*, 1978; *Voters and Media*, 1978. Fields: Political communications
and mass media in politics; electoral behaviour; political socialization.

[200]
BLUNT Michael Edward
18 June 1932, British. 53 Hawkstone Avenue, Whitefield, Manchester M25 7PR,
England. Degrees: BSc; PhD (London). Doctoral thesis: "Political Representation in
Multi-racial Societies with Special Reference to British East Africa". Lecturer in Pol, U
of Ife, Nigeria; Senior Lecturer, Dept of Soc and Pol Studies, U of Salford. Fields:
African history and politics; politics of education.

[201]
BOADEN Noel Thomas*
19 February 1934, British. Social Studies Building, The University, Liverpool L69 3BX, England. Degrees: BSc; MA (Essex), 1965; PhD (Liverpool), 1971. 1967-71 Research Fellow, Dept of Pol Theory and Inst, U of Liverpool; 1971- Lecturer in Social Administration, U of Liverpool. Publs: *Urban Policy Making*, 1971. Fields: Urban politics; social policy.

[202]
BOBBIO Norberto*
18 October 1909, Italian. Via Sacchi 66, 10128 Torino, Italy. Degrees: Dr iur; Dr phil. 1935-38 Professor, U of Camerino; 1938-40 Professor, U of Sienna; 1940-48 Professor, U of Padua; Professor, U of Turin. Publs: *Da Hobbes a Marx*, 1965; *Saggi sulla Scienza Politica in Italia*, 1969. Fields: Normative political theory.

[203]
BOCHEL John Main
14 January 1928, British. 106 Tay Street, Newport-on-Tay, Fife, Scotland. Degrees: BA; MA (Manchester), 1965. Lecturer in Government, Research Assistant, U of Michigan; Senior Lecturer in Pol Sci, U of Dundee. Publs: *Politics in the City*, 1973; *The Scottish Local Government Elections of 1974*, 1975; *The Scottish District Elections of 1977*, 1977; *Religion and Voting: A Critical Review and a New Analysis*, 1970; "The Impact of the Campaign on the Results of Local Government Elections", *BJPS*, 1972; "The Political Socialization of Activists in the British Communist Party", *BJPS*, 1973; "The Recruitment of Local Councillors", *Political Studies*, 1966; "Political Communication: Scottish Local Newspapers and the General Election of February 1974, *Scottish Journal of Sociology*, 1977. Fields: Local party activists; the selection of parliamentary candidates; local politics; political socialization and recruitment; local government elections; Scottish politics.

[204]
BOCK Hans Alfred
13 May 1940, German. 3504 Kaufungen 2, Rehheckenweg 6, FR Germany. Degrees: Dr phil (Marburg), 1968. Doctoral thesis: "Syndicalismus und Linkskommunismus von 1918 bis 1923. Zur Geschichte und Soziologie der Freien Arbeiter Union Deutschlands (Syndikalisten), der Allgemeinen Arbeiter-Union Deutschlands und der Kommunistischen Arbeiter-Partei Deutschlands". 1968-70 Lecturer of German Pol History, U de Paris; 1970-72 Maître de conférences associé, U de Paris, Inst d'Allemand Asnières; Professor of Pol Sci, Gesamthochschule, Kassel. Publs: *Syndikalismus und Linkskommunismus von 1918 bis 1923*, 1969; *Organisation und Taktik der proletarischen Revolution*, 1969; *Geschichte des "linken Radikalismus" in Deutschland*, 1976. Fields: French studies; European studies; history of the German working class; class movement; political theory.

[205]
BODDENDIJK Frank Roeland
13 May 1945, Dutch. Liszthof 12, Alphen aan den Rijn, The Netherlands. Degrees: Drs (Amsterdam). Lecturer in Pol Sci, Free U of Amsterdam. Fields: Women's studies; Marxist theories of the state; political philosophy; the politics of civilization or the new barbarism in an age of old non-decision makers and new mandarins.

[206]
BODE Erhardt
24 March 1948, German. Grosse Brunnenstrasse 93, 2000 Hamburg 50, FR Germany.
Degrees: Dipl Volkswirt. Fields: Political socialization; political psychology; political
economy.

[207]
BODIGUEL Jean-Luc
13 February 1937, French. 3 rue de la Méditerranée, 92160 Antony, France. Degrees:
Lic en droit (Grenoble), 1961; Dipl (IEP Grenoble), 1962; DES sci pol (Grenoble), 1962;
Dr de recherche en sci pol (Paris), 1966. Doctoral thesis: "La quatrième semaine de con-
gés payés et la réduction de la durée du travail en France". Attaché de recherche,
Chargé de recherche, CNRS; Directeur de séminaires, IEP Paris. Publs: *La réduction
de la durée du travail, enjeu de la lutte sociale; L'administration française* (with Mme
Kessler); *Les anciens élèves de l'Ecole Nationale d'Administration*, 1978. Fields: Administration and politics; high civil service for government members; court magistrates
in France.

[208]
BOEHRET Carl
30 July 1933, German. Am Egelsee 5, 6720 Speyer, FR Germany. Degrees: Dipl
Politologe, 1962; Dr rer Pol, 1966; Habilitation, 1970 (Free U of Berlin). Doctoral
thesis: "Aktionen gegen die kalte Sozialisierung 1926-30". 1971-74 Professor of Pol Sci
and Pol Econ, Free U of Berlin; 1974- Professor of Pol Sci, Graduate School of Administrative Sci, Speyer; 1970- Lecturer, Federal Academy of Public Administration,
Bonn. Publs: *Aktionen gegen die kalte Sozialisierung 1926/1930*, 1966; *Entschei-
dungshilfen für die Regierung*, 1970; *Simulation innenpolitischer Konflikte* (ed), 1972;
Das Planspiel als Methode der Fortbildung (co-author), 1975; *Grundriss der
Planungspraxis*, 1975; *Führungskonzepte für die öffentliche Verwaltung* (co-author),
1976; *Wörterbuch zur politischen Ökonomie* (ed and co-author), 1977; *Politik und
Wirtschaft* (ed and co-author), 1977. Fields: Policy science; planning and public administration; political economy; simulation and games; adult education.

[209]
BOETTCHER Winfried
11 March 1936, German. Walhornerstrasse 9, 5100 Aachen, FR Germany. Degrees: Dr
phil. Doctoral thesis: "The Image of Germany in the British Press 1960-1966". Professor of Pol Sci, U of Aachen. Publs: *The Image of Germany in Britain 1960-1972*,
1972; *British Ideas of Europe*, 1971-1975; *Peace Politics*, 1975; *The Political System of
the Federal Republic of Germany*, 1977. Fields: International politics, especially European politics; field between educational and political sciences.

[210]
BOGASON Peter
7 July 1947, Danish. Ved Højmosen 10-3, DK-2970 Hørsholm, Denmark. Degrees:
Cand phil, 1973; Cand mag, 1975. 1974- Assistant Professor, Research Fellow, Inst of
Pol Studies, U of Copenhagen. Publs: Articles in *Byplan; Juristen and Økonomen*;
"Regional Planning in Denmark", in *Intergovernmental Policy-Making* (K Hanf and F
Scharpf (eds)). Fields: Public planning; public administration; public policy.

[211]
BOGDANOR Vernon Bernard
16 July 1943, British. 17 Sunderland Avenue, Oxford, England. Degrees: BA; MA (Oxon), 1968. Fellow and Tutor in Pol, Brasenose Coll, Oxford. Publs: *The Age of Affluence 1951-64* (ed), 1970; *Disraeli: Lothair* (ed), 1975; *Devolution*, 1978; plus articles in *Political Studies, Political Quarterly, Parliamentary Affairs, Yale Law Journal, Oxford Review of Education*; contributor to *Corporatism: Myth or Reality?* (T Raison (ed)), 1977. Fields: British political thought since Hobbes; British constitutional thought since Dicey; British political history since 1865; federalism.

[212]
BOLLINGER Ernest
22 April 1932, Swiss. 37 Crêts-de-Champel, 1206 Genève, Switzerland. Degrees: Dr. Doctoral thesis: "La presse suisse: structure et diversité" (The Swiss Press: Structure and Diversity). Press and Public Relations, Vocational Training, Dept of Econ, U of Geneva. Publs: *Répertoire de la presse suisse*, 1969; *The Swiss Press and Local Politics*, 1978. Fields: Press affairs; mass communications; political systems and social communication.

[213]
BON Frédéric
30 January 1943, French. 10 Boulevard Maréchal Leclerc, 38000 Grenoble, France. Degrees: Dipl (Paris). Assistant de recherche, FNSP; Attaché de recherche, CNRS; Chargé de recherche, CNRS. Publs: *Les nouveaux intellectuels*, 1971; *Classe ouvrière et révolution*, 1971; *Attitudes et comportements politiques à Boulogne Billancourt*, 1971; *L'ouvrier français en 1970*, 1971; *Les sondages peuvent ils se tromper*, 1974; *Les élections en France*, 1978. Fields: Ideological studies; electoral studies; epistemology of social sciences.

[214]
BONANATE Luigi
17 August 1943, Italian. Via Andrea Doria 8, 10123 Torino, Italy. Degrees: Dr. Doctoral thesis: "La Teoria Critica della dissuasione". Professor of International Relations, Faculty of Pol Sci, U of Turin. Publs: *La Politica della Dissuasione*, 1971; *La Guerra Nella Societa Contemporanea, Scritti Scelti*, 1972; *Introduzione all'Analisi Politica Internazionale*, 1973; *Diritto Naturale e Relazioni tra gli Stati*, 1976; "Dimensioni del Terrorismo Politico", *Comunita*, 1977; "Eurocommunism: 'The Rules of the Game' ", *Scientia*, 1978; *Teoria Politica e Relazioni Internazionali*, 1976; *Il Sistema delle Relazioni Internazionali*, 1976. Fields: International relations theory; political theory; terrorism: national and international.

[215]
BOND Brian James
17 April 1936, British. Olmeda, Ferry Lane, Medmenham, Marlow, Buckinghamshire, England. Degrees: BA: MA (London), 1962. 1962-66 Lecturer in Modern History, U of Liverpool; Lecturer in War Studies, King's Coll, U of London; Visiting Professor, U of Western Ontario. Publs: *Victorian Military Campaigns*, 1967; *The Theory and Practice of War* (M Howard (ed)), 1965; *New Cambridge Modern History* (C L Mowat (ed)), 1969; *The Victorian Army and the Staff College 1854-1914*, 1972; *Chief of Staff: The Diaries of Lt Gen Sir Henry Pownall 1933-1944* (ed), 1973; *France and Belgium 1939-1940*, 1975; *Liddell Hart: A Study of His Military Thought*, 1977; *War and Society Yearbook* (ed), 1967. Field: British military policy, 1918-1939; the history and current role of the army in Pakistan; the education and training of army officers.

[216]
BONMARIAGE Joseph Louis*
1937, Belgian. BASS, Van Evenstraat 2A, B-3000 Louvain, Belgium. Degrees: Lic en sociologie (Louvain), 1967. Research Assistant, U of Louvain; Executive Director, Belgian Archives for the Social Sciences. Fields: Methodology of social research.

[217]
BONNEMAISON Antoine-Francois
14 April 1910, French. BP 46, 78001 Versailles-Cedex, France. Degrees: Dr en droit public; Dipl (IEP Paris); Dipl (Inst des Hautes Etudes Internationales Paris). Doctoral thesis: "L'armée internationale et le comité d'Etat-major". Fields: Philosophy and politics.

[218]
BONNET Serge
3 August 1924, French. Degrees: Dr. Doctoral thesis: "Sociologie politique et religieuse de la Lorraine". Directeur de Recherche, CNRS. Fields: Political sociology; sociology of catholicism; history of working class, especially the iron industry.

[219]
BOONSTRA Dick
1 August 1939, Dutch. Kennedaylaan 54, 2421 EP Nieuwkoop, The Netherlands. Degrees: Drs. Doctoral thesis: "Political Education and Youth Policy". Assistant, Dept of Pol Sci, Free U of Amsterdam. Fields: Political socialization; welfare policy; youth politics and policy.

[220]
BOOTH Ken
29 January 1943, British. 18 Maesyfelin, Penrhyncoch, Aberystwyth, Wales. Degrees: BA. Lecturer, Dept of Pol, U Coll of Wales, Aberystwyth. Publs: *The Military Instrument in Soviet Foreign Policy, 1917-1972*, 1974; *Soviet Naval Policy: Objectives and Constraints* (co-ed), 1975; *Contemporary Strategy: Theories and Politics* (co-author), 1975; *Navies and Foreign Policy*, 1977; *American Thinking about Peace and War* (co-ed and contributor), 1978. Fields: Strategic studies; Soviet foreign policy; theories of international politics.

[221]
BORCHARDT Wolfgang
27 February 1950, German. 2 Hamburg 26, Quellenweg 28, FR Germany. Degrees: Dipl Politologe. Wiss Referent im HWWA, Inst für Wirtschaftsforschung-Hamburg. Publs: "KSZE. Wirtschaftsbeziehungen im Entspannungsprozess", *Wirtschaftsdienst*, 1977; "Wirtschaftliche Komponenten der Entspannungspolitik', *Politik und Kultur*, 1978; "Der neue wirtschaftspolitische Kurs der VR China" (with U Dietsch), *Wirtschaftsdienst*, 1978; "Friedliche Koexistenz und Ost-West-Wirtschaftsbeziehungen", in *Hamburger Jahrbuch für Wirtschafts- und Sozialwissenschaften*, 1978. Fields: The economics and politics of East-West relations; the political and social systems of Eastern Europe, especially Hungary; the Communist parties of Western Europe (Euro-Communism); strategies and concepts for disarmament.

[222]
BORELLA Francois
1932, French. 9 rue de Badonviller, 54000 Nancy, France. Degrees: Dr d'Etat; Agrégé de droit public and sci pol. Doctoral thesis: "L'évolution politique et juridique de l'Union Française depuis 1946". 1955-62 Assistant, Chargé de cours, U de Nancy; 1962-66 Professeur, U de Alger; 1966- Professeur, U de Nancy II; 1973-78 Président de l'Université. Publs: *Le syndicalisme étudiant*, 1957; *L'évolution politique et juridique de l'Union Française depuis 1946*, 1958; *Le gouvernement des français*, 1963; *Les institutions politiques*, 1975; *Introduction au droit administratif algérien*, 1971; *Les partis politiques dans la France d'aujourd'hui*, 1977; *Les partis politiques dans l'Europe des Neuf*, 1978. Fields: Africa; international relations and international organizations; political and social powers in Western Europe.

[223[
BORG Olavi Allan
30 March 1935, Finnish. Näsilinnankatu 24 D 28, 33210 Tampere 21, Finland. Degrees: MA (Helsinki), 1958; Lic, 1961; Dr, 1964. Doctoral thesis: "Suomen Puolueideologiat" (Party Ideologies in Finland). 1958-66 Researcher and Lecturer, U of Helsinki; 1966-69 Assistant Professor of Soc Sci, U of Jyväskylä; 1969-73 Professor of Methodology of Soc Sci, U of Tampere; 1973- Professor of Pol Sci, U of Tampere. Publs: *Suomen Puolueet ja Puolueohjelmat 1880-1964*, 1965; *Mitä Puoluetta Äänestäisin*, 1970; *Puoluelaitos ja sen Kehityspiirteitä Itsenäisessä Suomessa*, 1977; "Basic Dimensions of Finnish Party-Ideologies: A Factor Analytical Study", *Scandinavian Political Studies*, 1966; *Communism — Finnish Style*. Fields: Political theory and ideologies; parties and party system; theory and methodology of social sciences; representation and functioning of parliaments.

[224]
BORGHORST Hermann
14 July 1947, German. Stubenrachstrasse 31a, 1 Berlin 37, FR Germany. Degrees: Dipl pol; Dr rer Pol. Doctoral thesis: "The Interdependence of the Federal Government and Local Communities in the Urban Renewal Program of the United States of America". Research Assistant, Free U of Berlin. Publs: *Bürgerbeteiligung in der Kommunal- und Regionalplanung*, 1976; "Citizens' Participation in the Process of Urban Renewal Exemplified by the US and the FRG" (with P Smith), *Problemcy Rad Norodowych*, 1977. Fields: Urban politics and administration; community power structure and political decision-making processes; community development and urban and regional planning; intergovernmental relationships and co-operative federalism.

[225]
BORLAND John Allison*
21 February 1941, British. Department of Social Theory, University College of North Wales, Bangor, Caerns, Wales. Degrees: BA. 1964-65 Research Student, U of Keele; 1965-67 Research Student, U of Salford; 1967-68 Senior Experimental Officer, U of Salford; Lecturer, U Coll of North Wales.

[226]
BORNSCHIER Volker
22 March 1944, German. In der Gand 1, CH-8126 Zumikon/Zürich, Switzerland. Degrees: Dr phil (Zürich); Habilitation (Zürich). Doctoral thesis: "Einige Determinanten des Firmenverhaltens im Industriesystem. Ein Beitrag zur Wirtschaftssoziologie". Research Assistant, Lecturer, Sociological Inst, U of Zürich. Publs: *Einige Determinanten des Firmenverhaltens im Industriesystem*, 1972; *Wachstum, Konzentration und Multinationalisierung von Industrieunternehmen*, 1976; "Statusinkonsistenz und Schichtung", *Zeitschrift für Soziologie*, 1977; "Abhängige Industrialisierung und Einkommensentwicklung", *Schweizerische Zeitschrift für Soziologie*, 1975; "Arbeitsteilung und soziale Ungleichheit", *Kölner Zeitschrift für Soziologie und Sozialpsychologie*, 1977. Fields: Economic sociology; world society and national development; multinational corporations.

[227]
BORRE Ole
23 September 1932, Danish. Ildervej 3, DK-8270 Højbjerg, Denmark. 1964- Assistant Professor, Professor in Sociology, Inst of Pol Sci, U of Aarhus. Publs: *Partistyrke og Social Struktur*, 1968; *Fire Folketingsvalg*, 1970; *Decembervalget 1973*, 1974; *Vaelgere i Toerne*, 1976; "Party Identification and its Motivational Base in a Multiparty System" (with D Katz), *Scandinavian Political Studies*, 1973; "The Changing Party Space in Danish Voter Perceptions" (with J Rusk), in *Party Identification and Beyond* (I Budge et al), 1975; "Recent Trends in Danish Voting Behaviour", in *Scandinavia at the Polls* (Cerny), 1977. Fields: Danish election surveys; models of voting behaviour; participation and protest behaviour; methodology; regression analysis; response error models; social indicators.

[228]
BORSA Giorgio
19 January 1912, Italian. Via Goito 5, 20121 Milano, Italy. Degrees: Laurea Giurisprudenza (Milan); Laurea Filisofia (Milan); Libera Docente. Doctoral thesis: "La Cessazione de Mandato Internazionale". Director, Far Eastern Section, Milan Inst for the Study of International Pol; Professor of Asian and African History, U of Milan; Professor of East Asian History; Professor of Modern History, U of Pavia; Director, Inst of Asian and African Studies; Director, Center for the Study of Non-European Peoples. Publs: *Gandhi e il Risorgimento Indiano*, 1942; *L'Estremo Oriente fra due Mondi*, 1961; *Italia e Cina nel Secolo XIX*, 1961; *La Nascita del Mondo Moderno in Asia Orientale*, 1977. Fields: Modernization in India, China and Japan.

[229]
BORTHWICK Robert Lambert
11 March 1941, British. Department of Politics, The University, Leicester LE1 7RH, England. Degrees: BA; PhD (Nottingham), 1968. Doctoral thesis: "The Standing Committees of the House of Commons: A Study of Membership, Procedure and Working Between 1945 and 1959". 1961-63 Research Student, U of Nottingham; 1973-74 Visiting Assistant Professor, Graduate School of Public Affairs, State U of New York at Albany; 1974- Lecturer in Pol, U of Leicester. Publs: "The Welsh Grand Committee", and other articles in *Parliamentary Affairs* (Walkland and Ryle (eds)), 1968; *The Commons in the Seventies*. Fields: Committee systems of both houses of the British parliament, especially the operation of standing (legislative) committees; British and American politics especially parliament and congress.

[230]
BOSC Robert Jean Marie
28 April 1909, French. 15 rue Raymond Marcheron, 92710 Vanves, France. Professor, Sociology of International Relations, Inst d'Etudes Soc, Inst Catholique de Paris. Publs: *Sociologie de la Paix* (ed), 1965; *Le Tiers Monde dans la politique internationale* (ed), 1968; *Guerres froides et affrontements*, 1973; "Maoisme et Léninisme et populisme", *Projet*, 1974; "Les régimes autoritaires de droite en Asie orientale", *Revue Française de Science Politique*, 1978; *L'Union Soviétique face aux revendications du Tiers-Monde*, 1976. Fields: International politics.

[231]
BOSCOLO Antonio Alberto
22 August 1920, Italian. Via Cimarosa 56, Cagliari, Sardegna. Degrees: Professore Ordinario. Consiglio Nazionale Ricerche. P delle Science 7 Roma. Publs: *I Parlamenti di Alfonso il Magnanimo*, 1953; *La Politica Italiana di Ferdinando I d'Aragona*, 1954; *La Politica Italiana di Martino il Vecchio re d'Aragona*, 1962; *I Conti di Capraia, Pisa e la Sardegna*, 1966; *Sibilla di Fortia Regina d'ARagona*, 1970; *Sardegna, Pisa e Genova nel Medioevo*, 1978. Fields: Medieval societies and institutions.

[232]
BOTZ Gerhard
14 March 1941, Austrian. Kleinstrasse 48, A-4045 Linz, Austria. Degrees: PhD (Vienna), 1967; Habilitation (Linz), 1977. Doctoral thesis: "Beiträge zur Geschichte der politischen Gewalttaten in Österreich 1918 bis 1933". 1966 Documentalist, Tagblawtt-Archiv, Vienna; 1968- Assistent, Dozent, U of Linz. Publs: *Die Eingliederung Österreichs in das deutsche Reich*, 1976; *Geschichte und Gesellschaft* (with H Hautmann and H Konrad (eds)), 1974; *Wohnungspolitik und Judendeportation in Wien 1938 bis 1945*, 1975; *Gewalt in der Politik*, 1976; *Internationale Tagung der Historiker der Arbeiterbewegung* (ed), 1976; *Im Schatten der Arbeiterbewegung. Zur Geschichte des Anarchismus in Österreich und Deutschland* (with G Brandstetter and M Pollak), 1977; *Der 13 März 1938 und die Anschlussbewegung*, 1978; *Wien vom Anschluss zum Krieg*, 1978. Fields: Austrian contemporary history; national socialism; theory of fascism; Austrian labour history; conflict research; political violence; quantification in history.

[233]
BOUDON Raymond
27 January 1934, French. GEMAS, Maison des Sciences de l'Homme, 54 Boulevard Raspail, 75006 Paris, France. Degrees: Dr d'Etat (Paris-Sorbonne), 1967. Doctoral thesis: "The Mathematical Analysis of Social Facts". 1964-67 Professor, U of Bordeaux; 1968-72 Director, Centre d'Etudes Sociologiques, CNRS; 1972-73 Fellow, Centre for Advanced Studies in Behavioural Sci, Stanford; 1967- Professor of Soc Sci Methods, Sorbonne; 1977 Foreign honorary member, American Academy of Arts and Sci. Publs: *L'analyse mathématique des faits sociaux*, 1970; *A quoi sert la notion de structure*, 1968; *Les méthodes en sociologie*, 1969; *Les mathématiques en sociologie*, 1970; *Mathematical structures in social mobility*, 1973; *L'inégalité des chances*, 1973; *Effets pervers et ordre social*, 1977. Fields: Methodology of social sciences; social mobility, inequality of opportunity; sociological theory; social change.

[234]
BOUILLON Jacques*
1931, French. 104 Avenue Saint-Exupéry, 92 Antony, France. Degrees: Agrégé d'histoire, 1953. Maître de conférences, l'Inst d'Etudes Pol, Paris. Publs: *Le monde contemporain* (with P Sorlin), 1971; *Munich 1938* (with G Vallette), 1965. Fields: Munich and the origins of the war, 1939-45.

[235]
BOUISSOU Michel*
28 July 1924, French. 72 Avenue de Versailles, Paris XVIème, France. Degrees: Dipl (IEP, Paris); Dr en droit et en sci pol; Agrégé des Facultés de Droit. Professeur, Faculté de Droit and l'Inst d'Etudes Pol, Toulouse; Professeur, U de Paris X. Publs: *La chambre des Lords au XXe siècle*, 1952; *La reconnaissance de la République Populaire de Chine*, 1967; *Cours de droit constitutionnel* (with R de Lacharrière), 1970. Fields: Parliamentary institutions; public opinion; the influence of mass media on opinion, and of opinion on the mass media.

[236]
BOURDEAUX Michael Alan
19 March 1934, British. Keston College, Heathfield Road, Keston, Kent BR2 6BA, England. Degrees: BA; BD (Oxon), 1968. Doctoral thesis: "Religious Ferment in Russia". 1969 Visiting Fellow, St Bernard's Seminary, USA; Research Fellow, Centre for International Studies, LSE; 1970- Director, Keston Coll, Centre for the Study and Religion and Communism. Publs: *Opium of the People*, 1965; *Religious Ferment in Russia*, 1968; *Patriarch and Prophets*, 1970; *Faith on Trial in Russia*, 1971; *Land of Crosses: The Catholic Church in Lithuania Today*, 1978. Fields: Religion in communist countries, especially the Soviet Union; Orthodox, Baptists and Roman Catholics in the Soviet Union.

[237]
BOURDET Yvon
1920, French. 11 place d'Orion, 92360 Meudon la Forêt, France. Degrees: Agrégé de l'Université; Dr ès lettres et sci humaines; Maître de recherche, CNRS; Chargé de conférences, EHESS; Président, Centre International de Coordination des Recherches sur l'Autogestion (CICRA). Publs: *Communisme et marxisme*, 1963; *Préjugés français et préjugés allemands*, 1967; *La Délivrance de Prométhée*, 1970; *Figures de Lukacks*, 1972; *Pour l'autogestion*, 1974; *Clefs pour l'autogestion*, 1975; *Qu'est-ce qui fait courir les militants?*, 1976; *L'éloge du patois ou l'itinéraire d'un occitan*, 1977.

[238]
BOURNAZEL Renata
1 June 1941, French. 4 rue de Chevreuse, 76006 Paris, France. Degrees: Dr (Paris 1). Doctoral thesis: "Le traité de Rapallo et son image en France". Attachée de recherche, FNSP. Publs: *Rapallo, naissance d'un mythe. La politique de la peur dans la France du Bloc National*, 1974; various articles in *Revue française de Science Politique*; *De Potsdam à Helsinki. La Politique soviétique en Allemagne 1945-1975*. Fields: International relations of the socialist countries; Soviet strategic concepts and Soviet foreign policy.

[239]
BOURRICAUD Francois
1922, French. 41 rue des Martyrs, 75009 Paris, France. Degrees: Agrégé phil, 1944; Dr ès lettres, 1961. Doctoral thesis: "Esquisse d'une théorie de l'autorité". 1968- Professor, U of Paris V. Publs: *Eléments pour une sociologie de l'action*, 1955; *Esquisse d'une théorie de l'autorité*, 1969; *Pouvoir et société dans le Pérou contemporain*, 1967; *Université à la dérive*, 1971; *L'individualisme institutionnel Essai sur la sociologie de Talcott Parsons*, 1977. Fields: General theory; science of organizations; education.

[240]
BOUZA-BREY VILLAR Luis
17 August 1945, Spanish. C Matilde Diez 10, Barcelona, Spain. Degrees: Dr in Law. Doctoral thesis: "La Contribucion de David Apter a la Teoria de la Modernizacion y el Desarrollo Politico: Nacia un Modelo Normativo-Estructural del Cambio Politico". Assistant Professor, U of Barcelona. Fields: Comparative politics; political change; political theory; political philosophy; Spanish political system and constitutional law.

[241]
BRAAM Gerard Pieter Adriaan
23 January 1930, Dutch. Kerkedennen 28, 7621 ED Borne (O), The Netherlands. Degrees: Drs: Senior Lecturer, U of Amsterdam; Senior Lecturer, U of Groningen; Professor of Sociology, Dept of Public Administration, Technical U of Twente. Publs: *Aging in Utrecht*, 1964; *Influence of Business Firms on the Government*, 1973; *Collective Actions* (co-author), 1976. Fields: Social change; social problems: political sociology.

[242]
BRACHER Karl Dietrich
13 March 1922, German. Bonn, Stationsweg 17, FR Germany. Degrees: PhD (Tübingen), 1948. Doctoral thesis: "Decline and Progress in Roman Thought after Augustus", 1950 Research Assistant, Inst für Pol Sci, Berlin; 1954- Lecturer, Hochschule für Politik and Free U of Berlin; 1958 Professor of Pol Sci, Berlin; 1959-Professor of Pol Sci and Contemporary History, Bonn. Publs: *Deutschland zwischen Demokratie und Diktatur*, 1964; *Theodor Heuss und die Wiederbegründung der Demokratie in Deutschland*, 1965; *The German Dictatorship*, 1970; *Nach 25 Jahren* (ed), 1970; *Bibliographie aus Politik* (with H Jacobsen (ed)), 1970; *The German Dilemma*, 1975; *Die Krise Europas*, 1917-75, 1976; *Zeitgeschichtliche Kontroversen*, 1976. Fields: Philosophy of history; theory of revolution; comparative analysis of political systems; nationalism; fascism; national socialism; history and structure of the second German democracy; history of political ideas.

[243]
BRADLEY John Francis Nejez*
16 January 1930, British. Department of Government, The University, Manchester M13 9PL, England. Degrees: MA (Cambridge), 1955; M Litt (Cambridge), 1959; Dr (Paris). Lecturer in Liberal Studies, U of Salford; Lecturer in Government, U of Manchester. Publs: *La Légion Tchecoslovaque en Russie, 1914-20*, 1965; *Allied Intervention Russia*, 1968; *Czechoslovakia: A History*, 1971; *Lidice: The Assassination of SS Obergrüppenführer R Heydrich*, 1971. Fields: Comparative communist systems, especially Czechoslovakia and the USSR; international politics, especially diplomatic history; human rights; Soviet history; comparative government.

[244]
BRAND John Arthur
4 August 1934, British. 6 Hughenden Terrace, Glasgow G12, Scotland. Degrees: MA (Aberdeen); PhD (London). Doctoral thesis: "Decision-making in a Local Government Education Authority in London". 1959-61 Assistant in Pol, U of Glasgow; 1961-63 Lecturer, U of Reading; 1963-64 Lecturer in Educational Administration, U of London; 1964- Senior Lecturer in Pol, U of Strathclyde; 1972- Director, Strathclyde Area Survey, U of Strathclyde. Publs: *Policies and Politics in Secondary Education in Greater London*, 1966; *Political Stratification and Democracy* (co-author), 1972; *Local Government Reform in England*, 1974. Fields: Nationalism; policy analysis.

[245]
BRÄNDSTRÖM Dan Agne
29 June 1941, Swedish. Nybruksvägen 15, S-90256 Umeå, Sweden. Degrees: MA (Umeå), 1969; PhD (Umeå), 1971. Doctoral thesis: "Nomineringsförfarande vid riksdagsval" (Nomination of Candidates to the Swedish Riksdag). 1965-71 Assistant Lecturer, Lecturer in Pol Sci, U of Umeå; 1975- Dean, Graduate School of Social Work and Public Administration; 1977 Regional Director, Umeå Regional Board of Higher Education. Publs: *Nomineringsförfarande vid riksdagsval*, 1972; *Län, landsting, kommun. Regional och lokal förvaltning i Sverige*, 1972; *Partierna Nominerar* (co-author), 1971; "Les Relations entre Saint-Barthétemy et la Suède entre 1784 et 1878", *Bulletin de la Société d'Histoire de la Guadeloupe*. Fields: Political recruitment; political parties; local government; political administration.

[246]
BRANDT Helmut Alfred
16 July 1911, German. 533 Königswinter-Thomasberg, Auf dem Mitschling 24, FR Germany. Degrees: Dr jur; Dr econ. Doctoral thesis: "Die Durchbrechung der Meistbegünstigung" (The Breach of the Most Favoured Nation Clause); Juridicial and Economic Expert and Adviser, German Bundestag; Lecturer in Pol Econ and Law of Econ, Free U of Berlin. Publs: "Internationales Wirtschaftsrecht. Begriff und System", *Weltwirtschaft*; "Herrschaftsordnung und Selbstverwaltung im viergeteilten Gross-Berlin", in *Memorial Publication in Honour of Hans Peters* (H Conrad *et al* (eds)), 1967. Fields: Economic and fiscal policy; law of economics; international political and economic relations.

[247]
BRASZ Henk A
17 February 1923, Dutch. Valentijn 8, Driebergen, The Netherlands. Degrees: Dr (Leiden). Doctoral thesis: "Changes in Dutch Communalism". 1939-49 Local Government; 1948-51 Provincial Government of Zuid-Holland; 1951-61 Senior Officer, Union of Dutch Local Authorities; Professor and Head of Dept of Public Administration, Free U of Amsterdam. Publs: *Changes in the Dutch Communalism*, 1961; *Introduction to Public Administration* (co-author), 1962; "Corruption", in *Political Corruption* (A J Heidenheimer (ed)), 1970; *Corruption* (co-author), 1960; *The Public Subsidy* (co-author), 1961; *Supervision of Local Government*, 1964; *The Study of Public Administration*, 1964; "Bureaucracy", *Political Reconnaissances*, 1971/72; *Methods of Public Administration (Praxiology)*, 1976. Fields: Methodology; development administration.

[248]
BRAUCH Hans Gunter
1 June 1947, German. Alte Bergsteige 47, D 695 Mosbach, FR Germany. Degrees: Dr phil. Doctoral thesis: "Structural Change and Armament Policy of the United States (1940-1950). World Power and its Domestic Preconditions". Research Associate, Inst für Pol Wissenschaft, Heidelberg. Publs: "Entwicklungen und Ergebnisse der Friedensforschung", *Neue Politische Literatur*, 1978; "Eurokommunismus und europäische Sicherheit aus der Sicht der USA", in *Sicherheit und Entspannung in Europa* (G Kiersch, R Seidelmann (eds)), 1977; "Atomare Diplomatie und der Beginn des kalten Krieges. Ein Literaturbericht", *Zeitschrift für Politik*, 1977. Fields: American foreign and defence policy; arms control and disarmament affairs; Eurocommunism; European security detente; new economic world order.

[249]
BREGNSBO Henning
29 January 1928, Danish. Holmesgaardsvej 19, DK-2920 Charlottenlund, Denmark. Degrees: MA (Aarhus), 1955; MA (Copenhagen), 1969. 1955-69 Secondary Teaching Positions; 1969-72 Senior Lecturer, U of Odense; 1972- Senior Lecturer, Inst of Pol Studies, U of Copenhagen. Publs: *Kampen om Skolelovene af 1958. En Studie i Interesseorganisationers Politiske Aktivitet*, 1971; *Interessegrupper*, 1975. Fields: Organizations; comparative/interorganizational analysis; interest organizations and interest groups.

[250]
BREITLING Rupert
19 February 1921, German. 6908 Wiesloch, Gerbersruhstrasse 131, FR Germany. Degrees: Dr phil (Heidelberg), 1954; Habilitation (Heidelberg), 1970. 1953-61 Research Assistant in Pol Sci, Heidelberg. Publs: *The German Federal Republic* (with K Deutsch), 1963; *Das Geld in der Politik, die Verbände in der Politik*, 1963; *Der Unternehmerbegriff*, 1967; *Unternehmerische Meinungspolitik in der Weimarer Republik*, 1968; *Politische Pression wirtschaftlicher und gesellschaftlicher Kräfte in der Bundesrepublik Deutschland*, 1970; *Partei und Wahlfinanzierung*, 1970; *Die nazionalsozialistische Rassenlehre*, 1971; *Auslandsgelder in der Innenpolitik*, 1971. Fields: Comparative political finance; comparative political ideologies; political bureaucracy and organization; political education and public relations.

[251]
BRESSERS Johannes Theodorus Antonius
22 December 1953, Dutch. Plataanstraat 9, Enschede (O), The Netherlands. Degrees: Drs. Research Assistant, Technische Hogeschool, Twente. Fields: Effectiveness of governmental policy in general, and environmental policy in particular.

[252]
BRETT Edwin Allan
18 September 1936, British. 142 Balfour Road, Brighton, Sussex, England. Degrees: BA; PhD. Doctoral thesis: "Development Policy in East Africa Between the Wars". 1960 Lecturer in Pol Sci, U of Witwatersrand; 1964-74 Lecturer in Pol Sci, U of Makerere, Uganda. Lecturer in Pol Sci, U of Sussex. Publs: *African Attitudes*, 1963; *Colonialism and Underdevelopment in East Africa*, 1973; "Politics, Economics and Rationality", *Social Science Information*, 1969; "Dependency and Development", *Cahiers d'Etudes Africaines*, 1972. Fields: Theories of development; agrarian change in Africa; political economy in advanced capitalism.

[253]
BREUNESE Jacob Nicholaas
14 February 1943, Dutch. Kringloop 179, Amstelveen, The Netherlands. Degrees: PhD. Doctoral thesis: "Bestuurskundig onderzoek" (Public Administration Research: A Methodological Study). Wetenschappelijk Medewerker, Dept of Public Administration, Free U of Amsterdam. Fields: Relevance of administrative research for policy; methods and methodology of applied social science research.

[254]
BRIMO Albert
19 December 1914, French. 96 rue de Longchamp, Neuilly Seine 92200, France. Degrees: Agrégé de Facultés de Droit; Lic ès lettres; Dipl (l'Ecole de sci Pol); Professeur titulaire. Doctoral thesis: "Pascal et le Droit". Professeur, Faculté de Droit, Toulouse; Professeur, IEP, Toulouse; Professeur, U de Paris II; Professeur, U de Droit d'Econ et de Soc Sci de Paris. Publs: *Pascal et le droit*; *Les grands courants de la philosophie du droit et de l'Etat*; *Les méthodes de la géosociologie electorale*; *Les méthodes des sciences sociales et politiques*. Fields: Electoral sociology; methods of political science; history of political ideas.

[255]
BRINKHORST Laurens Jan
Wildhoeflaan 2, The Hague, The Netherlands. Degrees: ME. Secretary of State, Foreign Affairs; Member of Parliament.

[256]
BRISCHETTO Maria Elisa*
16 April 1932, Italian. Via Rosso di San Secondo, Catania, Italy. Degrees: Degree in Law, 1958. Dr Assistant, Faculty of Pol Sci, U of Catania; Technical Dr, Faculty of Pol Sci, U of Catania. Fields: Penal law; political acculturation.

[257]
BROCK Lothar Joachim
30 January 1939, German. Mörchinger Strasse 130, D-1000 Berlin 37, FR Germany. Degrees: Dipl Politologe; Dr phil. Doctoral thesis: "Die Gründung der OAS als Problem der entwicklungspolitischen Instrumentalisierung internationaler Organisation durch die 'Dritte Welt' ''. Research Assistant, Dept of Legal Affairs, Pan American Union (OAS), Washington; Wiss Assistent, Otto-Suhr-Inst, Free U of Berlin; Akademischer Oberrat, Technische U Braunschweig. Publs: *Entwicklungsnationalismus und Kompradorenpolitik. Die Gründung der OAS und die Entwicklung der Abhängigkeit Lateinamerikas von den USA*, 1975; *Jahrbuch für Friedens- und Konfliktforschung* (co-ed), 1973; various articles on East-West relations, inter-American relations and EEC foreign policy. Fields: International relations with special reference to North-South relations and cooperation between countries with different social systems.

[258]
BROEKMEYER Marius Joseph
10 September 1927, Dutch. De Pauwentuin 22, 1183 MR Amstelveen, The Netherlands. Degrees: PhD. Doctoral thesis: "De Arbeidersraad in Zuidslavië 1950-1965". Europa Inst, U of Amsterdam. Publs: *Arbeiderszelfbestuur in een Joegoslavische Papierfabriek* (with J J Ramondt), 1971; *Arbeidersraad of Ondernemersstaat* (with I Cornelissen), 1969; *Yugoslav Workers' Self Management. Proceedings of a Symposium* (ed), 1970; *Het Wetenschapsbedrijf in de Sovjet Unie*, 1976; "Personeel en Management in de Sovjet Unie", *Intermediair*, 1978. Fields: Workers' self management and industrial management in Yugoslavia and the USSR; political development in Yugoslavia and the USSR.

[259]
BROMHEAD Peter Alexander
27 January 1919, British. Department of Politics, University of Bristol, 40 Berkeley Square, Bristol B58 1HY, England. Degrees: MA (Oxon), 1946; Dr phil (Oxon), 1950. Doctoral thesis: "Government Intervention in the Shipping Industry 1918-39". 1946-47 Lecturer, Wilton Park; 1947-62 Lecturer in Pol, U of Durham; 1963-64 Professor of Pol, U Coll, Swansea. Professor of Pol, U of Bristol. Publs: *Private Members' Bills in the British Parliament*, 1956; *The House of Lords and Contemporary Politics*, 1958; *Life in Modern Britain*, 1975; *Life in Modern America*, 1970; *Britain's Developing Constitution*, 1974; *The Great White Elephant of Maplin Sands*, 1973. Fields: British constitutional change; leisure and politics; transport politics.

[260]
BROUE Pierre
8 May 1926, French. 6 rue St Feraus, 38000 Grenoble, France. Degrees: Dr ès lettres. Doctoral thesis: "Bolchevisme, spartakisme et gauchisme face aux problèmes de la révolution prolétarienne en Allemagne". Professeur de lycée; Maître assistant, IEP, Grenoble; Chargé de maîtrise de conférences, IEP, Grenoble. Publs: *La révolution et la guerre d'Espagne*; *Le parti bolchévique*; *Révolution en Allemagne (1918-1923)*; *Le mouvement communiste en France*; *La révolution espagnole (1931-1939)*. Fields: International Communist movement.

[261]
BROWN Archibald Haworth
10 May 1938, British. 407 Banbury Road, Oxford OX2 7RF, England. Degrees: BSc; MA (Oxon), 1972. 1964-71 Lecturer in Pol, U of Glasgow; 1967-68 British Council Exchange Scholar, U of Moscow; 1971- Fellow, St Antony's Coll, Oxford and Lecturer in Soviet Inst, U of Oxford. Publs: *Soviet Politics and Political Science*, 1974; *The Soviet Union since the Fall of Krushchev* (with J Gray (co-ed)), 1977. Fields: Soviet politics; Czechoslovak politics, especially the Communist party of Czechoslavakia; comparative communism; leadership politics in Britain, especially the power of the prime minister; the Scottish and Russian enlightenment.

[262]
BROWN Neville George*
8 April 1932, British. Treetops, Hill Road, Watlington, Oxfordshire, England. Degrees: BSc (Econ); BA. 1957-60 Lieutenant, Royal Naval Weather Service; 1960-62 Lecturer in Modern Subjects, Royal Military Academy, Sandhurst; 1962-64 Research Associate, Inst for Strategic Studies; 1964-71 Lecturer in International Pol, U of Birmingham. Publs: *Strategic Mobility*, 1963; *Nuclear War: The Impending Strategic Deadlock*, 1965; *Arms without Empire*, 1967; *A History of the World in the Twentieth Century* (with D C Watt and F Spencer), 1970; *British Arms and Strategy, 1970-80*, 1969. Fields: European security, 1971-80; the world situation in the middle 1980s.

[263]
BRUNI-ROCCIA Giulio
20 December 1910, Italian. Via Rovighi 3, Bologna, Italy. Degrees: Premio Nazionale per le Pol Sci Sociali (Lincei); Cattedra di Filosofia del Diritto; Laurea in Giurisprudenza e Pol Sci. 1972-75 Preside della Facolta di Sci Pol, U di Milano; Direttore del Centro Documentazione e Studi per l'Unione Europea presso, U di Ferrara; Professore di Filosofia del Diritto e di Dottrina Generale della Stato, U di Ferrara; Professore Ord di Pol Sci, U di Milano; Direttore dell 'Istituto di Pol Comparata e Relazioni Internazionale, U di Milano. Publs: *Fondazione Della Scienza Delle Strutture Politiche* (Patron (ed)), 1976; *La Scienza Politica Nella Societa' In Trasformazione* (Giuffre (ed)), 1970;

La Ragion Puritana. Diritto e Stato Nella Coscienza Anglosassone, 1974; *La Dottrina del Diritto Naturale in America*; *Sociologia e Scienza Comparata del Diritto*. Fields: Political science; political systems; theory of political integration; European unity.

[264]
BRUNNER Georg
2 June 1936, German. Sonnleite 3, 87 Würzburg, FR Germany. Degrees: Dr jur, 1963; Habilitation, 1970. Doctoral thesis: "Die Grundrechte im Sowjetsystem". Wiss Referent am Bundesinstitut für Ostwissenschaftliche und internationale Studien, Köln; Professor für offentiliches Recht, Ostrecht und Politikwissenschaft, U of Würzburg. Publs: *Die Grundrechte im Sowjetsystem*, 1963; *Das Parteistatus der KPdSU 1903-1961*, 1965; *Die sowjetische Kolchosordnung*, 1970; *Die Problematik der sozialen Grundrechte*, 1972; *Kontrolle in Deutschland*, 1972; *Einführung in das Recht der DDR*, 1975; *Politische Soziologie der UdSSR*, 1977. Fields: Comparative government; Soviet and East European government and law; constitutional law and theory.

[265]
BRUNSCHWIG Henri
2 June 1904, French. 30 cours Marigny, 94 Vincennes, France. Degrees: Lic ès lettres et droit (Strasbourg), 1926-31; Agrégé histoire et géographie (Paris), 1946. Doctoral thesis: "La crise de l'Etat Prussien à la fin du 18ème siècle et la genèse de la mentalité romantique". Directeur d'Etudes, Ecole Pratique des Hautes Etudes; Professeur, IEP, Paris; Ecole des Hautes Etudes en Sci Soc. Publs: *La crise de l'etat prussien*, 1947; *La colonisation francaise*, 1949; *Mythes et réalités de l'impérialisme colonial francais*, 1960; *L'espansion allemande outre-mer du 15ème siècle à nos jours*, 1975; *L'avènement de l'Afrique Noire*, 1963; *Le partage des traités Makoko 1880*, 1972. Fields: African history from the 19th century to the present day.

[266]
BRUSCHI Alessandro
2 August 1942, Italian. Via 6 Prati 13, 50124 Florence, Italy. Professore incaricato of Methodology of Soc Sci, U of Florence. Publs: *La Teoria dei Modelli nelle Scienze Sociali*, 1971; *Relazioni Internazionali, Metodi e Techniche di Analisi* (with U Gori and F Attina), 1973. Fields: Logic of enquiry; survey design and analysis; Italy and Mediterranean area.

[267]
BRUUN Finn Gyes
16 April 1945, Danish. Skcering Hedevej 112, 8250 Egå, Denmark. Degrees: Cand sci pol (Aarhus), 1974. Assistant Professor, Inst of Pol Sci, U of Aarhus; 1974 Head of Section, Danish Ministry of Environment and Physical Planning; 1977 Associate Professor, Inst of Pol Sci, U of Aarhus. Publs: *Public Administration in Denmark* (with P Meyer *et al*), (in Danish), 1977; *Public Management* (in Danish), 1977. Fields: Public administration, especially public management; public finances; policy-making and participation; comparative administration.

[268]
BRUUN Hans Henrik
27 March 1943, Danish. Hammerensgade 3, 1267 Copenhagen K, Denmark. Degrees: Cand sci pol (Aarhus), 1971. 1971 Research Fellow, U of Aarhus; 1971-73 Secretary, Ministry of Foreign Affairs. Publs: *Science, Values and Politics in Max Weber's Methodology*, 1972. Fields: Methodology of social science; Max Weber; international relations theory; decision-making in foreign policy.

[269]
BRYDER Tom
18 January 1946, Danish. Forskarvägen 132, S-95163 Luleå, Sweden. Degrees: M soc sci; PhD. Doctoral thesis: "Power and Responsibility: Contending Approaches to Industrial Relations and Decision-Making in Britain 1963-1971". Associate Professor, U of Lulea. Publs: Articles in *Statsvetenskaplig Tidskrift*; *Systems Theory and Political Behaviour*, 1976. Fields: The social-psychology of political propaganda; industrial conflict and mediation; modern social theory from Marx to David Easton.

[270]
BÜCHI Willy
7 June 1907, Swiss. 24 Rue St-Barthélemy, 1700 Fribourg, Switzerland. Degrees: Lic and Dr en sci pol et soc (Louvain), 1930, 1938. 1932-50 Executive Manager, industrial associations (textile); 1950-73 Professor of Econ and Soc Policy, Faculté de Droit et des Sci Econ et Soc, U of Fribourg. Publs: Articles in *Civitas*; *Schweizerische Rundschau*; *Wirtschaft und Recht*; *Schweizerische Zeitschrift für Volkswirtschaft und Statistik*; *Neue Ordnung*; *Academia Friburgensis*; *Bulletin der EUBCU*.

[271]
BUCHLI Sylvia*
Swiss. CH Leisis, 1009 Pully, Switzerland. Degrees: Lic (Lausanne). First Assistant for Teaching and Research, Inst of Pol Sci, U of Lausanne; Scientific Adviser, Ecole Polytechnique Fédérale de Lausanne. Publs: *Les Elections Vaudoises de 1913 à 1966* (with R Ruffieux), 1973. Fields: Decision theory and policy sciences; applied systems approach in case studies for research policy; political advisory system of federal government; social forecasting versus technological forecasting.

[272]
BUCK Karl Hermann
30 August 1944, German. Kaiserstrasse 141, D-741 Reutlingen, FR Germany. Degrees: MA; Dr rer Soc. Doctoral thesis: "Die sozialistische Partei Chiles 1933-1973". Wiss Assistent, Inst für Pol Wissenschaft, U of Tübingen. Publs: *Griechenland und die EG Bonn*, 1978; "Die KPI", *Bürger im Staat*, 1976; "Die spanische Linke", *Bürger im Staat*, 1978; *Die italienischen und französischen Sozialisten und Kommunisten und ihre Haltung zur europäischen Integration 1958-77*; "Partito socialista Italiano" and "Pasok (Greece)", in *Die Sozialdemokratische Partei in Westeuropas im Wandel* (Paterson and Schmitz (eds)), 1978; "Die KPI", *Bürger im Staat*, 1977; "Systemwandel durch Eurokommunismus?", *Bürger im Staat*, 1978. Fields: Eurocommunism; direct elections of the European parliament; integration and/or development.

[273]
BUDGE Ian
21 October 1936, British. 4 Oxford Road, Colchester, England. Degrees: MA (Edinburgh), 1959; AM (Yale), 1961; PhD (Yale), 1966. Doctoral thesis: "Patterns of Democratic Agreement". Part-time Assistant, Temporary Lecturer, U of Edinburgh; Assistant Lecturer, Lecturer, U of Strathclyde. Lecturer, Senior Lecturer, Reader, U of Essex. Publs: *Scottish Political Behaviour* (with D W Urwin), 1966; *Agreement and Stability of Democracy*, 1970; *Political Stratification and Democracy* (with J Brand *et al*), 1972; *Belfast: The Approach to Crisis* (with C O'Leary), 1972; *Party Identification and Beyond* (with I Crewe and D Farlie (eds)), 1976; *Voting and Party Competition* (with D Farlie), 1977. Fields: Elections; political recruitment and careers; comparative politics and empirical and moral theory.

[274]
BUGGE Kjell
25 June 1944, Norwegian. Nordstien 16, N-6400 Molde, Norway. Degrees: Cand pol. Research Assistant, Inst of Soc and Pol Studies, U of Bergen; Lecturer, Møre & Romsdal Regional College, Molde. Publs: *Organization Structure in Central Government Administration*. Fields: Organization theory.

[275]
BUKSTI Jacob A
7 April 1947, Danish. Bragesvej 33, DK-8320 Åbyhøj, Denmark. Degrees: Cand mag. Lecturer, Inst of Pol Sci, U of Aarhus. Publs: *Et enigt Landbrug? Konflikt og samarbejde mellem landbrugets organisationer*; *Danske Organisationers Hvem Hvad Hvor* (with L N Johansen), 1977. Fields: Danish interest organizations; agricultural politics; labour market policy; public planning policy; EEC policy.

[276]
BULL Hedley Norman
10 June 1932, British. 5 Warnborough Road, Oxford, England. Degrees: BA; MA; BPhil (Oxon). 1963-67 Reader in International Relations, LSE; 1965-67 Director, Arms Control and Disarmament Research Unit, The Foreign Office; 1967-77 Professor of International Relations, Australian National U; 1977- Montague Burton Professor of International Relations, U of Oxford and Fellow of Balliol Coll. Publs: *The Control of the Arms Race* (ed), 1961; *Asia and the Western Pacific: Towards a New International Order?*, 1975; *The Anarchical Society: A Study of Order in World Politics*, 1977. Fields: Theory of international relations; history of the modern states system; arms control and disarmament.

[277]
BÜLLESBACH Alfred
29 July 1942, German. Connollystrasse 22, 8000 München 40, FR Germany. Degrees: Dipl Sci Pol. Doctoral thesis: "Planung und Gesetzgebund am Beispiel des Strafvollzugsgesetzes". 1972- Institut of Philosophy of Law and Rechtsinformatik, U of Munich. Publs: "Wahlfachgruppe: Rechtsphilosophie/Rechtssoziologie", *JUS*, 1975; "Inhalt und Grenzen der Wahlfachgruppe 'Rechtsphilosophie — Rechtssoziologie' ", *WEX*, 1976; "Rechtswissenschaft und Sozialwissenschaft", *Einführung in Rechtsphilosophie und Rechtstheorie der Gegenwart*, 1977; System-theoretische Ansätze und ihre Kritik", *Einführung in Rechtsphilosophie und Rechtstheorie der Gegenwart*, 1977; *Kommunikationstheorie im Recht* (co-author), 1978. Fields: Psycholinguistic and sociolinguistic methods of reconstruction of decisions of law; criminology; problems of right of privacy and data security; systems theory and cybernetics of law; the political and social aspects of decision making.

[278]
BURCH Martin Struan
13 October 1946, British. The Owlers, Whaley Bridge, Derbyshire, England. Degrees: BA: PhD (Glasgow), 1975. Doctoral thesis: "The Effects of Opposition Status Upon Certain Major Parties 1964-1970". 1972-75 Research Officer, Dept of Pol Sci, U Coll of Wales, Aberystwyth; 1975 Lecturer in Government, U of Manchester. Fields: Theory and methods of policy analysis; the politics and administration of taxes; Welsh politics.

[279]
BURGELIN Henri Louis Albert
4 August 1931, French. 55 rue Ste Geneviève, 91240 St Michel-sur-Orge, France. Degrees: Lic ès lettres; Agrégé (Sorbonne). Professor, Lycée Maréchal Ney, Saarbrücken; Lycée Fustel de Coulanges, Strasbourg; Assistant, Inst U des Hautes Etudes Internationales, Geneva; Faculté de Lettres, Paris; Maître de conférences, IEP, Paris. Publs: *La société allemande (1871-1968)*, 1964; *La première internationale*, 1962; contributor to *La grande encyclopédie Larousse*, 1966; *Dix leçons sur le nazisme*, 1976. Fields: Modern German history.

[280]
BURGENER Louis William
4 June 1917, Swiss, 81 Gesellschaftsstrasse, CH-3012 Berne, Switzerland. Degrees: Dipl des Höheren Lehramtes (Berne); Dr ès lettres (Genève). Doctoral thesis: "La Confédération suisse et l'éducation physique de la jeunesse". Professeur, Collège de la Chaux-de-Fonds; Professeur, College Neufeld, Berne; Lecturer in History, Genève and Zurich. Publs: *Communes et la Suisse*, 1941; *L'art militaire chez Villehardouin et chez Froissart*, 1943; *La Suisse dans la correspondance de Napoléon Ier*, 1944; *Die Schweizerische Eidgenossenschaft und die Körpererziehung, Quellen 1868-1962*, 1962; *Starke Jugend — freies Volk*, 1960; *Swiss Bibliography: Physical Education 1787-1896*, 1969; *L'éducation corporelle selon Rousseau et Pestalozzi*, 1973; *L'Education physique en Suisse: Histoire et situation actuelle*, 1974; *Sports and Politics*, 1978. Fields: Political science and history in the field of physical activities.

[281]
BURRI Nicholas
9 April 1948, Swiss. Rheinländerstrasse 6, 4056 Basel, Switzerland. Degrees: Lic phil. Publs: *UNO-Abstimmungsverhalten und bilaterale Beziehungen*, 1977. Fields: Foreign relations; international organizations; developing countries.

[282]
BURROUGHES Hugh Randall*
Department of Political Science, University College of Wales, Aberystwyth, Wales. Degrees: BSc; MA (Manchester), 1966. 1960-63 Administrative Work, CEGB; 1966-67 Tutorial Assistant, U of Manchester; 1967- Lecturer, U Coll of Wales. Publs: "Public Inquiries and Large Scale Development", *Public Law*, 1970; "Political and Administrative Problems of Development Planning", *Public Administration*, 1971. Fields: Amenity groups in Wales; non-departmental central government organizations in Britain.

[283]
BURTON John W
2 March 1915, Australian. Oxley Farm, Water Lane, Kent, England. Degrees: BA; PhD; DSc. Doctoral thesis: "Restrictive Intervention". Lecturer, U Coll London; Reader in Pol, U of Kent.

[284]
BUSCH Sibylle
25 October 1949, German. Leibnizstrasse 86, D-1 Berlin 12, FR Germany. Degrees: Dipl Pol. Publs: *Bestimmungsfaktoren, Möglichkeiten und Grenzen Internationaler Arbeitsteilung zwischen unterschiedlichen Gesellschaftssystemen am Beispiel der Beziehungen zwischen der EG und dem RGW*, 1977. Fields: Relations between EEC and COMECON: COMECON monetary relations; East-West and international monetary relations.

[285]
BUTLER David Edgeworth
17 October 1924, British. Nuffield College, Oxford, England. Degrees: MA (Oxon); D Phil (Oxon). 1947-48 Procter Visiting Fellow, U of Princeton, USA;. 1949-51 Student, Nuffield Coll; 1951-54 Research Fellow, Nuffield Coll; 1954-64 Dean and Senior Tutor, Nuffield Coll; 1955-56 Personal Assistant to H M Ambassador in Washington; Fellow, Nuffield Coll, Oxford. Publs: Six volumes in the *Nuffield Series of Election Studies*, 1951-70; *Political Change in Britain* (with D Stokes), 1969; *The Electoral System in Britain since 1918*, 1953; *British Political Facts 1900-1978*, 1978. Fields: British and Australian politics.

[286]
BUTLER Michael John Stewart
18 March 1943, British. 4 Glen Iris Close, Canterbury, Kent, England. Degrees: BSc. Lecturer in Pol and Government, Faculty of Soc Sci, U of Kent. Fields: Community politics, especially in Britain; constituency Labour party and attitudes of Labour party members at constituency level; redress procedures for individuals against administrative action by public authorities.

[287]
BUTLER Peter Freeman
26 July 1945, British. 6 Waverley Avenue, Exeter, England. Degrees: BSc. 1967-69 Research Student, Dept of International Pol, U Coll of Wales. Lecturer, Dept of Pol, U of Exeter. Fields: The significance for contemporary international theory of some aspects of the philosophies of Schopenhauer, Frege and Wittgenstein; history of international thought.

[288]
BUTT Richard Bevan
27 February 1943, British. 10a South Hill Park Gardens, London NW3, England. Degrees: BA; MA (Lancaster), 1969. Senior Research Associate, Inst of Local Government Studies, U of Birmingham; Principal, HM Treasury. Publs: "PPBS in Gloucestershire", *Local Government Studies*, 1972; "PPBS and Transportation", *Journal of Institution of Highway Engineers*, 1972. Fields: Planning, programming, budgeting, systems (PPBS) in British local government; political theory; public policy making.

[289]
BUTTNER Friedemann
18 May 1938, German. Franz Joseph Strasse 10, D-8000 München 40, FR Germany. Degrees: MA; Dr phil. Doctoral thesis: "The Crisis of Power and Authority in Islam. The Destruction of the Islamic Conception of Order in the Confrontation with Modern Europe" (in German). Wiss Assistent, Assistant Professor, Inst of Pol Sci, U of Munich. Publs: *Reform and Revolution in the Islamic World* (ed), 1972; *Social Progress Through Aid? Critical Essay on Western Development Policies* (ed), 1972; *Reform in Uniform? Military Rule and Development in the Third World* (with K Lindenberg *et al*), 1976. Fields: Political theory; political sociology; elite studies; problems of development; Middle Eastern Studies; Arab-Israeli conflict; modern Islam in Egypt.

[290]
BYRD Peter John
4 January 1945, British. 18 Greatheed Road, Leamington Spa, Warwickshire, England. Degrees: BA; PhD (Wales), 1971. Doctoral thesis: "Britain and the Anschluss 1931-1938: Aspects of Appeasement". 1969-72 Research Assistant, Lecturer, U of Glasgow; 1972- Lecturer in Pol, U of Warwick. Publs: Various articles on the history of the British nuclear science trade and commerce in British foreign policy, and Labour Party attitudes towards the European Community. Fields: British foreign policy; the making of foreign policy; the Labour Party; international relations theory.

C

[291]
CABATOFF Kenneth Herbert
30 October 1943, Canadian. Parc de Capeyron, Les Graves D-9, Mérignac 33700, France. Degrees: BA; MA; Dr phil. Doctoral thesis: "NIPA Lahore: An Institutional Case Study". Assistant Professor of Pol Sci, U of Waterloo, Ontario; Professor of Pol Sci, U du Québec, Montreal; Maître de Conférence Associé, IEP, U de Bordeaux 1. Publs: "Radio-Québec: A Case Study of Institution Building", *Canadian Journal of Political Science*, 1978; "Autorité et Syndicalisme à Radio-Québec", in *Programme d'études de cas en administration publique canadienne*; "Radio-Québec: Une Institution publique à la Recherche d'une mission", *Administration Publique du Canada*; "NIPA Lahore", in *Administrative Training and Development* (B B Schaffer (ed)). Fields: Public administration; organization theory; Third World politics.

[292]
CABOARA Lorenzo*
30 October 1905, Italian. Via XX Septembre 5, Genova, Italy. Degrees: Laurea in Giurisprudenza (Rome), 1928; Laurea in Filosofia (Genova), 1929; Libero Docente (Genova), 1943. 1944-68 Professor Incaricato of Constitutional Law, U of Genoa; 1968- Professor of Comparative Law, U of Trieste. Publs: *La Filosofia Politica di Romagnosi*, 1936; *Sulle Origini del Principio di Nazionalità*, 1942; *Autonomia della Filosofia Politica*, 1942; *Democrazia e Libertà nel Pensiero di Alexis de Tocqueville*, 1946. Fields: Italian enlightenment; constitutional politics.

[293]
CACIAGLI Mario
17 October 1938, Italian. Via dei della Robbia, 13, I-50132 Florence, Italy. Degrees: Laurea in Sci Pol (Florence), 1961. Doctoral thesis: "La lotta politica in Valdelsa dal 1892 al 1915". 1969-71 Assistente di scienza dell'administrazione, Facoltà di Sci Pol di Firenze; 1971-72 Professore incaricato di Sci Pol, Facoltà di Sci Pol di Padova, 1973; Professore incaricato di Sci Pol, Facoltà di Sci Pol di Catania; Professore stabilizzato di Sci Pol, Facoltà di Sci Pol, U di Catania. Publs: *Il movimento studentesco nella Germania Federale*, 1968; *Libertà di stampa e censura* (ed), 1970; *L'informazione di classe* (ed), 1972; *Un sistema politico alla prova* (with Spreafico), 1975; "La scienza politica nella Repubblica federale tedesca", 1976; *Democrazia cristiana e potere nel Mezzogiorno*, 1977. Fields: Political parties; elections; local politics.

[294]
CADART Jacques Gustave Eugene
11 February 1922, French. 6 Place Edmond Rostand, 75005 Paris, France. Degrees: Dr en droit; Agrégé de droit; Dipl (IEP); Dr d'Etat de droit public. 1951-69 Chargé de cours, Professor, Faculté de Droit et Sci Econ, Lyon; 1955-56 Professor, Faculté de Droit, U of Alger; 1968-69 Professor, Faculté de Droit et Sci Econ, U of Paris (Nanterre); 1969-70 Professor, Faculté de Droit et Sci Econ, Paris; 1970- Professor, UER de Sci Pol, U of Paris II. Publs: *Régime électoral et régime parlementaire en Grande-Bretagne*, 1948; *La régime électoral des Etats Généraux de 1789 et ses origines 1302-1614*, 1952; *Les tribunaux judiciaires et la notion de service public*, 1954. Fields: Elections and parties; federalism; British government; western political systems.

[295]
CAHIER Philippe
31 March 1932, French. 10 Pedro Meylan, 1208 Geneva, Switzerland. Degrees: Lic en droit (Paris), 1953; DES econ pol (Lyon), 1956; Dr sci pol (Geneva), 1959. 1958-60 Official, International Labour Office, Geneva; 1961-62 Research Fellow, U of Colombia, New York; 1964- Professor of International Law, Graduate Inst of International Studies, Geneva. Publs: *Etude des accordes de siège conclus entre les organisations internationales et les Etats ou elles résident*, 1959; *Le droit diplomatique contemporain*, 1962; "Le problème des effets des traités à l'égard des Etats tiers", *RCABI*, 1974. Fields: The law of treaties after the Vienna convention of 1969; international responsability of states; international arbitration.

[296]
CAHM Eric Selwyn Hilary
20 February 1933, British. School of Languages and Area Studies, Portsmouth Polytechnic, Hampshire Terrace, Portsmouth PO1 2EG, England. Degrees: BA. 1961-66 Assistant Lecturer, Lecturer in French Studies, U of Manchester; 1966-73 Lecturer in French Studies, Graduate School of Contemporary European Studies, U of Reading; 1973-77 Head of School of Languages and Area Studies, Portsmouth Polytechnic. Publs: *Voltaire's Correspondence* (Assistant Editor); *Politics and Society in Contemporary France 1789-1971: A Documentary History*, 1972; *Péguy et le nationalisme francais*, 1972. Fields: French history and political thought since 1870 with special reference to socialism and nationalism; the impact of the Dreyfus affair on French politics and the birth of the modern French political parties.

[297]
CALLOT Emile Francois
13 January 1933, French. 3 Avenue Chabalier, 07600 Vals les Bains, France. Degrees: DES; Dr (FNSP); Doctorat d'Etat. Doctoral thesis: "Le mouvement républicain populaire sous la IVème République- Contribution à l'étude du parti de Gouvernement". Maître-assistant, Sci Pol, U de Grenoble; Chargé de conférences, Faculté de Droit, Lyon. Publs: *Le cinquantenaire du parti démocrate populaire*; *L'importance du politique dans la compréhension des réalités sociales*; *Esquisse d'une theorie de parti de gouvernement*; *Géographie et sociologie électorales du département de la Haute-Savoie de 1956 à 1969*; *Etude d'un parti politique français, Le MRP*; *La conception du chef de l'Etat chez Benjamin Constant et ses rapports au régime politique*. Fields: Political parties; political regimes; institutional history; political methodology; political theory.

[298]
CALVERT Peter Anthony Richard

1936, British. Department of Politics, University of Southampton, Highfield, Southampton S09 5NH, England. Degrees: BA; AM (Michigan), 1961; MA; PhD (Cambridge), 1964. Doctoral thesis: "The Mexican Revolution 1910-14: The Diplomacy of Anglo-American Conflict". 1960-61 Teaching Fellow in History, U of Michigan; 1966 Visiting Lecturer, U of California at Santa Barbara; 1969-70 Research Fellow, Charles Warren Center for Studies in American History, Harvard U; 1964- Lecturer, Senior Lecturer, Reader in Pol, U of Southampton. Publs: *The Mexican Revolution 1910-14: The Diplomacy of Anglo-American Conflict*, 1968; *Latin America; Internal Conflict and International Peace*, 1969; *Revolution: Key Concepts in Political Science*, 1970; *A Study of Revolution*, 1970; *Mexico: Nations of the Modern World*, 1973; *The Mexicans: How They Live and Work*, 1975. Fields: Image-making in US presidential politics; the generation and transmission of political theory in Latin America and elsewhere; the concept of class.

[299]
CALVEZ Jean-Yves

3 February 1927, French. Borgo S Spirito 5, CP-9048, 00100 Roma, Italy. Degrees: Dipl (IEP Paris); Lic ès lettres, DES lettres (Paris); Dipl (Inst des Hautes Etudes Internationales Paris); Dipl (Ecole des Hautes Etudes Paris-Sorbonne). Professor of Soc Ethics and Phil, Faculté de Phil, Les Fontaines; Professor, IEP Paris; Président, Inst d'Etudes Soc, Inst Catholique, Paris; Director, CERAS (Soc Inst), Vanves; Ed, *Revue de l'Action Populaire*, *Projet*; Gen Assistant to the Superior General of the Society of Jesus. Publs: *La pensée de Karl Marx*, 1956; *Le revenu national en Union Soviétique*, 1957; *Droit international et souveraineté en URSS*, 1953; *Eglise et société économique*, 1959-61; *Introduction à la vie politique*, 1967; *Aspects politiques et sociaux des pays en voie de développement*, 1971. Fields: Political philosophy; Marxism; churches and social interests; sociology of religious organizations.

[300]
CAMARA Sylvain

1938. Guinean. 70 rue de Grenelle, 75007 Paris, France. Degrees: Dipl (Lyon); Dipl (Paris); Dr de recherches en sci pol. Doctoral thesis: "Le Conflit Franco-Guinéen". Rédacteur à l'hebdomadaire *Afrique Nouvelle*, Dakar; Chercheur à la FNSP. Publs: "Les Origines du Conflit Franco-Guinéen", *Revue Francaise d'Études Politiques Africaines*, 1975;. "Le Parti Démocratique de Guinée et la Politique des Investissements privés étrangers", *Revue Française d'Études Politiques Africaines*, 1976; "La Guinée et la Coopération Economique en Afrique de l'Ouest", *Cultures et Développement*, 1976; *Le conflit Franco Guinéen*, 1976. Relations between developed and underdeveloped countries; the Lomé convention.

[301]
CAMPA Riccardo

21 April 1934, Italian. Via Salaria 422, Rome, Italy. Professor, U of Bologna, U of Paris, U of London, U of Berlin, Lecturer and Professor at U of Madrid; Professor of Pol Theory, U of Naples. Publs: *Il Pensiero Politico Latinoamericano*; *L'Universo Politico Omogeneo*; *Inevitabilità e Congettura*; *Cultura Occidentale e Processo Politico Latinoamericano*; *Il Profetismo Laico*; *La Realtà e il Progetto Politico*; *El Caracter Secreto del Mundo*. Fields: Political theory; philosophy.

[302]
CAMPBELL Peter Walter
17 June 1926, British. Department of Politics, The University, Whiteknights, Reading RG6 2AA, England. BA; MA (Oxon), 1951. 1949-60 Lecturer, U of Manchester; 1954 Visiting Lecturer, Victoria U Coll, New Zealand; 1960-64 Professor of Pol Economy, U of Reading; 1964- Professor of Pol, U of Reading. Publs: *French Electoral Systems and Elections 1789-1957*, 1958; *Constitution of the Fifth Republic* (with B Chapman), 1958. Fields: Political institutions and sociology; British political culture.

[303]
CAMPBELL Thomas Douglas
3 March 1938, British. 5 Heathfield Drive, Glasgow, Scotland. Degrees: MA (Glasgow), 1962; PhD (Glasgow), 1969. Doctoral thesis: "Adam Smith's Sociology of Morals". 1964-70 Lecturer in Pol Philosophy, U of Glasgow; 1970-73 Lecturer in Moral Philosophy, U of Glasgow; Professor of Philosophy, U of Stirling. Publs: *Adam Smith's Science of Morals*, 1971. Fields: Adam Smith; rights; nationalism.

[304]
CAMUS Roger Gustave Hector
18 December 1928, Belgian. 70 Avenue de la Bugrane, 1020 Bruxelles, Belgium. Degrees: Lic en sci commerciales et financières. Chargé de mission au service spécial d'enquêtes budgétaires; Conseiller du Ministre des Finances de la République du Zaïre; Conseiller au cabinet du Secrétaire d'Etat au budget; Conseiller au cabinet du Secrétaire d'Etat à la coopération au développement; Chef de cabinet adjoint du Ministre de la Prévoyance Sociale; Membre de la Cour des Comptes; Commissaire aux comptes de l'agence de Coopération culturelle et technique (Paris); Chargé de cours, Inst Supérieur de Commerce St Louis (Bruxelles). Fields: Public finance.

[305]
CANAPA Marie-Paule
9 September 1938, French. 60 Quai Fernand Saguet, 94700 Maisons-Alfort, France. Degrees: Dipl (IEP Paris); Dipl de russe et serbocroate (Ecole des Langues Orientales). Doctoral thesis: "Problèmes agraires de la région de Valjevo (Yugoslavia)". Centre d'Etudes des Relations Internationales; FNSP; Attachée de recherche, CNRS. Publs: *Socialisme et réforme économique en Yougoslavie*, 1970. Fields: State, religion and agriculture in Yugoslavia; political institutions in Yugoslavia.

[306]
CANOVAN Margaret Evelyn
25 April 1939, British. 403 Durdar Road, Carlisle, Cumbria, England. Degrees: MA; PhD (Cantab). Doctoral thesis: "Political Thought of Joseph Priestley". 1964-71 Assistant Lecturer, Lecturer in Pol, U of Lancaster; Lecturer in Pol, U of Keele. Publs: *The Political Thought of Hannah Arendt*, 1974; *G K Chesterton-Radical Populist*, 1977. Fields: Modern political thought.

[307]
CAPDEVIELLE Jacques
28 May 1941, French. 37 rue de Grenelle, 75007 Paris, France. Degrees: Dipl (IEP), DES de sci pol; Lic en droit. Attaché de recherche, FNSP. Publs: *Les syndicats ouvriers en France* (with R Mouriaux); *L'ouvrier français en 1970* (with G Adam, F Bon and R Mouriaux); *Le point français- Etude des incidences politiques d'un conflit social* (with E Dupoirier and G Lorant). Fields: Political behaviour in the working classes; social class; power; strategies for an adaptation to crisis.

[308]
CAPITANCHIK David Bernard
5 November 1934, British. 564 King Street, Aberdeen AB2 1SR, Scotland. Degrees: BSc; MSc (Soton), 1967. Senior Lecturer in Pol, Kings Coll, U of Aberdeen. Publs: *The Eisenhower Presidency and American Foreign Policy*, 1969; plus various articles on attitudes and opinions on defence in Britain, including "Public Opinion and Popular Attitudes Towards Defence" in *British Defence Policy in a Changing World* (J Baylis (ed)), 1977. Fields: Political sociology, especially with reference to Israel; the relationship between social and political theory and public policy-making.

[309]
CAPLINGER James L
6 May 1938, American. Douzastraat 52, 2581 R2, The Hague, The Netherlands. Degrees: BA; JD (Law) (Ohio). Law Director, City of Springfield, Ohio, USA; City Manager, City of Springfield, Ohio, USA; City Manager, City of Kalamazoo, Michigan, USA; Adjunct Professor, Antioch Coll, Ohio, U of Western Michigan, Kalamazoo College, and Kalamazoo Valley Community Coll, Michigan, USA; Director, North American Urban Liaison Office, The Hague. Publs: Various articles on affirmative action, employee fringe benefits, international education. Fields: International education for practitioners; idea transfer (technology and management between Europe and North America; comparative local government; comparative local government; comparative central and regional government; citizen participation; internationalization of city management profession.

[310]
CAPURSO Marcello
9 January 1910, Italian. Via dei Colli della Farnesina 128, Rome, Italy. Degrees: Laurea (Perugia), 1931. 1953-70 Cattedratico di Dottrina dello Stato; Professor Incaricato di Filosofia del Diritto, U of Cagliari; 1971-74 Cattedratico di Filosofia del Diritto, U of Perugia; Cattedratico di Diritto Costituzionale Italiano e Comparato, U of Perugia; Incaricato di Dottrina dello Stato nella Scuola di Perfezionamento in Filosofia del Diritto, U of Rome. Publs: *Potere e Classi nella Francia della Restaurazione*, 1974; *Accentramento e Costituzionalismo*, 1959; *Che cosa è lo Stato*, 1966; *I Limiti della Sovranità negli Ordinamenti democratici*, 1967; *I Giudici della Repubblica*, 1977. Fields: Judiciary; community law; theory of interpretation.

[311]
CARLBOM Terry
22 December 1936, Swedish. Valloxvägen 41, S-74100 Knivsta, Sweden. Degrees: Dr fil. Doctoral thesis: "The Localization of University Education in Sweden 1950-1965. A Study in Political Influence". Lecturer, U of Uppsala and the U Coll of Journalism, Stockholm. Publs: articles on mass media. Fields: Mass media, especially the broadcasting companies of Scandinavia.

[312]
CARLING Alan Hugh
25 November 1949, British. 18 Sherborne Road, Bradford 7, West Yorkshire, England. Degrees: BA; MA (Essex). 1975-77 Lecturer in Soc, U of Manchester; Lecturer in Soc, School of Interdisciplinary Human Studies, U of Bradford. Publs: "The Unified Solution of the Cross-Coddington Model of the Bargaining Process", *Public Choice*, 1977. Fields: Political sociology; Marxist theory; sociology of organizations; mathematical models in the social sciences.

[313]
CARLSNAES Walter Emanuel
27 October 1943, Swedish. Gröfthöjparken 161, lejl 152, DK-826 Viby J, Denmark. Degrees: Fil kand (Uppsala); Fil lic (Uppsala); MA (Princeton); D Phil (Oxon). Doctoral thesis: "The Concept of Ideology and Political Analysis". Doctoral Fellow, U of Princeton and U of Uppsala; Kennedy Fellow, Harvard U; Florey Scholar, Oxford; Senior Lecturer in International Relations, Inst of Pol Sci, U of Aarhus. Publs: *The Concept of Ideology and Political Analysis*; *The Comparative Study of Foreign Policy and the Concept of Ideology*, 1978; "The Concept of African Nationalism", in *Idéer och Ideologier* (C A Hessler (ed)), 1969. Fields: Comparative foreign policy; conceptual analysis; regional integration; African politics; methodological aspects of political science.

[314]
CARRERE D'ENCAUSSE Hélène
French. 16 rue Raynouard, 75016 Paris, France. Degrees: Dr ès lettres (Sorbonne), 1976. Doctoral thesis: "Bolchevisme et nation 1917-1929". Maître de Recherches, FNSP; Professeur, IEP, Paris. Publs: *Le Marxisme et l'Asie*, 1965; *Réforme et révolution chez les musulmans de l'empire russe*, 1966; *L'URSS et la Chine devant la révolution des sociétés pré-industrielles*, 1970; *L'URSS, de Lénine à Staline*, 1972; *La politique soviétique au Moyen-Orient*, 1975; *Central Asia, a Century of Russian Rule* (Alworth (ed)), 1967. Fields: Marxism and the national question; Soviet national policy; bolshevism and international revolution; Soviet ideology and politics.

[315]
CARVER Terrell
4 September 1946, American. 4 Fulwood Park, Liverpool L17 5AG, England. Degrees: BA; B Phil; D Phil (Oxon). Doctoral thesis: "A Study of Marx's Methodology with Special Reference to the Grundrisse". Kellett Fellow, U of Columbia (held at Balliol Coll, Oxford); Lecturer, U of Liverpool. Publs: *Karl Marx: Texts on Method*, 1975. Fields: Marx; Marxism.

[316]
CASANOVA Jean-Claude*
11 June 1934, French. 32 rue du Vieux-Versailles, 78 Versailles, France. Degrees: Dr en sci econ (Paris); Dipl (IEP Paris); Agrégé des Facultés de Droit et Sci Econ. Doctoral thesis: "Essai sur quelques Tentatives d'Intégration de l'Economie". 1959-62 Chargé de recherche, Cabinet of Minister of Industry; 1965-69 Professeur, Faculté de Droit, U de Nancy; 1968-69 Professeur, Faculté de Droit, U de Paris-Nanterre; Professeur, Inst d'Etudes Pol; Directeur d'Etudes et Recherches, FNSP. Publs: *Politique Nationale de la Science: Etats Unis*, 1968; *Principes d'Analyse Economique*. Fields: Politics and economics in international relations.

[317]
CASES MENDEZ Jose Ignacio
9 July 1942, Spanish. Carretera al Plantio, Edificio Airesol 1, 3°B, Majadahonda, Madrid, Spain. Degrees: Dr en Derecho; Licenciado. Doctoral thesis: "Elecciones a Diputados y Partidos Politicos Baso Isabel II 1836-67". Professor in Electoral Soc, Spanish Public Law, Facultad Ciencias Pol, U de Madrid. Publs: Articles about electoral sociology and Spanish public law. Fields: Electoral sociology; Spanish history; Spanish public law.

[318]
CASTLES Francis Geoffrey
16 September 1943, British. 49 St Matthews Parade, Northampton, England. Degrees: BA. Assistant Lecturer in Pol, U of York; Lecturer in Pol, School of General Studies, Australian National U; Senior Lecturer in Pol Sci, Open U. Publs: *Pressure Groups and Political Culture*, 1967; *Politics and Social Insight*, 1971; *Decisions, Organizations and Society* (with D C Potter and D J Murray (ed)), 1976; *The Social Democratic Image of Society*, 1978. Fields: Scandinavian politics; comparative politics.

[319]
CATANZARO Raimondo
22 November 1942, Italian. Via Nizzeti 68, Catania, Italy. Degrees: Degree in Law (Catania), 1965. 1969-70 Assistente Incaricato, Faculty of Pol Sci, U of Catania; 1971-72 Honorary Lecturer in Sociological Studies, U of Sheffield; 1972- Lecturer in Soc of Econ, Faculty of Pol Sci, U of Catania. Publs: "Mobilizatione Sociale e Sviluppo Politico in Sicilia", *Rassegna Italiana di Sociologia*, 1973; *Community Power, Political Participation and Socio-economic Development* (with F C Bruhns *et al* (eds)); *Local Politics and Participation*, 1974; "Potere e Politica Locale in Italia", *Quaderni di Sociologia*, 1975; "Comportamento Collettivo e Mutamento Sociale", *Sociologia*, 1969; "Il Potere nella Communità", *Scienze Sociali*, 1971. Fields: Double working and class attitudes in southern Italy; welfare state and the reproduction of class structure; class structure in Italy; local government and politics in southern Italy; entrepreneurship in an underdeveloped Italian region.

[320]
CATHELINEAU Jean
5 April 1936, French. 40 Avenue Jeanne d'Arc, Bordeaux 33000, France. Doctoral thesis: "Le Contrôles des Finances Communales en France". Publs: *La fiscalité des collectivités publiques locales,* 1971; *Le contrôle des finances communales en France,* 1963; *Finances publiques,* 1975. Fields: Public finance; town planning and land development.

[321]
CAVALLI Luciano*
12 February 1924, Italian. Via Ricasoli 39, Firenze, Italy. Degrees: Laurea (Genoa); Libera Docenza in Sociologia. Direttore dell'Istituto di Sci Soziali; Professor Incaricato, Facoltà di Giurisprudenza, U of Genoa; Direttore dell'Istituto di Sociologia; Facoltà di Sci Pol; Professore ordinario di Sociologia, Facoltà de Sci Pol, U of Firenze. Publs: "La Democrazia manipolata", *Communità*, 1965; *La Città divisa*, 1965; *Max Weber: Religione e società*, 1968; *Il Mutamento sociale*, 1970. Fields: Social change; political sociology, leadership; history of sociology.

[322]
CAWSON Alan
3 February 1947, British. 83 Hollingbury Park Avenue, Brighton BN1 7JQ, England. Degrees: BA; Dr phil. Doctoral thesis: "Local Politics and Indirect Rule in Cape Coast, Ghana 1928-37". Lecturer in Social Policy, Preston Polytechnic; Lecturer in Pol, U of Sussex. Publs: "Pluralism, Corporatism and the Role of the State", *Government and Opposition*, 1978. Fields: Theories of the state; interest groups; politics and planning; local and urban politics.

[323]
CAYROL Roland Marc Gilbert

11 August 1941, French. 25 rue des Lilas, 75019 Paris, France. 1962-64 Secrétaire du Club Jean Moulin; 1964-65 Chargé d'études à l'ORTF; 1965-68 Assistant de l'Association Française de Sci Pol; Attaché de recherche, chargé de recherche, FNSP (Centre d'étude de la vie politique française contemporaine). Publs: "La Campagne Électorale", in *L'élection présidentielle de 1965* (in collaboration), 1970; "La Gauche", in *Les élections législatives de Mai 1967*, 1971; *"Histoire et Sociologie d'un parti"*, in *Le PSU et l'avenir socialiste de la France* (M Rocard *et al*), 1969; *François Mitterrand, 1945-1967*, 1967; *La presse écrite et audiovisuelle*, 1973; *Le député français* (with J L Parodi and C Ysmal), 1973; *La télévision fait-elle l'élection* (with J Blumler and G Thoveron), 1978. Fields: Study of political parties; political personnel; media and politics.

[324]
CAZENEUVE Jean

17 May 1915, French. 4 rue du Domaine, 78110 Le Vésinet, France. Degrees: Agrégé; Dr ès lettres. Directeur scientifique, CNRS; Professor, U of Paris; Director adjoint, Inst français de Presse; Président, Office des techniques modernes d'éducation; Vice-Président, Association internationale des sociologues de langue française; Président, Société Nationale de Télévision, TFI. Publs: *La mentalité archaique*, 1961; *Sociologie de la radio-television*, 1963; *Bonheur et civilisation*, 1966; *L'ethnologie*, 1967; *La sociologie*, 1970; *Sociologie du rite*, 1971; *Société de l'ubiquité*, 1972; *Guide alphabétique des mass-média*, 1973; *L'homme téléspectateur*, 1976. Fields. Mass media; anthropology.

[325]
CAZORLA José

29 March 1931, Spanish. Las Mercedes 31, Granada, Spain. Degrees: Dr of Law (Granada), 1964; Premio Extraordinario del Doctorado, 1963-65. Doctoral thesis: "Factores de la Estructura Socio-economica de Anadalucia Oriental". Professor Ayundante, Professor Adjunto, Professor Agregado, Dept de Derecho Politico, Facultad de Derecho, U of Granada; 1970-73 Director de Investigacion, Instituto de Ciencias de la Educacion, U de Granada; 1976 Visiting Professor, Oakland U, Michigan, USA; Catedratico de Derecho Politico, Facultad de Derecho, U de Granada; Vice-rector de la U. Publs: *Factores de la Estructura Socio-economica de Andalucia Oriental*, 1965; *Estructura Social de Andalucia* (co-author), 1970; *Problemas de Estratificacion Social En Espana*, 1973; *La Universidad de Granada a Comienzos de los Anos 70: un Analisi Sociopolitico*, 1977. Fields: Sociology of development; regional differences in Spain; political sociology; sociology of higher education.

[326]
CAZZOLA Franco

11 April 1941, Italian. Via Mollica 6, Cannizzaro, Italy. Degrees: Laurea; Libera Docenza. Doctoral thesis: "The Ruling Class in Maghreb". Professor of Pol Sci, U of Trento; Professor of Pol Sci and Legislative Behaviour, U of Catania. Publs: *Il Sistema Politico dell'Italia Contemporanea*, 1978; *Governo e Opposizione nel Parlamento Italiano*, 1975; *Il Partito come Organizzazione*, 1969. Fields: Government role in economic development; sociology of parties and elections.

[327]
CECIL Robert
25 March 1913, British. Barb Ridge, Hambledon, Hants PO7 6RU, England. Degrees: BA; MA (Cantab). 1968 Reader, Contemporary European History, U of Reading; 1970-73 Deputy Chairman, Graduate School of Contemporary European Studies, U of Reading; 1976- Chairman, Graduate School of Contemporary European Studies, U of Reading; Chairman, Institute for Culture Research. Publs: *Life in Edwardian England*, 1969; *The Myth of the Master Race: Alfred Rosenberg and Nazi Ideology*, 1972; *Hitler's Decision to Invade Russia*, 1975; *Hitler's War Machine* (ed adviser), 1975. Fields: Ideology; international cultural relations.

[328]
CHAMBRE Henri
13 January 1908, French. 15 rue Marcheron, 92 Vanves, France. Degrees: Ingénieur civil des Mines. 1957-69 Directeur d'Etudes, Ecole Pratique des Hautes Etudes, Section des Sci Econ et Soc, Paris-Sorbonne; 1968-73 Sous-Directeur, Collège de France, Laboratoire d'Analyse des Faits écon et soc; 1973- Membre du Comité de direction et Directeur de Recherches à l'Inst des Sci Math et Econ Appliquées. Publs: *Le Marxisme en Union Soviétique*, 1955; *L'aménagement du territoire en URSS*, 1959; *Union Soviétique et développement économique*, 1967; *L'Economie planifiée*, 1975; *L'Evolution du marxisme soviétique*, 1974; *De Karl Marx à Lénine et Mao-Tsé-Toung*, 1976. Fields: Economics of planning; mathematical economics and econometrics; economic activity analysis.

[329]
CHAPMAN Brian*
6 April 1923, British. Department of Government, University of Manchester, Manchester M13 9PL, England. Degrees: Dr phil. 1949-60 Department of Government, U of Manchester, and Visiting Professor at European Universities; 1960-61 Foundation Professor of Government, Director, Public Administration Programme, U of the West Indies; 1967-71 Dean, Faculty of Econ and Soc Studies, U of Manchester; 1972 Visiting Professor, Queen's U, Canada; Professor of Government, U of Manchester. Publs: *The Life and Times of Baron Haussman*, 1956; *The Profession of Government*, 1959; *The Fifth Constitution* (with P Campbell), 1959; *British Government Observed*, 1963; *The Police State*, 1970. Fields: Legal philosophy; military and police studies; military history.

[330]
CHAPMAN Jennifer P
Department of Politics, University of Strathclyde, McCance Building, Richmond Street, Glasgow C1, Scotland. Degrees: MA (Edinburgh). Assistant Lecturer, U of Strathclyde; 1967-68 Field Research in the Soviet Union; Lecturer, U of Strathclyde. Fields: The relationship of communist states; communist political systems.

[331]
CHAPMAN Richard Arnold
15 August 1937, British. 10 The Village, Brancepeth, Durham DH7 8DG, England. Degrees: BA; MA (Carleton), 1962; PhD (Leicester), 1966; MBIM, 1975. Doctoral thesis: "The Decision Making Process in British Government: A Case Study of the Decision to Raise the Bank Rate in September 1957". 1953-62 Civil Servant; 1961-62 Assistant in Pol Sci, U of Carleton; 1962-63 Assistant Lecturer in Pol, U of Leicester; 1963-68 Leverhulme Lecturer in Public Administration, U of Liverpool; 1968-71 Senior Lecturer in Local Government and Administration, U of Birmingham; 1971- Reader in Pol, U of Durham. Publs: *Decision Making*, 1969; *The Higher Civil Service in Britain*,

1970; *Style in Administration: Readings in British Public Administration* (A Dunsire (ed)), 1971; *The Role of Commissions in Policy Making* (contributor and ed), 1973; *Teaching Public Administration*, 1973. Fields: The British civil service; local government in England and Wales; development administration; administrative theory.

[332]
CHARLOT Jean
16 March 1932, French. 191 rue d'Alésia, 75014 Paris, France. Degrees: Dipl (IEP Paris), 1956; Dr, 1966; Dr ès lettres et soc pol, 1966; Doctoral thesis: "L'UNR-étude du pouvoir au sein d'un parti politique". Professor, IEP, Paris. Publs: *L'union pour la nouvelle République*, 1967; *Les Anglais devant la loi*, 1968; *Le phénomène gaulliste*, 1970; *Répertoire des publications des partis politiques français, 1944-67*, 1970; *Le gaullisme*, 1970; *Les partis politiques*, 1971; *Les Français et De Gaulle*, 1971; *Quand la Gauche peut gagner*, 1973. Fields: Political and party systems in Western countries.

[333]
CHARLOT Monica
31 March 1933, French. 191 rue d'Alésia, 75014 Paris, France. Degrees; BA (London); Agrégé d'anglais; Dr ès lettres. Doctoral thesis: "Les élections législatives en Grande-Bretagne depuis 1931". Lecturer, Nanterre; Professeur, Sorbonne (Paris III). Publs: *La démocratie à l'anglaise*, 1972; *Le syndicalisme en Grande-Bretagne*, 1970; *Le système politique britannique*, 1975; *La persuasion politique*, 1975; *Vivre avec la mort*, 1976; *Encyclopédie de civilisation britannique*, 1975; *Les femmes dans la société britannique*, 1977. Fields: French and British politics, especially voting behaviour; political persuasion; political elites.

[334]
CHARNAY Jean-Paul
18 July 1928, French. 20 rue de Beaune, 75005 Paris, France. Degree: Dr en droit (Paris), 1962; Dr ès sci pol (Paris X), 1977; Dr de recherche (Paris), 1962. Doctoral thesis: "Sociologie religieuse de l'Islam. Prolégomènes"; Chef de Travaux, Ecole Pratique des Hautes Etudes; Chargé de recherche, Maître de recherche, CNRS; Directeur du Centre d'Etudes et de Recherche sur les Stratégies et les Conflits, U de Paris-Sorbonne. Publs: *Société militaire et suffrage politique en France depuis 1789*, 1964; *La vie musulmane en Algérie d'après la jurisprudence de la première moitié du XXème siècle*, 1965; *Islamic Culture and Socio-economic Change*, 1971; *Essai général de stratégie*, 1973; *Réédition des écrits stratégiques de Guibert*, 1977; *De l'impérialisme à la décolonisation* (with J Berque et al), 1965; *Normes et valeurs dans l'Islam contemporain*, 1966; *L'ambivalence dans la culture arabe*, 1967. Fields: Voting in France; history and sociology of strategy; changes in contemporary muslim societies.

[335]
CHATELET Francois
27 April 1925, French. 7 ter rue Clauzel, 75009 Paris, France. Degrees: Dr ès lettres. Doctoral thesis: "La naissance de l'histoire. Essai sur la formation de la pensée historienne de la Grèce classique". Professeur de Lettres, Lycée Louis Le Grand; Professeur, U de Paris VIII; Directeur de l'UER de Phil; Chargé de cours d'histoire des idées pol, U de Paris I; Maître de conférences de Phil, Ecole polytechnique de Paris. Publs: *Périclès*, 1960; *La naissance de l'histoire*, 1972; *Platon*, 1965; *Hegel*, 1968; *Les marxistes et la politique* (co-author), 1975; *Histoire de la philosophie* (co-author), 1972-73; *Chronique des idées perçues*, 1977; *Histoire des idéologies*, 1978. Fields: Historical and philosophical origins of the State; theory of state power and relations with society; new forms of politics and the defence of freedom.

[336]
CHAZEL Francois Michel
10 December 1937, French. 266 Cours de l'Argonne, 33000 Bordeaux, France. Degrees: Dr ès lettres. Doctoral thesis: "La théorie analytique de la société dans l'oeuvre de Talcott Parsons: sa genèse et son apport". Lecturer, Harvard U; Attaché de recherche, CNRS; Maître Assistant, Faculté des Lettres et Sci Humaines, U de Bordeaux; Maître de Conférences de Soc Sci; Professeur de Sociologie, U de Bordeaux II. Publs: *L'analyse des processus sociaux* (with R Boudon and P Lazarsfeld), 1970; *Sociologie politique* (with P Birnbaum), 1971; *La théorie analytique de la société dans l'oeuvre de Talcott Parsons*, 1974; *Théorie sociologique* (with P Birnbaum), 1975; *Durkheim: les règles de la méthode sociologique*, 1975; "Power, Cause and Force", in *Power and Political Theory: Some European Perspectives* (B Barry (ed)), 1976. Fields: Conceptual and empirical analyses of power; political mobilization; political alienation; sociological theories: the processes of their construction and of their change.

[337]
CHENOT Bernard Marie Emile*
20 May 1909, French. 16 Avenue Pierre Ier de Serbie, Paris 16ème, France. Degrees: Lic en droit; Dipl. Auditeur, Maître des Requêtes, Conseiller d'Etat; Secrétaire général du Conseil économique; Ministre de la Santé Publique et Population; Ministre de la Justice; Vice-Président, Conseil d'Etat; Professeur, Inst d'Etudes Pol. Publs: *Histoire des idées politiques*, 1949; *Organisation économique de l'Etat*, 1965; *Les entreprises nationalisées*, 1970; *Etre ministre*, 1967; *Référendum*, 1969; *L'hôpital en question*, 1970. Fields: Social and economic policy; nationalized industries; economic and social administration.

[338]
CHESTER Norman (Sir)
27 October 1907, British. 136 Woodstock Road, Oxford, England. Degrees: MA (Oxon); MA; Hon Litt D (Manchester). 1935-36 Rockefeller Fellow; 1936-45 Lecturer in Public Administration, U of Manchester; 1940-45 Member Economic Section, War Cabinet Secretariat; 1945-54 Official Fellow, Nuffield Coll, Oxford; 1954- Warden, Nuffield Coll, Oxford. Publs: *Public Control of Road Passenger Transport*, 1936; *Central and Local Government Financial and Administrative Relations*, 1951; *The Nationalized Industries*, 1951; *Lessons of the British War Economy* (ed), 1951; *Organization of British Central Government, 1914-46* (ed), 1957; *Questions in Parliament* (with Mrs Browning), 1962; *The Nationalization of British Industry, 1945-51*, 1975. Fields: Public corporations and boards; history of British administration.

[339]
CHEVALIER Louis
29 May 1911, French. Collège de France, 11 Place M Berthelot, 75005 Paris, France. Publs: *Classes laborieuses, classes dangereuses à Paris pendant la première moitié du XIXème siècle*; *Les Parisiens*; *Histoire anachronique des français*; *L'assassinat de Paris*.

[340]
CHEVALLIER Jacques
2 July 1943, French. 57 rue Lhomond, 75005 Paris, France. Degrees: Dr en droit. Doctoral thesis: "L'élaboration historique du principe de séparation de la juridiction administrative et de l'administration active". 1966-69 Assistant, Faculté de Droit de Paris; 1970 Maître de conférences agrégé, Faculté de Droit de Nancy; 1970-74 Maître de conférences agrégé, Faculté de Droit d' Amiens; Professeur de Droit Public et Sci Pol, U d' Amiens. Publs: *Traité de science administrative* (with D Loschak), 1978; *La participation dans l'administration française*, 1975; *L'intérêt général dans l'administration française*, 1976; *Centre et périphérie dans l'analyse politique*. Fields: General theory of state; law; general theory of systems; administration and civil service.

[341]
CHEVALLIER Jean Jacques Joseph
15 February 1900, French. 45 Avenue des Cottages, 92340 Bourg la Reine, France. Degrees: Agrégé des Facultés de Droit; Dr ès sci pol et econ (Nancy), 1924; Dr ès sci juridiques (Nancy), 1925. Doctoral thesis: "L'instruction de service et le recours pour excès de pouvoir". 1926-42 Professeur, Faculté de Droit, U de Grenoble; 1943-70 Professeur, Faculté de Droit, U de Paris; 1942-67 Professeur, Ecole libre des Sci Pol, Inst d'Etudes Pol, U de Paris; Professeur honoraire, Faculté de Droit, U de Grenoble et U de Paris. Publs: *L'évolution de l'Empire Britannique*, 1931; *La société des nations britanniques*, 1939; *Les grandes oeuvres politiques de Machiavel à nos jours*, 1949; *Histoire des institutions politiques de la France moderne (1789-1845)*, 1952; *Histoire des institutions et des régimes de la France moderne (1789-1969)*, 1977. Fields: History of political ideas; institutions of the Fifth Republic.

[342]
CHEVRILLON Olivier
28 January 1929, French. 15 rue Maître Albert, 75005 Paris, France. Degrees: DES droit public; Dipl ENA (Paris). Maître des requêtes au Conseil d'État; Président-Directeur Général de *L'Express*; Président-Directeur-Général, Editorialiste du *Point*. Fields: USSR; USA; French domestic politics.

[343]
CHILDS David Hallam
25 September 1933, British. Department of Politics, University of Nottingham, University Park, Nottingham NG7 2RD, England. Degrees: BSc (Econ); PhD (LSE), 1961. Doctoral thesis: "The Development of German Socialist Thought". 1956-57 British Council Scholarship, U of Hamburg; 1961-64 Documentary TV; 1965-66 Bromley Technical Coll; 1966- Lecturer, Reader, Senior Lecturer in Pol, U of Nottingham. Publs: *East Germany*, 1969; *Germany Since 1918*, 1971; *Marx and the Marxists: An Outline History of Practice and Theory*, 1973; "The Ostpolitik and Domestic Politics in East Germany", in *The Ostpolitik and Political Change in Germany* (Tilford (ed)), 1975; "Sport in the German Democratic Republic", in *Sport Under Communism* (Riordan (ed)), 1978; "The British Communist Party and the War 1939-41", *Journal of Contemporary History*, 1977. Fields: Germany, especially parties; Labour and Communist movements; fascism; military and politics.

[344]
CHIROUX René
1936, French. 75 Avenue Jean Jaurès, 63400 Chamalières, France. Degrees: Dr. Doctoral thesis: "L'administration locale en Algérie". Fields: Electoral sociology; intercommunity relations; international relations, especially Southern Africa; constitutional law, especially Conseil Constitutionnel; international law of development and Third World countries.

[345]
CHOMBART DE LAUWE Paul-Henry
4 August 1913, French. Centre d'Ethnologie Sociale et de Psychosociologie, 1 rue du Onze Novembre, 92120 Montrouge, France. Degrees: Dr ès lettres (Sorbonne). Doctoral thesis: "La vie quotidienne des familles ouvrières". Maître de recherche, CNRS; Professor Ecole des Hautes-Etudes en Soc Sci (Pain) and Directeur du Centre d'Ethnologie Sociale (CNRS). Publs: *La culture et le pouvoir*, 1975; *Pour une sociologie des aspirations*, 1970; *Pour l'université avant, pendant et après Mai 1968*, 1968; *Des hommes et des villes*, 1965; *La vie quotidienne des familles ouvrières*, 1977; *Aspirations et transformations sociales* (co-author), 1970; *Transformation de l'environnement, des aspirations et des valeurs*, 1976. Fields: Research of social transformation and individual groups; relations between the processes of technical transformation and economy; the processes of transformation of social reports and the psychosocial processes; consequences of the definition of decision-making democracy.

[346]
CHRISTENSEN Jørgen Grønnegård
12 May 1944, Danish. Muslingevej 37, DK-8250 Egå, Denmark. Degrees: Cand sci pol. 1970-72 Assistant Professor, Inst of Pol Sci, U of Aarhus; 1972-76 Ministry of Finance, Dept of Administrative Organization and Dept of the Budget and Part-time Lecturer, Inst of Management, U of Aarhus; Assistant Professor, Inst of Management, U of Aarhus. Publs: "The Influence of Integration on National Administrative Structures in the EC" (in Danish), *Nordiske Administrativet Tidsskrift*, 1971; "The Administrative Consequences of New Legislation", *Nordiske Administrativet Tidsskrift*, 1974; *Decision-making on the Jurisdictions of Government Departments*, 1977. Fields: Public administration, especially the interaction between political and bureaucratic management at the central governmental level and the conditions of reform of governmental organization.

[347]
CHUBB Frederick Basil
8 December 1921, Irish. 19 Clyde Road, Ballsbridge, Dublin 4, Ireland. Degrees: BA; D Phil (Oxon), 1950; Litt D (Dublin), 1976. Doctoral thesis: "Financial Committees of the House of Commons". Lecturer and Reader in Pol Sci, Trinity Coll, U of Dublin; Professor of Pol Sci, Trinity Coll, U of Dublin. Publs: *The Control of Public Expenditure*, 1952; *The Constitution of Ireland*, 1970; *A Source Book of Irish Government*, 1964; *Economic Development and Planning* (co-ed with P Lynch), 1969; *The Government and Politics of Ireland*, 1970; *Cabinet Government in Ireland*, 1974. Fields: The government and politics of Ireland; comparative administration.

[348]
CIALDEA Basilio
May 1909, Italian. Via Appennini 25/B, 00198 Rome, Italy. Degrees: Dr in Law (Rome). Doctoral thesis: "Protezione di Minoranze Nazionali nella SDN". Professor, U of Genoa; Professor, Faculty of Pol Sci, U of Rome. Publs: *L'Equilibrio Europeo 1648-1789*; *Gli Stati Italiani e la Pace dei Pirenei*; *L'Italia e l'Equilibrio Europeo (1861-1867)*; *L'Ordinamento Marittimo nelle Relazioni Internazionali*; *La Chiesa tra i Concili Vaticani I e II*; *La Conferenza di Genova del 1922*; *L'Europa nelle Conferenze di Tehran, Yalta e Potsdam*; *La Cooperazione Europea*; *Il Sistema Coloniale tra le Due Guerre Mondiali*. Fields: International relations.

[349]
CLAES Lode*
17 June 1913, Belgian. Collegestraat 22, Brussels, Belgium. Degrees: Dr en droit (Catholic U of Louvain); Lic sci pol et soc. Barrister, Journalist, General Secretary of the Flemish Council for Econ Development; Senator for the Brussels Arrondissement; Director, Compagnie Lambert. Publs: Articles in *Streven*; *De Maand*; *Revue Nouvelle*. Fields: Economic policy.

[350]
CLAEYS BOUUAERT Ignace
9 January 1920, Belgian. Paul Fredericqstraat 13, 9000 Ghent, Belgium. Degrees: Dr en droit; Lic en notariat; Lic en sci pol; Dipl; Agrégé de l'enseignement supérieur. Professor, U of Ghent; Barrister. Fields: Comparative tax law.

[351]
CLAEYS Paul Henri
18 May 1937, Belgian. Avenue des martinets 36, 1160 Brussels, Belgium. Degrees: Dr; Lic. Doctoral thesis: "Groupes de pression en Belgique; les groupes intermédiaires socio-économiques". Aspirant, Fonds National de la Recherche Scientifique; Chargé de cours, U Libre de Bruxelles, Maître de recherche, Inst de Sociologie. Publs: "L'action des groupes de pression économiques et son institutionalisation", *Revue de l'Institut de Sociologie*, 1963; *Groupes de pression en Belgique*, 1973; "Les groupements européens de partis politiques" (with N Loeb-Mayer), *Res Publica*, 1977; *Pluralisme, politique et clivage linguistique: Le "cas" belge*, 1978. Fields: European political parties; political and social stratification; theories of negotiation.

[352]
CLAEYS VAN HAEGENDOREN Mieke*
8 January 1943, Belgian. Pleinstraat 5a, 3520 Zonhoven, Belgium. Degrees: Dr Pol Sci (Leuven), 1968. Doctoral thesis: "25 Jaar Belgisch Socialisme, Evolutie van de Verhouding van der Belgische Werkliedenpartij tot de Parlementaire Democratie in België". Researcher, Inst of Pol Studies, U of Leuven; Teacher, Economische Hogeschool, Limburg. Publs: *25 Jaar Belgisch Socialisme*, 1967. Fields: Political pluralism in Belgium.

[353]
CLAPHAM Christopher
20 March 1941, British. Chapel Cottages, Ellel, Lancaster, England. Degrees: BA; D Phil (Oxon), 1966; MA (Oxon), 1967. Doctoral thesis: "The Institutions of the Central Ethiopian Government, 1941-1966". Lecturer, Haile Selassie U, U of Manchester, U of West Indies; Lecturer, Senior Lecturer in Pol, U of Lancaster. Publs: *Haile Selassie's Government*, 1969; *Liberia and Sierra Leone: An Essay in Comparative Politics*, 1976; *Foreign Policy Making in Developing States*, 1977. Fields: Political explanation; comparative politics with special reference to Africa.

[354]
CLARK Martin
30 September 1938, British. Degrees: MA (Cantab); PhD (London). Lecturer, Dept of Pol, U of Edinburgh. Publs: *Antonio Gramsci and the Revolution that Failed*; "Italy-Regionalism and Bureaucratic Reform", in *The Failure of the State* (J Cornford (ed)); various articles on Italian politics in *Parliamentary Affairs*; on Sorel and the Futurist, *Futures* 1976, 1978; and on Gramsci in various journals. Fields: Modern Italian politics; eurocommunism; public order.

[355]
CLARKE David Kenneth
9 February 1912, British. The Dark House, Kingsbury, Milborne Port, Sherborne, Dorset, England. Degrees: MA (Cantab); CBE. 1935-38 Member of Conservative Research Dept; 1940-45 Civil Assistant, General Staff War Office; 1945-51 Director, Conservative Research Dept; 1951-61 Director, Research Administrative Staff Coll; 1961-67 Director of Management Studies, Research Fellow in Administration, U of Bristol; 1967-72 Principal, Swinton Conservative Coll; 1972- Retired, part-time Tutor, Open U. Publs: *The Conservative Faith in a Modern Age*, 1947; *Conservatism 1945-1950* (ed); *The Conservative Party*, 1975. Fields: Political parties in the UK; public administration.

[356]
CLEMENS-AUGUST Andre
5 March 1929, Austrian. A-6020 Innsbruck, Anton-Rauch-Strasse 13C, Austria. Degrees: Dr rer pol (Marburg), 1950; Habilitation (Köln), 1955; A Ord Professor (Innsbruck), 1958; Ord Professor (Innsbruck), 1962. Doctoral thesis: ''Finanzielle Stabilität als Richtschnur der Finanzpolitik''. Professor, Inst für Finanzwissenschaft, U of Innsbruck. Publs: *Finanztheorie* (with R Mauser), 1969; *Sündenbock Unternehmer* (with B Freudenfeld), 1973; *Finanzpolitik* (with K Schlögl), 1975. Fields: Money and finance politics; questions of law and middle class politics.

[357]
CLEMENTS Roger Victor
8 February 1925, British. Department of Politics, University of Bristol, 40 Berkeley Square, Bristol BS8 1HY, England. Degrees: BA; B Litt (Oxon), 1953; MA (Wisconsin), 1952. 1953-55 Research Assistant, U of Manchester; 1957- Assistant Lecturer, Lecturer, Senior Lecturer in Pol, U of Bristol. Publs: *Managers: A Study of their Careers in Industry*, 1957; *The Choice of Careers by Schoolchildren*, 1957; *Voting in Cities* (L J Sharpe (ed)), 1967; *Local Notables and the City Council*, 1969. Fields: Comparative local government.

[358]
CLIJSTERS Edi
15 August 1943, Belgian. Plantin en Moretuslei 85/5, B-2000 Antwerpen, Belgium. Researcher, U of Leuven. Publs: ''Guerilla Warfare as a Means of Confrontation in a Stabilizing Big Power Structure'' (in J Niezing (ed)); *Urban Guerilla: Studies on the Theory, Strategy and Practice of Political Violence in Modern Societies*, 1974; *Het Nut van een Miljoenenpropaganda* (with E De Graeve-Lismont and L Engelen), 1974; *L'ampleur et le coût des campagnes électorales en Belgique*, 1975. Fields: Regionalization in Belgium; public opinion on European integration; cost of election campaigns; coalition formation in multiparty systems; developments in Southern Europe, particularly in Portugal.

[359]
CLUTTERBUCK Richard Lewis
22 November 1917, British. Department of Politics, University of Exeter, England. Degrees: MA (Cambridge), 1939; PhD (London), 1971. Doctoral thesis: ''Riot and Revolution in Singapore and Malaya''. 1937-72 British Army. 1972- Senior Lecturer, Dept of Pol, U of Exeter. Publs: *Across The River*, 1957; *The Long Long War*, 1966; *Protest and the Urban Guerilla*, 1973; *Riot and Revolution in Singapore and Malaya*, 1973; *Living with Terrorism* (tr), 1975; *Guerillas and Terrorism*, 1977; *Britain in Agony*, 1978; *Kidnap and Ransom*, 1978. Fields: International politics; political violence.

[360]
COHAN Alvin Sanford*
15 December 1941, American. Flat 5, Furness College, The University of Lancaster, Lancaster, England. Degrees: BA; MA (Miami), 1965; PhD (Georgia), 1970. Doctoral thesis: "Revolutionary and Non-Revolutionary Elites: The Irish Political Elite in Transition 1919-69". 1966-70 Teaching Assistant, U of Georgia; 1970- Lecturer, U of Lancaster. Publs: *The Irish Political Elite*, 1972. Fields: Theories of revolution; political elites; political change in Ireland.

[361]
COHEN Robert
4 March 1930, Dutch. Avenue E Speeckaert 87, 1200- Brussels, Belgium. Degrees: Dr. Doctoral thesis: "The Corporation Between Socialist Parties in the European Community" (in Dutch). Director, Commission of the European Community. Publs: Various articles on political parties and the European Community, and on development and policy. Fields: Development policy; European parliament; political parties.

[362]
COHEN Robin
14 June 1944, British. Degrees: BA; MSc (LSE), 1966; PhD (Birmingham), 1971. Doctoral thesis: "The Role of Organized Labour in the Nigerian Political Process". 1967-69 Assistant Lecturer, Lecturer in Pol Sci, U of Ibadan, Nigeria; 1969-71 Research Fellow, U of Birmingham; 1971- Lecturer, Senior Lecturer, U of Birmingham; 1977-78 Visiting Professor, U of California, Mauritius and Toronto; Professor of Soc, U of the West Indies. Publs: *Labour and Politics in Nigeria*, 1974; *The Development of an African Working Class: Studies in Class Formation and Action* (co-ed), 1975; *Labour History in Africa* (co-ed), 1978. Fields: Comparative sociology/politics of labour; small island development; political economy.

[363]
COLEMAN Janet
11 May 1945, American. Department of Politics, Amory Building, Rennes Drive, U of Exeter, Exeter, England. Degrees: BA; M Phil; PhD (Yale); Dipl (Paris). Doctoral thesis: "Sublimes et Literati". Senior Member, St Edmund's House, U of Cambridge; Affiliate, Clarke Hall, U of Cambridge; Visiting Research Fellow, Churchill Coll, U of Cambridge; Lecturer, U of Cambridge; Senior Research Fellow, Warburg Inst, U of London; Post-Doctoral Fulbright Fellow, L'Ecole des Hautes Etudes, Paris; Lecturer, Dept of Pol, U of Exeter. Publs: "Jean de Ripa and the Oxford Calculators", *Medieval Studies*, 1975; *Medieval English Literature and Political History*, 1978. Fields: Ancient and medieval political thought; medieval philosophy and theology; Late medieval utopianism; 19th century idealist tradition; Hegel; Frankfurt school of critical sociology; political literature in the middle ages and early renaissance.

[364]
COLLIARD Jean-Claude
15 March 1946, French. 13 rue Thouin, 75005 Paris, France. Degrees: Lic en droit (Paris), 1966; Dipl (IEP Paris), 1967; DES de sci pol (Paris), 1967; DES de droit public (Paris), 1968; Dr en droit (Paris), 1972; Agrégé de droit public et sci pol, 1972. Doctoral thesis: "Gouvernements et majorités dans les régimes parlementaires contemporains", 1978. 1968-72 Assistant, Faculté de Droit de Paris I; Professeur, Faculté de Droit et de Sci Pol, U de Nantes; Maître de conférences, Institut d'Etudes Politiques de Paris. Publs: *Les républicains indépendants: Valéry Giscard d'Estaing*, 1971; *Gouvernements et majorités dans les régimes parlementaires contemporains*, 1972; *La désignation du*

Premier Ministre en régime parlementaire, 1977; "Louis Blanc", in *Les grands révolutionnaires*, 1977; *Les articles 49-50-51 de la Constitution de 1958*, 1978. Fields: Institutions in parliamentary governments; majorities and governments; European political parties; study of electoral behaviour.

[365]
COLLIGNON Jean-Guy
22 September 1941, French. 1 rue Rousselet, 75007 Paris, France. Degrees: Dr d'Etat; Dipl (IEP Paris); ENLOV (Russe); MA (Harvard). Doctoral thesis: "Les juristes en Union Soviétique". Assistant, Dept de Sci Pol, Sorbonne Paris I; Maître assistant, U de Droit, Economique et Sci Soc, Paris II. Fields: Socialist countries; administrative science.

[366]
COLLINS Neil
31 October 1948, Irish. Institute of Local Government Studies, University of Birmingham, England. Degrees: BA; MA (Liverpool). Research Fellow, U of Birmingham. Fields: Local government in the UK and Ireland.

[367]
COMBA Andrea Mario*
26 July 1936, Italian. Corse Re Umberto 94, 10128 Torino, Italy. Degrees: Libera Docenza in Diritto Internazionale; Laurea in Guirisprudenza. Doctoral thesis: "Rapporti fra e Patto Atlantico, l'Organizzazione Internazionale". Publs: *La Giuristizioni Amministrative delle Organizzazioni Internazionali*, 1967; *Profili della Strutturazione Organica della Comunità Internazionale*, 1971. Fields: The European process of integration from the political institution point of view.

[368]
COMPAGNA Luigi*
24 November 1948, Italian. Via Chiatamone 60, 80121 Naples, Italy. Degrees: Degree in Pol Sci (Naples), 1970. 1970 Co-operated with CESAS on research on Italian Socialism; 1969- Journalistic interest in historical evolution of European Marxism; Voluntary Assistant Professor of History of Pol Doctrines, U of Naples. Publs: Articles in *Nord e Sud*, *La Voce Repubblicana*. Fields: Political thought of Italian socialist thinkers of the 20th century.

[369]
CONAC Gérard
18 January 1930, French. 76 rue d'Assas, 75006 Paris, France. Degrees: Dr en droit; Dipl (IEP Paris). Doctoral thesis: "La fonction publique aux Etat-Unis". Directeur, Centre d'enseignement Supérieur de la Réunion; Directeur de la recherche, Inst International d'Administration Publique; Professeur, U de Paris I; Directeur au Centre d'Etudes Africaines des Université. Publs: *La constitution de la république française* (G Conac and F Luchaire (eds)), 1978; *Les institutions constitutionnelles des Etats d'Afrique*, 1978; *La fonction publique aux Etats-Unis*, 1968; Directeur de la collection *Politique comparée*. Fields: Comparative administration; African political institutions; political institutions in Western Europe; administration in the United States.

[370]
CONCOLATO Jean Claude
French. 1 Chemin de Ronde, 38000 Grenoble, France. Degrees: Dipl (IEP Grenoble); Lic en sociologie; DES sci pol; Dr d'Etat. Doctoral thesis: "Le Soudan: Politique et Accumulation Primitive". Khartoum (Sudan), 2nd Commercial Attaché, French Embassy, Algeria; Teaching Assistant, Faculty of Law, U of Constantine; CNRS, Inst d'Etudes Pol, Grenoble; Attaché de recherche, CNRS, Grenoble. Publs: "Le Système Politique Soudanais", *Revue Française d'Etudes Politiques Africaines*, 1977. Fields: Economic and political development in the Third World; military interventions and involvements in various political systems; main powers strategies and regional strategies.

[371]
CONSTANTIN Francois Guy
17 November 1941, French. Hameau Peboue, 25 rue Jacques Monod, 64000 Pau, France. Degrees: Dipl (IEP Paris), 1962; DES droit public, 1964; DES sci pol, 1970; Dr d'Etat, 1970 (all Bordeaux). Collaborateur technique, CNRS; Chargé de recherches, Centre d'Etudes d'Afrique Noire; Inst d'Etudes Pol, Bordeaux; Assistant, Faculté de Droit, Bordeaux; Maître assistant, IEP, Bordeaux. Maître assistant, Faculté de Droit, Pau; Directeur, Centre de Recherche et Etudes des Pays d'Afrique Orientale. Publs: *L'ONU et les territoires non autonomes*, 1970; *L'anti-colonialisme américain*, 1970; *Politique et administration de la nature: les parcs nationaux*, 1973; various articles on African international regionalism, Afro-Arab relations, cooperation between underdeveloped states, on African foreign policy; Politics in Zambia and Mozambique. Fields: African politics; international relations of the Third World, horizontal cooperation, North-South issue; concept of dependence; East African politics; local politics in rural French areas.

[372]
CONTI ODORISIO Ginevra
22 June 1938, Italian. Viale dell'Arte 13, Rome, Italy. Degrees: Laurea in Sci Pol. Doctoral thesis: "Il Partito Socialista Francese tra le Due Guerre". Assistente Ordinario di Storia delle Dottrine Politiche, Facoltà di Sci Pol, U di Roma; Professore Incaricato di Storia del Pensiero Politico, U di Roma. Publs: *S N H Linguet, Dall'Ancien Régime alla Rivoluzione*, 1976. Fields: History of political thought; women's studies.

[373]
CONTOGIORGIS George
1947, Greek. Gabriilidou 18, Athens (902), Greece. Degrees: BA; DES (Paris); Dr d'Etat (Paris II). Doctoral thesis: "La Théorie des Révolutions chez Aristote". Lecturer, Pantios School of Pol Sci, Athens. Publs: *La Théorie des Révolutions chez Aristote*, 1978; *La Crise du Pouvoir à Athènes au IV S*, 1973; In Greek: *The Negro's Political Rights and the Evolution of Federal System in USA*, 1976; *The President's Veto Power in USA*, 1976; *The "Politeia" of Lefcas in Antiquity*, 1977; *Political and Social Forces in Contemporary Greece*, 1978.

[374]
CORNFORD James Peters
25 January 1935, British. Brick House, Wicken Bonhunt, Saffron Walden, Essex CB11 3UG, England. Degrees: MA (Cambridge). 1960-64 Fellow of Trinity Coll, Cambridge; 1964-68 Lecturer in Pol Sci, U of Edinburgh; 1968-76 Professor of Pol, U of Edinburgh; Director, The Outer Circle Policy Unit, London. Publs: Contributions to *Cleavages, Ideologies and Party Systems* (Allardt and Littunen (eds)), 1964; *Ideas and Institutions in Victorian Britain* (R Robson (ed)), 1967; *International Guide to Electoral Statistics* (S Rokkan and J Meyriat (eds)), 1967; *Government and Nationalism in*

Scotland (J N Wolfe (ed)), 1969; *Mass Politics* (E Allard and S Rokkan (eds)), 1970; *Philosophy Politics and Society* (P Laslett *et al* (eds)), 1972; *The Failure of the State*, 1975. Fields: British political history in the 19th and 20th century; political theory; constitutional change in the UK.

[375]
CORRADINI Domenico
14 November 1942, Italian. Via Carlo Goldoni 2, 56100 Pisa, Italy. Degrees: Dr in Law; Libera Docenza. Doctoral thesis: "Filosofia e Sociologia nel Pensiero di Karl Mannheim" (Philosophy and Sociology in Karl Mannheim's Thought). Professor of Soc and Theory of Govt, U of Sassari; Professor of History of Pol Parties and Pol Sci, U of Pisa; Professor of Philosophy of Law, U of Catania; Professor of Philosophy of Law, U of Pisa. Publs: *Karl Mannheim; Il Criterio della Buona Fede e la Scienza del Diritto Privato*; *Garantismo e Statualismo*; *Politica e Dialettica*; *Croce e la Ragion Giuridica Borghese*; *Storicismo e Politicità del Diritto*; *Stato e Società*; *Per la Democrazia e il Socialismo*. Fields: Legal and political philosophy; theory of government; sociology; political science; psychology; history of political parties.

[376]
CORTIER Francoise*
5 November 1946, Belgian. 93 Avenue des Meuniers, 1160 Brussels, Belgium. Degrees: Lic en sci pol et sociale (Catholic U of Louvain), 1968. Part-time Assistant, Dept of Pol Sci, Catholic U of Louvain. Fields: The Israel-Arab conflict; foreign policy of the European Community.

[377]
COT Jean-Pierre*
23 October 1937, French. 3 bis Passage Landrieu, 75 Paris VIIème, France. Degrees: Agrégé de droit public et sci pol, 1966; Dr d'Etat (droit public), 1965. Doctoral thesis: "La conciliation internationale". 1962-66 Assistant, Faculté de Droit, U de Paris; 1967-69 Agrégé, Doyen, Faculté de Droit, U d'Amiens; Professeur de Droit International Public et Sociologie Pol, U de Paris I. Publs: *La conciliation internationale*, 1966; *L'analyse fractionnelle des phénomènes politiques*, 1971. Fields: The general theory of conflict; political socialization.

[378]
COTTERET Jean-Marie
30 July 1935, French. 11 bis Avenue Auber, 06 Nice, France. Degrees: Dr en droit; Dr en sci pol; Dipl du cycle supérieur d'études pol (Paris). Assistant de l'Assoc Française de Sci Pol; Professeur, Dept de Sci Pol, U de Paris I; Publs: *Lois électorales et inégalités de représentation*, 1960; *Les systèmes électoraux*, 1970; *Le pouvoir législatif*, 1962; *Les finances publiques*, 1970; *Le vocabulaire du Général de Gaulle*, 1970; *Gouvernants et gouvernés- La communication politique*, 1973; *Giscard-Mitterrand: 54774 mots pour convaincre*, 1978. Fields: Political communication; analysis of political vocabulary.

[379]
COUFFIGNAL Georges Philippe
1 September 1944, French. 5 Place de Gordes, 38000 Grenoble, France. Degrees: Lic en droit; Dipl (IEP Paris), 1969; DES droit public, 1970; DES sci pol, 1971; Doctorat de sci pol, 1977. Doctoral thesis: "Syndicalisme et système politique en Italie 1945-1973". Assistant, U de Grenoble II, Inst d'Etudes Pol. Publs: "La pédagogie dans l'enseignement supérieur, un exemple de recherche-action", *Orientations*, 1974; "Un sindacato autonomo — per che fare", in *AAVV Contrattazione, egalitarismo, autonomia, unità sindicale*, 1973. Fields: Italian and Spanish political systems; regionalism.

[380]
COULON Christian
6 September 1942, French. 29 rue Socrate, 33600 Pessac, France. Degrees: Doctorat d'Etat d'etudes pol (Paris). Doctoral thesis: "Pouvoir maraboutique et pouvoir politique au Sénégal". Research Assistant, African Studies Center, UCLA; Assistant de recherche, FNSP; Attaché de recherches, CNRS. Pubs: *Problèmes et perspectives de l'éducation dans un Etat du Tiers Monde: le cas du Sénégal* (with J L Balans and A Ricard), 1973; *Autonomie locale et intégration nationale au Sénégal* (with J L Balans and J M Gastellu), 1976. Fields: Islam and political development in Africa; African international relations; ethnicity, regionalism and political change in Western Europe and Africa.

[381]
COUTROT Aline
17 June 1927, French. 40 rue Boissonade, 75014 Paris, France. Degrees: Dr. Doctoral thesis: "Un courant de la pensée catholique: l'hebdomadaire Septembre 1934-37". Chargé de recherches, CNRS; Maître de conférences, Maître-assistant, IEP Paris. Publs: *Les forces religieuses dans la société française*, 1966. Fields: Political life in modern France; politics and religion; religious life; problems of youth; youth and politics.

[382]
COUWENBERG Servatius Wilhelmus
6 January 1926, Dutch. Akkerwinderstraat 23b, Rotterdam 12, The Netherlands. Degrees: Drs (Nijmegen), 1950; MA, 1950; Dr phil (Leiden), 1953. Doctoral thesis: "The Relationship between Government and Private Corporations in Public Administration". 1951-59 Political Editor of daily paper; 1960-62 Civil Servant; 1961-64 Lecturer in Soc Sci, Soc Academy of Rotterdam; 1962- Editor in Chief, *Civis Mundi*; Assistant Director, Oost-West Inst, The Hague; Lecturer in Pol Sci, Social Academy, The Hague; Professor of Constitutional and Administrative Law, Erasmus U of Rotterdam. Publs: *Oost en West op de drempel van een nieuw tijdperk*, 1966; *Herlevend Nationalisme*, 1967; *Modern Socialisme*, 1972; *Omstreden Staat*, 1974; *Democratische Rechtsstaat en het emancipatiestreven*, 1977; *Westers Staatsrecht als Emancipatieproces*, 1977; *Problemen der Democratie* (ed), 1967; *Tijdsein-peiling en perspectief van onze tijd*, 1972. Fields: Theory of development of modern constitutional law; human rights, especially in connection with East-West relations; problems of present-day corporatism.

[383]
COX William Harvey
1939, British. 32 Alton Road, Birkenhead, Merseyside, England. BA; MSc (London), 1964. Lecturer, U of Liverpool. Publs: *City Politics and the Press* (with D R Morgan), 1973; *Cities: The Public Dimension*, 1976. Fields: British and Irish politics; urban politics.

[384]
CRAIG James Alexander
27 March 1943, British. 23 Stonepail Close, Cheadle, Cheshire, England. Degrees: BA. Lecturer, Dept of Pol, U of Glasgow; Lecturer, Dept of Administrative Studies, U of Manchester. Fields: Politics of development; politics and planning in the Third World; politics of South East Asia with reference to Malaysia; politics and military governments.

[385]
CRANSTON Maurice William
8 May 1920, British. European University Institute, Badia Fiesolana, San Domenico di Fiesole, Florence, Italy. Degrees: BA; B Litt (Oxon), 1951; MA (Oxon), 1951. 1958-69 Lecturer, Reader in Pol Sci, LSE; 1969- Professor of Pol Sci, U of London. Publs: *John Locke*, 1957; *Sartre*, 1962; *What are Human Rights?*, 1963; *Western Political Philosophers*, 1964; *A Glossary of Political Terms*, 1967; *Political Dialogues*, 1969; *The New Left*, 1970; *The Mask of Politics*, 1974. Fields: Political philosophy; political ideology.

[386]
CREMIEUX-BRILHAC Jean-Louis
22 January 1917, French. 2 Boulevard St Germain, 75005 Paris, France. Degrees: DES. 1944 Sous Directeur, Ministère de l'Information, Paris; 1947- Sous Directeur, Directeur adjoint and Directeur de la Documentation Française au Secrétariat Général du Gouvernement; Professeur, Inst Français de Presse, U de Paris and Inst d'Etudes des Relations Internationales Contemporaines. Publs: *Retour par l'URSS*, 1945; *La documentation d'Etat aux Etat-Unis*, 1953; *L'éducation nationale* (co-author), 1965; *Les voix de la liberté*, 1975. Fields: Political, historical, social, economic, cultural and scientific problems.

[387]
CREWE Ivor Martin
15 December 1945, British. Department of Government, University of Essex, Wivenhoe Park, Colchester CO4 3SQ, Essex, England. Degrees: BA; MA (LSE), 1968. 1967-69 Lecturer, Dept of Pol, U of Lancaster; 1969-71 Junior Research Fellow, Nuffield Coll, U of Oxford; 1972- Lecturer, Senior Lecturer, Dept of Government, U of Essex; 1974-Director, SSRC Survey Archive, U of Essex. Publs: *Social Survey of the Civil Service* (with A H Halsey), 1969; *British Political Sociology Yearbook* (ed), 1975; *Party Identification and Beyond* (co-ed), 1976; *Two Cheers for Democracy: The Granada Survey on Public Attitudes to Parliament*; "Partisan Delignment in Britain, 1964-1974", *British Journal of Political Science*, 1977; "Do Butler & Stokes Really Explain Political Change in Britain?", *European Journal of Political Research*, 1974. Fields: Recruitment in the civil service; political attitudes and behaviour of the British middle-class; electoral behaviour and public opinion in western democracies, especially post-war Britain.

[388]
CRICK Bernard
16 December 1929, British. Degrees: BSc; PhD (London). Doctoral thesis: "The Origins and Conditions of the American Science of Politics". 1952-54 Teaching Fellow, U of Harvard; 1954-55 Assistant Professor, McGill U; 1957-65 Lecturer, Senior Lecturer, LSE; 1965-71 Professor of Pol Theory and Inst, U of Sheffield; 1971- Professor of Pol and Head of Dept, Birkbeck Coll, U of London. Publs: *In Defence of Politics*, 1962; *The Reform of Parliament*, 1964; *Essays on Reform*, 1967; *Protest and Discontent*, 1971; *Political Theory and Practice*, 1972; *Crime, Rape and Gin*, 1975; *Essays on Political Education* (with D Heater), 1978; *Political Literacy and Political Education* (with A Porter). Fields: Political theory; political education; politics in literature.

[389]
CRIDDLE Byron John
23 March 1942, British. 121 Blenheim Place, Aberdeen, Scotland. Degrees: BA; MA (Leicester), 1967. 1969- Lecturer in Pol, U of Aberdeen. Publs: *Socialists and European Integration: A Study of the French Socialist Party*, 1969; "The French Parti Socialiste", in *Social Democratic Parties in Western Europe* (W Paterson and A Thomas (eds)), 1977; various articles in *Parliamentary Affairs, The World Today*. Fields: Local political culture in a rural/small town milieu; the French party system since 1958; the French Socialist party; electoral politics and behaviour in France and Britain.

[390]
CROISAT Maurice
7 March 1935, French. 38 route de Chartreuse, 38000 La Tronche, France. Degrees: Dipl, 1959; Lic en droit; Dr en droit, 1964. Doctoral thesis: "Fédéralisme Canadien and autonomie du Québec". 1964-68 Professeur assistant, U de Montréal; 1968-Maître-assistant, Professeur, IEP Grenoble. Publs: *Fédéralisme canadien*, 1978; "Centralisation et décentralisation au sein des partis canadiens", *RFSP*; plus articles on Canadian political problems, planning and regionalism. Fields: Political organizations and behaviours; federalism; Canadian problems; political institutions.

[391]
CROLLEN Luc*
31 May 1942, Belgian. "Leeuwerikenvedl", Celestijnenlaan 39/113, 3030 Heverlee, Belgium. Degrees: Lic in de Pol en Sociale Wetenschappen (Catholic U of Leuven); MA (John Hopkins U, Washington). Assistant, Catholic U of Leuven; Teacher, Coll of Europe, Bruges. Publs: "Les flancs de l'alliance sont-ils menacés?" *Revue Générale Belge*, 1969; "Conventionele strijdkrachten en NAVO-strategie" (with D Bauwens), *Le Monde/De Atlantische Wereld*, 1970. Fields: Strategic studies; theories of international relations; international politics.

[392]
CROOK Richard Charles
24 August 1946, British. 73 Glasserton Road, Newlands, Glasgow G43 2LN, Scotland. Degrees: BA; MA (Durham); PhD (LSE). Doctoral thesis: "Local Elites and National Politics in Ghana: A Case Study of Political Centralization and Local Politics in Offinso Ashanti (1945-1966)". 1970-72 Junior Research Fellow, Inst of Commonwealth Studies, London; 1972-74 Lecturer in Pol, Huddersfield Polytechnic; 1974-76 Research Fellow, Centre of West African Studies, Dept of Pol, U of Birmingham; Lecturer in Pol, U of Glasgow. Publs: "Colonial Rule and Political Culture in Modern Ashanti", *Journal of Commonwealth Political Studies*, 1973; "Ghana: Recent History", in *Africa South of the Sahara*, 1975; "Political Centralization and Local Politics in Ghana", in *The Making of Politicians* (W H Morris-Jones (ed)), 1976. Fields: Politics of developing countries, especially Africa, West Africa; imperial history; political sociology.

[393]
CROSS John Arthur
10 May 1927, British. 58 Rhiwbina Hill, Cardiff CF4 6UQ, Wales. Degrees: BA; MA (Cambridge), 1952; BSc (London), 1956; PhD (London), 1965. Doctoral thesis: "The Dominions Department of the Colonial Office: Origins and Early Years, 1905-1914". 1950-54 Adult Education; 1954-61 Civil Service; 1961-64 Lecturer in Public Administration, CAT, Cardiff; 1964-75 Lecturer, Senior Lecturer, Reader in Pol, U Coll, Cardiff; 1976- Professor of Pol, U Coll, Cardiff. Publs: *Whitehall and the Commonwealth*, 1967; *The Tactics of Resignation* (with R K Alderman), 1967; *British Public Administration*, 1970; *Modern British Government*, 1972; *Sir Samuel Hoare; A Political Biography*, 1977. Fields: British politics and public administration.

[394]
CROUCH Martin
22 December 1943, British. Department of Politics, University of Bristol, Bristol BS8, England. Degrees: BA; MA (Wales), 1972. Lecturer in Soviet Pol Inst, U of Bristol. Publs: "Sejm Elections in Poland", *BJPS*, 1978. Fields: Aspects of Tsarist Russia 1905-17; Soviet transport, particularly urban transport; 1917 Russian revolution.

[395]
CROWE Sibyl Eyre
1 September 1908, British. St Hilda's College, Oxford, England. Degrees: BA; MA (Oxon), 1938; MA; PhD (Cambridge), 1938; 1938-41 Lecturer in Pol, St Hilda's Coll, Oxford; 1941- Tutor in Pol, St Hilda's Coll, Oxford; 1943- Fellow, St Hilda's Coll, Oxford; 1942-44 Research Assistant, F O; 1952- CUF Lecturer. Publs: *The Berlin West African Conference, 1884-85*. Fields: Biography of Sir Eyre Crowe.

[396]
CROZIER Michel
6 November 1922, French. 66 rue du Cherche-Midi, 75006 Paris, France. Degrees: Dr (Lille), 1949; Dr d'Etat (Paris), 1964. Doctoral thesis: "The Bureaucratic Phenomenon", 1947-48; 1964 Research Associate, Research Director, CNRS; 1959-60 Fellow, Center for Advanced Studies in the Behavioural Sciences, Dept of Soc Relations, Stanford, USA; 1967-68 Professor, Dept of Sociology, Nanterre; 1970- Director of Research, CNRS and Director, Centre de Sociologie des Organisations. Publs: *The Bureaucratic Phenomenon*, 1963; *The World of the Office Worker*, 1974; *L'acteur et le système*, 1977. Fields: Public administration and public policy; decision-making from a sociological point of view; the processes of human intervention within organizations and within broader systems; the importance of the intellectual input and of the varying concepts of rationality for the change process.

[397]
CRUISE O'BRIEN Donal Brian*
4 July 1941, Irish. Department of Economics and Politics, School of Oriental and African Studies, Senate House, London WC1, England. Degrees: BA; MA (Berkeley), 1964; PhD (London), 1969. Doctoral thesis: "The Monides of Senegal: the Socio-Economic Structure of an Islamic Order". 1967- Research Fellow and Lecturer in Pol, SOAS, U of London. Publs: *The Monides of Senegal: The Political and Economic Organization of an Islamic Brotherhood*, 1971. Fields: Constitution of a Senegalese peasantry under colonial rule, social and political aspects; politics and religion in Ireland.

[398]
CURRELL Melville Elizabeth
British. 28 York Avenue, Droitwich, Worcestershire, England. Degrees: BA; PhD (Birmingham). Doctoral thesis: "Women in Politics". Research Assistant, Research Associate, Faculty of Commerce and Soc Sci, U of Birmingham; Lecturer, Dept of Pol Sci, U of Birmingham. Publs: *The Gentle Anarchists* (with G N Ostergaard), 1971; *Political Women*, 1974. Fields: Political role of women, political socialization, British government and politics.

[399]
CUTURI Vittoria*
19 August 1944, Italian. Palazzo ESE, Via Beato Bernardo 5, Catania, Italy. Degrees: Degree in Pol Sci (Catania); Fellow in Pol Sci (Catania). Fields: Political elites; the meaning of power in political science; community power structure.

[400]
CZEMPIEL Ernst Otto
22 May 1927, German. 355 Marburg, Erfurterstrasse 14, FR Germany. Degrees: Dr phil (Mainz), 1956. Doctoral thesis: "Germany and the Affaire Dreyfus". 1966-70 Professor, U of Marburg; 1970- Professor, U of Frankfurt; 1970- Forschungsgruppenleiter, Hessische Stiftung Friedens- und Konfliktforschung. Publs: *Das Amerikanische Sicherheitssystem*, 1966; *Das deutsche Dreyfus-Geheimnis*, 1966; *Macht und Kompromiss, die Beziehungen der Bundesrepublik zu den Vereinten Nationen 1955-70*, 1970; *Schwerpunkte und Ziele der Friedensforschung*, 1972; *Friedenspolitik im südlichen Afrika*, 1976. Fields: Structure of foreign policy behaviour of the US; theoretical and analytical problems of peace research; American-European relations.

[401]
CZERNY Wilhelm Felix
4 September 1924, Austrian. Rauchfangkehrergasse 3, A-1150 Vienna, Austria. Degrees: PhD. Doctoral thesis: "Reichart Streun of Schwarzenau and the Austrian Liberty Letters". 1946 Member, Inst of Austrian Historical Research; 1948 Record Office of Parliament; 1949 Administration Office of Parliament; Member, Catholic Social Academy of Austria; Member of the Austrian Society for Pol Sci; Clerk, Austrian Parliament. Publs: *Catholic Social Encyclopedia* (contributor); *Encyclopedia for Theology and Church* (contributor); *Commentary on the Standing Orders of the Austrian National Council* (co-author); plus various articles and papers on political science and parliamentary systems. Fields: Theory of political science; parliamentary systems; party theory; history and critique of ideologies.

D

[402]
DAALDER Hans
4 May 1928, Dutch. 3, Piazza di San Franceico di Paola, 50124, Florence, Italy. Degrees: Dr (Amsterdam) 1960. Doctoral thesis: "Organisatie en Reorganisatie van de Britse Regering 1914-1963"; (Cabinet Reform in Britain 1914-1963). 1949-50 Assistant Professor of Journalism, U of Amsterdam; 1950-53 Assistant to Professor of Pol Sci, U of Amsterdam; 1958-63 Senior Lecturer in Pol Sci, Inst of Social Studies, The Hague; 1963- Professor of Pol Sci, U of Leiden; 1976-79 Professor of Pol Sci and Head of Dept of Pol and Soc Sci, European University Inst, Florence. Publs: *Cabinet Reform in Britain, 1914-1963*, 1963; "The Netherlands: Opposition in a Segmented Society", *Political Oppositions in Western Democracies* (A Dahl (ed)), 1966; "On Building Consociational Nations: The Cases of the Netherlands and Switzerland", *International Social Science Journal*, 1971; "Cabinets and Party Systems in Ten Smaller European Democracies", *Acta Politica*, 1971; "The Consociational Democracy Theme", *World Politics*, 1974; "Extreme Proportional Representation: the Dutch Experience", in *Adversary Politics and Electoral Reform* (S E Finer (ed)), 1975; *Politisering en Lijdelijkheid in de Nederlandse Politiek*, 1974; *Parlement en Politieke Besluitvorming in Nederland*, 1975. Fields: Dutch politics; comparative European politics; legislative behaviour; Marxism and nationality; university government.

[403]
DABEZIES Pierre Camille
9 February 1925, French. 11 rue de la Cerisaie, 75004 Paris, France. Degrees: Lic en droit; Dr de droit public; Agrégé de droit public et sci pol. Former Col, French Army; Assistant, U d'Amiens; Professeur, U de Caen; Professeur de Droit Public et Sci Pol, U de Paris 1; Directeur, Dept de Sci Pol, Sorbonne; Professeur, Inst d'Etudes Pol, ENA, Paris; Conseiller de Paris. Publs: *Forces politiques au Vietnam*, 1955; *Le développement des partis politiques malgaches*, 1959; *Fondement sociologique des partis en pays sous-développés*, 1959; *Evolution sociale et problèmes de commandement*, 1965; *Irregular Warfare in a Nutshell*, 1962; *Guerre révolutionnaire et conscience chrétienne*, 1963. Fields: Political parties; revolutionary warfare; ethnic, religious and social problems; military strategy; military sociology.

[404]
DAEMEN Henricus Hubertus Franciscus
27 February 1949, Dutch. Waalstraat 213, Enschede, The Netherlands. Degrees: Drs. Assistant Professor, Netherlands Organization for the Advancement of Pure Research; Assistant Professor, Twente U of Technology. Publs: "Political Culture", in *Kernthema's van de Politicologie* (M van Schendelen (ed)), 1976. Fields: Political culture; political opinion and attitudes; public administration political participation; parliaments.

[405]
DAETWYLER Martin Carl
23 May 1944, Swiss. Hasenmattweg 6, CH-3303 Jegenstorf, Switzerland. Degrees: Lic rer Pol, 1972; Dr rer Pol, 1975. Doctoral thesis: "Die Kandidaten und Gewählten bei den Nationalratswahlen von 1971 — ein Sozialprofil". Assistant Teacher, Swiss Centre for Pol Research; Information Officer, Swiss Housing Office. Fields: Political science; elections; housing; building and planning.

[406]
DAHLERUP Drude
3 February 1945, Danish. Solsikkevej 23, DK-8240 Risskov, Denmark. Degrees: Cand sci pol. Doctoral thesis: "Socialisme og Kvindefrigørelse i det 19 Arhundrede" (Socialism and Women's Liberation in the 19th century). Research Fellow, State Council for Social Research; Lecturer, Inst of Pol Sci, U of Aarhus. Publs: *Socialisme og Kvindefrigørelse i det 19 Århundrede,* 1973; "Netragtninger over de nye Kvindestudiers Baggrund, indhold og perspektiv", *Politica.* Fields: The women's movement and other women's organizations; social movements in general; theories of women's liberation.

[407]
DAMGAARD Erik
3 November 1943, Danish. Huedebjergvej 19, DK-8220 Brabrand, Denmark. Degrees: Cand sci pol (Aarhus), 1968; Dr sci pol (Aarhus), 1977. Doctoral thesis: "Folketinget Under Forandring" (Parliament in Change). 1968- Assistant Professor, Associate Professor, U of Aarhus. Publs: *Folketinget Under Forandring.* Fields: Legislative studies; coalition theory; public policy analysis; normative and empirical democratic theory.

[408]
D'AMICO Renato
9 April 1949, Italian. Via Conte Ruggero 11, Catania, Italy. Doctoral thesis: "Il Voto Elettorale a Catania: Analisi del Comportamento Elettorale dei Quartieri Catanesi en le Elezioni Regionali de 13.6.1971". Researcher at Isvi, Catania; Assistant Professor, Faculty of Pol Sci, U of Catania. Publs: "Catania. Le Elezioni del 1972 nella Storia Elettorale della Città", in *Um Sistema Politico alla Prova,* 1975; *Democrazia Cristiana e Potere nel Mezzogiorno* (with M Caciagli and A Spreafico), 1977; *Burocrazia e Ente Regione,* 1978. Fields: Bureaucracy; political system, political parties; elections.

[409]
DANAN Yves Maxime
2 January 1930, French. 40 Avenue du F Roosevelt, 92330 Sceaux, France. Degrees: Dr en sci pol; Dr en econ régionale et aménagement du territoire; Dipl d'études superieures de droit public; Dipl (IAE Nancy). Doctoral thesis: "La vie politique à Alger de 1940 a 1944". Chargé d'enseignement, U de Paris XII; Directeur d'études consultant auprès du Ministère de l'Environnement et de la qualité de la vie. Publs: *La vie politique à Alger de 1940 à 1944,* 1963; *Histoire postale et libertés publiques,* 1965; *Les agences d'urbanisme d'agglomération,* 1976; *Le droit de l'urbanisme* (co-author), 1978; "Le timbre et l'analyse quantitative en science politique"; "L'entreprise et la fonction de provision politique". Fields: Political history; urban law; town planning and local government.

[410]
DANKBAAR Bernard
29 July 1948, Dutch. De Clercqstraat 17, Amsterdam, The Netherlands. Degrees: Drs. Fellow of the Transnational Inst, Amsterdam. Fields: Military strategy and technology; unionization in the military.

[411]
DA POZZO Francois A
3 May 1943, Swiss. Kirchackerweg 10, 3123 Belp, Switzerland. Degrees: Dr rer pol. Doctoral thesis: "Elemente des politischen Systems der Schweiz in ausländischer Sicht". Research Assistant, Forschungszentrum für schweizerische Pol, Bern; Research Fellow, Dept of Pol Sci, U of California at Berkeley; Research Scholar, Schweizerischer Nationalfonds zur Förderung der wissenschaftlichen Forschung, U of Bern. Publs: *Die Schweiz in der Sicht des Auslandes. Ein Forschungsbericht über die Politikwissenschaftliche Literatur des Auslandes zum politischen System der Schweiz*, 1977; "Allgemeine Wirtschaftspolitik", "Kredit und Geld", "Energie" and "Verhehr", *Année Politique Suisse 1975*, 1976. Fields: Swiss politics; public policy making; comparative legislative research, Swiss parliament; comparative politics.

[412]
D'ARCY Francois
21 August 1940, French. 4 rue Dominique Villars, 38000 Grenoble, France. Degrees: Dipl (Paris); Lic; Dr (Paris). Doctoral thesis: "Structures administratives et urbanisation: La société centrale pour l'équipement du territoire". Professeur de Sci Pol, IEP; Directeur du CERAT. Publs: "Les communes rurales dans le département de Constantine", in *Essais sur l'économie de l'Algérie nouvelle*, 1965; "L'utilisation de la norme dans la domination", in *Prendre la ville*, 1977; "Le nouveau vocabulaire de l'Etat ou les avatars du droit administratif", in *Aménagement urbain et mouvement sociaux*, 1978. Fields: National and local administration; urban politics, political ideology in Quebec.

[413]
DAUDT Hans
12 January 1925, Dutch. Weerdestein 32, Amsterdam, The Netherlands. Degrees: Dr. Doctoral thesis: "Floating Voters and the Floating Vote: A Critical Analysis of American and English Election Studies". 1951-54 Journalist, Social-Economic Affairs, *Het Vrije Volk*; 1954-63 Staff Member, Inst for the Science of the Press, Amsterdam; 1967-71 Member, Royal Commission to Advise on Change to the Dutch Constitution; 1963- Professor of Pol Sci, U of Amsterdam. Publs: *Floating Voters and the Floating Vote. A Critical Analysis of American and English Election Studies*, 1961; *Enige recente ontwikkelingen in de wetenschap der politiek*, 1963; *Beeldreligie. Een kritische beschouwing naar aanleiding van reacties op de derde uitzending van 'Zo is het...'* (with B A Sijes), 1966; "Party-System and Voters' Influence in the Netherlands", in *Party Systems, Party Organization, and the Politics of New Masses* (O Stammer (ed)), 1968; "Legitimiteit en legitimatie", *Legitimatie*, 1974; "The Political Future of the Welfare State", *The Netherlands' Journal of Sociology*, 1977; "The Ostrogorski Paradox: A Peculiarity of Compound Majority Decision-making" (with D W Rae), *European Journal of Political Research*, 1976. Fields: Election studies; democratic process; problems of legitimacy.

[414]
DAUPHIN Joanne Coyle
31 March 1936, American. 86 rue d'Amsterdam, 75009 Paris, France. Degrees: BA; MA, 1958; MA LD, 1959; PhD (Tuft), 1963. Doctoral thesis: "Indochinese Administration and Education: French Policy and Practice, 1917-1945". U of Tufts; Mount Holyoke College; Committee on Oriental Studies, U of Columbia; American Coll in Paris; Inst of American Studies (SUNY), Paris; Southern Methodist U, Paris; U of Paris IV; Maître de conférences, IEP Paris and Chargé de cours, U of Paris XIII. Publs: *Inventaire des resources documentaires Africanistes à Paris* (co-ed), 1969; "French Provincial Centers of Documentation and Research on Africa", *African*

Studies Bulletin, 1966; "Belgian Centers of Documentation and Research on Africa", *African Studies Bulletin*, 1965. Fields: International relations; US foreign policy; US and comparative politics.

[415]
DAVEY Kenneth Jackson
9 December 1932, British. The Outlook, Worms Ash, Bromsgrove, Worcestershire, England. Degrees: MA (Oxon), 1957; M Soc Sci (Birmingham), 1971. 1957-64 Administrative Officer, Uganda Government; 1965-66 Senior Courts Adviser, Uganda; 1966-69 Chief Regional Inspector, Uganda; 1970-72 Director of Studies, East African Staff Coll; 1972- Lecturer, Associate Director, Inst of Local Government Studies, U of Birmingham. Publs: *Programme Budgeting for East Africa* (ed and contributor), 1972; *Developing Africa's Managers*, 1972; *Taxing a Peasant Society*, 1973. Fields: The operation of decentralized institutions of government in developing countries.

[416]
DAVID Dominique Jean Francois
20 April 1943, French. 147 rue de Bercy, 75012 Paris, France. Degrees: Lic droit (Paris), 1967; DES (Paris), 1968; Dipl (IEP Paris), 1968. 1968-69 Chargé de cours dirigés, Faculté de Droit de Paris; 1969-78 Assistant, U de Paris I. Publs: *Le marketing politique*, 1978; *ENA: réformisme ou révolution?*, *Revue politique et parlementaire*, 1968; "L'attitude de la République populaire de Chine à l'ONU 1971-73", *Problèmes politiques et sociaux*, 1974; "La République populaire de Chine et le droit des mers", *Revue française des problèmes asiatiques contemporains*, 1974; "La République populaire de Chine et les 'cinq Centres' ", *Annuaire du Tiers Monde*, 1975; "La décolonisation des Comores, de l'interdépendance des politiques à l'ambiguité des principes" *Annuaire français du Tiers Monde.*

[417]
DAVIES Christopher John*
30 January 1935, British. Institute of Local Government Studies, University of Birmingham, Birmingham B15 2TT, England. Degrees: BA; M Soc Sci (Birmingham), 1969. Administrative Officer, Education Department, London County Council; Lecturer, Inst of Local Government Studies, U of Birmingham. Publs: "The Re-organization of Local Government in England", *Canadian Public Administration*, 1970; "Comparative Local Government as a Field", in *Studies in Comparative Local Government*, 1970. Fields: Management theory applied to the public service, especially local government.

[418]
DAVIES Morton Rees
29 January 1939, British. Social Studies Building, The University, Liverpool L69 3BX, England. Degrees: BA. 1962- Lecturer; 1970 Leverhulme Lecturer in Public Administration; 1976 Director of Public Administration Studies, Dept of Pol Theory and Inst, U of Liverpool. Publs: *Models of Political Systems* (with V A Lewis), 1973. Fields: Public administration training; development administration.

[419]
DAVIES Robert William
23 April 1915, British. Centre for Russian and East European Studies, University of Birmingham, Birmingham B15 2TT, England. Degrees: BA; PhD (Birmingham), 1954. Doctoral thesis: "The Development of the Soviet Budgetary System, 1917-41". 1954-56 Senior Scholar, Assistant, U of Glasgow; 1956-63 Research Fellow, Lecturer, Senior Lecturer, U of Birmingham: Director, Centre for Russian and East European Studies;

Professor of Soviet Econ Studies, U of Birmingham. Publs: *The Development of the Soviet Budgetary System*, 1958; *Foundations of a Planned Economy, 1926-29* (with E H Carr), 1969; *Science Policy in the USSR* (co-author), 1969. Fields: Soviet economic history in the 1930s; research, developments and innovation in the USSR; comparative Soviet and East European politics.

[420]
DAWANCE-GOOSSENS Josette
14 November 1946, Belgian. Chaussée de Bruxelles 104, B-1900 Overijse, Belgium. Degrees: Lic en sci soc (Brussels), 1969. 1969-70 Chargée de recherches, Belgian Survey Inst; 1971- Chargée d'études, Inst U de Sondage d'Opinion Publique. Fields: Electoral sociology; methodology of the social sciences.

[421]
DAWISHA Adhid Isam
2 November 1944, Iraqi. Dept of International Relations, U of Keele, Keele, Staffordshire, England. Degrees: BA; PhD. Doctoral thesis: "Egypt and the Arab East, 1958-1963: A Foreign Policy Analysis". 1974-76 Lecturer in International Pol, U of Lancaster; 1976-77 Visiting Fellow in Pol, U of Southampton; 1977 Assistant Professor of Pol, U of British Columbia; 1977-78 Senior Research Fellow, International Institute of Strategic Studies; 1976-78 Part-time Lecturer in International Relations, U of Sussex; Lecturer in International Relations, U of Keele. Publs: *Egypt in the Arab World: The Elements of Foreign Policy: International Crisis Behaviour: The Syrian Intervention in Lebanon 1975-1976*; articles in *Asian Affairs*; *British Journal of International Studies*; *Government and Opposition*; *International Relations; Jerusalem Journal of International Relations*; *Middle East Journal*; *World Today*. Fields: Foreign policy analysis; Middle East politics; politics of international economic relations.

[422]
DAWISHA Karen Lea
2 December 1949, American. Degrees: BA: PhD (London), 1975. Doctoral thesis: "The Foundation, Structure and Dynamics of Soviet Policy Towards the Arab Radical Regimes 1955-61". 1973- Lecturer, U of Southampton; 1977 Visiting Professor, U of British Columbia; 1977-78 Academic Visitor, LSE. Publs: "The Roles of Ideology in the Decision-Making of the Soviet Union", *International Relations*, 1972; "Soviet Cultural Relations with Syria and Egypt, 1955-1970", *Soviet Studies*, 1975; "Soviet Policy in the Middle East", *Millenium*, 1977; "Soviet Crisis Behaviour", *Journal of International Relations*, 1978; *The Making of Soviet Foreign Policies*, 1978. Fields: Soviet foreign policy; comparative communist politics; decision-making theories.

[423]
DAY John
17 February 1931, British. Department of Politics, University of Leicester, University Road, Leicester LE1 7RH, England. Degrees: BA. Lecturer, Senior Lecturer in Pol, U of Leicester. Publs: *International Nationalism*, 1967. Fields: African nationalism in southern Rhodesia.

[424]
DEARLOVE John Norman
30 May 1944, British. 21 Clermont Terrace, Brighton, East Sussex, England. Degrees: BSc; MA (Sussex), 1966; D Phil (Sussex), 1972. Doctoral thesis: "Public Policy in a Royal Borough". 1966-Tutorial Fellow, Assistant Lecturer, Lecturer, U of Sussex; 1974-75 Visiting Associate Professor, Brooklyn Coll, SUNY and Senior Guest Scholar under the Fulbright Programme. Publs: "Councillors and Interest Groups in Kensington and Chelsea", *British Journal of Political Science*, 1971; "Voluntary Action: A National Perspective", in *Voluntary Action* (D Dickinson (ed)), 1973; *The Politics of Policy in Local Government*, 1973; "The Control of Change and the Regulation of Community Action, in *Community Work* (M Mayo and D Jones (eds)), 1974; "The BBC and the Politicians", *Index*, 1974; *The Reorganization of British Local Government*, 1978. Fields: Local politics in Britain and America; British politics; public policy and decision-making.

[425]
DEAS Malcolm Douglas
16 May 1941, British. St Antony's College, Oxford, England. Degrees: BA; MA (Oxon), 1966. 1962-66 Fellow, All Soul's Coll, U of Oxford; 1968-70, 1971-72 Acting Director, St Anthony's Coll, U of Oxford; 1966- Fellow, St Anthony's Coll, U of Oxford; U Lecturer in Latin American Pol and Government. Publs: "Guerillas in Latin America: a Perspective", *World Today*, 1968; "Colombian Prospects", *International Journal*, 1969; "Aldunas notas sobre la historia del caciquismo en Colombia", *Revista Occidente*, 1974; "A cundinamarca Hacienda- Santa Bárbara 1870-1914", in *Land and Labour in Latin America* (K Duncan *et al* (eds)), 1977. Fields: Colombian history and politics, 19th and 20th centuries; Venezuela.

[426]
DE BAECQUE Francis
11 March 1915, French. 13 Quai de Montebello, 75005 Paris, France. Degrees: Lic en droit; DES droit privé et econ pol; Dipl (IEP Paris). Auditeur au Conseil d'Etat; 1946 Sous-Directeur du contentieux des dommages de guerre; 1947-48 Directeur-adjoint du cabinet de René Coty (Ministré de la Reconstruction); 1949-54 Conseiller juridique du gouvernement tunisien; 1950-65 Maître des Requêtes; 1954-59 Directeur du secrétariat général de la présidence de la République; 1959-62 Conseiller juridique de l'Organisation commune des régions sahariennes; 1962-66 Directeur de cabinet de Louis Joxe; 1965- Conseiller; 1972- Membre, Vice President, Comite d'aménagement de la Région Parisienne; Président de la commission de coordination de la documentation administrative; 1972- Président de sous-section de la section du contentieux du Conseil d'Etat; 1975- Membre du Conseil Supérieur de la Magistrature. Publs: *Les superstructures des administrations centrales*, 1973; *L'administration centrale de la France*, 1973; *La situation des personnels enseignants des universités*, 1974; *Qui gouverne la France?*, 1976; *Rapport de la Commission de Coordination de la Documentation Administrative*, 1974, 1975, 1977. Fields: Politics and administration.

[427]
DE BAKKER Bert*
29 October 1946, Belgian. Heerenveld 144, B-2580 St Katelyne-Waver, Belgium. Degrees: Lic (Catholic U of Louvain), 1969. Assistant, Limburgh School of Econ. Publs: *De politieke zegginskracht van de gemeenteraadsverkiezingen* W Dewachter (ed)), 1970. Fields: Political options.

[428]
DEBBASCH Charles Arthur
22 October 1937, French. "La Bergerole", 2 Chemin de Bibémus, 13100 Aix en Provence, France. Degrees: DES droit privé; DES droit public; DES sci pol; Doctorat de droit public; Agrégé des Facultés de Droit. Doctoral thesis: "Procédure administrative contentieuse et procédure civile". Assistant; Chargé d'enseignement; Professeur agrégé, Faculté de Droit de Grenoble; Professeur agrégé de la Faculté de Droit et de Sci Econ, Aix-en-Provence; Président, U de Droit, Econ et Sci, Professeur de Sci admin et Droit admin, Faculté de Droit et Sci Pol, Doyen, Aix-Marseille; Professeur de Sci Pol, IEP Aix and Inst d'Etudes Françaises pour Etudiants Etrangers, Aix; Professeur de Sci Admin, Collège d'Europe, Bruges. Publs: *L'université désorientée*, 1970; *Pouvoir et administration au Maghreb* (co-author), 1970; *Science administrative*, 1971; *La France de Pompidou*, 1974; *Lexique de termes politiques* (co-author), 1975; *Contentieux administratif*, 1976; *Institutions et droits administratifs*, 1976; *Les chats de l'Emirat*, 1976. Fields: Administrative science; African political sociology; French political sociology and sciences; communications, media.

[429]
DEBOUTTE Jan Marie Joseph
18 December 1945, Belgian. Dassenstraat 27, B-3044 Haasrode (Oud Heverlee), Belgium. Degrees: Lic. 1973-76 Junior Professional Officer, United Nations Development Programme in Haiti; 1972- Research Assistant, Dept of Pol Sci, Catholic U of Leuven. Publs: *De houding van de Verenigde Staten tov de Europese Integratie 1960-1970*, 1971; "Tendensen in de Politieke Ontwikkeling van de DBr 1966-1972", *Politica*, 1972; *High Politics in the Low Countries — A Study of Foreign Policy Decision Making in Belgium and The Netherlands* (with A van Staden), 1978. Fields: International organizations, especially decision-making.

[430]
DEBRE Michel
15 January 1912, French. Assemblée Nationale, Place du Palais Bourbon, 75 Paris, France. Degrees: Dipl (IEP Paris); 1934-1935 Auditeur, Conseil d'Etat; 1944-45 Commissaire de la République; 1948-58 Senator; 1959-62 Prime Minister; 1966-73 Member of the French Government; 1963, 1967, 1968, 1973 Deputy, French Nat Assembly. Publs: *Ces princes qui nous gouvernent*, 1956; *Au service de la nation*, 1963; *Jeunesse, quelle France te faut-il?*, 1965; *Sur le gaullisme*, 1967; *Lettres à des militants sur la continuité, l'ouverture et la fidélité*, 1970; *Une certaine idée de la France*, 1972; *Combat pour les élections*, 1973; *Ancien ennemi du peuple*, 1976.

[431]
DE BRUIN Gerrit Pieter
7 November 1946, Dutch. Vincent van Goghweg 36, 1506 JC Zaandam, The Netherlands. Degrees: MA (Jak); MA (Amsterdam). Dept of Pol Sci, U of Amsterdam. Fields: Formal theory.

[432]
DE BRUIN Jan August Wilhelm
23 August 1943, Dutch. Houtzaagmolensingel 47, Bovenkarspel, The Netherlands. Degrees: Drs in Econ and Soc. Labour Analyst, AKZO; Economist, The Netherlands Institute of Econ; Assistant Professor, Free U of Amsterdam. Publs: "Policy Science and Policy Analysis", *Bestuurswetenschappen*, 1976; "Boundry Conditions: a note on the feasibility of goals" (with J A M Maarse), *Bestuurswetenschappen*, 1977. Fields: Policy sciences; policy analysis; policy development.

[433]
DE BRUYN Leonardus Petrus Johannes
19 August 1938, Dutch. Lange Kerkdam 99, Wassenaar, The Netherlands. Degrees: Drs (Nijmegen), 1964. 1965-1974 Scientific Researcher, Sociological Inst, Catholic U of Nijmegen; 1974- Civil Servant, Dept of Social Welfare and Culture, The Hague. Publs: *Party Selection, a Systematic Comparative Analysis of the Party Platforms for the 1971 Parliamentary Elections*, 1971; *De Nederlandse Kiezer 1971* (with others), 1972; *De Nederlandse Kiezer 1972* (with others), 1973; *De Nederlandse Kiezer 1973* (with others), 1974; *The Dutch Voter 1972/1973* (with W J Foppen), 1974. Fields: Decision-making; parties as communicators between government and voters; politicians and civil servants.

[434]
DE CASTRO-SARRIA Oskar*
8 November 1928, German. Postfach 1141, D-8058 Erding, FR Germany. Degrees: BA; MA (Borja), 1956; MA, 1967; PhD (Munich), 1971. Doctoral thesis: "Die politische Lehre von Jacques Maritain". 1971- Inst für Pol Wiss, Technical U of Munich. Publs: *Die politische Lehre von Jacques Maritain und die Problematik einer christlichen Politik*, 1971. Fields: Peace research on Germany; the image of the 'other' Germany in both countries.

[435]
DECHAMPS Bruno Josef Gerhard
4 April 1925, German. D-6072 Dreieichenhain, Ringstrasse 80, FR Germany. Degrees: MA (Fordham USA), 1949; Dr phil Soc Sci (Heidelberg), 1952. Doctoral thesis: "Die Verlagerung der parlamentarischen Arbeit und Entscheidung aus den Plenarversammlungen in die Ausschüsse". 1952-56 Editor, *Deutsche Zeitung and Wirtschafts-Zeitung*; 1956-65 Editor, *Frankfurter Allgemeine Zeitung*; 1966- Herasugeber, *Frankfurter Allgemeine Zeitung*. Publs: *Macht und Arbeit der Ausschüsse*, 1957; *Über Pferde*, 1957.

[436]
DE CLERCO Julian Bertrand*
14 February 1932, Belgian. Ravenstraat 112, 3000 Leuven, Belgium. Degrees: Lic (Catholic U of Louvain), 1963; Dr phil (Catholic U of Louvain), 1963. Doctoral thesis: "De atheistische arbeidsontologie van J. Vuillemin". Assistant, Faculty of Econ and Soc Sci, Catholic U of Louvain; Lecturer in Philosophy, Dominicum Studium Generale; Professor, Faculty of Soc Sci, Catholic U of Louvain. Publs: *Godsdienst en ideologie in de politiek*, 1968; *Socialisering en sociologie*, 1969; *Kritiek van der verzuiling*, 1969; *Politieke opties* (in collaboration), 1972. Fields: Political ethics; evolution and relevance of the 'Ideologiekritik' in sociology of knowledge and philosophy; influence of the religious evolution on established political structures in Western Europe; the Left-Right discussion.

[437]
DECRAENE Philippe
5 October 1930, French. 106 rue Haudan, 92330 Sceaux, France. Degrees: Lic ès lettres; DES; Certificat d'études supérieures d'ethnologie. African Affairs Editor, *Le Monde;* Editor-in-chief, *Revue francaise d'études politiques africaines*. Publs: *Le Panafricanisme*, 1977; *Tableau des partis politiques Sud-Sahariens*, 1963; *Lettres de l'Afrique Atlantique*, 1975; *L'expérience socialiste somalienne*, 1977. Fields: African political parties; panafricanism.

[438]
DEGEN Ulrich*
28 January 1943, German. 1 Berlin 41, Fregestrasse 8ʊ/11, FR Germany. Degrees: Dipl Pol Wiss (Berlin), 1970. Assistant for Pol Theory and Econ of Educational Planning, U of Berlin. Publs: "Zur Anwendung der kybernetischen System-theorie in den Sozialwissenschaften" (co-author), in *Planung und Information*, 1972; *Informationswissenschaft in der Lehrerausbildung-Inhalte-Methoden-Ziele-Gesellschaftliche Relevanz*, 1972. Fields: Programmed instruction and the influence of labour class in Germany; political planning and theory of planning in education theory; political economy and public interest; new political economy of computer learning in society and political education in industry.

[439]
DE GRAEVE-LISMONT Edith
30 March 1945, Belgian. Leopoldstraat 13, 3000 Leuven, Belgium. Degrees: Lic in pol and soc sci; Lic in econ sci; B phil. Doctoral thesis: "Power and Lack of Power of Parliamentary Opposition in Belgium". Assistant, Dept of Pol Sci, Catholic U of Leuven. Publs: *De Belgische Grondwet per 1 September 1970*, 1970; *De Belgische Grondwet van 1831 tot heden*, 1971; *Het nut van een miljoenenpropaganda* (with W Dewachter, E Clijsters and L Engelen), 1974. Fields: Public decision-making; opposition and minority; European integration.

[440]
DE HEER Maarten L
21 August 1929, Dutch. Frankenslag 386, The Hague, The Netherlands. Degrees: Drs (Amsterdam). Director, Agricultural Board. Fields: Agricultural policy; European integration.

[441]
DE JONGHE Eugeen*
14 December 1922, Belgian. Boskantlaan 1, 3030 Heverlee, 3000 Leuven, Belgium. Degrees: Dr en droit (Louvain); Dr ès philosophie (Louvain); Lic en sci écon (Louvain). Doctoral thesis: "The Liberalism of T H Green". 1961- General Secretary, Dean, Faculty of Econ and Soc Sci; Professor of Social Philosophy and Social and Pol Thought, U of Louvain. Publs: *Het arondissement Eeklo, sociaal-economische studie*, 1960; *Das Kapital (1867-1967)*, 1967; *Geschiedenis der Politieke en Sociale Theorieen — Hedendaagse periode Het Marxisme, deel 1 en deel 2*, 1967; *Geschiedenis der Politieke en Sociale Theorieen — Renaissance — XVIIIde eeuw*, 1968; *Geschiedenis der Politieke en Sociale Theorieen — Oudheid en Middeleeuwen*, 1969. Fields: Marxist thought; neo-anarchism; social philosophy.

[442]
DEKKER Henk
8 April 1949, Dutch. Esweg 46, Peize, The Netherlands. Degrees: Drs. 1971-1975 Maatschappijleer; 1973- Assistant Professor in Political Education, Dept of Political Education, U of Groningen. Publs: *Doelstellingen voor Maatschappijleer*, 1974; *Kernthema's voor Maatschappijleer*, 1976; "Films voor sociale en politieke vorming", *Stichting Burgerschapskunde*, 1978; "Lessen over macht" (co-author), *Stichting Burgerschapskunde*, 1978; plus various articles in *Intermediair* and *Sociale Vorming*. Fields: Political socialization; political interest, knowledge, behaviour of youth; political education; methods of political science; power-research.

[443]
DE KLEUVER Jan
20 December 1950, Dutch. Magdalenastraat 30, 3512 NH Utrecht, The Netherlands. Degrees: Drs. Doctoral thesis: "Multinational Companies and Employment". Policy-Assistant, Building and Wood-workers' Union, Christian National Federation of Trade-Unions. Fields: Labour-Market policy; labour relations; building policy; 'new political economy'; multinational companies.

[444]
DE LANGE Jan*
10 January 1936, Dutch. Julianaplantsoen 194, Diemen, The Netherlands. Degrees: Drs (Amsterdam), 1962. Civil Servant; Teaching Post, Inst of Pol Sci, U of Amsterdam. Publs: Articles in *Acta Politica*. Fields: Local politics, especially the relations of local systems to national political systems.

[445]
DE LANOO Ivan
26 February 1937, Belgian. Tiensesteenweg 229, 3042 Bierbeek, Belgium. Degrees: Lic; Dr; Aggregaat. Doctoral thesis: "Stratifikatieproblemen en Demokratisering van het Universitair Onderwijs" (Stratification Problems and Democratization of Higher Education). Geaggregeerde, U of Leuven. Publs: "De Sociale herkomst van de Leuvense Studenten", *Politica*, 1977. Fields: Education; methods and techniques of social sciences.

[446]
DELEECK Herman
29 August 1928, Belgian. Salvialei 9, 2540 Hove, Belgium. Degrees: Dr jur (Louvain), 1952; Dr econ (Louvain), 1966. Doctoral thesis: "Maatschappelijke zekerheid en Inkomensverdeling in Belgie" (Social Security and Income Redistribution in Belgium). Professor, U of Antwerp and U of Louvain; Senator. Publs: *Maatschappelijke zekerheid en Inkomensverdeling in België*, 1969; *Vermogensaanwasdeling en Investeringloon*, 1967; *Inleiding tot de sociale planning*, 1971; *Inkomensverdeling, sociale zekerleid en sociaal beleid*, 1972; *Ongelijkheden in de Welvaart staat*, 1977. Fields: Theory of social policy, especially social security; income distribution and redistribution; distribution of collective goods.

[447]
DE LEONE Enrico
9 May 1906, Italian. Degrees: Laurea in Giurisprudenza (Rome), 1929; Laurea in Sci Pol (Padova), 1930; Dipl in Diritti Orientali (Rome), 1934; 1933-43 Official Colonial Service, Professor "Storia e Istituzioni dell'Africa Mediterranea e del Vicino Oriente". Publ: *Le Prime Ricerche di una Colonia e la Esplorazione Politica, Geografica ed Economica*, 1955; *La Colonizzazione del L'Africa del Nord*, 1957-1960; *L'Impero Ottomano nel Primo Periodo delle Riforme (Tanzimat) Secondo Fonti Italiane*, 1967; *Riformatori Musulmani del XIX Secolo nell'Africa e nell'Asia Mediterranee*, 1973. Fields: North Africa, especially Maghreb nations.

[448]
DELLENBRANT Jan Åke
4 September 1946, Swedish. Eriksgatan 26, A S-75228 Uppsala, Sweden. Degrees: PhD, 1972. Doctoral thesis: "Reformists and Traditionalists: A Study of Soviet Discussions about Economic Reform, 1960-65". Senior Lecturer, U of Uppsala; Associate Professor of Soviet and East European Studies, U of Uppsala; Research Fellow, Dept of Pol, U of Stockholm. Publs: *Politik si Sovjetunionen*, 1971; *Reformists and Traditionalists: A Study of Soviet Discussions about Economic Reform 1960-1965*, 1972; *Regional Differences in the Soviet Union: A Quantitative Inquiry into the Development of the Soviet Republic*, 1977. Fields: Soviet politics; comparative politics; political parties; co-operative organizations.

[449]
DELLEY Jean-Daniel
9 February 1943, Swiss. 109 rue de Lausanne, 1202 Geneva, Switzerland. Degrees: Lic en philosophie; Lic en sci pol; Dr. Doctoral thesis: "L'initiative populaire en Suisse. "Mythe et réalité de la démocratie directe". Chef de travaux, Faculté de Droit, U de Genève. Fields: System of Swiss politics; theory of democracy; sociology of law.

[450]
DELMARTINO Franck
31 October 1939, Belgian. L'Beosierlaan 20, B-3200 Kessel-Lo, Belgium. Degrees: Lic pol and soc sci (Louvain), 1967; Dr Medieval Studies (Louvain), 1968; Dr soc sci (Louvain), 1975. Doctoral thesis: "Schaalvergroting en bestuurskracht" (Scale Increase and Administrative Power). Assistant, Dept of Pol Sci, U of Louvain. Publs: *De fusie van kleine gemeenten*, 1967; *Inspraak in opsraak*, 1977. Fields: Amalgamation of municipalities; comparative local government; history of administrative institutions; citizen participation and community building.

[451]
DELORME Helene
17 January 1940, French. Maison des Sciences de l'Homme, 54 Boulevard Raspail, 75006 Paris, France. Doctoral thesis: "Les paysans de Bruxelles-étude de l'appareil de représentation des agriculteurs dans l'Europe des six (1958-71)". Attachée de recherche, FNSP. Fields: International relations.

[452]
DELPEREE Albert
23 April 1912, Belgian. 46 rue d'Espagne, 1060 Brussels, Belgium. Degrees: Lic en sci financières, 1933; Dr en sci commerciales, 1935. Doctoral thesis: "Les conventions collectives du travail". Professeur, Catholique U de Louvain. Publs: *Politique sociale et intégration européene*, 1956. Fields: Social policy; social security.

[453]
DELRUELLE Nicole
26 January 1939, Belgian. Avenue Louise 418, B-1050 Bruxelles, Belgium. Degrees: Lic en sci soc, 1960; Dr en sci soc (Free U Brussels), 1970. Doctoral thesis: "Les notables en Belgique". 1960 Chargée de recherche, Inst de Sociologie, Free U of Brussels; 1970 Maître de recherches, Inst de Sociologie, Free U of Brussels; 1965- Assistante, Faculté des Sci Soc; 1970- Chargée de cours, Free U of Brussels; Director, Inst U de Sondage d'Opinion Publique; Chargée de cours, U of Liège. Publs: *Le Comportement électoral des électeurs belges* (co-author), 1970; *La mobilité sociale en Belgique*, 1971; *Les notables en Belgique*, 1972. Fields: Electoral sociology; social mobility; philosophical problems of sociological research.

[454]
DE MALAFOSSE Jehan
6 April 1921, French. 121 rue Magne, 91 Etampes, France. Degrees: Lic ès lettres, 1946; Agrégé de droit, 1951. Faculté de Droit et de Sci Econ, U de Tunis; Faculté de Droit et de Sci Econ, U de Toulouse; Professor, Faculté de Droit d'Econ et Sci Soc, U de Paris. Publs: *La protection possessoire au Bas-Empire*, 1951; *Histoire du droit privé* (with P Ourliac), 1964; *Le régime juridique de la chasse*, 1971; *Le droit de l'environnement: le droit à la nature*, 1973; *Histoire des institutions et des régimes politiques de la Révolution à la IVème République*, 1975. Fields: Parliamentary institutions of the 19th and 20th centuries; public administration; politics of the environment.

[455]
DEMICHEL André
18 March 1935, French. 6 rue de la Plaine, 75020 Paris, France. Degrees: Agrégé de droit. Doctoral thesis: "Le contrôle de l'Etat sur les entreprises privées". Publs: *Les dictatures européennes*; *Les réformes parlementaires européennes*; *Institutions et pouvoirs en France*; *Libertés et pouvoir en France*; *Grands services publics et entreprises nationales*; *Le Droit administratif*. Fields: Constitutional and administrative law.

[456]
DEMOULIN Robert Leon
8 May 1911, Belgian. Séminaire d'Histoire Contemporaine, Faculté de Philosophie et Lettres, 3 Place Cocherill, 4000 Liège, Belgium. Degrees: PhD (Liège), 1932; Agrégé de l'Enseignement Supérieur (Liège), 1938. Doctoral thesis: "Les journées de septembre 1830 à Bruxelles et en province". Dean, Faculty of Philosophy and Letters, U of Liège; Professor of Contemporary History, U de Liège. Publs: *Les journées de Septembre 1830 à Bruxelles et en province. Etude critique d'après les sources*, 1934; *Guillaume Ier et la transformation économique des provinces belges 1815-1830*, 1938; *La révolution de 1830*, 1950. Fields: Political and social evolution in 19th and 20th centuries; diplomatic relations, 1789-present; economic history.

[457]
DENNI Bernard
20 March 1949, French. 150B Galerie de l'Arlequin, 38100 Grenoble, France. Degrees: Dipl (IEP). Doctoral thesis: "La competition des Droites dans la région Rhône-Alpes sous la V République, analyse politique sociologique et stratégique". Assistant, IEP, Grenoble. Publs: "Réduction de la partie: analyse des forces politiques dans la région Rhône-Alpes", in *Espace et Politique*; "Les circonscriptions électorales dans la région Rhône-Alpes", *Les Dossiers de l'Insée*, 1978. Fields: Religion and traditional politics; Rhône-Alps problems.

[458]
DE NOLF Rigo F*
12 August 1940, Belgian. Talingstraat 16, Capelle a/d Yssel, The Netherlands. Degrees: Lic (Louvain), 1964. 1965-66 Editor, *De Standaard*; 1966-67 Adjunct Chief, Service Social, Louvain; 1967-68 Graduate Assistant, Dept of Pol Sci, Kent State U, Ohio; 1968- Lecturer, Rotterdam School of Econ. Publs: *Het Federalisme in België als grondwettelky vraagstuk*, 1968. Fields: Terror and government; past and present.

[459]
D'ENTRÈVES Alexander Passerin*

26 April 1902, Italian. Strada al Ronchi 48, Cavoretto, Torino, Italy. Degrees: Dr of Law (Turin), 1922; D Phil (Oxon), 91932. 1929 Lecturer, U of Turin; 1934 Professor, U of Messina; 1935 Professor, U of Pavia; 1938 Professor, U of Turin; 1946-57 Serena Professor of Italian Studies, U of Oxford; Fellow, Magdalen Coll, U of Oxford; 1957 Visiting Professor, Harvard U; 1960-64 Visiting Professor, Yale U; Professor of Pol Theory, U of Turin. Publs: *The Medieval Contribution to Political Thought*, 1939; *Reflections on the History of Italy*, 1947; *Natural Law, An Introduction to Legal Philosophy*, 1951; *Dante as a Political Thinker*, 1952; *The Notion of the State, An Introduction to Political Theory*, 1967.

[460]
DENVER David Trodden

2 October 1944, British. 41 Belle Vue Terrace, Lancaster, England. Degrees: MA (Glasgow); B Phil (Dundee). Lecturer, Dept of Pol, U of Lancaster. Publs: *Scottish Local Government Elections*, 1974. Fields: Political parties; elections; political sociology.

[461]
DEPPE Frank

23 September 1941, German. 355 Marburg/Lahn, Heusingerstrasse, 3 FR Germany. Degrees: Dr phil; Habilitation. Doctoral thesis: "Zum Verhältnis von politischer Theorie und politischer Praxis bei L. A. Blanqui". 1968-70 Assistant, U of Marburg; 1970-72 Akademischer Rat, U of Marburg; Professor of Pol Sci, Philipps-U, Marburg/Lahn. Publs: *Verschwörung, Aufstand und Revolution*, 1969; *Kritik der Mitbestimmung*, 1969; *Die neue Arbeiterklasse*, 1970; *Das Bewusstsein der Arbeiter*, 1971; *Europäische Wirtschaftsgemeinschaft. Zur politischen Ökonomie der westeuropäischen Integration*, 1975; *Arbeiterbewegung und westeuropäische Integration*, 1976; *Geschichte der deutschen Gewerkschaftsbewegung*, 1977. Fields: Problems of capitalist integration (EEC); the internationalization of the economic and political systems of modern capitalist societies; history and theory of trade union policy; history and theory of the state.

[462]
DEPRE Roger

26 June 1929, Belgian. Acacialaan 24, 3300 Tienen, Belgium. Degrees: Dr. Doctoral thesis: "Topambtenaren van de Ministeries in België" (Top Civil Servants in Belgian Ministries). Professor, Dept of Pol Sci, Catholic U of Leuven. Publs: *Innovations in Local Government*, 1972; "Career Patterns of Higher Civil Servants in Belgium", *Res Publica*, 1973; *Les effectifs de personnel dans les villes et les communes belges*, 1974; *La préparation aux functions publiques administratives par les universités en Europa accidentale*; *Gemeentebeleid na de fusies*. Fields: Public administration; management of local government; organizational theory and practice.

[463]
DE RAEYMAEKER Omer Joseph

25 October 1911, Belgian. Leopoldstraat 2, 3000 Leuven, Belgium. Degrees: Dr jur; Dr rer pol. Doctoral thesis: "Belgie's international beleid 1919-1939" (Belgium's International Policy Between the Two World Wars). Ord Professor, Faculty of Soc Sci, Catholic U of Leuven; Dean, Faculty of Econ and Soc Sci, Catholic U of Leuven; Chairman, Inst of Pol and Soc Sci, Catholic U of Leuven; Chairman, Dept of Pol Sci, Catholic U of Leuven; Professor, Dept of Pol Sci, Catholic U of Leuven; 1961-65 Vice-President, Belgian National Foundation for Sci Research; Em Professor, Catholic U of

Leuven. Publs: *Belgian International Policy 1919-1939* (in Dutch), 1945; *Small Powers and International Co-operation* (in Dutch), 1947; *International Relations* (in Dutch), 1954; *La Belgique et les nations unies*, 1958; *Internationale Instellingen*, 1975; *UNO Operations for Maintenance of Peace* (in Dutch) (with L van Depoele *et al*), 1972; *Small Powers in Alignment* (with W Andries *et al*), 1974. Fields: International relations; international institutions, especially UNO; history of international relations; Belgian foreign policy.

[464]
DERATHE Robert Felix Emile
20 December 1905, French. 19 rue du Calvaire, 92 St Cloud, France. Degrees: Agrégé de philosophie, 1931; Dr ès lettres (Paris), 1950. Professeur de philosophie dans divers lycées; 1935-38 Pensionnaire, Inst français, Berlin; 1938-39 Professeur, Inst français de Vienne; 1948-49 Chargé d'enseignement, Faculté des Lettres, U de Dijon; 1949-51 Chargé d'enseignement, Faculté des Lettres, U de Nancy; Professeur de philosophie, U de Nancy II; Directeur, UER de Philosophie-Psychologie-Sociologie. Publs: *Le rationalisme de Jean-Jacques Rousseau*, 1948; *Jean Jacques Rousseau et la science politique de son temps*, 1950; *Montesquieu, de l'esprit des lois*, 1973; *Hegel, principe de la philosophie du droit ou droit naturel et science du droit en abrégé*, 1975. Fields: Jean Bodin and the political philosophy of the 16th century.

[465]
DE REUCK Anthony Vivian Smith
3 September 1923, British. 6 The Mall, East Sheen, London SW14, England. Degrees: MSc; MSc (Econ); DIC; ARCS. Editor of *Nature*; Deputy Director, CIBA Foundation for Medical Research, London; Research Associate, Centre for the Analysis of Conflict, London; Chairman, Conflict Research Society, London. Senior Lecturer in International Relations, Dept of Linguistic and International Studies, U of Surrey. Publs: *Conflict in Society*, 1966; *Caste and Race*, 1967; *Communication in Science*, 1968; *Weil wir Überleben Wollen*, 1970; "Controlled Communication: Rationale and Dynamics", in *The Human Context*, 1974; "Value Systems and Value Change", in *Proceedings 3rd International Conference on Unity of the Sciences*, 1974; *The Study of World Society* (with J W Burton *et al*). Fields: Conflict analysis and conflict resolution; group dynamics of diplomatic negotiation; exchange theory of international relations.

[466]
DE RHAM Gerard
19 May 1946, Swiss. Av Ramuz 115, CH-1009 Pully, Switzerland. Degrees: Dr ès sci pol. Doctoral thesis: "La politique étrangère de la République de Zambie". Inst de Sci Pol, U de Lausanne; Dept de Sociologie, U de Genève. Publs: *La politique étrangère de la République de Zambie*, 1977; *Xénophobie?* (with U Windisch and J M Jaeggi), 1978; articles in *Annuaire Suisse de Science Politique*; *Journal of Peace Research*. Fields: Sociology of development and imperialism; immigrant workers in Switzerland; ideology and politics in Switzerland.

[467]
DERIVRY Daniel Henri*
25 March 1936, French. 19 rue de la Mare aux Fées, 95 Franconville, France. Degrees: Dipl (IEP). 1960-69 Collaborateur technique, CNRS; 1969- Attaché de recherche, Groupe d'Étude de Méthodes de l'Analyse Sociologique, CNRS. Publs: "Analyse Ecologique du Vote Paysan", in *Les Paysans et la Politique* (H Mendras (ed)), 1971. Fields: Political sociology.

[468]
DERLIEN Hans Ulrich
20 July 1945, German. Am Sooren 21, 2000 Hamburg 73, FR Germany. Degrees: Dipl Soziologe; Dr rer Pol. Doctoral thesis: "Evaluation of Public Policymaking — Organization, Methods and Politics of Programme Evaluation" (in German). 1972-73 Assistant, Research Inst, Advanced College of Public Administration, Speyer; 1973-76 Assistant, Inst of Applied Social Research, Cologne. 1976- Professor, Hochschule der Bundeswehr, Hamburg. Fields: Public administration, especially ministerial bureaucracy; local government; organization theory.

[469]
DERRIENNIC Jean-Pierre*
22 December 1943, French. 76 rue Lecourbe, Paris XVème, France. Degrees: Dipl (IEP Paris), 1964. Assistant de recherche, Centre d'Etudes de Relations Internationales. Publs: "Relations Interétatiques inégales et conflits" *Revue Française de Science Politique*, 1971. Fields: Relations between internal and international conflicts.

[470]
DESCAMPS Eugène Paul
17 March 1922, French. 3 Avenue des Noëls, 95230 Soisy-sous-Montmorency, France. 1950-61 Secrétaire général du Syndicat de la Sidérurgie et de la Fédération Nationale de la Métallurgie; 1961-71 Secrétaire général de la Confédération Française des travailleurs chrétiens; 1971-74 Chargé d'enseignement, Paris X Nanterre; 1972-77 Chargé de cours, Ecole Nationale d'Administration et Inst d'Etudes Sociales; 1977- Professeur associé, Paris X Nanterre. Publs: *Militer*, 1971; *Les conflits sociaux en Europe* (contributor), 1971; *Industry's democratic revolution* (Ch Levison (ed)), 1974. Fields: Collective bargaining; social conflicts; industrial relations in multi-nationals; organization of international unionism.

[471]
DE SOTO Jean
14 January 1915, French. 1 rue de Goff, 75005 Paris, France. Degrees: Agrégé droit public, 1945; Dr en droit. Professeur, Faculté de Droit, U de Strasbourg; Professeur, Faculté de Droit, U de Paris. Fields: Relations between European law and French public law; history of political ideas in the 19th and 20th centuries.

[472]
DESSELBERGER Hermann
13 July 1943, German. Hammer Strasse 58, D-4400 Münster, FR Germany. Degrees: Dr phil (Giessen). Doctoral thesis: "Schools and Ujamaa. An Inquiry into the Economic Development and the Extension of Primary Schools of the Tanga Region/Tanzania". Assistant Professor, Pädagogische Hochschule Westfalen-Lippe, Münster. Publs: "Physical Regions of Africa", in *Meyers Kontinente und Meere*, 1968; *Schools and Ujamaa*, 1975; "Regional Planning and Functional Administrative Reforms", (Tranhardt (ed)), *Functional Administrative Reform*, 1978. Fields: Development politics; adult education; social geography; Africa South of the Sahara.

[473]
DE SWAAN Abraham
8 January 1942, Dutch. Keizersgracht 752, 1017 Amsterdam, The Netherlands. Degrees: PhD. Doctoral thesis: "Coalition Theories and Cabinet Formations". 1971-1973 Senior Lecturer, U of Rotterdam; 1973- Senior Lecturer, Full Professor of Soc, Sociological Institute, U of Amsterdam. Publs: "Coalition and Cabinet Formations, *Elsevier*, 1973; "Testing Coalition Theories: The Combined Evidence" (with R K Mokken), in *Politics as Rational Action*, 1977; *Coalitions: The Case of The Netherlands* (J Dreijmanis and E Browne (eds)); "A Classification of Parties and Party Systems According to Coalition Options", *European Journal of Political Research*, 1975; "On the Sociogenesis of the Psychoanalytic Setting", in *Human Figurations (Essays in Honour of Norbert Elias)*, 1976; "Terror as a Government Service", in *Repression and Repressive Violence* (M Hoefnagels (ed)), 1977. Fields: Coalition theory; history of the psychoanalytic movement and techniques; welfare state; state control and repression.

[474]
DEUBNER Christian
12 June 1942, German. Amalienstrasse 97, D-8000 München 40, FR Germany. Degrees: Dipl Pol, 1968; Dr rer Pol, 1975; Doctoral thesis: "Die Atompolitik der Westdeutschen Industrie und die Gründung von EURATOM". Assistant, Free U of Berlin; Research Assistant, U of Constance; Researcher, Stiftung Wisenschaft und Politik, Ebenhausen. Publs: *Die Atompolitik der Westdeutschen Industrie und die Gründung von EURATOM*, 1977; "The Expansion of Capital and the Genesis of International Nuclear Politics in West Germany", *International Organization*, 1979; "Deutsch-Französische Wirtschaftsbeziehungen im Rahmen der weltwirtschaftlichen Arbeitsteilung: Interdependent, Divergenz oder strukturelle Dominanz?" (with Rehfeldt and Schlupp), in *Deutschland-Frankreich-Europa* (Picht (ed)), 1978. Fields: International and German nuclear politics; German foreign economic politics and structures of interdependence in Western Europe; effects of internationalization of capital in FR Germany and Western Europe; Mediterranean politics.

[475]
DEUTSCH Karl Wolfgang
21 June 1912, American. 1000 Berlin 33, Höhmannstrasse 8, FR Germany. Degrees: Dr (Charles U, Prague); PhD (Harvard); DA (Geneva); LLD (Michigan); LLD (Illinois); PhD (Mannheim). Professor, MIT; Professor, Yale; President of the International Pol Sci Association; Stanfield Professor of International Peace, Dept of Govt, Harvard U, and Director, International Inst for Comparative Social Research, Science Centre, West Berlin. Publs: *The Nerves of Government*, 1966; *France, Germany and the Western Alliance* (with L J Edinger, R C Macridis and R L Merritt); *Problems of World Modelling* (with B Fritsch, H Jaguaribe and A Markovits). Fields: Political science.

[476]
DE VROEDE Paul
16 October 1919, Belgian. Leopoldstraat 33, 2800 Mechelen, Belgium. Degrees: Dr in Law (Brussels); Dr in History (Ghent); Lic in Pol Sci (Brussels). Professor, Faculty of Law, Faculty of Pol and Soc Sci, Free U of Brussels. Publs: Articles in *Rechtskundig Weekblad Journal des Tribunaux*; *Revue de Droit Intellectuel*; *Tijdschrift voor Privaatrecht*; *Tijdschrift voor Europees Recht*; *Belgische Rechtspraak in handelszaken*; *Prijsregeling*, 1976; *handboek van Belgisch Economisch recht*, 1978.

[477]
DEWACHTER Wilfried Franz Josef
5 March 1938, Belgian. Jachthoorn 10, 3202 Linden, Belgium. Degrees: MA, PhD (Leuven). Doctoral thesis: "The General Elections as a Process of Power Achievement in the Belgian Political System". Research Assistant, Centrum voor Politieke Studiën, Catholic U of Leuven; Professor of Pol Soc, Catholic U of Leuven. Publs: *De wetgevende verkiezingen als proces van machtsverwering in het Belgisch politiek bestel*, 1967; *Carte politique de la Belgique. Atlas des élections législatives du 31 Mars 1968*, 1970; *De politieke zeggingskracht van de Gemeenteraadsverkiezingen*, 1970; *De Belgische grondwet van 1831 tot heden*, 1971; *Het nut van een miljoenenpropaganda*, 1974. Fields: Political sociology, especially power distribution at the national and international level; political parties and pressure groups; elite studies.

[478]
DHONDT Jan*
22 January 1915, Belgian. Blandijnberg 2, Ghent, Belgium. Degrees: PhD (Ghent), 1939. Doctoral thesis: "King Henry I". 1939-42 Research Fellow; 1942-44 Record Office; Professor of Contemporary History, U of Ghent. Fields: Political and social history of Belgium since 1940.

[479]
DIAS Patrick Venantius
18 May 1934, German. 7800 Freiburg, Hohlenstrasse 1, FR Germany. Degrees: Lic (Theological College, Poona, India), 1958; Dr (Tübingen), 1965. Doctoral thesis: "Vielfalt der Kirche in der Vielfalt der Jünger, Zeugen und Diener". 1958-60 Professor of Ethics and Civil Law, Rachol College, Goa, India; 1963-65 Research Scholar, Alexander von Humboldt-Stiftung; 1966 Associate Research Fellow, Arnold Bergsträsser Inst, Freiburg; Research Officer, Senior Staff Member, Senior Research Associate, Arnold Bergsträsser Inst, Freiburg. Publs: *Vielfalt der Kirche in der Vielfalt der Jünger, Zeugen und Diener*, 1968; *Kirche. In der Schrift und im zweiten Jahrhundert*, 1974; *Situation et Perspectives de la Faculté des Sciences de l'Education à l'université Nationale du Zaire*, 1973; *Erziehung in Indien zwischen sozialer Reproduktion und Revolution. Theoretisch-methodischer Ansatz und Bibliographie*, 1975; *Education: an Obstacle to Development? Some remarks about the political functions of education in Asia and Africa* (co-author), 1975; *Reproduktionseffekt oder Wandelsrelevanz der Bildung*, 1975; *La formation des enseignants au Zaire*, 1976; *Indien: Populistischer Sozialismus und blockabhängige Neutralitätspolitik*, 1976; *Soziale Bedingungen religiöser Erscheinungen am Beispiel der katholischen Kirche*, 1977. Fields: Sociology of religion and education; political sociology of developing countries; politics and policy making in education; social psychology of political groups.

[480]
DIEDERICH Nils
24 May 1934, German. Wilkistrasse 54a, 1000 Berlin (Zahlendorf), FR Germany. Degrees: Dipl Volkswirt, 1959; Dr rer Pol, 1964; Venia Legendi, 1970. Doctoral thesis: "Empirische Wahlforschung". 1957 Zentralinst für Sozialwissenschaftliche Forschung; 1970 Professor in Pol Sci, Fachbereich Pol Wissenschaft (Otto-Suhr-Inst), Free U of Berlin; 1971-76 Head of the Planning Division of the Governing Mayor of Berlin; 1976-Member of Deutscher Bundestag; Professor in Pol Sci, Free U of Berlin. Publs: *Empirische Wahlforschung*, 1965; *Verbände und Gesetzgebung* (co-author), 1965. Fields: Political sociology; political parties; interest groups; electoral analysis; mass political behaviour; planning; political economy.

[481]
DIEM Peter
7 April. 1937, Austrian. Kramergasse 3, 1010 Vienna, Austria. Degrees: Dr jur (Vienna), 1960; MSc (Southern Illinois), 1961. Doctoral thesis: "American Catholics as a Political Pressure Group 1945-60". Chief of Party Organization, OEVP; Director of Pol Research, OEVP; Market and Media Research. Publs: *Zeit zur Reform* (with H Neisser), 1969. Fields: The ideological development of Christian-democrat parties; reform of political party structure; election campaigns; voting behaviour; reform of parliamentary system; RTV-audience research; book-market research.

[482]
DIEZ DEL CORRAL Luis*
5 July 1911, Spanish. Madrid 1, Jorge Juan 7, Spain. Ord Professor, U of Madrid. Publs: *El Liberalismo Doctrinario*, 1945; *De Historia y Politica*, 1957; *The Rape of Europe* (tr), 1959; *La Mentalidad Politica de Tocqueville*, 1964. Fields: Tocqueville; liberalism.

[483]
DILLON George Michael
15 July 1945, British. Department of Politics, University of Lancaster, Fylde College, Lancaster LA1 4YE, England. Degrees: BA; MA (Dalhousie); PhD (Lancaster). Doctoral thesis: "Policy Implementation: A Case Study of the Polaris Executive". Lecturer in Pol, U of Lancaster. Publs: *Canadian Naval Policy since World War II: A Decision-Making Analysis*, 1972; "Defence and Security (with P Nailor), in *Britain in the EEC* (D Evans (ed)), 1973; Defence Decision-Making", in *British Defence Policy* (J Baylis (ed)); "Policy and Dramaturgy: A Critique of Current Conceptions of Policy Making", *Policy and Politics*, 1976. Fields: Policy science; defence analysis, management and procurement.

[484]
DIMITRIJEVIC Vojin
9 July 1932, Yugoslavian. Bulevar JNA 139, 11040 Beograd, Yugoslavia. Degrees: MA; Dr. Doctoral thesis: "Territorial Asylum". Research Assistant, Inst for International Pol and Econ, Beograd. Assistant Professor, Associate Professor, U of Beograd. Publs: *Utociste na teritoriji strane drzave*, 1970; *Medvnarodne organizacije*, 1978; *Pojam bezbednosti u medunarodnium odnosima*, 1973; *Osnovi teorije medunarodnih odnisa*, 1977. Fields: International organizations; terrorism; international relations theory.

[485]
DINWIDDY John Rowland
16 May 1939, British. Little St Anne's Coach House, Englefield Green, Surrey, England. Degrees: BA; MA (Oxon), 1965; PhD (London), 1971. Doctoral thesis: "Parliamentary Reform as an Issue in English Politics, 1800-10". Senior Lecturer in History, Royal Holloway Coll, London; Associate Research Fellow, U Coll, London; Joint General Ed *Collected Works by Jeremy Bentham*. Publs: *Christopher Wyvill and Reform 1790-1820*, 1971; plus various articles in *History, Historical Journal, Journal of the History of Ideas, International Review of Social History,* and others. Fields: Early 19th century radicalism; political ideas of the late eighteenth century, especially the thought of Burke and Bentham.

[486]
DITTBERNER Jürgen*
1 December 1939, German. 1 Berlin 22, An der Bastion 46, FR Germany. Degrees: Dipl Soziologe (Free U of Berlin), 1965; Dr rer Pol (Free U of Berlin), 1969. 1965-69 Assistant, Inst für Pol Wiss, Free U of Berlin; 1969-73 Assistant Professor, Zentralinst für Sozialwissenschaftliche Forschung, Free U of Berlin. Publs: *Die Bundesparteitage der Christlich Demokratischen Union und der Sozialdemokratischen Partei Deutschlands, von 1946 bis 1968*, 1969. Fields: Problems of class structure and party system in FR Germany; political elections; non-party articulation in politics; political sociology.

[487]
DODD Clement Henry
6 April 1926, British. Department of Political Studies, University of Hull, Kingston-upon-Hull, England. Degrees: BA; MA (Edinburgh), 1955. 1957-63 Lecturer in Pol, U of Leeds; 1959-62 Visiting Professor of Public Administration, East Technical U, Ankara; 1963-67 Lecturer in Middle Eastern Pol, U of Durham; 1967-70 Senior Lecturer in Government, U of Manchester. Publs: *Studies in University Government and Administration* (ed), 1963; *Politics and Government in Turkey*, 1969; *Israel and the Arab World* (with M Sales), 1970; *Political Development*, 1972. Fields: Turkish politics; the politics of Persia and Pakistan.

[488]
DOEKER Günther
30 August 1933, German. 1 Berlin 33, Winklerstrasse 15, FR Germany. Degrees: LLM (Tulane School of Law), 1958; PhD (Tulane), 1964; Habilitation, Aggregation (Berlin), 1970. Professor, Free U of Berlin; Member, Institute of Strategic Studies, London. Publs: *The Treaty-Making Power in the Commonwealth of Australia*, 1966; *Vergleichende Analyse Politischer Systeme*, 1971; *Festschrift für Karl Löwenstein* (co-author), 1971; *Festschrift für Ernst Fraenkel* (co-author), 1974; *Parlamentarismus and Föderalismus*, 1977; *Die Vereinten Nationen*, 1976. Fields: Constitutional and international law; international organizations; comparative politics and international relations; administrative planning and organization.

[489]
DOERR Werner
17 December 1948, German. Paulinstrasse 69, D-5500 Trier, FR Germany. Degrees: Dr (Frankfurt), 1973. Doctoral thesis: "American Foreign Policy Towards the Soviet Union 1961-72". 1973-75 Akademischer Tutor, Gesamthochschule Kassel; 1975- Assistant Lecturer, Lecturer in International Relations, U of Trier. Fields: US foreign policy; external relations of the European Community; cultural exchanges and foreign policy.

[490]
DOGAN Mattei
16 October 1920, French. 72 Boulevard Arago, 75013 Paris, France. Degrees: Dr ès lettres; Dipl (IEP Paris); DES History, DES Phil (Sorbonne), 1953; Visiting Professor, U of Indiana, U of Yale; Inst of Statistical Mathematics, Tokyo; Recurring Visiting Professor, U of California; Research Director, CNRS, Paris; Director, Bureau d'Analyses européennes, Paris. Publs: *Les Françaises face à la politique*, 1956; *Partiti politici e strutture sociali in Italia* (with Petrocca), 1968; *Quantitative Ecological Analysis in the Social Sciences* (with Rokkan), 1969; *European Politics* (with R Rose), 1971; *The Mandarins of Western Europe* (ed), 1975; "Political Cleavage and Social Stratification in France and Italy", in *Party Systems and Voter Alignment*, 1967; "Political Ascent in a Class Society", in *Political Decision Makers*, 1961; *Les clivages politiques dans la classe ouvrière*, 1962. Fields: Political elites; legislatures and executives; mass political behaviour.

[491]
D'OLIVIERA E SOUZA Jorge Manuel*
5 October 1945, Belgian. Van Monsstraat 85, 3000 Leuven, Belgian. Degrees: Lic in pol sci (Catholic U of Louvain), 1970. Assistant, Catholic U of Louvain. Publs: "Sociale communicatiermiddelen en opvoeding", *De Maand*, 1967; "L'enjeu de la guerre", *Revue Nouvelle*, 1971. Fields: Epistemological analysis of methods in peace and conflict research; semantics and conflict, a definition of a semantic theory of bargaining.

[492]
DOMENACH Claude
8 January 1938, French. Chemin de la Tour de Chiens, Corenc, 38700 La Tronche, France. Degrees: Dipl (IEP Paris); ENA. Administrateur civil, Ministère de l'Equipement; Directeur, Professeur associé, IEP Grenoblé. Fields: Town planning; social politics; public administration.

[493]
DOMES Jürgen Otto
2 April 1932, German. Scheidterstrasse 6, 6601 Saarbrücken-Scheidter Berg, FR Germany. Degrees: PhD (Heidelberg), 1960; Habilitation (Berlin), 1967. Doctoral thesis: "Das Freiwilligengesetz im II. Deutschen Bundestag — eine Studie zum Oppositionsverhalten des Parlaments". 1959-62 Research Assistant, Inst of Pol Sci, U of Heidelberg; 1963-64 Visiting Professor, National Chengchi U, Taiwan; 1964-67 Assistant Professor, Otto-Suhr-Inst, Free U of Berlin; 1967 Junior Associate, Free U of Berlin; 1968-69 Senior Associate Professor, Free U of Berlin; 1970-75 Professor of Pol Sci and Director, Research Unit on Chinese and East Asian Politics, Free U of Berlin; Professor and Chairman of Pol Sci and Director, Research Unit on Chinese and East Asian Politics, U des Saarlandes. Publs: *Kulturrevolution und Armee*, 1967; *Vertragte Revolution — Die Politik der KMT in China, 1923-37*, 1969; *Die Kuomintang-Herrschaft in China*, 1970; *Die Ära Mao Tse-tung — Innenpolitik in der VR China*, 1971; *Internal Politics in China 1949-72*, 1973; *China nach der Kulturrevolution*, 1975; *China after the Cultural Revolution*, 1977; *Sozialismus in Chinas Dörfern*, 1977. Fields: Typology of political systems and comparative politics; Chinese politics since 1919; problems of parliamentary democracy in Germany.

[494]
DONALD David
28 September 1940, British. 3 Elm Road, Killearn, Stirlingshire, Scotland. Degrees: BA. Principle Lecturer in Pol and Government, Glasgow Coll of Technology. Fields: Policy studies, especially social policy in the UK and USA.

[495]
DONEGANI Jean-Marie
2 December 1948, French. 127 rue Marcadet, 75018 Paris, France. Degrees: Dr. Doctoral thesis: "Militantisme politique et univers religieux". Chercheur, Centre d'Etudes des Parlements, U de Paris I; Assistant de recherche, FNSP; Attaché de recherche, CNRS. Publs: *Mouvement de libération du peuple 1942-1957, de l'action catholique au combat politique*, 1972; *Le conseil d'administration des établissements secondaires* (with A Percheron et E Landowski); *La prise de décision en France* (with M Sadoun *et al*), 1975; *La réforme de l'enseignement secondaire en France*, 1976. Fields: Religion and politics in individual behaviour.

[496]
DONELAN Michael Denis
2 August 1932, British. London School of Economics and Political Science, Houghton Street, Aldwych, London WC2, England. Degrees: BA; MA (Oxon). Lecturer, Senior Lecturer in International Relations, LSE. Publs: *The Ideas of American Foreign Policy*, 1963; *International Disputes: The Political Aspects* (co-author), 1971; *International Disputes: Case Histories* (co-author), 1973; *The Reason of States* (ed), 1978. Fields: The political aspects of international economic relations; history of international thought; national honour.

[497]
DONNISON David Vernon
19 January 1926, British. Supplementary Benefits Commission, New Court, Carey Street, London WC2, England. Degrees: BA; D Litt (Bradford), 1973. 1950 Lecturer in Social Administration, U of Manchester; U of Toronto; Reader, Professor of Soc Administration, LSE; Chairman, Supplementary Benefits Commission; Visiting Professor, LSE and UCL. Publs: *The Neglected Child and the Social Services*, 1954; *Welfare Services to a Canadian Community*, 1958; *The Government of Housing*, 1965; *Social Policy and Administration* (with V Chapman), 1967; *London: Urban Patterns, Problems and Policies* (co-ed), 1973; *An Approach to Social Policy*, 1975; *Social Policy and Administration Revisited*, 1975. Fields: Social policy and administration, particularly housing and education; urban studies and planning; social security.

[498]
DONOUGHUE Bernard
8 September 1934, British. 7 Brookfield Park, London NW5, England. Degrees: MA (Oxon), 1960; D Phil (Oxon), 1963. Doctoral thesis: "British Politics and the American Revolution". Research Student, Nuffield Coll, U of Oxford; Henry Fellow, Harvard U; Editorial Staff, *The Economist*, *The Sunday Times*, *The Sunday Telegraph*; Senior Research Officer, PEP; 1974- Senior Policy Adviser to the Prime Minister. Publs: *Wage Policies in Public Sector*, 1962; *Structure and Organization of British Trade Unions*, 1963; *Trade Unions in a Changing Society*, 1963; *British Politics and the American Revolution*, 1964; *People into Parliament*, 1966. Fields: Contemporary British politics and history.

[499]
DOORNBOS Martin R
19 December 1934, Dutch. Tuinfluiterlaan 3A, The Hague, The Netherlands. Degrees: PhD (California), 1973. Doctoral thesis: "Conflict and Change in Ankole Society ". 1965-67 Research Fellow, Makerere Institute of Social Research and Lecturer, Dept of Pol Sci, U of Makerere; 1971 Visiting Associate Professor, U of Syracuse; 1973-76 Visiting Senior Lecturer, U of Leiden; 1976- Senior Lecturer in Pol Sci, Inst of Soc Studies, The Hague. Publs: *Regalia Galore: The Decline and Eclipse of Ankole Kingship*, 1975; *Political Identity: A Case Study from Uganda* (with M Segall and C Davis), 1976; *Government and Rural Development in East Africa: Essays on Political Penetration* (with L Cliffe and S Coleman (eds)), 1977; *Not All the King's Men: Inequality as a Political Instrument in Ankole, Uganda*, 1978. Fields: Comparative politics; political sociology; political anthropology; African politics and society; development studies; local politics; ethnicity; political inequality; development administration; bureaucracy and development, especially rural development.

[500]
DORMANN Manfred E*
31 December 1939, German. Fachbereich Politische Wissenschaft, 775 Konstanz, Universität, FR Germany. Degrees: Dr phil. 1967-71 Wiss Assistent, Fachbereich Pol Wissenschaft, U of Konstanz; Visiting Assistant Professor, Dept of Pol Sci, State U of New York at Binghampton, USA; Wiss Assistent, Fachbereich Pol Wissenschaft, U of Konstanz. Publs: *Demokratische Militärpolitik*, 1970. Fields: Foreign policy decision-making; planning, organization and administration of W German foreign policy.

[501]
DÖRR Manfred August Georg Heinrich*
23 March 1936, German. Kropbacher Weg 33, D-6300 Giessen, FR Germany. Degrees: Dr phil (Marburg/Lahn), 1964. Doctoral thesis: "Die Deutschnationale Volkspartei 1925-28". Wiss Assistent; Studienrat im Hochschuldienst. Publs: *Die Deutschnationale Volkspartei 1925-28*, 1966. Fields: American and German policy in relation to the restoration of the liberal economic policy; problem of the liberal-socialist coalition in West Germany.

[502]
DOUXCHAMPS Alain*
19 March 1948, Belgian. Avenue des Eperviers 115, B-1150 Bruxelles, Belgium. Degrees: Lic en sci commerciales et consulaires, 1969; Dipl (Inst Européen des Hautes Etudes Internationales, Nice), 1971. 1971-72 Assistant, ICHEC; Chargé de cours, Inst d'Enseignement Supérieur de Namur. Publs: *L'Europe des syndicats*, 1972; *La Cogestion dans le statut des sociétés anonymes européennes*, 1972. Fields: Europe and trade unions.

[503]
DOWSE Robert Edward
17 April 1933, British. 148 Heavitree Road, Exeter, England. Degrees: BSc; PhD (LSE), 1962. Doctoral thesis: "The ILP, 1918-32". Assistant Lecturer, U of Edinburgh; Lecturer, U of Hull; Lecturer, U of Ghana; Lecturer, Reader, U of Exeter. Publs: *Left in the Centre*, 1966; *Readings on British Politics and Government* (co-ed), 1968; "Attlee as a Prime Minister", in *The Role of the Prime Minister* (J Mackintosh (ed)), 1978; *The Labour Ideal*, 1976; "Military and Police Rule in Ghana", in *Ghana and the Return to Civilian Rule* (D Austin (ed)), 1971; *Political Sociology: A Textbook*, 1972. Fields: Political sociology; political economy; political development, especially Ghana.

[504]
DRAGO Roland
22 June 1923, French. 15 rue Jean Boulogne, 75016 Paris, France. Degrees: Dr en droit, 1948; Agrégé en droit, 1950. 1950-54 Professeur, Inst des Hautes Etudes, U de Tunis; 1954-65 Professeur, Faculté de Droit, U de Lille; Professeur, Faculté de Droit, U de Paris II. Publs: *Les crises de la notion d'éstablissement public,* 1950; *Traité de contentieux administratif* (with J Auby), 1975; *Traité du droit de la presse* (with R Blin and A Chavanne), 1970; *Science administrative*, 1977. Fields: Administrative law; administrative science.

[505]
DREITZEL Hans Peter*
3 January 1935, German. 1 Berlin 12, Goethestrasse 69, FR Germany. Degrees: PhD (Göttingen), 1961; Habilitation, Dr of Soc Sci (Göttingen), 1967. Assistant Professor, U of Göttingen; Visiting Professor, U of California at Berkeley; Assistant Professor, New School U of New York; Professor of Soc, Free U of Berlin. Publs: *Elitebegriff und Sozialstruktur*, 1962; *Die gesellschaftlichen Leiden und das Leiden an der Gesellschaft*, 1968; *Einsamkeit als soziologisches Problem*, 1970; *Entwicklungsaspekte der Industriegesellschaft*, 1972. Fields: Social stratification; social classes and elite groups in industrial societies; theories of evolution and revolution; role theory; deviant behaviour; political socialization; integration of some paradigms developed in stratification theory and role theory.

[506]
DREWRY Gavin Richard
11 June 1944, British. 43 Sandringham Crescent, South Harrow, Middlesex HA2 9BP, England. Degrees: BSc. 1966-69 Research Assistant, Assistant Research Officer, Dept of Soc, Bedford Coll; 1969- Lecturer in Government, Bedford Coll. Publs: *Final Appeal: A Study of the House of Lords in its Judicial Capacity* (with L Blom-Cooper), 1972; *Law and Morality* (with L Blom-Cooper), 1976; *Law, Justice and Politics*, 1975. Fields: The legislative process, with particular reference to the purpose and content of public bill legislation in Britain; the development of legal dimensions to the study of British public administration; appellate courts.

[507]
DREYFUS Francoise Anita*
11 May 1942, French. 2 Square Adanson, Paris Vème, France. Degrees: DES droit public (Paris), 1967; DES sci pol (Paris), 1968; Dr en droit public (Paris), 1971. Doctoral thesis: "Le principe de la liberté du commerce et de l'industrie dans la jurisprudence du Conseil d'Etat". Assistante, U de Paris I. Publs: *L'intervention économique*, 1971. Fields: Administrative law; law and politics from a psychoanalytic viewpoint.

[508]
DREYFUS Francois Georges
13 September 1928, French. 63 Avenue des Vosges, F-67000 Strasbourg, France. Degrees: Agrégé d'histoire; Dr ès lettres. Doctoral theses: "Société et mentalité à Mayence au XVIIIème siècle". 1952-58 Professeur de lycées; 1958-61 Attaché de recherche, CNRS; 1961- Maître assistant, Maîtres de conférences, Professeur d'Histoire Contemporaine et Sci Pol, U de Strasbourg; Directeur, Inst d'Etudes Pol; Directeur, Centre d'Etudes Germaniques de Strasbourg. Publs: *Documents d'histoire contemporaine*, 1976; *Les forces religieuses dans la société française*, 1965; *Sociétés et mentalités à Mayence au XVIIIème siècle*, 1968; *La vie politique en Alsace 1918-1936*, 1969; *Le temps des révolutions*, 1969; *Histoire des Allemagnes*, 1972; *Histoire des Gauches en France 1940-1974*, 1975. Fields: French political life since 1930; politics, economy, religion and society in Germany since 1870; politics, religion and economy in the judeochristian world.

[509]
DREYFUS Jacques
13 January 1920, French. 33 rue des Tournelles, 92290 Chatenay-Malabry, France. Degrees: Dipl (Ecole Polytechnique, Ingénieur des Ponts et Chaussées); Dr ès lettres. Doctoral thesis: "L' urbanisme comme idéologie de la rationalité- le refus de l'ordre de la différence". Ministère de l'Equipement, Paris; Enseignant, IEP and UER "Urbanisation et Aménagement", U de Grenoble. Publs: *La ville disciplinaire*, 1976; *Implication ou neutralité des méthodes statistiques appliquées aux sciences humaines: l'analyse des correspondances*, 1975; *Les méthodes quantitatives dans le processus de normalisation* (co-author), 1977. Fields: Rationality and normalization; Resistance to standardization and the non structural in the social system.

[510]
DRUCKER Henry Matthew
29 April 1942, American. 31 Buccleuch Place, Edinburgh EH8 9JT, Scotland. Degrees: BA; PhD (LSE). Doctoral thesis: "The Nature of Ideology and its Place in Modern Political Thought". Lecturer, U of Edinburgh. Publs: "Just Analogies: The Place of Analogies in Political Thought", *Political Studies*, 1970; "Marx's Concept of Ideology", *Philosophy*, 1971; *The Political View of Ideology*, 1974; *The Scottish Government Yearbook* (with M G Clarke), 1977, 1978; *A Study of the Scottish Labour Party*, 1977; "Leadership Elections in the Labour Party", *Parliamentary Affairs*, 1976; "Devolution vs Cooperation", *Government and Opposition*, 1977. Fields: Normative political theory; Scottish politics; Labour politics.

[511]
DUBBELDAM-DE VRIES Ada
22 April 1938, Dutch. Ruimzicht 304, Amsterdam-Osdorp, The Netherlands. Degrees: Drs (Amsterdam), 1965. Civics teacher, Academy for Teachers, Dordrecht; Pol Teacher, Academy for Social Workers, Baarn; Lecturer in Pol; 1968 Staff member, U of Amsterdam; Lecturer in Pol, Netherlands Inst for Business Studies. Publs: "52 Secretaries of State", *Acta Politica*, 1967/68; articles in *Intermediair* and *Didahtiek der Sociale Wetenscheppen*. Fields: Social policy in the Common Market; policy towards handicapped people, mental and physical.

[512]
DUCHROW Ulrich
13 June 1935, German. 18 Avenue des Amazones, CH-1224 Genève, Switzerland. Degrees: Habilitation. Doctoral thesis: "Christenheit und Weltverantwortung. Traditionsgeschichte und systematische Struktur der Zweireichelehre". Member of staff, Forschungsstätte der Evangelischen Studiengemeinschaft, Heidelberg; Privatdozent, Theologischen Fakultät, U of Heidelberg; Director, Dept of Studies of the Lutheran World Federation, Geneva. Publs: *Zwei Reiche und Regimente: Ideologie oder evangelische Orientierung? Fall-und Hintergrundstudien zur Theologie und Praxis lutherischer Kirchen im 20, Jahrhundert* (ed), 1977; *Texte zur Kirchen-und Theologiegeschichte* (ed), 1972, 1975, 1976; *Marxismusstudien*, 1969. Fields: Social ethics and the history of church and society.

[513]
DUCLAUD-WILLIAMS Roger
5 December 1943, British. 25a Sherbourne Place, Leamington Spa, Warwickshire, England. Degrees: BA; D Phil (Sussex). Doctoral thesis: "The Politics of Housing in Britain and France". Temporary Lecturer, U of Glasgow; Lecturer, Dept of Pol, U of Warwick. Publs: *The Politics of Housing in Britain and France*, 1978. Fields: French politics; policy making.

[514]
DUCLOS Louis Jean
30 November 1925, French. 13 rue de la Cité Universitaire, 75014 Paris, France. Degrees: Dipl (Ecole des Langues Orientales Vivantes, Paris). Brevet du Centre des Hautes Etudes Administratives pour l'Afrique et l'Asie moderne (Paris); Maîtrise de droit privé; 1952-56 Officier des Services des Affaires indigènes, protectorat de la République française au Maroc; 1957-62 Conseiller militaire et administratif dans le Maroc indépendant; Rédacteur, Section "Monde Arabe", Secrétariat Général de la Défense Nationale (Paris); Chercheur, FNSP. Publs: *Les nationalismes maghrébins* (co-author), 1966; *L'impasse israélienne*, 1968; *La guerre d'usure israélo-arabe*, 1970; *La bataille d'Octobre*, 1974; *La Jordanie*, 1977. Fields: The Middle-East, especially the evolution of the Israel-Arab conflict.

[515]
DUHAMEL Olivier Edouard
2 May 1950, French. 39 rue Claude Bernard, 75005 Paris, France. Degrees: DES droit public; DES sci pol. Assistant de droit public; Directeur, *Pouvoirs*. Publs: *Chili ou la tentative, révolution légalité*, 1974; "L'organisation du pouvoir au Portugal, 1974-75", *Revue Française d'Etudes Politiques Méditérranéennes*, 1975; "L'AUPELF et la coopération universitaire, de la franconie au dialogues des cultres", *Revue Française d'Etudes Politiques Africaines*, 1976. "Le parti démocratique gabonais: études des fonctions d'un parti unique africain", *Revue Française d'Etudes Politiques Africaines*, 1977; "Chronique des partis politiques (Amérique Latine)", in *L'Annuaire du Tiers Monde*, 1975, 1976, 1977; "La constitution de la Vème République et l'alternance", *Pouvoirs*, 1977; "Fidel Castro", in *Les grands révolutionnaires* (Martinsart (ed)), 1978. Fields: Political parties; Communist movement; elections; television.

[516]
DUKE Victor
27 July 1948, British. Department of Sociological and Political Studies, University of Salford, Salford, Manchester MS 4WT, England. Degrees: BA; MSc (Strathclyde). Lecturer, Dept of Soc and Pol Studies, U of Salford. Publs: *The Middle Class Left in Britain and Australia* (with D Jary and M Goldsmith). Fields: Middle class radicalism; working class conservatism; comparative politics, particularly Britain, Australia and Western Europe; methodological problems.

[517]
DUNCANSON Denis John
26 May 1917, British. 26 Leinster Mews, London W2, England. Degrees: MA (London). Colonial Administrative Service, Malaya, Singapore, Hong Kong; Diplomatic Service, London and Vietnam; Fellow in International Relations, LSE; Reader in South East Asian Studies, U of Kent. Publs: *Government and Revolution in Vietnam*, 1968; "Pacification and Democracy in Vietnam", *World Today*, 1967; "Dilemmas of Counterinsurgency", *Foreign Affairs*, 1969; "The Triumph of Leninism", *Lugano Review*, 1976; *The Peacetime Strategy of the Chinese People's Republic*, 1977; "From Bolshevism to People's War", in *Anatomy of Communist Take Overs* (T T Hammond (ed)), 1978. Fields: Comparative government in the Chinese world; national liberation and other Leninist techniques of revolution in Asia.

[518]
DUNMORE Timothy
29 July 1948, British. 23 Lugano Close, Westlands, Newcastle-under-Lyme, Staffordshire, England. Degrees: BA; MA (Essex), 1971. Doctoral thesis: "Soviet Economic Policy-Making during the Fourth Five Year Plan Period 1946-50". Lecturer in Pol, U of Keele. Fields: Soviet politics, particularly role of CPSU and industrial decision-making and implementation; Soviet politics in relation to comparative politics.

[519]
DUNN John Montfort
9 September 1940, British. 3 Tennison Avenue, Cambridge CB1 2DX, England. Degrees: BA. 1965-66 Fellow of Jesus Coll, U of Cambridge; 1966-68 Fellow and Coll Lecturer, King's Coll, U of Cambridge; 1968-69 Visiting Lecturer in Pol Sci, U of Ghana; 1972-77 Lecturer in Pol Sci, U of Cambridge; 1977- Reader in Pol, U of Cambridge. Publs: *The Political Thought of John Locke*, 1969; *Modern Revolutions: An Introduction to the Analysis of a Political Phenomenon*, 1972; *Dependence and Opportunity: Political Change in AHAFO* (with A F Robertson), 1974; *West African States: Failure and Promise* (ed and contributor), 1978. Fields: Political philosophy; history of political ideas; revolution; post-colonial states; philosophy of the social sciences; analysis of social and political change in modern Africa.

[520]
DUNSIRE Andrew
29 November 1924, British. 7 College Road, Copmanthorpe, York, England. Degrees: MA (Edinburgh). 1952-53 Assistant Lecturer in Government, LSE; 1953-57 Lecturer in Government, U of Exeter; 1957-59 Temporary Principal, Ministry of Transport and Civil Aviation; 1959-64 Lecturer in Pol, U of Exeter; 1964- Senior Lecturer, Reader in Pol, U of York. Publs: *The Making of an Administrator* (ed), 1956; *Management Training Survey* (co-ed), 1967; *Style in Administration: Readings in British Public Administration* (co-ed), 1971; *Administration: The Word and the Science*, 1973; *The Execution Process: Implementation in a Bureaucracy*; *The Execution Process: Control in a Bureaucracy*, 1978. Fields: Public administration; machinery of central government; organization theory.

[521]
DUPEUX Louis
28 July 1931, French. 36 Boulevard de Lyon, 67 Strasbourg, France. Degrees: Agrégé d'histoire; Dr ès lettres, 1974. Doctoral thesis: "Stratégie communiste et dynamique conservatrice. Essai sur les différents sens de l'expression 'National-bolchevisme' dans l'Allemagne de Weimar". IEP, Strasbourg. Publs: various articles in *Revue d'Allemagne*. Fields: Germany; nationalism; fascism; communism.

[522]
DUPRAT Jean-Pierre Yves
3 February 1941, French. Le Grand Chêne A, rue Lamartine, 33400 Talence, France. Degrees: Dr en droit; Dipl (IEP Bordeaux); DES; Lic ès lettres. Doctoral thesis: "Politique et religion dans le Léviathan ou Th. Hobbes'. Assistant, Maître-assistant, U de Bordeaux; Maître de conférences agrégé de Droit Public, IEP Bordeaux. Publs: *La débudgétisation*, 1972; *La Banque de France- Situation juridique*, 1976; *Notes de jurisprudence*. Fields: History of political thought; public finance and economic law.

[523]
DUPRAT Pierre Gérard
25 June 1933, French. 8 allée Spach, 67000 Strasbourg, France. Degrees: Agrégé; Dr ès lettres (Paris), 1971. Doctoral thesis: "Le socialisme algérien d'autogestion rurale". Professeur de Sci Pol, U de Strasbourg III. Publs: *Révolution et autogestion en Algérie*; *Marx, Proudhon, théorie du conflit social*; *Justice et politique*, 1975. Fields: History of political thought; contemporary French political thought.

[524]
DUPUIS Georges*
27 April 1932, French. 85 Boulevard Pasteur, Paris XVème, France. Degrees: Dr d'Etat; Agrégé des Facultés de Droit; Maître de conférences; Professeur, Faculté de Rennes; Professeur, U de Paris; Directeur des Etudes de l'ENA. Publs: *La Politique de Chateaubriand*, 1967; *Eléments de sociologie politique*, 1966; *L'ORTF*, 1970; *Organigrammes des institutions françaises*, 1971. Fields: The 'management' of public service; the making of top civil servants.

[525]
DUPUY René-Jean*
7 February 1918, French. Faculté de Droit et des Sciences Economiques, Université de Nice, 14 rue Louis de Coppet, Nice, France. Degrees: Dr en droit (Paris), 1948; Agrégé des Facultés de Droit, 1950. 1951-56 Professeur, U d'Alger; 1956-62 Professeur, U d'Aix-en-Provence; 1962- Professeur, Faculté de Droit et des Sci Econ, U de Nice. Publs: *Le nouveau panaméricanisme*, 1956; *Le droit des rapports entre les organisations internationales*, 1960; *Le droit international*, 1963; *L'enseignement du droit international*, 1967; *Politique de Nietzsche*, 1969; *Le fond des mers* (with C A Colliard, J Polveche and R Vayssière), 1971; *L'organisation des Etats Americains*, 1971; *La Souveraineté au XXème siècle* (ed), 1971.

[526]
DUVERGER Maurice*
5 June 1917, French. 24 rue des Fossés St Jacques, 75005 Paris, France. Professeur, Agrégé des Facultés de France; Professeur, Faculté de Droit de Bordeaux; Professeur, U de Paris-I — Sorbonne; Directeur, Dept de Sci Pol, Sorbonne. Publs: *Les partis politiques*, 1951; *La démocratie sans le peuple*, 1967; *Institutions politiques et droit constitutionnel*, 1971; *Janus — les deux faces de l'occident*, 1972. Fields: Analysis of comparative political systems; structure of organizations, especially political parties.

[527]
DUYNSTEE Frans Josef Ferdinand Marie*
11 February 1914, Dutch. Groesbeekseweg 215, Nijmegen, The Netherlands. Degrees: Drs in Law (Nijmegen), 1941. Advocaat-Procureur; Counsellor, Ministry of Justice; Dean, Faculty of Law, U of Nijmegen; Professor in Constitutional Law and Comparative Constitutional Law. Publs: *Revision of the Netherlands Constitution in 1953*, 1954; *Netherlands New Guinea*, 1961; *The Netherlands Formations of Cabinets 1946-65*, 1966. Fields: General theory of law and state; comparative constitution of law; constitutional history.

[528]
DVORAK Johann
17 April 1946, Austrian. A-1040 Vienna, Karolinengasse 24/11, Austria. Degrees: Dr phil. Doctoral thesis: "Staat, Recht und Agrarpolitik während der Englischen Revolution 1642-53" (State, Law and Agrarian Policy during the English Revolution 1642-65). Ministry of Education, Dept for Adult Education. Fields: Political theory; development of state, law and bureaucracy.

[529]
DYSON Kenneth Herbert Fewster
10 November 1946, British. Social Studies Building, The University, Liverpool
L69 3BX, England. Degrees: BSc; MSc (LSE), 1969. 1969- Lecturer, Dept of Pol
Theory and Institutions, U of Liverpool. Publs: *Party, State, and Bureaucracy in
Western Germany*, 1977. Fields: Organization theory; public administration; German
politics; theories of the state.

E

[530]
EAGLESTONE Alexander
1 April 1929, British. 16 Shooters Hill Road, Blackheath, London SE3, England.
Degrees: Lic Phil (Rome); MA (Oxon); Dip Ed (London). 1952 Lecturer, U of Madrid;
1959-62 British Council, Kuwait; 1962-66 Regional Director, British Council, Brasil;
1966- Principal Lecturer, Royal Naval Coll, Greenwich; 1972 Visiting Lecturer, City U,
London. Publs: *Brasil* (World Survey), 1968; *Mexico* (World Survey), 1969; plus articles in *International Affairs, The Tablet*. Fields: European parliament; European
defence; history of political theory.

[531]
EBBIGHAUSEN Rolf
2 March 1937, German. Apostel-Paulus-Strasse 18, 1000 Berlin 62, FR Germany.
Degrees: Dipl Soziologie, 1963; Dr rer Pol, 1968; Habilitation, 1972. Doctoral thesis:
"Parteiensoziologie. Demokratietheorie: Eine Studie über M. Ostrogorski, R. Michels
und die neuere Entwicklung der Parteienforschung". 1972- Professor of Pol Soc, Inst
für Soziologie and Zentralinst für sozialwissenschaftliche Forschung, Free U of Berlin.
Publs: *Die Krise der Parteiendemokratie und die Parteiensoziologie*, 1969; *Parteiensystem in der Legitimationskrise — Studien und Materialien für Soziologie der Parteien
in der BRD*, 1973; *Monopol und Staat*, 1974; *Bürgerlicher Staat und politische
Legitimation*, 1976; *Politische Soziologie — Für Geschichte und Ortsbestimmung*,
1978. Fields: Political theory; political sociology; comparative political research on
changing patterns and functions of government in Western democracies, especially on
the role of party systems; interest groups, unions etc.

[532]
EBERT Theodor
6 May 1937, German. Münchenerstrasse 36e, 1 Berlin 49, FR Germany. Degrees: Dr
phil. Doctoral thesis: "Gewaltfreier Aufstand. Alternative zum Bürgerkrieg". Professor of Pol Sci, Free U of Berlin. Publs: *Demokratische Sicherheitspolitik* (ed), 1975;
Gewaltfreie Aktion (ed); *Vierteljahreshefte für Frieden und Gerechtigkeit*. Fields: Peace
research, non-violent action; ecological movements.

[533]
EBERWEIN Wolf Dieter
27 December 1943, German. Hoenersweg 24, D-48 Bielefeld 1, FR Germany. Degrees:
Dipl Pol (Berlin), 1970; Dr Soz Wiss (Bielefeld), 1976. Doctoral thesis: "Auswärtiges
Amt und Strukturwandel der Aussenpolitik 1956-1973". Research Assistant, U des
Saarlandes; Wiss Assistent, Fakultät für Soziologie, Bielefeld. Publs: *Friedens- und
Konfliktforschung — Eine Einführung* (with P Reichel), 1976; "Untersuchung über
rechtliche und bürokratische Behinderungen empirischer Forschung" (co-author),
Kriminologisches Journal, 1977; "Personelle und institutionelle Anpassung des

Auswärtigen Amtes", *PVS Sonderheft*, 1978; "Crisis Research: A Western View", in *Crises and Crisis Management — An East-West Symposium* (D Frei (ed)), 1978. Fields: International relations, crises, conflict; public administration and planning; ethical and legal problems of social science research.

[534]
ECCLESHALL Robert Richard
26 April 1946, British. 2 University Street, Belfast 7, Northern Ireland. Degrees: BA; PhD. Doctoral thesis: "Order and Reason in Politics: Divergent Trends in Traditional Political Thought in England During the Early Modern Period". 1971-72 Temporary Lectureship in Pol Sci, U Coll, Aberystwyth; 1973 Temporary Lectureship in Philosophy, U of Sussex; 1973- Lecturer in Pol Sci, Queens U, Belfast. Publs: *Order and Reason in Politics: Theories of Absolute and Limited Monarchy in Early Modern England*, 1978; "The Undivided Self", in *The Concept of Socialism* (B Parekh (ed)), 1975; "Technology and Liberation", *Radical Philosophy*, 1975; "Richard Hooker's Synthesis and the Problem of Allegiance", *Journal of the History of Ideas*, 1976; "English Conservatism as Ideology", *Political Studies*, 1977. Fields: History of political thought; political theory; ideology.

[535]
EDMEAD Frank
15 June 1919, British. 11 Varney Close, Hemel Hempstead, Herts HP1 2LH, England. Degrees: BA; MSc (London), 1968. 1950-67 Editorial Staff, *The Guardian*; 1968-70 Research Associate, Centre for the Analysis of Conflict, U Coll, London; Lecturer in International Relations, City U, London. Publs: *Analysis and Prediction in International Mediation*, 1971. Fields: Systems models of international conflict; international mediation.

[536]
EHLERT Wiking*
29 June 1942, German. 4801 Jöllenbeck, Schildescherstrasse 34, FR Germany. Degrees: Dipl Pol (Free U of Berlin). Assistant, U of Bielefeld. Fields: The function of public planning for administration.

[537]
ELCOCK Howard James
6 June 1942, British. 30 Mizzen Road, Beverley High Road, Hull HU6 7AG, England. Degrees: BA; B Phil (Oxon), 1966; MA (Oxon), 1968; PhD (Hull), 1973. Doctoral thesis: "Britain and the Russo-Polish Frontier, 1919-21". 1966- Lecturer, Senior Lecturer in Pol, U of Hull. Publs: *Administrative Justice*, 1969; *Portrait of a Decision: The Council of Four and the Treaty of Versailles*, 1972; *Political Behaviour*, 1976; "J M Keynes at the Paris Peace Conference", in *Essays on John Maynard Keynes*, 1975. Fields: Judicial behaviour; the citizen and the administration; local government; treaty of Versailles, 1919; studies of political elites.

[538]
ELDER Neil Colbert McAulay
7 September 1925, British. Department of Political Studies, University of Hull, N Humberside, England. Degrees: BA; B Litt (Oxon), 1954. 1951-53 Lecturer in Pol, Brasenose and St John's Colls, U of Oxford; 1953-56 Lecturer in Pol, St John's and University Colls, U of Oxford; 1956-67 Lecturer and Head of Dept, Queen's Coll, U of Dundee; 1967-Senior Lecturer in Pol Studies, U of Hull. Publs: *Government in Sweden*, 1970. Fields: Government and politics in Scandinavia; trends in the Scandinavian party system; regional government in Sweden; longer-term trends in the British political system.

[539]
ELIASSEN Kjell Arnold
18 May 1946, Norwegian. Lystrupvej 354, DK-8520 Lystrup, Denmark. Degrees: Cand polit (Bergen), 1971. Research Assistant, Inst of Soc, U of Bergen; Hon Research Fellow, Harvard U; Visiting Fellow, U of California, Berkeley; Assistant Professor, Associate Professor, Inst of Pol Sci, U of Aarhus. Publs: "Statssekretaerenfagmann eller Politiker", *Tidsskrift for Samfunnsforskning*, 1972; "Politische Beteilung und Parteipolitische Bindung der Gewerkschaften in Westeuropa: ein Überblick", *Soziale Welt*, 1974; "The Formation of Mass Political Organizations: An Analytical Framework" (with L Svaasand), *Scandinavian Political Studies*, 1975; "Professionalization of the Legislatures: Long Term Change in Political Recruitment in Denmark and Norway", in *Comparative Studies in Society and History*, (with M Pedersen) 1978. Fields: Comparative studies of political development and elite recruitment; political mobilization and the institutionalization of political cleavages; studies of trade union-labour party relationships in Western Europe; relationship between interest organizations and the state; the formation of public policy.

[540]
ELKLIT Jørgen
12 October 1942, Danish. Fredensvang Runddel 3, DK-8260 Viby J, Denmark. Degrees: Cand phil (Aarhus), 1970. Research Scholar, U of Aarhus; Lecturer, Senior Lecturer, Inst of Pol Sci, U of Aarhus. Publs: *Folketaellingen 1845*, 1970; *National Tilhørsforhold i Nordlesvig* (with Noack and Tonsgaard), 1978. Fields: Social and political development in the late 19th century; national minorities; election law; voting behaviour 1870-1939; policies of higher education.

[541]
ELLEMERS Jo Egbert
12 January 1930, Dutch. Troelstralaan 60, 9722 JM Groningen, The Netherlands. Degrees: Cand (Amsterdam), 1952; Drs (Amsterdam), 1954; Dr (Utrecht), 1967. Doctoral thesis: "Van Idee tot moderne Staat" (From Idea to Modern State: A Study of Social Change in Israel). 1951-1954 Assistant, U of Amsterdam; 1953-1956 Research Associate, Inst of Social Research in the Netherlands; 1956-1958 Research in Israel and Research Fellow, Hebrew U of Jerusalem; 1958-1967 Senior Lecturer, U of Amsterdam; 1967- Professor of Soc, U of Groningen; 1970- Professor Extraordinary of Soc, Free U of Brussels. Publs: *Studies in Holland Flood Disaster*, 1955; *De Februari-Ramp*, 1956; *Van Idee Tot Moderne Staat*, 1967; *Macht en Sociale Verandering*, 1968. Fields: Social change; politics; power and decision-making; general and theoretical sociology; political science; race and ethnic relations.

[542]
ELLIOTT Sydney
7 October 1943, British. 6 Chesterbrook Crescent, Newtownards, Co Down, Ireland. Degrees: BA; PhD (Belfast), 1971. Doctoral thesis: "The Electoral system in Northern Ireland since 1920". Lecturer in Pol Sci, Queen's U, Belfast. Publs: *Northern Ireland Parliamentary Election Results 1921-72*, 1973; *The Northern Ireland Border Poll* (with R J Lawrence), 1975; *The Northern Ireland General Elections of 1973* (with R J Lawrence and M J Laver), 1975; *Northern Ireland Government Elections of 1977* (with F J Smith), 1978. Fields: Northern Ireland politics; electoral systems and party pay-offs.

[543]
ELLUL Jacques César*
6 January 1912, French. La Marierre, 33 Pessac, Gironde, France. Degrees: Lic de lettres (Bordeaux), 1932; Lic de droit (Bordeaux), 1931; Dr de droit (Bordeaux), 1936. 1937-40 Chargé de cours d'histoire du droit; 1943-71 Agrégé puis Professeur Titulaire, Faculté de Droit, U de Bordeaux; Professeur, IEP, U de Bordeaux 1. Publs: *La technique ou l'enjeu du siècle*, 1964; *Propagandes*, 1965; *Histoire des institutions*, 1966; *L'illusion politique*, 1964; *Autopsie de la Révolution*, 1969. Fields: Contemporary society; sociological, political, psychological, religious study.

[544]
ELLWEIN Thomas
16 July 1927, German. 8165 Fiselbachau, FR Germany. Degrees: Dr jur (Erlangen), 1950. Doctoral thesis: "Der Einfluss der Nordamerikanischen Bundesverfassungsrechts auf die Verhandlungen der deutschen Nationalversammlung 1848-1849". Leiter der Bayerischen Landeszentrale für Pol Bildung; Direktor des Seminars für Pol Bildung, U of Frankfurt. Direktor des Sozialwissenschaftliche Inst der Bundeswehr, München; Prof für Pol Wissenschaft, U of Konstanz. Publs: *Einführung in die Regierungs- und Verwaltungslehre*; *Politische Verhaltenslehre*; *Gesetzgebung und politische Kontrolle*; *Regierung als politische Führung*; *Politik und Plannung*; *Wertheim I. Fragen an eine Stadt*; *Berufsbeamtentum-Anspruch und Wirklichkeit*; *Zur Entwicklung der öffentlichen*, *Aufgaben in der BRD*; *Regieren und verwalten*. Fields: Civil service; political behaviour; socialization.

[545]
ELOVAIN, Mauri Kalevi
4 July 1936, Finnish. Vuorimiehenk 13 A, Helsinki 14, Finland. Degrees: MA, 1962. Assistant in Pol Sci, U of Turku; 1965-66 Member of Finnish delegation to the 20th and 21st UN General Assembly; Second Secretary, Committee of Foreign Relations of the Finnish Parliament; Member of Finnish delegation to UNESCO's 19th General Conference; 1975 Member of the Finnish National Commission to UNESCO; 1977 Board Member of the Finnish Peace Research Trust of Tampere. Publs: *Finnish Foreign Policy*, 1963; *A Bibliography of Literature on Questions concerning International Relations in Denmark, Finland, Norway and Sweden 1945-60* (with R Lehtinen). Fields: International politics; human rights in the UN; political and economic integration in Europe; European security problems.

[546]
ELVANDER Nils
16 April 1928, Swedish. Tuvängsvägen 12, 752 45 Uppsala, Sweden. Degrees: PhD (Uppsala), 1961. 1956-60 Assistant Lecturer, U of Uppsala; 1961-67 Docent, U of Uppsala; 1967- Associate Professor, U of Uppsala. Publs: *Harald Hjärne och konservatismen, Konservativ idédebatt i Sverige 1865-1922*, 1961; *Intresseorganisationerna i dagens Sverige*, 1966; *Skattepolitiken 1945-70. En Studie i partiers och organisationers funktioner*, 1972; *Konfliktlösning på Arbetsmarknaden*, 1974. Fields: Political influence of the Swedish interest organizations; comparative analysis of the 'interest articulation and aggregation' functions of Swedish political parties and interest organizations; comparative analysis of labour relations and the development of the Social Democratic parties in the Scandinavian countries; Swedish health policy.

[547]
EMERI Claude Georges
6 September 1933, French. 25 rue Laharde, 33110 Le Bouscat, France. Degrees: Dipl
sup d'études et recherches pol, FNSP (Paris), 1958; Dr en droit public (Bordeaux),
1964. Doctoral thesis: "De la responsabilité de l'administration à l'égard de ses col-
laborateurs". Professeur de Droit public et Sci Pol, U de Bordeaux I; Directeur, IEP
Bordeaux. Publs: *Les systèmes électoraux* (with J M Cotteret), 1978; *Le budget de
l'Etat*, 1975; *Giscard d'Estaing- Mitterrand, 54000 mots pour convaincre* (with J M Cotteret *et al*), 1976. Fields: French political parties; political life in Latin America, French
parliamentary law; political communication.

[548]
ENGELSING Rolf
9 October 1930, German. Carstennstrasse 25d, 1 Berlin (West) 45, FR Germany.
Degrees: Dr phil; Habilitation. Doctoral thesis: "Bremen als Auswandererhafen
1683-1880". Professor, Free U of Berlin. Publs: *Albertino Mussato: Der Tyrann*, 1967;
Deutsche Bücherplakate des 17. Jahrhunderts, 1971; *Analphabetentum und Lektüre*,
1973; *Der Bürger als Leser*, 1974; *Arbeit, Zeit und Werk im literarischen Beruf*, 1976;
Sozial und Wirtschaftsgeschichte Deutschlands, 1976; *Zur Sozialgeschichte deutscher
Mittel- und Unterschichten*, 1978. Fields: History.

[549]
ENKE Edo*
16 March 1940, German. c/o HSFK, Eschersheimer Landstrasse 14, 6 Frankfurt am
Main, FR Germany. Degress: Diplom rer oec (Mannheim), 1967; Dr phil (Mannheim),
1971. Doctoral thesis: "Upper Class and Political System. Empirical Analysis of 800
West German Top Positions". 1967-70 Research Assistant, Inst for Soc Sci, U of Mannheim; 1970-71 Research Fellow, U of Aberdeen; 1971- Hessische Stiftung Friedens-
und Konfliktforschung (HSFK), Frankfurt am Main. Publs: "Oberschicht und
Politisches System", in *Sozialwissenschaftliches Jahrbuch für Politik*, 1973. Fields:
Theory of interest and conflict; theory of mass communication; methods of survey
research.

[550]
ERMACORA Felix*
13 October 1923, Austrian. 1 Karl Lügerring, Vienna, Austria. Degrees: Dr jur. 1949-51
Assistant Professor of Public Law, U of Innsbruck; 1951-57 Senior Officer in the
Federal Chancellery/Vienna Constitutional Dept; 1957-64 Professor of Public Law, U
of Innsbruck; Professor of Public Law, U of Vienna; Member of the European Commission on Human Rights; Delegate of Austria on the UN Human Rights Commission.
Publs: *Neutrality and Austrian State Treaty*, 1957; *Human Rights and Fundamental
Freedoms in Austria*, 1963; *Minority Protection in the UN*, 1964 *Austrian Constitutional Theory*, 1970; *General Theory of Law and State*, 1970; *Prevention of Discrimination through UN*, 1971. Fields: General theory of law; Marxism and Leninism; human
rights; federalism; European integration; peace and neutrality; comparative government; international organization.

[551]
EROS John Stephen
21 November 1905, British. Department of Politics, The University, Keele, Staffordshire, England. Degrees: Dr phil (Heidelberg), 1931; PhD (Manchester), 1951. Doctoral
thesis: "Economic Imperialism and Capital Exports 1931: The Economic and Social
Policies of the Powers at the Paris Peace Conference 1918, and the Second 1919-25,
with special reference to Austria and Hungary". 1931 Cultural-Education Dept of

Budapest Municipality; 1945-49 Cultural Dept of Hungarian Foreign Office; 1952-53 Economic Research Dept, LSE; Senior Lecturer in Government, Dept of Pol, U of Keele. Publs: *K Mannheim's Systematic Sociology* (co-ed), 1957; "Hungary", in *European Fascism* (S J Woolf (ed)), 1968. Fields: Social, cultural and economic origins of European fascism; history of political ideas, 1871-1971.

[552]
ERRERA Roger
3 December 1933, French. 147 Avenue de Suffren, 75015 Paris, France. Degrees: Lic; DES; Dipl (IEP, ENA Paris). Maître de conférences, IEP, Paris; Maître des requêtes au Conseil d'Etat. Publs: *Les libertés à l'abandon*, 1975; plus various articles in *Esprit, Critique, Communications, Le Monde, La Quinzaine Littéraire, La Croix, Projet, Index, The Human Rights Review*. Fields: Political philosophy; civil liberties; judicial review.

[553]
ESCHENBURG Theodor*
24 October 1904, German. 74 Tübingen, Am Apfelburg 15, FR Germany. Degrees: Dr phil (Berlin), 1928. Doctoral thesis: "Das Kaiserreich am Scheideweg — Basserman, Bulow und der Block". 1929-45 Wiss Referent, Geschäftsführer, Industrieverband; Professor of Pol Sci, U of Tübingen. Publs: *Die deutsche Frage*, 1959; *Der Sold des Politikers*, 1959; *Das isolierte Berlin*, 1961; *Ämterpatronage*, 1961; *Probleme der modernen Parteifinanzierung*, 1961; *Zur politischen Praxis in der Bundesrepublik*, 1963; *Über Autorität*, 1965. Fields: Constitutional and domestic politics of the Federal Republic of Germany.

[554]
ESKELINEN Anne Anja Anneli
25 November 1949, Finnish. Näsilinnankatu 36 E 38/2, 33200 Tampere 20, Finland. Degrees: MSc soc sci (Tampere), 1973. 1975-76 Assistant in International Pol, U of Tampere; 1976- Teacher and Research Associate in International Pol, U of Tampere. Publs: articles in *Ulkopolitiikka*. Fields: Arms control and disarmament, especially nuclear-free zones.

[555]
ESSER Josef
12 April 1943, German. 7750 Konstanz 16, Adenauerstrasse 4, FR Germany. Degrees: Dr rer Soc. Doctoral thesis: "Zum Verhältnis von Politik und Ökonomie im entwickelten Kapitalismus". Wiss Assistent. Publs: *Einführung in die materialistische Staatsanalyse*, 1975; *Gesellschaftsplanung in kapitalistischen und sozialist Systemen* (co-author), 1972; *Verwaltungswissenschaft in Konstanz* (co-author), 1977; *Die sozialen Kosten einer modernisierten Volkswirtschaft. Strukturelle Arbeitslosigkeit und gesellschaftliche Desintegration* (co-author), 1978. Fields: Government theory; political economy; trade unions.

[556]
EVANS Judith Ann
13 February 1946, British. 3 Lucena House, 348 Hornsey Road, London N7, England. Degrees: BA; MSc (LSE), 1969. Lecturer, Dept of Pol Studies, Queen Mary Coll, U of London. Fields: Political sociology; political theory; women's studies.

[557]
EVANS Michael
24 February 1936, British. 69 Westgage, Hale, Cheshire, England. Degrees: BA; MA (Manchester). 1961-62 Lecturer in Pol Sci, U of Makerere, Kampala; 1963- Assistant Lecturer, Lecturer, Senior Lecturer in Government, U of Manchester. Publs: *Karl Marx*, 1975. Fields: Intellectual development of Karl Marx; contemporary political theory.

[558]
EVERTS Philip Pelgrim
22 January 1938, Dutch. Wasstraat 59, Leiden, The Netherlands. Degrees: Master in Law. Doctoral thesis: "Houdingen en Activiteiten van de Nederlandse Kerken aangaande het Oorlogsvraagstuk" (Attitudes and Activities of the Dutch Churches with Respect to War and Peace). 1962-70 Research Associate, Inst for Peace Research, U of Gröningen; Director, Inst for International Studies, U of Leiden. Publs: *Thailand, een Tweede Vietnam? De Amerikaanse Bestrijding van het communisme in Zuid-Oost Azië*, 1968; *The European Community in the World*, 1972; *International Repertory of Institutions for Peace and Conflict Research*, 1973; *De Elite en de Buitenlandse Politiek* (with others), 1968; "A Survey of International Studies in the Netherlands", in *International Studies in Six European Countries*, 1976; *Developments and Trends in Peace and Conflict Research*, 1971; "A Survey of Institutions", *Journal of Conflict Resolution*, 1972. Fields: Peace research; international relations.

F

[559]
FABER Styze
22 January 1937, Dutch. Kooikamp 57, Hardegarijp, The Netherlands. Degrees: Dr. Doctoral thesis: "Burgomaster and Democracy". Member of Parliament. Publs: *Burgomaster and Democracy*; *Friesland and Public Administration*. Fields: Political leaders; political process; public administration; regionalism/devolution.

[560]
FABRE Michel Henri
29 September 1916, French. 5 bis Cours de la Trinité, 13100 Aix-en-Provence, France. Degrees: Agrégé des Facultés de Droit, 1946; Dr en droit, 1941. 1946-52 Professeur, Faculté de Droit, U d'Alger; 1958-61, 1967-71 Doyen, Facultés de Droit, Sci Econ, U d'Aix; 1961-11 Recteur, U of Madagascar; Professeur, U d'Aix. Publs: *Théorie des démocraties populaires*, 1948; *Le soldat des Etats-Unis*, 1951; *Les nouveaux principes du droit public*, 1956; *Principes républicains du droit constitutionnel*, 1967. Fields: French constitutional law; constitutional law of popular democracies.

[561]
FABRIS Hans Heinz
5 June 1942, Australian. c/o Institut für Publizistik und Kommunikationstheorie, Sigmund-Haffner Gasse 18, 5020 Salzburg, Austria. Degrees: Dr phil. Doctoral thesis: "Demokratische Auswahl". Universitätsassistent und Lehrebeauftragter, U of Salzburg; Assistant, Inst für Publizistik und Kommunikationstheorie, U of Salzburg. Publs: *Demokratische Auswahl*, 1968; *Das Selbstbild von Redakteuren an Tageszeitungen*, 1971; "Das österreichische Mediensystem" (H Fischer (ed)), in *Das politische System Österreichs*, 1974; *Medienforschung in Österreich*, 1975. Fields: Politics of communication; local politics; process of innovation; futurism; journalism.

[562]
FALCHI Maria Antonietta
3 July 1944, Italian. Corso Firenze 9/ɔ, 16136 Genova, Italy. Degrees: Doctor of Law. Doctoral thesis: "Aspetti della Metodologia Giuridica nell'Analisi di Hart". Assistant of Sociology, Dept of Pol Sci, U of Genova. Publs: "The Conspiracy to Corrupt Public Morals", in *Annali Fac Giurisprudenza*, 1970; "Metodologia Analitica e Problematica della Responsabilità Giuridica, in H. L. A. Hart", in *Annali Fac Scienze Politische*, 1973; "Il Fondamento Sociale e Politico del Diritto nell' Analisi di Hart", *Annali Fac Scienze Politiche*, 1974; "Legalità, Legittimità e Obbligazione Politica nel Giuspositivismo Analitico", in *Annali Fac Scienze Politiche*, 1975. Fields: Sociology of law; jurisprudence; legal philosophy; political philosophy.

[563]
FALTER Jürgen W
22 January 1944, German. Valleystrasse 34, 8 München 70, FR Germany. Degrees: Dipl; Dr rer Pol. Doctoral thesis: "Die säarländischen Landtagswahlen vom 14 Juni 1970 — eine wahlsoziologische Analyse" (The 1970 Saar Elections). Wiss Assistent, Inst für Politikwissenschaft, U des Saarlandes; Professor of Pol Soc and Methodology of Soc Sci, Hochschule der Bundeswehr, Münich. Publs: *Faktoren der Wahlentscheidung — Eine wahlsoziologische Analyse am Beispiel der saarländischen Landtagswahl*, 1970; *Psychische und soziale Determinanten des politischen Verhaltens im Saarland* (with V Trommsdorff), 1972; *Der 'Positivismusstreit' in der amerikanischen Politikwissenschaft*, 1978; *Methoden der Kausalanalyse von Kontingenztafeln* (with R Pelka and K Ulbricht), 1978. Fields: Voting behaviour; the translation of epistemological into methodological prescriptions; political behaviour in the Weimar Republic, with special emphasis on nazi voting behaviour; multilevel analysis; philosophy of the social sciences.

[564]
FANTOZZI Pietro*
21 July 1947, Italian. c/o Università di Calabria, ANAPLI, via Montevideo 55, 87100 Cosenza, Italy. Degrees: Dr (Urbino), 1970. Instructor, U of Ancona; Assistant Professor, U of Calabria. Fields: Underdevelopment in Southern Italy; new classes in Italy; local power in Southern Italy.

[565]
FARNETI Paolo Andrea
5 February 1936, Italian. Strada Castelvecchio, Moncalieri, Turin, Italy. Degrees: Laurea Jurisprudence (Turin), 1961; PhD (Columbia), 1968. Doctoral thesis: "Attitudes of Businessmen in Economic Development: The Case of Piedmont in Italy". Professor of Pol Sci, U of Turin. Publs: *Theodor Geiger e la Coscienza della Società Industriale*, 1966; *Imprenditore e Società*, 1969; *Sistema Politico e Società Civile*, 1971; *Il Sistema Politico Italiano* (ed), 1973; "Partiti e Sistema di Potere", in *L'Italia Contemporanea* (V Castronovo (ed)), 1976; *Politica e Società* (ed), 1978. Fields: Political behaviour; political elites in Europe; analysis of political structures through aggregate data; Italian political thought since 1861.

[566]
FARRELL Brian
9 January 1928, Irish. Room G3-02, Arts Block, University College, Dublin 4, Ireland. Degrees: BA; MA (Dublin), 1956. 1955-67 Administrative Staff, U Coll, Dublin; 1967-Lecturer, Pol Institutions, U Coll, Dublin. Publs: *Chairman or Chief? The Role of Taoiseach (Prime Minister) in Irish Government*, 1971; *The Origins of the First Dail: Parliament and Nation-building*, 1971. Fields: Irish politics; political communication.

[567]
FAURBY Ib
21 February 1941, Danish. Agatvej 16, DK-8541 Skoedstrup, Denmark. Degrees: MA (Aarhus), 1969. Doctoral thesis: "The Common Market Policy of the British Labour Party, 1958-68". 1969- Lecturer in International Relations, Inst of Pol Sci, U of Aarhus; 1976 Fulbright-Hays Scholar, The School of International Relations, U of Southern California. Publs: "The Lack of Cumulation in Foreign Policy Studies: The Case of Britain and the European Community", *European Journal of Political Research*, 1976; "Premises, Promises and Problems of Comparative Foreign Policy", in *Cooperation and Conflict*, 1976; various articles in international relations. Fields: Comparative foreign policy; foreign policy decision-making; crisis management; energy policy; British foreign policy; Chinese foreign policy; the foreign policies of the Scandinavian countries.

[568]
FAURE Yves-André
2 April 1948, French. Chemin de Boscarn, Macau, 33460 Margaux, France. Degrees: Lic ès lettres; Maître ès lettres; Lic en droit public; DES sci pol; DES d'histoire institutionelle et sociale. Doctoral thesis: "Histoire et politique en Afrique noire". Professeur de Lettres; Chargé de cours complémentaire, Faculté de Droit, Bordeaux; Assistant de recherche, IEP, Bordeaux. Publs: "Vicissitudes des organisations sous-regionales de l'OERS et l'OMUS", *Revue Française d'Etudes Politiques Africaines*, 1977; "Chroniques du Senégal de la Côte d'Ivoire de la Guinée et du Bénin", *Annuaire de legislation française et étrangère*, 1977; "l'Afrique noire et les provinces extérieures", in *l'Année Africaine*, 1977. Fields: Political process and change; international relations.

[569]
FEJTÖ Francois
31 August 1909, French. 49 Boulevard Victor Hugo, 92 Neuilly/Seine, France. Degrees: Dipl de Professeur de littérature hongroise et allemande (Budapest), 1932, 1935-38 Co-Director, Szep Szö, Hungary; 1950- Commentator, Agence France-Presse; Dirige séminaires, IEP. Publs: *Histoire des démocraties populaires*, 1952; *Tragédie hongroise*, 1956; *Chine-URSS: Les origines du schisme*, 1964; *Le conflit*, 1966; *Histoire des démocraties populaires après Staline*, 1969; *Dictionnaire des partis communistes et mouvements révolutionnaires*, 1971; *Le coup de Prague*, 1976; *L'héritage de Lénine*, 1977. Fields: History of the communist world; Sino-Soviet relations.

[570]
FEMIA Joseph Vincent
17 December 1946, American. 22 Warwick House, Central Avenue, Levenshulme, Manchester 19, England. Degrees: BA; B Phil (Oxon), 1971. 1973-74 Lecturer in Pol Philosophy, St Hugh's Coll, U of Oxford; 1974-75 Lecturer in Government, U of Manchester; 1975- Lecturer in Pol Theory and Inst, U of Liverpool. Publs: "Barrington Moore and the Preconditions for Democracy", *British Journal of Political Science*, 1972; "Hegemony and Consciousness in the Thought of Antonio Gramsci", *Political Studies*, 1975; "Gramsci and the via Italiana", *Government and Opposition*, 1978; "Elites Participation and the Democratic Creed", *Political Studies*, 1978. Fields: The thought of Gramsci; Marxism in general; democratic theory; Italian communism.

[571]
FENGER Pim
7 October 1940, Dutch. Lomanstraat 12, Amsterdam, The Netherlands. Degrees: Dr. Paradiso Director; Boemanstichting; Research Dept, Ministry of Education and Sciences. Publs: *Protest in an Established Society*, 1974; *Beleidsanalyse Beeldende Kunsten, toestand en processen*, 1976. Fields: Arts and culture; arts policy; science policy; research policy.

[572]
FENNEMA Meindert
21 May 1946, Dutch. Baard 19, Friesland, The Netherlands. Degrees: BA; MA. Doctoral thesis: "The Multinational Corporation and the European Communities". Research Fellow, Netherlands Organisation for the Advancement of Pure Research; Lecturer in Pol Sci, Inst for Pol Sci, U of Amsterdam. Publs: *De multinationale onderneming en de nationale staat*, 1975; "Konzentrationsbewegungen in der westeuropäischen Automobilindustrie" (with K P Tudyka (ed)), 1974; "Graven naar macht; enkele opmerkingen bij de theorie en praktijke van het onderzoek naar de machtspositie van de economica en politieke elite in Nederland", *De Gids*, 1976; "Internationale vervlechting van industrie en bankwezen" (with P de Jong), in *Herstrukturering van de Nederlandse industrie* (A Teulings (ed)), 1978. Fields: Internationalization of capital and the state; interlocking directorates/network analysis; nationalism and regional development.

[573]
FENNER Christian
16 August 1942, German. Carmerstrasse 10, D-1000 Berlin, FR Germany. Degrees: Dipl Pol, 1969; Dr phil, 1974. Doctoral thesis: "Die Auseinandersetzung um den demokratischen Sozialismus. Möglichkeiten und Grenzen sozialistischer Gegeninterpretation in der Bundesrepublik Deutschland. Eine Historisch-Kritische Verlaufsanalyse". 1969-76 Assistant Professor; 1976- Assistant Professor, Inst für Innenpolitik und Komparatistik, Fachbereich Pol Wiss, Freie, U of Berlin. Publs: "Liberalisierung und Demokratisierung des Sozialismus in der CSSR", in *Aus Politik und Zeitgeschichte*, 1970; "Die deutsche Studentenrevolte und das Modell der jugoslawischen Arbeiterselbstverwaltung", in *Marxistische Praxis* (O K Flechtheim and E Grassi (ed)), 1973; "Vergesellschaftung und Demokratisierung", in *Systemwandel und Demokratisierung* (Fenner and Blanke (eds)), 1975; "Das Parteisystem der Bundesrepublik Deutschland seit 1969 — Normalisierung und Polarisierung", in *Das Parteiensystem der Bundesrepublik* (D Staritz (ed)), 1976; *Demokratischer Sozialismus und Sozialdemokratie. Realität und Rhetorik der Sozialismusdiskussion in Deutschland*, 1977; "Das schwedische Parteiensystem", in *Handbuch westeuropäischer Parteiensystem* (J Raschke (ed)), 1977. Fields: Comparative political systems — party systems; theory of democratic socialism; the party system of Germany — "Innenpolitik".

[574]
FERDINAND Charles Ian Peter
30 September 1947, British. 62 Cannon Park Road, Coventry CV4 7AY, England. Degrees: BA; MSc (London). 1976- Lecturer in Pol, U of Warwick. Fields: Comparative communism; political systems.

[575]
FERNS Henry Stanley
16 December 1913, Canadian. 1 Kesteven Close, Sir Harry's Road, Birmingham B15 2UT, England. Degrees: BA; MA (Queens); MA; PhD (Cambridge). Doctoral thesis: "The Development of British Enterprise in Argentina 1806-1895". 1945-49 Assistant Professor of History, U of Manitoba; 1949-50 Fellow, Soc Sci Research Council of Canada; 1950-56 Lecturer, Modern History and Government; 1956-60 Senior Lecturer; 1961- Professor of Pol Sci, U of Birmingham. Publs: *The Age of Mackenzie King* (with B Ostry), 1976; *Britain and Argentina in the XIX Century*, 1960; *Argentina*, 1969; *National Economic Histories: Argentina*, 1973; *The Disease of Government*, 1978. Fields: The problem of limiting the power of governments.

[576]
FETSCHER Iring
4 March 1922, German. Ganghoferstrasse 20, Frankfurt/M, FR Germany. Degrees: Dr phil, 1950; Habilitation, 1959. Doctoral thesis: "Rousseau's politische Philosophie". 1950-1975 Assistent, Dozent, Tübingen; 1975-76 Professor of Social Philosophy, U of Nijmegen; 1976- Professor für Politikwissenschaft, J W Goethe U, Frankfurt a-M. Publs: *Hegels Lehre vom Menschen*, 1970; *Karl Marx und der Marxismus.* 1967; *Rousseaus politische Philosophie*, 1960; *Grossbritannien, Gesellschaft-Staat-Ideologie*, 1978; *Modelle der Friedenssicherung*, 1972; *Herrschaft und Emanzipation, zur Philosophie des Bürgertums*, 1976; *Der Marxismus — seine Geschichte in Dokumenten* (ed), 1976. Fields: History of political philosophy; Marxism; problems of peace research.

[577]
FEUER Guy René
10 December 1925, French. 9 rue de Montessuy, 75007 Paris, France. Degrees: Dr en droit (Paris), 1953; Agrégé des Facultés de Droit, 1960. Doctoral thesis: "Des causes d'exonération ou de limitation de la responsabilité internationale des Etats". U de Bordeaux, Poitiers, Strasbourg, Paris, Paris V. Publs: *Les problèmes juridiques de l'assistance technique dans le cadre des Nations Unies et des institutions spécialisées*, 1957; *Le Moyen-Orient contemporain, guide de recherches*, 1975; Articles in *Annuaire Française de Droit International; La Revue Générale de Droit International Public, Le Journal du Droit International*. Fields: International public law; international laws; problems of the Third World; relations between industrialized and developing countries.

[578]
FICHTER Tilman
1 August 1937, German. 1 Berlin 19, Klausenerplatz 4, FR Germany. Degrees: Dipl Pol. Doctoral thesis: "Continuity and Discontinuity of Political and Social Elites in Germany 1943-1953". Wiss Assistent, Zentralinstitut, Free U of Berlin. Publs: *Der ergwungene Kapitalismus* (with M Schmidt), 1971; *Kampf um Bosch*, 1974; *Historische-empirische Politikforschung in Berlin* (with S Lonnendonker), 1975; *Aspekte der Parteiengeschichte in den ersten Nachkriegsjahren (1945-49)* (with M Schmidt), 1977. Fields: Working class parties; political and social elites.

[579]
FIJALKOWSKI Jürgen
29 August 1928, German. Asternplatz 1, 1000 Berlin 45, FR Germany. Degrees: Dr phil; Habilitation. Doctoral thesis: "Die Wendung zum Führerstaat — Ideologische Komponenten in der Politischen Philosophie Carl Schmitts". 1959-70 Research Fellow in Soc and Pol Sci, Inst für Soziologie und Inst für Pol Wissenschaft, Free U of Berlin; 1971-76 Professor für Politikwissenschaft und Pol Bildung, Pädagogische Hochschule Berlin; Professor für Innenpolitik und Pol Soziologie, Fachbereich Politikwissenschaft, Free U of Berlin. Publs: *Die Wendung zum Führerstaat*, 1958; *Politologie und Soziologie* (ed), 1965; "Das politische Problem der Feindschaft", *PVS*, 1965; *Berlin, Hauptstadtanspruch und Westintegration*, 1967; "Methodologische Grundorientierungen", in *Enzyklopädie geisteswissenschaftlicher Arbeitsmethoden* (M Thiel (ed)), 1967; "Bemerkungen zur Rätediskussion", in *Probleme der Demokratie heute*, 1971; "Structure of German Society", in *Germany today* (Payne (ed)), 1971; "Pluralistische und antagonistische Gesellschaft", in *Soziologie, Festangabe für König*, 1973. Fields: Sources of conflict in social structure; social history of civil service; constitutional theory; constitutional and administrative reform; domestic affairs of German Federal Republic and Berlin; comparative theory of West European and East German political and social developments.

[580]
FILESI Teobaldo
17 January 1917, Italian. Via Luigi Credaro 19, 00135 Rome, Italy. Degrees: Laurea in Giurisprudenza (Rome), 1935. Professor, U of Naples, Pontificia U, Urbaniana (SCV); Director, *Africa*; Direttore dell 'Institute Storico-politico della Facoltà di Sci Pol, U degli Studi di Napoli. Publs: *Nazionalismo e Religione nel Congo all'Inizio del 1700*; *La Setta degli Antoniani*, 1972; *China and Africa in the Middle Ages*, 1972; *The Public Archives of Campania with Special Reference to the Archive of State in Naples*, 1973; *Il Dey d'Algeri a Napoli e a Livorno (1824-1833)*, 1974; *Profilo Storico-politico dell'Africa*, 1976; *Realtà e Prospettive della Storiografia Africana*, 1978; *Quadro Storico e Guida delle Fonti della 'Missio Antiqua' dei Cappuccini italiani nell'Antico Regno del Congo (1645-1835)*, 1978. Fields: History of Africa; politics in modern Africa; history of Catholic missions in Africa; family law in Africa; political institutions of independent Africa.

[581]
FINER Samuel Edward*
22 September 1915, British. All Soul's College, Oxford, England. Degrees: BA; BA(Hist); MA (Oxon), 1946. 1946-50 Lecturer in Pol, Junior Fellow, Balliol Coll, U of Oxford; 1950-55 Professor of Government, U of Keele; 1957-59 Visiting Professor, Inst of Social Studies, The Hague; 1962 Cornell U; 1969 Hebrew U of Jerusalem; 1966- Professor of Government, U of Manchester; All Soul's Coll, Oxford. Publs: *A Primer of Public Administration*, 1950; *The Life and Times of Sir Edwin Chadwick*, 1952; *Local Government in England and Wales* (with Sir John Maud), 1953. *Anonymous Empire: A Study of the Lobby in Britain*, 1966; *Backbench Opinion in the House of Commons* (co-author), 1955; *Private Enterprise and Political Power*, 1958; *Man on Horseback: The Role of the Military in Politics*, 1962; *Pareto: Sociological Writings*, 1966; *Comparative Government*, 1970.

[582]
FINLAYSON Donald Alexander MacAulay
27 September 1936, British. 10 Crossways, Houston, Renfrewshire, Scotland. Degrees: BA; BSc (London); MSc (Strathclyde). Senior Lecturer in Government, Paisley Coll. Publs: "Scottish Members of Parliament: The Problems of Devolution", *Parliamentary Affairs*, 1975. Fields: Policy studies; local government.

[583]
FIOCCO, Laura*
27 March 1942, Italian. c/o INAPLI, University of Calabria, 87100 Cosenza, Italy. Dr (Ancona). 1970-72, Instructor U of Ancona; 1972- Assistant Professor, U of Calabria. Fields: Economic development in Italy since the war.

[584]
FIRPO Luigi
4 January 1915, Italian. Corso Moncalieri 69, Turin, Italy. Degrees: Dr jur. Doctoral thesis: "The Political Thought of Thomas Campanella". 1946- Professor of History of Pol Thought, U of Turin. Publs: *Bibliografia di T. Campanella*, 1940; *Ricerche Campanelliane*, 1947; *Il Processo di G. Bruno*, 1949; *Lo Stato Ideale della Controriforma*, 1957; *Il Pensiero Politico del Rinascimento*, 1964. Fields: History of political thought, with special interest in humanism, renaissance and counter reformation; history of utopian thought; political debates on the reformation.

[585]
FISCHER Heinz
9 October 1938, Austrian. Josefstädterstrasse 21/20, A-1080 Wien, Austria. Degrees: Dr jur. 1971- Member of Parliament; Chairman of the Socialist group of the Austrian Parliament; Member of the Executive Committee of the Socialist Party of Austria. Publs: "Zum Wort gemeldet: Otto Rauer" (H Fischer (ed)), 1968; "Kommentar zur Geschäftsordnung des Nationalrates" (with W Czerny), 1968; "Karl Renner. Porträt einer Evolution" (H Fischer (ed)), 1970; "Das politische System Österreichs" (H Fischer (ed)), 1974; "Positionen und Perspektiven", 1977.

[586]
FISTIÉ Pierre*
16 July 1923, French. 22 'Le Parc', 91 Evry, France. Degrees: Dipl l'Ecole Pratique des Hautes Etudes, 1966. 1960- Chercheur, FNSP. Publs: *Singapour et la Malaisie*, 1960; *La Thailande*, 1971; *L'évolution de la Thailande contemporaine*, 1967; *Sous-développement et utopie au Siam*, 1969. Fields: Contemporary history of the Far East; contemporary political development in Singapore and Malaysia; international relations of Japan; British policy East of Suez.

[587]
FLECHTHEIM Ossip Kurt
5 March 1909, 1 Berlin 33, Kohlfsstrasse 18, FR Germany. Degrees: Dipl (Inst des Hautes Etudes Internationales, Geneva); Dr jur (Köln), 1934; Dr phil (Heidelberg), 1947. 1939-40 Assistant Research Associate, Columbia, NY, USA; 1940-43 Visiting Professor, Free U of Berlin; 1952-59 Professor, Deutsche Hochschule für Pol, Berlin; 1961-74 Professor of Pol Sci, Free U of Berlin. Publs: *Dokumente zur Parteipolitischen Entwicklung in Deutschland*, 1962-71; *Von Hegel zu Kelsen*, 1963; *Eine Welt oder keine?*, 1964; *Weltkommunismus im Wandel*, 1965; *History and Futurology*, 1966; *Bolschewismus 1917-57*, 1967; *Futurologie-der Kampf um die Zukunft*, 1970; *Die Bundesrepublik*, 1973; *Zeitgeschichte und Zukunftspolitik*, 1974. Fields: Theory and history of communism, and its future; political parties in the USA and Germany since 1945; ideology and utopia; future research and futurology.

[588]
FLEURY Antoine
2 May 1943, Swiss. 2 rue des Rois, CH-1204 Genève, Switzerland. Degress: Lic ès lettres (Geneva), 1967; DES (Paris), 1966; Dr ès sci pol (Geneva), 1974. Doctoral thesis: "La politique allemande au Moyen-Orient 1919-1939. Etude comparative de la pénétration de l'Allemagne en Turquie, en Iran et en Afghanistan". 1969-74 Assistant, Inst des Hautes Etudes Internationales, Geneva; 1975- Maître assistant, Faculté des Lettres, U de Genève; 1976- Chargé de recherche, Inst U des Hautes Etudes Internationales, Geneva; Secrétaire général de l'Association européenne d'Histoire contemporaine; Secrétaire de la Commission nationale pour la publication de Documents diplomatiques suisses. Publs: *La pénétration allemande au Moyen-Orient, 1919-1939: le cas de la Turquie, de l'Iran et de l'Afghanistan*, 1977; *Documents diplomatiques suisses, 1918-1920*, 1978. Fields: History of international relations in the 20th century; problems of political independence and economic interdependence or economic alignment; case studies: the countries of the Middle East and the Mediterranean area; Switzerland; origins and steps of international concentration in economic and social matters.

[589]
FLORY Maurice
19 June 1925, French. 15 rue Roux Alpheran, 13100 Aix en Provence, France. Degrees: Dr en droit (Paris), 1950; Agrégé droit public, 1952. 1952-56 Professeur, Faculté de Droit, Rabat, Morocco; 1957-67 Professeur, Faculté de Droit, U d'Aix-Marseille; 1967-71 Chef de la mission culturelle, Ambassade de France, Morocco; 1971- Professeur, Faculté de Droit et Sci Pol, U d'Aix-Marseille; Directeur, Centre de recherches et d'études sur led sociétés méditerranéennes. Publs: *Le statut international des gouvernements réfugiés et le cas de la France libre*, 1952; *La notion de protectorat et son évolution en Afrique du Nord*, 1955; "L'ONU", in *Jurisclasseurs*, 1956; *Le régime politique des pays arabes*, 1968; *Droit international du dévelopement*, 1977; *L'Annuaire de l'Afrique du Nord* (ed). Fields: International public law; international organizations; international law of development; North Africa; the United Nations development system.

[590]
FLOTO Inga
26 October 1937, Danish. Lystbådevej 6, Jyllinge, 4000 Roskilde, Denmark. Degrees: Cand mag; Dr phil. Doctoral thesis; "Colonel House in Paris. A Study of American Policy at the Paris Peace Conference 1919". Assistant Professor in Contemporary History, U of Copenhagen. Publs: *Colonel House in Paris. A Study of American Policy at the Paris Peace Conference*, 1973. Fields: American history and politics; Danish and American historiography.

[591]
FLYNN Peter*
30 December 1935, British. Institute of Latin-American Studies, The University, Glasgow G12 8QH, Scotland. Degrees: MA (Oxon), 1964; Dr phil (Oxon). Doctoral thesis: "Brazil: From Revolution to Civil War: A Study of the Vargas Revolution of 1930 and the Sao Paulo Revolt of 1932". Senior Scholar, St Anthony's Coll, U of Oxford; Lecturer in Latin American History, U of Glasgow; Lecturer in Latin American Pol, U of Liverpool; 1972- Director, Inst of Studies, U of Glasgow. Publs: *Modern Brazil* (with H Carless), 1971. Fields: Contemporary political history of Brazil; clientage and "boss politics" in Brazil; political mobilization; relation between clientage and party formation.

[592]
FOLEY Charles Frederick William*
12 August 1944, British. 18 Radley Road, Pedmore Hill, Stourbridge, Worcestershire DY9 8XX, England. Degrees: MBA (Liverpool), 1970. 1965-68 Statistician, English Electric Ltd; 1970-72 Part-time Lecturer, U of Liverpool; 1972- Senior Research Associate, U of Birmingham. Fields: Management style; local government.

[593]
FONTAINE André-Lucien-Georges
30 March 1921, French. 6 rue Gounod, 75017 Paris, France. Degrees: Lic ès lettres; DES droit public et econ pol. 1947- *Le Monde*; 1949- Foreign editor, Chief Editor, *Le Monde*. Publs: *L'alliance atlantique à l'heure du dégel*, 1960; *Histoire de la guerre froide*, 1966; *La guerre civile froide*, 1969; *Le dernier quart de siècle*, 1976. Fields: History; foreign policy; society and politics in general.

[594]
FONTANET Joseph Paul Marie
9 February 1921, French. 36 Boulevard Emile Augier, 75016 Paris, France. Degrees: Dipl des hautes études commerciales; Dr en droit. Doctoral thesis: "Le dépérissement de l'actif des entreprises en période d'inflation". Membre du Parlement; Ancien Ministre; Directeur d'une Société de Financement. Publs: *Le Social et le Vivant*, 1977. Fields: General theory of systems; social and economic questions; political science.

[595]
FONTEIN Herman
22 December 1950, Dutch. Ahornstraat 10, 6523 JJ Nijmegen, The Netherlands. Inst of Pol Sci, U of Nijmegen. Publs: "Koude Oorlog en Bewapening", in *Oost Europa Verkenningen*, 1978; "Een gemeenschappelijke buitenlandse politiek: machtsmiddel van een Verenigd Europa?", *Dosschrift*, 1978. Fields: Problems of war and peace, especially the arms dynamic in the Soviet Union; external relations of the EEC; socialism (Eurocommunism).

[596]
FOPPEN J Wil
27 April 1946, Dutch. Aardappelmarkt 27, 3311 BA Dordrecht, The Netherlands. Degrees: Drs. Netherlands Organisation for Pure Scientific Research (ZWO). Publs: *De Nederlandse Kiezer* (co-author), 1972, 1973; *The Dutch Voter* (with L P de Bruyn), 1972, 1973; *National Electoral Data Project*, 1974. Fields: Historical trends in election results; voters' preferences, opinions and attitudes; the sense of legality and legitimacy of voters; election surveys in general.

[597]
FORNLEITNER Luise*
7 October 1945, Austrian. Wien XI, Zippererstrasse 14/8/34, Austria. Degrees: Dr Rechtswiss Fak (Vienna), 1970. Practice at Courts of Justice; Assistant for Constitutional Law, World Trade U, Vienna; Scholar, Inst of Advanced Studies, Vienna. Fields: Sociology of law systems; political socialization and political education; theory of power structures.

[598]
FORSELL Harry Amos*
31 July 1928, Swedish. Postlåda 4074, S-902 54 Umeå, Sweden. Degrees: MA (Umeå), 1969; PhD (Umeå), 1972. Doctoral thesis: "Transformation of Society and Decision-making Capacity of Local Governments". 1965-72 Research Assistant, U of Umeå; Assistant Professor of Pol Sci, U of Umeå. Publs: "Size and Organization of Electoral Campaigns", in *Den kommunala självstyrelsen*, 2, 1971; "Communal Support for Political Parties", in *Statens offentliga utredningar*, 1972. Fields: Party finance; election campaigns; environmental politics.

[599]
FORSYTH Murray Greensmith*
30 October 1936, British. Department of Politics, The University, Leicester LE1 7RH, England. Degrees: BA; MA (Oxon), 1964; 1960-64 Research Officer, PEP, London; 1964-71 Lecturer in Pol, U of Leicester; Reader in International Pol, U of Leicester. Publs: *The Parliament of the European Communities* (with G Denton and M MacLennan), (PEP); *Economic Planning and Policies in Britain, France and Germany*, 1968. Fields: Institutions of, and economic policy in the Common Market; theory of integration.

[600]
FORTIN Carlos
29 April 1940, Chilean. 9 Freshfield Place, Brighton, Sussex, England. Degrees: BA; MA (Yale). Doctoral thesis: "The International Politics of Nationalization: The Case of Chilean Copper". 1966-71 Associate Professor, Assistant Professor of Pol, Latin American School of Pol Sci and Public Administration, Santiago; 1971-73 Head of the European Bureau of the Chilean Copper Corporation, London; 1973-74 Lecturer in Government and History, U of Essex; 1974- Research Fellow, Inst of Development Studies, U of Sussex. Publs: "Principled Pragmatism in the Face of External Pressure: The Foreign Policy of the Allende Government", in *Latin America: The Search for a New International Role*, 1975; "Compensating the Multinationals: Chile and the US Copper Companies", *IDS Bulletin*, 1975; "The State, MNCs and Natural Resources in Latin America", *IDS Bulletin*, 1977; "Law and Economic Coercion as Instruments of International Control", in *The Nationalization of Multinationals in Peripheral Economics* (S Picciotto and J Faundex (eds)), 1978. Fields: The international politics of natural resources; the state and capital accumulation in Latin America.

[601]
FOSTER Alan Joseph
22 February 1939, British. 45 Park House Gardens, East Twickenham, Middlesex, England. Degrees: BA; Dip Ed (Oxon); MSc (London). Senior Lecturer in Pol, Thames Polytechnic. Fields: Comparative politics; political economy; defence.

[602]
FOTHERINGHAM Peter
10 December 1938, British. Department of Politics, The University, Glasgow, Scotland. Degrees: MA (Glasgow), 1961; MA (Manitoba), 1962. 1962- Lecturer, U of Glasgow; 1969-70 Visiting Assistant Professor, State U of NY at Buffalo, USA. Publs: *American Government and Politics* (with J Kellas and A M Potter), 1978. Fields: American politics; international politics; marine pollution control.

[603]
FOTIA Mauro
19 October 1939, Italian. Largo Vessella, 31-00199 Rome, Italy. Degrees: Laurea in Sci Pol; Laurea in Giurisprudenza; Libera Docenza in Dottrina dello Stato; Premio Nazion dell'Accademia dei Lincei, per le Sci Pol e Soc, 1969. Doctoral thesis: "Il pensiero politico di Gaetano Mosca". Professore di Sci Pol, U di Messina; Professore di Sci Pol, U di Trieste; Professore di Sci Pol, La Medesima U; Professore di Sci della Pol e del diritto, La Libera U, Internaz degli Studi Sociali di Roma; Professore di Sci Pol, L'Instituto Superiore Internaz per le Relazione Publiche di Roma; Professore di Sci Pol, Professore di Antropologia Pol, per la Scuola di Perfezionamento in Statistica e Ricerca Sociale della Facoltà di Sci Statistiche e Demografische, U di Roma. Publs: *Ideologia e Scienza Politica*, 1971; *Ruoli di Dominio e Classe Politica*, 1972; *Partiti e Movimento Politico di Massa*, 1974; *Assiologia Classe al Potere e Scienza Politica*, 1970; "Classe Politica, Liberalismo, Democrazia in Gaetano Mosca", *Rivista di Sociologia*, 1966; "Intellectuels et Politique selon Gaetano Mosca", *Politique*, 1963; "Les nouvelles élites politiques dans le processus de développement économique du continent Africain", *Revue Juridique et Politique. Indépendance et Coopération*, 1967; "Ideologies Elites politiques", *l'Homme et la Société*, 1967. Fields: Socialism; liberalism; Eurocommunism.

[604]
FOUGERE Louis Eugene Dominique
9 October 1915, French. 6 rue Chanoiseau, 75004 Paris, France. Degrees: Lic en droit, lettres et phil; Dipl (IEP Paris). Conseiller d'Etat. Publs: *La fonction publique*, 1966; *Le Conseil d'Etat. Son histoire à travers les documents d'époque* (ed), 1974. Fields: History of the French administration; administrative science; modern history; Europe; political economic and social evolution of the Third World.

[605]
FOURASTIE Jean
15 April 1907, French. 10 rue Gésar Franck, 75015 Paris, France. Degrees: Ingenieur des Arts et Manufactures, 1930; Dipl (IEP Paris), 1933; Dr en droit, 1936. Professeur, Conservatoire National des Arts et Métiers, IEP Paris; Directeur d'études, Ecole des Hautes Etudes; Membre élu, Inst de France. Publs: *Le grand espoir du XXème siècle; La planification en France*, 1963; *Les 40000 Heures*, 1965; *Les conditions de l'esprit scientifique*, 1966; *Comment mon cerveau s'informe*, 1968. *Essais de morale prospective*, 1968; *Faillite de l'université?*, 1971; *Le long chemin des hommes*, 1975; *Pouvoir d'achat, prix et salaires*, 1977. Fields: Children's background and ability; economics: prices, salaries, purchasing power, economic growth, productivity; sociology: education, evolution of behaviour and political ideas; methodology of thought.

[606]
FOVERSKOV Peter
30 July 1946, Danish. Hunderupvej 91, 5230, Odense M, Denmark. Degrees: Cand phil. Publs: "Women in Parliament: the Causes of Under-representation Exemplified by Denmark and Norway in the 1960s", *European Journal of Political Research*, 1978; "Den Politiske Rekrutterings proces: Teoretiske Betragtninger of en Tentain Model", *Statsvetenskaplig Tidskrift*, 1978. Fields: Political recruitment; comparative politics.

[607]
FRAGA IRIBARNE Manuel
23 November 1922, Spanish. Ministro Ibañez Martin 5, Residencia para Profesores, Ciudad universitá, Madrid 3, Spain. Degrees: Lic; Dr in Law, 1968. Professor, Faculty of Law, U of Valencia; 1953 Professor, Faculty of Pol Sci and Sociology, U of Madrid. Publs: *Horizonte Espanol*, 1966; *Cinco Loas*, 1965; *El Desarrollo Politico*, 1971; *Legislividad y Representación*, 1973; *La Republica; Los Tempos*, 1975; *Canovas, Maestu y Offus des Curses*, 1976; *La Monarquia y el Pais*, 1977; *Los Nucos dia 'Cops'*, 1977; Fields: Political change and development.

[608]
FRANCK Louis
28 April 1906, French. 31 Boulevard du Commandant Charcot, 92200 Neuilly-sur-Siene, France. Degrees: Dr en droit. Ancien Directeur des Prix et des Enquêtes Econ, Ministère de l'Economie et des Finances, Paris; Ministère Plénipotentiaire Conseiller Financier près l'Ambassade de France, Londres; Ancien Professeur, IEP Paris; Président Honoraire, Société Commerciate de Réassurance, Paris. Publs: *L'économie corporative fasciste en doctrine et en fait- ses origines et son évolution*, 1934; *L'expérience Roosevelt et le milieu social américain*, 1937. *Démocrates en crise — Roosevelt, Van Zeeland, Leon Blum*, 1937; *Les étapes de l'économie fasciste italienne- du corporatisme à l'économie de guerre*, 1939; *Histoire économique et sociale des Etats-Unis de 1919 à 1949*, 1950; *Les prix*, 1958; *La libre concurrence*, 1963; *La politique économique des Etats-Unis*, 1966. Fields: Governmental interaction in economic life.

[609]
FRANK Peter John
6 May 1934, British. Department of Government, University of Essex, Wivenhoe Park, Colchester, Essex, England. Degrees: BA. 1944-5 Assistant Lecturer in Russian History, U of Leeds; 1965-8 Lecturer in Soviet History, U of Leeds; 1968- Lecturer, Senior Lecturer in Soviet Government, U of Essex. Fields: Russian and Soviet political and social history; Communist party of the Soviet Union.

[610]
FRANKEL Joseph
1913, British. The Old Rectory, Avington, Near Winchester, Hampshire, England. Degrees: LL M (Lvov), 1935; LL M (Western Australia), 1948; PhD (LSE), 1950. 1951-52 Temporary Assistant Lecturer, U Coll, London; 1953-63 Lecturer and Senior Lecturer in Pol, U of Aberdeen; 1963- Professor of Pol, U of Southampton. Publs: *The Making of Foreign Policy*, 1967; *International Relations*, 1970; *International Politics: Conflict and Harmony*, 1969; *National Interests*, 1970. Fields: British foreign policy; international theory.

[611]
FRANKLIN Mark N
29 January 1942, British. Department of Politics, University of Strathclyde, McCance Building, Richmond Street, Glasgow C1, Scotland. Degrees: MA (Oxon); PhD (Cornell). Doctoral thesis: "Voice of the Backbench: Patterns of Behaviour in the British House of Commons". 1974-75 Senior Study Director, National Opinion Research Center and Visiting Assistant Professor, U of Chicago; Lecturer, U of Strathclyde. Publs: *DAEDAL: A Data Archiving, Editing, Describing and Analysing Language*, 1973; "A Non-Election in America?", *BJPS*, 1971; "Computers and the Modern Member of Parliament", *The Parliamentarian*, 1973; "Patterns of Opposition Behaviour in Modern Legislatures" (with A Milnor), in *Legislatures in Comparative Perspective* (Kornberg (ed)) 1973; "Aspects of Coalition Payoffs in European

Parliamentary Democracies" (with E Browne), *APSR*, 1973; "Early Day Motions as Unobtrusive Measures of Backbench Opinion in Britain" (with M Tappin), *BJPS*, 1977; "The Decline of Class Voting in Britain" (with A Mugham), *APSR*, 1978. Fields: American and British politics, especially legislative behaviour; computer applications to political data.

[612]
FREDDI Giorgio
14 April 1932, Italian. Vic Bagni di Mario 10, 40136 Bologna, Italy. Degrees: Laurea in Giurisprudenza; MA (Berkeley), 1959; PhD (Berkeley), 1959; Doctoral thesis: "Legitimacy and Opposition in the Italian Judiciary: A Study of Organizational Conflict". 1962-67 Lecturer, Higher School for Administrative Sci, Bologna; 1968-69 Assistant Professor, U of Trento; 1970- Associate Professor, Professor, U of Bologna; 1976-77 Visiting Professor, Dept of Pol Sci, Berkeley; 1978 Royer Fellow of Econ and Pol Sci, Berkeley. Publs: "Per uno Studio Politico del Federalismo", *Rassegna Italiana di Sociologia*, 1965; *Attività Burocratica e Rapporto fra Politica e Amministrazione*, 1966; *L'Analisi Comparata di Sistemi Burocratici Pubblici*, 1968; "La Magistratura come Organizzazione Burocratica", *Politica del Diritto*, 1972; "Teoria dell'Organizzazione", *Dizionario di Politica*, 1975; "Le Agenzie negli USA", *Studi Parlamentari e di Politica Costituzionale*, 1975; *Conflitto e Tensioni nella Magistratura*, 1977. Fields: Organization theory; comparative politics and bureaucracy; judicial behaviour.

[613]
FREEMAN Michael
14 October 1946, British. Department of Government, University of Essex, Wivenhoe Park, Colchester CO4 3SQ, Essex, England. Degrees: BA; LL B (Stanford), 1960; PhD (Essex), 1970. Doctoral thesis: "Political Participation". 1966-67 Temporary Lecturer, U of Edinburgh; Lecturer, U of Essex. Publs: "Revolution", *British Journal of Political Science*, 1972. Fields: Contemporary political theory, especially theories of revolution.

[614]
FREI Daniel
24 October 1940, Swiss. Hohlgrasse 34, CH-5000 Aarau, Switzerland. Degrees: Dr phil (Zürich), 1964; Dipl (Graduate Inst of International Studies, Geneva) 1967. 1968- Lecturer, U of Zürich; 1971 Visiting Professor, The Bologna Center, The John Hopkins U; 1971- Professor of Pol Sci, U of Zürich. Publs: *Neutralität-Ideal oder Kalkull ? Aussenpolitisches Denken in der Schweiz*, 1967; *Dimensionen neutraler Politik*, 1969; *Kriegsverhinderung und Friedenssicherung*, 1970; *Theorien der internationalen Beziehungen*, 1977; *Sicherheit — Weltpolitische Probleme*, 1977. Fields: International relations theory; applied peace research, disengagement, de-escalation, neutralization, etc; foreign policy analysis and planning; foreign policy indicators; theory of security; theory of international relations.

[615]
FRENKEL Max
14 April 1938, Swiss. Haltenrain 1, CH-4528 Zuchwil, Switzerland. Degrees: Dr jur. (Utrecht). Doctoral thesis: "Institutionen der Verwaltungskontrolle". Secretary General of Swiss Conference on Forecasting; Visiting Fellow, Australian National U, Canberra; Director, Joint Centre for Federal and Regional Studies, Riehen. Publs: *Partnership in Federalism* (ed); various papers on questions of federalism. Fields: Constitutional law and issues; federalism.

[616]
FRERK Carsten
24 October 1945, German. Erdmannstrasse 11, D-1000 Berlin 62, FR Germany. Degrees: Dipl Politologe. Assistant, Dept of Pol, Free U of Berlin. Fields: Party theory; international party federations; parties and pressure groups; political process.

[617]
FRESCO-KAUTSKY Edith Jakobine
22 February 1925, Dutch. Grote Houw 128, 4817 RJ Breda, The Netherlands. Degrees: MD; PhD. Doctoral thesis: "Kissingers Denkwereld: Restauratie of vernieuwing". Scientific Assistant, U of Leiden. Fields: International affairs.

[618]
FREUND Julien
9 January 1921, French. 5 Chemin de la Schrann, 67220 Ville, France. Degrees: Dr. Doctoral thesis: "Essence du politique". Professeur de Soc; Directeur de l'Inst de Polimologie. Publs: *Qu'est ce que la politique*, 1968; *Le Nouvel age*, 1970; *Pareto*, 1974; *Utopie et violence*, 1978. Fields: Conflict and violence; human behaviour and behavioural patterns; research on war and peace.

[619]
FREYMOND Jacques*
1911, Swiss. Institut Universitaire de Hautes Etudes Internationales, 132 rue de Lausanne, CH 1211 Geneva 21, Switzerland. Degrees: Dr ès lettres. Director, Graduate Inst of International Studies; Professor of Contemporary History, U of Geneva. Publs: *La politique de Francois Ier à l'égard de la Savoie*, 1939; *Lénine et l'impérialisme*, 1951; *De Roosevelt à Eisenhower. La politique américaine, 1945-52*, 1953; *Le conflit sarrois, 1945-55*, 1959; *La première internationale* (ed), 1962; *Western Europe since the War*, 1964; *Etudes et documents sur la première internationale en Suisse*, 1964; *Contributions à l'histoire du Comintern*, 1965.

[620]
FREYSSINET-DOMINJON Jacqueline
25 January 1938, French. Les Martinets A, 38610 Gières, France. Degrees: Dr. Doctoral thesis: "Les manuels d'histoire de l'enseignement privé de la IIIème à la Vème Républi-que 1881-1959". Assistant, Maître-Assistant en Sci Pol. Publs: "Exploring political space: a study of French voters' preferences" (with G Mauser), in *Party Identification and Beyond* (I Budge *et al (eds))*, 1976; *La publicité, institution et discours*, 1978. Fields: Communications; political behaviour.

[621]
FRIEDBERG Erhard
13 April 1942. Austrian. Helmstedterstrasse 15, 1000 W Berlin 31, FR Germany. Degrees: Dipl (Paris); Dipl supérieur de recherche (FNSP). 1968-74 Research Fellow, Centre de Sociologie des Organisations, Paris; 1974-77 Research Fellow, International Inst of Management, Berlin; 1978- Chargé de Recherche, CNRS. Publs: *L'analyse sociologique des Organisations; L'Acteur et le Système* (with M Crozier); plus various articles on French industrial policy. Fields: Industrial policy and public policy; sociology of organized action.

[622]
FRIEDRICH Manfred*
7 January 1933, German, 3141 Octmissen, FR Germany. Degrees: Dipl rer Pol (Frankfurt), 1956. 1960-66, Scientific Assistant; 1966- Professor of Pol Sci, U of Hamburg. Publs: *Philosophie und Ökonomie beim jungen Marx*, 1960; *Opposition ohne Alternative?*, 1962; *Zwischen Positivismus und Materialismus*, 1971. Fields: German constitutional history; history of German public law; theory and practice of modern parliaments.

[623]
FRIEDRICH Paul Joachim
5 August 1938, German. Hopmannstrasse. 2/221, 5300 Bonn 2, FR Germany. Degrees: MA. Doctoral thesis: 1974-75 Research Associate, IISS, London; Assistant, U of Freiburg; Assistant, Ministry of Defence, Bonn; SPD Parliamentary Party, Bundestag, Bonn; 1966-68 Research Fellow, Hoover Inst, Stanford; Research Fellow, Forschungsinstitut, Deutsche Gesellschaft für Auswärtige Politik, Bonn. Publs: Articles in *Esprit, Neue Gesellschaft, Journal of Common Market Studies, Survival*; five chapters on Communist parties in Western Europe (France, Austria, GDR, Switzerland, West Berlin), in *Yearbook on International Communist Affairs 1968*, 1969; *Rüstungskontrolle und Sicherheit in Europa*, 1978. Fields: French Left; Western European Left and communism; defence and security policy of France and Germany; Atlantic Alliance politics; arms control; nuclear energy and nuclear nonproliferation.

[624]
FRITSCH Bruno
24 July 1926, Swiss. Aussichtsstrasse 13, CH-8704 Herrliberg, Switzerland. Degrees: Dr rer Pol (Basel); Habilitation (Basel). Doctoral thesis: "Die Geld und Kredittheorie von Karl Marx". Professor of Econ, Technical U of Karlsruhe; Professor of Econ and Head, Econ Dept, South Asia Inst, U of Heidelberg; Professor of Econ and Director, Centre for Econ Research, Swiss Federal Inst of Technology, Zürich. Publs: *Geschichte und Theorie der amerikanischen Stabilisierungspolitik 1933-39 und 1946-53*, 1959; *Die Vierte Welt*, 1973; *World Trade Flows, Integrational Structure and Conditional Forecasts* (co-author), 1971; *Bildung, Luxus oder Überlebenschance?*, 1973; *Wachstumsbegrenzung als Machtinstrument*, 1974; *Een nieuw machtsmiddel ?* "Grenzen aan de grooei", 1975; *Growth Limitation and Political Power*, 1976; *Problems of World Modelling, Political and Social Implications* (with K W Deutsch et al (eds)), 1977. Fields: International economics; international aspects of ecology; economic development; systems theory; future research.

[625]
FROGNIER André Paul
17 December 1944, Belgian. 20 Rue Florémond, 5890 Chaumont-Gistoux, Belgium. Degrees: Dr en droit; Dr en sci pol et soc. Doctoral thesis: "Changement Electoral, Distances entre Partis et Participation Politique. Etude comparative des 3 Regions Belges: La Wallonie, La Flandre et Bruxelles" (Electoral Change, Party Distances and Political Participation. Comparative Study of the 3 Belgian Regions: Walloon, Flanders and Brussels). Chargé de cours, Catholic U of Louvain. Publs: "Party Preference Spaces and Voting Change in Belgium", in *Party Identification and Beyond* (I Budge and I Crewe (eds)), 1975; "Vote, classe sociale et religion/pratique religieuse", *Res Publica*, 1978; "L'axe gauche/droite", *Res Publica*, 1976; "Parties and Cleavages in the Belgian Parliament", *Legislative Studies Quarterly*, 1978; "Le pouvoir des partis belges à la Chambre des Représentants. Un Essai de mesure de pouvoir basé sur la theorie des jeux", in *Cahiers du Crisp*, 1972. Fields: Electoral behaviour in Belgium/EEC; Belgian politics; methodology.

[626]
FROMME Friedrich Karl
10 June 1930, German. 6242 Kronberg 1, Doppesstrasse 7, FR Germany. Degrees: Dr phil (Tübingen), 1958. Doctoral thesis: "Die verfassungspolitischen Folgerungen des Parlamentarischen Rats aus Weimarer Republik und National-sozialistischer Diktatur". 1958-1964 Assistant Lecturer of Pol Sci, U of Tübingen; 1962-1964 Redakteur Süddeutscher Rundfunk Stuttgart, Frankfurt; 1964-1968 Politischer Redakteur *Frankfurter Allgemeine Zeitung*, Frankfurt; 1968-1974 Korrespondent Bonn; 1974- Redakteur *Frankfurter Allgemeine Zeitung*, Verantwortlich für Innenpolitik. Publs: *Von der Weimarer Verfassung zum Bonner Grundgesetz*, 1962; *Gesetzgebung im Widerstreit*, 1976. Fields: Comparative government; institutions; constitutional law.

[627]
FRY Geoffrey Kingdon
22 October 1937, British. 9 East Moor Road, Rundmay, Leeds LS8 9JT, England. Degrees BSc; PhD. Doctoral thesis: "The Changing Role of the Administrative Class of the British Home Civil Service 1853-1966". Civil Service; 1968- Lecturer in Pol, U of Leeds. Publs: *Statesmen in Disguise*, 1969; *The Growth of Government*, 1978; Articles in *Public Administration, Political Studies, Political Quarterly, Bulletin of Economic Research, Public Administration Bulletin, Public Law*. Fields: Modern British public administration, especially British central government; administrative history; the role of the state; comparative public administration.

[628]
FURLONG Paul Francis
22 February 1948, British. 150A Cottingham Road, Hull, North Humberside, England. Degrees: PhL (Rome); BA. Doctoral thesis: "The Capacity of Mass-Mobilization of the Catholic Church in Italy". Lecturer in Pol, Dept of Pol, U of Hull. Publs: "Il Voto Preferenza e L'Elettoraid Romano, Elezioni Politiche 1976", *Rivista Italiana Di Scienza Politica*, 1977. Fields: The Catholic church in Italy; Italian state intervention in the economy; Italian voting patterns; religion and politics in Western Europe.

[629]
FÜRST Dietrich
2 March 1940, German. Erlenweg 16, D-7752 Reichenau 2, FR Germany. Degrees: Dipl Volkswirt; Dr rer Pol; Habilitation. Doctoral thesis: "Local Contributions to Countries". Assistant, German Inst for Urban Studies, Berlin; Assistant, U of Cologne; Associate Professor, U of Konstanz. Publs: *The Fees* (with K H Hansmeyer), 1968; *The Equipment of Central Places With Infrastructure* (with K H Hansmeyer), 1970; *Industrial Location — An Empirical Investigation* (with K Zimmerman), 1973; *Community Decision Making*, 1975; *Regional Policy* (with P Klemmer and K Zimmerman), 1975; *Urban Economics*, 1977. Fields: Local and regional planning and policy making; intergovernmental relations; regional and sectoral policy making; process of urban agglomeration and its consequences on intergovernmental relations.

[630]
FURTAK Robert Karl
26 July 1930, German. Ringstrasse D 7801 Stegen üb Freiburg, Germany. Degrees: Dipl Dolmetscher (Heidelberg), 1956; Juristische Staatsprüfung (Heidelberg), 1961; Dr rer Pol (Technische Hochschule Aachen), 1965. Doctoral thesis: "Die zentrifugalen Tendenzen im Weltkommunismus, dargestellt am Beispiel der kubanischen Revolution". Lecturer for Russian Language and Soviet Studies, U of Heidelberg;

Akademischer Rat, Dept of Pol Sci, U of Freiburg; Professor of Pol Sci, Erziehungswissenschaftliche Hochschule Rheinland-Pfalz, Landau. Publs: *Kuba und der Weltkommunismus*, 1967; *Revolutionspartei und politische Stabilität in Mexico*, 1969 and 1973; *Jugoslawien: Politik, Gesellschaft, Wirtschaft*, 1975. Fields: Comparative politics, especially socialist countries and Latin-American countries; international politics, especially East-West relations; international communism.

[631]
FUSILIER Reymond
2 October 1927, French. 11 rue de Département, Paris XIXe, France. Degrees: Dr en droit; DES. Doctoral thesis: "Le parti social-démocrate suédois". Attaché, Maître de recherches, CNRS. Publs: *Le parti social-démocrate suédois — son organisation*, 1954; *Les monarchies parlementaires*, 1960; *Les pays nordiques*, 1965; *Traité sur l'organisation des services d'incendie et les corps de sapeurs-pompiers,* 1967/68; *L'âge en droit*, 1973. Fields: History of political and social change in Scandinavia.

G

[632]
GAASHOLT Øystein
3 December 1936, Norwegian. Hedeskovvej 19, 8520 Lystrup, Denmark. Degrees: BA; MA (Oregon), 1968; MA (Oregon), 1969; PhD (Oregon), 1974. Doctoral thesis: "Dissatisfaction Among Prison Inmates: A Political Perspective". 1972- Adjunkt, Lecturer, Inst of Pol Sci, U of Aarhus. Fields: Political psychology; political socialization; minorities and subcultures in the political system.

[633]
GABRIEL Jürg Martin
29 April 1940, Swiss. In der Au 42, 8706 Meilen, Switzerland. Degrees: BA; MA, 1968; PhD, 1971. Doctoral thesis: "Clausewitz Revisited". 1972-75 IRIC, U of Yaoundé, Cameroon; Lecturer, U of Zürich; Lecturer, Handelsschule KV, Zürich. Publs: *Das politische System der Schweiz*, 1977. Fields: Swiss government; African governments; comparative government.

[634]
GABRIEL Oscar W
11 July 1947, German. Eltvillerstrasse 2, 6507 Ingelheim/Rh, FR Germany. Degrees: Dipl Pol (Hamburg), 1972; Dr rer Pol (Hamburg), 1975. Doctoral thesis: "Herbert Marcuses Thesen zur Universalität der Herrschaft in der industriellen Gesellschaft". Inst für Kommunalwissenschaften, Konrad Adenauer Stiftung, St. Augustin; Inst für Politikwisschschaft, Johannes Gutenberg U, Mainz. Publs: "Strukturprobleme des lokalen Parteiensystems", in *Strukturprobleme des lokalen Parteiensystems* (O W Gabriel *et al* (eds)), 1976; "Bürgerinitiativen im lokalpolitischen Entscheidungsprozess. Entstehungbedingungen und Aktionsmuster", in *Bürgerinitiativen und repräsentatives System* (B Guggenberger and U Kempf (eds)), 1978; "Methodologie der Politikwissenschaft", in *Grundkurs Politische Theorie* (O W Gabriel (ed)), 1978; "Systemtheories", in *Grundkurs Politische Theorie* (O W Gabriel (ed)), 1978; "Mängelanalyse des politischen Willenbildungsprozesses auf lokaler Ebene", in *Partizipation und Representation* (with L Albertin *et al*), 1978. Fields: Modern political theory; local politics; political economy/sociology; methods of empirical social research.

[635]
GALIZIA Mario*
14 November 1921, Italian. Via Stefano Jacini 30, 00191 Rome, Italy. Degrees: Laurea in Giurisprudenza. 1947-65 Judge; 1965 Professor, U of Siena; 1966-70 Professor, U of Pavia; Lawyer and Professor of Public Law, U of Florence. Publs: *La Teoria della Sovranità dal Meolivero alla Rivoluzione Francese*, 1951; *Scienza Giuridica e Diritto Costituzionale*, 1954; *Profili Storico-comparativi della Saluza del Diritto Costituzionale*, 1963; *La Libertà di Circolazione e Joggiorno*, 1967; *Studi sui Rapporti fra Parlamento e Governo*, 1972.

[636]
GALLHOFER Irmtraud Nora
16 August 1945, Dutch. Blauwburgwal 201, Amsterdam, The Netherlands. Degrees: PhD (Vienna), 1968; Dr (Amsterdam), 1973. Doctoral thesis: "Der Damenfriede von Cambrai, 1529". Research Assistant, Free U of Amsterdam. Publs: "L'application d'un modèle de décision à des données historiques" (with W E Saris), *Revue Française de Science Politique*, 1975; "Recente ontwikkelingen op het gebied van geautomatiseerde inhoudsanalyse" (with W E Saris), *Acta Politica*, 1975; "Een begrippenapparaat voor de beschrijving van redeneringen van Politici" (with W E Saris), *Acta Politica*, 1978; "In Search of Semantic Characteristics for Machine Coding" (co-author), *Methoden en Data Nieuwsbrief*, 1978; "Coders' Reliability in the Study of Decision-Making Concepts, Replications in Time and Across Topics", *Methoden en Data Nieuwsbrief*, 1978; "A Validation Study of Hoesti's Dictionary" (with W E Saris and E Morton), *Quantity and Quality*, 1978. Fields: Content analysis; decision-making.

[637]
GALNOOR Itzhak
5 December 1940, Israeli. Department of Political Science, Hebrew University, Jerusalem, Israel. Degrees: BA; MPA (Syracuse); PhD (Syracuse). Doctoral thesis: "Programme Budgeting in Institutions of Higher Education". Prime Minister's Office, Unit for Social Welfare; Analyst, Ministry for Foreign Affairs, Dept of International Cooperation; 1979- Chairman, Dept of Pol Sci, Hebrew U of Jerusalem and Director, Public Administration Graduate Programme, Hebrew U of Jerusalem. Publs: "New Systems Budgeting and the Developing Nations" (with B M Gross), *International Social Science Journal*, 1969; *Social Information for Developing Countries* (ed), 1971; "The Influence of Inquiry Commissions on Government Policy-making", *Netivei Irgaun U'Minhal*, 1973; "Social Indicators for Social Planning: The Case of Israel", *Social Indicators Research*, 1974; "Reforms of Public Expenditure in Great Britain", *Canadian Public Administration*, 1974; "Values and Ideology in National Planning" (with R Bilski), in *Towards More Systematic Thinking on Israel's Future* (C Sheffer (ed)); "Government Secrecy: Exchanges, Intermediaries and Middlemen", *Public Administration Review*, 1975; *Government Secrecy in Democracies* (ed), 1977. Fields: Israeli politics and administration; comparative politics and administration; public administration; government secrecy.

[638]
GAMBLE Andrew Michael
15 August 1947, British. 4 College Street, Sheffield S10 2PH, England. Degrees: BA; MA (Durham), 1969; PhD (Cambridge), 1975. Doctoral thesis: "The Conservative Nation: Electoral Perspectives within the British Conservative Party 1945-1970". Lecturer, Dept of Pol Theory and Inst, U of Sheffield. Publs: *The Conservative Nation*, 1974; *From Alienation to Surplus Value* (with P Walton), 1972; *Capitalism in Crisis: Inflation and the State* (with P Walton), 1976. Fields: Political economy; British politics; political theory; the development of political studies.

[639]
GANTZEL Klaus Jürgen
21 February 1934, German. Ludolfstrasse 42, D-2000 Hamburg, FR Germany. Degrees: Dr rer Pol (Cologne), 1961; Habilitation (Mannheim), 1970. Doctoral thesis: "Wesen und Begriff der mittelständischen Unternehmung". 1958-63 Research Assistant, Cologne; 1964-70 Assistant in Pol Sci, Mannheim; 1971-75 Research Group Leader, Peace Research Inst, Frankfurt; 1972-76 Honorary Professor, U of Frankfurt; 1975- Professor of Pol Sci, U of Hamburg. Publs: *System und Akteur — Beiträge zur vergleichenden Kriegsursachenforschung*, 1972; *Konflikt-Eskalation-Krise: Sozialwissenschaftliche Studien zum Ausbruch des Ersten Weltkrieges* (co-ed), 1972; *Internationale Beziehungen als System* (ed), 1973; *Herrschaft und Befreiung in der Weltgesellschaft* (ed), 1975; *Kapitalistische Penetration in Europa* (ed), 1976; *Zur Multinationalisierung des Kapitals* (ed), 1976; *Afrika zwischen Kolonialismus und Neo-Kolonialismus* (ed), 1976. Fields: International relations, structural history and political economy of the international system since the 14th century; armament dynamics and disarmament; causes of war; East-West conflict and detente; under-development and structural dependency; theory and analysis of modern state functions.

[640]
GARDNER John*
8 December 1939, British. Department of Government, University of Manchester, Manchester M13 9PL, England. Degrees: BA. 1962-66 Research Postgraduate Student, School of Oriental and African Studies, U of London; 1963 Visiting Fellow, Inst of Modern Asian Studies, Hong Kong; Lecturer in Government, U of Manchester. Publs: "The Wu-fan Campaign in Shanghai", in *Chinese Communist Politics in Action* (A D Barnett (ed)), 1971. Fields: Political participation in China; mass mobilization and education in the Chinese revolution.

[641]
GARLICHS Dietrich
29 December 1947, German. Breite Strasse 14, 1000 Berlin 41, FR Germany. Degrees: Diplom in Verwaltungswissenschaften (Konstanz); MPA (Harvard). Research Fellow, International Inst of Management, Berlin. Fields: Governmental reorganization; intergovernmental relations; federal regulation and control.

[642]
GÄRTNER Heinz
7 March 1951, Austrian. Olsa 45, A-9360 Friesach/Ktn, Austria. Degrees: Dr phil. Doctoral thesis: "The Communist Party in Austria: Elements of Dependence". Publs: "Towards a Project Oriented Political Science", *Österreichische Zeitschrift für Politikwissenschaft*, 1976; "The Communist Party in Austria", *Österreichische Zeitschrift für Politikwissenschaft*, 1978. Fields: World communism; dependence analyses; Third World.

[643]
GARVIN Thomas C
7 July 1943, Irish. Ardeevin, Upper Kilmacud Road, Dublin 14, Ireland. Degrees: BA; MA (Ireland), 1966; PhD (USA), 1974. Doctoral thesis: "Political Parties in Dublin". Administrative Officer, Government of Ireland; Teaching Assistant, U of Georgia; Assistant Lecturer, Lecturer, U Coll, Dublin. Publs: Articles in *Economic and Social Review, Political Studies, British Journal of Political Science, European Journal of Political Research, Social Studies*. Fields: Political parties; voting behaviour; political development; legislatures; political ideology; Irish politics generally.

[644]
GASTEYGER Curt
20 March 1929, Swiss. 38 Crêts-de-Champel, 1206-Genève, Switzerland. Degrees: Dr jur (Zürich), 1954. Doctoral thesis: "Die politische Homogenität als Faktor der Föderation". 1964-68 Director of Programmes, International Inst for Strategic Studies, London; 1968-74 Deputy Director, Atlantic Inst for International Affairs, Paris; 1974- Professor for International Relations and Strategic Studies, Graduate Inst of International Studies. Publs: "New Dimensions of Conflict and Order", in *International Relations in a Changing World*, 1977; "The Traffic of Arms: Between Facts and Fictions", *Information*, 1977; *Die beiden deutschen Staaten in der Weltpolitik*, 1976; "Konfrontation und Koexistenz mit den Vereinigten Staaten", *Osteuropa-Handbuch 'Sowjetunion: Aussenpolitik 1953-1973'*, 1976; "Sicherheitspolitik", *Handbuch der Schweizerischen Aussenpolitik*, 1975. Fields: International relations, strategic and international security studies.

[645]
GAUDEMET Paul Marie
15 May 1914, French. 31 Boulevard Suchet, 75016 Paris, France. Degrees: Dr en droit. Professeur, Faculté de Droit, U de Nancy; Directeur, Dept de Sci Pol, Centre Universitaire Européen, U de Nancy; Professeur, U de Paris. Publs: *Le pouvoir exécutif dans les pays occidentaux*, 1956; *Précis de finances publiques*, 1974-77. Fields: Financial and political reports; administrative science.

[646]
GAZIE Daniel Charles
10 February 1947, French, 41 rue du Théâtre, 75014 Paris, France. Degrees: Dr d'Etat. Doctoral thesis: "Indifférence et politisation-l'intérêt pour la politique dans les sociétés occidentales". 1971- Maître-assistant, Dept de Sci Pol, U de Paris I. Publs: *Les professionnels de la politique*, 1973; "Economie des partis et rétribution du militantisme", *Revue Française de Science Politique: Droit constitutionnel et institutions politiques*, 1976. Fields: Political participation; political involvement; political parties; political recruitment, political elites; electoral sociology.

[647]
GEBHARDT Jürgen
27 July 1934, German. D-8012 Ottobrunn, Bozenestrasse 7, 463 Bochum Hustadtring 81/903, FR Germany. Degrees: Dr phil (Munich), 1961; Habilitation (Munich), 1969. Doctoral thesis: "Politik und Eschatologie-Studien zur Geschichte der Hegelschen Schule 1830-40". 1959-1961 Wiss Assistent, U of Munich; 1962-1963 Research Associate in Government, Harvard U: 1963-1965 Associate Professor of Pol Sci, Western Reserve U; 1965-1969 Wiss Assistent und Lehrebeauftragter, U of Munich; 1969 Visiting Associate Professor of Pol Sci, East Texas State U; 1969-1971 Universitätsdozent, U of Munich; 1971 Ordentlicher Professor für Pol Wissenschaft, Ruhr-U, Bochum. Publs: *Politik und Eschatologie* (ed), 1963; *Die Revolution des Geistes* (J Harrington (ed)), 1968; *Die Krise des Amerikanismus*, 1976. Fields: Politics, theory and philosophy; history of political ideas; comparative politics.

[648]
GEILING Martin
27 July 1938, German. 1 Mueckendell, 6602 Saarbrücken-Dudweiler, FR Germany. Degrees: Dipl Pol Sci; PhD (Free U of Berlin). Doctoral thesis: "The Development of American Strategic Thinking and its Impact on US Security Policy Towards the USSR, 1945-1963". 1964-1965 Research Assistant, Free U of Berlin; 1965-1967 Visiting Research Fellow, MIT, Cambridge, Mass, USA; Lecturer in Pol Sci, Saar U; Vice-Chairman, Inst of Educational and Social Research, Saarbrücken. Publs: *Aussenpolitik und Nuklearstrategie*, 1975; *Politik in der fragmentieren Gesellschaft: sozialer Konflikt und politische Kultur in den Niederlanden, Belgien, Österreich und der Schweiz*, 1978. Fields: Comparative politics; elite studies; organizational behaviour; democratic theory and political influence; European integration; local and regional politics.

[649]
GEISMANN Georg*
11 February 1935, German. 69 Heidelberg, Freiburger Strasse 62, FR Germany. Degrees: Dipl Kaufmann (Köln), 1959; Der rer Pol (Köln), 1964. Doctoral thesis: "Political Structure and Governmental System of the Netherlands". 1969- Assistant, Inst für Sozialwissenschaften, U of Mannheim. Publs: *Politische Struktur und Regierungssystem der Niederlande*, 1964. Fields: Theory of the social sciences; theory of political philosophy, especially democratic elitism, traditional and modern liberalism, property, Karl Marx.

[650]
GÉLARD Patrice*
3 August 1938, French. 12 Route d'Octeville, 76310 Sainte-Adresse, France. Degrees: Lic en droit, 1960; DES droit public, 1965; DES sci pol, 1961; Dipl de droit comparé; Dipl de l'Ecole Nationale des Langues Orientales Vivantes, 1960; Dr d'Etat en sci pol, 1962; Dr en Etudes Slaves, 1962. 1965-68 Assistant, Faculté de Conférences Agrégé, U de Lille II; 1973- Professor of Public Law and Pol Sci, U of Lille. Publs: *Les organisations de masse en Union Soviétique*, 1965; *Lénine: L'Etat et la révolution*, 1971; *L'administration locale en URSS*, 1972. Fields: Soviet Union; socialist states; comparative politics; models of political development; new states; modern political analysis of political systems.

[651]
GEMZELL Carl-Axel Uno
20 October 1931, Swedish. Mantalskroken 10, S-222 47 Lund, Sweden. Degrees: Dr fil (Lund). Doctoral thesis: "Raeder, Hitler und Skandinavien: Der Kampf für einen Maritimen Operationsplan". 1965-77 Assistant Professor of History, U of Lund; Professor of Contemporary History, Roskilde U Centre. Publs: *Raeder, Hitler und Skandinavien: Der Kampf für einen maritimen Operationsplan*, 1965; *Organization, Conflict, and Innovation: A Study of German Naval Strategic Planning, 1888-1940*, 1973; "En tysk operationsstudie mot Sverige", *Historisk Tidskrift*, 1975; "Tysk militär planläggning: fall Sverige", *Scandia*, 1976; "Första världskriget och den irländska konflikten", in *Festskrift till Sverker Rosén*, 1975; "Lucius, Wallenberg och Ryssland: Storfinans och politik under första världskriget", *Aktuellt och Historiskt*, 1976. Fields: Foreign policy and international relations; organizations; political protest; historiography.

[652]
GENTILE Roraria Maria
19 August 1946, Italian. Via S Euplio 13, Catania, Italy. Degrees: Laurea. Doctoral thesis: "Partito Comunista e Lotte Contadine in Sicilia". Researcher, Isvi, Catania; Tutor, Lecturer, Faculty of Pol Sci, U of Catania. Publs: *Democrazia Cristiana e Potere nel Mezzogiorno* (with M Caciagli *et al*), 1978. Fields: The formation of the fascist political class after 1929 in Sicily; the reconstruction of the Italian Communist party in Catania in the post war period.

[653]
GEORGE David Alexander*
20 December 1940, British. 42 Jesmond Park Court, Newcastle-upon-Tyne NE7 7BN, England. Degrees: BSc. 1967- Lecturer in Pol, U of Newcastle-upon-Tyne. Fields: Fascist ideology 1918-45 in Italy, France, Germany.

[654]
GEORGE Stephen Alan
14 October 1949, British. 21 Tullibardine Road, Sheffield, S11 7GL, England. Degrees: BA; M Phil (Leicester). 1971-72 Research Assistant, Dept of Contemporary Studies, Huddersfield Polytechnic; Lecturer, Dept of Pol Theory and Inst, U of Sheffield. Publs: "Paul-Henri Spaak and a Paradox in Belgian Foreign Policy", *British Journal of International Studies*, 1975; "The Reconciliation of the 'Classical' and 'Scientific' Approaches to International Relations", *Millennium*, 1976; "Schools of Thought in International Relations", in *The Reason of States* (M Donelan (ed)), 1978. Fields: The European community; the development of the study of politics and international relations as distinct academic disciplines.

[655]
GEORGEL Jacques
2 October 1932, French. Degrees: Dr d'Etat. Doctoral thesis: "La quatrième République à la recherche d'une politique gouvernementale". Professor, U of Rennes; Professor, Inst Universitaire Européen, Florence. Publs: *Sociologie politique* (co-author), 1966; *Politique de Chateaubriand* (co-author), 1966; *Le sénat dans l'adversité*, 1967; *Le franquisme*, 1970; *Critiques et réformes des constitutions de la République, 1959-60*; *Le Conseil constitutionnel* (co-author), 1972; *La direction collégiale en Union Soviétique* (co-author), 1973; *Centenaire de la 3ème République*, 1975. Fields: Political institutions; Spain and Portugal.

[656]
GÉRARD-LIBOIS J
3 December 1923, Belgian. 28 Avenue du Houx, 1170 Bruxelles, Belgium. Degrees: Dr Law (Liège), 1946. Chairman, CRISP; President, CEDAF. Publs: *Sécession au Katanga*, 1963; *Congo*, 1965; *L'an 40, la Belgique occupée* (co-author). Fields: Political socialization; contemporary Belgian history; decolonization: myth and reality, Central Africa.

[657]
GERAS Norman Myron
25 August 1943, British. 14 Mayville Drive, Manchester M20 9RB, England. Degrees: MA. 1965-67 Studentship, Nuffield Coll, Oxford; Lecturer in Government, U of Manchester. Publs: "Political Participation in the Revolutionary Thought of Leon Trotsky", in *Participation in Politics* (G Parry (ed)), 1972; *The Legacy of Rosa Luxemburg*, 1976; articles in *Ideology in Social Science* (R Blackburn (ed)), 1972; *Western*

Marxism: A Critical Reader, 1977; *Revolution and Class Struggle* (R Blackburn (ed)), 1977. Fields: Political thought of Leon Trotsky; history of contemporary Marxist theory; structuralism in modern social theory; Marxism.

[658]
GERBAUD Francoise
16 August 1944, French. 170 Galerie de L'Arlequin, Appt 8503, 38100 Grenoble, France. Attachée de recherche. Publs: *Evaluation de la préoccupation "environnement cadre de vie dans l'administration française"* (co-author), 1975; *Administration et population face aux transformations du cadre de vie* (co-author), 1978; *Schéma d'orientation et d'aménagement des Alpes du Nord* (co-author), 1977. Fields: Environment; space and politics; country planning in mountain regions.

[659]
GERDES Dirk
9 February 1945, German. Schlosswolfsbrunnenweg 5a, D-6900 Heidelberg, FR Germany. Degrees: Dr rer Soz. Doctoral thesis: "Abschreckung und Entspannung-Legitimatorische Folgeprobleme bundesrepublikanischer Entspannungspolitik". Tutor, Inst für Politikwissenschaft, U of Tübingen; Studienreferendar am Studienseminar, Tübingen; Wiss Assistent, Inst für Pol Wissenschaft, Heidelberg. Publs: *Legitimationsprobleme und Aussenpolitik-Ein Unterrichtsmodell*, 1978; "Die Relevanz der Ostpolitik für gesellschaftliche Veränderungen in der BRD-Entspannung und Zerfall normativer Kontrolle in einer penetrierten Entspannungsgesellschaft", in *Die Ostpolitik der Bundesrepublik* (Jahn/Rittberger (eds)), 1974; "Europäische Direktwahlen", *SOWI*, 1978. Fields: Theory of international relations; European integration; regionalism; national minorities; "ethnicity" in Western Europe.

[660]
GERIN Paul E A
22 September 1933, Belgian. 5 rue J Hermesse, B-4500 Jupille-sur-Meuse, Liège, Belgium. Degrees: Dr en philosophie et lettres. Doctoral thesis: "Les courants de pensée et d'action sociales". Chef de travaux, Chargé de cours, U de Liège; Maître de conférences, U de Louvain. Publs: *Catholiques liégeois et question sociale (1833-1914)*, 1959; *Bibliographie de l'histoire de Belgique (1789-21 Juillet 1914)*, 1960; *Initiation à la documentation écrite de la période contemporaine (fin du XVIIème siècle à nos jours)*, 1970; *La presse liégeoise de 1850 à 1914* (with M L Warnotte), 1971; *Presse populaire catholique et presse démocrate chrétienne en Wallonie et à Bruxelles (1830-1914)*, 1975. Fields: Contemporary institutions; information; bibliography.

[661]
GERLACH Herbert Wolfgang
19 November 1942, German. Sternwaldstrasse 31, D-78 Freiburg, FR Germany. Degrees: Dr phil (Freiburg). Doctoral thesis: "Die Berlinpolitik der Kennedy-Administration, eine Fallstudie zum aussenpolitischen Verhalten der Kennedy-Regierung in der Berlinkrise". 1968 DAAD Research Fellowship, U of Harvard; 1976 Adenauer Research Fellowship; 1976 Presidential Campaign; 1976- Wiss Assistent, Pädagogische Hochschule Esslingen. Publs: *Die Berlinpolitik der Kennedy-Administration, eine Fallstudie zum aussenpolitischen Verhalten der Kennedy-Regierung in der Berlinkrise 1961*, 1977; *The American Presidential Campaign 1976*, 1978. Fields: Foreign policy of the USA; Western European states; international relations.

[662]
GERLICH Peter
17 December 1939, Austrian. Pokornygasse 23, A-1190 Vienna, Austria. Degrees: MA Comparative Law (Columbia), 1962; Dr jur (Vienna), 1964. 1966-73 Head Assistant, Dept of Pol, Inst of Advanced Studies, Vienna; 1974 Assistant Professor, Technical U of Brauschweig, FR Germany; 1975- Professor of Pol Sci, U of Vienna. Publs: *Nationalratswahl*, 1966; *Vienna: Jugend und Volk* (co-ed), 1966; *Abgeordnete in der Parteiendemokratie* (with H Kramer), 1969; *Parlamentarische Kontrolle im politischen System*, 1973. Fields: Comparative politics; legislative studies; Austrian politics.

[663]
GERMANN Raimund E
18 January 1940, Swiss. 19 Avenue Petit-Senn, CH-1225 Chêne-Bourg, Genève, Switzerland. Degrees: Dr (Fribourg), 1968; MA (Wisconsin), 1971; Agrégé (Fribourg), 1975. Doctoral thesis: "Verwaltung und Einheitspartei in Tunesien". 1971- Chargé de recherches, U de Genève; 1975 Rédacteur en chef, *l'Annuaire Suisse de Science Politique*; 1975- Chargé de cours, U de St-Gall; 1976- Chargé de cours, U de Fribourg. Publs: *Verwaltung und Einheitspartei in Tunesien*, 1968; *Verwaltung im Umbruch* (co-author), 1972; *Pouvoir et administration au Maghreb* (co-author), 1975; *Politische Innovation und Verfassungsreform*, 1975; *Fédéralisme en action: l'aménagement du territoire* (co-author), 1978. Fields: Comparative politics; public administration; planning; policy analysis.

[664]
GERSHUNY Jonathan Israel
16 September 1949, British. 17 Sudeley Street, Brighton, Sussex, England. Degrees: BSc; MSc (Strathclyde); D Phil (Sussex). Doctoral thesis: "Rationality and the Choice of Public Policy". Research Associate, Dept of Transport Technology, Loughborough; Fellow, Science Policy Research Unit, U of Sussex. Publs: *After Industrial Society?*, 1978; "The Myth of the Service Economy", *Futures*, 1977; "Technology Assessment: Oversold and Underachieving", *Futures*, 1977; *Towards a Social Assessment of Technology*, 1976; "Social Justice and Public Policy Making", in *Socio-technics* (A B Cherns (ed)), 1976; "The Choice of Scenarios", *Futures*, 1976; "The Non-Paradox of Swing", *Journal of Political Science*, 1974; "Superconductivity: Transport Technology with Nowhere to go", *Lloyds List*, 1976. Fields: Post industrial society; technology assessment; social and technological forecasting.

[665]
GERSTENBERGER Heide
21 July 1940, German. Schwachhauser Ring 6, 2800 Bremen, FR Germany. Degrees: Dipl Sozialwirt (Göttingen), 1964; Dr disc Pol (Göttingen), 1969. Doctoral thesis: "Die konservative Revolution", 1969; "Zur politischen Ökonomie der bürgerlichen Gesellschaft", 1972; 1966- Wiss Assistent in Seminar Wissenschaft von der Pol, U of Göttingen; 1972 Privatdozentin, U of Göttingen. Publs: *Die konservative Revolution*, 1969; *Zur politischen Ökonomie der bürgerlichen Gesellschaft*, 1972. Fields: Political theory; theory of the capitalist state; theory and history of bourgeois society.

[666]
GERSTLE Jacques Georges
9 July 1948, French. 32 rue Falguière, 75015 Paris, France. Degrees: Lic en droit; DES sci pol; DES information et communication; Dr d'Etat. Doctoral thesis: "Permanence et changement du langage socialiste". Assistant, Dept de Sci Pol, U de Paris I. Publs: *Giscard d'Estaing- Mitterrand-54774 mots pour convaincre*, 1976; "Qui réforme ce

message?'', *Projet*, 1978; *Lexique de sociologie politique*, 1978. Fields: Political communication; mass media: content analysis; persuasion and propaganda; symbolic aspects of political life.

[667]
GIBBENS John Richard
29 October 1945, British. Almgill, 64 Water End, Brompton, Northallerton, North Yorkshire, England. Degrees: BSc; MA (Durham), 1969. Doctoral thesis: "John Grote's Philosophy of Practice". 1969-77 Part-time Lecturer, Newcastle Polytechnic; 1977- Lecturer in Pol and Philosophy, Teeside Polytechnic. Fields: Political theory, especially Victorian thought and the origins of idealism in England; political philosophy, especially contemporary political analysis.

[668]
GIBBS Norman Henry
17 April 1910, British. Flexneys House, Stanton Harcourt, Oxford OX8 1RP, England. Degrees: MA; D Phil. Doctoral thesis: "The Administration of the Mediaeval Borough of Reading". Fellow and Tutor in Modern History and Pol, Merton Coll, Oxford; 1953-77 Chichele Professor of the History of War, U of Oxford; Fellow, Emeritus Professor, All Souls Coll, Oxford. Publs: *The British Cabinet System* (ed); *Grand Strategy: British Rearmament Policy 1933-39*. Fields: 19th and 20th century; military history and strategic thought.

[669]
GIDDINGS Philip James
5 April 1946, British. Department of Politics, University of Reading, Whiteknights, Reading RG6 2AA, England. Degrees: BA; MA; D Phil (Oxon), 1972. Doctoral thesis: "Agricultural Marketing Boards as Political and Administrative Instruments". 1970-72 Temporary Lecturer in Public Administration, U of Exeter; 1972- Lecturer in Pol, U of Reading. Fields: Nondepartmental organizations in British government; the politics of public expenditure; the impact of recent changes in the machinery of government in Britain and the civil service; policy-making in the Conservative party; redress of citizens' grievances.

[670]
GIDLUND Gullan
14 December 1945, Swedish. Törnskatevägen 1, 90237 Umeå, Sweden. Degrees: BA. Assistant Lecturer, U of Umeå. Publs: "Partimål — en Studie av Målprioriteringar Bland Företrädare för små Partier", *Politik*, 1977; "Politiska Poster och Partiaktivitet. En Undersökning bland Socialdemokratiska Politiker i Västerbotten 1978" (with J Gidlund); *Arbetslivet i ett Politiskt Perspektiv. Översikt och Bibliografi rörande Svensk Statsvetenskaplig forskning*. Fields: Party finance; work and political behaviour.

[671]
GIDLUND Janerik
7 June 1947, Swedish. Törnskatevägen 1, S-902 37 Umeå, Sweden. Degrees: BA. Consultant, UN Association in Sweden; Acting Research Assistant, Dept of Pol Sci, U of Umeå. Publs:. *Småpartier i den Kommunala Demokratin*, 1975; *Planering och Medinflytande. Ett Forskningsprogram om Beslutsprocessen vid fysisk Planering på Kommunal Nivå*, 1976; *Politiska Poster och Partiaktivitet. En Undersökning bland Socialdemokratiska Politiker i Västerbotten* (with Gidlund), 1978. Fields: Local government; grassroots organizations and small parties.

[672]
GILBERT Claude
8 September 1948, French. 6 rue Fantin-Latour, 38 Grenoble, France. Degrees: Dr d'Etat. Doctoral thesis: "Vitry, municipalité communiste". Chercheur contractuel, CERAT; Chargé de cours, IEP and Attaché de recherche, CNRS. Publs: Various articles on the nouvelle petite bourgeoisie urbaine.

[673]
GILG Peter
17 March 1922, Swiss. Haspelweg 50, CH-3006 Berne, Switzerland. Degrees: Dr phil. Doctoral thesis: "Die Entstehung der demokratischen Bewegung und die soziale Frage". 1950-55 Librarian, Stadt- und Universitätsbibliothek; 1955-65 Foreign affairs editor, *Der Bund*, Berne; Assistant director, Forschungszentrum für schweizerische Pol, U of Berne; Professor of contemporary history, Inst of History, U of Berne. Publs: *Die Erneuerung des demokratischen Denkens im Wilhelminischen Deutschland*, 1965; *Jugendliches Drängen in der schweizerischen Politik*, 1974; *Année politique suisse* (co-author), 1965. Fields: Swiss political parties and movements; elections and referenda in 20th century Switzerland.

[674]
GILHOLDES Pierre
23 February 1932, French. 2 Allée Rembrandt, 94800 Villejuif, France. Degrees: Agrégé (Paris), 1964. Researcher, FNSP. Publs: *Tableaux des partis politiques en Amérique du Sud* (co-author); *Agrarian problems and peasant movements* (co-author), 1970; *Politics and violence, the agrarian question in Colombia* (co-author); *Paysans de Panama*; *Colombia*; *La terre et l'homme*. Fields: Latin-America; Colombia; Central America; peasants, military and violence.

[675]
GILL Peter
26 February 1947, British. 85 Entwistle Heights, Liverpool L8 7AW, England. Degrees: BSc; MA (Essex), 1970. 1970-73 Lecturer, Fareham Technical Coll, Hants; 1973-74 Temporary Lecturer, Dept of Government, U of Essex; Lecturer, Dept of Soc Studies, Liverpool Polytechnic. Fields: Politics of the United States; relationship of law and politics; teaching methods in politics.

[676]
GILLESPIE Richard Henry Charles
18 February 1952, British. 11 Clayton Park Square, Brandling Village, Newcastle-upon-Tyne NE2 4DP, England. Degrees: BA. Doctoral thesis: "The Peronist Left of Argentina". Temporary Lecturer, Dept of Pol, U of Newcastle-upon-Tyne. Publs: "Armed Struggle in Argentina", in *Latin American Politics Reader*. Fields: Latin American politics; Argentina; Peronism; Latin American left.

[677]
GILLI Jean Paul
4 October 1930, French. 12 rue du Regard, 75006 Paris, France. Degrees: B of Law (Aix-Marseille), 1952; MA Law (Paris), 1959; LLD (Paris), 1960; PhD (Paris), 1960. 1954-60 Barrister, Court of Appeal, Paris; 1958-60 Instructor, Law School, U of Paris; 1960-62 Assoc Professor, Law School, U of Grenoble; 1962-64 Assoc Professor, Law School, U of Nice, U of Aix-Marseille; 1964- Professor, Law School, U of Nice; 1965-68 Professor, Nat Museum of Arts and Crafts, Nice; 1968- Director, Centre of Admin Studies; 1970-71 Président, U of Paris-Dauphine. Publs: *The Judicial Cause of Action*, 1962; *The Cooperation between Government and Organizations of Employers*

and Workers in France; The National Property, 1962; *Casebook in the Field of Urbanism,* 1974; *The Administrative Aspects of Regionalization,* 1975; *Towards a New Definition of Property Rights,* 1976. Fields: Administrative science; local and university administration.

[678]
GIRARD Alain*
13 March 1914, French. Institut National d'Etudes Démographiques, 27 rue du Commandeur, Paris XIVème, France. Degrees: Dr ès lettres. Professeur, Sorbonne; Conseiller technique, Inst National d'Etudes Démographiques; Directeur, *Sondages.* Publs: *Manifestations et mesure de l'opinion publique,* 1958; *L'opinion publique et la presse,* 1964; *La réussite sociale en France,* 1961; *Problèmes contemporains de population,* 1967. Fields: Public opinion; political demography; sociology of education.

[679]
GIROD Roger
24 March 1921, Swiss. 1232 Confignon, Genève, Switzerland. Degrees: PhD (Geneva), 1952. Doctoral thesis: "Attitudes collectives et relations humaines: tendances actuelles des sciences sociales américaines". 1949-51 UNESCO, Paris; 1952 Professeur de Sociologie, U de Genève; Member, Research Committee on Pol Sci, International Sociological Association; Professeur de Sociologie, U de Genève. Publs: *Attitudes collectives et relations humaines: tendances actuelles des sciences sociales américaines,* 1952; *Etudes sociologiques sur les couches salariées: ouvriers et employés,* 1961; *Milieu social et orientation de la carrière des adolescents* (with J F Rouillier), 1961-68; *Mobilité sociale,* 1971; *L'étude de la politique sociale: enseignement et recherche dans quelques pays d'Europe* (with P de Laubier), 1974; *Inégalité — Inégalités: Analyse de la mobilité sociale,* 1977; *L'école et la vie,* 1977. Fields: Political power and social stratification; social mobility.

[680]
GLADDISH Kenneth Raymond
17 October 1928, British. Department of Politics, The University, Whiteknights, Reading RG6 2AA, England. Degrees: BA. 1952-61 Colonial Administrative Service, East Africa; 1962- U of Reading; 1965-74 Sub-Dean, Faculty of Letters and Soc Sci; 1967- Senior Lecturer in Pol; 1974- Director of Studies, Combined Soc Sci Programme. Publs: "The Yield of African Politics", *Political Studies,* 1965; "Evolving Systems of Government", *Africa; Journal of Contemporary History,* 1969; "Two-Party versus Multi-Party: Britain and the Netherlands", *Acta Politica,* 1972; *Parliamentary Affairs,* 1974. Fields: African politics, changing systems and their analysis; separatism and minorities; politics in the Netherlands and in Denmark.

[681]
GLAESSNER Gert Joachim
13 September 1944, German. Konstanzer Strasse 57, D-1000 Berlin 31, FR Germany. Degrees: Dr rer Pol; Dipl Pol. Doctoral thesis: "Gesellschaftliche Leitung und Kaderpolitik in der DDR, dargestellt am Beispiel des Staatsapparates". Wiss Mitarbeiter, Zentralinstitut für sozialwissenschaftliche Forschung, Free U of Berlin. Publs: *Herrschaft durch Kader. Leitung der Gesellschaft und Kaderpolitik in der DDR am Beispiel des Staatsapparates* (with I Rudolph), 1977; *Macht durch Wissen. Zum Zusammenhang von Bildungspolitik, Bildungssystem und Kaderqualifizierung in der DDR,* 1978. Fields: Political sociology; East Europe, DDR; education, economy and planning.

[682]
GLASS Stanley Thomas
7 September 1932, British. Department of Politics, University of Keele, Staffordshire, England. Degrees: BA; B Litt (Oxon), 1963. 1960-63 Assistant Lecturer, Dept of Pol, Queen's U, Belfast; 1963- Assistant Lecturer, Lecturer, Dept of Pol, U of Keele. Publs: *The Responsible Society*, 1966. Fields: History of political ideas.

[683]
GLASTRA VAN LOON Jan Frederik*
16 March 1920, Dutch. Molenstraat 27, The Hague, The Netherlands. Degrees: M of Law (Leiden), 1949; Dr of Law (Leiden), 1958. Clerk, Permanent Committee for Justice, Second Chamber, States General, The Netherlands; Professor of Law, U of Leiden. Publs: *Begrip van Het Recht*, 1964; *Norm En Handleiding, Bydrage tot de Kentheoretische Fundering der Sociale Wetenschappen*, 1958; *Guide to Foreign Legal Materials, Belgium, Luxembourg, Netherlands* (co-editor, co-author), 1968. Fields: Epistemology and methodology of the social sciences; the role of belief systems in social change.

[684]
GLEDITSCH Nils Petter
17 July 1942, Norwegian. International Peace Research Inst, Oslo, Raadhusgt 4, Oslo 1, Norway. Degrees: Magister (Oslo), 1968. 1964-68 Research Assistant; 1968- Research Fellow; 1972, 1977-78 Executive Director, International Peace Research Inst, Oslo; 1976 Ed, *Journal of Peace Research*. Publs: Kamp uten Våpen (ed), 1965; *Norge i Verdenssamfunnet: en Statistisk Håndbok*, 1970; *Krigsstaten Norge* (with S Lodgaard), 1970; *De Utro Tjenere. Embetsverket i EF-kampen* (with J Elster and Ø Østerud (ed)), 1974; *Kampen om EF* (with O Hellevik), 1977. Fields: Military policy; international interaction patterns.

[685]
GOETSCHIN Pierre
20 May 1923, Swiss. Ecole des Hautes Etudes Commerciales, Dorigny, 1015 Lausanne, Switzerland. Degrees: Dr Pol Sci (Lausanne); Lic Econ (Lausanne). Employed in industry and banking in Switzerland and abroad; Professor, IMEDE Management Development, Inst and U of Lausanne. Publ: *L'évolution du marché monétaire de Londres — Institutions et politique monétaire*, 1958. Fields: Private and public management; international business; impact of politics on business planning and international strategy.

[686]
GOGUEL Francois
3 February 1909, French. 1 rue Récamier, 75007 Paris, France. Degrees: Dip (IEP Paris), 1929; Dr en droit (Paris), 1938; 1948-71 Professor, IEP Paris; 1954-58 Secrétaire Général, Comité de la République; 1958-71 Secrétaire Général du Sénat; 1971- Membre du Consel Constitutionnel; Président, FNSP. Publs: *La politique des partis sous la IIIème République*, 1946; *La régime politique français*, 1954; *La politique en France* (with A Grosser), 1962; *Géographie des élections françaises*, 1972; *Modernisation économique et comportement politique*, 1970; *France under the Fourth Republic*, 1952. Fields: Electoral geography and sociology; History of the Third Republic; French political institutions.

[687]
GÖHRING Walter
20 February 1936, Austrian. Universitätsstrasse 8/6, 1090 Wien, Austria. Degrees: Dr phil. Doctoral thesis: "Die Illegalen Jugendverbände im Widerstand gegen den Nationalsozialismus". Lecturer, U of Salzburg and Klagenfurt; Director, Austrian Inst of Pol Education, Vienna. Publs: *Arbeitsbuch Zeitgeschichte* (with F Hirt); "Gründungsparteitag der Österreichischen Sozieldemokratie", in *Jugend und Volk*; *Neuensetze kulturellen Erwachsenenbildung* (with F Hirt). Fields: International problems of political education.

[688]
GOIO Franco
30 April 1948, Italian. Via Rosselli I, Pavia, Italy. Degrees: Degree in Pol (Pavia); Doctoral thesis: "Sistema Politico e Lotta per il Potere: Critica della Teoria Politica di David Easton". Teaching and Research Assistant in Pol Sci; Assistant Professor of Pol Sci, U of Pavia. Publs: "Appunti Critici sulla Teoria Politica di David Easton", *Il Politico*, 1973; "Introduzione" to *La Violenza Politica*, H L Nieburg, 1974; "Struttura del Potere e 'Outputs' Decisionali nella Comunità Locale", *Rivista Italiana di Scienza Politica*, 1977; "Sistemi Politici Locali e *Outputs* Decisionali: una Rassegna", *Il Politico*, 1977; "Decentramento Urbano e Interessi Collettini a Milano: Due Processi Decisionali", 1979. Fields: Systems theory and local politics; violence and political movements.

[689]
GOLDMANN Kjell
24 June 1937, Swedish. Lupinvägen 2 A, 191 47 Sollentuna, Sweden. Degrees: PhD, 1971. Doctoral thesis: "International Norms and Wars between States: Three Studies in International Politics". 1964-70 Research Associate, 1967-77 Research Director, Swedish Institute of International Affairs; 1969-70 Research Fellow, Center for International Affairs, Harvard U; 1972-77 Associate Professor, 1977- Professor of Pol Sci, U of Stockholm. Publs: *Peace-keeping and Self-defence*, 1968; *Strategi i väst och öst* (ed), 1965; *International Norms and War between States*, 1971; *Tension and Détente in Bipolar Europe*, 1974; *Det internationella Systemet: en Teori och dess Begränsningar* (1978). Fields: International politics; peace and conflict studies; Swedish foreign and defence policy.

[690]
GOLDSMITH Maurice Marks
15 May 1933, American. Degrees: AB; PhD (Columbia), 1964. Doctoral thesis: "The Political Philosophy of Thomas Hobbes". 1960-68 Instructor, Assistant Professor in Government, U of Columbia; 1969- Professor of Pol Theory, U of Exeter. Publs: *Hobbes's Science of Politics*. 1966; "Allegiance", in *The Study of Politics* (P T King (ed)), 1977; "Public Virtue and Private Vices: Bernard Manderille and English Political Ideologies in the Early Eighteenth Century", *Eighteenth Century Studies*, 1976; "Manderille and the Spirit of Capitalism", *Journal of British Studies*, 1977; "The New American Conservatism" (with M Hawkins), *Political Studies*, 1972. Fields: Political philosophy; history of political thought especially in the 17th and 18th centuries.

[691]
GOLDSMITH Michael James Frederick
20 June 1939, British. 51 Park Road, Leyland, Lancashire, England. Degrees: BA; MA. 1963-73 Lecturer in Pol, U of Salford; 1970-72 Visiting Professor, Dept of Pol Studies, Queen's U, Kingston, Ontario; 1973- Senior Lecturer in Pol, U of Salford. Publs: Various articles and monographs in the fields of urban politics, planning and political sociology. Fields: Urban politics and public policy; politics of planning, housing and transport; political sociology.

[692]
GOLDTHORPE John Harry*
27 May 1935, British. Nuffield College, Oxford OX1 1NF, England. Degrees: BA; MA (Cantab): MA (Oxon). 1957-60 Junior Research Fellow, U of Leicester; 1960-62 Fellow, King's Coll, Cambridge; 1962-69 Assistant Lecturer, Lecturer, U of Cambridge; Official Fellow, Nuffield Coll, Oxford. Publs: *The Affluent Worker* (co-author), 1969. Fields: Occupational and social mobility.

[693]
GOMORI George Thomas*
3 April 1934, British. 55 Eltisley Avenue, Cambridge, England. Degrees: BA; B Litt (Oxon), 1962. 1963-64 Lecturer in Polish and Hungarian, U of California at Berkeley; 1964-65 Research Fellow, U of Harvard; 1965-69 Research Associate, Senior Research Associate, Centre for Russian and East European Studies, U of Birmingham; Assistant Lecturer in Polish, U of Cambridge; Fellow of Darwin Coll, Cambridge. Publs: *Polish and Hungarian Poetry, 1945-56*, 1966; *New Writing of East Europe* (co-ed), 1968; *Histoire du soulevement hongrois 1956* (P Gosztony (ed)), 1966; *Kultura Essays* (L Tyrmand (ed)), 1970; *The Soviet Union and Eastern Europe. A Handbook* (contributor), 1970. Fields: Literature and politics in Poland and Hungary; South-East Asian writers as members of a professional pressure group in Eastern Europe.

[694]
GONIDEC Pierre Francois
6 May 1914, French. 17 rue d'Anjou, 75008 Paris, France. Degrees: Dr en droit (Paris), 1943; DES econ pol; Agrégé de droit et sci écon. Directeur, Centre d'Études Pol Tiers Monde; Professeur de Sci Pol, U of Paris I. Publs: *Droit du travail des territoires d'Outre Mer*, 1958; *Droit d'Outre Mer*, 1959; *Les droits Africains*, 1968; *L'Etat Africain*, 1970; *Les systèmes politiques africains*, 1971. Fields: Political and judicial problems in Africa and the Third World; international relations.

[695]
GONNET Paul
1920, French. 3 rue des Oeillets, 06000 Nice, France. Degrees: Agrégé; Dr ès lettres. Doctoral thesis: "La société dijonnaise au XIXème siècle, esquisse de l'évolution économique, sociale et politique d'un milieu urbain contemporain". Professeur, Lycée Parc Impérial, Nice; Maître assistant, Collège U à Nice de la Faculté d'Aix; Maître de conférences, Professeur sans chaire, U de Nice; Directeur du Laboratoire d'Histoire économique et soc. Publs: *Un grand préfet de la Côte-d'Or sous Louis-Philippe: la correspondance d'Achille Chaper (1831-1840)*, 1970; *Histoire de Nice et du pays niçois* (co-author), 1976; *Régions et régionalisme en France du XVIIIème siècle à nos jours*, 1977; *Villes du littoral* (ed), 1975; *Inventaire des oeuvres d'Edgar Quinet et des travaux publiés sur elles* (ed), 1977. Fields: Urban history: studies in urbanism, economy, social history and analysis of political life; radical thought; Edgar Quinet; tourism and international cooperation.

[696]
GONZALEZ-CASANOVA José Antonio
2 December 1935, Spanish. 10 Reina Elisenda, 34 Barcelona, Spain. Degrees: Dr in Law. Doctoral thesis: "The People's Committee of the Yugoslav Commune". Professor, Dept of Pol Sci, U of Barcelona. Publs: *El régimen Político de Televisión*, 1967; *Los Derechos Humanos*, 1968; *Comunicación Humana y Comunidad Política*, 1968; *Elecciones en Barcelona 1931-36*, 1968; *Federalismo i Autonomía a Catalunya 1868-1939*, 1974; *La Republica*, 1976; *Que son los Estatutos de Autonomia*, 1977. Fields: Constitutional law.

[697]
GOODIN Robert Edward
30 November 1950, American. Department of Government, University of Essex, Colchester, Essex, England. Degrees: BA; D Phil (Oxon), 1974. Doctoral thesis: "Political Rationality". 1974-75 U of Strathclyde; 1975-78 U of Maryland; 1977 Visiting Professor, U of Oslo; 1978- Lecturer in Pol Theory, U of Essex. Publs: *Politics of Rational Man*, 1976. Fields: Political economy; political theory, empirical and normative.

[698]
GOODMAN David Stephen Gordon
19 February 1948, British. 11 Clayton Park Square, Newcastle-upon-Tyne NE2 4DP, England. Degrees: BA. Doctoral thesis: "Central-Provincial Relations in the Peoples Republic of China: The South West, 1955-1966". 1971-74 Research Fellow, Contemporary China Inst, U of London; 1974- Lecturer in Pol, U of Newcastle-Upon-Tyne. Publs: *A Research Guide to Chinese Provincial and Regional Newspapers*, 1976; *China: The Politics of Public Security* (with T Bowden), 1976; *A Provincial Handbook of the Peoples Republic of China* (co-ed), 1978. Fields: The spatial distribution of political power and decision-making; communist politics; Chinese politics.

[699]
GOODWIN Geoffrey Lawrence
14 June 1916, British. London School of Economics and Political Science, Houghton Street, London WC2A 2AE, England. Degrees: BSc. 1945-48 Foreign Office (London); 1948- Teaching Staff, LSE; Montague Burton Professor of International Relations, LSE. Publs: *The University Teaching of International Relations* (ed), 1952; *Britain and the United Nations*, 1958; *World Institutions and World Order*, 1964; *Research in International Organizations* (with S Strange), 1969; *New Dimensions of World Politics,* (ed) 1975. Fields: International institutions; external relations of the European Community.

[700]
GORDON Ian Andrew
28 December 1943, British. 10 Avenue Road, Kingston-upon-Thames, Surrey, England. Degrees: BA; MA (McMaster), 1967. Doctoral thesis: "The Recruitment of Local Political Leaders". 1968-69 Teaching Assistant, U of Essex; 1969-71 Temporary Lecturer, U of Exeter; 1971- Senior Lecturer in Politics, Kingston Polytechnic. Publs: "Political Ideology of Labour Councillors", *Policy and Politics*, 1977; "Direct Elections to the European Parliament: The British Debate", *The London Review of Public Administration*, 1977. Fields: Urban politics; British politics; political behaviour with special reference to Europe.

[701]
GORI Umberto
4 October 1932, Italian. Piazza della Signoria 6, 50122 Firenze, Italy. Degrees: Libera Docenza. Assistant Professor of International Law, U of Macerata; Professor of International Relations and Director, Inst of Pol Sci, U of Florence. Publs: *L'Università e la Comunità Europea*, 1964; *L'Organizzazione Internazionale dalla SdN alle NU*, 1969; *La Diplomazia Culturale Multilaterale dell'Italia*, 1970; *Relazioni Internazionali-Metodi e Tecniche di Analisi* (co-author), 1974. Fields: Forecasting techniques in foreign policy; international integration theory.

[702]
GORLICH Ernest Joseph*
16 November 1905, Austrian. A-1030 Vienna, Arsenal, Obj, V/III/III8, Austria. Degrees: Dr phil (Vienna), 1930. 1932-38 Headmaster, Girl Teachers' Coll; 1945-68 Headmaster, Technical Coll; Professor Emeritus. Publs: *Handbuch des Österreichers*, 1948; *Geschichte Österreichs*, 1970; *Grundzüge der Geschichte der Habsburgermonarchie und Österreichs*, 1970; *Gegenwartskunde*, 1962; *Die österreichische Nation und der Widerstand*, 1968. Fields: Austrian history; history of the Hapsburg monarchy from Maria Theresa to the present day.

[703]
GÖRLITZ Axel
20 August 1935, German. Am Wolfsberg 29, D-7000 Stuttgart 70, FR Germany. Degrees: Dr Int, 1965; Habilitation (Frankfurt), 1971. Doctoral thesis: "Die Erledigung des Verwaltungsrechtsstreits in der Hauptsache". 1965-1970 Wiss Assistent, U of Frankfurt; 1970- Professor of Pol Sci, Pädagogische Hochschule Ludwigsburg; Privatdozent, U of Frankfurt. Publs: *Parlament und Verwaltung*; *Gesetzgebung und politische Kontrolle*, 1967; *Demokratie im Wandel*, 1969; *Verwaltungsberichtsbarkeit in Deutschland*, 1970; *Handlexikon zur Politikwissenschaft* (co-ed)), 1972; *Politikwissenschaftliche Propädeutik*, 1972; *Politische Funktionen des Rechts*, 1976; *Politische Sozialisationsforschung*, 1977. Fields: Methodology; political theory; law and politics.

[704]
GORMAN Jonathan Lamb
14 January 1946, British. 53 Marlborough Park South, Belfast, BT9 6HR, Northern Ireland. Degrees: MA (Edinburgh); PhD (Cambridge). Doctoral thesis; "The Possibility of Objectivity in History". Research Fellow, U of Birmingham; Lecturer in Social Philosophy, The Queen's U, Belfast. Publs: "Objectivity and Truth in History", *Inquiry*, 1974; "A Problem in the Justification of Democracy", *Analysis*, 1978. Fields: Analytical political philosophy; historicism; philosophy of social and political science.

[705]
GOSSES Antoinette Helene
17 July 1944, Dutch. Amstel 264, Amsterdam, The Netherlands. Degrees: Dr. Ministry of Finance; Ministry of Foreign Affairs; Editor/Producer/Director, Radio Nederland, the Dutch World Broadcasting system; member of the Third World Desk. Fields: Development aid policy, especially in Africa.

[706]
GOTTMAN Jean Iona
10 October 1915, French. School of Geography, Mansfield Rd, Oxford OX1 3TB, England. Degrees: Lic ès lettres (Paris), 1932; DES (Sorbonne), 1934; MA (Oxon), 1968; Dr ès lettres (Paris), 1970. 1942-65 Member, Inst for Advanced Studies, Princeton, NJ; 1946-47 Director of Studies and Research, United Nations Secretariat, NY, USA; 1948-56 Professor, IEP Paris; 1956-60 Research director, XXth Century Fund, NY, USA; 1960- Professor, Ecole des Hautes Etudes, Sorbonne; 1968- Professor of Geography, Head of School of Geography, U of Oxford; Fellow, Hertford College, Oxford; Fellow, British Academy. Publs: *L'Amérique*, 1960; *A Geography of Europe*, 1969; *La politique des Etats et leur géographie*, 1952; *Marché des matières premières*, 1957; *Megalopolis*, 1961; *Essais sur l'aménagement de l'espace habité*, 1966; *The Renewal of the Geographic Environment*, 1969; *The Significance of Territory*, 1973. Fields: Evolution of the concept and significance of territory; urban and local government, especially in Western Europe and North America; geographical factors in international relations.

[707]
GOUGH John Wiedhofft*
23 February 1900, British. 28 Hill Top Road, Oxford OX4 1PE, England. Degrees: BA; MA, 1926; D Litt, 1965 (all Oxon). 1923-32 Lecturer in History, U of Bristol; 1929-30 Visiting Lecturer, Western Reserve U, Cleveland, Ohio; 1932-67 Fellow and Tutor, Oriel Coll, Oxford; Emeritus Fellow, Oriel Coll. Publs: *The Social Contract*, 1957; *John Locke's Political Philosophy*, 1973; *Fundamental Law in English Constitutional History*, 1971; *Locke, Second Treatise of Government* (ed), 1966; *John Locke, Epistola de Tolerantia* (co-ed), 1968.

[708]
GOURDON Alain André
16 October 1928, French. 5 Passage Doisy, 75017 Paris, France. Degrees: Dipl (Paris). 1956-60 Conseiller du Government du Cambodge; 1961-63 Haut Conseiller à la Cour Suprême du Maroc; 1964 Consultant de l'OCDE; 1965 Professeur, Inst d'Administration de Saigon; Visiting Professor aux Ecoles Nationales d'Administration de Bogota, Alger, Abidjan, Bamako et Vientiane; Conseiller à la Cour des Comptes de France; Vice-President de la Foundation Culturelle et Scolaire à vocation internationale. Publs: *Eloge du colonialisme*, 1962; *Les deux stratégies du communisme*, 1964; *Les cadres*, 1967; *Haro sur la Démocratie*, 19732; *Sexologie de l'occident*, 1976; *Mendés France*, 1977; *Les matriarches*, 1978. Fields: Crisis analysis.

[709]
GOURNAY Bernard*
31 May 1930, French. Fondation Nationale des Sciences Politiques, 27 rue St Guillaume, Paris VIIème, France. Degrees: Ancien élève Ecole Nationale d'Administration. 1962-66 Directeur d'Etudes et de Recherches, FNSP; Professeur, Inst d'Etudes Pol, Paris, Inst International d'Administration Publique, Paris. Publs: *L'administration*, 1962; *Introduction à la science administrative*, 1966; *Administration publique*, 1967. Fields: Public administration; governmental decision-making.

[710]
GOWAN Ivor Lyn
23 April 1922. Department of Political Science, University College of Wales. Llandinman Building, Aberystwyth, Cardiganshire, Wales. Degrees: BA; MA (Oxon), 1951. 1949-65 Lecturer, Senior Lecturer in Public Administration, U of Nottingham; Vice-Principal, Head of Dept, Dept of Pol Sci, U Coll, Wales. Publs: *Government of Wales*

in the Twentieth Century in Welsh Studies in Public Law, 1970. Fields: Central, regional and local government; government and politics of Wales; European government.

[711]
GOYARD Claude A H
19 December 1929, French. 29 Avenue Georges Mandel, 75016 Paris, France. Degrees: Dr. Doctoral thesis: "La compétence judiciaire en matière administrative". Former doyen, Faculté de Droit, Abidjan, Côte d'Ivoire; Séminaire annuel d'administration régionale et territoriale de 3ème cycle (doctorat), U de Paris II. Publs: *Le gouvernement du Portugal*, 1964; *L'affaire du Santa-Maria*, 1962; *Séparatisme et autonomisme*, 1977; *Maurras et la 3ème République. 1977; Les idées de Ch Eisenmann sur la théorie du contrôle de la légalité des motifs*, 1974; *Coordination et consultation*, 1974; *Les épurations administratives*, 1978; *Le statut de Paris*, 1978. Fields: Regional and territorial administration; control of legality in acts; motivations; destabilization of Africa; political crimes; autonomous regions.

[712]
GRABENDORFF Wolf
1 June 1940, German. Am Buchet 8, 8021 Icking, FR Germany. Degrees:. Dipl Pol. 1964-66 Assistant, Latin American Dept, Free U of Berlin; 1970-71 and 1975- Research Associate, Latin American Affairs, Stiftung Wissenschaft und Politik, Ebenhausen; 1972-74 Latin American Correspondent, German TV system (ARD) in Buenos Aires, Argentina. Publs: *Lateinamerika — wohin? Informationen und Analysen*, 1974; *Bibliographie zur Politik und Gesellschaft der Dominikanischen Republik*, 1973; *Lateinamerika — Kontinent in der Krise* (ed), 1973; *Brasilien: Entwicklungsmodell und Aussenpolitik* (co-author with M Nitsch), 1977. Fields: Latin American politics; inter-Latin American relations; Latin American foreign policies.

[713]
GRAF KIELMANSEGG Peter
27 June 1937, German. Ackerstrasse 13, 5060 Bergisch-Gladbach 3, FR Germany. Degrees: Dr phil (Bonn), 1963. Doctoral thesis: "Stein und die Zentralverwaltung 1813-14". Wiss Assistent, Privatdozent, Professor, Seminar für Pol Wissenschaft, U of Köln. Publs: *Stein und die Zentralverwaltung 1813-14*, 1964; *Deutschland und der Erste Weltkrieg*, 1968; *Legitimationsprobleme politischer Systeme* (ed), 1976; *Volkssouveränität*, 1977; *Regierbarkeit* (ed), 1977. Fields: Modern German history; comparative government; theory of democracy.

[714]
GRAHAM Bruce Desmond
3 November 1931, British. School of African and Asian Studies, University of Sussex, Falmer, Brighton BN1 9QQ, Sussex. Degrees: BA; MA (Auckland); PhD (Australian National U), 1959. Doctoral thesis: "The Formation of the Australian Country Parties". 1960-64 Research Fellow, Dept of Pol Sci, Inst of Advanced Studies, Australian National U; 1964-67 Lecturer in Pol; 1967-68 Reader in Pol; 1968- Professor of Pol, U of Sussex. Publs: *The French Socialists and Tripartisme, 1944-47*, 1965; *The Formation of the Australian Country Parties*, 1966; *A Handbook of Australian Governments and Elections* (co-ed), 1968. Fields: The ideology of the Bharatiya Jana Sangh, a Hindu Nationalist party; factional systems within the Uttar Pradesh unit of the Indian National Congress.

[715]
GRALHER Martin Theodor
29 November 1939, German. Auf dem Backenberg 7, 4630 Bochum 1, FR Germany. Degrees: Dr phil (Heidelberg). Doctoral thesis: "Repräsentation und Revolution in der Englischen Revolution". Wiss Assistent, Inst für Pol Wissenschaft, U of Heidelberg; Wiss Assistent, Lehrstuhl für Pol Wissenschaft, Ruhr-U, Bochum; Akademischer Rat, Professor für Pol Wissenschaft, Abteilung für Sozialwissenschaft, Rhur-U, Bochum. Publs: *Demokratie und Repräsentation in der Englischen Revolution*, 1973; *Qualifikation und Repräsentation*, 1974; *Der Bundesrat als eine föderale Lösung*, 1975; *Räson des Verfassungsstaates*, 1977; *Ruhendes Mandat und Repräsentationsverständnis*, 1977; *Politische und soziale Kontrolle- Zur Funktion der Verfassungsberichtsbarkeit im politischen System der Bundesrepublik Deutschland*, 1977; "Mitte-Mischung-Mässigung-Strukturen, Figuren, Bilder und Metaphern in der Politik und im politischen Denken", *Res Publica*, 1977. Fields: Constitutional development; change and revision in Germany, Switzerland, Japan and other countries; constitutional theory as part of comparative politics; political theory.

[716]
GRAN Thorvald
26 May 1943, Norwegian. Loddefjorden 4, 5071 Loddefjord pr Bergen, Norway. Degrees: Mag pol sci. Lecturer in Pol Sci, U of Bergen. Fields: International agricultural developments; international organizations; state planning of higher education in Norway and other European countries; structure of the central administration in postwar Norway.

[717]
GRANGÉ Jean Pierre
20 August 1925, French. 78 Boulevard Arago, 75013 Paris, France. Degrees: DES sci pol (Paris), 1963. Chef de service adjoint au Sénat, Paris. Publs: *Etudes sur le Parlement de la Ve République: la fixation de l'ordre du jour*, 1965. Fields: Constitutional and parliamentary law; working of the French Parliament; comparative studies on governments with two chambers.

[718]
GRANSOW Hans Volker
29 April 1945, German. Rolandstrasse 30, D-4800 Bielefeld 1, FR Germany. Degrees: Dipl Pol (Free U of Berlin), 1970; D Phil (Free U of Berlin), 1974. Doctoral thesis: "Zur Kulturpolitischen Entwicklung in der DDR bis 1973" (On the Development of Cultural Policy in the GDR up to 1973). 1970-71 Wiss Mitarbeiter, Soziologie, Technische U, Berlin; 1971-76 Wiss Assistent, Publizistik Wissenschaft, Free U of Berlin; Lehrbeauftragter, Pol Wiss, U of Bremen; Wiss Assistent, Pol Wiss, U of Bielefeld; Lehrbeauftragter, Soziologie, U of Paderborn. Publs: *Kulturpolitik in der DDR*, 1975; *Aspekte des Freizeitsverhaltens in der DDR*, 1974; *Die DDR und die politische Wissenschaft*, 1976; "Ursprünge der politischen Ökonomie des Sozialismus", *Sozialistische Politik*, 1976; *Dialektik und Kultur*, 1976. Fields: Communism , especially GDR and political economy of socialism.

[719]
GRANT Wynford Paul
11 January 1947, British. 36 Cowdray Close, Leamington, Warwickshire, England. Degrees: BA; MSc (Strathclyde), 1969; PhD (Exeter), 1973. Doctoral thesis: "Independent Local Political Parties: The Origins, Development and Consequences of Ratepayer and Similar Movements". 1971- Lecturer in Pol, U of Warwick. Publs: *The Confederation of British Industry* (with D Marsh), 1977; *Independent Local Politics in England*

and Wales, 1977. Fields: Industrial policy; interest groups; nonpartnership in local politics; proportional representation in local government elections.

[720]
GRAS Christian
2 April 1935, French. 5 rue Soultz, 67100 Strasbourg, France. Degrees. Agrégé, 1959; Dr d'Etat, 1970. Doctoral thesis: "Alfred Rosmer (1877-1964) et le mouvement révolutionnaire international". CNRS, Paris; Professeur, U Sci Humaines, Strasbourg. Publs: *Alfred Rosmer et le mouvement révolutionnaire international*, 1971; *Régions et régionalisme en France depuis la fin du XVIIIème siècle* (ed); *Les Etats marxistes et léninistes de 1917 à nos jours*. Fields: Regional and ethnic problems in Western Europe compared with USA and Canada; the international Communist movement.

[721]
GRASZ Hendrikus Andries*
17 February 1923, Dutch. 40 Handellaan, The Hague, The Netherlands. Degrees: Dr Soc Sci (Leiden), 1956; Dr of Law (Leiden); 1960. Senior Staff Member, Dutch Union of Local Authorities; Professor of Public Administration, Head of Dept, Free U of Amsterdam; Professor Extraordinarius, Sociology, Inst of Technology, Twente Enschede. Publs: *Veranderingen in Nederlands Communalisme*, 1960; *Inleiding bestuurswetenschap*, 1969; *Studie van het openbaar bestuur*, 1964; *Toezicht op gemeentebsturen*, 1964. Fields: International relations; bureaucratization of society; government in Zambia; the Dutch Council of State.

[722]
GRAUHAN Rolf-Richard
21 December 1934, German. Modersohnweg 12, D-2800 Bremen, FR Germany. Degrees: Dr jur, Referendarexamen, Oberlandsgericht Schleswig, 1957; Dr jur (Heidelberg), 1959; Jur Assessorexamen, Justizministerium (Stuttgart), 1963. Doctoral thesis; "Gibt es in der Bundesrepublik einen pouvoir neutre?". 1961-1965 Wiss Assistent, Inst für Pol Wissenschaft, U of Heidelberg; 1965 Visiting Research Associate, Joint Center for Urban Studies, MIT and Harvard U; 1965-1967 Städtischer Rechtsrat, City Administration, Munich; 1967-1969 Akademischer Rat, U of Konstanz; 1969-1971 Wiss Rat, Fachbereich Pol Wissenschaft, U of Konstanz; Professor of Pol Sci, U of Bremen. Publs: "Die Verschwisterung deutscher und französischer Gemeinden", in *Politische Dimensionen der europäischen Gemeinschaftsbildung*, (Carl J Friedrich (ed)), 1968; *Modelle politischer Verwaltungsführung*, 1969; *Politische Verwaltung: Auswahl und Stellung der Oberbürgermeister als Verwaltungschefs deutscher Grossstädte*, 1970; *Politik der Verstädterung* (with W. Linder), 1974; *Grenzen des Fortschritts-Widersprüche der gesellschaftlichen Rationalisierung*, 1975; *Grossstadt-Politik. Texte zur Analyse und Kritik lokaler Politik* (ed), 1972; *Lokale Politikforschung* (ed), 1975; *A Reader in Planning Theory*, 1973; "Policy Analysis Illustrated by the Problem of Urbanization" (with W Linder *et al*), in *German Political Studies* (K Beyme (ed)), 1974. Fields: Constitutional theory; political planning and decision-processes; inter-systemic politics.

[723]
GRAVIER Jean-Francois
14 April 1915, French. 51 Avenue de la Motte-Picquet, 75015 Paris, France. Degrees: Agrégé d'histoire et géographie. Conseiller au Commissariat Général au Plan; Membre du Conseil économique et social; Professeur, Conservatoire National des Arts et Métiers. Publs: *Paris et le désert français*; *L'aménagement du territoire*; *La question régionale*; *Economie et organisation régionale*. Fields: Town and country planning; regional planning; regional organization.

[724]
GRAWITZ Madeleine
10 September 1910, French. 14 bis rue du Bois de Boulogne, 92 Neuilly/Seine, France. Degrees: Lic ès lettres; Agrégée de droit public; Dr de droit. 1952-67 Professeur de Droit Public, U de Lyon; 1967- Professeur de Droit Public, U de Paris; Directrice du Centre d'Education Ouvrière de Lyon; Professeur, Directrice, Dept Sci Soc, U de Paris I. Publs: *Méthodes des sciences sociales*, 1964. Fields: Methodology of the social sciences; political sociology; psychology.

[725]
GRAY Andrew Garrard
31 July 1947, British. Eliot College, University of Kent, Canterbury, Kent, England. Degrees: BA. 1972-78 Lecturer, Senior Lecturer in Public Administration, Manchester Polytechnic; 1978- Lecturer in Administration Studies, U of Kent. Fields: Organizations and administration of government.

[726]
GRAY John Nicholas
17 April 1948, British. 3B Woodstock Road, Oxford, England. Degrees: MA (Oxon); D Phil (Oxon). Doctoral thesis: "Liberty and Human Nature in the Liberal Tradition". 1973-76 Lecturer in Pol Theory, Dept of Government, U of Essex; Fellow and Tutor in Pol, Jesus Coll, Oxford. Fields: Philosophical aspects of liberalism; 19th century English political thought; philosophical problems of the social sciences.

[727]
GRAY Timothy Stuart*
1 April 1940, British. Department of Politics, University of Newcastle-upon-Tyne, Newcastle-upon-Tyne NE1 7RU, England. Degrees: BA. 1963-66 Temporary Lecturer, U of Newcastle; 1966- Lecturer, U of Newcastle. Fields: Herbert Spencer's political theory.

[728]
GRAZIANO Luigi
19 September 1939, Italian. Via Bramante 39, Milan, Italy. Degrees: Laurea in Sci Econ and Commerciali (Rome), 1963; Dipl (Inst d'Etudes Pol, Paris), 1966; PhD (Princeton), 1977. Doctoral thesis: "Clientelism and the Italian Political System. A Theoretical and Empirical Study". 1968-71 U Fellow, Dept of Pol, Princeton U; 1972-76 Professore Incaricato, U of Catania; 1976- Professore Incaricato Stabilizzato (Pol Soc), U of Turin. Publs: *La PoliticanEstera rofessore Incaricato, U of Catania; 1976- Professore Incaricato Stabilizzato (Pol Soc), U of Turin. Publs: La Politica Estera Italiana nel Dopoguerra*, 1967; *Clientelismo e Mutamento Politico* (ed), 1974; "A Conceptual Framework for the Study of Clientelism", in *Cornell University Western Societies Occasional Papers*, 1975; "Bentley e la Scienza Politica Comportamentista", in *Annali della Fondazione Luigi Einaudi*, 1975; *Territorial Politics in Industrial Nations* (with S Tarrow & P Katzenstein (eds)), 1978. Fields: Clientelism; group theory; logic of comparative research; centre-periphery relations.

[729]
GREAVES Harold Richard Gorin
17 November 1907, British. London School of Economics and Political Science, Houghton Street, Aldwych, London WC1, England. Degrees: BSc. Lecturer, Reader, U of London; Emeritus Professor of Pol Sci, U of London. Publs: *The League Committees and World Order*, 1931; *The Spanish Constitution*, 1933; *Reactionary England and other Essays*, 1936; *The British Constitution*, 1938; *Federal Union in Practice*,

1940; *The Civil Service in the Changing State*, 1947; *The Foundations of Political Theory*, 1958. Fields: Public administration; legal studies; regionalism and local government; political theory.

[730]
GREENAWAY John Robert
12 April 1947, British. 58 Sandringham Road, Norwich, England. Degrees: BA; MA (Cambridge); PhD (Leeds). Doctoral thesis: "The Local Option Question and British Politics 1864-1914". Research Assistant, U of Durham; Lecturer, U of East Anglia. Fields: Administrative reform in Britain, 1850-1970; the political system in late Victorian Britain.

[731]
GREENWOOD Royston
29 October 1944, British. 61 Sellywick Drive, Sellypark, Birmingham, England. Degrees: B Soc Sci; M Soc Sci; PhD (Birmingham). Doctoral thesis: "Strategies of Organizational Control". Lecturer, Inst of Local Government Studies, U of Birmingham. Publs: *Corporate Planning in English Local Government: 1967-1972* (with J D Stewart (eds)), 1974; "The Politics of the Budgetary Process in English Local Government", *Political Studies*, 1977; "Contingency Theory and Public Bureaucracies", *Policy and Politics*, 1976; "Contingency Theory and the Organization of Local Authorities", *Public Administration*, 1975; *In Pursuit of Corporate Rationality*, 1976; "Institute of Local Government Studies Centralization Revisited", *Administrative Science Quarterly*, 1976. Fields: The politics of budgeting; organization theory with special reference to the structure of intra-organizational conflict in public bureaucracies.

[732]
GREGORY Francis Edward Coulton
11 June 1945, British. Department of Politics, The University, Southampton SO9 5NH, England. Degrees: BA; MSc (Southampton). 1968-70 Research Assistant, U of Southampton. 1970- Lecturer, Dept of Pol, U of Southampton. Publs: "West European Collaboration in Weapons Procurement" (with J Simpson), *ORRIS*, 1972; "Protest and Violence: The Police Response", *Conflict Studies*, 1976. Fields: The comparative study of the police systems of the EEC states.

[733]
GREGORY Roy George
7 March 1935, British. Department of Politics, The University, Whiteknights Park, Reading, Berks, England. Degrees: BA; D Phil (Oxon). Doctoral thesis: "The Miners and British Politics, 1906-14". Professor of Politics, U of Reading. Publs: *The Miners and British Politics 1906-14*, 1968; *The Price of Amenity: Five Studies in Conservation and Control of Administrative Action*, 1975. Fields: Political history of the British Labour movement; parliamentary surveillance over the executive, especially the British parliamentary commissioner.

[734]
GREIFFENHAGEN Martin Otto Werner
30 September 1928, German. Rottannenweg 4, D-7000 Stuttgart 1, FR Germany. Degrees: Dr phil. Doctoral thesis: "Skepsis und Naturrecht in der Theologie Jeremy Taylors (1613-1667)". Professor für Pol, Pädagogische Hochschule Lüneburg; Direktor, Inst für Politikwissenschaft, U of Stuttgart. Publs: *Das Dilemma des Konservatismus in Deutschland*, 1977; *Der neue Konservatismus der siebziger Jahre*, 1974;

Freiheit gegen Gleichheit?, 1975; *Demokratisierung in Staat und Gesellschaft*, 1973; *Emanzipation*, 1973; *Zur Theorie der Reform*, 1978. Fields: History of political ideas; democratic theory.

[735]
GREMION Pierre René Joseph
19 February 1937, French. 50 rue R Marcheron, 92 Vanves, France. Degrees: Lic ès lettres; Dipl (Paris). Doctoral thesis: "Pouvoir local, pouvoir central-essai sur la fin de l'Administration Républicaine". 1964-66 Chercheur sous contrat; 1966- Attaché de recherches, Maître de recherches, CNRS. Publs: *La mise en place des institutions régionales*, 1966; *La structuration du pouvoir au niveau départemental*, 1969; *Les services extérieurs du Ministère des Finances dans le système de décision déparemental* (with F d'Arcy), 1970; *Où va l'administration française* (with Crozier *et al*), 1974; *Le pouvoir périphérique*, 1976; *L'ordinateur au pouvoir* (co-author), 1978. Fields: State and society.

[736]
GREVEN Michael T
7 March 1947, German. Ludwigstrasse 22, 4790 Paderborn, FR Germany. Degrees: MA (Bonn), 1972; Dr phil (Bonn), 1973. Doctoral thesis: "Systemtheorie und Demokratie". 1972-73 U of Bonn; 1973-77 U of Paderborn; 1977-78 Visiting Lecturer, U of Ife; Professor of Pol Sci, Philipps-U of Marburg. Publs: *Systemtheorie und Gesellschaftsanalyse*, 1974; *Krise des Staates?*, 1976; *Parteien und politische Herrschaft*, 1977. Fields: Political theory and philosophy; political sociology; neomarxism and anarchism.

[737]
GREWE Hartmut
7 May 1945, German. Nächstenbacher Berg 10, D-6940 Weinheim, FR Germany. Degrees: BA; MA (Duke), 1971; PhD (Duke), 1973. Doctoral thesis: "Comparative Politics and Political Development: Analytic and Normative Dilemmas in Research". 1978 Visiting Assistant Professor, Dept of Government, U of Texas at Austin; Assistant Professor, Dept of Pol Sci, U of Mannheim. Publs: "Staatliche Wirtschaftspolitik zwischen Ordnungssicherung und Konjunktursteuerung", in *Probleme der Modernisierungspolitik* (Zapf (ed)), 1977; *Macht und Motivation im politischen Prozess: Zwei Austauschtheoretische Erklärungsmodelle*, 1977. Fields: Comparative politics; political development; political economy; transnational relations; Western Europe.

[738]
GRIMLUND Bengt Emil
5 November 1919, Swedish. Axtorpsvägen 28, 902 34 Umeå, Sweden. Degrees: Fil kand (Lund), 1942; Pol mag (Lund), 1947; Fil lic (Uppsala), 1953. 1958-67 Rektor, Västerbottens läns folkhögsköla; 1967-74 Rektor, School of Social Work and Public Administration, Umeå; 1974- Rektor, School of Education, Umeå. Publs: *Hur Danmark styrs*, 1949; *Den nya Riksdagen* (with L Ricknell), 1970; *Län, landsting, kommun* (with D Brändström and L Ricknell), 1978. Fields: History of political ideas, especially socialism in France; Supreme Court of the United States; comparative government.

[739]
GRIMM Dieter
11 May 1937, German. Fallerslebenstrasse 16, D-6000 Frankfurt M, FR Germany. Degrees: Referendar, 1962; Assessor, 1967; LLM (Harvard), 1965; Dr jur (Frankfurt), 1971. Doctoral thesis: "Zur Rechts- und Staatslehre Léon Duguits". Research Fellow, Max-Planck-Inst, Frankfurt; Lecturer, Constitutional Law and Pol Sci, U of Trier.

Publs: *Solidarität als Rechtsprinzip*, 1973; *Rechtswissenschaft und Nachbarwissenschaften*, 1976. Fields: Law and politics; constitutional law; constitutional history, especially 19th century; political theory; government.

[740]
GRIMSSON Olafur Racnar*
14 May 1943, Icelandic. University of Reykjavik, Reykjavik, Iceland. Degrees: BA; PhD (Manchester), 1970. Doctoral thesis: "Political Power in Iceland Prior to the Period of Class Politics, 1845-1918". Research, SED Project; Tutorial Assistant, U of Manchester; Lecturer, U of Iceland. Publs: "Iceland", in *International Guide to Electoral Statistics* (S Rokkan and J Meyrial (eds)), 1969. Fields: Icelandic politics; comparative politics.

[741]
GROOM Arthur John Richard
5 July 1938, British. 8 Cherry Avenue, Canterbury, Kent, England. Degrees: BSc; MA (Lehigh); Dr ès Sci Pol (Geneva). Doctoral thesis: "British Thinking About Nuclear Weapons 1940-62". Lecturer, U Coll, London; Reader in International Relations, U of Kent, Canterbury. Publs: *The Management of Britain's External Relations* (with R Boardman), 1973; *British Thinking About Nuclear Weapons*, 1974; *Functionalism* (with P Taylor), 1975; *The Study of World Society: A London Perspective* (with J W Burton *et al*), 1975; *Peacekeeping*, 1973; *International Organization* (with P Taylor), 1978. Fields: Theory of international relations; strategy and conflict; international organization.

[742]
GROSSER Alfred
1 February 1925, French. 8 rue Dupleix, 75015 Paris, France. Degrees: Agrégé, Dr ès lettres et sci pol. 1964-65 Kratter Visiting Professor of Modern European History, U of Stanford, USA; Director, Graduate programme, Professor, IEP Paris. Publs: *Hitler, la presse et la naissance d'une dictature*, 1959; *La quatrième République et sa politique extérieure de la Vème République*, 1965; *Au nom de quoi? Fondements de notre temps 1946-70*, 1970; *L'explication politique*, 1972; *La politique en France* (with F Boguez), 1975; *Gegen den Strom*, 1975; *La passion de comprendre*, 1977. Fields: German contemporary history and politics; French politics; comparative politics; international relations; comparative political development of European countries since 1945.

[743]
GRUNER Erich
5 January 1915, Swiss. 3084 Wabern, Nr Berne, Switzerland. Degrees: Dr phil (Berne), 1942; Dr hc (Lausanne). 1941-61 Professor, College of Basle; 1961- Professor of Sociology of Pol and Social History, U of Berne; Director, Forschungszentrum für Geschichte und Soziologie der schweizerischen Politik. Publs: *Wetgeschichte des 20. Jahrhundert* (with E Sieber), 1976; *Die Arbeiter in der Schweiz im 19 Jahrhundert*, 1968; *Bürger, Staat und Politik in der Schweiz* (with B Junker), 1978; *Die Parteien in der Schweiz*, 1977; *Die Schweizerische Bundesversammlung 1920-68*, 1970; *Die Wahlen in den schweizerischen Nationalrat (1848-1919)*, 1978; *Les élections au Conseil national suisse (1848-1919): Droit et système électoral, participation au scrutin, comportement de l'électorat et des partis, thèmes dominants et données majeures des campagnes électorales*, 1978; *Die Finanz- und Steuergesinnung des Schweizervolks*, 1977. Fields: Swiss politics and contemporary history; historical statistics; history of emigration/immigration; elections; trade unions; strikes; employers' organizations.

[744]
GRÜNFELD Frederik
21 June 1949, Dutch. Reitdiepstraat 4 III, Amsterdam, The Netherlands. Degrees: Dr. Doctoral thesis: "Influences on the Foreign Policy of Israel". Researcher in Soc Sci. Publs: *Political Attitudes in Lelystad*, 1977. Fields: International relations; public administration.

[745]
GUELKE Adrian Blanchard
15 June 1947, British. 65 Fitzwilliam Street, Belfast BT9 6AS, Northern Ireland. Degrees: BA; MA (Cape Town). 1969 Temporary Lecturer in Comparative African Government and Law, U of Cape Town; Lecturer in Pol Sci, Queen's U of Belfast. Publs: "Force, Intervention and Internal Conflict", in *The Use of Force in International Relations* (F S Northedge (ed)), 1974; "Africa as a Market for South African Goods", *The Journal of Modern African Studies*, 1974; *Is State Control of Labour in South Africa Effective?* (with S Siebert), 1973. Fields: Politics in Southern Africa; imperialism; politics in the Third World; comparative political violence; international relations.

[746]
GUIDICINI Paolo
17 August 1933, Italian. Bentini 42, Bologna, Italy. Doctoral thesis: "Struttura Urbana e Comunicazione delle Idee". Direttore Istituto di Sociologia, U di Bologna.

[747]
GUILLANEUF Raymond
15 October 1932, French. 181 rue Ordener, 75018 Paris, France. Degrees: Dr 3ème cycle. Doctoral thesis: "La presse en Côte d'Ivoire: La colonisation et l'aube de la décolonisation (1906-1952)". Maître-assistant, UER de Sci Pol, U de Paris I. Publs: "La gauche non conformiste dans le Puy de Dôme de 1945 à 1960", *Revue d'Auvergne*, 1977. Fields: Foreign policy; history of the press; political history.

[748]
GUILLAUME Pierre Andre
26 June 1933, French. 26 Résidence du Pontet, 33600 Pessac, France. Degrees: Agrégé d'histoire, 1957; Dr 3ème cycle, 1965; Dr d'Etat, 1970. Doctoral thesis: "La population de Bordeaux au XIXème siècle". 1958-60 Agrégé répétiteur, Ecole Norm Sup, St Cloud; 1962-72 Assistant, Maître-assistant, Chargé d'enseignement, Maître de conférences, U de Bordeaux; 1972- Professeur, IEP, Bordeaux III. Publs: *La compagnie des mines de la Loire*, 1966; *La population de Bordeaux au XIXème siècle*, 1972; *Le monde colonial*, 1974; *Histoire économique du XXème siècle*, 1976. Fields: France in 20th century; contemporary Canada; contemporary Africa.

[749]
GULBRANDSEN Lars
19 February 1946, Norwegian. Disenveien 25, Oslo 5, Norway. Degrees: Cand pol. Doctoral thesis: "Marked og Politikk. Boligmarked og Boligpolitikk: Oslo i det tyvende Arhundre". Research Fellow, Inst for Pol Sci, U of Oslo; Researcher, Inst for Applied Soc Research, Oslo. Publs: "Market Interest and Moral Indignation: the Political Psychology of Housing Price Regulations in Postwar Oslo" (with U Torgevsen) *Scandinavian Political Studies,* 1974; "Concern with Redistribution as an Aspect of Postwar Norwegian Housing Policy" (with U Torgevsen), *Acta Sociologica,* 1978. Fields: Public policies in the housing sector, especially market regulation and individual market behaviour.

[750]
GUNN Lewis Arthur
10 April 1935, British. 7 Rosslyn Terrace, Glasgow G12 9NB, Scotland. Degrees: MA (Aberdeen), 1957. 1957-59 Teaching Assistant, Cornell U; 1959-66 Lecturer, U of Manchester; 1966-72 Senior Lecturer in Pol, U of Glasgow; 1969-70 Tutor in Public Administration, Civil Service Coll, London; Civil Service Professor of Administration, U of Strathclyde and Civil Service Coll. Publs: *Government and Allocation of Resources to Science*, 1966; "Politicians or Officials; Who is Answerable?", *The Political Quarterly*, 1972; "Government, Technology and Planning in Britain", in *Meaning and Control: Essays in Social Aspects of Science and Technology* (Edge and Wolfe (eds)), 1973; "The Assembly and its Servants", *New Edinburgh Review*, 1976; "Devolution and the Civil Service", in *Devolution and the Media in the United Kingdom*, 1977; "Devolution: A Scottish View", *The Political Quarterly*, 1977; "The Debate About Devolution", *The Times Educational Supplement*, 1976; "Six Questions about Management Training", in *Civil Service Training* (R A W Rhodes (ed)), 1977. Fields: Public policy and administration; policy analysis; management training.

[751]
GUNNMO Alf Olav
19 February 1942, Swedish. Lagmansvägen 133, 830 20 Brunflo, Sweden. Degrees: MA (Umeå), 1971. Lecturer in Pol Sci, U of Umeå. Fields: Regional and local government; public administration.

[752]
GURNY Ruth
27 March 1948, Swiss. Langacherstrasse 2, 8127 Forch, Switzerland. Degrees: PhD. Doctoral thesis: "Nationalism Today". U of Ottawa; U of Zurich. Publs: *Nationalismus heute- 3 Versuche einer soziologischen Klärung*, 1976. Fields: Minority-majority relations.

[753]
GUSTAFSSON Frans Agne Samuel
1 September 1925, Swedish. Ferievägen 11, 22367 Lund, Sweden. Degrees: Fil lic. 1951-Assistant Teacher, Teacher, Amanuens, Inst of Pol Sci, U of Lund; 1964 Expert, Dept of Justice and Secretary; 1965-68 Expert, Royal Commission on County Communal Democracy. Publs: *Författningsreform — nytt Alternativ* (co-author), 1963; *Demokratisk Författning*, 1976; *Försvar för Folkstyret*, 1970; *Hur går det med Demokratin?*, 1971; *Modern Demokrati* (co-author), 1976; *Kommunal självstyrelse*. *Kommunerna i det politiska systemet*, 1977; *Företagsdemokratin och den offentliga sektorn* (co-author), 1978; *Local Government in Sweden*, 1978. Fields: Constitutional problems and the problems of local government.

[754]
GUSTAFSSON Gunnel
4 July 1943, Swedish. Rödhakevägen 52 A, S-902 37 Umeå, Sweden. Degrees: MA (Umeå), 1969; PhD (Umeå), 1972. Doctoral thesis: "Transformation of Society and Political Socialization". Acting Professor, U of Umeå. Publs: "Tid och Politik", *Statsvetenskaplig Tidskrift*, 1971; "Environmental Influence on Political Learning", in *The Politics of Future Citizens* (R G Nieme (ed)). Fields: Political socialization and political recruitment; physical planning; problems of municipal boundaries and amalgamation.

[755]
GUSTAFSSON Mervi Anita
1 January 1950, Finnish. Jänislahdenkatu 6 E 72, SF-33410 Tampere 41, Finland. Degrees: M Pol Sci (Tampere), 1974. 1975 Lecturer, Dept of Pol Sci, U of Tampere; 1976 Research Assistant, International Food Politics Project, Academy of Finland; 1976 Research Fellow, Tampere Peace Research Inst; 1977 Research Assistant, International Food Politics Project, Academy of Finland. Publs: *Migrant Workers in European Economic Community*, 1974; *US Food Aid Policy in Political Economy of Food*, 1976; *Food Aid in International Relations: The Case of the United States*, 1977. Fields: Migrant workers in the EEC; international food aid; food problem in developing countries and the new international economic order.

[756]
GUTTERIDGE William Frank
British. 26 St Mark's Road, Leamington Spa, Warwickshire CV32 6DL, England. Degrees: MA. 1949-63 Lecturer, Senior Lecturer, Royal Military Academy, Sandhurst; 1963-67 Head of Dept of Languages and Soc Sci/Modern Studies, Lanchester Polytechnic; 1967- Director of Complementary Studies and Professor of International Studies, U of Aston in Birmingham. Publs: *Armed Forces in New States*, 1962; *Military Institutions and Power in the New States*, 1965; *The Military in African Politics*, 1969; *Military Regimes in Africa*, 1975. Fields: Civil-military relations; political role of the military; politics of nuclear proliferation and the arms trade; the military situation in Africa.

[757]
GYSELINCK Leon Marie Hippolyte
11 July 1891, Belgian. 37 Berkenlaan, 2610 Wilrijj, Belgium. Degrees: Dr en droit (Free U of Brussels), 1919. Avocat honoraire (Antwerp); Juge suppléant honoraire, Tribunal de 1ère Instance d'Anvers; Professeur ém, U of Brussels, U of Antwerp; Président Honoraire, Banque d'Anvers; Ancien Président, Association Belge des Banques; Ancien President, Commission de Droit Monétaire, International Law Association; Vice-Président, Centre d'Etudes pour l'Expansion d'Anvers; Trésorier, Association Belge de Droit Maritime. Publs: *L'enseignement des relations internationales*, 1951. Fields: International law; international relations.

H

[758]
HAAVIO-MANNILA A Elina
3 August 1933, Finnish. Mariankatu 15 A 22, 00170 Helsinki, Finland. Degrees: Dr (Helsinki), 1958. Doctoral thesis: "Village Fights". 1956-61 Researcher and Teacher, College of Nursing; 1962-71 Research Fellow, Soc Sci Research Council; 1965-71 Docent of Sociology, U of Helsinki; 1971- Associate Professor of Sociology, U of Helsinki. Publs: *Kylätappelut*, 1958; *Läkärit Tutkittavina*, 1964; *Suomalainen Nainen ja Mies*, 1968; *Women in the Economic, Political and Cultural Elite in Finland*, 1977; "Changes in Sex Roles in Politics", *International Journal of Sociology*, 1978; "How Women Become Political Actors", 1978. Fields: Sex roles in politics in comparative perspective; services given by family vs public service organizations.

[759]
HABERL Othmar Nikola
4 December 1943, German. Nockwinkel 85, D-4300 Essen 14, FR Germany. Degrees: Dipl Pol (Free U of Berlin), 1969; Dr phil (Free U of Berlin), 1974. Doctoral thesis: "Party Organization and the National Question in Yugoslavia". Assistant Professor, U of Essen. Publs: *Emanzipation der KPJ von der Kontrolle der Komintern/KPdSU 1941-1945*, 1976; *Parteiorganisation und nationale Frage in Jugoslawien*, 1976; *Abwanderung von Arbeitskräften aus Jugoslawien*, 1978. Fields: Contemporary history of Eastern Europe; East-West relations during the Cold War 1947-1953; migrant workers in Europe.

[760]
HABICHT Max
6 March 1899, Swiss. 3 Rebwiesstrasse, 8702 Zollikon, Switzerland. Degrees: Dr of Law (Zürich), 1924; Dr of Juridical Sci (Harvard), 1926. Doctoral thesis: "Die Erbschaftsteilung im schweizerischen Recht". 1928-39 member of the Legal Section of the League of Nations Secretariat; 1942 Delegate of the Swiss Legation for War Prisoners, Washington; 1963 Professor of International Law, International Christian U, Tokyo, Japan; 1964-International Legal Advisor. Publs: *Post-War Treaties for the Pacific Settlement of International Disputes*, 1931; "The Special Position of Switzerland in International Affairs", *International Affairs*, 1953; *The Proposals of World Federalists for United Nations Charter Revisions*, 1954; *Consultation between the United Nations and Non-Governmental Organizations*, 1949; *Conflict Resolution by Peaceful Means*, 1966; "Weltfriede durch neues Weltrecht ", *Der Quäker*, 1969; "Über den Frieden", *Der Quäker*, 1975. Fields: Peace research.

[761]
HACCOÛ Huibert
17 April 1950, Dutch. Kerveltuin 6, 2353 PN Leiderdrop, The Netherlands. Degrees: Dr. Doctoral thesis: "Methods of Policy Development". Local Government Planner; Central Government Planner, Ministry of Health and Environment Protection. Publs: "Causes of Failure of Government Policy", *Bestuurswetenschappen*, 1978. Fields: Planning theories and techniques; welfare economics.

[762]
HAECKLE Erwin
21 March 1941, German. Fachbereich Politik, Universität Konstanz, Postfach 7733, D-7750 Konstanz, FR Germany. Degrees: MA (Minnesota), 1965; Dr rer Soc (Konstanz), 1970; Habilitation (Konstanz), 1976. 1969-70 Research Associate, International Inst for Strategic Studies, London; 1970- Wiss Assistent, Privatdozent, U of Konstanz. Publs: *Military Manpower and Political Purpose*, 1970; *Kritik der Jungen Linken in Europa* (co-author), 1973; *Afrikanischer Nationalismus*, 1974; *Multinationale Konzerne und europäische Integration*, 1975; *Demokratische Aussenpolitik?*, 1977. Fields: International integration; international organization; history of international relations; West European politics; military sociology.

[763]
HAENSCH Dietrich
1937, German. Seminar für Wissenschaft von der Politik, Schneiderberg 50, 3 Hannover 1, FR Germany. Degrees: Dr rer Pol; Dipl Pol. Doctoral thesis: "Familienpolitik als Staatspolitik". Professor of Pol Sci, Technische U, Hannover. Publs: Several publications concerning rationalization and reform of the public service in The Federal Republic of Germany. Fields: Public service; state railways in Germany; labour movement in Germany, France; working classes.

[764]
HAESTRUP Jørgen*
9 August 1909, Danish. Svendstrupvej 66, 5260 Hjallese, Denmark. Degrees: Cand mag (Copenhagen), 1934; Dr phil (Aarhus), 1954. 1934-60 Lektor, Sct Knuds Gymnasium, Odense; 1966- Lektor, U of Odense. Publs: *Kontakt med England 1940-43*, 1954; *Hemmelig alliance*, 1959; *Hilsen til Vera*, 1956; *Table Top*, 1961; *Kilder til Modstandsbevaegelsens Historie*, 1962; *From Occupied to Ally*, 1963; *Besaettelsens hvem, hvad, hvor*, 1965; *Til Landets Bedste*, 1971. Fields: Denmark during the occupation 1940-45; resistance movements during the Second World War.

[765]
HAFTENDORN Helga
9 September 1933, German. Heisterweg 8, D-2000 Schenefeld, Bz Hamburg, FR Germany. Degrees: Dr phil (Frankfurt), 1960; Venia Legendi (Hamburg), 1972. Doctoral thesis: "Das Problem von Parlament und Öffentlichkeit, dargestellt am Beispiel der Parlamentsberichterstattung". 1960-63 Associate Editor, *Europa-Archiv*; 1963-69 Research Fellow, Deutsche Gesellschaft für Auswärtige Politik; 1969-73 Wiss Rat, U of Hamburg; 1973-77 Professor of Pol Sci, Hochschule der Bundeswehr, Hamburg. Publs: *Militärhilfe und Rüstungsexporte der Bundesrepublik Deutschland*, 1971; *Abrüstung- und Entspannungspolitik zwischen Sicherheitsbefriedigung und Friedenssicherung; Zur Aussenpolitik der Bundesrepublik Deutschland*, 1974; *Theorien der Internationalen Politik*, 1975; *Verwaltete Aussenpolitik Sicherheits- und Entspannungspolitische Entscheidungen in Bonn*, 1977. Fields: German foreign policy; US foreign policy; arms control and security policy; foreign policy decision making; theories of international relations.

[766]
HAKOVIRTA Harto Kalevi
16 December 1941, Finnish. Välimaankatu 1-5 D-58, 33500 Tampere, Finland. Degrees: M soc sci (Tampere), 1968; Lic soc sci (Tampere), 1973; Dr soc sci (Tampere), 1976. Doctoral thesis: "Puolueettomuus ja Integraatiopolitiikka — Tutkimus Puolueettoman Valtion Adaptaatiosta Alueelliseen Integraatioon Teorian, Vertailujen ja Suomen Poikkeavan Tapauksen Valossa". 1971-73 Acting Assistant in International Pol, U of Tampere; 1975-76 Professor of International Pol, U of Tampere; 1973- Assistant in International Pol, U of Tampere. Publs: *Suomen Turvallisuuspolitiikka*, 1971; *Suomen Hallitukset ja Hallitusohjelmat 1945-1973* (co-ed and co-author), 1973; *Suomettuminen*, 1975; *Suomen Ulkopolitiikka* (co-ed and co-author); *Puolueettomuus ja Integraatiopolitiikka*, 1976. Fields: Finnish foreign policy; theory and practice of neutrality; regional integration; theory of foreign policy; international migration and politics.

[767]
HALE William Mathew
17 November 1940, British. 9 Victoria Terrace, Durham, England. Degrees: MA (Oxon); PhD (ANU). Doctoral thesis: "Afghanistan, Britain and Russia, 1905-21". Joint Research Dept, FO/CRO; Lecturer in Middle East Pol, Dept of Pol, U of Durham. Publs: "CENTO RCD and the Northern Tier", *Middle Eastern Studies*, 1972; "Aspects of the Turkish General Election of 1969", *Middle Eastern Studies*, 1972; "Anglo-Turkish Relations: An Historical Conspectus", *Foreign Policy*, 1971; "Modern Turkish Politics: An Historical Introduction", " Particularism and Universalism in Turkish Politics", "Labour Unions in Turkey: Progress and Problems", in *Aspects of Modern Turkey* (W Hale (ed)), 1976; "Turkey and the Cyprus Crisis", *World Today*, 1974; "Turkish Democracy in Travail: The Case of the State Security Courts", *World Today*, 1977; "Cyprus in Perspective", *Contemporary Review*, 1977; "Turkey's Inconclusive Election", *World Today*, 1977. Fields: Modern Turkish politics and history.

[768]
HALLE Louis Joseph
17 November 1910, Swiss. Chemin de Botterel 18, CH-1222 Vésenaz, Switzerland. Degrees: BSc (Harvard), 1932. Professor Emeritus, Graduate Inst of International Studies, Geneva, and Visiting Professor, Bologna Center, John Hopkins School of Advanced International Studies. Publs: *Civilization and Foreign Policy*; *Dream and Reality*; *Aspects of American Foreign Policy*; *Men and Nations*; *The Society of Marx*; *The Ideological Imagination*; *Out of Chaos*.

[769]
HALVORSEN Kjell Harald
4 May 1946, Norwegian. Daelenengaten 9, Oslo 5, Norway. Degrees: MA. Doctoral thesis: "Colonial Work and Foreign Labour. An Analysis of the Proletarianization of Algerian Peasants". Research Associate, Inst for Pol Sci, U of Oslo. Fields: International political economy and problems of development in developing countries.

[770]
HAMILTON Keith Alexander
20 September 1942, British. Pen-v-Wern Lodge, New Cross, Aberystwyth, Dyfed, Wales. Degrees: BSc; PhD (London). Doctoral thesis: "The Embassy of Sir Francis Bertie in Paris During the Period 1905-1914". Lecturer, Dept of International Pol, U Coll of Wales, Aberystwyth. Publs: "An Attempt to Form an Anglo-French Industrial Entente", *Middle Eastern Studies*, 1975; "Great Britain and France, 1905-1911" and "Great Britain and France 1911-1914", in *British Foreign Policy Under Sir Edward Grey* (with F H Hinsley (ed)), 1977. Fields: International history in the 19th and 20th centuries, especially Anglo-French relations.

[771]
HAMMAR Karl Thomas Gilius
24 December 1928, Swedish. Bergavägen 19, S-182 33 Danderyd, Sweden. Degrees: Pol mag, 1954; Fil lic, 1959; Fil dr, 1964 (all Stockholm). Doctoral thesis: "Sverige åt svenskarna: Invandringspolitik, utlänningskontroll och asylrätt 1900-32". 1959-62 Assistant teacher, Dept of Pol Sci, U of Stockholm; 1962-63 Director, Inst for English-speaking Students, U of Stockholm. 1964- Docent, Assistant Professor, Dept of Pol Sci, U of Stockholm. Publs: *Sverige åt svenskarna: Invandringspolitik, utlänningskontroll och asylratt 1900-32*, 1964; *Leva i Sverige*, 1971; *The First Immigrant Election*, 1977; "Immigrants and Politics", in *Finns in Södertälje*, 1973.

[772]
HAMON Léo
1908, French. 12 rue de la Glacière, 75013 Paris, France. Degrees: Lic en lettres; Dr en droit; Agrégé de droit public. Doctoral thesis: "Le conseil d'Etat juge du fait". Professor, U of Dijon, U of Orléans, U of Paris I. Publs: *La stratégie contre la guerre*, 1967; *Acteurs et données de l'histoire*, 1972; *La révision*, 1974; *Socialisme et pluralité*, 1975; *Une République présidentielle*, 1978. Fields: Sociological theory; political science theory; socialist theory; new forms of power.

[773]
HAMPSHER-MONK Iain William
1 November 1946, British. 33 Portland Street, Exeter EX1 2EG, England. Degrees: BA. Lecturer in Pol Theory, Dept of Pol, U of Exeter. Publs: "Political Theory of the Levellers: Putney Property and Professor Macpheson", *Political Studies*, 1976; "Resistance and Economy in Dr Angtim's Locke", *Political Studies*, 1978; *Tacit concept of consent in Locke: a note on citizens, levellers and patriarchalism in Locke's 2*

Treatises, 1978; "The Society of the Friends of the People: Late Eighteenth Century Civic Humanists?", *Journal of British Studies*, 1978. Fields: English political thought, especially 17th and 18th century; methodology of history of ideas; political economy.

[774]
HAMPTON William Albert
26 July 1929, British. Division of Continuing Education, University of Sheffield, 85 Wilkinson Street, Sheffield S10 2GS, England. Degrees: BSc; PhD (Sheffield). Doctoral thesis: "Democracy and Community: A Study of Politics in Sheffield". 1944-60 Industrial Worker in Printing; 1963 Temporary Research Assistant, LSE; 1963- Reader, Division of Continuing Education, U of Sheffield. Publs: *Democracy and Community: A Study of Politics in Sheffield*, 1970. Fields: Mass values and political participation in public administration.

[775]
HANDLEY David H
27 August 1938, American. 19 Chemin de la Planche d'Aire, CH-1212 Grand Lancy, Switzerland. Degrees: Lic ès sci pol (Graduate Inst of International Studies), 1968; Dr ès sci econ et soc (Geneva), 1975. Doctoral thesis: "Public Support for European Integration: Conceptual Formulation, Methodological Approaches and Secondary Analysis of 1971 Survey Data in Five Common Market Countries, with Special Reference to Regional Economic Context"; Professeur Suppleant, Assistant, U de Genève; Research Assistant, Carnegie Endowment for International Peace; Professeur Assistant, Dept of Sci Pol, U de Genève. Publs: "Mini et Micro Informatique: Une Revolution Permanente", *Chefs. Revue Suisse de Management*, 1978; "Opinion Public et Integration Européene", *Economie et Humanisme*, 1975; "Conflit de generations et politique etrangère en Suisse", in *Annuaire Suisse de Science Politique* (with H Kerr), 1974; *Economic Problem Regions and Attitudes Towards the EEC and European Unification*, 1975. Fields: European integration; mass political behaviour; methodology; computer applications.

[776]
HANDS Hugh Thomas Gordon
7 September 1944, British. 1 Bedford Place, Lancaster, England. Degrees: BA; B Phil (Oxon). Lecturer in Pol, U of Lancaster; Head of Dept of Pol. Publs: "Roberto Michels and the Study of Political Parties", *Journal of Political Science*, 1971; "Turnout and Marginality in Local Elections: A Comment", *British Journal of Political Science* (with D T Denver), 1972; "Marginality and Turnout in British General Elections", *British Journal of Political Science* (with D T Denver), 1974; "Differential Party Votes in Multi-Member Electoral Divisions", *Political Studies*, 1975. Fields: Political sociology; sociological theory; Robert Michels, local politics.

[777]
HANF Kenneth I
9 November 1937, American. Pfeddersheimer Weg 25, 1000 Berlin 38, FR Germany. Degrees: MA (California); PhD (California). Doctoral thesis: "The Higher Civil Service in West Germany: Administrative Leadership and the Policy Process". 1964-66 Research Assistant, Academy of Administrative Sci, Speyer; 1966-72 Assistant Professor, Dept of Pol Sci, U of California; Senior Fulbright Research Professor; 1973 Free U of Berlin; 1973-77 Research Fellow, International Inst of Management, Berlin; Visiting Professor of Pol Sci, John F Kennedy Inst for North American Studies, Free U of Berlin. Publs: "Environmental Concern and Lake Tahoe: A Study of Elite Perceptions, Backgrounds and Attitudes" (with E Costantini), *Environment and Behaviour*, 1972; "Administrative Developments in East and West Germany", *Political Studies*,

1973; "Sozialplanung in der entwickelten Sozialistischen Gesellschaft", *Sonderheft Deutschlandarchiv*, 1975; "Joint Decision-Making in the GDR: An Interorganizational Perspective on Policy and Planning", *Organization and Administrative Sciences*, 1977; "Cooperative Arrangements for the Delivery of Public Services in the GDR", *Urban Affairs Annual Review*, 1977. Fields: Comparative politics and administration; comparative policy analysis; organization theory.

[778]
HANF Theodor
20 March 1939, German. 31 Jacobistrasse, 78 Freiburg, FR Germany. Degrees: Dr phil (Freiburg), 1966. Doctoral thesis: "Das Erziehungswesen in Gesellschaft und Politik des Libanon" (Education, Society and Politics in Lebanon). 1971 Professor of Pol Sci, U of Regensburg; 1967 Visiting Professor, U of Stanford; 1968 Visiting Professor, U of Lovanium, Zaire; 1970 Visiting Professor, U of Michigan; Visiting Professor, American U of Beyrout; Professor of Sociology, German Inst for International Pedagogical Research, Frankfurt; Honorary Professor of Pol Sci, U of Freiburg; Director, Arnold-Bergstraesser-Institut, Freiburg. Publs: *Erziehungswesen in Gesellschaft und Politik des Libanon*, 1969; *Les étudiants universitaires Congolais. Une enquête sur leurs attitudes socio-politiques* (with P Dias and others), 1971; *Education et développement au Rwanda. Problèmes, apories, perspectives* (with P Dias and others), 1974; *Südafrika: Friedlicher Wandel? Möglichkeiten demokratischer Konfliktregelung. Eine empirische Untersuchung* (with W Weiland and others), 1978; *Sozialer Wandel* (co-ed), 1975; *Education and Politics* (ed), 1975; "Le Comportement politique des étudiants libanais", *Travaux et Jours*, 1973; "Der Libanonkrieg: Von der Systemkrise einer Konkordanzdemokratie zum Spanischen Bürgerkrieg der Araber?", in *Friedensanalysen*, 1978. Fields: Conflict regulation in segmented societies; education and politics.

[779]
HANISCH Rolf
10 November 1942, German. 2 Hamburg 19, Bismarckstrasse 12, FR Germany. Degrees: Dipl Pol (1968); Dr rer Pol (1973). Doctoral thesis; "Der Handlungsspielraum eines Landes der Peripherie im internationalen System. Das Beispiel Ghana's" (The Scope of Action of a Country of the Periphery in the International System. The Case of Ghana). 1970-73 Wiss Mitarbeiter, Arbeitsstelle Politik Afrika, Free U of Berlin; 1973-76 Wiss Assistent, Inst für Ausländische Landwirtschaft, Georg-August U of Göttingen; 1976-Wiss Rat, U of Hamburg. Publs: *Bürgerkrieg in Afrika? Biafra und die inneren Konflikte eines Kontinents*, 1970; *Der Handlungsspielraum eines Landes der Peripherie im internationalen System. Das Beispiel Ghana's*, 1975; "Confrontation Between Primary Commodity Producers and Consumers: The Cocoa Hold-up of 1964-65", *Journal of Commonwealth and Comparative Politics*, 1975; *Ghana and the Cocoa World Market. The Scope of Action of a Raw Material Exporting Country of the Periphery in the World Market (up to 1966)*, 1976; "Decision-making Processes and Problems of Implementation of Land Reform in the Philippines", *Asia Quarterly*, 1977. Fields: International relations and development policy of LDC's, especially international commodity policy and agricultural policy.

[780]
HANNAFORD Ivan William
21 March 1931, British. 14 Twickenham Road, Teddington, Middlesex, England. Degrees: BSc; MSc (LSE). 1969-72 Assistant Professor, Dept of Pol Studies, U of Lakehead, Canada; 1972- Assistant Director (Academic) Kingston Polytechnic, Surrey. Publs: "Machiavelli's Concept of Virtue Reconsidered", *Political Studies*, 1972. Fields: University development.

[781]
HANSEN Holger Bernt
3 January 1936, Danish. Mellemvang 11, DK-3640 Birkeroed, Denmark. Degrees: BA;
M Th (Copenhagen). Doctoral thesis: "Mission, Church and State in a Colonial Setting
— a Case Study from Uganda". Research Fellow and Lecturer, U of Makerere, Uganda; Senior Lecturer, Inst of Pol Studies, U of Copenhagen. Publs: *Ethnicity and
Military Rule in Uganda*, 1977. Fields: Religion and politics, church and state; ethnicity
as a political factor; military rule as a political phenomenon.

[782]
HANSEN Peter
2 June 1941, Danish. Langelinie 171, 5230 Odense, Denmark. Degrees: Cand sci pol.
1966-70 Associate Professor, U of Aarhus; 1970-71 Danish Member, UN Delegation;
1971-73 Associate Professor, U of Aarhus; 1973-76 Senior Research Fellow, U of
Aarhus; Professor, U of Odense. Publs: *Verdenspolitik (co-author), 1969; International Organisation*, 1975; various articles in *International Studies Quarterly, International Journal of Comparative Sociology, Journal of Common Market Studies, International Review of Administrative Sciences*. Fields: International organization; European integration; development; foreign policy studies; political attitudes.

[783]
HANSEN Tore
3 September 1942, Norwegian. Munkedamsveien 98, Oslo 2, Norway. Degrees: BA;
Cand pol (Oslo). Research Fellow, Inst of Pol Sci, U of Oslo; Lecturer in Pol Sci, U of
Oslo. Publs: *Lokale Beslutningsprosesser* (with F Kjellberg), 1978; "Budgetary
Strategies and Success at Multiple Decision Levels in the Norwegian Urban Setting"
(with A T Cowart and K E Brofoss), *American Political Science Review*, 1975;
"Municipal Expenditures in Norway" (with F Kjellberg), *Policy & Politics*, 1976;
"Central Controls and Local Budgeting Behaviour", *Policy & Politics*, 1978. Fields:
Local finances; budgeting and local planning; methodology/statistics.

[784]
HANSSON Rolf B*
29 January 1947, Swedish. University of Lund, 220 05 Lund 5, Sweden. Degrees: BA.
Fields: Soviet Union.

[785]
HARARI Bhund
27 July 1935, Israeli. 25A Mizan Street, Tel-Baruch, Tel-Aviv, Israel. Degrees: BSFS
(Georgetown); MA (California); PhD (California). Doctoral thesis: "The Politics of
Labour Legislation in Japan". 1968-73 Lecturer, Dept of Pol Sci, Tel-Aviv; 1973-74
Foreign Research Scholar, Inst of Soc Sci, U of Tokyo; 1975 Center Associate, Center
for Japanese and Korean Studies, U of California, Berkeley; Senior Lecturer, Depts of
Pol Sci and E Asian Studies, the Hebrew U of Jerusalem. Publs: *The Politics of Labour
Legislation in Japan: National-International Interaction*, 1973; "Japanese Politics of
Advice in Comparative Perspective", *Public Policy*, 1974; "Limitations and Prospects
of Planned Change in Multinational Corporations", *Human Relations* (with Y Zeira),
1976; "Attitudes of Japanese and Non-Japanese Employees: A Cross-National Comparison in Uninational and Multinational Corporations", *International Journal of
Comparative Sociology* (with Y Zeira), 1977; "Unemployment in Japan: Policy and
Politics", *Asian Survey*, 1978. Fields: Japanese politics and foreign policy; organization
theory with special emphasis on Japan; human resources development in multinational
corporations.

[786]
HARDER Hans Joachim
24 November 1943, German. Sautierstrasse 55, D-7800 Freiburg im Breisgau, FR Germany. Degrees: Dr phil. Doctoral thesis: "Der Kanton Jura. Ursachen und Schritte zur Lösung eines Schweizer Minderheitenproblems" (The Canton of Jura. Reasons and Steps to the Solution of a Swiss Minority Problem). Historian and Staff Officer, German Service of Military History, Freiburg. Fields: Federalism and minorities; political systems of the United States, Switzerland, France.

[787]
HARDING Gordon Neil
14 March 1942, British. 5 Church Park, Mumbles, Swansea, Wales. Degrees: BA; MSc (LSE). Lecturer in Pol and Russian Studies, U Coll, Swansea. Publs: "Lenin's Early Writings — The Problem of Context", *Political Studies*, 1975; "Lenin and his Critics: Some Problems of Interpretation", *European Journal of Sociology*, 1976; "Socialism and Violence", *The Concept of Socialism*, 1974; *Lenin's Political Thought*, 1977; *Marxism and the Labour Movement in Russia: Key Documents*, 1978. Fields: European socialist thought; Russian social and political thought.

[788]
HARLE Vilho
21 May 1947, Finnish. Lehvänkatu 24 D-33, 33820 Tampere 82, Finland. Degrees: Dr (Tampere), 1975. Doctoral thesis: "International Tension: An Application of Cohesion Theory and Event Analysis to East-West Relations during the Post-War Years". Lecturer in Pol Sci, U of Tampere; Research Fellow, National Research Council for Soc Sci, Academy of Finland. Publs: In Finnish: *Armament and Disarmament* (co-author), 1972; *'White Book': Facts and Figures on Finnish Defence Policy* (co-author), 1978; *Leko-70 and HS 1182 Hawk*, 1978; In English: *The Political Economy of Food* (ed), 1978. Fields: Peace research; theories of international conflicts; arms race and disarmament; events data research; Finnish defence policy; international food/agricultural policy.

[789]
HARLOFF Eileen Marie
9 October 1927, American/Dutch. Laan van Meerdervoort 1285, The Hague, The Netherlands. Degrees: BA: MPA (Michigan), 1957. 1957-58 Fulbright Fellow in Public Administration, International Union of Local Authorities; 1958-59 Editorial work, IULA; Research Officer, IULA. Publs: *Local Government Throughout the World* (co-author), 1961; *The Structure of Local Government: A Comparative Survey of 81 Countries* (co-author), 1969; "Organization and Administration of Environment Programmes", in *Organization and Administration of Environmental Programmes*, 1974. Fields: Long-term planning in local decision-making; regional planning and regional government; urban problems; urban land policies; metropolitan government; citizen participation in local government.

[790]
HARMEL Pierre
16 March 1911, Belgian. University of Liège. Degrees: Dr in Law; Agrégé de l'enseignement supérieur. Professor, U of Liège; 1946-71 Representative, Belgian House of Representatives; 1971- Senator, Belgian Senate; 1950-72, various posts in Belgian government; 1965-66 Prime Minister; 1973-77 President, Belgian Senate. Publs: *Le principe "Non bis in idem"*, 1942; *Culture et profession*, 1944; *La famille et l'impôt en Belgique*, 1945; *Traité élémentaire de droit notarial*, 1961; *L'acte notarié*, 1961; *Organisation et déontologie du notariat*, 1977.

[791]
HARRISON Brian Howard
9 July 1937, British. Corpus Christi College, Oxford, England. Degrees: BA; MA; D Phil (Oxon), 1966. 1961-64 Senior Scholar, St Anthony's Coll, U of Oxford; 1964-67 Junior Research Fellow, Nuffield Coll, U of Oxford; 1970 Visiting Professor, U of Michigan, Ann Arbor; 1967- Fellow and Tutor in Modern History and Pol, Corpus Christi Coll, U of Oxford. Publs: *History at the Universities* (with George Barlow); *Drink and Sobriety in an Early Victorian Country Town* (with Barrie Trinder), 1969; *Drink and the Victorians*, 1971. Fields: The history of pressure groups and reforming movements in the 18th and 19th centuries; British women's organizations, 1900-1940.

[792]
HARRISON Martin
1930, British. Department of Politics, University of Keele, Keele, Staffordshire, England. Degrees: BA; DES (Paris), 1960; D Phil (Oxon), 1960. 1957-62 Research Fellow, Nuffield Coll; 1962-66 Lecturer, Senior Lecturer, U of Manchester; Professor, Head of Dept, U of Keele. Publs: *Trade Unions and the Labour Party Since 1945*, 1960; *De Gaulle's Republic* (with P M Williams), 1971. Fields: Contemporary French politics; British political parties; financing of political parties; radio and TV in politics.

[793]
HARRISON Reginald James
14 May 1927, British. Department of Politics, University of Lancaster, Bailrigg, Lancaster, England. Degrees: BA: BSc; PhD (Ohio), 1964. Doctoral thesis: "Organization and Procedure of the New Zealand Parliament". 1954-56 Assistant, Dept of Pol, Ohio State U; 1957-66 Lecturer, Senior Lecturer, Victoria U of Wellington, New Zealand; 1967- Lecturer, Senior Lecturer, U of Lancaster. Publs: "Government — Parliament", in *An Encyclopaedia of New Zealand* (McLintock (ed)); "New Zealand Foreign Policy", in *The Other Powers* (R P Barston (ed)), 1973; *Europe in Question: Theories of Regional International Integration*, 1974; "Testing Functionalism", in *Functionalism* (P Taylor and J Groom (eds)), 1975; "Neo-functionalism", in *International Organization: A Conceptual Approach* (Groom and Taylor (eds)), 1978; "Harmonization" (with S Mungall), in *International Organization: A Conceptual Approach*; *Politics of Advanced Industrial Societies*, 1978. Fields: European community politics; integration theory.

[794]
HARRISON Royden John
3 March 1927, British. 4 Wilton Place, Sheffield S10 2BT, England. Degrees: BA; MA (Oxon), 1955; D Phil (Oxon), 1955. Doctoral thesis: "England Positivists and Labour Movements 1859-85". 1955-63 Lecturer in Industrial Studies, U of Sheffield; 1964 Visiting Professor in English and European History, U of Wisconsin, USA; 1967-70 Senior Lecturer, Reader in Pol Theory and Inst, U of Sheffield; Professor of Soc History, Director, Post-Graduate Centre for the Study of Soc History, U of Warwick. Publs: *Before the Socialists: Studies in Labour and Politics, 1881-1961*, 1965; *The English Defence of the Commune*, 1971; *Labour in Modern British Politics*, 1971. Fields: Labour history; institutions and policies; comparative studies; social history of crime.

[795]
HART Jennifer Margaret
29 January 1914, British. 11 Manor Place, Oxford, England. Degrees: MA (Oxon). 1936-48 Home Office; 1948-50 Supervisor of Studies, Dept of Extra-Mural Studies, U of Oxford; 1950-51 Research Fellow, Nuffield Coll, U of Oxford; 1951- Tutor in Modern History and Pol and Fellow, St Anne's Coll, U of Oxford. Publs: *The British Police*; "Religion and Social Control", in *Social Control* (A Donajgrodski (ed)). Fields: Police; social and administrative history; emancipation of women; social and political influence of religion.

[796]
HART Thomas G
6 December 1936, Swedish. Falkvägen 6, S-19060 Bålsta, Sweden. Degrees: AB (Pennsylvania), 1959; MA (Stockholm), 1962; PhD (Stockholm), 1971. Doctoral thesis: "The Dynamics of Revolution: A Cybernetic Theory of the Dynamics of Modern Social Revolution with a Study of Ideological Change and Organizational Dynamics in the Chinese Revolution". Research Associate, Swedish Inst of International Affairs; Docent, Dept of Pol Sci, U of Stockholm. Publs: *The Cognitive World of Swedish Security Elites*, 1976. Fields: International relations; comparative politics and foreign policy; Chinese politics and foreign policy; conflict theory and peace research.

[797]
HARTJENS Peter Garre
14 January 1944, American. Ostlandstrasse 49, 5 Köln 40, FR Germany. Degrees: AB (Franklin and Marshall U Coll), 1965; PhD (N Carolina), 1972. Doctoral thesis: "Varieties of Democratic Political Development: The German Experience". 1969-75 Assistant Professor, Franklin and Marshall Coll, Lancaster, Pa; 1975-77 Director of Evaluation, Governor's Commission on Crime Prevention and Control, State of Minnesota; Research Scientist, Zentralarchiv für empirische Sozialforschung, U of Cologne. Publs: "Secondary Analysis in the Social Sciences" (with W M Chandler), in *Social Science Information; Representation in the US Congress 1973*, 1974; *Minnesota Crime Watch: An Evaluation*, 1976. Fields: Evaluation research; public policy; socialization; voting behaviour.

[798]
HARTLEY Owen Arthur
21 September 1943, British. Department of Politics, The University, Leeds LS2 9JT, England. Degrees: BA; D Phil (Oxon), 1969. Doctoral thesis: "Housing Policy in Four Lincolnshire Towns 1919-59". 1968- Lecturer in Pol, U of Leeds. Fields: Public administration, especially local government; British government and politics; theory of war and military history since 1914.

[799]
HARTMANN Dieterr-Dirk
13 October 1935, German. Weissdornweg 14W34, D-7400 Tübingen, FR Germany. Degrees: Dr jur; Dr rer Soc. Doctoral thesis: "Ausreisefreiheit"; 'Volksinitiativen". Lehrauftrag, Pol Sci, U of Tübingen. Publs: *Gleichheitsgebot und Willkürverbot*, 1972; *Volksinitiativen*, 1967. Fields: National socialism; democratic theory; political psychology; Federal German political system.

[800]
HAUNGS Peter Joachim*
12 April 1939, German. 55 Trier, Merianstrasse 12, FR Germany. Degrees: Dr phil (Heidelberg). Doctoral thesis: "Reichspräsident und parlamentärische Kabinetsregierung. Eine Studie zum Regierungssystem der Weimarer Republik in den Jahren 1924-29". Wiss Assistent, Inst für Pol Wissenschaft, U of Heidelberg; 1972- Wiss Rat, Professor für Pol, U of Trier-Kaiserslautern. Publs: *Wahlkampf und Wählertradition. Eine Studie zur Bundestagswahl von 1961* (with B Vogel), 1965; *Reichspräsident und parlamentärische Kabinettsregierung*, 1968. Fields: The German and the French political system (of the Fifth Republic); political parties; elections and election campaigns.

[801]
HAUS Wolfgang
26 July 1927, German. D-1000 Berlin 33, Tauberstrasse 23a, FR Germany. Degrees: Dr phil (Free U of Berlin), 1955. Doctoral thesis: "England, Russia and the Near East 1907-8 — The Development of an Entente". Wiss Referent des Geschäftsfygrebdeb Oräsuduaknutgkuedes des Deutschen Städtetages; 1963-67 Bezirkverordneter von Berlin-Wilmersdorf; Vorsitzender der SPD-Fraktion der Bezirksverordnetenversammlung von Berlin-Wilmersdorf; Geschäftsführer des Kommunalwissenschaftlichen Forschungszentrums des Vereins für Kommunalwissenschaften e. V. Berlin; Lehrbeauftragter der Free U of Berlin; Mitglied des Abgeordnetenhauses von Berlin; Stellvertretender Fraktionsvorsitzender der SPD; Vorsitzender des Rundfunkrates des Senders Freies Berlin; 1973-77 Vorsitzender der SPD-Fraktion; 1973 Intendant des Deutschen Instituts für Urbanistik; 1978 Intendant des Senders Freies Berlin. Publs: *Kommunalwissenschaftliche Forschung*, 1966; *Gemeindeordnungen in Europa* (with A Krebsbach), 1967; *Quellen des Gemeinderechts* (with C Engeli). Fields: Municipal systems of government; history of municipal administration; decision-making in administration; problems of municipal development and reform of administration.

[802]
HÄUSSERMANN Hartmut*
6 July 1943, German. 1000 Berlin 62, Insbrucker Strasse 4, FR Germany. Degrees: Dipl Soziologe. Wiss Assistent, Inst für Soziologie, Free U of Berlin.

[803]
HAYWARD Jack Ernest Shalom
18 August 1931, British. 'Hurstwood', Church Lane, Kirkella, Humberside HU10 7TA, England. BSc; PhD (LSE), 1958. Doctoral thesis: "The Idea of Solidarity in French Social and Political Thought in the Nineteenth Century and Early Twentieth Century". 1959-63 Assistant Lecturer, Lecturer in Pol, U of Sheffield; 1968-69 Senior Research Fellow, Nuffield Coll, U of Oxford; Senior Lecturer in Pol, U of Keele; Professor of Pol, U of Hull. Publs: *Private Interests and Public Policy. The Experience of the French Economic and Social Council*, 1966; *The One and Indivisible French Republic*, 1973; *Planning, Politics and Public Policy: The British, French and Italian Experience* (co-ed), 1975. Fields: The French left; government-industry relations in western Europe; comparative economic planning; interest groups; administrative relations in France.

[804]
HAYWARD Keith
17 January 1948, British. 59 Ness Grove, Cheadle, Staffordshire, England. Degrees:

BA; MA. Senior Lecturer, Dept of International Relations and Pol, North Stafford-shire Polytechnic. Publs: "Politics and European Aerospace Collaboration", *Journal of Common Market Studies*, 1976. Fields: The politics of science and technology.

[805]
HEADEY Bruce Wyndham*
14 November 1943, British. 39 Rossie Crescent, Bishopbriggs, Glasgow, Scotland. Degrees: BA; MA (Wisconsin), 1968; PhD (Strathclyde), 1973. Doctoral thesis: "The Job of Cabinet Minister". Lecturer, U of Strathclyde. Publs: "Trade Unions and Na-tional Wages Policies", *Journal of Politics*, 1970; "What is a Strong Minister?", *New Society*, 1970; "Indicators of Housing Satisfaction: A Castlemilk Pilot Study", in *Strathclyde University Occasional Papers*. Fields: Political leadership.

[806]
HEIDAR Knut
29 April 1949, Norwegian. Eventyrveien 34, Oslo 8, Norway. Degrees: MA (Oslo), 1973. Doctoral thesis: "The Institutionalization of the Norwegian Labour Party 1887-1940". 1972-74 Research Assistant, Inst for Social Research, Oslo; Research Associate, Inst of Pol Sci, U of Oslo. Publs: several articles on developments in the Norwegian Labour party, on oligarchy and on the debate on the deradicalization of European Social Democratic parties. Fields: Working class parties; social movements; 19th and 20th century Norwegian social and political history.

[807]
HEINRICH Hans-George
26 January 1942, Austrian. A-1090 Wien, Ferstelgasse 6/19, Austria. Degrees: Dr jur (Vienna), 1964. Research and teaching Assistant, School of Law and Pol Sci, U of Vien-na. Publs: "Zur sowjetischen Wirtschaftsrechtstheorie", *Osteuroparecht*, 1970; "Politische Sozialisation, politische Kultur und Systemtheorie", *Österreichische Zeitschrift für Politikwissenschaft*, 1972; "Chinesische und sowjetische Wirt-schaftstheorie: Vergleich zweier Modell", *China-Report*, 1972; "Zum Politologenbedarf in Österreich" (with H Fabris *et al*), *Österreichische Zeitschrift für Politikwissenschaft*, 1973; "Zur Funktion der Rechtssprache in 'Kaderverwaltung' und 'Bürokratie' ", *Österreichische Zeitschrift für Politikwissenschaft*, 1974. Fields: East European politics; linguistic pragmatics.

[808]
HEINTZ Peter
6 November 1920, Swiss. Ruchenacker 5, CH-8126 Zumikon, Switzerland. Degrees: PhD. Doctoral thesis: "Beitrag zur Theorie der Inflation". 1950-59 Assistant, Sociological Seminar, U of Cologne; 1955-65 UNESCO Expert in Costa Rica, Colom-bia, Santiago de Chile; 1958-65 Professor of Sociology, Director of Latin American Faculty of Soc Sci, Santiago de Chile; 1966- Member, Departamento de Sociologia, San Carlos; Professor of Sociology, U of Zürich and Director of the Sociological Inst, U of Zürich. Publs: *Die Autoritätsproblematik bei Proudhon*, 1957; *Soziale Vorurteile*, 1957; *Einführung in die Soziologische Theorie*, 1968; *Ein soziologisches Paradigma der Entwicklung*, 1969; *A Macrosociological Theory of Societal Systems* (ed), 1972; *The Future of Development* (with S Heintz), 1973. Fields: Development; stratification; in-ternational relations; construction of macrotheoretical theories.

[809]
HEINZIG Dieter
6 June 1932, German. Stettinerstrasse 42, D-5042 Erftstadt, FR Germany. Degrees: PhD. Doctoral thesis: "Moscow's Alliance with the Kuomintang and Soviet Military Advisers with the South China Govenment 1922-1927" (in German). Research Associate, Seminar for Pol and Law of Eastern Europe, U of Kiel; Head, Section for the Study of Sino-Communism, Federal Inst for East-European and Int Studies, Cologne. Publs: *Disputed Islands in the South-China Sea*, 1976; *Die Anfänge der kommunistischen Partei Chinas im Lichte der Memoiren Chang Kuo Taos*, 1972; *Die Krise der kommunistischen Partei Chinas in der Kulturrevolution*, 1969; *Sowjetische Militärarbeiter bei der Kuomintang 1923-1927*, 1978. Fields: Foreign policy of the People's Republic of China; Sino-Soviet relations; Soviet policy towards Asia.

[810]
HEISKANEN Ilkka Juhani
23 December 1935, Finnish. Urheilukatu 22 A-12, Helsinki 25, Finland. Degrees: MA (Helsinki), 1960; PhD (Helsinki), 1967. Doctoral thesis: "Theoretical Approaches and Scientific Strategies in Administrative and Organizational Research. A Methodological Study". 1962-67 Research Fellow, National Research Council for Soc Sci in Finland; 1967- Associate Professor of Administrative Research, Professor of Pol Sci, U of Helsinki. Publs: Dissertation, 1967; "Valtioneuvoston asema Suomen Poliittisessa Järjestelmässä", *Valtioneuvoston Historia*, 1975; "Defining the Objectives of Cultural Development: Empirical Assessment via the Analysis of its Major Economic, Political and Social Determinants" (with R Mitchell), in *Planning for Cultural Development: Methods and Objectives*, 1976; *Julkinen, Kollektiivinen ja Markkinaperusteinen*, 1977. Fields: The status and role of public management systems within the systems of societal control and guidance; informal networks of power in society; public goods and control of people; the national and international impacts of culture industries.

[811]
HELENIUS Ralf Harry
19 October 1938, Finnish. Villebrådsstigen 1 A 8, Esbo 10, Finland. Degrees: Dr, 1969. Doctoral thesis: "The Profile of Party Ideologies". 1971-74 Lecturer, Finnish School of Econ, Helsinki; 1972-74 Acting Professor, Swedish School of Econ, Supervising Teacher, Swedish School of Social Work and Local Administration; 1973 Acting Professor, U of Helsinki; 1977- Professor of Pol Sci, Swedish School of Econ, Helsinki. Publs: *Suuret ismit 1970-luvun politiikassa*, 1972; *Konsumera allt och alla*, 1974; *Akademikernas fackliga organisationsberedskap*, 1975. Fields: Political ideologies; methodology; consumer affairs; labour market.

[812]
HELLBLING Ernst Carl
2 January 1901, Austrian. Volkgasse 12, 1130 Wien, Austria. Degrees: Dr der Rechte. Obersenatsrat der Stadt Wien; Professor der Deutschen und Österreichischen Rechtsgeschichte, Salzburg. Publs: *Kommentar zu den Verwaltungsverfahrengesetzen*, 1954; *Österreichische Verfassungs und Verwaltungsgeschichte*, 1956. Fields: History; philosophy.

[813]
HELLEVIK Ottar
20 June 1943, Norwegian. Ostadalsvejen 56, Oslo 7, Norway. Degrees: Magistergrad (Oslo), 1968. 1964-70 Research Assistant, Researcher, Peace Research Inst, Oslo; Amanuensis, Inst of Pol Sci, U of Oslo. Publs: *Stortinget — en Sosial elite?*, 1969; *Forskningsmetode i Sosiologi og Statsvitenskap*, 1977; *Gallupdemokratiet. Bruk og Misbruk av Meiningsmålingar*, 1972; *Kampen om EF* (with N P Gleditsch), 1977. Fields: Methodology; organizational democracy; political participation of women.

[814]
HELLSTERN Gerd Michael
19 August 1947, German. Adolfstrasse 8, 1 Berlin 41, FR Germany. Degrees: Dipl Pol Sci. Research Assistant, Pol Sci Dept, Free U of Berlin. Publs: *Sanierungsmassnahmen*. *Städtebauliche und stadtstrukturelle Wirkungen* (with H Wollmann), 1978; "Sozialwissenschaftliche Untersuchungsregeln und Wirkungsforschung", *Res Publica; Festschrift für Dolf Sternberger* (P Haungs (ed)), 1977; "Perspektiven einer praxisnahen politikwissenschaftlichen Forschung auf der und für die lokale Ebene" (with H Wollmann and P Kevenhörster), in *Politikforschung und lokale Praxis*, 1978; "Analyse kommunaler Entscheidungsprozess", in *Vorstudien zum Stadtforschungsprogramm* (R Bosch (ed)), 1978. Fields: Public policy; public administration; regional and urban policy; community politics; interorganizational and network theory.

[815]
HENIG Stanley
7 July 1939, British. 10 Yealand Drive, Lancaster, England. Degrees: BA. 1964-66 Lecturer in Pol, U of Lancaster; 1964-72 Assistant Editor, 1972- Acting Editor, *Journal of Common Market Studies*; 1966-70 Member of Parliament; 1970-71 Lecturer in Pol, U of Warwick; 1971-72 Consultant, European Movement; Lecturer in Public Administration, Civil Service Coll, London. Publs: *European Political Parties* (contributing ed), 1970; *External Relations of the European Community*, 1971; "Mediterranean Policy of the European Community", in *The New Politics of European Integration*, 1972. Fields: Impact of enlargement on institutions of the European community, and the functioning of the Council of Ministers of the European community.

[816]
HENNIG Eike
1 April 1943, German. Thüringer Strasse 2, 6231 Schwalbach, Germany. Degrees: MA (Marburg), 1971; Dr phil (Marburg), 1973; Habilitation (Hannover), 1976. Doctoral thesis: "Zur Darstellung des Verhältnisses von Nationalsozialismus und Industrie". Mitarbeiter der Forschungsstelle des Seminars für Pol Bildung; Wiss Mitarbeiter, Fachbereich Gesellschaftswissenschaften, U of Frankfurt. Publs: *Massenmedien und Meinungsbildung*, 1970; *Thesen zur deutschen Sozial- und Wirtschaftsgeschichte 1933 bis 1938*, 1973; *Bürgerliche Gesellschaft und Faschismus in Deutschland*, 1977. Fields: Mass communication; social history of Germany since 1870; German fascism.

[817]
HENNING Roger
16 August 1947, Swedish. John Ekströmsväg 4, 184 00 Åkersberga, Sweden. Degrees: PhD. Doctoral thesis: "The State as Entrepreneur. A Study of Statsföretag AB's goal, Organization Effectively". Research Assistant. Publs: *Business and Politics. On Selective Economic Policies and Government-Company Relations*. Fields: Industrial policy; economic policy.

[818]
HENNINGSEN Sven
2 February 1910, Danish. Dantesplads 4, Copenhagen 1556, Denmark. Degrees: Mag art (Copenhagen), 1937; Dr phil (Göteborg), 1944. Doctoral thesis: "A Study of Early Danish Economic Liberalism". 1943-53 Assistant Professor; 1944-45 Associate Professor; 1953- Professor of Contemporary History and Pol Sci, U of Copenhagen. Publs: *The Foreign Policy of the Powers 1830-90*, 1936; *The Far East and the Conflict of the Powers*, 1941; *A Study of Early Danish Economic Liberalism*, 1944; *World Politics*, 1946; *The North Atlantic Treaty*, 1952; *Danish Foreign Policy 1939-41*, 1967; *Atomic Policy 1939-1945*, 1971; *International Politics*, 1976. Fields: 20th century history; the development of political ideas in the 20th century.

[819]
HENNIS Wilhelm
18 February 1923, German. Seminar für Wissenschaft Politik Universität, D-78 Freiburg/Breisgau, FR Germany. Degrees: Dr jur (Göttingen), 1951; Habilitation (Frankfurt), 1960. 1960-62 Professor of Pol Sci, Pädagogische Hochschule, Hannover; 1962-67 Professor of Pol Sci, U of Hamburg; Professor of Pol Sci, U of Freiburg/Br. Publs: *Verfassung und Verfassungswirklichkeit*, 1968; *Politik als praktische Wissenschaft*, 1968; *Grosse Koalition ohne Ende?*, 1968; *Die deutsche Unruhe*, 1969; *Demokratisierung*, 1970; *Die missverstandene Demokratie*, 1973; *Organisierter Sozialismus*, 1977; *Regierbarkeit* (ed), 1977. Fields: Politics and religion; conservation and modernity; the political theory of the New Left; governability.

[820]
HENRIET Paul Oscar Louis
7 March 1948, Belgian. 25 Avenue Antoine Depage, B- 1050 Brussels, Belgium. Degrees: Lic; Lauréat, 1972. 1972- Conseiller-adjoint, Conseil Central de l'Economie. Publs: "La pensée politique de Theordore Herzl", *Res Publica*, 1971; "La presse française et la guerre des six jours. Essai d'analyse", *Res Publica*, 1973. Fields: Political strategy of management; relations between state services and social groups; political aspects of industrial relations; right-wing movements in Belgium.

[821]
HERETH Michael Wolfgang*
1 December 1938, German. 463 Bochum, Hustadtring 53, FR Germany. Degrees: Dipl Volkswirt (München), 1952; PhD (Erlangen), 1968. Doctoral thesis: "Parlamentarische Opposition in der Bundesrepublik Deutschland am Beispiel der SPD-Bundestagsfraktion, 1949-66". Dozent, Volkschochschule; Assistant, Ruhr U of Bochum. Publs: *Mobilisierung der Demokratie* (co-ed), 1966; *Junge Republik* (ed), 1966; *Parlamentarische Opposition in Deutschland, 1949-66*, 1968; *Parlamentarische Opposition in der Bundesrepublik*, 1969; *Die Reform des Deutschen Bundestages*, 1971. Fields: Intra-party democracy; neo-Marxist thought; relationship between political thought and theology.

[822]
HERMAN Valentine Mark
15 October 1946, British. Marathon 22, Krimpen a/d Ijssel, The Netherlands. Degrees: BA; MA (Essex), 1969. 1971-77 Lecturer, U of Essex; 1977- Visiting Lecturer, U of Aarhus; 1977- Lecturer, Erasmus U, Rotterdam. Publs: *Parliaments of the World: A*

Reference Compendium, 1976; *The European Parliament and the European Community* (with J Lodge), 1978; *Workbook for Comparative Government* (with J Blondel), 1972; *The Backbencher and Parliament* (with D Leonard (co-ed)), 1972; *Cabinet Studies* (with J Alt (co-ed)), 1975. Fields: European, comparative and British politics; the political institutions of the European community; comparative political performance; legislative behaviour, parliamentology and parliamentrics; politics and sport.

[823]
HERMENS Ferdinand Alois*
20 December 1906, American. 5 Köln 41, Schallstrasse 6, FR Germany. Degrees: Dipl Volkswirt (Bonn), 1928; Dr rer Pol (Bonn), 1930. Doctoral thesis: "Demokratie und Kapitalismus. Ein Versuch zur Soziologie der Staatsformen". 1930-34 Research Fellowships and Assistantships; 1935-38 Assistant Professor of Econ, Catholic U of America; 1938-45 Associate Professor of Pol, U of Notre Dame; 1945-50 Professor of Pol Sci, U of Notre Dame; 1950- Professor of Pol Sci, U of Köln; Director of Seminar for Pol Sci, and U Inst for Pol Research. Fields: The relation between domestic political institutions and foreign policy, and between economics and politics; peace and conflict research.

[824]
HERMERÉN Bengt John Henrik
5 June 1943, Swedish. Degrees: PhD. Doctoral thesis: "Government Formation in Multiparty Systems". Assistant Professor, Educational Manager. Publs: "Government Formation in Multiparty Systems", *Scandinavian Political Studies*. Fields: Comparative politics; public administration.

[825]
HERMET Guy Andre Roger
14 June 1934, French. 8 Square Monteverdi, 91450 Soisy/Seine; France. Degrees: Dr en soc (Sorbonne); Dipl (IEP Paris). Doctoral thesis: "Fonctions politiques du catholicisme dans l'Espagne franquiste". Chargé de recherches, FNSP; Maître de conférences, IEP Paris; Chargé de cours, U de Paris-Sorbonne; Directeur, Centre d'Etudes et de recherches internationales, FNSP. Publs: *Emigrants saisonniers espagnols en France*, 1961; *Le problème méridional de l'Espagne*, 1965; *Les Espagnols en France*, 1967; *Les communistes en Espagne*, 1971; *La politique dans l'Espagne Franquiste*, 1971; *L'Espagne de Franco*, 1974; *Elections without a Choice*, 1978; *Des élections pas comme les autres*, 1978. Fields: Spanish political system; authoritarian systems.

[826]
HERNANDEZ LAUFUENTE Adolfo
31 March 1946, Spanish. Fuencarral 126, 7°-1, Madrid 10, Spain. Degrees: Lic. Doctoral thesis: "Autonomia e Integracion en la II Republica Espanola". Professor Encargado de Curso de Comportamiento Pol, Partidos y Grupos de Presion, Seminario de Derecho Pol, U Complutense, Madrid. Fields: Electoral sociology; political sociology; public law.

[827]
HERNES Gudmund
25 March 1941, Norwegian. Øyjordsveien 71, 5000 Bergen, Norway. Degrees: PhD (John Hopkins), 1971. Doctoral thesis: "Interest, Influence and Cooperation — A Study of the Norwegian Parliament". 1969- Assistant Professor, Professor of Soc, U of Bergen; 1978- Research Director, Centre for Advanced Training and Research, Inst of Econ and Public Policy. Publs: *Makt og Avmakt*, 1975; *Utdanning og Ulikhet*, 1976; *Om Ulikhetens Reproduksjon*, 1974; *Dynamikk i Borehullene* (with A Selvik), 1977;

"A Markovian Approach to Measures of Association", *American Journal of Sociology*, 1970; "Political Resource Transformation", *Scandinavian Political Studies*, 1974; "Structural Change in Social Processes", *American Journal of Sociology*, 1976. Fields: Political economy; legislatures; political theory; methodology.

[828]
HERNES Helga Maria
16 January 1938, American. Øyjordsveien 71, Bergen, Norway. Degrees: BA; PhD (John Hopkins), 1970. Doctoral thesis: "Concepts of Community in Modern Theories of International Law". Senior Lecturer, U of Bergen. Publs: "The Visible Hand of the Multinational Corporation", *EJPR*, 1972; "Formal Theories of International Relations", *EJPR*, 1975; *The Multinational Corporation: an annotated bibliography*, 1977. Fields: Political theory of organizations; women's studies.

[829]
HERREMANS Maurice Pierre
3 June 1914, Belgian. Avenue Defré 31, 1180 Brussels, Belgium. Degrees: Dr. Doctoral thesis: "La Constitution des Indes Britanniques". Vice President, Centre de Recherche et d'Information Socio-Politiques. Publs: *La question des Flandres,* 1948; *La Wallonie,* 1952; *Personnes déplacés,* 1952. Fields: Language problems; nationality problems.

[830]
HERZ Thomas Aage
20 April 1938, Swedish. Klerschweg 5, 5000 Köln 51, FR Germany. Degrees: Dr rer Pol (Köln), 1973. Doctoral thesis: "Soziale Bedingungen für Rechtsextremismus in der Bundesrepublik und in den Vereinigten Staaten". Research Assistant, Zentralarchiv für empirische Sozialforschung, U of Köln; Professor of Sociology/Methodology, Gesamthochschule Siegen. Publs: *Soziale Bedingungen für Rechtsextremismus in der Bundesrepublik und in den Vereinigten Staaten,* 1975; *Öffentliche Meinung und Europäische Integration,* 1978; "Effekte beruflicher Mobilität", *Zeitschrift für Soziologie,* 1976; *Berufliche Mobilität in der Bundesrepublik* (with M Wieken-Mayser), 1976. Fields: Voting behaviour; right-wing extremism; European integration; occupational mobility; values and value change; research methods.

[831]
HERZFELD Hans
22 June 1892, German. 1 Berlin 33, Buchsweilerstrasse 5, FR Germany. Degrees: PhD, 1923. 1923-29 Privatdozent, Halle; 1929-38 Professor, Halle; 1946-49 Professor, U of Freiburg; 1949-60 Professor, Free U of Berlin; 1960 Professor Emeritus, Free U of Berlin. Publs: *Die Weimarer Republik*, 1966; *Der Erste Weltkrieg*, 1968; *Berlin und die Provinz Brandenburg im 19. und 20. Jahrhundert*, 1968. Fields: Contemporary history since 1910; German and comparative history since 1862.

[832]
HERZOG Dietrich
28 July 1931, German. Marienplatz 6, 1 Berlin 45, FR Germany. Degrees: Dipl Pol, 1955; Dr phil; Habilitation, 1972 (all Free U of Berlin). 1959 Research Assistant; 1965 Lecturer in Pol Soc; 1968 Akademischer Rat; 1972- Professor of Pol Sci, Free U of Berlin. Publs: *Klassengesellschaft ohne Klassenkonflikt; Politische Karrieren: Selektion und Professionalisierung politischer Führungsgruppen*, 1975; *The Study of Elites in West Germany*, 1977. Fields: Political sociology; elites; parties; parliaments.

[833]
HESSE Paul Hermann Konrad
29 January 1919, German. Schlossweg 29, 7802 Merzhausen über Freiburg in Breisgau, FR Germany. Degrees: Dr Law (Göttingen), 1950. 1955-56 Privatdozent, U of Göttingen; 1956- Professor, U of Freiburg; Head of Department, Inst für öffentliches Recht. Publs: *Der Rechtsschutz durch staatliche Gerichte im kirchlichen Bereich*, 1956; *Die normative Kraft der Verfassung*, 1959; *Der unitarische Bundesstaat*, 1962; *Grundzüge des Verfassungsrechts der Bundesrepublik Deutschland*, 1977. Fields: Constitutional theory and law; constitutional politics.

[834]
HESSLER Carl Arvid
10 February 1907, Swedish. Degrees: Dr fil (Göteborg), 1937; Geijer som politiker I. 1937-47 Docent in Pol Sci, U of Göteborg; 1947-72 Professor in Pol Sci, U of Uppsala. Publs: *Geijer som politiker I*, 1947; *Engelskt statsliv*, 1940; *Staten och konsten i Sverige*, 1942; *Stat och religion i Upplysningstidens Sverige*, 1956; *Statskyrkodebatten*, 1964. Fields: History of political ideas; relations between social structure and political ideas; the Confucian tradition in China and its relation to the thoughts of Mao Tse-Tung.

[835]
HEUNKS Felix
21 May 1936, Dutch. Durendaaldreef 78, Oisterwijk, The Netherlands. Degrees: PhD (Tilburg). Doctoral thesis: "Alienation and Voting-Behaviour" (in Dutch). 1962-1966 Social Researcher, Agricultural-Econ Institute, The Hague; Social Researcher, U of Tilburg. Publs: *Alienation and Voting-Behaviour* (in Dutch), 1973; *The Dutch Voter 1972-73* (co-author, in Dutch), 1977; *Kernthema's van de Politicologie* (co-author), 1976. Fields: Social and political attitudes and behaviour; methods for social research.

[836]
HEURLIN Bertel*
18 October 1935, Danish. Magnoliavej 27, 3630 Jaegerspris, Denmark. Degrees: Cand mag (Copenhagen), 1962. 1962-64 Secretary, Ministry of Foreign Affairs; 1964-65 Research Associate, Inst of Contemporary History and Pol Sci, U of Copenhagen; 1965-70 Lecturer in Modern History; Assistant Professor, Lecturer, Inst of Contemporary History and Pol Sci, U of Copenhagen. Publs: *The Problem of Disarmament in International Politics*, 1968; *Disarmament*, 1970; *International Disarmament negotiations after World War II*; *Disarmament Negotiations 1919-37*; *The Foreign Policy of Denmark*, 1970; *The Policy of Disarmament*, 1971. Fields: International politics; disarmament and arms control; small-power problems.

[837]
HIESTER Daniel W
29 May 1944, American. 11 Nursery Walk, Forty Acres Road, Canterbury, Kent CT2 7TF, England. Degrees: BA: MA (South Carolina), 1973. Lecturer, U of Kent. Fields: International relations; comparative analysis of foreign policy; nuclear weapons and strategic analysis; European integration; American foreign policy.

[838]
HILGER Dietrich*
22 April 1926, German. Universität Hamburg, Seminar für Sozialwissenschaften, Von-Melle-Park 15, Hamburg 13, FR Germany. Degrees: Dr phil (Hamburg), 1958. Wiss Assistent, Wiss Rat, Wiss Oberrat, Professor, U of Hamburg. Publs: *Edmund Burke und seine Kritik der fransösischen Revolution*, 1960; *Die Eigentumslogen* (co-ed), 1965. Fields: Political philosophy; history of political ideas; social and economic history.

[839]
HILL Christopher John
20 November 1948, British. 82 Lordship Park, London N16, England. Degrees: BA. Doctoral thesis: "The Decision-Making Process in Relation to British Foreign Policy 1938-41". Lecturer in International Relations, LSE. Publs: "The Credentials of Foreign Policy Analysis", *Millennium*, 1974; "Theories of Foreign Policy-Making for the Developing Countries", in *Foreign Policy-Making in Developing States* (C Clapham (ed)), 1977; "A Theoretical Introduction", in *Foreign Policy-Making in Western Europe* (W Paterson and W Wallace (eds)), 1978; "Foreign Policy Analysis" (with M Light), in *International Theory: A Bibliography* (C Mitchell and A T R Groom (eds)), 1978. Fields: Foreign policy analysis; comparative study of decision-making; political culture and public opinion; foreign policies of Western European states; international theory.

[840]
HILL Christopher Richard
4 March 1935, British. Alcuin College, Heslington, York, England. Degrees: MA (Cantab).

[841]
HILL Dilys Mary
8 September 1935, British. 127 Bursledon Road, Hedge End, Southampton SO3 4BU, England. Degrees: BA; PhD (Leeds), 1966. Doctoral thesis: "Democracy in Local Government: A Study in Participation and Communication". Assistant Lecturer, Lecturer, Senior Lecturer, Dept of Pol, U of Southampton. Publs: "Four Constituency Campaigns: Leeds West", in *The British General Election of 1964* (with P Nette) (D E Butler and A King (eds)), 1965; "Leeds", in *Voting in Cities* (L J Sharpe (ed)), 1967; *Participating in Local Affairs*, 1970; *The Planning and Management of Human Settlements with Special Emphasis on Participation*, 1975; "American Metropolitanism and the Ambiguity of 'Mild Chaos' ", *Urban Studies*, 1976; "Political Ambiguity and Policy: The Case of Welfare", *Social and Economic Administration*, 1978; "Neighbourhood Councils", *Planning and Administration*, 1978; "Privacy and Social Welfare", in *Privacy* (J Young (ed)), 1978. Fields: Local government; urban planning; participation; urban problems in Third World countries.

[842]
HILL Ronald James
4 July 1943, British. 23 Dun Emer Road, Dundrum, Dublin 14, Ireland. Degrees: BA; MA (Essex), 1968; MA (Dublin), 1973; PhD (Essex), 1974. Doctoral thesis: "Tiraspol: A Study of a Soviet Town's Political Elite". 1965-69 Research Assistant, Dept of Government, U of Essex; 1967-68 Post-graduate Exchange Student, Academy of Sciences, Kishinev, USSR; 1969- Junior Lecturer, Lecturer, Dept of Pol Sci, Trinity Coll, Dublin. Publs: *Soviet Political Elites: The Case of Tiraspol*, 1977; "Patterns of Deputy Selection to Local Soviets", *Soviet Studies*, 1973; "Soviet Literature on Electoral Reform", *Government and Opposition*, 1976; "The CPSU in a Soviet Election Campaign", *Soviet Studies*, 1976. Fields: Soviet government and society, particularly local government and politics; the CPSU; Soviet political science.

[843]
HILL Trevor Keith*
28 July 1943, British. Department of Politics, University of Strathclyde, McCance Building, Richmond Street, Glasgow G1 1XQ, Scotland. Degrees: BA. 1966-68 Tutorial Assistant, U of Leicester; 1968-69 Belgian Government Scholar, U of Brussels: 1969-Research Assistant, Lecturer in Pol, U of Strathclyde. Publs: "Belgium", in *European Political Parties* (S Henig and J Pinder (eds)), 1970; "Belgium: Political Change in a Segmented Society", in *Electoral Behaviour: A Comparative Handbook* (R Rose (ed)), 1973. Fields: Belgium: religion in politics; comparative electoral behaviour.

[844]
HINE David John
29 March 1949, British. 13 Queen's Terrace, Jesmond, Newcastle-upon-Tyne NE1 7RU, England. Degrees: BA. Lecturer in Pol, U of Newcastle-upon-Tyne. Publs: "Divorce: Italian Style", in *Parliamentary Affairs* (with M Clark and R E M Irving), 1974; "Italian Socialism and the Centre Left Coalition", *Journal of Common Market Studies*, 1975; "Italy: The Search for Stability", *Current Affairs Bulletins*, 1975; "The Labour Movement and Communism in France and Italy", in *Social and Political Movements in Western Europe* (M Kolinsky and W E Paterson (eds)), 1976; "Italian Compromises: Historical and Necessary", *Contemporary Review*, 1976; "Social Democracy in Italy", in *Social Democratic Parties in Western Europe* (W E Paterson and A H Thomas (eds)), 1977; "Socialists and Communists in Italy: Reversing Roles?", *West European Politics*, 1978. Fields: Italian party politics; the Italian Socialist party; Italian public administration.

[845]
HIRSCH Joachim*
22 April 1938, German. 6078 Neu Isenburg 2, Schwalbenstrasse 6, FR Germany. Degrees: Diplom-Kaufmann (Frankfurt), 1961; Dr rer Pol (Frankfurt), 1965. Doctoral thesis: "Die öffentlichen Funktionen der Gewerkschaften". 1963-70 Wiss Assistent, U of Frankfurt; 1971 Kommissarischer Direktor des Seminars für die Wissenschaft von der Pol, U of Göttingen; 1971- Professor für Pol Wiss, Fachbereich Gesellschaftswissenschaften, U of Frankfurt. Publs: *Die öffentlichen Funktionen der Gewerkschaften*, 1966; *Parlament und Verwaltung: Haushaltsplanung und Haushaltskontrolle in der Bundesrepublik Deutschland*, 1968; *Wissenschaftlichtechnischer Fortschritt und politisches System*, 1970; *Materialien und Analysen zur Wissenschafts- und Bildungspolitik* (with S Liebfried), 1971. Fields: Parliamentarism in West Germany; budgetary process; public administration and economic process; theory of the state; science policy in West Germany.

[846]
HIRSCH-WEBER Wolfgang
20 July 1920, Germany. Am Grossen Wald, 6901 Gaiberg, FR Germany. Degrees: Dr phil. Doctoral thesis: "Gewerkschaften in der Politik". Inst für Pol Wissenschaft, Free U of Berlin; Lateinamerika Inst, Free U of Berlin; Ordentlicher Professor, U of Mannheim. Publs: *Wähler und Gewählte. Eine Untersuchung der Bundestagswahl* (with K. Schütz), 1957; *Gewerkschaften in der Politik. Von der Massenstrekdebatte zum Kampf um das Mitbestimmungsrecht*, 1959; *Politik als Interessenkonflikt*, 1969; *Lateinamerika: Abhängigkeit und Selbstbestimmung*, 1972; *Verbände und Gesetzgebung. Die Einflussnahme der Verbände auf die Gestaltung des Personalvertretungsgesetzes*, 1965; "Die SPD im Weimarer Parteiensystem und in der Bundesrepublic", *Die Neue Gesellschaft*, 1958; "Gesellschaftliche Konflikte in einigen ländern Südamerikas", *Moderne Welt*, 1965. Fields: Comparative politics; Latin America; interest groups; parties; labour movement; political theory.

[847]
HIRSZOWICZ Lukasz*

18 February 1920. 17 Harefields, Oxford, England. Degrees: MA (Hebrew U, Jerusalem); PhD (Polish Academy of Sciences, Warsaw); Habilitation (Polish Academy of Sciences, Warsaw). Doctoral thesis: "Iran 1951-53. Oil-Imperialism-Nationalism". 1954-62 Adjunctur, Associate Professor, Inst of History, Polish Academy of Sciences, Warsaw; 1964-69 Associate Professor, Oriental Inst, U of Warsaw; 1965-70 Visiting Fellow, St Anthony's Coll, U of Oxford; 1970- Research Fellow, Centre for International Studies, LSE. Publs: *Iran 1951-53. Oil-Imperialism-Nationalism*, 1958; *The Third Reich and the Arab East*, 1966. Fields: Arab nationalism; problems of contemporary Eastern Europe; international relations in the Middle East; Soviet policy in the Middle East.

[848]
HIRTZ Colette Therese

14 July 1929, French. 6 rue Champ Rochas, 38240 Meylan, France. Degrees: Agrégé d'histoire; Dr 3ème cycle. Doctoral thesis: "L'Est Républicain, naissance et développement d'un grand quotidien régional (1889-1914)". Maître-Assistant, IEP Grenoble. Fields: History of mass media; religious organizations; contemporary history of social and ideological problems.

[849]
HJELLUM Torstein*

21 December 1940, Norwegian. Institute of Sociology, U of Bergen, Christiesgate 19, 5000 Bergen. Norway. Degrees: Magistergrad (Oslo), 1965. Research Assistant, Christian Michelsen Inst, Bergen; Lecturer, U of Bergen. Publs: *Partiene i Lokalpolitikken*, 1967; *Vestlandsplanen*, 1970. Fields: Political economy; state and industry; class structure in Norway.

[850]
HJULSTAD Roar

2 January 1945, Norwegian. Skinnveien 5, 4000 Stavanger, Norway. Degrees: Cand Pol. Doctoral thesis: "How to make a Traffic-Trap". Amanuensis, Rogaland Regional College, Stavanger. Publs: *An Evaluation of Central Policy-areas in Stavanger*; *The Budgetary Process in Local Governments*. Fields: The theory of organizations; local government activity.

[851]
HODDER-WILLIAMS Richard

18 March 1943, British. Department of Politics, 40 Berkeley Square, Bristol BS8 1HY, England. Degrees: BA; MA (Oxon), 1969. 1965-67 Teaching, Research Fellow, U Coll of Rhodesia. 1967- Lecturer, U of Bristol; Member, Standing Committee on U Studies of Africa; Contributing Ed, *International Journal of Politics*. Publs: *Public Opinion Polls and British Politics*, 1970; *East African Politics* (ed)), 1975; *An Introduction to African Politics: A Study Guide*, 1976. Fields: The development of political attitudes among rural Europeans in Rhodesia; East African politics, especially the nature of peasant demands and identification; the Supreme Court of the USA.

[852]

HOETJES Bernardus Johanna Simon

1 September 1945, Dutch. Waterruit 54, 2804 PD Gouda, The Netherlands. Degrees: Dr (Leiden), 1977. Doctoral thesis: "Political and Administrative Corruption in Developing Countries — An Exploration of Theory and Research, with Special Reference to Post-Independence India". 1971-74 Assistant Professor of Pol Sci, U of Amsterdam; 1974-76 Erasmus U of Rotterdam; Assistant-Professor of Pol Sci, U of Leiden. Publs: "Politics and Government — A Background to Corruption in Public Administration in Developing Countries", *Sociologia Neerlandica*, 1976; "India, noodtoestand, verkiezingen, machtswisseling", *Internationale Spectator*; "Het openbaar bestuur in ontwikkelingslanden — problemen van bestuur en bestuurswetenschap", *Acta Politica*, 1978; "De Nederlandse ontwikkelingshulp" (with M Rozendaal), *Intermediair*, 1977. Fields: Comparative politics and public administration; comparative federalism; South Asia, especially India.

[853]

HOFF Rudolf Hendrik

30 December 1949, Dutch. Commelinstraat 401, Amsterdam, The Netherlands. Degrees: Dr (Free U of Amsterdam). Doctoral thesis: "De buitenlandse Politiek van Israël 1970-1974" (The Foreign Policy of Israel). Teacher, History and Constitutional Law. Publs: "Politieke Propaganda", in *Politieke Strategie, Aspecten en Voorbeelden*, 1971. Fields: International relations; history of political ideas.

[854]

HOFFMANN-NOTWOTNY Hans-Joachim

17 March 1934, German. Rütistrasse 5, CH-8903 Birmensdorf, Switzerland. Degrees: Dipl Volkswirt (Köln); Dr phil (Zürich). Doctoral thesis: "Migration. A Contribution to a Sociological Explanation". Research Assistant, U of Cologne; Research Assistant, Head Assistant, Associate Professor, Full Professor, Director of the Soc Inst, U of Zürich. Publs: *Migration-Ein Beitrag zu einer soziologischen Erklärung*, 1970; *Soziologie des Fremdarbeiterproblems-Eine theoretische und empirische Analyse am Beispiel der Schweiz*, 1973; "Poverty and Disadvantaged Minorities: Some Considerations Concerning Socio-Psychological Indicators and Social Structure", in *Subjective Elements of Well-Being* (Burkhard and Strumpel (eds)), 1974; *Politisches Klima und Planung, Soziale Indikatoren V* (ed), 1977; *Umwelt und Selbstverwirklichung als Ideologie*, 1977. Fields: Minority/majority relations; political institutions; social indicators.

[855]

HOFOSS Dag

21 March 1946, Norwegian. Ollevejen 5, Oslo 11, Norway. Degrees: Cand pol (Oslo), 1971. 1971-74 Scientific Assistant, U of Oslo; 1974- Head, Dept of Local Government, Norwegian State School of Local Government and Social Work. Publs: *Introduction to Organization Theory*; *Political Norway*. Fields: Public administration; sociology of knowledge; history of ideas.

[856]

HOFSTETTER Viktor A

13 July 1942, Swiss. Hadlaubstrasse 121, CH-8006 Zürich, Switzerland. Degrees: Lic theol (Fribourg); MA (Rochester NY). 1972-73 Research Assistant, U of Northern Illinois; 1973-76 Teaching and Research Assistant, Instructor, U of Rochester; 1976- Mittelschullehrer, Kantonsschule Zürich. Publs: *Values in Recruitment*, 1973; *A Critique of the Concept of Ideology in Empirical Research* (co-author), 1975. Fields: Political philosophy; comparative legislative studies; social choice theory; ethics and politics; political recruitment.

[857]
HOGWOOD Brian Walter
29 June 1950, British. 21 Birkhill Avenue, Bishopbriggs, Glasgow G64 2LP, Scotland. Degrees: BA; PhD (Keele), 1977. Doctoral thesis: "The Politics of Industrial Change: Government Involvement in the UK Shipbuilding Industry 1959-73". Econ Sub Editor, Cambridge U Press; Lecturer, Dept of Pol, U of Strathclyde. Publs: "Monitoring of Government Involvement in Industry: The Case of Shipbuilding", *Public Administration*, 1976; "Government Involvement in the UK Shipbuilding Industry: The Implications for Industrial Consent", *Journal of the Conflict Research Society*, 1977; "Intergovernmental Structures and Industrial Policy in the UK", *Studies in Public Policy*, 1977; "Models of Industrial Policy: The Implications for Devolution", *Studies in Public Policy*, 1977. Fields: Government involvement in UK shipbuilding; political and economic models of regional policy; political economy of devolution and independence in Scotland.

[858]
HØIVIK Tord
19 February 1942, Norwegian. Rådhusgatan 4, Oslo 1, Norway. Degrees: Cand real (Oslo), 1969. 1969-72 Research Fellow, International Peace Research Inst, Oslo; 1972-76 Lecturer, U of Oslo; 1974-75 Senior Tutor, Cooperative College, Moski; 1977-Research Director, International Inst of Peace Research, Oslo. Publs: *Mål og Metode*, 1974; articles in *Journal of Peace Research* and *Quality and Quantity*. Fields: Peace research; applied statistics; development theory; Mediterranean studies.

[859]
HOLDEN Barry Barfield
14 July 1936, British. Department of Politics, The University, Whiteknights, Reading RG6 2AA, England. Degrees: BA. 1962-63 Temporary Assistant Lecturer, U of Southampton; Lecturer, Senior Lecturer in Pol, U of Reading. Publs: *The Nature of Democracy*, 1974. Fields: Democratic theory and practice; the nature of political analysis with special reference to the modern role of traditional political philosophy.

[860]
HOLDSWORTH Mary*
1908, British. St Mary's College, University of Durham, Old Shire Hall, Durham, England. Degrees: BA. 1948-62 Secretary and Senior Research Officer, Inst of Colonial (later Commonwealth) Studies, U of Oxford; 1962 Principal, St Mary's Coll; Honorary Lecturer, Dept of Pol, U of Durham. Publs: *Turkestan in the Nineteenth Century*, 1959; "Africa", in *The Cold War* (Luard (ed)), 1964; "Lenin and the Nationalities Question", in *Lenin The Man, The Theorist, The Leader* (Schapiro and Reddaway (eds)), 1967. Fields: Minorities in the Soviet Union; protest literature in Asian and African colonial countries; Russian 19th century expansion into Asia and problems of culture contact; peasant and peasant agriculture in transition; Soviet contact with Africa; Soviet politics.

[861]
HOLGER Mirek
23 July 1947, German. Turmstrasse 23, D-5300 Bonn 2, FR Germany. Degrees: Dipl Pol. Geschäftsführer des Arbeitskreises Europäische Integration e V Fields: West-European integration; development politics.

[862]
HÖLL Otmar
21 February 1948, Austrian. Speisingerstrasse 76/1, A-1130 Wien, Austria. Degrees: Dr jur. Wiss Angestellter, Inst für Höhere Studien, Vienna. Publs: "Kritische Ammerkungen zur Kleinstaatentheorie", *Österreichische Zeitschrift für Politikwissenschaften*, 1978; *Die Europäische Integration und Österreich* (with M Dillinger and P M Arsoner); "Österreich im internationalen System 1955-1975" (with H Kramer), *Neue Entwicklungs- Politik*, 1976; *Kleinstaaten und Abhängigkeit* (with H Kramer), 1977. Fields: International relations; small states theory; dependence of nations; technology; international division of labour; European integration; peace research; university didactics.

[863]
HOLLOWAY John Patrick
26 July 1947, Irish. Collielaw Cottages, Oxton, Landerdale, Scotland. Degrees: BA; PhD. Doctoral thesis: "The Legal and Political Implications of the Coordination and Harmonization of Social Security in the European Communities". 1968-69 Assistant, Judicial Section, Coll of Europe, Bruges; Lecturer, Dept of Pol, U of Edinburgh. Publs: *The State and Capital* (co-ed), 1978. Fields: Marxist theory of the state; state expenditure; social policy.

[864]
HOLM Hans Henrik
29 October 1951, Danish. Frodesvej 18, 8230 Åbyhøj, Denmark. Degrees: Cand phil. Adjunkt, Inst for Statskundskab, U of Aarhus. Publs: *Johan Galtung, Superstar eller Vaekkelsespraedikant*; articles in *Politica*, 1977, and in *Macro-analysis* (Heiestad (ed)), 1978. Fields: International relations; transgovernmental policies; peace and conflict research; development problems.

[865]
HOLMBERG Sören Birger
11 October 1943, Swedish. Skårsgatan 4, S-412 69 Göteborg, Sweden. Doctoral thesis: "Riksdagen Representerar Svenska Folket, Empiriska Studier, Representativ Demokrati" (The Riksdag Represents the Swedish People. Empirical Studies in Representative Democracy). Associate Professor in Pol Sci, U of Göteborg. Publs: *Väljarna och Kärnkraften*, 1977. Fields: Electoral behaviour; representative democracy.

[866]
HOLST Johan Jørgen
29 November 1937, Norwegian. Midtskogveien 22a, 2020 Skedsmokorset, Norway. Degrees: AB (Columbia), 1960; Magistergrad (Oslo), 1965. Doctoral thesis: "Arms Stability in the Cold War". 1961-62, 1963-67 Research Associate, Systems Analysis Group, Norwegian Defence Research Establishment; 1962-63 Research Associate, Center for International Affairs, Harvard U; 1967-69 Senior Staff Member, Hudson Inst, New York; 1970 Visiting Professor, Chair of Strategic Studies, Carleton U, Canada; Director of Research, Norwegian Inst of International Affairs; Ed, *Cooperation and Conflict*. Publs: *Norsk Sikkerhetspolitikk i Strategisk Perspektiv*, 1967; *Why ABM? Policy issues in the Missile Defence Controversy*, 1967; *Ef-Norges Vei?*, 1972; *Hvorfor Ja Til Ef*, 1972. Fields: Theory of international relations; strategic analysis; arms control; foreign policy.

[867]
HOLT Stephen Campbell
1935, British. Nab Field, 12 Nab Lane, Shipley BD18 4HJ, England. Degrees: BA; MA (Cantab), 1963; PhD (Manchester), 1966. Doctoral thesis: "The Relations between the Executive and Consultative Organs of the European Community". 1963-69 Lecturer in Pol Theory and Inst, U of Sheffield; 1969-70 Visiting Professor of Pol Sci, U of Colorado, USA; Professor of European Studies, U of Bradford. Publs: *The Common Market: The Conflict of Theory and Practice*, 1967; *Six European States: The Countries of the European Community and their Political Systems*, 1970; *Europe from Below: An Assessment of Franco-German Popular Contacts* (with J E Farquharson), 1975. Fields: Political aspects of the European community and the political systems of the member states.

[868]
HOLVOET Luc Raphael
19 February 1953, Belgian. Kerkstraat 28, 3200 Kessel-Lo, Leuven, Belgium. Degrees: Lic. Research Assistant, Dept Pol Wetenschappen, Catholic U of Leuven. Publs: *Omrekening van de uitslagen van de gemeenteraadsverkiezingen van 11 oktober 1970 naar de gefusioneerde gemeenten in Vlaanderen*, 1976; "De nieuwe politieke kaart van België, *Res Publica,* 1976; "Simulatie van een meerderheidsstelsel in België, *Res Publica,* 1977. Fields: Political sociology; political parties; social movements and social actions; unconventional political behaviour; elections; the federalization of Belgium.

[869]
HOOD Christopher
5 March 1947, British. 5E Cleveden Place, Kelvindale, Glasgow G12 0HG, Scotland. Degrees: BA; B Litt (Glasgow), 1971. Doctoral thesis: "The Development of Betting Taxes in Britain". 1972-77 Lecturer in Pol, U of Glasgow; 1977- Research Fellow, SSRC Machinery of Government Project, Inst of Soc and Econ Research, U of York. Publs: *The Limits of Administration,* 1976; chapters in *Political Questions* (A M Potter and B Chapman (eds)), 1975; *Public Policy and Private Interests* (W J M Mackenzie *et al* (eds)), 1975; *Policy Dynamics*, 1976; plus articles in *Public Administration, Political Studies.* Fields: Machinery of government theory; administrative analysis; policy implementation analysis; development of quantitative indices in public administration.

[870]
HOOGERWERF Andries
11 March 1931, Dutch. Schumannlaan 30, Enschede, The Netherlands. Degrees: Dr. Doctoral thesis: "Protestantisme en progressiviteit". 1960-69 Free U of Amsterdam; 1969-75 Catholic U of Nijmegen; Professor of Policy Studies, Dept of Public Administration, U of Technology, Twente. Publs: *Politicologie: Begrippen en Problemen*, 1972; *Beleid Belicht* (ed), 1972; *Verkenningen in de Politiek* (ed), 1976; *Gelijkheid en Ongelijkheid in Nederland* (with J van den Doel (eds)), 1975. Fields: Policy studies, especially the study of policy impact.

[871]
HÖPFL Harro Maximilian Wilhelm
12 September 1943, German. Department of Politics, University of Lancaster, Bailrigg, Lancaster, England. Degrees: BSc; MSc (LSE). 1967- Lecturer, Dept of Pol, U of Lancaster; 1973-74 Visiting Lecturer, San Francisco State U. Fields: Political science and traditional political theory; the political thought of Jean Calvin.

[872]
HÖPFLINGER Francois
6 June 1948, Swiss. Seestrasse 227, 8810 Horgen, Switzerland. Degrees: Dr phil. Doctoral thesis: "Industriegewerkschaften in der Schweiz. Eine soziologische Untersuchung". University Assistant, Soziologisches Inst, U of Zürich. Publs: *Industriegewerkschaften in der Schweiz*, 1976; *Das umheimliche Imperium. Wirtschaftsverflechtung in der Schweiz*, 1977; "Probleme der strukturellen Differenzierung in kleinen Gesellschaften" (with H Geser), in *Schweiz Zeitschrift für Soziologie*, 1976; "Staatsverwaltung und Sozialstruktur: Ein Vergleich zwischen vier Kantonen" (with H Geser), in *Schweiz Jahrbuch für Politische Wissenschaft*, 1977. Fields: Trade unions; organizations; small states.

[873]
HOPPE Robertus
23 June 1950, Dutch. De Loet 216, Castricum, The Netherlands. Degrees: Dr. Staff Member, Dept of Pol Sci, Free U of Amsterdam. Publs: "Organski's Fasen van Politieke Ontwikkeling", *Acta Politica*, 1971; "Het Surinaamse Politiek Systeem: Elite-Kartel Demokratie", *Acta Politica*, 1976; "Surinam" (with C F Wittebrood), in *Handbuch der Dritten Welt*, 1976; *Vademecum bestaande methoden van Beleidsontwikkeling*, 1977. Fields: Policy analysis; policy science; modern political philosophy; development planning.

[874]
HÖRBERG Karl Thomas
15 October 1949, Swedish. Rudbecksgatan 101, S-216 22 Malmö, Sweden. Degrees: FK; FM; PM; CE. Research Assistant, U of Lund. Publs: *Internationella Framtidsbilden*, 1975; *Aktörer i Internationell Politik* (ed), 1977; *Sverige i Världen — Tankar om Framtiden* (ed), 1978. Fields: International politics; future studies.

[875]
HORN Hannelore Hildegard
19 November 1929, German. Wachstelstrasse 16b, 1 Berlin 33, FR Germany. Degrees: Dipl Pol (Berlin), 1954; Dr phil (Free U of Berlin), 1958. Doctoral thesis: "Der Kampf um den Bau des Mittellandskanals. Eine politologische Untersuchung über die Rolle des Bundes der Landwirte im Preussen Wilhelms II". 1956-60 Wiss Mitarbeiterin, Osteurop-Inst, Free U of Berlin; 1960-64 Assistentin, 1964-71 Akademische Rätin/Oberrätin, Otto-Suhr-Inst, Free U of Berlin; Professor/Hochschullehrer, Fachbereich Pol Wissenschaft, Free U of Berlin. Publs: *Der Kampf um den Bau des Mittellandkanals. Eine politologische Untersuchung über die Rolle einer wirtschaftlichen Interessenverbandes im Preussen Wilhelms II*, 1964; contributor to *Politik im 20. Jahrhundert*, 1964-73. Fields: History and theory of international relations; government and political system of the USSR; comparative communism.

[876]
HORN Klaus Ernst
30 April 1934, German. Friedrichstrasse 50, D 6 Frankfurt/Main, FR Germany. Degrees: Dipl, 1974; Dr, 1971. Doctoral thesis: "Elements of a Political Psychology". Assistant, Head, Dept of Social Psychology, Sigmund Freud Inst, Frankfurt/Main. Publs: *Dressur oder Erziehung*, 1973; *Der Kranke in der modernen Gesellschaft* (co-ed), 1970; *Gruppendynamik und der subjektive Faktor* (ed), 1972; *Kritik der Hochschuldidaktik* (ed), 1978; various articles on psychoanalysis, social and political psychology and medical sociology. Fields: Political psychology; medical sociology.

[877]
HORN Wolfgang
4 November 1939, German. Halferstein 14, 4300 Essen 14, FR Germany. Degrees: Dr phil (Mannheim), 1970. Doctoral thesis: "Führergedanke und Parteiorganisation in der NSDAP". Akademischer Oberrat for Pol Sci, U of Essen. Publs: *Führerideologie und Parteiorganisation in der NSDAP 1919-1933, 1972; Kandidaten im Wahlkampf. Kandidatenaufstellung, Wahlkampf und lokale Presse 1975 in Essen* (with H Kühr), 1978. Fields: German contemporary history; constitutional policy; political sociology.

[878]
HORNUNG Klaus
26 June 1927, German. Reutlingen, Rossnagelweg 11, FR Germany. Degrees: Dr phil (Tübingen), 1955; Habilitation (Freiburg), 1974. Doctoral thesis: "Der Jungdeutsche Orden — Ein Beitrag zur deutschen politischen Überlieferung". Professor für Pol, Pädagogische Hochschule, Reutlingen and Privatdozent, U of Freiburg. Publs: *Der Jungdeutsche Orden*, 1958; *Etappen der politischen Pädagogik in Deutschland*, 1965; *Politik und Zeitgeschichte in der Schule*, 1966; *Wohin geht Deutschland? Aufsätze zur Politik und Zeitgeschichte*, 1967; *Staat und Armee — Studien zur Befehls- und Kommandogewalt und zum politisch-militärischen Verhältnis in der Bundesrepublik Deutschland*, 1975; *Der faszinierende Irrtum — Karl Marx und die Folgen*, 1978; "Sozialismus und Kommunismus in Griechenland — innenpolitisches Kräftefeld und aussen- politische Positionen", in *Die sozialistischen und kommunistischen Parteien in Westeuropa* (D Oberndörfer (ed)), 1978. Fields: Political theory and theory of political education; government and comparative government; political-military relations; contemporary history; international politics.

[879]
HORTON John
1 September 1951, British. Alcuin College, University of York, Heslington, York YO1 5DD, England. Degrees: BSc; MSc (Wales). Lecturer in Pol, U of York. Fields: Political philosophy; philosophy of the social sciences.

[880]
HOSKING Geoffrey A*
28 April 1942, British. Department of History, University of Essex, Wivenhoe Park, Colchester CO4 3SQ, Essex, England. Degrees: MA, 1963; PhD (Cambridge). Doctoral thesis: "Government and Duma in Russia, 1907-14". Lecturer, U of Essex. Publs: *Government and Duma in Russia, 1907-14*, 1972. Fields: Government and Duma in Russia; the Liberal party in Britain, 1905-14; voting in the late years of the Weimar Republic; the Russian peasant revolution, 1917.

[881]
HOUTART Francois
7 March 1925, Belgian. Avenue Sainte-Gertrude 5, B-1348 Ottignies, Louvain-la-Neuve, Belgium. Degrees: Dipl (Institut Supérieur d'Urbanisme Appliqué); PhD (Louvain). Doctoral thesis: "Religion and Ideology in Sri Lanka". Secretary, International Conference of Sociology of Religion; Secretary-General, International Federation of Inst for Socio-Religious Research; Director, Research Centre for Socio-Religious Research, U of Louvain. Publs: *Aspects sociologiques du catholicisme américain*, 1957; *El Cambio social en America latina*, 1964; *L'éclatement d'une église*, 1969; *The church and revolution* (with A Rousseau), 1971. Fields: Sociology of religion; sociology of development; Asia; Latin-America.

[882]
HOWARTH Jolyon Michael*
4 May 1945, British. 22 rue du Four, 75006 Paris, France. Degrees: BA. 1967-70 Research Student, U of Reading; Assistant, UER des Pays Anglophones, U de Paris III. Publs: "La Propagande Socialiste d'Edouard Vaillant 1880-1884", *Le Mouvement Social*, 1970; "Edouard Vaillant", *International Review of Social History*, 1972. Fields: International socialist movement 1905-14; Edouard Vaillant's letters to the Bureau socialiste international; the relationship between the British and the French trades union movements in the period leading up to World War I.

[883]
HOWELL David
12 December 1945, British. 132 Egerton Road South, Manchester 21, England. Degrees: BA; PhD (Manchester), 1971. Doctoral thesis: "The Restatement of Socialism in the British Labour Party 1947-61". 1971- Lecturer in Government, U of Manchester. Publs: *British Social Democracy: A Study in Development and Decay*, 1976; plus articles in *Dictionary of Labour Biography*, 1976 and 1977, *Government and Opposition*, *The Historian*, *Political Studies*. Fields: Emergence of working class political organizations; problems of social democracy.

[884]
HØYER Svennik
3 August 1931, Norwegian. Ingar Nilsensvei 5b, Oslo 2, N-1002, Norway. Degrees: Magister Artium (Oslo), 1959. Research Assistant, Research Fellowship, Norwegian Research Council and U of Oslo; Associate Professor in Communication, U of Oslo; 1972-74 Royal Commission on the Press; 1972-74 British Council, Academic Interchange with Europe Scheme. Publs: "The Political Economy of the Norwegian Press", *Scandinavian Political Studies*, 1968; *The Politics and Economics of the Press: A Developmental Perspective* (with S Hadenius and L Weibull), 1975; "Temporal Patterns and Political Factors in the Diffusion of Newspapers", *Scandinavian Political Studies*, 1975; "The Politics of Professionalization in Scandinavian Journalism" (with P E Lorentzen), in *Current Theories in Scandinavian Mass Communications Research* (M Berg *et al* (eds)), 1977. Fields: Techniques of content analysis; the comparative study of press systems; comparative political communication; journalism; community studies with reference to local media.

[885]
HRBEK Rudolf
23 September 1938, German. D-7400 Tübingen, Philosophenweg 17, FR Germany. Degrees: Dr phil (Tübingen), 1968; Habilitation (Tübingen), 1973. Doctoral thesis: "Die SPD, Deutschland und Europa; Die Haltung der Sozialdemokratie zum Verhältnis von Deutschland-Politik und West- integration (1945-1957)". 1964-66 Lecturer in Pol Education; 1966-68 Wiss Assistent, Inst für Politikwissenschaft, U of Tübingen; 1969 Akademischer Rat; 1973 Dozent; 1974 Wiss Rat und Professor; 1976- Professor, Inst für Politikwissenschaft, U of Tübingen. Publs: *Die SPD, Deutschland und Europa, 1972; Die Haltung der Sozialdemokratie zum Verhältnis von Deutschland-Politik und West- integration (1945-1957)*, 1972; *Gesellschaft und Staat in Grossbritannien*, 1971; *Das Problem der Neugliederung des Bundesgebietes*, 1971; *Eine neue politische Infrastruktur? Zum Problem transnationaler Kooperation und Koalition politischer Parteien in der EG*, 1976. Fields: European integration in the EC; European Parliament; comparative government and politics of some western European democracies; federalism; German foreign policy.

[886]
HUANG FUNG LEE Oey Hong Lee*
3 March 1924, Indonesian. 7a Mill Beck Court, Cottingham, Hull, E Yorks, England.
Degrees: Cand Soc Sci (Amsterdam), 1950; Dr Soc Sci (Amsterdam), 1955; PhD
(Amsterdam), 1971. Doctoral thesis: "Indonesian Government and Press during Guid-
ed Democracy". 1955-57 Head of State Libraries Bureau, Min of Education, Indonesia;
1957-59 Lecturer, U of Macassar, Indonesia; 1960-65 Reader in Mass Communication
Sci, U of Indonesia; 1965- Fellow, Lecturer in Pol of S E Asia, Centre of S E Asian
Studies, U of Hull. Publs: *The China-Japanese War, 1937-45*, 1959; *The Chinese Civil
War, 1945-49*, 1960; *The Secret Story of the Korean War*, 1961; *Asia wins at Dienbien-
phu*, 1962; *Mass Communication of the Press*, 1965;. *Indonesian Government and
Press during Guided Democracy*, 1971. Fields: Politics of South East Asia, especially
Indonesia.

[887]
HUBER Jakob
22 November 1947, Austrian. A-9201 Krumpendorf, Berthastrasse 45, Austria. Doctoral thesis: "Philosophie und Wissenschaftstheoretische Fragen an eine mögliche
Sozialtheorie". Publs: *Zeit im Alltagsverständnis und als philosophisches Problem*,
1977; *Gruppendynamik und Gruppenpädagogik — Ihr Beitrag zur politischen Bildung*,
1976; *Gruppe und Bildung*, 1975; *Soziale Indentität und Gruppendynamik*, 1978.
Fields: Time and individuals; collective identities; philosophy; fascism.

[888]
HUFNAGEL Gerhard L
2 April 1939, German. Kleine Trift 11, 5905 Freudenberg, FR Germany. Degrees: Dr
phil (Tübingen). Doctoral thesis: "Kritik als Beruf. Der kritische Gehalt im Werk Max
Webers". 1962-64 Lecturer in German, St John's Coll, U of Cambridge; 1966-67 Lecturer of German, U of East Anglia; 1968-74 Assistant, Inst for Contemporary History, U
of Tübingen; 1975- Professor of Pol Sci, U of Siegen. Publs: *Kritik als Beruf. Der
kritische Gehalt im Werk Max Webers,* 1971; Editor and translator of works by K Eins-
tein (*Geschichte und Geschichtswissenschaft im 20. Jahrhundert*), 1972; S de Madariaga
(*Morgen ohne Mittag. Erinnerungen 1921-36*), 1972; B Ward (*Sind die Wirtschaftswissenschaften am Ende? Aporien und Argumente*), 1976; J P Harrison (*Der
Lange Marsch zur Macht. Die Geschichte der Kommunistischen Partei Chinas*), 1978;
various articles on contemporary German history and political theory. Fields: Political
theory and history of political ideas; comparative politics; contemporary history;
political sociology.

[889]
HUGHES Christopher John
6 March 1918, British. Cedar Lodge, Saddington, Leicester LE8 0QT, England.
Degrees: MA (Oxon), 1939; B Phil (Oxon), 1947; D Litt (Oxon), 1974. Lecturer, U of
Glasgow; Foreign Office, Cultural Relations Branch, Germany; Lecturer, U of
Leicester; Professor of Pol, U of Leicester. Publs: *The Federal Constitution of
Switzerland*, 1954; *The British Statute Books*, 1956; *The Parliament of Switzerland*,
1962. Fields: Political philosophy; Switzerland; federalism and confederalism.

[890]
HULTÉN Bengt Evert
19 April 1936, Swedish. Dr Forselis gata 2, S 413 26 Göteborg, Sweden. Degrees: Fil
kand, 1961; Fil mag, 1967. 1961-65 Amanuensis of Philosophy, 1967-69 of Pol Sci;
1969-72 U Lecturer in Pol Sci, U of Göteborg; 1965- Lecturer in Econ, Philosophy, Pol
Sci, U of Göteborg. Publs: "A Commentary on Education in Political Theory and

History of Political Ideas'', *Statsvetenskaplig tidskrift*, 1972. Fields: Party programmes and platforms and their function within and outside the parties.

[891]
HUMBLE Stephen John
28 October 1947, British. Institute of Local Government Studies, University of Birmingham, Box 363, Birmingham B15 2TT, England. Degrees: BA. Senior Research Associate, Centre for Applied Research in Education, U of East Anglia; Senior Research Associate, Inst of Local Government Studies, U of Birmingham; Research Fellow, Inst of Local Government Studies, U of Birmingham. Publs: *Conditions of Innovation*, 1973; *From Council to Classroom* (with H Simon), 1978. Fields: Local government; neighbourhood councils; the voluntary sector; the local educational system.

[892]
HUNTZINGER Jacques Gabriel
8 January 1943, French. 72 rue de Rennes, 75006 Paris, France. Degrees: Dr d'Etat. Doctoral thesis: "L'emploi de l'arme atomique et le Droit international public''. 1971-74 Maître de conférence- délégué, U de Lille; 1974-78 Maître de conférence, U de Besançon; Professeur, U de Paris X; Directeur de Séminaire à l'Ecole Nationale d' Administration. Publs: "L'entreprise de la réeducation des forces en Europe'', *Revue générale Droit International Public*, 1975; *Controlling Future Arms Trade*, 1977; "The French Socialist Party and Western Relations'', in *The Foreign Policies of West European Socialist Parties*, 1978; plus various articles in *Le Monde, Le Nouvel Observateur, Politique Etrangère*. Fields: International relations; defence policy; problems of security.

[893]
HUOPANIEMI Jukka Tapani
16 July 1936, Finnish. Sarvimaentie 16 as 27, 04200 Kerava, Finland. Degrees: Master of pol sci, 1961; Lic pol sci, 1971. 1961-71 Assistant, U of Helsinki; 1973 Acting Assistant Professor, U of Jyvaskyla; 1974-75 Acting Professor of Pol Sci, U of Helsinki; 1975- Lecturer in Pol Sci, U of Helsinki. Publs: *The Roles of Non-Alliance*, 1971; "Finland and the New International Economic Order'', in *Yearbook of Finnish Foreign Policy*, 1976. Fields: International politics; political systems; politics of development.

[894]
HURTIG Serge
16 April 1927, French. 8 Passage du Guesclin, 75015 Paris, France. Degrees: Dip (IEP Paris), 1950. 1956-69 Associate Director, Documentation services, FNSP; 1961-67 General Secretary, International Pol Sci Association; 1951- Staff member, Secretary General, FNSP; 1971- Professor, IEP Paris; Directeur d'études et recherches, Cycle Supérieur d'Etudes Pol; 1963- Ed, *International Political Science Abstracts/Documentation politique internationale*. Publs: *Eléments de science politique* (co-author), 1971. Fields: US politics; French politics; socialism.

[895]
HURWITZ Harold
13 January 1924, American. Kilstetter Straße 30v, 1 Berlin 37, FR Germany. Degrees: BA; MA (Columbia), 1954; D phil (Berlin), 1963; Habilitation (Berlin), 1972. Doctoral thesis: "Der Heimliche Leser: Beiträge zur Soziologie des Geistigen Widerstands''. 1946-49 Research Analyst, Ed, *Information Control*, US Military Government; 1950-52 Research Consultant to Mayor of Berlin; Ed, *Berlin Briefings*; Professor of Pol Sci, Otto-Suhr-Inst, Free U of Berlin. Publs: *Der Heimliche Leser: Beiträge zur Soziologie*

des Geistigen Widerstands, 1966; *Die Stunde Null der Deutschen Presse — Die Amerikanische Presse-politik in Deutschland 1945-49*, 1971. Fields: Change and resilience of political attitudes; time-series analysis of comparable opinion research surveys.

[896]
HUYSE Lucien Georges
18 November 1937, Belgian. Berkenlaan 8, 3202 Linden, Belgium. Degrees: Dr Pol and Soc Sci (Louvain), 1970. Doctoral thesis: "Passiviteit, pacificatie en verzuiling in de Belgische politiek". 1962-65 Research Assistant, U of Louvain; 1965-66 British Council Scholar, Inst of Education, U of Oxford; 1966-70 Research Assistant, Assistant Professor, Professor, Dept of Sociology, U of Louvain. Publs: *De niet-aanwezige staatsburger*, 1969; *L'apathie politique*, 1970; *Passiviteit, pacificatie en verzuiling in de Belgische politiek*, 1970; *De justitiebegrotingen van 1966 tot 1975*, 1975; *In de buiten-baan: arbeiderskinderen, universitair onderwys en sociale ongelykheid*, 1976. Fields: The politics of accommodation in Belgium; the recruitment of political elites in Belgium; language conflict and language policy; the recruitment and selection of practising lawyers.

I

[897]
IGNAZI Piero
15 February 1951, Italian. Corso Mazzini 54/3, 48018 Faenza, Italy. Degrees: Laurea in Pol Sci (Bologna), 1974; 1976- Researcher, Dept of Pol and Soc Sci, European U, Florence. Publs: *I Nuovi Radicali* (with M Teodori and A Panebianco), 1977. Fields: Political participation; attitudes of party members; methodology.

[898]
ILLY Hans F
16 April 1940, German. Stockmattenweg 22, D-7800 Freiburg, FR Germany. Degrees: Dipl Kaufmann, 1965; Dr phil, 1975. Doctoral thesis: "Politik und Wirtschaft in Kamerun. Bedingungen, Ziele und Strategien der staatlichen Entwicklungspolitik". 1965-67 Konrad Adenauer Foundation, Bonn; 1967-70 Lecturer, Panafrican Inst for Development, Douala, Cameroon; Research Fellow and Deputy Head of Dept, Arnold Bergsträsser Inst for Socio-political Research; Lecturer in Pol Sci, U of Freiburg. Publs: *Kamerun — Strukturen und Probleme der sozio-ökonomischen Entwicklung* (ed), 1974; *Politik und Wirtschaft in Kamerun. Bedingungen, Ziele und Strategien der staatlichen Entwicklungspolitik*, 1976. Fields: Comparative government, especially authoritarian regimes; comparative public administration; urbanization in developing countries; francophone black Africa, the Caribbean, the Philippines and Kenya.

[899]
INGHELS Francis Marie*
8 May 1943, Belgian. 7 rue A Mockel, Liège, Belgium. Ingénieur Commercial, U of Mons; Grad en Sci Actuarielles, U of Louvain; Assistant, Belgian Archives for Soc Sci, U of Louvain. Fields: Statistics for human sciences; regression and factor analysis; elaborating a general software system applied to statistical methods.

[900]
INGLE Stephen James
6 November 1940, British. 114 Westbourne Avenue, Hull, Yorkshire, England. BA; MA (Econ); D Phil. Doctoral thesis: "Politics of Education". Lecturer, U of Hull. Publs: "Party Politics and the Decline of Ideology in New Zealand: The Example of Education", *Journal of Commonwealth Political Studies*, 1970; "A Comparative Study of Two Educational Pressure Groups", in *The Anatomy of Influence* (ed), 1972; "Socialism and Literature: The Contribution of Imaginative Writers to the Development of the British Labour Party", *Political Studies*, 1974; "Socialist Man: William Morris and Bernard Shaw", in *The Concept of Socialism* (Parekh (ed)), 1975; "Politics and Literature: An Unconsummated Relationship", *Political Studies*, 1977. Fields: British politics; politics and literature.

[901]
INGLEHART Ronald*
5 September 1934, American. Department of Political Science, University of Geneva, Geneva, Switzerland. Degrees: BA; MA (Chicago), 1962; PhD (Chicago), 1967. Doctoral thesis: "The Socialization of 'Europeans' ". 1966- Assistant Professor, U of Michigan, USA; 1969- Chargé de recherches, U of Geneva. Publs: Articles in *American Political Science Review, Comparative Studies in Society and History, International Organization, Comparative Politics, Il Politico*. Fields: Political socialization; comparative political behaviour.

[902]
IN'T VELD Roeland Jaap
20 July 1942, Dutch. Duyvendakstraat 5, Leiden, The Netherlands. Degrees: Dr. Doctoral thesis; "Majority Rule and Welfare Theory" (in Dutch). Ordinarius in Public Administration, Catholic U of Nijmegen. Publs: Articles in *De Economist, Statistica Neerlandica, Bestuurswetenschappen, Openbare Financiën*. Fields: New political economy; local government; planning theory; economics of education.

[903]
IONESCU George Ghita
8 March 1913, British. 36 Sandileigh Avenue, Manchester 20, England. Degrees: Lic droit and sci pol (Bucharest). Doctoral thesis: "The Politics of Industrialization". Nuffield Fellow, LSE; Reader, U of Manchester; Professor of Government, U of Manchester; Ed, *Government and Opposition*. Publs: *Communism in Rumania*, 1964; *The Break-up of the Soviet Empire*, 1965; *The Politics of the European Communist States*, 1967; *Opposition* (co-author), 1968; *Populism* (co-author), 1969; *The New Politics of European Integration* (ed), 1971; *Centripetal Politics*, 1975; *The Political Thought of Saint-Simon*. Fields: The governability of European industrial countries.

[904]
IRVING Ronald Eckford Mill*
14 July 1939, British. Centre of European Governmental Studies, Old College, South Bridge, Edinburgh 8, Scotland. Degrees: BA; MA (Oxon), 1968; D Phil (Oxon), 1968. Doctoral thesis: "The MRP and French Policy in Indonesia, 1945-54". 1961-68 Schoolmaster; 1968-69 Lecturer in Pol, U of Bristol; 1970- Lecturer, Centre of European Governmental Studies, U of Edinburgh. Publs: *Christian Democracy in France*, 1972. Fields: French politics; French electoral studies; Christian democracy as a political phenomenon in the European communities.

[905]
IRWIN Galen Arnold
14 January 1942, American. Kagertuinen 108, Sassenheim, The Netherlands. Degrees:
AB (Kansas); MA (Florida State); PhD (Florida State), 1967. Doctoral thesis: "Two
Methods for Estimating Voter Transition Probabilities". 1967-68 Instructor, Florida
State U; 1968-73 Assistant Professor, U of Iowa; Senior Lecturer, U of Leiden.
Publs: *De Nederlandse Kiezer*, (ed), 1977; *Political Participation in the Netherlands: A
Preliminary Report*, 1972; "Issue Consensus in a Multi-Party System: Voters and
Leaders in the Netherlands", *Acta Politica*, 1975; "Party, Accountability and the
Recruitment of Dutch Municipal Councilmen", in *Elite Recruitment in Democratic
Politics* (Eulan and Gudnowski (eds)), 1976; "Compulsory Voting Legislation: Impact
on Voter Turnout in the Netherlands", *Comparative Political Studies*, 1974. Fields:
Comparative political behaviour; research methods; American politics.

[906]
ISAMBERT Francois André*
5 October 1924, French. 122 Avenue Aristotle Briand, 92 Montrouge, France. Degrees:
Agrégé de philosophie, 1947; Dr ès lettres (Sorbonne), 1967. Doctoral thesis: "Religion,
Politique et Science Sociale chez P J B Buchez, 1798-1865". 1950-54 Assistant, Sorbonne; 1954-65 Chercheur, CNRS; 1965-70 Professeur, U de Lille, U de Nanterre;
1971- Directeur d'études, Ecole Pratique des Hautes Etudes. Publs: *Christianisme et
classe ouvrière*, 1960; *De la Charbonnière au Saint Simonisme*, 1966; *Buchez, ou l'âge
théologique de la Sociologie*. Fields: Religion and politics.

[907]
ISBERG Nils Magnus Albert
7 July 1939, Swedish. Docentbacken 3, 104 05 Stockholm, Sweden. Degrees: Fil kand
(Stockholm), 1965; Civ Ek, 1966; Dr fil (Stockholm), 1975. Doctoral thesis: "Partierna
inför väljarna" (Parties Facing the Voters). 1969-76 Lecturer, Graduate School of
Social Welfare and Public Administration and Inst for English-speaking Students, U of
Stockholm; 1975- Secretary, Parliamentary Standing Committee on the Constitution.
Publs: "A Technique for Structural Content Analysis of Party Propaganda" (co-
author), *Scandinavian Political Studies*, 1972; *Partierna inför väljarna* (co-author),
1974. Fields: Political parties; voting behaviour and elections; legislative behaviour;
public administration.

[908]
ISMAYR Wolfgang
11 December 1942, German. Musstrasse 52, D-8600 Bamberg, FR Germany. Degrees:
Dr phil. Doctoral thesis: "Das politische Theater in Westdeutschland". Wiss
Mitarbeiter, Erziehungswiss Fakultät, U of Munich; Dozent, Wiss Assistent für
Politikwissenschaft, Fachbereich Sozialwissenschaften, U of Bamberg; 1974- Mitglied
des Senats. Publs: *Das politische Theater in Westdeutschland*, 1977; "Kulturpolitik,
und politische Kultur", in *Beilage zur Wochenzeitung Das Parlament'*, 1978;
"Hochhuths politisches Theater", in *Rolf Hochhuth, Text und Kritik*.

[909]
IWAND Wolf Michael
17 June 1941, German. Salvator Strasse 10, 51 Aachen, FR Germany, Degrees: Dipl Pol; Dr rer Pol. Doctoral thesis: "Political Aspects of the Image of the United States of America in the West-German Press. German-American Relations at the Beginning of the Seventies". Lecturer, Inst für Pol Wissenschaft, Technische Hochschule. Publs: *Wählerfluktuation in der Bundesrepbulik*, 1972; *Politische Aspekte des Amerikabildes in der überregionalen Westdeutschen Presse*, 1974; *Nationenbilder als Gegenstand der Massenkommunikationsforschung*, 1977. Fields: Political sociology; political psychology; political socialization; political culture; parties, parliaments, voting behaviour.

J

[910]
JACCARD Marianne
6 December 1945, Swiss. 3 rue de Bourg, 1003 Lausanne, Switzerland. Degrees: Lic, 1968; Dipl, 1974. 1968-69 Assistante d'enseignement, Inst de Sci Pol, U de Lausanne; 1971-74 Assistante, Office d'Orientation Professionnelle de Lausanne; Conseillère en Orientation Professionnelle, Office cantonal d'Orientation Professionnelle. Fields: Adolescent psychology; professional information and career choice.

[911]
JÄCKEL Hartmut
30 September 1930, German. Seehofstrasse 118, 1000 Berlin 37, FR Germany. Degrees: Dr jur (Freiburg); LLM (Yale). Doctoral thesis: "Grundrechtsgeltung und Grundrechtssicherung". 1970 Professor of Pol Sci, Free U of Berlin; 1974-77 Vice President, Free U of Berlin; Senatsdirektor, Senatsverwaltung für Wissenschaft und Forschung, Berlin. Publs: Two books, various articles and papers on political/legal questions. Fields: Domestic and comparative politics; political parties; elections; constitutions and government.

[912]
JACOBS Benet Lawrence
16 February 1918, British. Horseshoe House, Beckley, Near Rye, Sussex, England. 1947-61 Colonial Administrative Service, Director of Studies in Public Administration, U of Makerere, Uganda; 1961-65 Visiting Fellow, Head of School of Economic and Soc Studies, U of Botswana, Lesotho and Swaziland; 1965-67 Civil Service Training Adviser to Botswana, Lesotho and Swaziland Governments; 1967 Civil Service Training Adviser to Government of Bahamas; 1967-69 Visiting Fellow, Head of School of Public Administration, U of Mauritius; 1969-71 Administrative Secretary, Inst of Development Studies, U of Sussex; 1973 Visiting Professor, U of Michigan; 1971- Director of Studies, Inst of Development Studies, U of Sussex. Publs: *A Guide for Administrators Working in Ministries*, 1969; *Training Needs of the Government of Swaziland* (with B B Schaffer), 1974; *IDEP/UNICEF Cooperation*, 1974; *Administrative Problems of Small Countries* (P Selwyn (ed)), 1975; *The Case Study Approach* (G. Hyden (ed)), 1975; *Third Country Training Prospects and Attitudes*, 1977; *Evaluation of UK Technical Cooperation in Botswana and Mauritius*, 1977; *Manpower Training Plan for the Cook Islands*, 1977. Fields: Developing countries; civil service training programmes and their evaluation; ethics and corruption; public administration; factors inhibiting efficiency in public services; the evaluation of technical assistance programmes.

[913]
JACOBS Everett Mayer
3 July 1941, American. Department of Economic and Social History, University of Sheffield, Sheffield S10 2TN, England. Degrees: BA; MSc (LSE), 1966. 1968-70 Research Fellow, Centre of Russian and East European Studies, U Coll, Swansea; 1970- Lecturer, Senior Lecturer in Economic and Soc History, U of Sheffield. Publs: "Jewish Representation in Local Soviets, 1959-1973", *Soviet Jewish Affairs*, 1976; "Rent and the Change for Public Services in Soviet Urban Public Housing", *Canadian Slavonic Papers*, 1977; "Recent Developments in Organisation and Management of Agriculture in Eastern Europe", in *Joint Economic Committee Congress of the US, East European Economics Post-Helsinki*, 1977. Fields: Soviet and East European agriculture; economic and social history; Soviet local government.

[914]
JACOBSEN Hanns-Dieter
10 May 1944, German. 74 Hauptstrasse, 1000 Berlin 41, FR Germany. Degrees: Dipl Volkswirt; Dr rer Pol. Doctoral thesis: "Bestimmungsgründe der wirtschaftlichen Beziehungen zwischen West- und Osteuropa". 1970-74 Wiss Assistent, Fachbereich Wirtschaftswissenschaft, Free U of Berlin; 1974-78 Wiss Referent, Stiftung Wissenschaft und Pol, Ebenhausen bei Münche; 1978 J F Kennedy Fellow, Center for European Studies, Harvard U. Publs: *Die wirtschaftlichen Beziehungen zwischen West und Ost*, 1975; *Kritische Einführung in die Aussenhandelstheorie* (with W. Bärtschi), 1976; *Die wirtschaftlichen Beziehungen zwischen Ost und West als Problem der europäischen und atlantischen Gemeinschaft*, 1975; "CMEA and the World-Economy — Institutional Concepts" (with M Baumer), in *East European Economics Post-Helsinki*, 1977; *Strategie und Schwerpunkte der aussenwirtschaftlichen Beziehungen der DDR*, 1978; plus various articles in *Konjunkturpolitik, Die Neue Gesellschaft, Aussenpolitik, Deutschland Archiv, Journal of World Trade Law, Osteuropa-Wirtschaft*. Fields: East-West economic relations; integration problems in Eastern and Western Europe; conflicts in transatlantic relations; economic policy of the US.

[915]
JACOBSEN Hans-Adolf
16 November 1925, German, Klosterweg 26, 53 Bonn-Buschdorf, FR Germany. Degrees: Dr phil, 1955; Habilitation (Bonn), 1966. 1956-61 Dozent für Zeitgeschichte, Schule der Bundeswehr füt innere Führung (Koblenz); 1961-64 Direktor, Forschungsinstitut, Deutsche Gesellschaft für Auswärtige Pol, Bonn; U Professor, Direktor des Seminars für Pol Wissenschaft, Bonn. Publs: *Strategie der Abrüstung*, 1962; *Zur Konzeption einer Geschichte des 2. Weltkrieges 1939-45*, 1964; *Der Zweite Weltkrieg*, 1965; *Nationalsozialistische Aussenpolitik 1933-38*, 1968; *Deutsche Ostpolitik 1919-70*, 1970; *Wie Polen und Deutsche einander sehen*, 1973; *KSZE*, 1973, 1977; *Von der Strategie der Gewalt zur Politik der Friedenssicherung*, 1977; *Karl Haushofer. Leben und Werk*, 1978. Fields: Theory and contemporary history of international relations; German, Japanese and Soviet foreign policy; disarmament; the military and society; problems of war and peace; peace research.

[916]
JACOBSEN Knut Dahl*
University of Bergen, Christiesgatan 19, N-5000 Bergen, Norway. Professor of Public Administration, U of Bergen. Publs: *Technical Assistance in Agriculture*. Fields: Role of state administration in agricultural development; processes of planning; university organization.

[917]
JACOBSEN Kurt Harald
4 March 1933, Norwegian. Roheim, 3800 Bø, Norway. Degrees: BS; Magister Artium (Oslo), 1967. 1967-72 Researcher, International Peace Research Inst, Oslo); 1972-Telemark Regional College. Publs: "Voting Behaviour of the Nordic Countries in the General Assembly", *Cooperation and Conflict*, 1967; "Some Aspects of UN Voting Patterns", in *Proceedings of the IPRA Second Conference*, 1968; "Sponsorships in the United Nations — A Systems Analysis", *Journal of Peace Research*, 1969; "Some Behavioural Characteristics in the United Nations as a Function of Rank", in *Proceedings of the IPRA Third Conference*, 1970; "Sponsorships in the United Nations Negotiating Process", *Cooperation and Conflict*, 1970; "Representation at the United Nations", *Bulletin of Peace Proposals*, 1971; *The United Nations System — A Quantitative Analysis of Conflict, Inequality and Relevance*, 1978. Fields: United Nations; local government.

[918]
JÄGGI André P
4 February 1954, Swiss. Im Schönbühl 1 B, CH-8700 Küsnacht, Switzerland. Assistant, Dept of Pol Sci, U of Zürich. Publs: *Nationale Minderheiten im zwischenstaatlichen Spannungsfeld*, 1976; *Die Chefbeamten des EPD. Eine Untersuchung zur Personalstruktur* (with V Schmid and B Hugentobler), 1978; *Aussenpolitik und Öffentlichkeit ini der Sicht der EPD-Chefbeamten*, 1978. Fields: Foreign policy decision-making; public policy; interest aggregation; minorities.

[919]
JAFFRE Jérome
27 July 1949, French. 20 rue du Cherche-Midi, 75006 Paris, France. Degrees: Dipl (IEP Paris); DES. 1973-75 Chercheur, FNSP; 1975- Directeur des Etudes Pol, SOFRES. Publs: *L'opinion francaise en 1977*; various articles in *Revue Française de Science Politique, Projets, Pouvoirs*. Fields: Public opinion; electoral behaviour.

[920]
JAGSCHITZ Gerhard
27 October 1940, Austrian. A-1180 Vienna, Messerschmidtgasse 28, Austria. Degrees: Dr phil (Vienna), 1968. Doctoral thesis: "Die Jugend des Bundeskanzlers Dr Engelbert Dollfuss". Assistant Lecturer, Inst of Contemporary History, U of Vienna; Secretary General, Association of Austrian Sound Archives. Publs: *Der Putsch. Die Nationalsozialisten 1934 in Österreich*, 1976; *Die Stunde Null, Niederösterreich 1945*, 1975; "Österreichische Innenpolitik 1945-1965", in *Zwei Jahrzehnte Zweite Republik*, 1965; "Von der Demokratie zum Ständestaat", in *Österreich 1918-1938*, 1970; "Filmpropaganda im Dritten Reich", in *Propaganda und Gegenpropaganda im Film 1933-1945*, 1972; "Bundeskanzler Engelbert Dollfuss", in *Vom Justizpalast zum Heldenplatz*, 1975; "Zur Methodik historischer Tondokumentation", in *Das Schallarchiv*, 1977; "NSDAP und Anschluss in Wien 1938", in *Wien 1938*, 1978. Fields: History of the Austrian National Socialist party 1918-1945; Austrian fascism; Austrian domestic policy, 1945-present; audiovisual media; diplomatic history since 1945; Austrian-German relations.

[921]
JAHN Egbert
26 May 1941, German. Hünerbergstrasse 9, 6242 Kronberg 2, FR Germany. Degrees:
Dr phil (Marburg), 1969. Doctoral thesis: "Die Deutschen in der Slowakei 1918-1929.
Ein Beitrag zur Nationalitätenproblematik". Wiss Assistent, U of Marburg;
1974-Forschungsgruppenleiter; 1975- Professor, U of Frankfurt. Publs: *Die Deutschen
in der Slowakei 1918-29. Ein Beitrag zur Nationalitätenproblematik*, 1971; *Die
Ostpolitik der BRD* (with V Rittberger (ed)), 1974; *Sozioökonomische Bedingungen der
sowjetischen Aussenpolitik*, 1975; *Kommunismus — und was dann?*, 1974. Fields:
Soviet societal structure; peace movements; Eurocommunism and East-West détente.

[922]
JAMES Alan Morien
20 January 1933, British. 23 Park Lane, Congleton CW12 3DG, Cheshire, England.
Degrees: BSc. 1955-57 UK Civil Service; 1957 Assistant Lecturer, Lecturer, Senior Lecturer, Reader, LSE; 1968 Rockefeller Research Fellow in International Organizations,
Inst of War and Peace Studies, U of Columbia, New York; 1971- Professor of International Relations, U of Keele. Publs: *The Politics of Peace-keeping*, 1969; *The Bases of
International Order* (ed), 1973. Fields: International society, with special reference to
the contemporary meaning and significance of sovereignty as it is applied to the state in
its international aspects; political aspects of the United Nations, with special reference
to UN peace-keeping.

[923]
JAMES Michael Henry*
5 December 1943, British. Department of Political Science, The Queen's University of
Belfast, Belfast BT7 1NN, Northern Ireland. Degrees: BA. Part-time Tutor in History
of Pol Thought, U of Durham; Research Assistant to the Bentham Project, U Coll,
London; Part-time Lecturer in History of Pol Thought, Regent Street Polytechnic; Lecturer in Pol Sci, Queen's U of Belfast. Fields: The industrial class in French political
thought, 1789-1825.

[924]
JÄNICKE Martin
15 August 1937, German. 33 Patschkauerweg 51, 1000 Berlin, FR Germany. Degrees:
Dr phil; Dipl Soz. Doctoral thesis: "Totalitäre Herrschaft" (Totalitarian Rule). Professor of Comparative Pol, Dept of Pol Sci, Free U of Berlin. Publs: *Der Dritte Weg*,
1964; *Totalitäre Herrschaft*, 1971; *Herrschaft und Krise*, 1973; *Politische Systemkrisen*,
1973; *Umweltpolitik*, 1978. Fields: Comparative politics; political theory; environmental policy; East-European studies; futurology.

[925]
JANNE Henri
20 February 1908, Belgian. Institut de Sociologie, U de Bruxelles, 44 Avenue Jeanne,
1050 Bruxelles, Belgium. Degrees: Dr en philosophie et lettres, 1932. Doctoral thesis:
"La diffusion du christianisme sous le principat de Claude". 1949-56 Director, Inst de
Sociologie, U de Bruxelles; 1949- Professeur, Faculté des Soc Sci, Pol et Econ; Président,
Comité Directeur, Inst d'Etudes européennes, U de Bruxelles. Publs: *Le système social
— Essai de théorie générale*, 1968; *Le temps du changement*, 1970. Fields: Sociology of
education; function of the education system; relations between socio-cultural and
educational changes; democratization studies.

[926]
JANSE Christiaan Samuel Leendert*
30 July 1943, Dutch. Voortwÿk 8, Brenkelen, The Netherlands. Degrees: B Pol Sci (Free U of Amsterdam), 1965; M Pol Sci (Free U of Amsterdam), 1969. Assistant Lecturer, Inst of Soc Sci, Amsterdam. Publs: Chapters in *Het Socialisme* (J Fetscher (ed)), 1970; *Verkenningen in de Politiek* (A Hoogerwerf (ed)), 1971. Fields: History of political ideas, especially the 19th and 20th centuries.

[927]
JANSEN Alf-Inge*
30 December 1939, Norwegian. Institute of Sociology, University of Bergen, Christiesgate 19, N-5000 Bergen, Norway. Degrees: Master of Publ Admin (Indiana); Mag art (Oslo). Research Fellow, NAVF; Research Fellow, U of Bergen; Research Fellow, Inst of Sociology, U of Bergen. Fields: Public planning; public administration and policy; science policy.

[928]
JANSEN Claude Georges Alexis*
4 May 1943, Belgian. Avenue G E Lebon 127, 1160 Brussels, Belgium. Degrees: Lic in pol and diplomatic sci (Free U of Brussels), 1971. Candidate for competitive examination of Belgian Foreign Office, or other functions in minister's office. Publs: *Memoir on the Foreign Relations of the European Communities*, 1971. Fields: Relations between NATO and Gaullist France; relations between France and the European Communities: difficulties with integration.

[929]
JANSEN Max
22 July 1932, Dutch. Gentiaanstraat 46, Bassum, The Netherlands. Degrees: Dr. Senior Lecturer, Europa Institute, U of Amsterdam. Publs: *History of European Integration 1945-1975*. Fields: History of European integration; political aspects of European integration; European policies of European states.

[930]
JANSSON Jan-Magnus*
24 January 1922, Finnish. Ramsays strand 1, Helsinki 33, Finland. Degrees: Dr of Pol Sci (Helsinki), 1950. 1966-70 Chairman, Finnish Council of Peace Research; 1954- Professor of Pol Sci, U of Helsinki; 1959- Chairman, Finnish Inst of Foreign Affairs; 1966-Leader of the Swedish People's Party in Finland; 1971- Dean, Soc Sci Faculty, U of Helsinki. Publs: *Hans Kelsens Statsteori*, 1950; *Frihet och Jämlikhet*, 1952; *Grundlagsutskottets Funktioner*, 1954; *Politikens Teori*, 1969. Fields: Scientific political theory, especially systems theory; political ideologies, especially ideas of democracy; Finnish foreign policy and the role of neutrality in the international system.

[931]
JAQUET Louis George Martin*
20 January 1912, Dutch. c/o NATO Defence College, Viale della Civiltà del Lavoro 38, 00144 Rome, Italy. Degrees: Dr of Law (Leiden), 1935. Doctoral thesis: "The Industrialization of Japan". 1952-64 Ministry of Foreign Affairs; 1964-72 Director, Netherlands Inst of International Affairs; Director, Postgraduate Course of International Relations; Ed in Chief, *International Spectator*; 1972- Civil Deputy Commandant, NATO Defence Coll, Rome. Publs: *De Industrialisatie van Japan in Verband met de Japanse Handelsexpansie naar Nederlandsch-Indië*, 1935; *Japan's Come-back, Effects on Eastern and Western Countries*, 1952; "Opgenomen", in *Eastern and Western World, Selected Readings*, 1953; "Afrika in de Wereldpolitiek", in *De Groeiende*

Gestalte van Tropisch Afrika (co-author), 1967; *Nederlandse Buitenlandse Politiek,* 1970; *Intervention in International Politics* (ed), 1971; *Internationale Verkenningen: Flitsen uit de Ontwikkelingen in Europa, Azie en Amerika.*

[932]
JARLOV Carsten
16 May 1948, Danish. Degrees: Cand Sci Pol. Publs: *Underbeskaeftigelse og Underuddannelse* (with C Jarlov and L Togeby), 1975; "Korporatismebegrebet of Studiet af Samspillet mellem Politiske Institutioner" (with D Dahlerup *et al*), *Økonomi og Politik,* 1975; "Arbejdsløshed og Uddannelsesløshed blandt unge. Et socialt problem" (with C Jarlov and L Togeby), *Socialt Tidsskrift,* 1976; *The Danish Committee System* (with C Jarlov *et al*), 1976; "Unge og politik" (with C Jarlov and L Togeby) , in *Idésamling vedrørende fremtidig ungdomsforskning* (with C Jarlov and L Togeby), 1977; "Holdningsdannelse og politisk involvering (with L Togeby), in *Festskrift til Erik Rasmussen,* 1977; *Offentlige Udvalg* (with O P Kristensen, L N Johansen), 1977; "Electoral Mobility and Social Change in Denmark" (with O P Kristensen), *Scandinavian Political Studies,* 1978.

[933]
JARY David William
17 December 1938, British. 21 Framingham Road, Brooklands, Sale, England. Degrees: BSc. Principal Lecturer in Soc, Manchester Polytechnic. Senior Lecturer in Soc, U of Salford. Publs: *The Middle Class in Politics* (with J Garrard *et al* (eds)), 1978; plus various articles in *British Journal of Sociology*, *Sociological Review*. Fields: Political sociology; social stratification; sociological theory; modes of explanation.

[934]
JAUMIN-PONSAR Anne M
13 October 1939, Belgian, 1 Avenue de Longueville, B-1200 Brussels, Belgium. Degrees: Dr in Law; MA (Madison); Dr in Pol Sci. Doctoral thesis: "La Policy Science: une nouvelle école de la décision publique". 1964-68 Barrister; Assistant, Dept of Pol Sci, U of Louvain; Associate Professor, Faculty of Econ, Pol and Soc Sci, U of Louvain. Fields: Decision making problems in the public sector; theories of organization applied to government and public administration; evaluation of the efficiency of public administration and indicators of administrative capacity; status of women in industrial society.

[935]
JAY Richard
16 December 1946, British. 17 Chlorine Gardens, Belfast 9, Northern Ireland. Degrees: BA; B Phil (Oxon). 1970-71 Lecturer, St Catherine's Coll, U of Oxford; Temporary Lecturer, Dept of Government, U of Essex; Lecturer, Dept of Pol Sci, The Queens U, Belfast. Publs: "The Lincoln By-Election" (with C Cooke and J Ramsden (eds)), in *By-Elections in British Politics*, 1973; *British Politics*, 1973; *Joseph Chamberlain*, 1978. Fields: Modern British and Irish politics; political theory and philosophy; theories of social conflict.

[936]
JEANNENEY Jean-Noël*
2 April 1942, French. 115 rue Notre-Dame des Champs, 75006 Paris, France. Degrees: Dipl (IEP Paris), 1964; Agrégé d'Histoire, 1965; Dr de recherche, 1970. 1969 Assistant, Maître Assistant en Histoire contemporaine, U de Paris-X, Nanterre. Publs: *Le Riz et le Rouge, Cinq Mois en Extrême-Orient*, 1969; "Jules Jeanneney", in *Journal Politique 1939-42* (ed), 1972. Fields: 20th century French politics, especially the Right; pressure groups.

[937]
JENKINS William Ieuan

22 August 1941, British. Darwin College, The University, Canterbury, Kent, England. Degrees: BSc; PhD (London), 1966. 1966-67 Acting Senior Scientific Officer, British Council, London; 1967-70 Research Fellow, Dept of Soc Sci, U of Loughborough; 1970-71 Research Associate, U of Loughborough; Lecturer, Senior Lecturer, Interdisciplinary Studies, U of Kent. Publs: *Social Science and Government: Policies and Problems* (co-ed), 1972; *Policy Analysis: A Political and Organizational Perspective*, 1978. Fields: Public administration; policy analysis; organizational behaviour; political aspects of decision-making techniques; science and public policy; the social implications of science technology.

[938]
JENSEN Hans Støttrup*

7 August 1944, Danish. Engdalgårdsvej 162, 8330 Beder, Denmark. Degrees: Cand sci pol (Aarhus), 1970. Lecturer, Inst of Pol Sci, U of Aarhus. Fields: Political socialization; political parties.

[939]
JENSEN Poul-Erik Daugaard

7 May 1944, Danish. Aafloejen 26, 1 TH, 2700 Broenshoej, Denmark. Degrees: MSc. Research Fellow, Assistant Professor, Inst of Organizational and Industrial Sociology, Copenhagen School of Econ and Soc Sci. Publs: *Politiske Sagers Opstaen og Udvikling*, 1976; *Magt og Deltagelse*, 1978; *Kommune, Borger, Presse*, 1978. Fields: Power and participation in local politics; structure and functions of political parties and interest organizations.

[940]
JERVÅS Gunnar Emanuel

1 July 1938, Swedish. Sandelsgatan 11, 115 33 Stockholm, Sweden. Degrees: BA; MA; PhD. Doctoral thesis: "Security Policy as a Process". Senior Lecturer, U of Umeå; Associate Professor of International Pol, U of Umeå; Associate Professor, Head of International Pol Studies, National Defence Research Inst, Stockholm. Publs: *Security Policy as a Process*, 1971; *From Guerilla to Nuclear Warfare*, 1972; *International Conflict Processes*, 1963; *Foreign Policy in the North*, 1973; *How to Study Politics*, 1974; *Theories of War*, 1975; *The American Political System*, 1977. Fields: Conflict theory; security policy; policy analysis; political theory; American politics; American foreign policy.

[941]
JESSE Eckhard

26 July 1948, German. Thomasstrasse 9, 5501 Franzenheim, FR Germany. Degrees: Dipl pol (Free U Berlin), 1976. Wiss Mitarbeiter, U of Trier. Publs: *Die Demokratie der Bundesrepublik Deutschland*, 1978; *Parteiendemokratie und Parteiensystem der Bundesrepublik Deutschland*, 1977; *Die Parlamentarische Demokratie*, 1976. Fields: Elections; parties; parliamentary affairs; radicalism.

[942]
JESSOP Bob
3 March 1946, British. The Old Manse, Pierce Lane, Fulbourn, Cambridge CB1 5DJ England. Degrees: BA; MA (Cantab); PhD (Cantab). Doctoral thesis: "Traditionalism, Conservation, and British Political Culture with Special Reference to Five English Constituencies". Research Fellow in Soc and Pol Sci, Downing Coll, U of Cambridge; Lecturer, U of Essex. Publs: *Social Order, Reform and Revolution*, 1972; *Traditionalism, Conservatism and British Political Culture*, 1974; "Recent Theories of the Capitalist State", *Cambridge Journal of Economics*, 1977. Fields: State theory; corporatism; social democracy.

[943]
JOBERT Bruno
20 July 1940, French. 1000 Galerie de l'Arlequin, 38000 Grenoble, France. Degrees: Dr en sci pol. Doctoral thesis: "La planification urbaine: de la production de règles à la rationalisation de l'influence étatique". Researcher, CNRS CERAT, Inst Etudes Pol de Grenoble. Fields: Political theory, social policy, especially welfare policy; national planning.

[944]
JOENNIEMI Pertti
28 December 1942, Finnish. Kaupinkatu 20 B 56, Tampere 50, Finland. Degrees: Lic. Doctoral thesis: "On the Future of Neutrality". Senior Research Fellow, Tampere Peace Research Inst. Publs: Various on the dynamics of armament, problems of disarmament; Finnish foreign policy; military manpower systems.

[945]
JOHANSEN Lars Nørhy
16 August 1949, Danish. Langelinie 169, Dk-5230 Odense M, Denmark. Degrees: Cand phil, 1973. Doctoral thesis: "Preferential Voting at the Elections to the Folheting in the 1960s". 1973-74 Assistant Professor, U of Aarhus; 1974-77 Assistant Professor, U of Odense; 1977- Assistant Professor, European University Inst, Florence. Publs: *Samfundsfaglig Metocrebog*, 1977; *Danske organisationers huem-huad-huor* (with A Buksti), 1977. Fields: The relationship between the state and interest organizations; corporatism; social science research methods; political parties.

[946]
JOHANSSON Folke V
17 December 1943, Swedish. Östra Gunnesgärde 6 C, 417 43 Göteborg, Sweden. Degrees: PhD (Göteborg). Doctoral thesis: "Sverige Partipolitiseras. Dagspressen som en Spegel av Politisk Utveckling 1896-1908". Research Associate, Dept of Pol Sci, U of Göteborg. Fields: The role of royal commissions in government decision-making; political communication and mass media studies.

[947]
JOHANSSON Leif
5 December 1942, Swedish. Småskolevägen 43, 223 67 Lund, Sweden. Degrees: PhD. Doctoral thesis: "Landstingskommunerna. Organisation Beslutsprocess och Serviceutbud". Lecturer, Dept of Pol Sci, U of Lund. Publs: *Statsvetenskapliga Analysinriktningar i Teori och Praktik* (ed), 1974; *Självstyrelsen 5: Landstingskommunerna* (with Leif *et al*), 1975. Fields: Political Science as a profession; public policy; methodology in the social sciences.

[948]
JOHANSSON Olaf C A
31 January 1950, Swedish. Skolgatan 75, 902 40 Umeå, Sweden. Degrees: Fil kand. Assistant Lecturer in Pol Sci, U of Umeå, and Director of Studies in Administrative Techniques. Fields: Political socialization; mass communication, public administration.

[949]
JOHN Ieuan Gwilym
19 February 1915, British. Creuddyn, Plas Avenue, Aberystwyth, Wales. Degrees: BA; MSc (London), 1939. 1939-40 WEA Part-time Tutor, South Wales; Assistant Lecturer, Lecturer, Senior Lecturer in International Pol, U Coll of Wales; Wilson Professor of International Pol, U Coll of Wales, Aberystwyth. Publs: "France, Germany and the Saar Problem" *World Affairs*, 1950; *EEC Policy Towards Eastern Europe* (contributor and ed), 1975; *International Politics 1919-1939* (contributor), 1972. Fields: Political aspects of European integration; foreign policy of the Federal German Republic, 1957-68; international relations; European integration; external relations of the European community; Soviet attitudes and policy towards the EEC; foreign policy of Germany particularly the Federal Republic.

[950]
JOHNSON Keith
5 July 1953, British. 9 Berrington Close, 'Greenvale', Redditch, Worcester, England. Degrees: BSc; MSc, 1975; Dipl in International Studies, 1975. Part-time Tutor, Dept of Extra Mural Studies, U of Cambridge; Lecturer in Government, Birmingham Polytechnic. Fields: Politics and policy making in the EEC; foreign policy analysis; international politics and theory.

[951]
JOHNSON Nevil
6 February 1929, British. Nuffield College, Oxford, England. Degrees: BA; MA. Reader in the Comparative Study of Inst; Fellow, Nuffield Coll, U of Oxford. Publs: *Parliament and Administration*, 1967; *Government in the Federal Republic of Germany*, 1973; *In Search of the Constitution: Reflections on State and Society in Britain*, 1977. Fields: British government and administration with particular reference to parliamentary institutions; the West German political system; comparative analysis of local governmental processes in Britain and West Germany; theory of institutions.

[952]
JOHNSON Richard William*
British. Magdalen College, Oxford, England. Degrees: BA; B Phil; MA. Lecturer, School of Social Studies, UBA; Fellow in Pol and Soc, Magdalen Coll, U of Oxford. Publs: *African Perspectives* (with C Allen (eds)), 1970. Fields: Social and political change in Guinea; political cleavages; British political elite studies.

[953]
JOHNSTON Larry D
7 November 1932, British. 44 Cedar Drive, Hatch End, Pinner, Middlesex, England. Degrees: BA; MA (Kansas), 1955; PhD (California), 1961. Doctoral thesis: "A Study of Judicial Review in Australia". 1959-61 Lecturer, Dept of Pol Sci, Wellesley Coll, Wellesley, Mass; 1961-63 Lecturer and Assistant Professor, Hunter Coll of the City U, New York; 1964-65 Lecturer, Dept of Pol Theory and Inst, U of Sheffield; 1966-73 Lecturer, Dept of Government, U of Essex; 1973-74 Senior Sci Officer, Soc Sci Research Council; 1974-76 Lecturer, New Coll, U of Oxford; 1977 Visiting Lecturer, Dept of History, U of Warwick; 1976- Lecturer in Pol, U Coll at Buckingham. Publs: *The Presi-*

dent: Roles and Powers (with D Haught (eds)); *The American Democrat* (with G Dekker (eds)); *International Studies in Europe* (contributor). Fields: Political theory and jurisprudence; British government and politics; American government and politics.

[954]
JOLL James Bysse
21 June 1918, British. 24 Ashchurch Park Villas, London W12 9SP, England. Degrees: MA (Oxon). 1947-50 Fellow and Tutor in Pol, New Coll, U of Oxford; 1950-67 Fellow and Sub-Warden, St Antony's Coll, and U Lecturer in Modern History and Pol, U of Oxford; Stevenson Professor of International History, U of London. Publs: *The Second International 1889-1914*, 1974; *Three Intellectuals in Politics*, 1960; *The Anarchists*, 1964; *Europe Since 1870*, 1976; *Gramsci*, 1977. Fields: European history 19th and 20th centuries; history of Germany; intellectual history; history of revolutionary ideas and movements.

[955]
JOLLIVET Marcel*
30 May 1934, French. Groupe de Recherches Sociologiques, Université de Paris-X, Bâtiment G, 92000 Nanterre, France. Degrees: Lic ès lettres (Sorbonne), 1958; Dipl sci pol (IEP), 1956; Dipl d'études supérieures de philosophie (Sorbonne), 1959. Chercheur, CNRS, Paris; Maître de recherche, CNRS. Publs: *Les Collectivités Rurales Françaises*, 1971. Fields: Village social life; agricultural trade unions; agricultural policy; political and social life of the peasantry; economic transformations of rural life.

[956]
JOLY Jacques
13 August 1938, French. 7 Place Jean Moulin, 38000 Grenoble, France. Degrees: Agrégé. Maître-assistant d'histoire. Fields: Town Planning; country planning; territorial administration; political geographies.

[957]
JONES George William
4 February 1938, British. Department of Government, London School of Economics and Political Science, Houghton Street, Aldwych, London WC2, England. Degrees: BA; MA (Oxon), 1965; D Phil (Oxon), 1965. Doctoral thesis: "The Political Structure of the Wolverhampton Borough Council since 1900". 1963-66 Lecturer in Government, U of Leeds; 1966-71 Lecturer, Senior Lecturer, Reader, Professor of Government, LSE. Publs: *Borough Politics*, 1969; *Herbert Morrison: Portrait of a Politician* (with B Donoughue), 1973. Fields: Administrative organization and political pressures; forms of administrative structure; local government; prime ministers and cabinets.

[958]
JONES Peter Mervyn
5 January 1945, British. 142 Hamilton Road, Reading RG1 5RE, England. Degrees: BA. 1970 Temporary Lecturer in Pol, U of Aberdeen; Lecturer in Pol, U of Reading. Publs: *International Yearbook of Foreign Policy Analysis* (ed), 1975; *British Foreign Secretaries since 1945* (co-author), 1977. Fields: Evolution of British defence and foreign policy objectives in the post World War II era.

[959]
JONES Peter Nigel
19 December 1945, British. 3 Cavendish Place, Jesmond, Newcastle upon Tyne, NE2 2NE, England. Degrees: BSc; MSc (London). 1971-72 Temporary Lecturer, U of Sheffield; 1972- Lecturer, Dept of Pol, U of Newcastle-upon-Tyne. Fields: Contemporary political philosophy; history of political thought.

[960]
JONES Robert John Barry
16 February 1946, British. 5 Ilex Close, Sonning Common, Reading, RG4 9LG, England. Degrees: BA; D Phil (Sussex). Doctoral thesis: "Challenge and Response in International Politics: An Analysis of the Development of British Policy Towards Germany During 1935 and Early 1936". Lecturer in Pol, U of Reading. Publs: "The Study of 'Appeasement' and the Study of International Relations", *British Journal of International Studies*, 1975. Fields: International political economy; theory of international relations; foreign policy analysis; collective political psychology.

[961]
JONES Roy Elliott
British. 76 Pencisely Road, Llandaff, Cardiff, Wales. Degrees: BA; MA. Lecturer in International Pol, U Coll of Wales; Lecturer in Pol, U of York; Reader in Pol, U Coll, Cardiff. Publs: *The Functional Analysis of Politics*, 1967; *Nuclear Deterrence*, 1968; *Analysing Foreign Policy*, 1970; *The Changing Structure of British Foreign Policy*, 1974. Fields: Foreign policy studies.

[962]
JÖNSSON Sven Christer
16 May 1944, Swedish. Näktergalsvägen 44, S-240 17 S Sanby, Sweden. Degrees: PhD (Lund), 1975; Docent (Lund), 1976. Doctoral thesis: "The Soviet Union and the Test Ban: A Study in Soviet Negotiating Behaviour". 1971-72 Administrative Assistant, Dept of Pol Sci, U of Lund; 1975-76 External Lecturer, Inst of Pol Studies, U of Copenhagen; 1976- Forskar-assistent, Dept of Pol Sci, U of Lund. Publs: *Sovjets Utrikespolitik* (ed), 1972; *Soviet Bargaining Behaviour*, 1978. Fields: International politics; comparative foreign policy; bargaining theory; Soviet politics.

[963]
JORION Edmond Jean Armand
9 May 1917, Belgian. 10 rue de Neufchatel, 1060 Brussels, Belgium. Degrees: Dr en droit (Brussels), 1942. Civil Servant, Ministries of Economic Affairs, National Education; Professor, Free U of Brussels. Publs: *De la sociologie juridique*, 1967; *Théorie générale de l'administration publique*, 1977; "De l'administration des affaires du peuple par le peuple", *Revue Administration Publique*, 1977. Fields: Public administration; sociology of law.

[964]
JOST Hans Ulrich
29 July 1940, Swiss. Kramgasse 32, 3011 Bern, Switzerland. Degrees: Dr phil. Doctoral thesis: "Linksradikalismus in der deutschen Schweiz". Oberassistent/Lektor, Historischen Inst, U of Bern. Publs: *Die Altkommunisten. Linksradikalismus und Sozialismus in der Schweiz 1919-21*, 1977; "Politisches System und Wahlsystem der Schweiz unter dem Aspekt von Integration und Legetimität", in *Jahrbuch für politische Wissenschaft*, 1976; "Protestbewegung und politischer Radikalismus. Über die Funktion von sozialer Devianz und Stigma im politischen System der Schweiz", in *Jahrbuch für politische Wissenschaft*, 1973. Fields: History and politology of Switzerland.

[965]
JOUBERT Jean-Paul
2 April 1946, French. 3 Boulevard des Diables Bleus, 38000 Grenoble, France. Degrees: Dipl (IEP Grenoble); Lic; Dipl d'études et recherches (FNSP); Dr d'Etat. Doctoral thesis: "Marceau Pivert-Etude d'un courant socialiste révolutionnaire". Assistant, Maître assistant, IEP Grenoble. Publs: *Revolutionnaires de la SFIO*. Fields: History of political ideas; labour movements.

[966]
JOUVE Edmond
14 September 1937, French. 3 rue Marie Davy, 75014 Paris, France. Degrees: Lic en droit (Paris), 1960; DES en droit public (Paris), 1961; DES sci pol, 1962; Dr sci pol (Paris), 1966; Doctoral thesis: "Le Général de Gaulle et la construction de l'Europe, 1940-66". 1963-68 Assistant, Faculté de Droit et Sci Econ, Paris; 1968-Maître assistant, Dept de Sci Pol, U de Paris I. Publs: *Le Général de Gaulle et la construction de l'Europe, 1940-66,* 1967; *La République du Mali,* 1975; *Relations internationales du Tiers Monde,* 1976. Fields: Problems of the Third World, especially international relations; administrative dependence; budgetary law.

[967]
JUDGE David
22 May 1950, British. 10 Spiers Road, Lochwinnoch, Renfrewshire, Scotland. Degrees: BA. Lecturer in Pol, Paisley Coll. Publs: "Backbench Specialization: A Study in Parliamentary Questions", *Parliamentary Affairs,* 1974; "Scottish Members of Parliament: Problems of Devolution", *Parliamentary Affairs,* 1975; "Public Petitions and the House of Commons", *Parliamentary Affairs,* 1978. Fields: British politics; legislatures; European politics.

[968]
JUKOLA-AHO Marja Helena
13 November 1949, Finnish. Paperitehtaankatu 8 A 3, 33230 Tampere 23, Finland. Degrees: MSc pol sci (Tampere), 1972. 1975- Assistant, Inst of Pol Sci, U of Tampere. Fields: Political socialization; political parties and interest groups.

[969]
JUNKER Beat
27 September 1928, Swiss. Ferenbergstrasse 24, CH-3066 Stettlen, Switzerland. Degrees: Dr phil. Doctoral thesis: "Eidgenössische Volksabstimmungen über Militärfragen um 1900". Staatliches Lehrerseminar Bern; Ausserordentlicher Professor für Geschichte und Soziologie der schweizerischen Pol, U of Bern. Publs: *Die Bauern auf dem Wege zur Politik,* 1968; *Kampf und Verantwortung, die bernische Bauern-, Gewerbe- und Bürgerpartei 1918-1968* (with R Maurer), 1968; *Staat und Politik in der Schweiz* (with E Gruner), 1978; "Mouvements paysans et problemes agraires en Suisse de la fin du XVIIIè siècle a nos jours" (with E Gruner), in *Les mouvements paysans dans le monde contemporain,* 1976; "Bauernparteien in der Schweiz", in *Europäische Bauernparteien im 20. Jahrhundert,* 1977. Fields: Peasant parties.

[970]
JUNNE Gerd
15 January 1947, German. Tägermoosstrasse 24, D-7750 Konstanz, FR Germany. Degrees: Dipl Pol, 1970; Dr rer Pol, 1975. Doctoral thesis: "Der Eurogeldmarkt. Seine Bedeutung für Inflation und Inflationsbekämpfung". 1970-72 Research Assistant, Free U of Berlin; 1972-74 Lecturer, Pädagogische Hochschule Berlin and U of Bremen; 1974- Assistant, Dept of Pol Sci, U of Konstanz. Publs: *Spieltheorie in der internationalen Politik,* 1972; *Internationale Abhängigkeiten* (with S Nour), 1974; *Kritisches Studium der Sozialwissenschaften,* 1976. Fields: International relations; development problems; multinational corporations; international banking; international monetary relations; didactical problems.

[971]
JURRJENS Rudolf Theodoor*
26 April 1938, Dutch. Ter Braaklaan 21, Uithoorn, The Netherlands. Degrees: Cand Ex (Free U of Amsterdam), 1960; Dr Ex (Free U Amsterdam), 1965. Assistant Professor, Free U of Amsterdam. Publs: *Final Report of the Simulation Course. European Security Conference* (co-author), 1970. Fields: Cultural policy between East and West.

K

[972]
KAARSTED Tage
27 May 1928, Danish. Rosenvaenget 7 A, 5250 Odense SV, Denmark. Degrees: Cand mag (Aarhus), 1955; Dr phil (Aarhus), 1968. Doctoral thesis: "Paaskekrisen 1920" (The Easter Crisis 1920). 1955-68 Grammar School Master; 1961-68 Part-time Lecturer in Pol Sci, U of Aarhus; 1968- Professor of Contemporary History; 1967-73 Consultant to Ministry of Education on Social Studies in Danish Grammar Schools; 1971-Historiographer to Her Majesty Queen Margrethe. Publs: *Hvad Skal det Nytte?*, 1958; *Ove Rode I-II*, 1971; *Regeringskrisen 1957*, 1964; *Paaskekrisen 1920*, 1968; *Danks Politik i 1960 erne. Taktik og Strategi*, 1969; *Storbritannien or Danmark 1914-20*, 1974; *De Danske Ministerier 1929-53*, 1977; *Great Britain and Denmark*, 1978. Fields: Political and parliamentary trends in Denmark since 1945.

[973]
KAASE Max Willy
14 May 1935, German. Ludwig-Beck-Strasse 22, 68 Mannheim 1, FR Germany. Degrees: Dipl Volkswirt (Köln), 1959; Dr rer Pol (Köln), 1964; Habilitation (Mannheim), 1972. Doctoral thesis: "Wechsel von Parteipräferenzen. Eine Analyse am Beispiel der Bundestagswahl". 1962-64 Assistant, U of Köln; 1964-65, 1967-71 Assistant, U of Mannheim; 1965-66, 1971-72 Research Fellow, U of Michigan and other American Universities; 1972-73 Privatdozent, U of Mannheim; Executive Director, Zentrum für Umfragen, Methoden und Analysen (ZUMA), Mannheim; Professor of Pol Sci, U of Mannheim. Publs: *Wechsel von Parteipräferenzen*, 1967; "Demokratische Einstellungen in der Bundesrepublik Deutschland", in *Sozialwissenschaftliches Jahrbuch für Politik*, 1971; *Expectations and Political Action* (with H Barnes (ed)), 1978; *Wahlsoziologie heute. Analysen aus Anlass der Bundestagswahl*, 1976. Fields: Democratic theory; voting behaviour; political participation and social movements; political institutions and governability; social science research methodology.

[974]
KAFKA Gustav Eduard*
4 February 1907, Austrian, Alberstrasse 8, A-8010 Graz, Austria. Degrees: Dr jur (Leipzig), 1933. 1933-38 Wirtschaftsjurist; 1938-45 Emigration and arrest for political attitudes; 1945-52 Provisional Inspector of Police; 1952-55 Head of Styria Publishers; 1955 Lectureship, U of Graz; 1956-61 in charge of Zentralkomitee der Deutschen Katholiken, Bad Godesberg; 1961-65 Assistant Professor, Hochschule für Welthandel, Vienna; 1965- Ord Professor, U of Graz; Head, Inst of Pol Theory and Austrian Constitutional Law; Dean, Faculty of Law, U of Graz. Publs: *Die Katholiken vor der Politik*, 1958; *Der freiheitliche Sozialismus in Deutschland*, 1960; *Der gesetzgebende Richterspruch, Grundprobleme der Verfassungsgerichtlichen Normenkontrolle in Österreich*, 1967. Fields: Constitutional and administrative law; comparative government; history of political ideas.

[975]
KAISER Herman Jozef
24 March 1954, Dutch. Graaf Janstraat 161, 2713 CK Zoetermeer, The Netherlands. Scientific Assistant, Ministry of Culture, Recreation and Social Welfare. Fields: Public policy evaluation; administrative problems of decentralization; community policy in overspill-towns.

[976]
KAISER Karl
8 December 1934, German. Kronprinzenstrasse 68, 53 Bonn, Bad Godesberg, FR Germany. Degrees: Dipl Kfm; DES; Dr rer Pol. Doctoral thesis: "EEC and Free Trade Area; England and the Continent in European Integration". Director, Research Inst of the German Society for Foreign Affairs, Bonn; Professor of Pol, U of Cologne. Publs: *German Foreign Policy in Transition. Bonn between East and West*, 1968; *Friedensforschung in der Bundesrepublik*, 1970; *Europe and the United States. The Future of the Relationship*, 1973; *Jahrbuch — Die Internationale Politik 1968/69* (with D Mende *el al* (eds)), 1974; *Kernenergie und internationale Politik. Zur friedlichen Nutzung der Kernenergie* (with B Lindemann (eds)), 1975; *Sicherheitspolitik vor neuen Aufgaben* (with K M Kreis (eds)), 1977; *Auto und Umwelt* (co-author), 1973; *Umweltgutachten* (co-author), 1978.

[977]
KÄKÖNEN Jyrki Kalevi
23 January 1943, Finnish. Kustavintie 9 J 82, 20310 Turku 31, Finland. Degrees: MA. 1974 Research Fellow, Tampere Peace Research Institute; 1976- Assistant, Dept of Pol Sci, U of Turku. Publs: "World Bank: A Bridgehead of Imperialism", *Instant Research on Peace and Violence*, 1975; "Effects of the EEC Association on Foreign Trade and Diplomatic Relations of the African States", 1976. Fields: Development problems; African development; international conflicts; development and international organizations.

[978]
KALDOR Mary Henrietta
11 March 1946, British. Flat 14, 35 Sussex Square, Brighton BN2 5HD, Sussex, England. Degrees: BA. Research Fellow, Institute for the Study of International Organizations; Visiting Fellow, Otto Suhr Institute, Free U of Berlin; Visiting Fellow, Centre for International Studies, MIT; Scholar, Stockholm International Peace Research Institute; Fellow, Science Policy Research Unit, U of Sussex. Publs: *The Disintegrating West*, 1978; *The Arms Trade and The Third World* (co-author), 1971; *European Defence Industries: National and International Implications*, 1972; "The Armaments Sector", *IDS Bulletin*, 1977; "Military Technology and Social Structure: The Weapon System as a Product of Advanced Industry and its Impact on Underdevelopment", *Bulletin of Atomic Scientists*, 1977; "The Significance of Military Technology", *Bulletin of Peace Proposals*, 1977. Fields: Military technology; arms control and disarmament.

[979]
KALTEFLEITER Werner
21 April 1937, German. 2303 Tüttendorf (Gettorf), FR Germany. Degrees: Dipl Volkswirt; Dr rer Pol. 1961- Assistant, Privatdozent, Ausserplanmässiger Professor, U of Köln; 1971- Ordentlicher Professor, Inst für Pol Wissenschaft, Christian-Albrechts U, Kiel; 1970-75 Director, Soc Sci Research Inst, Konrad Adenauer-Foundation; 1975- Vice President, U of Kiel. Publs: *Funktion und Verantwortung in den Europäischen Organisation,* 1964; *Wirtschaft und Politik in Deutschland*, 1966; *Die Funktion des*

Staatsoberhauptes in der parlamentarischen Demokratie, 1970; *Zwischen Konsens und Krise — Eine Analyse der Bundestagswahl 1972*, 1973; *Vorspiel zum Wechsel. Eine Analyse der Bundestagswahl 1976*, 1977. Fields: Comparative government; political system of the Federal Republic; election studies; problems of mass communication.

[980]
KAMMLER Hans
7 December 1935, German. Deutscher Ring 2, D-5030 Hurth-Hermühleim, FR Germany. Degrees: Dipl Handelslehrer (Hamburg), 1960; Dr rer Pol (Köln), 1966; Habilitation (Köln), 1972. Doctoral thesis: "Der Ursprung des Staates. Eine Kritik der Überlagerungslehre". 1963-66 Teacher, Berufsbildende Schulen Wipperfrith; 1966-72 Assistant, Forschungsinst für Pol Wissenschaft und Europäischen Fragen, U of Köln; 1972 Akademischer Oberrat, Forschungsinst für Pol Wissenschaft und Europäische Fragen, Köln. Publs: *Der Ursprung des Staates*, 1966; "Zur antropologischen Fundierung der Theorie der Institutionen", *Politische Vierteljahresschrift*, 1968; *Die Feudalmonarchien*, 1974; "Formal Models vs Real Models: Tools of Inquiry in International Relations", in *General Systems*, 1974; *Logik der Politikwissenschaft*, 1976; "Territories and People as Scarce Resources", *Zeitschrift für die gesamte Staatswissenschaft*, 1977. Fields: Theory and history of political systems; international relations; philosophy and methodology of the behavioural sciences.

[981]
KAPTEYN Paul Joan George
31 January 1928, Dutch. Van Lennepweg 65, The Hague, The Netherlands. Degrees: Dr in Law (Leiden), 1960. Doctoral thesis: "The Common Assembly of the European Coal and Steel Community, an Experiment in International Parliamentarism". 1953-60 Assistant Lecturer, Law Faculty, U of Leiden; 1960-63 Dutch Foreign Office; 1963-74 Professor of the Law of International Organizations, U of Utrecht; 1974-76 Member of the Council of State of the Netherlands. Publs: *L'Assemblée Commune de la CECA*, 1961; *An Introduction to the Law of the European Communities* (with Verhoven van Themaat), 1970; *The United Nations and the International Economic Order*, 1977; *The New International Economic Order*, 1977. Fields: Decision-making process in the European Communities; functions of the European Parliament; legal aspects of European integration; external relations of European communities; international economic organizations.

[982]
KAPUR Harish
21 February 1929, Indian. Institute of International Studies, 132 rue de Lausanne, Geneva, Switzerland. Degrees: BA; MA (Bombay); LL B (Bombay); PhD (Geneva). Doctoral thesis: "Soviet Russia and Asia 1917-27". 1957-61 Assistant Legal Adviser to the United Nations High Commissioner for Refugees, Geneva; 1961-62 Research Associate, Harvard Research Center; Professor of International Relations, Graduate Inst of International Studies; Director, Asian Centre, Geneva. Publs: *Soviet Russia and Asia 1917-27*, 1966; "Soviet Relations with Asia", in *The Soviet Union, A Half-Century of Communism* (ed), 1968; *Soviet Union and Emerging Nations*, 1971; *China in World Politics*, 1975. Fields: Comparative communist systems; strategic studies; theory of international relations; Soviet and Chinese foreign policies; China and the Third World; Eurocommunism.

[983]
KARHAUSEN Mark*
13 April 1940, German. Zentralarchiv für empirische Sozialforschung, Universität zu Köln, Bachemer Strasse 40, 5 Köln 41, FR Germany. Degrees: Dipl Kaufmann (Köln), 1969. Doctoral thesis: "Zur Technik der Prüfung und Bereinigung von Umfragedaten". Zentralarchiv, Köln. Fields: Development of programmes for data processing and data cleaning; applications of simulation techniques in social research.

[984]
KASTARI Paavo Kristian
13 November 1907, Finnish. Puistokatu 3 B 26, Helsinki 14, Finland. Degrees: Lic jur; Dr. Doctoral thesis: "Dissolution of Parliament According to the Finnish Law". 1943 Docent; 1946 Assistant Professor; 1956 Professor of Constitutional Law; 1952-56 Ombudsman of the Parliament; 1957-58 Minister of Communications; Emeritus Professor of Constitutional Law. Publs: *Dissolution of the Parliament*, 1940; *Privileged Position of the Central Bank of Finland*, 1955; *La Présidence de la République en Finland*, 1956; *Legal Foundations of the Political System in Finland*, 1969; *Constitutional Protection of Civil Rights in Finland*, 1971; *Finnish Constitutional Law*, 1977. Fields: Comparative law and sociology of law.

[985]
KASTELEIN Johan
3 January 1927, Dutch. Mozartstraat 59, 2324 XR Leiden, The Netherlands. Degrees: PhD. Doctoral thesis: "Tasks and Task- Contacts". Work Analyst; Management Consultant; Deputy Head, Organization Dept, Organization Researcher, Inst of Public Administration, U of Amsterdam. Publs: *Tasks and Task-Contacts*, 1977; *Points for Consideration When Organizing Projects*, 1975; *Interdepartmental Policy Co-ordination* (with R H P W Kottman), 1975; *Management in de Rijksdienst*, 1977; *Zelfmanagement*, 1977. Fields: Comparison between private and public management and organization; centralization/decentralization, heteronomy/autonomy and the functions of information systems.

[986]
KASTENDIEK Hans D
10 December 1942, German. Niebuhrstrasse 76, 1000 Berlin 12, FR Germany. Degrees: Dipl Pol (Berlin), 1969; Dr rer Pol (Berlin), 1976. Doctoral thesis; "Zur Analyse wissenschaftlichen Wandels. Gesellschaftlich-politische Vorraussetzungen und Bedingungen der Herausbildung und Entwicklung der (West) deutschen Politikwissenschaft". 1970-76 Assistant Lecturer, Free U of Berlin; 1976- Assistant Professor, Free U of Berlin. Publs: "Zur neueren marxistischen Diskussion über die Analyse von Form und Funktion des bürgerlichen Staates", *Politische Vierteljahresschrift*, 1975; *Kritik der politischen Wissenschaft* (co-author), 1975; "Zur Politologie-Kritik Ossin K Flechtheims", in *Systemwandel und Demokratisierung* (Fenner/Blanke (eds)), 1975; *Die Entwicklung der westdeutschen Politik-Wissenschaft*, 1977. Fields: Society and social science; development of political science as a discipline.

[987]
KAUFMAN Gianni
20 April 1947, Italian. Via M de Taddei 10, Milan, Italy. Degrees: Laurea. Doctoral thesis: "Il Problema dei Valori in Max Weber". Research Assistant of Pol Sci, Catholic U of Milan; Associate Professor of Pol Sci, U of Calabria. Publs: *Il Sistema Globale — Immagini e Modelli*, 1974. Fields: International relations; capitalist political systems; international dependency.

[988]
KAVANAGH Dennis Anthony
27 March 1941, British. 39 Ashton Lane, Sale, Cheshire, England. Degrees: BA; MA (Manchester), 1966. 1965-67 Assistant Lecturer, U of Hull; 1969-70 Ford Foundation Fellow, U of Stanford; Lecturer, U of Manchester; 1977- Visiting Professor, European U Inst, Florence; 1974- Senior Lecturer, U of Manchester. Publs: *Constituency Electioneering*, 1970; *Political Culture*, 1972; *The British General Election of February 1974*, 1974; *The British General Election of October 1974 (with D E Butler)*, 1975; *New Trends in British Politics* (with R Rose), 1977. Fields: Political leadership; parties and elections; political culture.

[989]
KEATING Michael James
2 February 1950, British. 52 Station Road, Stone, Staffordshire ST15 8ES, England. Degrees: BA; MA (Oxon), 1975; PhD (CNAA), 1975. Doctoral thesis: "The Role of the Scottish MP". 1972-75 Part-time Lecturer, Glasgow Coll of Technology; 1975-76 Senior Research Officer, U of Essex; 1976- Lecturer in Pol, North Staffordshire Polytechnic. Publs: various articles on parliamentary behaviour, local Government reform, devolution; Scottish nationalism, environmental politics. Fields: Scottish nationalism; devolution; political parties.

[990]
KEATINGE Neil Patrick
21 March 1939, Irish. 19 Palmerston Gardens, Dublin 6, Ireland. Degrees: BA; MSc (LSE), 1963; PhD (Trinity Coll, Dublin), 1968. Doctoral thesis: "The Formulation of Irish Foreign Policy". 1963- Junior Lecturer, Lecturer in Pol Sci, Trinity Coll, Dublin. Publs: *The Formulation of Irish Foreign Policy*, 1973; *A Place Among the Nations: Issues in Irish Foreign Policy*, 1978. Fields: International relations; foreign policy analysis; European community.

[991]
KEDOURIE Elie*
London School of Economics and Political Science, Houghton Street, London WC2A 2AE, England. Degrees: BSc. 1936-65 Lecturer, Reader, LSE; 1965- Professor of Pol, LSE. Publs: *England and the Middle East: The Destruction of the Ottoman Empire 1914-21*, 1956; *Nationalism*, 1971; *Afghani and Adburk: an Essay on Religious Unbelief and Political Activism in Modern Islam*, 1966; *The Chatham House Version and other Middle-Eastern Studies*, 1970. Fields: Political thought in England in the 19th and 20th centuries; European political thought; intellectual and political history of the Middle East in modern times; British relations in the Middle East after 1914.

[992]
KEIR Malcolm McLaren
British. 14 Hurst Lodge, 25 Coolhurst Road, London N8 8ES, England. Degrees: BA; MA (Essex). Part-time Tutor (extra-mural) in Pol, The Open U; Visiting Lecturer in Pol, U of Syracuse; Senior Lecturer in Pol, Ealing Coll of Higher Education. Fields: British government and politics; political sociology of advanced industrial societies.

[993]
KEITH-LUCAS Bryan
1 August 1912, British. Darwin College, The University, Canterbury, Kent, England. Degrees: MA (Cambridge); MA (Oxon). 1948-65 Senior Lecturer in Local Government, U of Oxford; 1950-65 Fellow of Nuffield Coll, U of Oxford; 1956-70 Chairman, National Association of Parish Councils; 1965-77 Professor of Government; 1970-74

Master of Darwin Coll, U of Kent. Publs: *The English Local Government Franchise*, 1952; *History of Local Government in England*, 1971. Fields: Local government; constitutional change in Africa; regionalism.

[994]
KELIDAR Abbas Rashid*
15 May 1936, Iraqi. 1 Benyon House, Myddelton Passage, London EC1, England. Degrees: BA; MA (Nottingham), 1963; PhD (SOAS, London), 1966. Doctoral thesis: "Shaykh Ali Yusuf, Political Journalist and Islamic Nationalist. A Study in Egyptian Politics 1880-1913". Lecturer in Pol, SOAS, U of London. Publs: "Syria", in *The Middle East: A Handbook*, 1971. Fields: Politics of integration; the role of ministries in the politics of the new states: the case of Iraq.

[995]
KELLAS James Grant
16 May 1936, British. Department of Politics, University of Glasgow, Glasgow W 2, Scotland. Degrees: MA (Aberdeen), 1958; PhD (London), 1962. Doctoral thesis: "The Liberal Party in Scotland, 1885-95". 1961-62 Tutorial Fellow in History, Bedford Coll, U of London; 1962-64 Assistant in History, U of Aberdeen; Lecturer, Reader in Pol, U of Glasgow. Publs: *Modern Scotland*, 1968; *The British General Election of 1970* (contributor) (D E Butler and M Pinto-Duschinsky (eds)), 1971; *The Scottish Political System*, 1975; *The Political Economy of Change* (contributor) (J J W Alexander (ed)), 1975; *Social Class in Scotland* (contributor) (M G Clarke and H M Drucker), 1976; *The Future of Scotland* (contributor) (R Underwood (ed)), 1977; *The British People: Their Voice in Europe* (contributor), 1977; *American Government and Politics* (with A M Potter and P Fotheringham), 1978. Fields: Scottish political system; American federalism; smaller European democracies; British House of Commons.

[996]
KELLER Wilhelm Gottfried Sebastian
8 November 1952, German. Schulweg 8, 7603 Oppenau, FR Germany. Degrees: Dr. Doctoral thesis: "Der Meinungshörer. Ein psycho-politisches Modell zur Erforschung von Meinungsfeldern". Journalist. Publs: "Meinungshörer-Studie" (with G Keller), *Psychologie Heute*, 1976. Fields: Political psychology; foreign policy; opinion research.

[997]
KELLERHALS Jean
24 May 1941, Swiss. 353 rue de Bernex, 1233 Bernex, Switzerland. Degrees: Lic ès sci écon; Lic en soc; Dr en sociologie. Doctoral thesis: "Formes et fonctions de la participation aux associations" (Forms and Functions of Participation in Voluntary Associations.) 1964-66 Assistant, Dept of Sociology, U of Geneva; 1967-70 Chef de travaux, Faculty of Law, U of Fribourg; 1972-77 Assistant Professor, Dept of Sociology, U of Geneva; 1975 Visiting Professor, Dept of Sociology, U of Neuchâtel; 1977- Professor, Dept of Sociology, U of Geneva. Publs: *Jeunesse et société* (with P Arnold et al), 1972; *Les associations dans l'enjeu démocratique: étude sur la participation aux associations*, 1974; *Familles urbaines et fécondité* (with M Bassand), 1975; *Le sens de l'avortement: étude psychosociologique* (with W Pasini), 1976. Fields: Sociology of associations; sociology of the family; sociology of law.

[998]
KELLY Petra K*
29 November 1947, German. Economic and Social Committee of the European Communities, 2 rue Ravenstein, Office 512, 1000 Bruxelles, Belgium. Degrees: BA; MA (Europa Inst Amsterdam), 1971. 1966-70 Pol Staff of Senators R F Kennedy, Hubert Humphrey; 1969-70 Taught World Pol Seminar, American U, Washington; 1971- EEC Administrator, Social Policy Section, Econ and Social Committee, EEC. Publs: *Revolutionism* (with A A Said), 1971. Fields: Europeanization of national political parties; social policy; role of the economic and social committee within EEC policy.

[999]
KELSTRUP Morten*
27 April 1942, Danish. Vaeldegaardsvej 28, Gentofte, Denmark. Degrees: Cand pol sci (Aarhus). Research Assistant, Danish Inst of International Studies; Part-time Lecturer, U of Copenhagen. Publs: "Kommissionens Rolle i Faellesmarkedets Beslutningsproces", *Økonomi og Politik*, 1968; *David Easton's Systemteori*, 1969. Fields: European integration; systems theory; critical theory; Marxism.

[1000]
KEMAN Joh Engelbertus
20 August 1948, Dutch. Verspronckweg 301, Haarlem, The Netherlands. Degrees: BA; MA. Doctoral thesis: "Political Science and Contemporary History: Symbiose or Synthesis?" (in Dutch). Assistant in Contemporary History, Free U of Amsterdam; Lecturer in Pol Sci, U of Amsterdam. Publs: *The Cold War Revisited* (in Dutch), 1975; *The Military Apparatus as a State-Apparatus* (in Dutch), 1977; *The Military as a Theoretical and Methodological Problem* (in Dutch), 1977; *The Economics of the Military: The Dutch Experience (1945-1972)*, 1978. Fields: Theories of the state and its functioning; Marx and Weber and the study of politics; industrial relations; wage-policies and unemployment.

[1001]
KEMP Betty*
5 November 1916, British. St Hugh's College, Oxford, England. Degrees: MA (Oxon), 1947. 1945-46 Lecturer, U of Manchester; 1946- Fellow and Tutor, St Hugh's College, U of Oxford. Publs: *King and Commons, 1600-1832,* 1957; *Sir Francis Dashwood: an Eighteenth Century Independent,* 1967; *Votes and Standing Orders of the House of Commons: the Beginning,* 1972. Fields: British parliament; parliamentary procedure; comparative constitutional history, especially 18th and 19th centuries.

[1002]
KEMP Udo
29 March 1943; German. Am Schmiedacker 1, D7815 Kirchzarten, FR Germany. Degrees: PhD (Tübingen). Doctoral thesis: "Kandidatenaufstellung in Frankreich". Professor of Pol Sci, Pädagogische Hochschule, Freiburg. Publs: Books and articles on the political system of France, USA and the Federal Republic of Germany. Fields: Comparative politics.

[1003]
KEMPERS Frans
12 July 1926, Dutch. Watteaustraat 8A hs, Amsterdam, The Netherlands. Degrees: MA. Ed, *Eastern European Affairs* of Keesing's Historisch Archief; Acting Director, Inst for Science of the Press, U of Amsterdam. Publs: *Mass Communications Research in the Netherlands* (in Dutch), 1973; *Editorial Democracy* (in Dutch), 1974; *Journalists*

and Press Concentration (with J Wieten (ed)) (in Dutch), 1976; *Media Politics and Media Research* (in Dutch), 1977. Fields: Communism; press concentration; editorial democracy; mass media.

[1004]
KENNEDY William Vincent
30 November 1945, American. Kantstrasse 154a, 1 Berlin 12, FR Germany. Degrees: BA; MA (Colorado), 1972. Assistant Director of Environmental Education, Western Pennsylvania Conservancy; Instructor, Penn State U; Research Fellow, International Inst for Environment and Society. Fields: Environmental impact assessment.

[1005]
KERBLAY Basile
1920, French. 56 rue Vaneau, 75007 Paris, France. Degrees: Dr ès lettres (Sorbonne); Dipl (IEP Paris); Dipl (Ecole Nat des Langues Orientales, Paris). Doctoral thesis: "Les marchés paysans en URSS; l'isba russe d'hier et d'aujourd'hui". Research Assistant, UN Econ Commission for Europe, Geneva; Chargé de mission, Direction d'Europe, Ministère des Affaires Estrangères, Paris; Directeur d'Etudes, Ecole Pratique des Hautes Etudes, Sorbonne; Professeur titulaire de la chaire de civilisation russe et soviétique, Paris IV; Chargé de cours d'économie soviétique, IEP Paris. Publs: *Les marchés paysans en URSS,* 1968; *L'isba d'hier et d'aujourd'hui,* 1973; *La société soviétique contemporaine,* 1977; *The Theory of Peasant Economy* (with A Chayanov), 1966. Fields: Soviet economics and society; Russian agrarian history in the 19th and 20th centuries.

[1006]
KERR Henry H (Jr)
1 December 1936, American. 12 Chemin Colladon, 1209 Geneva, Switzerland. Degrees: BA; MA (Michigan), 1966; PhD (Michigan), 1970. 1964-66 Assistant Study Director, Inst for Soc Research, U of Michigan; 1967-69 Doctoral Fellow, Soc Sci Research Council and Rackham School of Graduate Studies; 1969-70 Assistant Professor, U of Virginia; 1970- Lecturer, Research Fellow, Assistant Professor, U of Geneva. Publs: *Wir und die Welt* (with D Frei), 1973; *Switzerland: Social Cleavages and Partisan Conflict,* 1974; *Les Suisses et la politique* (with D Sidjanski, Ch Roig *et al*), 1975; *Parlement et société en Suisse,* 1978. Fields: Comparative political sociology and behaviour, particularly protest behaviour; survey research analysis; comparative parliamentary studies.

[1007]
KERVER Johan C M
4 June 1952, Dutch. Kolmschotlanden 93, Enschede, The Netherlands. Degrees: BA; MA (Leiden). Assistant Professor in Pol Sci, Twente. Fields: Theoretical political science; Dutch politics; tax policy.

[1008]
KESLET Jean-Francois
1932, French. 65 rue Brillat Savarin, 75013 Paris, France. Degrees: Lic ès lettres; Dipl (IEP); Dipl ENA. Ancien pensionnaire de la Fondation Thiers; Administrateur civil; Maître de conférences, Professeur, U René Descartes, Paris V; Directeur, Dept Carrières Soc, IUT Paris V. Publs: *L'administration publique; sociologie des fonctionnaires* (co-ed); "Les origines sociales des fonctionnaires" (contributor), in *Traité de science administrative,* 1966; "L'influence de l'ENA sur la rénovation de l'administration et ses limites", in *Tendances et volontés de la société française,* 1966; "Les opinions politiques des anciens élèves de l'ENA", in *Les fonctionnaires et la politique,* 1976. Fields: Political parties; the Socialist movement.

[1009]
KESSLER Marie-Christine
1940, French. 159 Boulevard Bineau, 92200 Neuilly/Seine, France. Degrees: Dipl (IEP Paris), 1962; Lic en droit, 1963; Dr de 3ème cycle, 1967. Doctoral thesis: "Le conseil d'Etat". 1964-68 Assistante de recherche, FNSP; Attachée de recherche, Chargée de recherche, CNRS. Publs: *Le conseil d'Etat*, 1968; *L'expérience française des villes nouvelles* (co-ed), 1970; *Les superstructures des administrations centrales* (co-ed), 1972; *L'ENA et la politique de la haute fonction publique depuis 1945*, 1978. Fields: Civil service appointments, training and appointment of civil servants; financial and management control; the civil service in political thought.

[1010]
KEVENHÖRSTER Paul Johannes*
5 June 1941, German. 5303 Bornheim/Kardorf, Buchenstrasse 11, FR Germany. Degrees: Dipl Volkswirt (Köln); Dipl Kaufmann (Köln); Dr rer Pol (Köln), 1968. Doctoral thesis: "The Japanese Political System". 1967-69 Research Assistant, Konrad-Adenauer-Foundation; Research Assistant, IWUG Inst, Stotzheim. Publs: *Das politische System Japans*, 1969; *Der Überdruss an der Demokratie*, 1970; *Im Wechselspiel der Koalitionen*, 1970. Fields: Direct democracy in industrial societies; Jugoslav self-management system; Japanese economic policy.

[1011]
KEWENIG Wilhelm A
20 June 1934, German. 23 Kiel 1, Bismarckallee 9, FR Germany. Degrees: Dr jur (Köln), 1962; LLM (Harvard Law School), 1966. Doctoral thesis: "The Coexistence of Religious Communities in the Lebanon". Professor, Director, Inst for International Law, U of Kiel. Fields: International organizations, especially UN; international economic law; peace research.

[1012]
KHO Frans*
30 November 1925, Indonesian. c/o Institute of Political Science, University of Nijmegen, Verlendge Groenestraat 43, Nijmegen, The Netherlands. Degrees: Dr (Leiden), 1957. Consultant Adviser to the Indonesian Govt on Technical Assistance; Lecturer and Research, Centre of Peace Research, U of Nijmegen; Adviser, U Atma jaya, Djakarta, Indonesia. Publs: *Les églises chrétiennes et la décolonisation*, 1964. Fields: Political problems of the Third World; peace problems, especially formation; peace education.

[1013]
KIENZLE Rolf
6 December 1939, German. Eman-Geilbelstrasse 3, D 62 Wiesbaden, FR Germany. Degrees: MA (Mainz). 1970- Assistant, Inst of Pol Sci, U of Mainz. Publs: *Das Selbstverständnis der CDU; Einheit von Planung, Entscheidung und Kontrolle; Informationen suchen und finden — Leitfaden zum Studien der Politologie, Publizistik, Soziologie*, 1976; "Parteien im Wahlkampf", *Politische Studien*, 1978. Fields: Empirical theory of democracy; parliamentarism; political sociology of subsystems; data collecting techniques.

[1014]
KIERSCH Karl Wilhelm Gerhard
2 May 1939, German. Steinmetzstrasse 37, D1000 Berlin 30, FR Germany. Degrees: Dipl Pol; Dr rer Pol; Habilitation. Doctoral thesis: "Parlament und Parlamentarier in der Aussenpolitik der IV Republik". Assistant Professor, Professor of Pol Sci, Free U of Berlin. Publs: *Parlament und Parlamentarier in der Aussenpolitik der IV Republik*,

1971; *Bestimmungsfaktoren der Aussenpolitik in der zweiten Hälfte des 20. Jahrhunderts,* (with G Ziebura and F Ansprenger), 1974; *Sicherheit und Entspannung in Europa. Die Antwort des Demokratischen Sozialismus* (with R Seidelmann), 1977; plus several articles on French internal and external politics. Fields: Theories of international politics; the international system since 1945; European integration; foreign policy; decision-making processes; internal and external politics of France; Western European social democratic parties.

[1015]
KILROY-SILK Robert*
19 May 1942, British. Social Studies Building, The University, Liverpool L69 3BX, England. Degrees: BSc. 1966- Lecturer, Dept of Pol Theory and Inst, U of Liverpool. Publs: *Socialism Since Marx,* 1972; *The Role of Commissions in Policy Making* (contributor), 1973. Fields: Industrial relations; theories of socialism.

[1016]
KIMBER Richard
1 August 1940, British. Department of Politics, The University, Keele, Staffordshire, England. Degrees: BA. Lecturer in Pol, U of Keele. Publs: *Political Parties in Modern Britain* (with J D Lees), 1972; *Campaigning for the Environment* (with J J Richardson), 1974; *Pressure Groups in Britain* (with J J Richardson), 1974. Fields: Pressure groups.

[1017]
KINDBLAD Britt-Marie
11 January 1943, Swedish. Morkullevägen 12K, 902 37 Umeå, Sweden. Degrees: BA. 1974-75 Amanuensis, Dept of Pol Sci, U of Umeå; 1975- Assistant Researcher, U of Umeå. Fields: Citizen participation in regional public administration.

[1018]
KINDERSLEY Richard Kerr
9 September 1922, British. The Dover House, Easington, Watlington, Oxford OX9 5AZ, England. Degrees: BA; PhD (Cambridge), 1957. Doctoral thesis: "Legal Marxism in Russia". 1954-56 Lecturer in Russian and French, Royal Navy Coll, Dartmouth; 1957-67 HM Foreign Office; Faculty Lecturer in International Communism, St Anthony's Coll, U of Oxford. Publs: *The First Russian Revisionists,* 1962. Fields: The Yugoslav Federal Assembly; history of the communist international.

[1019]
KING Anthony Stephen
17 November 1934, Canadian. Department of Government, University of Essex, Wivenhoe Park, Colchester C04 3SQ, England. Degrees: BA; D Phil (Oxon), 1962. Doctoral thesis: "Some Aspects of the History of the British Liberal Party, 1906-14". 1961-65 Fellow, Magdalen Coll, U of Oxford; 1967 Visiting Professor, U of Wisconsin, USA; 1966 Senior Lecturer, Reader, Professor, U of Essex; 1977-78 Fellow, Center for Advanced Study in the Behavioural Sciences, Stanford, California. Publs: *British Politics: People, Parties and Parliament* (ed), 1966; *The British General Election of 1964* (with D E Butler), 1965; *The British General Election of 1966* (with D E Butler), 1966; *The British Prime Minister* (ed), 1969; *Britain Says Yes: The 1975 Referendum on the Common Market,* 1977. Fields: Comparative executives; comparative policy analysis; US and British government and politics.

[1020]
KINNAS John
24 August 1938, Greek. 2 Akronos Street, Athens 506, Greece. Degrees: PhD (London); Dr ès sci pol (Panteios Graduate School of Pol Sci, Athens). Doctoral thesis: "The Politics of Association of European Organizations; A Comparative Approach". Professor, Centre of Higher Technical and Professional Training, Athens. Publs: *The Commonwealth and European Unification*, 1967; *International Cooperation in Space Communications. The Case of Intelsat*, 1971; *The International System and Foreign Policy*, 1976 (all in Greek); "Association", in *International Organization: A Conceptual Approach* (P Taylor and A J R Groom (eds)), 1978. Fields: International organizations; international economic relations; international systems theory.

[1021]
KIPE Rüdiger Richard
5 February 1942, German. Europaring 92, D-5300 Bonn 1, FR Germany. Degrees: Dr jur. Doctoral thesis: "Die Prinzipien und Grundlagen des Föderalismus in der Tschekoslowakischen Sozialistischen Republik". Wiss Referent, SPD-Fraktion, Deutscher Bundestag; Wiss Assistent, Gesamthochschule Siegen und Abgeordneten-Mitarbeiter, Deutscher Bundestag. Publs: *Föderalismus in der CSSR; Stellung Ostberlins zur DDR; Deutsche und Europäische Option im Grundgesetz; Der Bundesrat als Gesetzgebungsorgan*. Fields: Political system of the FRG; constitutional law; system comparison; East-West relations.

[1022]
KIRBY Stephen*
7 March 1943, British. 207 Victoria Avenue, Hull, East Yorks, England. Degrees: BA; MSc (LSE), 1966. 1966- Assistant Lecturer, Lecturer in International Relations, U of Hull. Fields: UN peacekeeping; Britain and NATO; national interest and ideology.

[1023]
KIRCHHOFF Hans
9 October 1933, Danish. Soendermarken 39, 3060 Espergaerd, Denmark. Degrees: MA, 1961; Dr phil, 1978. Doctoral thesis: "The August Rising 1973: The Fall of the Policy of Collaboration. A Study in Collaboration and Resistance". Associate Professor, Inst of Contemporary History, U of Copenhagen. Publs: Various articles and papers on Danish-German relations 1970-75. Fields: Mass movements; group psychology; the individual versus the state.

[1024]
KIRCHNER Emil Joseph
19 March 1942, German. 20 Lammas Way, Wivenhoe, Essex, England. Degrees: BA; MA (Case Western Reserve); PhD (Cleveland). Doctoral thesis: "An Empirical Examination of the Functionalist Concept of Spillover". Lecturer in Government, U of Essex. Publs: *Trade Unions as a Pressure Group in the European Community*, 1977; "An Empirical Examination of the Functionalist Concept of Spillover", in *International Organization*, 1978. Fields: European integration: theoretical, methodological and conceptual problems in the study of European integration; Western European politics; developments in industrial democracy; social and environmental policy; USA-Europe relations; relationship between the EEC and the developing countries.

[1025]
KIRK-GREENE Anthony Hamilton Millard*
16 May 1925, British. St Anthony's College, Oxford, England. Degrees: MA (Cambridge) 1954. 1957-61 Senior Lecturer in Government, Inst of Administration, Zaria, Nigeria; 1962-66 Reader in Government, Ahmadu Bello U, Nigeria; 1967- Senior Research Fellow in African Studies, St Anthony's Coll, Oxford. Publs: *Adamaura Past and Present*, 1958; *The Principles of Native Administration in Nigeria*, 1965; *Lugard and the Amalgamation of Nigeria*, 1968; *Crisis and Conflict in Nigeria*, 1971. Fields: Political history of anglophone Africa; Africanization of the bureaucracies in West and East Africa; nature and quality of leadership in Africa; the impact of independence on the first two generations of African civil servants.

[1026]
KISKER Gunter
20 February 1925, German. Wadlstrasse 74, 6301 Linden/Am Mühlberg, FR Germany. Degrees: Dr jur, 1963; Habilitation, 1967. Doctoral thesis: "Die Rückwirkung von Gesetzen im anglo-amerikanischen Recht" (1963). Professor of Public and International Law, U of Giessen. Publs: *Gruppenmitbestimmung in der öffentlichen Verwaltung*, 1972; *Vertrauensschutz im Verwaltungsrecht*, 1973; *Die Beziehungen des Bundesrats zu den Ländern*, 1974; *Bundesstaatliches Kompetenzgefüge und Bund-Länder-Planung*, 1975; *Abbau politischer Konfliktüberlastung durch Dezentralisierung*, 1976; *Neue Aspekte im Streit um den Vorbehalt des Gesetzes*, 1977; *Kooperation zwischen Bund und Ländern*, 1977; *Zuständigkeit des Parlaments für politische Leitenscheidungen*, 1978. Fields: Federalism; international organization; administration; parliamentarism.

[1027]
KISS Alexandre Charles
2 June 1925, French. 29 rue du Conseil des XV, 67 Strasbourg, France. Degrees: Dipl (IEP Paris), 1949; Dipl (Hague Academy of International Law), 1950; Dr (IEP Paris), 1951. 1951- Researcher, CNRS: 1963- Teacher, Faculté de Droit, U de Strasbourg; 1968-Teacher, Faculté Internationale pour l'Enseignement du Droit Comparé; Teacher, Collège d'Europe, Bruges; Directeur de Recherche, CNRS; Professeur, IEP, U de Strasbourg. Publs: *L'abus de droit en droit international*, 1952; *Répertoire de la pratique française en matière de droit international*, 1962. Fields: International law: international protection of the environment; human rights; East-West relations.

[1028]
KITZINGER Uwe
12 April 1928, British. Standlake Manor, Nr Witney, Oxon, England. Degrees: MA; B Litt. Dean of INSEAD, Fontainebleau, and Emeritus Fellow of Nuffield Coll, U of Oxford; Ed, *Journal of Common Market Studies*; 1973-75 Adviser to Sir Christopher Soames, Commission of the European Communities. Publs: *German Electoral Politics*, 1960; *The Challenge of the Common Market*, 1961; *Britain, Europe and Beyond*, 1964; *The European Common Market and Community*, 1967; *The Second Try*, 1969; *Diplomacy and Persuasion*, 1973; *The 1975 Referendum* (with D Butler), 1976. Fields: EEC; politics of international trade.

[1029]
KJELLBERG Francesco
19 August 1935, Norwegian. Institute of Political Science, University of Oslo, PO Box 1097 Blindern, Oslo 3, Norway. Degrees: Magister artium; Dr phil. Doctoral thesis: "Political Institutionalization". 1962- Fellow, Assistant Professor, Associate Professor, Inst of Social Research, Oslo. Publs: *Kommunalpolitikk*, 1971; *Political Institu-*

tionalization, 1975; plus several articles on public policy and local government. Fields: Study of public policy; local government; neighbourhood government in Norway and Italy; municipal finances in Norway.

[1030]
KLANDERMAN Jacob Egbertus
18 August 1946, Dutch. Vergierdeweg 240, Haarlem, The Netherlands. Degrees: Dr. Institute of Public Administration, U of Amsterdam. Publs: *Management in de Rijksdienst* (contributor). Fields: Public administration; management science.

[1031]
KLEINSTEUBER Hans J
5 June 1943, German. Otterbekallee 21, 2000 Hamburg 19, FR Germany. Degrees: Dr rer Pol; Dipl Pol. Doctoral thesis: "Staatsintervention in den USA: Die Interstate Commerce Commission" (State Intervention in the USA: The Interstate Commerce Commission). Assistant, Free U of Berlin; Professor of Pol Sci, U of Hamburg. Publs: *Staatsintervention in den USA: Die Interstate Commerce Commission*, 1977; *Die USA-Politik, Wirtschaft, Gesellschaft: Eine Einführung*, 1974; *Fernsehen und Geschäft*, 1973. Fields: Comparative government: USA, Great Britain, France, Italy, GDR, USSR; mass media; new communication technologies, especially cable television.

[1032]
KLINGEMANN Hans D
3 February 1937, German. Friedrichsplatz 14, 68 Mannheim 1, FR Germany. Degrees: Dr rer Pol. Doctoral thesis: "Bestimmungsgründe der Wahlentscheidung" (Determinants of Voting Behaviour). 1961-64 Wiss Hilfskraft, Forschungsinstitut für Pol Wiss und Europäische Fragen, U of Cologne; 1965-66 Instructor, Zentralarchiv für empirische Sozialforschung, U of Cologne; 1966-74 Wiss Assistent, Zentralarchiv für empirische Sozialforschung, U of Cologne; 1974- Direktor, Zentrum für Umfragen, Methoden und Analysen, Hilfseinrichtung der Deutschen Forschungsgemeinschaft (DFG), Mannheim. Publs: "Issue-Orientierung, Issue-Kompetenz und Wahlverhalten aus kommunal politischer Perspektive" (with P Kevenhörster *et al*), in *Kommunales Wahlverhalten*, 1976; "Politische Ideologie und politische Beteiligung: Bericht über ein Forschungsprojekt und ein Forschungsseminar" (with M Kaase), *Mannheimer Berichte*, 1975; "Politische Bestimmungsgründe der Wahlentscheidung?", *Politische Bildung*, 1972; *Politischer Radikalismus* (with F U Pappi), 1972; "Testing the Left-Right Continuum on a Sample of German Voters", *Comparative Political Studies*, 1972; *Bestimmungsgründe der Wahlentscheidung*, 1969, in *Techniken der empirischen Sozialforschung* (van Koolwijk and Wieken-Mayser (eds)), 1975; "Computerunterstützte Inhaltsanalyse als Instrument zur Vercodung offener Fragen" (with K Schonbach), 1977. Fields: Political sociology.

[1033]
KLOSS Günther
20 December 1933, British. 33 Old Broadway, Manchester M20 9DH, England. Degrees: Staatsexamen (Tübingen). Lecturer, Dept of German, U of Nottingham; Lecturer, Senior Lecturer, Dept of European Studies and Modern Languages, UMIST. Publs: *West Germany: An Introduction*, 1976; articles in *German Life and Letters*, *Minerva*, *Konstanzer Blätter für Hochschulfragen*, *Wiener Library Bulletin*, *Journal of Common Market Studies*. Fields: German politics and administration; higher education planning and administration; local government administration.

[1034]
KNAPP Manfred
14 April 1939, German. Kurt-Schumacher-Ring 33, 6200 Wiesbaden, FR Germany. Degrees: Dr phil (Marburg), 1971. Doctoral thesis: "Der US-Informationsdienst als Instrument der amerikanischen Aussenpolitik während der Präsidentschaft John F. Kennedys". 1967-68 Kennedy Memorial Followship, U of Harvard; 1968-70 Teaching and Research Assistant, U of Marburg; 1970-72 Lecturer, U of Frankfurt/M; 1972- Dozent for International Relations, U of Frankfurt/M. Publs: *Die Stimme Amerikas — Auslandspropaganda der USA unter der Regierung John F Kennedy*, 1972; *Die deutsch -amerikanischen Beziehungen nach 1945* (ed), 1975. Fields: Foreign relations of the USA and the Federal Republic of Germany; German-American relations after World War II; international political communication; international organizations; the impact of technological innovations on international relations.

[1035]
KNAPP Wilfrid Francis
4 December 1924, British. St Catherine's College, Oxford, England. Degrees: BA; MA (Oxon), 1949. Fellow and Tutor in Pol, St Catherine's Coll, U of Oxford; Lecturer in Pol, U of Oxford. Publs: *A History of War and Peace 1939-65*, 1967; *Tunisia*, 1969; *North West Africa: A Political and Economic Survey*, 1977. Fields: United States' presence in the Middle East since 1945; North African politics.

[1036]
KNAPPE Eckhard
20 May 1943, German, Sundgauallee 4/22, 78 Feiburg, FR Germany. Degrees: Dr rer Oec. Doctoral thesis: "Möglichkeiten und Grenzen dezentraler Umweltschutzpolitik". Wiss Assistent, Inst für Sozialpolitik, Ruhr-U, Bochum; Wiss Assistent, Inst für Allgemeine Wirtschaftsforschung, Abteilung Sozialpolitik, U of Freiburg. Publs: *Verteilungstheorie*, 1974; *Problembereiche der makroökonomischen Analyse und Entscheidung*, 1975; *Wohlfahrtsökonomik*, 1975/76. Fields: Economic theory of politics; economics of social welfare; foreign affairs.

[1037]
KNEEN Peter Hugh
6 February 1945, British. 4 Cross Row, Hunwick, Crook, Co Durham, England. Degrees: BA; MA. 1974-76 Temporary Lecturer, Research Fellow, Centre for Russian and East European Studies, U of Birmingham; 1976- Lecturer in Pol, U of Durham. Publs: "Why Natural Scientists are a Problem for the CPSU", *British Journal of Political Science*, 1978; "Higher Education and Cultural Revolution in the USSR", *Centre for Russian and East European Studies Discussion Papers*, 1976; "The Ambivalence of Soviet Science", *New York Times*, 1975. Fields: History and politics of Russia and the USSR.

[1038]
KNEI-PAZ Baruch
8 August 1937, Israeli. 26 Rashba Street, Jerusalem. Israel. Degrees: BA; MA (Manitoba); B Phil (Oxon); D Phil (Oxon). Doctoral thesis: "The Social and Political Thought of Leon Trotsky". Senior Lecturer, Dept of Pol Sci, Hebrew U of Jerusalem. Publs: *The Social and Political Thought of Leon Trotsky*, 1978. Fields: Political thought and theory; mass politics; theories of revolution; modern ideologies.

[1039]
KNEUCKER Raoul Friedrich
13 February 1938, Austrian. Haymogasse 82/2, 1238 Vienna, Austria. Degrees: Dr jur (Graz), 1961. Civil Servant, Styria; Research Assistant, U of Vienna; Secretary General of the Austrian Rectors' Conference. Publs: Various articles on higher education, Austrian constitutional and administrative questions; "Austria: An Administrative State", *ÖZP*, 1973. Fields: Higher education; public administration.

[1040]
KNUDSEN Olav
31 July 1943, Norwegian. Konvallveien 32 A, 1301 Sandvika, Norway. Degrees: MA (Denver), 1969; PhD (Denver), 1972. Doctoral thesis: "The Politics of International Shipping: Interaction and Conflict in an International Issue-area, 1946-68". 1967-68 Research Assistant, U of Denver; 1968-69 Teaching Fellow, Temple Buell Coll, Denver; 1970- Sessional Lecturer, Assistant Professor, Associate Professor, Inst of Pol Sci, U of Oslo. Publs: *The Politics of International Shipping*, 1973; "Political Engineering in Liner Shipping", *Arkiv for Sjørett*, 1975; *Foreign Affairs Coverage and Selective Reporting in Politically Committed Newsmedia: A Study of two Norwegian Newspapers*, "Capabilities, Issue-areas, and Inter-State Power", "The Power of Multinational Corporations in Industrialised Countries", both in *Power, Capabilities, Interdependence: New Perspectives on International Power* (K Goldmann and G Sjøstedt (eds)), 1978. Fields: Quantitative comparative studies of foreign policy behaviour; relations between governments and non-territorial international actors; inter-state influence in specialized issue-areas and organizational interaction settings; news media coverage of foreign affairs; multinational corporations in industrialized countries.

[1041]
KNÜTTER Hans-Helmuth*
9 May 1934, German. 53 Bonn, Helmholtzstrasse 1, FR Germany. Degrees: Dr phil (Bonn), 1960. Doctoral thesis: "Ideologien des Rechtsradikalismus im Nachkriegsdeutschland". 1960-67 Wiss Assistent, U of Bonn; Akademischer Rat, Seminar für Pol Wissenschaft, U of Bonn. Publs: *Ideologien des Rechtsradikalismus im Nachkriegsdeutschland*, 1962; *Bonner Studenten über ihre Wohnheime*, 1967; *Geistige Grundlagen und politische Richtung der Deutschen National- und Soldatenzeitung*, 1964. Fields: Political theory; political parties; pressure groups; Jews and the Left; political education.

[1042]
KOCHER Gerhard
7 February 1939, Swiss. Jonas-Furrer-Strasse 21, 8046 Zürich, Switzerland. Degrees: Dr rer Pol (Berne). Doctoral thesis: "Verbandseinfluss auf die Gesetzgebung" (Influence of Interest Groups on Legislation). Swiss Office for the Development of Trade, Zürich; Independent research. Publs: *Zukunftsforschung in der Schweiz*, 1970; *Zukunftsaspekte unseres Gesundheitswesens*, 1974; *Kosteneindämmung im Gesundheitswesen*, 1977-78. Fields: Interest groups; futurism; health policy; evaluation.

[1043]
KODALLE Klaus M
18 October 1943, German. Diesterwegstrasse 27, D-208 Pinneberg, FR Germany. Degrees: Dr phil. Doctoral thesis: "Thomas Hobbes — Logik der Herrschaft und Vernünft des Friedens". Dept of Theology, U of Hamburg. Publs: *Thomas Hobbes — Logik der Herrschaft und Vernunft des Friedens*, 1972; *Politik als Macht und Method. Carl Schmitts Politische Theologie,* 1973; "Negative Dialektike" (with T Koch and H

Schweppenhäuser), in *Idee der Versönnung. Eine Kontroverse über Th W. Adorno*, 1973; *Stubehagen am Jesus. Eine Herausforderung der Psychonalayse an die Theologie*, 1978. Fields: Political philosophy; history of ideas; social philosophy; metaphysics; ethics/philosophy of religion.

[1044]
KOHLENBERGER Helmut Karl
26 October 1942, German. Herklotzgasse 10, A-1150 Wien, Austria. Degrees: Dr phil (Tübingen). Doctoral thesis: "Similitudo und Ratio. Überlegungen zur Methode bei Anselm von Canterbury". Wiss Assistent, Leibniz Kolleg, U of Tübingen; Philos Inst, U of Wien; Lecturer, U of Wien and München. Publs: *Similtiudo und Ratio*, 1972; "Geschichtstheorie", *Wissenschaft und Weltbild*, 1975; *Ortsbestimmung der praktischen Philosophie*, 1976; *Sola ratione*, 1970; *Virtus politica*, 1974; *Die Verantwortung der Wissenschaft*, 1975; *Die Wahrheit des Ganzen*, 1976; *Von der Notwendigkeit der Philosophie in der Gegenwart*, 1976. Fields: Philosophy of politics; philosophy of history; ethics; theology; psychoanalysis.

[1045]
KOHLER Beate
28 December 1941, German. c/o Technische Hochschule, D 61 Darmstadt, Schloss, FR Germany. Degrees: PhD (Köln). Director, Research Inst on European Affairs, Bonn; Professor, Technische Hochschule, Darmstadt; Visiting Professor, Center of Advanced International Studies, John Hopkins U, Bologna. Publs: *Ein Markt und eine Währung* (with G Schlaeger), 1971; *Die Zukunft Europas* (with R Nagel), 1968; *Erfolge und Krisen der Integration*, 1970; *Der Vertrag über die Nichtverbreitung von Kernwaffen und das Problem der Sicherheitsgarantien*, 1972; *Modelle für den Bildungsurlaub. Lehren und Lernen in der Arbeiterbildung* (with Lauritzen, Otten, Trenheit), 1977; *Die Süd-Erweiterung der EG* (ed), 1977. Fields: International organizations; European integration; European foreign policy.

[1046]
KOJA Friedrich*
29 January 1933, Austrian. Lederwaschgasse 22, 5020 Salzburg, Austria. Degrees: Dr jur; Dr rer Oec. 1957-68 Sekretär des Österreichischen Verfassungsgerichtshofes; Ord Professor, Vorstand des Inst für Verfassungs- und Verwaltungsrecht, U of Salzburg. Publs: *Das Verfassungsrecht der österreichischen Bundesländer*, 1967; *Die Rechtsprechung des Verwaltungsgerichthofes 1946-59* (co-author), 1963; *Die Rechtsprechung des Verwaltungsgerichthofes 1960-64* (co-author), 1968. Fields: Austrian federalism; parliamentarism; constitutional law.

[1047]
KOLINSKY Martin
24 June 1936, British. 12 Sellywick Drive, Birmingham B29 7JH, England. Degrees: BA; PhD (LSE), 1966. Doctoral thesis: "Social Structure in France 1930-58". 1966-70 Lecturer in Soc, U of Birmingham; 1970-72 Hebrew U of Jerusalem; 1972- Lecturer, Senior Lecturer in Pol Sci, U of Birmingham. Publs: *Continuity and Change in European Society*, 1974; *Social and Political Movements in Western Europe* (co-ed), 1976; *Regional Assertion and European Integration* (ed), 1978. Fields: Social change in France; fascism; socio-political movements; European integration.

[1048]
KÖNIG Klaus
21 April 1934, German. Wimphelingstrasse 5, D-6720 Speyer, FR Germany. Degrees: Ass jur; Dr jur; Dr rer Pol; Habilitation. Doctoral thesis: "Die Anerkennung ausländischer Verwaltungsakte"; Erkenntnisinteressen der Verwaltungswissenschaft. Research Associate, Research Inst for Public Administration, Speyer; Regierungsdirektor, Office of the Prime Minister, Rheinland-Pfalz; Professor of Administrative Science and Public Law, Hochschule für Verwaltungswissenschaften, Speyer. Publs: *Die Anerkennung ausländischer Verwaltungsakte*, 1965; *Verwaltungsverfahrensgesetze des Auslandes*, 1967; *Erkenntnisinteressen der Verwaltungswissenschaft*, 1970; *Koordination und intergrierte Planung in den Staatskanzleien* (ed), 1976; "Civil Service Reforms in Europe", *Speyerer Arbeitshefte*, 1977; "Education for Public Administration: Developments in Western Europe", *Speyerer Arbeitshefte*, 1977; "Curriculumentwicklung zur Fachhochschule für öffentlliche Verwaltung", *Speyerer Arbeitshefte*, 1977; "Aspects of Workers' Participation in the Public Sector", in *Aspects of Development, Essays in Honour of J N Khosla*, 1977; "Entwicklungen der inneren Verwaltungsorganisation in der Bundesrepublik Deutschland", *Speyerer Arbeitshefte*, 1978. Fields: Theory and study of public administration; social, political, economical context of public administration; public policy and planning; public personnel and civil service; organization of government and administration; administrative development and co-operation.

[1049]
KOOIMAN Jan
12 November 1931, Dutch. Juliana van Stolberglaan 45, The Hague, The Netherlands. Degrees: Dr (Leiden), 1971. Doctoral thesis: "Besturen is Beslissen" (To Govern Is To Decide). 1962-65 Assistant in American Studies, Inst of American Studies, U of Amsterdam; 1966-67 Harkness Fellow Commonwealth Fund, Yale U, Harvard U, U of Michigan, U of California at Berkeley; 1967-70 Secretary to the Leader of the Dutch Labour Parliamentary Faction; 1971-73 Assistant Professor, U of Leiden; 1973- Professor in Public Administration, Graduate School of Management, Delft. Publs: *Besturen is Beslissen*, 1971; *Over de Kamer gesproken*, 1976. Fields: Policy-making; parliamentary politics; governmental organization; public management.

[1050]
KOOPS Wolter
24 January 1921, Dutch. Oosteinde 27, 2271 EB Voorburg, The Netherlands. Degrees: Dr (Leiden). Doctoral thesis; "Federalisme; de Canadese Variëteit". Research Assistant; 1954 Clerk-Assistant, Second Chamber of the States-General; 1973- Clerk of the Second Chamber of the States-General. Fields: Constitutional law; political history.

[1051]
KOPP Hans W
12 June 1931, Swiss. Haus Drei-Eichen, CH-8126 Zumikon, Switzerland. Degrees: Dr (Zürich), 1957; Master of Law (Michigan), 1958. Doctoral thesis: "Substance and Forms of Statutory Law". Senior Partner of Kopp & Vetsch, Zürich. Publs: *Substance and Forms of Statutory Law*, 1958; *Parliaments*, 1966; *Legal Problems of the Next Generation*, 1966; *Analysis of our Time*, 1973; *Crisis and Democracy*, 1974; *Communication in Democracy*, 1976 (all in German); *Ein Mann ging verlegen im Regen*, 1975. Fields: History: rise and fall of Napoleon; futurology; parliamentarism; media-politics.

[1052]
KORANY Bahgat Mohamed*

10 May 1939, Egyptian. Graduate Institute of International Studies, 132 rue de Lausanne, Geneva, Switzerland. Degrees: BA; MA (Sussex), 1966. 1961-63 State Dept of Information, Cairo; 1963-70 Presidency of the Republic, Cairo; 1970- Simultaneous Interpreter, Annual Conference, International Labour Organization; Assistant, Graduate Inst of International Studies, Geneva. Publs: "Non-alignment: Its Conflict-reducing Function in the International System", *Annals of International Studies*, 1972. Fields: Political behaviour and political sociology in the development of Third World states; the applicability of the structural-functional model to Third World political systems.

[1053]
KORITZINSKY Theo*

2 November 1941, Norwegian. Ammerudgrenda 153, Oslo 9, Norway. Degrees: Mag art (Oslo), 1968. 1969-70 Assistant Professor; 1971-72 Research Fellow; 1972- Assistant Professor, Inst of Sociology, U of Oslo. Publs: *Velgere, Partier og Utenrikspolitikk*, 1970; *Samfunnsfag og Påvirkning* (ed), 1972. Fields: Ideologies and legitimating problems; social policies and welfare; local government and decentralization problems; Marxism; education and indoctrination.

[1054]
KOSKIAHO Tapio Juhani

14 January 1940, Finnish. Pyynikintori 8 A 10, 33230 Tampere 23, Finland. Degrees: Dr (Tampere). Doctoral thesis: "Vaaliliittoutuminen Eduskuntauaaleissa" (The Electoral Alliances in the Finnish Parliamentary Elections in 1907-1975). 1974-75 Acting Associate Professor in Soc Sci, U of Oulu; 1967- Assistant, Lecturer, Docent of Pol Sci, U of Tampere. Publs: *Vaaliliittoutuminen Eduskuntauaaleissa*, 1977; *Suomen Hallitukset pä Hallifurohjelmat 1945-1973* (with H Hakovirta), 1973; *Women in Local Politics: The Case of Finland*, 1977. Fields: Parliamentary elections; women in politics; Communist parties in Western Europe; parties' conventions in Finland; small parties in Finland and in northern countries.

[1055]
KOUBA Ernst

19 June 1944, Austrian. Metternichgasse 11/15, 1030 Vienna, Austria. Degrees: Dr. Inst for Advanced Studies; Verwaltungsakademie des Bundes. Publs: *Verwaltung in der Demokratie*, 1978. Fields: Public administration; interaction between bureaucracy and the public.

[1056]
KRAGH Jens

1 December 1950, Danish. Mellemhaven 6, Korinth, 5600 Fåaborg, Denmark. Degrees: Cand sci pol. Teacher, U Centre of Roskilde; Researcher, U of Copenhagen. Publs: *Opbrud påa Venstreflöjen 1956-1960*, 1976; *Folkesocialisme*, 1977. Fields: Political parties.

[1057]
KRAMER Heinz

29 March 1945, German. Winibaldstrasse 1, D-8190 Wolfratshausen, FR Germany. Degrees: Dipl Volkswirt; Dr rer Pol. Doctoral thesis: "Nuklearpolitik in West-Europa und die Forschungspolitik der Euratom" (Nuclear Politics in Western Europe and Research Policy of Euratom). U des Saarlandes, Saarbrücken; Stiftung Wissenschaft

und Pol, Ebenhausen/Isar. Publs: *Nuklearpolitik in Westeuropa und die Forschungspolitik der Euratom*, 1976. Fields: Development and structure of the EEC; theory of regional processes of integration; non-governmental participants in the EEC; social and economic structural developments in Italy and France.

[1058]
KRAMER Helmut
7 December 1940, Austrian. Alszeile 3/3, 1170 Vienna, Austria. Degrees: PhD (Vienna), 1964. Doctoral thesis: "Die Vogtei in der deutschen Verfassungsgeschichte des 11 und 12. Jahrhunderts". 1965-66 Research Assistant, U of Stanford; Assistant, Chairman, Dept of Pol Sci, Inst of Advanced Studies; 1971- Lecturer, U of Vienna and Salzburg. Publs: *Abgeordnete in der Parteiendemokratie* (with P Gerlich), 1969; articles on political socialization, foreign policy analysis, problems of empirical research. Fields: International relations; methodology; political socialization; democratization of social science.

[1059]
KRAMER-FISCHER Dorit Friederike Karin
21 May 1943, Austrian. Pilgramgasse 11/18, A-1050 Vienna, Austria. Degrees: Dr phil. Doctoral thesis: "Die christliche Sozialreform Anton Orels" (The Christian Social Reform of Anton Orel). Documentation Centre of Urban Studies, Vienna; Inst for Advanced Studies, Vienna; Volunteer, Aid in Educator. Publs: *Das politische Bewusstsein der Jugend* (with H Ornauer), 1971; "Das Politische Interesse der Jugend", in *Motivation und Engagement* (J Radlegger and H Schön (eds)), 1972; "Jugend und Gesellschaft in Österreich" (with H Kramer), in *Das politische System Österreichs* (H Fischer (ed)), 1974; "Sozialtechnologie und soziale Bewegungen. Am Beispiel neuerer Arbeiten zur Jugend- und Studentenforschung", (co-author), *Leviathan*, 1976. Fields: Political socialization; urban studies; imperialism and problems of developing countries.

[1060]
KREILE Michael
11 October 1947, German. Neckarhangweg 1, 69 Heidelberg, FR Germany. Degrees: PhD (Tübingen), 1977. Doctoral thesis: "Osthandel und Ostpolitik. Zum Verhältnis von Aussenpolitik und Aussenwirtschaft in den Beziehungen der Bundesrepublik Deutschland zu den RGW-Ländern". Wiss Assistent, Inst für Pol Wissenschaft, U of Heidelberg. Publs: "Ostpolitik und ökonomische Interessen", in *Die Ostpolitik der BRD* (E Jahn/V Rittberger), 1974; "Kapitel: Bundesrepublik Deutschland", in *Die Ostbeziehungen der Europäischen Gemeinschaft*, 1977; "West Germany: the Dynamics of Expansion", *International Organization*, 1977. Fields: Political economy of international relations; foreign policy of the Federal Republic; Italian politics.

[1061]
KREIS Georg
14 November 1943, Swiss. Schalerstrasse 26, CH-4054 Basel, Switzerland. Degrees: Dr phil. Doctoral thesis: "Zensur und Selbstzensur. Die schweizerische Pressepolitik im Zweiten Weltkrieg". Assistent am Historischen Seminar, U of Basel; Gastprofessor, U of Neuchâtel; Research-Fellow, Fondation Nationale Suisse de la Recherche Scientifique. Publs: *Juli 1940. Die Aktion Trump*, 1973; *Zensur und Selbstzensur. Die schweizerische Pressepolitik im Zweiten Weltkrieg*, 1972; *Auf den Spuren von "La Charité". Die schweizerische Armeeführung im Spannungsfeld des deutsch-französichen Gegensatzes*, 1977; "Problemi della stampa in un paese neutrale, *Archivio Storico Ticinese*, 1971; "Die Schweiz und der Zweite Weltkrieg. Bilanz und bibliographischen Überblick nach dreissig Jahren", in *La Seconda Guerra Mondiale Nella Prospettiva Storica a Trent 'Anni dall' Epilogo*, 1975; "General Guisan, Minister

Frölicher und die Mission Burckhardt 1940", *Schweizerische Zeitschrift für Geschichte*, 1977; "Die Schweiz im Jahre 1940. Von der Beschäftigung mit Bundesrat Pilet-Golaz", *Schweizer Monatshefte*, 1978; "Entartete Kunst in Basel. Eine Chronik ausserordentlicher Ankäufe im Jahre 1939", *Basler Zeitschrift für Geschichte und Altertumskunde*, 1978. Fields: National socialism; fascism; Swiss history 1914-1945; French history 1870-1914; interdependence of home and foreign politics.

[1062]
KRELL Gert
1 July 1945, German. Bienerstrasse 17, 6238 Hofheim/TS, FR Germany. Degrees: Dr phil. Doctoral thesis: "Rüstungsdynamik und Rüstungskontrolle. Die gesellschaftlichen Auseinandersetzungen um Salt in den USA, 1969-1975". Wiss Mitarbeiter, Peace Research Institute, Frankfurt; Wiss Mitarbeiter, Abteilung internationale Beziehungen, Fachbereich Gesellschaftswissenschaften, U of Frankfurt. Publs: *Rüstungsdynamik und Rüstungskontrolle. Die gesellschaftlichen Auseinandersetzungen um Salt in den USA, 1969-1975*, 1977; *Zur Diskussion über die taktischen Nuklearwaffen in Europa. Analyse und Dokumentation* (with P Schlotter), 1978; several articles on arms race theory, US and FRG defence policy, and arms control. Fields: Arms race theory; the arms race and the East-West conflict; arms control; deterrence theory and military strategy; US foreign policy; peace research in general.

[1063]
KREUTZBERGER Wolfgang Michael*
11 May 1939, German. Beim Steinernen Kreuz 1, 28 Bremen 1, FR Germany. Degrees: MA (Freiburg), 1969; Dr phil (Freiburg), 1970. 1967-69 Wiss Hilfskraft; 1969-73 Wiss Assistent, U of Erlangen-Nürnberg; Akademischer Rat, Technical U of Hannover. Publs: *Studenten und Politik 1918-33*, 1972. Fields: West German foreign policy towards Eastern Europe; functions and structures of the military-industrial complex in West European societies; problems of a materialist theory of the state.

[1064]
KRIEBEL Suzanne*
6 May 1911, German. Dreililienplatz 1, 6200 Wiesbaden, FR Germany. Degrees: Dr rer Nat. Official in the Personal Dept of the Land Hessen. Publs: *Gegenwartsaufgaben der Öffentlichen Verwaltung* (F Morstein-Marx (ed)); *Hessische Hochschulwerke für Staatwissenschaftliche Fortbildung* (contributor). Fields: Political science; sociology; administration; management.

[1065]
KRIEGEL Annie*
9 September 1926, French. 67 rue de Caumartin, Paris IXème, France. Degrees: Agrégée, 1948; Dr d'Etat, 1964. Doctoral thesis: "Aux origines du communisme français". Professeur, Faculté de Lettres, U de Reims; Professeur, U de Paris — Nanterre; Directeur, l'UER de Soc Sci. Publs: *1920. Le congrès de Tours. Naissance du Parti communiste français*, 1964; *Les internationales ouvrières, 1864-1943*, 1964; *1914: La guerre et le mouvement ouvrier français*, 1964; *Aux origines du Communisme français*, 1964; *La croissance de la CGT (1918-21)*, 1966; *Le socialisme français et le pouvoir* (with M Perrot), 1966; *Le pain et les roses. Jalons pour une histoire des socialismes*, 1968; *Les communistes français*, 1970. Field: European ideas on communism.

[1066]
KRIESI Hanspeter
10 December 1949, Swiss. Röschibachstrasse 77, 8037 Zürich, Switzerland. Degrees: Lic rer Pol (Bern); MA (Chicago); Dr (Zürich). Doctoral thesis: "A Model for the Flow of Students through the Swiss University System". Assistant Researcher, U of Zürich. Fields: Corporatism; interest group politics; pre-parliamentary decision-making; influence processes in pre-parliamentary decision-making.

[1067]
KRIPPENDORF Ekkehart R A
22 March 1934, German. Via Belmeloro 11, 40126 Bologna, Italy. Degrees: Dr phil, 1959; Habilitation (Tübingen), 1972. 1961-62 Assistant Instructor, Yale U; 1962-63 Research Fellow, Inst of War and Peace Studies, U of Columbia, New York; 1963-68 Assistant, Kennedy Inst für Amerikastudien, Otto-Suhr-Inst, Free U of Berlin; 1968-69 Visiting Professor, Queens Coll, City U of NY, Columbia U Summer School; 1972- Kennedy Inst, Free U of Berlin; 1969- Professor of International Relations, John Hopkins U; 1972-76 Privatdozent, U of Tübingen; 1976- Professor of Phil and History, U of Urbino, Italy. Publs: *Die LDPD in der SBZ 1945-48*, 1960; *Erziehungswesen und Judentum*, 1961; *Political Science* (ed), 1965; *Friedensforschung* (ed), 1968; *Die amerikanische Strategie*, 1970; *Probleme der Informationalen Beziehungen*, 1972; *Internationale Beziehungen*, 1972; *Internationales System als Geschichte, Internationale Beziehungen als Wissenschaft*, 1977. Fields: Theory of international relations; imperialism; political economy and history of the international system; philosophy of history.

[1068]
KRISTENSEN Ole Preben
1 October 1946, Danish. Ellebnaekvej 18, Lystrup, Denmark. Degrees: Cand mag. Assistant Professor, Associate Professor, Inst of Pol Sci, U of Aarhus. Publs: *Den sikre kreds: Operationalisering og empirisk relevans*, 1973; "Sikre kredse og personlig stemmeafgivning ved folketingsvalgene i tresserne og halvfjerdserne" (with L Johansen), *Skrifter fr institut for historie og samfundsvidenskab*, 1977; "Electoral Mobility and Social Change in Denmark" (with C Jarlov), *Scandinavian Political Studies*, 1978. Fields: Relationship between public sector and private sector; interest organizations; "corporatism"; public sector growth; political recruitment; methodology.

[1069]
KRÖGER Klaus
7 July 1929, German. Hölderlinweg 14, 6300 Giessen, FR Germany. Degrees: Dr jur (Freiburg/Br), 1961; Habilitation (Giessen), 1970. Doctoral thesis: "Das Recht der freien Meinungsäusserung der Beamten im politischen Bereich". 1957-64 Wiss Assistent, U of Freiburg/Br; 1964-66 Wiss Assistent und Lehrbeauftragter; 1966-70 Dozent, Abteilung für Erziehungswissenschaften, U of Giessen; 1971- Professor für Verfassungsrecht, Verwaltungsrecht und Politische Wissenschaft, U of Giessen. Publs: *Widerstandsrecht und demokratische Verfassung*, 1971; *Die Ministerverantwortlichkeit in der Verfassungsordnung der Bundesrepublik*, 1972; *Grundrechtstheorie als Verfassungsproblem*, 1978. Fields: Constitutional law; political theory; domestic problems of the Federal Republic of Germany; constitutional history.

[1070]
KRONVALL Kai Folke
17 September 1939, Swedish. Norrgärdsvägen 49, 18400 Akersberga, Sweden. Degrees: MA (Lund), 1969; Dr phil (Lund), 1975. Doctoral thesis: "Political Mass Communications in a Multiparty System — Sweden, a Case Study". 1969-71 Research Assistant, Political Party Research Group, U of Stockholm; 1970-75 Assistant Teacher, Dept of Pol Sci, U of Lund; 1972-75 Scholarship, Dept of Pol Sci, U of Lund; 1976 Investigative Secretary of the Royal Commission on Mass Media Research; Secretary of the Executive Committee, Municipality of Vaxholm. Publs: *Partipressen idag*, 1971; *Opinion Formation: News, Mass Media, and Propaganda*, 1977; *Mass Media Research in Sweden*, 1977. Fields: The propaganda output of political parties in the 1970 Swedish election campaign; political mass communication, especially the relationship between political parties and mass media in the Swedish political system.

[1071]
KRUMHOLZ Rolf-Walter
6 April 1924, German. Markgrafenstrasse 88, 1000 Berlin 28, FR Germany. Degrees: Dipl (Deutsche Hochschule für Politik), 1952; Dr phil, 1967; Hon-Prof, 1974. 1949-64 Leiter der Abteilung Dokumentation der Deutschen Hochschule für Pol, Berlin, later Otto-Suhr Inst, Free U of Berlin; 1965-67 Sekretär der Deutschen Vereinigung für politische Wissenschaft; Wiss Geschäftsführer der Leitstelle Politische Dokumentation, Free U of Berlin. Publs: *Die politische Dokumentation in der BRD*, 1969. Fields: Information processes and communication channels in politics.

[1072]
KRUSIUS-AHRENBERG Helene-Charlotte Lolo
21 June 1909, Finnish. V Aaltonenv 2C, Helsinki 57, Finland. Degrees: MA (Helsinki), 1932; PhD (Helsinki), 1934. Doctoral thesis: "Der Durchbruch des nationalismus und iberalismus im Politischen Leben Finnlands 1856-63". 1945-49 Assistant Professor, U of Helsinki; 1949-52 Acting Professor, Dept of Pol Sci, U of Helsinki; 1945-48 Assistant Professor, Dept of Pol Sci, Swedish School of Economics; 1948-73 Full Professor, Dept of Govt and History, Swedish School of Economics; 1946-60 Professor of Pol Sci and Economic Pol, Inst of Economy and Soc Sci, Swedish School of Economics. Publs: *Der Durchbruch des nationalismus und Liberalismus im Politischen Leben Finnlands 1856-63*, 1937; *Tyrannmördaren C. F. Ehrensvärd*, 1947; *Studies in Finnish Constitutional Development and the History of the Finnish Diet*, 1977. Fields: Political theory; economic politology; workers' participation in management.

[1073]
KUEHR Anton Herbert
18 September 1937, German. D-4200 Oberhausen 11, Zur Ludwighütte 7, FR Germany. Degrees: Dr phil (Cologne). Doctoral thesis: "Parteien und Wahlen im Stadt- und Landkreis Essen in der Zeit der Weimarer Republik". Akademischer Oberrat; Professor of Pol Sci, U of Essen. Publs: "Parteien und Wahlen im Stadt- und Landkreis Essen in der Zeit der Weimarer Republik — Unter besonderer Berücksichtigung des Verhältnisses von Sozialstruktur und politischen Wahlen", *Beiträge zur Geschichte des Parlamentarismus und der politischen Parteien*, 1973; "Demokratie und Obligarchie in der CDU — Eine Fallstudie", *RCDS-Schriftenreihe*, 1975; "Kandidaten im Wahlkampf", in *Kandidatenauslese, Wahlkampf und lokale Presse* (co-author), 1975; *Sozialwissenschaftliche Studien zur Stadt- und Regionalpolitik*, 1978. Fields: Political sociology, especially political parties, German party system; social studies; political and social education.

[1074]
KUHNL Rheinhard
25 May 1936, German. Eichen 33, 355 Marburg, FR Germany. Degrees: Habilitation, 1971; D phil. Professor, Inst fur Wiss Pol, U of Marburg. Publs: *Die nazionalistische Linke 1925-30*, 1966; *Das Dritte Reich in der Presse der Bundesrepublik*, 1966; *Die NPD. Struktur, Ideologie und Funktion einer neofaschistischen Partei*, 1969; *Deutschland zwischen Demokratie und Faschismus*, 1969; *Formen bürgerlichen Herrschaft- Liberalismus und Faschismus*, 1971; *Der deutsche Faschismus in Quellen und Dokumenten* (ed), 1975; *Die Zerstörung der Weimar Republik* (ed), 1977. Fields: Analysis of international fascism.

[1075]
KUHNLE Stein
22 November 1947, Norwegian. 5066 Hjellestad, Norway. Degrees: Cand pol. Doctoral thesis: "Social Mobilization and Political Participation: The Nordic Countries c. 1850-1970". 1974-76 Research Associate, U of Bergen; 1977 Ford Fellowship; 1978- University Fellow, U of Bergen, Norway. Publs: *Patterns of Social and Political Mobilization: A Historical Analysis of the Nordic Countries*, 1975. Fields: Comparative politics; history of the welfare state; nation building and citizenship.

[1076]
KUIPER Dirk Theodoor
25 December 1938, Dutch. Nieuwmarkt 20ᵃ, Amsterdam, The Netherlands. Degrees: Dr (Free U of Amsterdam). Doctoral thesis: "The Calvinist Leaders, a Sociological Study of Ideology, Conflict and Coregroup Formation within the Reformed World Between 1820 and 1930". 1972 Lecturer in Sociology, Subfaculty of Socio-Cultural Sci, Free U of Amsterdam; 1972- Vice-Chairman of Anti-Revolutionary Party. Fields: Study of elites; changes in Dutch political system; sociology of religion; sociology of socio-cultural sciences.

[1077]
KUKAWKA Pierre
3 April 1943, French. La Maladière, St Vérand, 38160 St Marcellin, France. Degrees: Lic; DES. Fields: Local community; urban policy.

[1078]
KULKE Eckehard
26 June 1942, German. Am Hörchersberg 13, 78 Freiburg/Breisgau, FR Germany. Degrees: PhD. Doctoral thesis: "The Parsees in India — A Minority as Agent of Social Change". 1969-75 Research Associate, Arnold-Bergsträsser-Inst; 1973-74 Visiting Lecturer, U of Singapore; Lecturer, Dept of Pol Sci, U of Freiburg and Arnold-Bergsträsser-Inst. Publs: *The Parsees in India: A Minority as Agent of Social Change*, 1974; *Die Abwahl einer Diktatur — Hintergründe und Auswirkungen der indischen Parlamentswahlen*, 1977. Fields: Election research in South-Asia; urbanization and local government in Asia.

[1079]
KÜLP Bernhard
10 April 1933, German. 78 Freiburg, Kapellenweg 34, FR Germany. Degrees: Dr rer Pol. Doctoral thesis: "Der Anteil der Arbeiter und Unternehmer am Sozialprodukt". Director, Inst für Sozialpolitik, Ruhr-U, Bochum; Director, Inst für Allgemeine Wirtschaftsforschung, Abteilung Sozialpolitik, U of Freiburg. Publs: *Lohnbildung im Wechselspiel von politischen und wirtschaftlichen Kräften*, 1965; *Streik und Streikdrohung*, 1969; *Verteilungspolitik*, 1971; *Soziale Sicherheit*, 1971;

Arbeitsökonomik, 1972; *Verteilungstheorie*, 1974; *Wohlfahrtsökonomik*, I and II, 1975/76. Fields: International relations; sociology; economics of social welfare.

[1080]
KUMAR Krishan
11 August 1942, British. 51 Black Griffin Lane, Canterbury, Kent, England. Degrees: MA (Cambridge); MSc (London); PhD (Kent). Doctoral thesis: "Prophecy and Progress: Sociological Perspectives on the Past, Present, and Future of Industrial Societies". 1972-73 Producer, Talks and Documents Dept, BBC; Senior Lecturer in Soc, U of Kent at Canterbury. Publs: *Revolution: The Theory and Practice of a European Idea* (ed), 1971; *Prophecy and Progress: The Sociology of Industrial and Post-Industrial Society*, 1978. Fields: Social movements; political sociology; historical sociology; social change in advanced industrial societies.

[1081]
KUYPERS Gijsbert
18 May 1921, Dutch. Beethovenlaan 15, 3781 TL Voorthuizen, The Netherlands. Degrees: MA (Free U of Amsterdam), 1943; Dr (Free U of Amsterdam), 1954. Doctoral thesis: "De Russische Problematiek in het Sowjet-staatsbeeld" (Russian Elements in the Idea of the Soviet State). 1945-54 Foreign Ed, *Trouw*; 1954-60 Legal Adviser, Life Insurance Company; 1960- Professor of Pol Sci, Free U of Amsterdam. Publs: *De Russische Problematiek in het Sowjet-staatsbeeld*, 1954; *Het Voorschrift en de Macht*, 1960; *De Nederlandse Kiezers in 1967*, 1967; *Het Politieke Spel in Nederland*, 1967; *Grondbegrippen van Politiek*, 1973; *Beleidsontwikkeling en de Vaagheid van Idealen*, 1976. Fields: Political theory; policy analysis; policy making.

[1082]
KYRÖLÄINEN Hannu Veikko
9 January 1952, Finnish. Sammonkatu 33 C 40, SF-33540 Tampere 54, Finland. Degrees: M Pol Sci (Tampere), 1976. 1975-76 Research Fellow, Tampere Peace Research Inst; 1976-77 Research Assistant, Dept of Pol Sci, U of Tampere; 1977- Research Assistant, Research Fellow, Tampere Peace Research Inst. Publs: "Suomen ja Neuvostoliiton välinen funktionaalinen yhteistyö 1918-1974", *Rauhan- ja konfliktintutkimuslaitos*, 1977. Fields: Functional cooperation between socialist and capitalist countries.

L

[1083]
LABOA GALLEGO Juan Maria
15 August 1939, Spanish. Raimundo Fernandez Villaverde 10, Madrid 3, Spain. Degrees: Dr en Historia; Lic en Filosofia. Doctoral thesis: "Rodrigo Sanchez de Arevald: Primer Humanista Español". Assistant Professor of Spanish Pol Law, Facultad de Ciencias Pol/Soc, U Complutense de Madrid. Fields: Political law; sociology of religion.

[1084]
LABOUCHEIX Henri
1909, French. 14 route de Versailles, 78530 Chateaufort, France. Degrees: Dr d'Etat. Doctoral thesis: "Richard Price — Theorist of the American Revolution, the Scientist, the Economist, the Philosopher". Chairman, Training Coll for Secondary School

Teachers in Paris; Chairman, Center of Research on the History of Ideas in the Anglo-American World; Professor, U of Sorbonne, Paris. Publs: *Richard Price, Scientist and Philosopher*; *The Political Ideas of Jefferson*; *Physics and Metaphysics in Newton*; *Chemistry, Philosophy and Theology in Joseph Priestley*; *Natural Law and Historical Law in Edmund Burke*; *The Political Ideas of John Adams*; *Sociological Stereotypes, Rational Archetypes and the Structures of the Brain*; *The Political Theory of Hobbes and the Civilization of Today.* Fields: Correlation between political philosophy and sciences; correlation between ideologies and psychology; correlation between rational creativity and the structure of the brain; correlation between stereotyped systems and the structure of the brain.

[1085]
LABROUSSE Jeanne*
11 November 1935, French. 3 rue Alfred de Vigny, 92 Courbevoie, France. Degrees: Dr (Paris), 1963. Doctoral thesis: "Le quartier des halles à Paris". 1959- Attachée au Cabinet du Préfet de la Seine; 1960-64 Attachée de recherches, CNRS, Paris; Chef du Département Pol, Inst Français d'Opinion Publique; Maître de conférence, IEP, Paris. Publs: Articles in *Sondages*, *Revue Française de Science Politique*, *Cahiers de la Fondation Nationale des Sciences Politique*. Fields: Political and urban sociology; study of political attitudes.

[1086]
LACHENAL Francois Paul
31 May 1918, Swiss. CH-1249 Sézegnin, Geneva, Switzerland. Degrees: Dr jur (Basel). Doctoral thesis: "La Parti Politique. Sa fonction de droit public". 1942-44 Attaché à la légation de Suisse, Vichy; 1944-45 Attaché à la légation de Suisse, Berlin; 1945-46 Attché au Dept Pol Suisse, Berne; Attached to the Board of C H Boehringer Sohn for International Relations and Director of *Internationale Tage*, Ingelhelheim am Rhein. Fields: International cultural relations.

[1087]
LACOUR Claude
10 July 1940, French. 57 Place des martyrs de la Résistance, 33000 Bordeaux, France. Degrees: Agrégé. Doctoral thesis: "Revenus agricoles et croissance régionale en France". Professeur, U de Limoges; IEP Bordeaux, U de Bordeaux I. Publs: "Croissance urbaine et coûts de la croissance urbaine", *Revue Economique du Sud Ouest*, 1975. "Malaise paysan et politique agricole commune d'exception" (with J G Mérigot), *Revue de la Défense Nationale*, 1975; "Grands desseins et réalités quotidiennes: Réflexions sur le bilan de la politique agricole commune', *Revue Economique du Sud-Ouest*, 1975; "La croissance urbaine en Aquitaine", *Economie et Humanisme*, 1976; "La détermination des aires d'attraction et d'animation des villes moyennes en Aquitaine", *Revue économique du Sud-Ouest*, 1976; *Urbanisation et urbanisme en Aquitaine-d'une métropole dominante à un système urbain d'équilibre*, 1977; "Les besoins sociaux culturels des personnes âgées-Eléments de réflexion à propos d'une enquête en Dordogne et en Gironde" (with M Baratra), *Revue Economique du Sud- Ouest*, 1976. Fields: Space and urban analysis; development and regional analysis; political and economic foundations of regional and urban analysis.

[1088]
LACOUTURE Jean
9 June 1921, French. 143 rue d'Alésia, 75014 Paris, France. Degrees: Dr en soc. Doctoral thesis: "Personnalisation de pouvoir dans les nouveaux états". 1966 Research Fellow, Harvard U; Professeur, IEP Paris. Publs: *Egypt in Transition*; Political biographies of *De Gaulle, Nasser, Ho Chi Minh, Malraux*, 1973; *Léon Blum*, 1977. Fields: Middle East; North China; Indochina; contemporary France.

[1089]
LAGROYE Jacques
13 June 1936, French. Degrees: Agrégé d'histoire; Dr en études pol; Agrégé de sci pol. Doctoral thesis: "Société et politique: Chaban-Delmas à Bordeaux". 1965-68 Professeur de Ière Supérieure; 1968-72 Assistant agrégé d'Histoire, U de Bordeaux I; 1972-Maître assistant, Professeur, IEP, Bordeaux; Directeur scientifique du Centre d'Etude et de Recherche sur la Vie Locale. Publs: *Société et politique: Chaban-Delmas à Bordeaux*. 1973; "Etude d'une catégorie dirigeante en milieu urbain", *ADTR*, 1974; "Trois fédérations de partis politiques", *RFSP*, 1974; *Les militants politiques dans trois partis français*, 1976; *Local Government in France and Great Britain* (with V Wright (eds)), 1978; "Le pouvoir local", *Collectivités Locales* (F Benoit (ed)), 1978. Fields: Local politics; urban politics; interest groups; political parties in the French political system; political theory.

[1090]
LAKEMAN Enid
28 November 1903, British. 37 Culverden Avenue, Tunbridge Wells, Kent TN4 9RE, England. Degrees: BSc. Director, Electoral Reform Society. Publs: *How Democracies Vote*, 1974. Fields: Electoral systems.

[1091]
LALOY Jean Leonard
1 April 1912, French. 25 rue Ernest Renan, 92190 Meudon, France. Degrees: Lic ès lettres; Dipl (Ecole libre des Sci Pol). 1952-68 Professeur, l'Ecole Nationale d'Administration; Professeur invité, l'Inst U des Hautes Etudes Internationales, Geneva; Professeur, IEP, U de Paris. Publs: *Entre Guerres et Paix (1945-1965)*, 1966; *Le Socialisme de Lénine*, 1967. Fields: International relations, especially Soviet Russia; Second World War and after.

[1092]
LAMB Geoffrey Boyd
11 February 1944, South African. 70 Havelock Road, Brighton, Sussex, England. Degrees: BA; MA (Sussex), 1966; D Phil (Sussex), 1970. Doctoral thesis: "Politics and Rural Development in Murang's District, Kenya". 1968-70 Research Officer, Royal Inst of Public Administration; 1970-71 Research Fellow, School of African and Asian Studies; 1971- Fellow, Inst of Development Studies, U of Sussex. Publs: *Peasant Politics*, 1974; *Public Inquiries as an Instrument of Government* (with R E Wraith), 1971; "Marxism, Access and the State", *Development and Change*, 1975; "The Neocolonial Integration of Kenyan Peasants", *Development and Change*, 1977; "Rural Institutions, Public Services and Employment", in *ILO* (with B B Schaffer *et al*), 1978. Fields: Housing, employment and political relations in Trinidad; comparative country studies on growth, distribution and basic needs; political relations and theories of the state.

[1093]
LAMBELET Jean Christian
18 December 1938, Swiss. Ch de Vaugueny 10, CH-1066 Epalinges, Switzerland. Degrees: Lic ès sci pol (Lausanne), 1962; MA (Harvard), 1965; PhD (Harvard), 1969. Doctoral thesis: "Labor Supply and Price Stability in Switzerland". 1964-67 Teaching Fellow, Dept of Econ, U of Harvard; 1968-69 Consultant, OECD, Paris; 1969-70 Research Associate, Center for Middle Eastern Studies, U of Harvard; 1970-72 Assistant Professor, Department of Econ and Near East Center, U of Pennsylvania;. 1972- Professor of Econ, U of Lausanne; 1977- Associate Professor, Graduate Inst of International Studies, Geneva. Publs: "A Dynamic Model of the Arms Race in the Middle

East, 1953-1965", *General Systems*, 1971; "Towards a Dynamic Two-Theater Model of the East-West Arms Race", *Journal of Peace Science*, 1973; "The Anglo-German Dreadnought Race, 1905-1914", *Papers of the Science Society*, 1975; "Do Arms Races Lead to War?" *Journal of Peace Research*, 1975; "A Numerical Model of the Anglo-German Dreadnought Race", *Papers of the Peace Science Society*, 1975; "A Complementary Analysis of the Anglo-German Dreadnought Race", *Papers of the Peace Science Society*, 1977; "Une analyse statistique de la votation du 25 septembre 1977 sur l'initiative populaire 'pour la solution du délai' " (with Auterbacher), 1978; *Dynamics of Arms Races: Mutual Stimulation vs Self-Stimulation,* forthcoming. Fields: Arms races; aspects of the Swiss political system.

[1094]
LAMBERT Jacques Edouard
5 March 1901, French. 30 Place Bellecour, 69007 Lyon, France. Degrees: Dr en droit (Lyon), 1924. 1925-38 Faculté de Droit, U de Lyon; 1938-39 Faculté Phil, Porto Alegre, Brazil; 1939-45 Professor, Faculdade Nacional de Phil, Rio; 1945- Professeur, Faculté de Droit, U de Lyon. Publs: *Histoire constitutionnelle des Etats-Unis*, 1934; *La vengeance privée et les fondements du droit international public*, 1936; *Problèmes démographiques contemporains*, 1949; *Le Brésil*, 1953; *Os Dois Brasis*, 1959; *Amérique latine*, 1964. Fields: Latin American political institutions; demography.

[1095]
LANCELOT Alain*
12 January 1937, French. 12 rue d'Alembert, 92 Issy-les-Moulineaux, France. Degrees: Dipl (Paris), 1958; Dipl supérieur de recherches et d'études pol, 1963; Dr (Sorbonne), 1967. Doctoral thesis: "Abstentionnisme Electoral en France". Researcher, CNRS; Maître de conférences, IEP; Visiting Professor, U of Montreal, Canada; Visiting Professor, IEP, Algiers; Directeur d'Etudes et de Recherches, FNSP; Professor, IEP, Paris; Secretary-general, Association Française de Sci Pol. Publs: *Les Attitudes Politiques*, 1969; *L'Abstentionnisme Electoral en France*, 1968; *Atlas des Circonscriptions Electorales depuis 1875* (co-author), 1970; *La Participation des Français à la Politique*, 1971. Fields: Electoral studies along ecological lines; comparative political behaviour; political alienation in France and in Canada.

[1096]
LANCELOT Marie-Thérèse*
25 March 1935, French. 12 rue d'Alembert, 92 Issy-les-Moulineaux, France. Degrees: Dipl, IEP 1958. 1960-62 Assistante de recherches, FNSP; 1962-64 Assistante, Association Française de Sci Pol; 1969-70 Ingénieur Chargée d'Etudes, Société Française d'Etudes par Sondages; 1964- Collaboratrice Technique, Centre d'Etude de la Vie Pol Française Contemporaine; 1970- Assistante du Cycle Supérieur de Specialisation en Etudes de Marché et d'Opinion par Sondages, Inst d'Etudes Pol. Publs: *L'organisation armée secrète*, 1963; *L'administration française: Administrations locales* (with B Gournay), 1967; *Atlas des circonscriptions électorales en France depuis 1875* (co-author), 1970; *Les élections législatives de mars 1967* (co-author), 1971. Fields: Electoral geography and political ecology; survey research and public opinion.

[1097]
LANDAU Jacob
1924, Israeli. PO Box 8065, Jerusalem, Israel. Degrees: MA (Jerusalem), 1946; PhD (London), 1949. Doctoral thesis. "Parliaments and Parties in Egypt, 1866-1924". Visiting Appointments at Us of Brandeis, California, Columbia, Wayne State (Detroit), Ankara, Texas, Candido Mendes, Rio de Janeiro; Professor of Pol Sci; The Hebrew U of Jerusalem. Publs: *Parliaments and Parties in Egypt*, 1953; *Jews in Nineteenth —*

Century Egypt, 1969; *The Arabs in Israel: A Political Study*, 1969; *The Hejaz Railway and the Muslim Pilgrimage: A Case of Ottoman Political Propaganda*, 1971; *Middle Eastern Themes: Papers in History and Politics*, 1973; *Radical Politics in Modern Turkey*, 1974; *The Arabs and the Histadrut*, 1976; *Politics and Islam; the National Salvation Party in Turkey*, 1976. Fields: The politics and government of the Middle East.

[1098]
LANDOWSKI Eric Ladislas
1 May 1942, French. 10 rue de la Chaise, CEVIPOF, 75007 Paris, France. Degrees. Lic en droit; Lic en lettres; Dipl (IEP), 1963. Attaché de recherche, CNRS, Paris. "Formes et pratiques de la représentation dans le Vème Plan", *Planification et Société*, 1975; "La mise en scène des sujets de pouvoir", *Langages*, 1976; "Le débat parlementaire et l'écriture de la loi", *Revue Française de Science Politique*, 1977. Fields: Ideology and politics; semiotics of socio-political discourse.

[1099]
LANE Jan Erik
23 May 1946, Swedish. Hammargatan 21, S-911 00 Vännäs, Sweden. Degrees: PhD. Doctoral thesis: "Action and System Studies in Political Theory". Docent, Dept of Pol Sci, U of Umeå; Director, Center for Administrative Studies. Fields: Public Administration.

[1100]
LANGROD Georges
20 September 1903, French. 88 Boulevard Pereire, 75017 Paris, France. Degrees: MA; LLD, PhM (Jagelonnian). Doctoral thesis: "Judicial Administrative Control in Europe, especially in Poland". Professor, Jagelonnian U; Professor, U of the Saar; UN Lecturer, Brazilian School of BA, Rio de Janeiro; Consultant of OECD; Visiting Professor, U of Wyoming, USA, U of Turin, U of Bologna, U of Toulouse; Professor, Polish U Abroad, London; Research Director Em, CNRS, Paris; Reader, Ecole des Hautes Etudes, Sorbonne; Professor Em, Law Faculty, U of Saar. Publs: *Comparative Studies in Judicial Administrative Control*, 1964; *Comparative Administrative Law*, 1950; *French Administration Today*, 1964; *Internal Civil Service*, 1964; *Treatise of Administrative Science* (ed), 1967; *European Civil Service* (ed), 1956; *Consultative Administration* (ed), 1971.

[1101]
LANZA Orazio
26 November 1951, Italian. Via Milo 28, Catania, Italy. Doctoral thesis: "Comportamento Politico e Clientelismo a Messina". Researcher, ISVI, U of Catania. Publs: "Gli Enti del Settore Agricolo nel Sistema Politico Italiano", *Rassegne Italiane di Sociologia*, 1977; *Agricoltura e Sistema Politico*, 1978. Fields: Government role in agricultural development; problems of state intervention; problems of political systems.

[1102]
LAPIERRE Jean-William
17 April 1921, French. La Rêverie, Avenue Bieckert, 06000 Nice, France. Degrees: Agrégé de philosophie, 1946; Dr ès lettres (Paris), 1969. Doctoral thesis: "Essai sur le fondement du pouvoir politique". 1953-57 Professeur de Philosophie, Lycées Marseille, Aix-en-Provence; 1957-62 Maître Assistant de Soc, U d'Aix-en-Provence; 1962-65 Chargé d'enseignement de Soc, U of Tananarive; 1965- Maître de conférences de Soc, Professeur de Soc, U de Nice. Publs: *Le pouvoir politique*, 1953; *Une recherche sur le civisme des jeunes à la fin de la IV ème République*, 1961; *Essai sur le fondement*

du pouvoir politique, 1968; *L'information sur l'Etat d'Israel dans les grands quotidiens français en 1958*, 1968; *L'analyse des systèmes politiques*, 1973; *Vivre sans Etat? Essai sur le pouvoir politique et l'innovation sociale*, 1977. Fields: Systems analysis and dialectics; political anthropology; French urbanization and local government; political power in the field of culture and sport.

[1103]
LAROQUE Pierre
2 November 1907, French. 124 Avenue Victor Hugo, 75016 Paris, France. Degrees: Dr en droit (Paris), 1933; Dipl (Ecole Libre des Sci Pol, Paris), 1927; Dr en droit honoris causa (Colombia), 1954. 1930 Auditeur au Conseil d'Etat; 1940 Maître des Requêtes au Conseil d'Etat; 1951 Conseiller d'Etat; Professeur, IEP Paris; 1944-51 Directeur Général de la Sécurité Sociale; 1953-67 Président, Conseil d'Administration, Caisse Nat de Sécurité Sociale; Président, Section Sociale du Conseil d'Etat. Publs: *La tutelle administrative*, 1930; *Les usagers des services publics industriels*, 1933; *Les conventions collectives du travail*, 1934; *Les rapports entre patrons et ouvriers*, 1938; *Réflexions sur le problème social*, 1953; *Les classes sociales*, 1959; *Succès et faiblesses de l'effort social français*, 1961; *Politique de la vieillesse*, 1962; *Les institutions sociales de la France*, 1962. Fields: Public administration in France and abroad; administrative law; social and demographic policy.

[1104]
LARSEN Knud*
17 October 1936, Danish. Institut for Samtidshistorie og Statskündskab, Rosenborggade 15², 1130 Copenhagen, Denmark. Degrees: Cand mag (Copenhagen), 1963. Lecturer, U of Copenhagen; Associate Professor, U of Copenhagen. Publs: *Oversigt over nogle Hovedlinier i den Europaiske Forfaluingshistorie efter 1815*, 1968; *Imperialismin og Afrika*, 1968; *Afrikas Afkolonisering*, 1969; *Afkolonisering*, 1968; *Mennesheit i Sampundet*, 1970. Fields: The Danish disarmament proposals during and after the First World War.

[1105]
LARSEN Stein Ugelvik
17 March 1938, Norwegian. J L Mowinckelsvei 122, 5033 Fyllingsdalen, Norway. Degrees: Mag art. Assistant, U of Oslo; Amanuensis, U of Bergen. Fields: Comparative politics; local politics; politics of fascism.

[1106]
LARSSON Björn Gustaf Reidar*
17 May 1936, Swedish. Kungsgatan 32, 902 45 Umeå, Sweden. Degrees: Fil lic (Uppsala), 1965; Fil dr (Uppsala), 1970. Doctoral thesis: "Theories of Revolution, from Marx to the First Russian Revolution". 1964-65 Lecturer in Pol Sci, U of Uppsala; 1971- Docent Associate Professor, Dept of Pol Sci, U of Umeå; 1971- U Lecturer in Pol Sci, Graduate School of Social Work and Public Administration, Stockholm. Publs: *Theories of Revolution, from Marx to the First Russian Revolution*, 1970; *Politiska Idealogier. En Antologi*, 1971. Fields: Socialist concepts of democracy; minorities and politics; ethnic and linguistic minorities in Sweden with an international comparative aspect.

[1107]
LASLETT Peter
1915. British. Trinity College, Cambridge, England. Degrees: MA (Cambridge). Reader in Pol and the History of Social Structure, U of Cambridge; Fellow of Trinity College; Director, Cambridge Group for the History of Population and Social Structure. Publs: Founder and General Editor (with W S Runciman, Q R D Skinner, J Fishkin), *Philosophy, Politics and Society*; *Locke's Two Treatises of Government*, 1978; *The World We Have Lost*, 1965. Fields: Political philosophy; history of political theory; theory of social structure.

[1108]
LAUFER Heinz
22 April 1933, German. 8000 München 90, Schweigerstrasse 4, FR Germany. Degrees: Juristische Staatsprüfung, 1958; PhD (Würzburg), 1961; Habilitation (Munich), 1967. Doctoral thesis: "Das Kriterium politischen Handelns". 1958 Assistant, U of Würzburg; 1959 Assistant, U of Munich; 1962 Lecturer in Pol Sci, U of Munich; 1967 Assistant Professor, U of Munich; 1968- Professor of Pol Sci, U of Munich; Professor of Pol Sci and Legal Theory, U of Munich. Publs: *Regieren im Verfassungsstaat*, 1970; *Der Bundesrat*, 1972; *Das föderative System der Bundesrepublik Deutschland*, 1977; *Föderalismusstudien*, 1973; *Die Landesvertretungen*, 1974; *Der Föderalismus der Bundesrepublik Deutschland*, 1974; *Freizeitpolitik von Bund, Ländern und Gemeinden*, 1976; *Der sozialisierte Mensch*, 1977. Fields: Government of the Federal Republic of Germany; comparative government; legal studies; legislatures and executives; political parties; pressure groups; public administration; political theory; regionalism, local government and federalism.

[1109]
LAUTMAN Jacques
7 May 1934, French. 126 Boulevard Raspail, 75006 Paris, France. Degrees: Dr ès lettres. Doctoral thesis: "Fortunes quelconques, logement et devenir urbain". Researcher, CNRS; Professor, Paris IX (Nanterre). Publs: *Années sociales* (co-author), 1973; *Les architectes, métamorphoses d'une profession libérale* (co-author), 1973. Fields: Social change.

[1110]
LAUWERYSEN Staf
10 October 1951, Belgian. Ursulinensetraat 21, 3020 Wygemaal-Leuven, Belgium. Research Assistant, Catholic U of Leuven. Fields: Local and regional government; problems of the Third World.

[1111]
LAVER Michael John
3 August 1949, British. 19 Annesley Road, Liverpool 17, England. Degrees: BA; MA (Essex), 1971. 1971-72 Research Assistant, Dept of Government, U of Essex; 1972-73 Lecturer in Pol, Dept of Pol Sci, Queens U, Belfast; 1973- Lecturer in Pol, Dept of Pol Theory and Inst, U of Liverpool. Publs: *The Theory and Practice of Party Competition*; *The Northern Ireland General Elections of 1973*. Fields: Strategic interaction.

[1112]
LAVIGNE Pierre Jean Bernard
28 December 1922, French. 94 rue Broca, 75013 Paris, France. Degrees: Lic ès lettres (Rennes), 1942; Dr en droit (Rennes), 1946; Agrégé de droit, 1950. Doctoral thesis: "Le travail dans les constitutions françaises 1789-1945". 1946-47 U de Rennes; 1948-50 U de Strasbourg; 1950-54 Professeur, Fort de France, Martinique; 1954-67 Professeur, U de

Strasbourg; 1959-64 Directeur, IEP; 1964-68 Directeur, Centre de Recherches sur l'URSS et les Pays de l'Est; 1967- Professeur, Directeur, UER Admin publique et droit public interne, U de Paris I (Panthéon- Sorbonne). Publs: *Le travail dans les constitutions françaises 1789-1945, Climats et sociétés*, 1966. Fields: French university administration.

[1113]
LAWRENCE Reginald James
14 June 1914, British. Department of Political Science, Queen's University, Belfast, BT7 1NN, Northern Ireland. Degrees: BSc. Doctoral thesis: "The Government of Northern Ireland". Professor of Pol, U of Belfast. Publs: *The Government of Northern Ireland*, 1965. Fields: Public administration; politics and government in Northern Ireland.

[1114]
LAYTON-HENRY Zygmunt
28 August 1942, British. 12 Arbour Close, Kenilworth CV8 2BA, England. Degrees: B Soc Sci; PhD (Birmingham), 1973. Doctoral thesis: "Political Youth Movements in Britain". 1967-68 Senior Research Assistant, U of Brunel; 1968- Lecturer in Pol, U of Warwick. Publs: Articles in *Journal of Contemporary History, Parliamentary Affairs, Political Quarterly, New Community, New Society.* Fields: Political sociology in political parties; politics and race relations.

[1115]
LECA Jean
20 March 1935, French. 20 Quai des Allobroges, 38000 Grenoble, France. Degrees: Dr en droit; Dipl (IEP). 1962-65 Directeur, IEP, Alger; 1972-73 Visiting Professor, U of Wisconsin; 1969- Professor, U of Grenoble. Publs: *L'Algérie politique-institutions et régime politique* (with J C Vatin), 1975; "Pour une analyse comparative des systèmes politiques médidterranéens", *Revue Française de Science Politique;* various articles on Algeria and political development, in *Annuaire de l'Afrique du Nord*, and on international cooperation in *Etudes Internationales.* Fields: Comparative political systems; role of the international system in the foundation and functioning of internal political systems.

[1116]
LECLERIC Jacques
1935, French. 54 Boulevard Raspail, 75006 Paris, France. Degrees: DES; Dr d'histoire; Dipl d'indonésien. Doctoral thesis: "La pensée des communistes indonésiens: l'indonésisation du marxisme à travers les textes d'Aidit, président du PC Indonésien, 1962-65"; Lecturer, Nat Inst of Oriental Languages and Civilisations, U of Paris III; Research Fellow, CNRS, Paris. Publs: "Iconologie politique du timbre post indonésien, 1950-70, *Archipel*, 1973; "Vocabulaire social et répression politique: un exemple indonésien", in *Annales ESC*, 1973; "La circonscription: remarques sur l'idéologie du territoire national en Indonésie", *Cultures et Développement*, 1975; *Syndicalistes en Indonésie*, 1975; "Blason de la révolution: sens et contre sens dans le discours d'Aidit, 1962-63", *Revue Française de Science Politique,* 1978; "La condition des partis révolutionnaires indonésiens à la recherche de leur identité, 1028-48", *Cultures et Développement*, 1978; *Cinq principes pour un Etat: Le Pantjasila indonésien*, 1978. Fields: State ideology and state ideological supports in Indonesia; ideologies and organization of the "working class" in Indonesia since independence; class and nation in the political values of newly independent countries.

[1117]
LECOMTE Patrick
12 February 1948, French. Le Clairfontaine, rue de la Libération, 38610 Gières, France. Degrees: Dipl (IEP Grenoble); Dipl (FNSP); Dr. Doctoral thesis: "The Gaullist Party in Isère. Contribution to the Study of the 'Rallying' Party". Lecturer, IEP, Grenoble; Assistant Teacher, Law Inst of Constantine, Algeria; Assistant Teacher, Pol Studies Inst of Grenoble. Publs: "L'UDR et la réforme régionale", in *La réforme régionale et le référendum de 27 Avril 1969* (J L Quermonne *et al*), 1970; *L'Union des Démocrates pour la République dans l'Isère- les hommes*, 1970; "Les groupes d'action municipale dans le système politique local" (with J P Bernard and J M Blancherie), *Revue Française de Science Politique*, 1972; *L'Union des Démocrates pour la République dans l'Isère- contribution à l'étude du Parti de Rassemblement*, 1974; "Le parti selon la Charte Nationale" (with J L Bernelas), *Maghreb-Machrek*, 1977; *Cours de sociologie*, 1976; *Cours de sociologie politique*, 1977; "La politique d'arabisation de l'enseignement: le cas de l'Institut de Droit de Constantine", *Maghreb-Machrek*, 1978. Fields: Political organizations; political militarism; social change and political modernization.

[1118]
LEE John Michael
29 March 1932, British. Department of Politics and Sociology, Birkbeck College, 7-15 Gresse Street, London W1P 1PA, England. Degrees: BA; B Litt (Oxon), 1957. 1958-67 Lecturer, Senior Lecturer, U of Manchester; 1967-69 Temporary Principal, Treasury/CSD; 1969-72 Senior Lecturer, Inst of Commonwealth Studies; Reader in Pol, Birkbeck Coll, U of London. Publs: *Social Leaders and Public Persons*, 1963; *Colonial Development and Good Government*, 1967; *African Armies and Civil Order*, 1969; *The Scope of Local Initiatives* (with B Wood *et al*), 1974. Fields: Policy studies; central administration in Britain and Canada; administrative history.

[1119]
LEEMANS Arne F
22 January 1920, Dutch. Institute of Public Administration, 526 Herengracht, Amsterdam, The Netherlands. Degrees: MA (Leiden), 1946; Dr in Law. Doctoral thesis: "De eenheid van het bestuur der grote stad" (Integration of Policy-Making in a Large City). 1949-61 International Union of Local Authorities; 1958- Assistant Secretary-General; 1961-70 Reader in Public Administration, Chairman, Master's Programme in Public Administration, Inst of Soc Studies; Professor of Public Administration, U of Amsterdam; Director, Inst of Public Administration, U of Amsterdam. Publs: *De eenheid in het bestuur der grote stad*, 1967; *Changing Patterns of Local Government*, 1970; *Administrative Reform* (ed), 1971; "Amsterdam", in *The Great Cities of the World* (W A Robson (ed)), 1971; "De totstandkoming van het beleid", in *Beleid Belicht* (A Hoogerwerf (ed)), 1973; *The Management of Change in Government* (ed), 1976. Fields: Policy-making; administrative reform; relationship between levels of government; teaching of public administration.

[1120]
LEES John David
27 August 1936, British. 25 Larchwood, Keele University, Staffordshire ST5 5BB, England. Degrees: BA; MA (Michigan); PhD (Manchester). Doctoral thesis: "Appropriations Politics: A Study of the Role of the Congressional Appropriations in the American Political Process". Teaching Fellow, U of Michigan; Lecturer, Senior Lecturer, Reader, U of Keele. Publs: *The Political System of the United States*, 1975; *The Committee System of the US Congress*, 1967; *Political Parties in Modern Britain* (co-ed), 1972; *Committees in Legislatures: a Comparative Analysis* (co-ed and contributor), 1978. Fields: American politics; comparative government; political behaviour.

[1121]
LEFEBVRE Henri*
1 June 1901, French. 30 rue Rambuteau, Paris IIIème, France. Degrees: Dr ès lettres (Sorbonne), 1954. Directeur de Recherche, CNRS; 1961-65 Professeur de Soc, U de Strasbourg; 1965- Professeur de Soc, U de Paris X. Publs: *Le droit à la ville*, 1968; *La vie quotidienne dans le monde moderne*, 1968; *L'Irruption: de Nanterre au Sommet*, 1968; *Logique formelle et logique dialectique*, 1969; *Du rural à l'urbain*, 1970; *Manifeste différentialiste*, 1970; *Urbanisme et révolution urbaine*, 1970; *La fin de l'histoire*, 1970. Fields: Sociology, especially urban.

[1122]
LEFTWICH Adrian
24 March 1940, British. Kings Manor, Exhibition Square, York YO1 2EW, England. Degrees: BA; D Phil (York). Doctoral thesis: "Colonialism and the Constitution of Cape Society under the Dutch East India Company". Junior Lecturer, School of African Studies, U of Cape Town; Lecturer in Pol, U of Lancaster; Lecturer in Pol, U of York. Publs: *South Africa. Economic Growth and Political Change*. Fields: Political change; politics in plural societies; interdisciplinary studies; Marxism; social science and history; social and economic change in Third World countries.

[1123]
LEGENDRE Pierre*
15 June 1930, French. 13 Boulevard des Invalides, Paris VIIème, France. Degrees: Agrégé des Facultés de Droit et des Sci Econ, 1957. Doctoral thesis: "L'histoire du système de droit ecclésiastique". Attaché au Centre National de la Recherche Scientifique; 1957-68 Professeur, U de Lille; 1968- Professeur, U de Paris I; Professeur, U de Paris X. Publs: *Histoire de l'administration de 1750 à nos jours*, 1968; *L'administration du XVIIIe siècle à nos jours*, 1970. Fields: National assemblies; legal history; psychology.

[1124]
LEHMANN Hans Georg
13 October 1935, German. Im Bonnet 23, 5300 Bonn 3, FR Germany. Degrees: Dr phil, 1966. Doctoral thesis: "Die Agrarfrage in der Theorie und Praxis der deutschen und internationalen Sozialdemokratie. Vom Marxismus zum Revisionismus und Bolschewismus". 1966-74 Mitarbeiter und Mitherausgeber der *Akten zur deutschen auswärtigen Politik 1918-1945* im Auswärtigen Amt in Bonn; 1970- Lehrbeauftragter, Dozent für Pol, Pädagogische Hochschule Rheinland, Bonn. Publs: *Der Reichsverweser-Stellvertreter, Horthys gescheiterte Planung einer Dynastie*, 1975; *In Acht und Bann. Politische Emigration, NS-Ausbürgerung und Widergutmachung am Beispiel Willy Brandts*, 1976; *Carlo Schmid Bibliographie*, 1977; *Der Oder-Neisse-Konflikt*, 1978. Fields: European politics; formation politics; conflict research.

[1125]
LEHMBRUCH Gerhard
15 April 1928, German. Brunnenstrasse 30, D-7400 Tübingen, FR Germany. Degrees: Dr phil (Tübingen), 1962; Habilitation (Tübingen), 1969. Doctoral thesis: "Studien zur Theorie der Parteiensystem". 1960-69 Wiss Assistent, Privatdozent, U of Tübingen; 1969-73 Wiss Rat, Professor, U of Heidelberg; 1973- Professor, U of Tübingen. Publs: *Proporzdemokratie: Politisches System und politische Kultur in der Schweiz und in Österreich,* 1967; *Einführung in die Politikwissenschaft,* 1971; *Parteienwettbewerb im Bundesstaat,* 1976. Fields: Western European politics; political parties and interest groups; neo-corporatism; federalism.

[1126]
LEHNER Franz*
14 July 1946, Swiss. Zum Dornbusch 20, 68 Mannheim 81, FR Germany. Degrees: Dipl (Mannheim), 1970. 1967-70 Research Assistant in Social Psychology; 1970- Assistant in Pol Sci, U of Mannheim. Fields: Theory of political behaviour in democracies; problems of philosophy of science in political science.

[1127]
LEHNING Percy B
23 June 1944, British. Keizersgracht 537, Amsterdam, The Netherlands. Degrees: Dr (Amsterdam), 1971. Lecturer in Pol Sci, U of Amsterdam. Publs: "De Rechtvaardigheidstheorie van Rawls", *Acta Politica* (with R J van der Veen), 1977; "Social Contract and Property Rights: A Comparison Between John Rawls and James M Buchanan", in *Democracy, Consensus and Social Contract* (P Birnbaum *et al* (eds)), 1978; "Een filosoof van de vrijheid protesteert tegen gelijkheid", *De Gids*, 1976. Fields: Analytical political philosophy; political theory; political thought and the history of political ideas; methodology.

[1128]
LEIBHOLZ Hermann Gerhard
15 November 1901, German/British. Herzberger Landstrasse 57, 3400 Göttingen, FR Germany. Degrees: Dr phil (Heidelberg), 1921; Dr jur (Berlin), 1925. Doctoral thesis: "Fichte und der demokratische Gedanke". 1929 Professor of Public and International Law, U of Greifwald; 1931-35 U of Göttingen; 1951-71 Associate Justice of the Federal Constitutional Court, Karlsruhe; 1939-48 Fellowship of the World Council of Churches, and Magdalen College, U of Oxford; Professor Em, U of Göttingen. Publs: *Das Wesen der Repräsentation in der Demokratie*, 1973; *Die Strukturprobleme der modernen Demokratie*, 1974; *Verfassungsstaat — Verfassungsrecht*, 1973; *Kommentar zum Grundgesetz der Bundesrepublik Deutschland* (with Rinck), 1975; *Kommentar zum Bundesverfassungsrecht — Gesetz* (with Rupprecht), 1971; *An der Schwelle zum gespaltenen Europa*, 1974. Fields: Law; politics; economics.

[1129]
LEIRER Herbert
12 March 1942, Austrian. Castelligasse 5/7, A-1050 Wien, Austria. Degrees: Dr jur (Vienna), 1971. 1970-72 Inst for Advanced Studies; 1972- Wiss Mitarbeiter des Instituts für Kriminalsoziologie. Publs: *Politologie in der Politischen Bildung* (co-author), 1972; *Richter als Diagnostiker* (co-author), 1973. Fields: Criminology, criminal statistics; political socialization; sociology of organizations.

[1130]
LELEU Claude
22 July 1924, French. 18 rue Marcel Peretto, 38100 Grenoble, France. Degrees: Dr. Doctoral thesis: "Les élections dans le département de l'Isère de 1936 à 1969". Publs: *Géographie des elections françaises de 1936 à 1967*; *The French Referendum*, 1972; plus various papers and articles on elections. Fields: Electoral sociology.

[1131]
LE LOHÉ Michel Julian*
30 December 1928, British. 229 Queen's Road, Bradford BD2 4BT, England. Degrees: BSc; MSc (London), 1963. Lecturer in Pol, U of Bradford. Publs: *Voting in Cities* (co-author), 1967. Fields: English local government; ethnic voting behaviour.

[1132]
LE-MAY Godfrey Hugh Lancelot*
7 September 1920, British. 38 Sandfield Road, Headington, Oxford, England. Degrees: BA; MA (Oxon). 1947-48 Lecturer in History, Rhodes U Coll; 1951-53 Lecturer in Pol, Balliol Coll, U of Oxford; 1953-67 Professor of Pol Studies, U of the Witwatersrand, Johannesburg; Fellow and Tutor in Pol, Worcester Coll, Oxford. Publs: *British Government*, 1914-53: *Select Documents*, 1964; *British Supremacy in South Africa, 1899-1907*, 1965; *Black and White in South Africa*, 1971. Fields: English constitutional history from 1865.

[1133]
LENARDIĆ Marek
29 June 1947, Yugoslavian. Anzbachgasse 56, A-1140 Wien, Austria. Degrees: Dipl; D Phil (Zagreb); Dr Soc (Zagreb). Doctoral thesis: "Political Parties and Pressure Groups, Lobbies and Interest Groups". Publs: *Rasna diskriminacija*, 1969; *United Nations Efforts for the Solution of Social and Economic Problems in the Developing Countries*, 1970; *Political Parties and Pressure Groups, Lobbies and Interest Groups*, 1978; "Essay über Ökologie", 1977. "Politische Organisationen"; *Journal für Wiss Soz Forschung*, 1978; "Questions of Industrial Society", in *Nase teme*, 1977. Fields: Political organizations; Political parties; pressure groups.

[1134]
LEPSIUS Rainer
8 May 1928, German. Mozartstrasse 23, 6940 Weinheim, FR Germany. Degrees: Dr Oec Publ (Munich), 1955. Doctoral thesis: "Zur soziologischen Theorie der Sozialpolitik". 1963 Privatdozent, U of München; 1966 Temple U, Philadelphia; 1968 and 1970 U of Pittsburgh; 1977 Visiting Professor Stanford U; 1964- Professor of Soc, U of Mannheim. Publs: *Denkschrift zur Lage der Soziologie und Politischen Wissenschaft*, 1961; *Extremer Nationalismus*, 1966; "Parteiensystem und Sozialstruktur", in *Wirtschaft, Geschichte und Wirtschaftsgeschichte* (Abel (ed)), 1966; "Wahlverhalten, Parteien und politische Spannungen", *Politische Vierteljahresschrift*, 1973; "The Collapse of an Intermediary Power Structure; Germany 1933-34", *International Journal of Comparative Sociology*, 1968; "Social Structure and Political Order, in *Sozialwissenschaftliches Jahrbuch für Politik*, 1976; "Modernisierungspolitik als Institutionenbildung", in *Probleme der Modernisierungspolitik* (W Zapf (ed)), 1977; "Gesellschaftliche, kulturelle und politische Übereinstimmungen und Gegensätze in beiden deutschen Staaten", in *Zur Sache*, 1977. Fields: Comparative research on Western democracies; processes of institution building; party structure and social structure; national socialism.

[1135]
LERNO Paul
29 December 1933, Belgian. Damstraat 131, 2958 Weerde, Belgium. Degrees: Lic pol sci. Lecturer in General Soc, HSLI, Brussels. Publs: "Doelstellingen van de Sociale Vorming", *Nova et Vetera*. Fields: Political and social education.

[1136]
LERUEZ Jacques
4 May 1931, French. 32 rue de la Colonie, 75013 Paris, France. Degrees: Lic; DES d'anglais; Lic en droit; DES sci pol; Dr, 1971. Doctoral thesis: "The Ideology of Planning in Britain 1930-70". Chargé de recherches, CNRS, FNSP. Publs: *Planification et politique en Grande-Bretagne 1945-71*, 1972; *Economic Planning and Politics in Britain 1945-74*, 1975; *Histoire de la Grande-Bretagne. III Les temps difficiles* (with J Surel),

1978; plus various articles in *Revue Française de Science Politique, Etudes, Défense Nationale, Documentation Française*. Fields: British politics; incomes policy; government-union relationships; industrial democracies; ethnicity; the politics of emigration; devolution and nationalism, especially in Scotland; the Northern Ireland problem.

[1137]
LESER Norbert Franz
31 May 1933, Austrian. Bauernfeldgrasse 714, 1190 Vienna, Austria. Degrees: Dr (Vienna), 1958. 1960-63 Legal Adviser, Ministry of Transport; 1963-66 Assistant of Pol Sci, Inst for Advanced Study and Sci Research, Ford Foundation, Vienna; 1967 Dozent for the Philosophy of Law and State, U of Graz; 1971- Professor of Pol Sci, U of Salzburg. Publs: *Zwischen Reformismus und Bolschewismus. Der Austromarxismus als Theorie und Praxis*, 1968; *Die Odyssee des Marxismus. Auf dem Weg zum Sozialismus*, 1971; *Sozialismus zwischen Relativismus und Dogmatismus*, 1974; *Als Zaungäste der Politik* (with R Berczeller), 1976. Fields: Political science; philosophy; theology; literature.

[1138]
LESOURNE Jacques Francois
26 December 1928, French. 52 rue de Vaugirard, Paris, France. Degrees: Dipl (Ecole Polytechnique). Professeur, Ecole Nat de la Statistique et de l'Administration Econ et Ecole des Mines, St Etienne; Professeur d' Econ, Conservatoire Nat des Arts et Métiers. Director, Interfutures Project, OECD. Publs: *Technique économique et gestion industrielle*, 1958; *Le calcul économique*, 1966; *Le calcul économique-théorie et applications*, 1972; *Modèles de croissance de l'entreprise*, 1973; *Cost benefit analysis and economic theory*, 1975; *A theory of the individual for economic analysis*, 1977; *Les systèmes du destin*, 1976. Fields: Systems theory and its application to socio-political systems; economic theory; policy analysis.

[1139]
LESSNOFF Michael Harry
23 January 1940, British. Department of Politics, University of Glasgow, Glasgow W2, Scotland. Degrees: MA (Glasgow), 1963; B Phil (Oxon), 1965. Assistant Principal, Dept of Education and Sci, U of London; Lecturer, Dept of Pol, U of Glasgow. Publs: Articles in *Sociological Review; Political Studies; Philosophical Quarterly; The Structure of Social Science*, 1974; *Philosophy and Public Affairs*. Fields: Philosophy of the social sciences; political philosophy.

[1140]
LETTEBOER Johannes Frederik Anton
12 February 1945, Dutch. Stadionweg 138, The Netherlands. Degrees: Dr. Doctoral thesis. "Is Slum Clearance a Political Problem?". Secretary, Employers Union. Fields: Housing; slum clearance; urban renewal.

[1141]
LETWIN William
14 December 1922, American. 3 Kent Terrace, London NW1, England. Degrees: BA; PhD. Doctoral thesis: "The Origins of Scientific Economics: English Economic Thought, 1660-1776". 1955-66 Assistant Professor, Associate Professor of Econ History, Massachusetts Inst of Technology; 1966- Professor of Pol Sci, LSE. Publs: *The Origins of Scientific Economics*, 1963; *Law and Economic Policy in America*, 1965; *Documentary History of American Economic Policy*, 1972. Fields: Public policy; American economic policy; US government and politics; constitutional law in USA; comparative federalism.

[1142]
LEURDIJK Jan Hendrik
17 August 1939, Dutch. Hazelaarlaan 30, Hilversum, The Netherlands. Degrees: Drs (Amsterdam). Assistant Professor of International Relations, U of Amsterdam. Publs: Articles on the foreign policy of The Netherlands; theoretical aspects of international politics. Fields: International relations.

[1143]
LEVEAU Rémy
6 July 1932, French. 14 rue Maurice Berteaux, 92310 Sevres, France. Degrees: Dr en sci pol; Maître de conférence agrégé de sci pol. Doctoral thesis: "Le rôle politique des élites rurales dans le Maroc indépendant". 1957-58 Chargé de recherches de sociologie rurale, CNRS; 1958-59 Assistant, Faculté de Droit, U de Rabat; 1960-65 Conseiller Technique, Cabinet du Ministère de l'Intérieur du Maroc, Chargé de cours, Faculté de Droit, U de Rabat; 1965-67 Attaché à la Direction, IEP, U de Paris; 1967-68 Visiting Associate Professor, U of Michigan; 1968-71 Conseiller Culturel de Coopération Technique auprès de l'Ambassade de France en Libye; 1971-74 Chargé de recherches, Centre d'Etudes des Relations Internationales, FNSP; 1974-76 Professeur, Faculté de Droit, WSJ Beyrouth; Maître de conférences agrégé de sci pol, Professeur, IEP, Paris. Publs: *Le fellah Marocain*, 1976; plus articles in *Revue Française de Science Politique*, *Annuaire d'Afrique du Nord*, *Revue de Géographie du Maroc*, *Analyse et Prévision*, *La Revue Mahgreb*. Fields: Contemporary Asian world.

[1144]
LEVI Lucio
31 August 1938, Italian. Via V Vela 35, 10128 Turin, Italy. Doctoral thesis: "The Political Thought of Alexander Hamilton". Assistant, Chair of Dottrina dello Stato, U of Turin; Assistant, Chair of Filosofia della Pol; Professor, Faculty of Pol Sci, U of Turin. Publs: *Alexander Hamilton e il Federalismo Americano*, 1965; *Il Problema della legittimità nel Parlamento dell'Italia Repubblicana*, 1970; *Trent'anni di Vita del Movimento Federalista Europea* (with Pistone (eds)), 1973; *Crisi dello Stato Nazionale, Internazionalizzazione del Processo Produttivo e Internazionalismo Operaio*, 1976; *Federalismo e Integrazione Europea*, 1978. Fields: Historical materialism; the theory of raison d'Etat vis-à-vis the general theory of political process; education and internationalism; European integration.

[1145]
LEVIN Michael Martin John
4 October 1940, British. 3 Trefor Road, Aberystwyth, Wales, England. BA; MSc (LSE), 1965; PhD (Leicester), 1971. Doctoral thesis: "Uses of the Social Contract Method: Locke to Paine". 1965-66 Tutorial Assistant, U of Leicester; 1966-67 Temporary Assistant Lecturer, U of Leeds; Lecturer in Pol Sci, U Coll of Wales, Aberystwyth. Publs: Articles in *Journal of the History of Ideas*, *Political Studies*, *Planet*, *Dictionary of the History of Ideas*, *Political Science Quarterly*, 1973. Fields: Political theory since the 18th century; German politics; socialism.

[1146]
LEVY Denis Marchand Gérard
19 July 1920, French. 90 Boulevard Raspail, 75006 Paris VIème, France. Degrees: Ing Civ Aéron; Lic lettres (Paris); Dipl (IEP Paris); Dr en droit (Paris). Doctoral thesis: "La responsabilité de la puissance publique et de ses agents en Angleterre". 1959-62 Lecturer, U of Dakar; 1962-69 Professor, U of Nancy; 1967-68 Visiting Professor, U of Edinburgh; Guest Professor, U of Saarbrücken; Professor of Public Law, U of Paris II. Publs: *Absolutism, Custom and Conventions in Politics*. Fields: Constitutional law; electoral systems; political parties.

[1147]
LEVY Paul Michel Gabriel
27 November 1910, Belgian. Ferme d'Enée, Chaussée de Tirlemont 49, 5800 Gembloux sur Ormeau, Belgium. Degrees: Ingénieur Commercial (Free U Brussels), 1931; Lic (Free U Brussels), 1932. School of International Studies, Geneva; 1931-34 Professor of Statistics, Ecole des Hautes Etudes, Ghent; 1935-51 Professor of Statistics, Inst des Hautes Etudes de Belgique, Brussels; 1933-49 Head of Information Services, Belgian Broadcasting; 1946 Member, Belgian House of Representatives; 1949-66 Director of Press and Information, Council of Europe, Strasbourg; 1939 Member, Upper Council for Statistics of Belgium; 1954-72 Professeur, Centre des Hautes Etudes Européennes, Strasbourg; 1966-72 Associé Professeur, Inst de Soc, U de Strasbourg; Director, Inst of Polemology; 1968- Professor, U of Louvain and Dean, Faculty of Econ Soc and Pol Sci. Publs: *Psychologie sociale et propagande politique*, 1934; *La bataille de l'index*, 1938; *La statistique des langues en Belgique* (co-author), 1940; *Héros et martyrs, nos fusillés*, 1946; *Les heures rouges des Ardennes*, 1946; *La querelle du recensement*, 1960; *Une paix pour notre temps*, 1975; *Polémologie, recherche sur la paix, irénologie*, 1977. Fields: Sociology of communication; polemology; linguistics; border problems; international organizations.

[1148]
LEWIN Leif Gunnar Torbjörn
28 March 1941, Swedish. Skytteanum, 75120 Uppsala, Sweden. Degrees: PhD. Doctoral thesis: "Planhushållningsdebatten" (The Debate on the Planned Economy). 1967-72 Assistant Professor, Pol Sci; 1972- Johan Skytte Professor of Eloquence and Government. Publs: *Planhushållningsdebatten*, 1967; *Folket och Eliterna*, 1970; *The Swedish Electorate*, 1972; *Statskunskapen, Ideologierna och den Politiska Verkligheten*, 1972; *Hur styrs facket?*, 1977; *Åsiktsjournalistiken och den fackliga Demokratin*, 1977. Fields: Rational choice theory; democratic theory.

[1149]
LEWIN Moshe
6 November 1921, French. 27 Selly Wick Drive, Selly Park, Birmingham 29, England. Degrees: BA; Dr en histoire (Sorbonne), 1964. Directeur d'Etude Suppleant, Ecole Pratique des Hautes Etudes, Paris; Senior Fellow, Russian Inst, U of Columbia, USA; Member, Inst for Advanced Study, Princeton, USA; Fellow, Kennan Inst for Russian Studies, Woodrow Wilson International Center for Scholars, Washington; Professor of Soviet History and Pol, Centre for Russian and East European Studies, U of Birmingham. Publs: *La paysannerie et le pouvoir soviétique 1928-30*, 1968; *Le dernier combat de Lénine*, 1968; *Political Undercurrents in Soviet Economic Debates*, 1974. Fields: Social and political history of the Soviet thirties; the dynamics of ruling monopolistic parties, especially the Communist party of the Soviet Union.

[1150]
LEWIS Paul Geoffrey
28 March 1945, British. 11 Dells, Olney, Buckinghamshire MK46 5HY, England. Degrees: B Soc Sci; PhD. Doctoral thesis: "The Politics of Polish Peasantry, 1956-70". Lecturer in Government, Open U. Publs: *The Practice of Comparative Politics* (with D C Potter (eds)); *The Politics of Revolt*, 1974; *Questions in Soviet Government and Politics* (with F Castles and S Saunders), 1976; *Options in Soviet Government and Politics* (with R Clifton and M Glenny), 1976; *The Practice of Comparative Politics* (with F Castles and D Potter (eds)), 1978. Fields: East European politics; comparative politics.

[1151]
LEYS Roger Temple
30 January 1938, Danish. Grønnegade 33, Isal, DK-1107 Copenhagen K, Denmark. Degrees: BA; MA (California). Lecturer, Inst for Samfundsfag, U of Copenhagen. Publs: *Dualism and Rural Development in East Africa*, 1973; "Gold Mining in 1974: the Gold of Migrant Labour", *African Affairs*, 1975. Fields: African politics; imperialism and the peripheral state.

[1152]
L'HUILLIER Fernand Pierre
24 July 1905, French. 20 rue d'Oslo, 67000 Strasbourg, France. Degrees: Agrégé; Dr ès lettres. Doctoral thesis: "Recherches sur l'Alsace napoléonienne — la mise en vigueur des décrets de Trianon et de Fontainebleau dans le grand-duché de Bade". Professeur honoraire de l'Université; President de l'Association Européenne d'Histoire Contemporaine. Publs: *De la sainte alliance au Pacte Atlantique*, 1955; *Les institutions internationales et transnationales*, 1961; *Dialogues franco-allemands 1925-1933*, 1970; *La libération de l'Alsace*, 1975. Fields: Contemporary history of Germany; Franco-German relations; De Gaullism.

[1153]
LIEBERT Ulrike
30 January 1951, German. Kapellenweg 37, 8131 Berg, FR Germany. Degrees: MA (Munich). Doctoral thesis: "Spain's Integration in the European Community: The Regional Problem". Fields: Comparative politics; ethnomethodology; political culture; regional movements; political economy; supranational organization.

[1154]
LIEPELT Klaus
6 September 1931, German. Friedrichsallee 19, Bonn 2, FR Germany. Degrees: MA (Michigan), 1954.

[1155]
LIGEUX Paul Marie*
20 February 1909, Belgian. 13 rue Lambermont, 1330 Rixensart, Belgium. Dr en droit (Louvain), 1932. Directeur, *Le XXe Siècle*; Dir Gen, Ministry of Justice; Directeur, Office de l'Information du Congo Belge; Professeur, Faculté des Sci Econ, U de Louvain; Dir, Inst Belge d'Information; Président, Société d'Etudes Pol et Soc, Louvain; Professeur, U Lovanium Kinshasa, Congo. Publs: *Le passage de l'Iraty*. Fields: Information, development and peace; future of the press; copyright law; higher education.

[1156]
LIGHT Margot
9 January 1940, British. 83 Muswell Hill Road, London N10 3HS, England. Degrees: BSc. Lecturer, Dept of Linguistic and International Studies, U of Surrey. Fields: International relations theory; conflict analysis; Soviet politics and foreign policy.

[1157]
LIJPHART Arend
17 August 1936, Dutch. Schaepmanlaan 4, Noordwijkerhout 2438, The Netherlands. Degrees: BA; MA (Yale), 1959; PhD (Yale), 1963. 1961-63 Instructor in Pol Sci, Elmira Coll; 1963-68 Assistant and Associate Professor of Pol Sci, U of California at Berkeley; Professor of International Relations, U of Leiden. Publs: *The Trauma of Decolonization: The Dutch and West New Guinea*, 1966; *The Politics of Accommodation:*

Pluralism and Democracy in the Netherlands, 1975; *World Politics* (ed), 1971; *Politics in Europe: Comparisons and Interpretations* (ed), 1969; *Democracy in Plural Societies: A Comparative Exploration*, 1977. Fields: International relations, especially integration and the development of theory; comparative analysis of democratic politics.

[1158]
LINDBLAD Ingemar
4 September 1932, Swedish. Fjärde Villagatan 31, 502 44 Borås, Sweden. Degrees: Fil kand, 1954; Fil lic, 1957; Fil dr, 1960. Doctoral thesis: "The Swedish Municipal Workers' Union — A Study in Trade Unionism". Secretary, Royal Commission on Broadcasting; Assistant to Director-General, Swedish Radio; Docent, Dept of Pol Sci, U of Stockholm. Publs: *The World of Broadcasting*, 1970; *Fundamentals of Political Science*, 1972; *Scandinavian Politics* (contributor), 1972. Fields: Mass communication; local government; aspects of political behaviour.

[1159]
LINDER Wolf Joseph
26 May 1944, Swiss. Habsburgstrasse 33, 8037 Zürich, Switzerland. Degrees: Dr rer Soc (Konstanz); Lic jur (Zürich). Doctoral thesis: "Der Fall Massenverkehr — Verwaltungsplanung und städtische Lebensbedingungen". U of Konstanz; ORL Inst, Zürich. Publs: *Politik der Verstädterung* (with R Grauhan), 1974; *Erzwungene Mobilität* (with U Maurer and H Resch), 1975; *Verwaltungsreform als Ausbildungsreform* (with H Treiber), 1976; "Raumordnungspolitik in den Strukturproblemen von Umwelt und Wachstum", in *Werdende Raumplanung*, 1974; "Möglichkeiten und Grenzen politischer Planung in der Schweiz", *DISP*, 1977; "Regierung und Verwaltung vor den Anforderungen politischer Planung", in *Schweizerisches Jahrbuch für Politische Wissenschaft*, 1977; "Plädoyer für ein allgemeines Verkehregestz", *DISP*, 1978; *Planung in der schweizerischen Demokratie*, 1978. Fields: Public policy; political planning; constitutional law; participation; processes of democracy.

[1160]
LINDMAN Sven Olof Gustav
19 August 1910, Finnish. Puolalaparrken 4a, 2010 Åbo 10, Finland. Degrees: Mag phil (Åbo), 1932; PhD (Åbo), 1937; PhD (Uppsala), 1974. 1937-42 Docent, Swedish U of Åbo; 1956-62 Vice-Chancellor, Swedish U of Åbo; 1942-73 Professor of Pol Sci, Swedish U of Åbo; 1974- Director, Research Inst of the Åbo Akademi Foundation. Publs: *Parlamentarismens Införande i Finlands Statsförfattning*, 1935; *Studier över Parlamentarismens Tillämpning i Finland 1919-26 med Särskild Hänsyn till Regeringsbuldningens Problem*, 1937; *Statsskick och Förvaltning i Finland. En Översikt*, 1941; *Johan Jacob Nordström. Hans Samhällssyn och Politiska Personlighet. Tiden intill 1854*, 1948; *Partistudier*, 1957; *Eduskunnan Aseman Muuttuminen 1917-19* (Suomen Kansanedustuslaitoksen historia VI), 1968; *Från Storfurstendöme till Republik. Tillkomsten av 1919 års Regeringsform*, 1969; *Some Forms of Party Activity*, 1974. Fields: Constitutional history; 19th century political ideas.

[1161]
LINDSTRÖM Ulf A
30 March 1952, Swedish. Stipendiegränd 14 F 4, S-902 40 Umeå, Sweden. Degrees: Fil kand. Publs: *The Scandinavian Party System* (with S Berglund), 1978. Fields: Political sociology; right-wing extremism in western nations.

[1162]
LINES Colin Leonard
22 November 1941, British. 196 London Road, St Leonards-on-Sea, Sussex, England. Degrees: BSc; MSc (London). Principal Lecturer and Head of the Division of Pol, Thames Polytechnic. Fields: History of political thought.

[1163]
LINHARD José
29 May 1939, German. Tapiauer Allee 24, 1000 Berlin 19, FR Germany. Degrees: Dipl Pol. Clinical Research, Schering AG, Berlin. Publs: *Oral Contraception, 40 years of Development*, 1972-73; "Familienplanungspolitik in Lateinamerika" in *Bevölkerungswissenschaft — Bevölkerungspolitik*, 1974; *Bevölkerungspolitik und Familienplanung in der Volksrepublik China*, 1975; "Familienplanungspolitiken in Lateinamerika" in *Berichte zur Entwicklung in Spanien, Portugal, Lateinamerika*, 1975; "Bevölkerungspolitik in Lateinamerika — Auswirkungen der Bukarester Weltbevölkerungskonferenz" in *Weltmarkt und Entwicklungsländer* (J Linhard and K Voll, (eds)), 1976; "Die chinesische Bevölkerungsentwicklung", *Sexualmedizin*, 1976; "Akzeptabilität moderner Kontrazeptiva am Beispiel der Papierpille", *Österreichische Apotheker-Zeitung*, 1977; "Bevölkerungsproblematik der Volksrepublik China" in *Entwicklungsprobleme und Lösungsversuche in der Volksrepublik China*, 1977. Fields: Contraceptive methods; demography; family planning; population policies and theories.

[1164]
LINK Werner
14 July 1934, German. Wendelinusstrasse 45, 5500 Trier, FR Germany. Degrees: PhD (Marburg), 1961; Habilitation (Mannheim), 1970. Doctoral thesis: "Die Geschichte des Internationalen Jugendbundes (IJB) und des Internationalen Sozialistischen Kampfbundes (ISK)". 1971-75 Professor of Pol Sci, U (Gesamthochschule) of Kassel; 1973 Visiting Professor, School of Foreign Service, U of Washington; 1975- Professor of Pol Sci, U of Trier. Publs: *Mit dem Gesicht nach Deutschland. Eine Dokumentation über die sozialdemokratische Emigration* (with E Matthias), 1968; *Die amerikanische Stabilisierungspolitik in Deutschland 1921-1932*, 1970; *Das Konzept der friedlichen Kooperation und der Beginn des kalten Krieges*, 1971; *Procedures and Outcomes of Detente Policy*, 1974; *Deutsche und amerikanische Gewerkschaften und Geschäftsleute 1945-1975. Eine Studie über transnationale Beziehungen*, 1978. Fields: International relations and foreign policies, especially German-American relations; European and American relations; West European integration; international conflicts and regional structures.

[1165]
LINTONEN Raimo Kalevi
13 December 1945, Finnish. Kauppiaank, 13 D 24, 00100 Helsinki 10, Finland. Degrees: MA. 1967-1970 Secretary, Finnish Inst of International Affairs; 1972 Researcher, Organization Project, Dept of Pol Sci, U of Helsinki; 1973- Assistant, Dept of Pol Sci, U of Helsinki. Publs: *The Nordic Transnational Association Network: Structure and Correlates* (co-author), 1975; *Valtio Japanin taloudesllisessa hyteiskuntamuodostumassa: johdatusta teoreettiseen ja konkreettiseen analyysiia* (co-author), 1975. Fields: National and international networks of associations; military organization and society; transgovernmental relations.

[1166]
LIPSCHITS Isaac
19 November 1930, Dutch. Kraneweg 17, Groningen, The Netherlands. Degrees: Dipl supérieur d'études et de recherches pol (FNSP), 1958; PhD (Amsterdam), 1962. Doctoral thesis: "La politique de la France au Levant, 1939-41". 1961-66 Lecturer in Pol Sci, U of Amsterdam; 1966-68 Visiting Senior Lecturer, U of Haifa; 1967-68 Visiting Senior Lecturer, Hebrew U of Jerusalem; 1968-70 Senior Lecturer in International Relations; U of Leiden; Senior Lecturer in Pol Sci, Rotterdam Economic U; Lecturer, International Relations, Dutch Airforce Staff Coll; 1945- Full Professor of Contemporary History, Inst of History, U of Groningen; Director, Centre for Study and Documentation of Political Parties. Publs: *La politique de la France au Levant, 1939-41*, 1963; *Honderd jaar NIW. Het Nieuw Israelietisch Weekblad 1865-1965*, 1966; *Links en Rechts in de Politiek*, 1969; *Simulaties in de Internationale Politiek*, 1971; *Politieke Stromingen in Nederland*, 1977; *Onstaansgeschiedenis van de Nederlandse Politieke Partijen, Deel I: De Protestants-Christelijke Stroming tot 1940*, 1977; *Verkiezingsprogramma's 1977*, 1977. Fields: Dutch politics; history of international relations since 1945; political parties: theory and history.

[1167]
LITT Jean-Louis*
6 October 1935, Belgian. Centre d'Etudes du Développement Régional, Université Catholique de Louvain, Louvain, Belgium. Degrees: Lic in Chemical Philology (Louvain), 1959; Lic in Philosophy (Inst Comizius, Kimhors), 1962; Lic in Soc (Louvain), 1970. Teacher in Secondary School; Assistant, Centre d'Etudes du Développement Régional, U de Louvain. Fields: Relations between social class structure and regional development.

[1168]
LITTLE Richard
26 October 1944, British. 6 Parkhill Road, London NW3, England. Degrees: BSc; PhD (Lancaster). Doctoral thesis: "External Involvement in Civil War". 1969-77 Lecturer, Dept of Pol, U of Lancaster; 1977- Lecturer in Government, Open U. Publs: *Intervention: External Involvement in Civil Wars*, 1975. Fields: International relations theory; third party mediation and conflict resolution.

[1169]
LITTLE Walter
18 June 1945, British. 16 Pelham Grove, Liverpool 17, England. Degrees: BA; MA (John Hopkins); PhD (Cambridge). Doctoral thesis: "Political Mobilization in Peronist Argentina". Publs: "Party and State in Peronist Argentina", *Hispanic American Historical Review*, 1973; "Electoral Aspects of Peronism", *Journal of Inter-American Studies*, 1973; "Popular Origins of Peronism", in *Argentina in the Twentieth Century* (D Rock (ed)); "Teaching Politics at Liverpool", in *Teaching Politics*. Fields: Populism; political violence; role of the state in development; Latin American politics; militarism.

[1170]
LIVELY John Frederick
15 June 1930, British. 203 Myton Road, Warwick, England. Degrees: BA; MA (Oxon and Cambridge). 1956-58 Research Fellow, St Anthony's Coll, U of Oxford; 1958-62 Lecturer in Pol, U Coll of Swansea; 1962-65 Lecturer in Pol, U of Sussex; 1965-75 Fellow and Tutor in Pol, St Peter's Coll, U of Oxford; Professor of Pol, U of Warwick. Publs: *Social and Political Thought of Alexis de Tocqueville*, 1962; *The Works of*

Joseph de Maistre (ed), 1965; *The Enlightenment*, 1966; *Democracy*, 1975; *Utilitarian Logic and Politics* (with J C Rees), 1978; *Democracy, Consensus and Contract* (with P Birnbaum and G Parry), 1978. Fields: Democratic theory; de Tocqueville.

[1171]
LLOYD Lorna W H
British. Department of International Relations, University of Keele, Keele, Staffordshire, England. Degrees: BSc. Doctoral thesis: "Britain and Compulsory Arbitration with special reference to the Optional Clause of the Permanent Court of International Justice, 1914-31". Lecturer in International Relations, U of Keele. Fields: Inter-war British and dominion foreign policy; League of Nations; peaceful settlement of disputes.

[1172]
LLOYD-JONES Ioan David
19 April 1932, British. 6 North Gardner Street, Glasgow G11 5BT, Scotland. Degrees: BA; MA (Cantab), 1956; PhD (Cantab), 1962. Doctoral thesis: "Charles Fourier's Conception of a Social Science". Part-time supervisor, St John's Coll, U of Cambridge; Assistant Lecturer, U of Glasgow; Visiting Professor, Coll of Wooster, Ohio, USA; Senior Lecturer, U of Glasgow. Publs: Articles in *History Today, New Society*. Fields: Utopian socialism; rhetoric/persuasion in politics.

[1173]
LOCK Grahame Edwin
27 August 1946, British. Langebrug 13, Leiden, The Netherlands. Degrees: BA; PhD (Cambridge). Doctoral thesis: "Theories of Ideology". Research Officer, Ecole Normale Supérieure, Paris; Lecturer in Pol Theory, U of Leiden. Publs: *Politieke Theorieen* (with H Van Gunsteren), 1977; *Ideology and the State*, 1978. Fields: Theories of the state; socialism and communism; ideology; politics and production.

[1174]
LODGE Juliet
British. 137B Ella Street, Hull HU5 3AJ, England. Degrees: BA; MA; M Phil. Lecturer in West European Pol, U of Auckland, New Zealand; Visiting Fellow, Centre for International Studies, LSE; Lecturer, Dept of Pol, U of Hull. Publs: *The European Parliament and The European Community*; *The European Policy of the SPD*; *Small State Diplomacy: New Zealand and The European Community*. Fields: West European politics; European integration, EEC institutions, policies and politics; international relations; comparative politics.

[1175]
LOEB-MAYER Nicole
6 October 1927, Belgian. 21 rue Langeveld- Bte 12, 1180 Bruxelles, Belgium. Degrees: Lic en sci soc; Dr en sci soc (Bruxelles). Doctoral thesis: "Socialisation et consensus européen en Belgique". Chercheur, Centre National d'Etudes des Problèmes de Sociologie et d'Economie Européennes; Chercheur, sociologie du travail, Inst de Sociologie, U Libre de Bruxelles; Chercheur, U Libre de Bruxelles. Publs: *Le patronat industriel belge et la CEE*, 1965; *Les trois grands partis politiques belges et l'intégration européenne*, 1969; "Chronologie d'une équivoque: les 'sommets' et l'Europe politique", *Res Publica*, 1977; "Les partis et l'Europe: perspectives de renouveau?", in *Textes et Documents*. Fields: European integration; political parties; socialization; nationalism.

[1176]
LOENNENDONKER Siegward
18 April 1939, German. 186 Bundesallee, 1000 Berlin 31, FR Germany. Degrees: Dipl Soziologie. Doctoral thesis: "Die Gründung der freien Universität Berlin — Entstehung einer politischen Universität". Wiss Assistent; Wiss Angesteller, F U Berlin. Publs: *Freie Universität Berlin 1948-1973 - Hochschule im Umbruch* (with T Fichter), 1975; *Kleine Geschichte des SDS- Der sozialistische deutsche Studentenbund von 1946 bis zu seiner Selbstauflösung*, 1977. Fields: Student movements; theory development of leftwing student movements; history of the German university.

[1177]
LOERTSCHER Clive
17 October 1948, Swiss. Place Chauderou 20, 1003 Lausanne, Switzerland. Degrees: Lic en sci pol. Assistant, Inst de Sci Pol, U de Lausanne. Publs: "Pourquoi et comment étudier l'Etat", in *Annuaire Suisse du Science Politique*, 1976; *Le parti communiste suisse et les syndicats 1920-1921. Stratégie du front unique en suisse*, 1977. Fields: State theories; fiscal crisis; state activities; labour movements.

[1178]
LOEW Konrad Maria
25 December 1931, German. Kirchenstrasse 17, 8021 Baierbrunn, FR Germany. Degrees: Dr jur. Doctoral thesis: "Der Grundrechtsbegriff der Bayerischen Verfassung und ihre Grundrechte". 1972-75 U of Erlangen; 1975- U of Bayreuth. Publs: *25 Jahre Grundgesetz — ein Zwischenzeugnis* (ed and co-author), 1974; *Freiheit und Gleichheit oder die Quadratur des Kreises* (ed and co-author), 1974; *Konrad Adenauer — Leben und Werk* (co-author), 1976; *Ausbeutung des Menschen durch Menschen*, 1977; *Die Grundrechte — Verständnis und Wirklichkeit in beiden Teilen Deutschlands*, 1977.

[1179]
LOIODICE Aldo*
20 May 1941, Italian. Via Nicolai 29, Bari, Italy. Degrees: Dr of Law (Bari), 1964. Assistant Professor of Constitutional Law, U of Bari; Member, Special Committee on Comparative Urban Planning; Professor of Public Law and School Legislation, U of Sassari; Professor of Public Law, U of Bari. Publs: *Revoca di Incentivi Economici ed Eccesso di Potere Legislativo*, 1967; *Contributo allo Studio sullo Libertà di Informazione* (Torene (ed)), 1969. Fields: Parliament and public opinion; radio and television; hospital and school legislation; local and regional governments.

[1180]
LOMER Margaret Anna
18 November 1932, British. 20 Raglan Road, Edgbaston, Birmingham B5 7RA, England. Degrees: BA. Research Associate, Inst of Local Government, U of Birmingham. Publs: "The Chief Executive in Local Government 1974-76", *Local Government Studies*, 1977. Fields: Local government structure and management organization.

[1181]
LOMPE Klaus
6 January 1937, German. Department of Political Science, Technical University of Braunschweig, Braunschweiger Strasse 50a, 3301 Gross Schwulper, FR Germany. Degrees: Dipl Kaufmann; Dr rer Pol; Habilitation. Lecturer, Dept of Soc Sci, U of Köln; Lecturer, Technical U of Berlin; Professor of Pol Sci, Technical U of Braunschweig. Publs: *Wissenschaftliche Beratung der Politik. Ein Beitrag zur Theorie anwendender Sozialwissenschaften*, 1972; *Wissenschaftler und Politiker-Partner oder Gegner?* (co-ed), 1967; *Gesellschaftspolitik und Planung. Probleme politischer Planung*

in der sozialstaatlichen Demokratie, 1976. Fields: Political planning in democracies; problems of policy sciences; empirical research of the decision-making processes in political institutions; reform of government and the civil service.

[1182]
LONG Joyce Ruth
3 July 1924, British. Institute of Local Government Studies, University of Birmingham, Birmingham B15 2TT, England. Degrees: B Com; PhD (Leeds), 1948. Doctoral thesis: "Industrial Economics: The Factors Governing the Locating of Industry". 1948-52 Research Fellow, Dept of Econ, U of Birmingham; 1959-62 Free-lance Editorial and Consultancy Work; 1961-63 Tutor, Faculty of Commerce, U of Birmingham; 1963-66 Research Fellow, Dept of Education, U of Birmingham; 1966 Research Fellow, Senior Research Associate, Inst of Local Government Studies, U of Birmingham. Publs: *Labour Turnover Under Full Employment*, 1951; *The Wythall Inquiry: A Planning Test Case* (ed), 1961; *Universities and the General Public*, 1968; *Administration in a Large Local Authority: A Comparison with Other County Boroughs* (co-author), 1969; *Setting up the New Authorities* (with A Norton), 1972; *Employee Participation and Local Government*, 1976; *A Consumer's Guide to Local Government* (M Minogue (ed)), 1977. Fields: Management in local government.

[1183]
LOPEZ NIETO Lourdes
18 March 1953, Spanish. O'Donnel 42, Madrid 9, Spain. Degrees: Lic (Madrid); Dipl. Research Fellow, Assistant Professor in Electoral Soc, Seminar Derecho Pol, Facultad Pol y Soc, U Complutense de Madrid. Publs: "Polemicas Sobre la Geografia Electoral", *Historia*, 1977; "Un Hombre un Voto: Mito y Realidad", in *Argomentos* (co-author), 1977; "Un Dilema Para las Leyes Electorales: C Partidos O Candidatos?", in *Cuadernos Economicos de Informacion Comercial Española*, 1977; *Legislacion Politica del Estado Español 1936-75*, 1978. Fields: Political law; political sociology; electoral sociology.

[1184]
LOPEZ-PINA Antonio
4 June 1937, Spanish. Calle Colombia 32, Madrid 16, Spain. Degrees: Dr en Derecho (Madrid). Doctoral thesis: "The 'Interessenverbände' in the German Federal Republic". 1963-64 Post-doctoral Research, IEP, U de Paris; 1964-66 Associate Visiting Research Scholar, Inst for Soc Research, U of Michigan; Center for International Affairs, Harvard U; 1966- Catedrático de Derecho Pol, U Autónoma de Madrid. Publs: *Estructuras Electorales Contemporáneas*, 1970; *La Cultura Política de la España de Franco*, 1976; *Sociología Política*, 1976; *La España Democrática y Europe* (ed), 1977; *Poder y Clases Sociales* (ed), 1978. Fields: Comparative politics; intellectual history; history of sociological theory; political theory; modern history; ideology; theory of the state; constitutional law; political sociology.

[1185]
LORENZ Hanns Friedrich*
31 May 1936, German. Erlenstrasse 8, CH-8280 Kreuzlingen, Switzerland. Degrees: BS (Brigham Young U, Utah); MPA (Harvard); LLB; Dr jur (Würzburg). Doctoral thesis: "Security of Employment in France". Civil Service, Bonn; Personal Assistant, Cambridge, Mass; Lecturer, U of Freiburg; Senior Lecturer, U of Konstanz. Publs: *Moderne Verwaltung durch Fortbildung*, 1968; *Verwaltung in der Demokratie*, 1972. Fields: Government influence on industries' expansion policy; content and methods of new political science curricula.

[1186]
LOSCHAK Danièle
5 April 1946, French. 59 rue Lhomond, 75005 Paris, France. Degrees: Dr en droit. Doctoral thesis: "Le rôle politique du juge administratif français". Professeur de droit public et sci pol, U d'Amiens. Publs: *Traité de Science administrative* (with J Chevallier), 1978; plus various articles on public law and administrative science. Fields: General theory of state and law; civil service; epistemology; analysis of speech and semiology.

[1187]
LOUBET DEL BAYLE Jean-Louis
29 April 1940, French. 14 Hameau des Bosquets, 151 route de Seysses, 31300 Toulouse, France. Degrees: Dipl (IEP Toulouse), 1962; Dr en droit (Toulouse), 1968. Doctoral thesis: "Les nonconformistes des années 30, une tentative de renouvellement de la pensée politique française". Chercheur, CNRS; Assistant, Maître assistant de sci pol, U de Toulouse; Directeur, Centre d'Etudes et de Recherches sur la Police, IEP, Toulouse. Publs: *Les nonconformistes des années 30, une tentative de renouvellement de la pensée politique française*, 1969; *Introduction aux méthodes des sciences sociales*, 1977. Fields: History of political thought; electoral sociology; methodology; policy.

[1188]
LOVENDUSKI Joni
19 May 1945, American. 25 Fairmount Drive, Loughborough, Leicestershire, England. Degrees: BA; MA (Manchester). Lecturer in Pol, Dept of European Studies, U of Loughborough. Fields: Women and politics; politics of advanced industrial society; revolutionary theory.

[1189]
LÖWENHARDT Johan Herman Louis
22 August 1947, Dutch. Baljuw 66, Hoorn, The Netherlands. Degrees: Dr. Doctoral thesis: "Decision-Making in the Soviet Union". 1973-74 Junior Fellow, The Russian Inst, U of Columbia, New York; 1974-75 Pol Sci Editor, *Great Spectrum Encyclopedia*. Staff Member, Inst for Eastern European Studies, U of Amsterdam. Publs: "The Tale of the Torch, Scientist-Entrepreneurs in the Soviet Union", *Survey*, 1974; "De Vervuiling van het Bajkalmeer", *Internationale Spectator*, 1972; "Het Sovjetcolofon — een sleutelgat voor de Kremlinoloog?" *Internationale Spectator*, 1977. Fields: Comparative politics; political theory; politics in the Soviet Union; science policy; methodology of sovietological research.

[1190]
LUBER Burkhard
29 December 1944, German. Postfach 4029, D-4952 Porta Westfalia, FR Germany. Degrees: Dr phil. Doctoral thesis: Events Analysis and International Politics". Director, Adult College, International Friendship House. Publs: *Frieden auf dem Land*. Fields: Peace research; education.

[1191]
LUCAS Noah
30 June 1927, British. 18 Broad Elms Lane, Sheffield S11 9RQ, England. Degrees: MA (Glasgow), 1951; PhD (Washington), 1961. Doctoral thesis: "Histadrut: The Israeli Labour Movement as a Nationalist and Socialist Movement: A Study in Ideologies and Behaviour". 1961-63 Assistant Professor, Southern Illinois U, USA; 1965 Associate Professor, Southern Illinois U, USA; 1963-66 Research Fellow, Hebrew U of Jerusalem; 1966-67 Visiting Lecturer, U of Glasgow; Lecturer in American Government

and Pol, U of Sheffield; 1975-76 Research Fellow, Visiting Fellow, U of Oxford; Centre for Postgraduate Hebrew Studies and Senior Associate Member, St Anthony's Coll, U of Oxford; 1976- British Academy Overseas Visiting Fellow, Harvard U. Publs: *The Modern History of Israel*, 1974. Fields: Modern Israeli political history; American social and political history since the New Deal; problems of revolutions; comparative development.

[1192]
LUCHAIRE Francois*
1 January 1919, French. 11 rue Saint-Lazare, Paris IXème, France. Degrees: Dr en droit (Caen), 1942; Agrégé des Facultés de Droit, 1945. 1945 Professeur, Faculté de Droit, U de Nancy; 1960 Directeur, Inst des Hautes Etudes d'Outre-Mer; 1964 Professeur, Faculté de Droit, U de Paris; 1966 Membre du Conseil Constitutionnel; 1971 President, U de Paris I. Publs: books and articles on constitutional law, administrative science, under-developed countries, European problems. Fields: Europe; developing countries; the constitution and political life.

[1193]
LUCIFREDI Pier Giorgio
15 November 1939, Italian. Via S Luca D'Albaro 4, 16146 Genoa, Italy. Degrees: Laurea in Giurisprudenza (Genoa), 1961; Abilitazione Assistente Ordinario (Genoa), 1964; Libera Docenza in Diritto Costituzionale, 1968. Doctoral thesis: "Crisis of Government in a Parliamentary System". 1961-64 Volunteer Assistant, U of Rome; 1964-68 Ord Assistant, U of Rome; 1968-72 Chargé de Cours, U of Rome; Ord Professor of Constitutional Law, U of Genoa. Publs: *L'Iniziativa Legislativa Parlamentarie*, 1968; *Il Sistema Costituzionale Francese*, 1972; *Il Sistema Statunitense*, 1974; *Il Sistema Britannico*, 1977. Fields: Constitutional law, especially the constitutional machinery of government; parliamentary organization and working; comparative government.

[1194]
LUDZ Peter Christian
22 May 1931, German. Thurn-und-Taxis-Strasse 7, 8133 Feldafing, FR Germany. Degrees: Dipl Volkswirt (Munich), 1953; PhD (Free U of Berlin), 1956; Habilitation (Free U of Berlin), 1967. Doctoral thesis: "Der Ideologie-begriff des jungen Marx und seine Fortentwicklung im Denken von Georg Lukacs und Karl Mannheim". 1956-69 Assistant Associate Professor of Pol Soc, Full Professor of Pol Sci, Free U of Berlin; 1960-69 Head of Dept of East German and East European Affairs, Research Inst for Pol Sci; 1969-73 Full Professor of Pol Sci and Soc, U of Bielefeld; 1973- Professor of Pol Sci, U of Munich. Publs: *G Lukács, Werkauswahl* (ed), 1961 and 1967; *Studien und Materialien zur Soziologie der DDR* (ed), 1971; *Parteielite im Wandel*, 1968;. *The Changing Party Elite in East Germany*, 1972; *Two Germanies in One World*, 1973; *Alienation as a Concept in the Social Sciences*, 1975; *Materialien zum Bericht zur Lage der Nation, 1971, 1972, 1974* (director of studies and co-author), 1971-1975; *Ideologiebegriff und marxistische Theorie*, 1976; *Die DDR zwischen Ost und West*, 1977. Fields: Political theory; comparative analysis of political and social systems; East and West Germany; history of secret societies since 1780.

[1195]
LUIF Paul
7 May 1948, Austrian. Josef-Kainz-Strasse 3/30, A-5020 Salzburg, Austria. Degrees: Dr jur (Vienna); Absolvent (Vienna). Assistant, Inst for Pol Sci, U of Salzburg. Publs: "Zur wirtschaftlichen Situation von Presse und Rundfunk in Österreich", *Publizistik*, 1976; "Kriegsursachen als Gegenstand der Friedensforschung", *Zeitgeschichte*,

1977/78. Fields: International relations; peace research; national security; military and militarism; police; causes of war; parliament and mass media; methodology and methods of empirical social research.

[1196]
LUKES Steven Michael
8 March 1941, British. 18 Beaumont Buildings, Oxford, England. Degrees: BA; MA, 1965; D Phil, 1968. Doctoral thesis: "Emile Durkheim: An Intellectual Biography". Temporary Assistant, Lecturer in Moral and Pol Philosophy, U of Keele; Research Fellow, Nuffield Coll, U of Oxford; Fellow and Tutor in Soc and Pol, Balliol Coll, U of Oxford. Publs: *The Good Society: A Book of Readings* (with A Arblaster), 1971; *Emile Durkheim: His Life and Work*, 1973; *Individualism*, 1973; *Power: A Radical View*, 1974; *Essays in Social Theory*, 1977. Fields: Political sociology; the history of sociology; the philosophy of the social sciences.

[1197]
LUND Reinhard
8 March 1933, Danish. Øksnebjergvej 42, 5000 Odense, Denmark. Cand pol (Copenhagen), 1959. 1960-67 Research Associate; 1967-71 Director of Research, Danish National Inst of Social Research; Director of Management Studies, U of Odense. Publs: *45 timers ugens indforelse*, 1960; *Tillidsmandsinstitutionen*, 1963; *Tillidsmandskursus, Danmarks Radio*, 1969; *Arbetslivet i Kris och Förvandling*, 1971; *Indflydelse og samarbejde* (author), 1971; *Beslutningsprocesser*, 1971; *De Ansattes Indflydelse*, 1972; *Sammenslutningen og Centralorganisationen*, 1972; *Organisationsstrukturens Centralisering Inden For Jern og Metal*, 1974; *Skal Virksomheden Overleve* (with B Ranning), 1975. Fields: Participation of employees in management; centralization and bureaucratization of labour market organizations; decision-making.

[1198]
LUNDMARK Kjell
22 April 1944, Swedish. Trastvägen 8 D, S-902 37 Umeå, Sweden. Degrees: MA (Umeå), 1972. Research Assistant, U of Umeå. Fields: Public administration; regional and local government.

[1199]
LUNDQUIST Lennart Harald Sture
13 February 1938, Swedish. Sandgatan 12, S-22350 Sweden. Degrees: Fil dr, 1972. Doctoral thesis: "Means and Goals of Political Decentralisation". Professor in Pol Sci, Inst of Pol Studies, U of Copenhagen. Publs: *Förvaltningen i det politiska sesrement*, 1971; *Means and Goals of Political Decentralization*, 1972; articles in *Scandinavian Political Studies*; *Nordisk Administrator Tidskrift*; *Statsvetenskaplig Tidskrift*. Fields: Public administration; democratic theory; planning.

[1200]
LUYKX P Theo
14 October 1913, Belgian. Laneaustraat 12, 1020 Bruxelles, Belgium. Degrees: Lic phil et lettres; Lic History, 1938; Dr phil et lettres, 1940; Cand jur. Doctoral thesis: "Johansson van Constantinopel". Professor, U of Ghent. Publs: *Contemporary Political History of Belgium*, 1977; *International Relations since the Vienna Congress*, 1972; *Historical and Political Development of Mass Media*, 1917. Fields: Contemporary political history; mass media organizations and structure.

[1201]
LYON Peter Hazelip
4 April 1934, British. 14 Sydney Road, Guildford, Surrey, England. Degrees: BSc; PhD (London), 1961. Doctoral thesis: "Neutralism: Its Meaning and Significance in Contemporary International Politics". 1955-56 Ministry of Defence; 1957-63 Lecturer in Pol, U of Leicester; 1963-69 Lecturer in International Relations, LSE; 1967 Visiting Professor of Pol Sci, U of California; 1970 U of Pennsylvania; 1973 U of Cornell; 1976 U of Illinois; 1969- Inst of Commonwealth Studies. Publs: *Neutralism*, 1963; *War and Peace in Southern Asia*, 1969; *New Orientations* (ed), 1970; *Britain and Canada* (ed), 1976. Fields: New states in world politics; foreign policy-making diplomacy; international relations, theories, syllabi and methods; Australia and Canada.

M

[1202]
MAARSE Johannes Antonius Maris
16 May 1948, Dutch. Tibbertlanden 9, Enschede, The Netherlands. Degrees: Drs. Assistant Professor of Soc, Free U of Amsterdam; Assistant Professor of Public Administration, Technische Hogeschool Twente. Publs: "Traditionale en Ekonomische Bestuurskunde", *Beleid en Maatschappij*, 1975; "Randvoorwaarden en Beleid" (with J A W de Bruin), *Bestuurswetenschappen*, 1977. Fields: Public administration; policy effects.

[1203]
MABILEAU Albert
12 September 1927, French. 38 Boulevard du Président Wilson, 73000 Bordeaux, France. Degrees: Dr d'Etat. Doctoral thesis: "Le parti libéral britannique". Directeur, IEP, Bordeaux; Professeur de Sci Pol, U de Bordeaux. Publs: *Les partis politiques en Grande-Bretagne* (with M Merle); *La personnalisation du pouvoir (with L Hamon); Les facteurs locaux de la vie politique nationale* (ed); *La décolonisation en Afrique Noire* (with J Meyriat). Fields: Local government and local administration; British political system; political systems in North Africa; political leadership.

[1204]
MacFARLANE Leslie John
22 August 1924, British. 14 Crick Road, Oxford, England. Degrees: BSc; MA (Oxon); PhD (London). Doctoral thesis: "The British Communist Party 1920-27". 1941-57 London County Council Administration Posts; 1957-63 Lecturer in Government, Birmingham Coll of Commerce; 1963-69 Tutor in Pol, Ruskin Coll, Oxford; 1969- Fellow and Tutor in Pol, St John's Coll, U of Oxford; Lecturer in Pol Theory, U of Oxford. Publs: *British Communist Party: Origins and Development until 1929*; *British Politics 1918-64*; *Modern Political Theory*; *Political Disobedience*; *Violence and the State*; *Issues in British Politics Since 1945*. Fields: Political obligation; rights.

[1205]
MACHIN Howard
22 May 1947, British. Degrees: BA; PhD (LSE). Doctoral thesis: "The Prefects of the Fifth French Republic 1958-69". Lecturer in French Public Administration, 1977. Fields: French government; politics; political parties; local politics.

[1206]
MACKIE Thomas Taylor
23 March 1942, British. 146 Fergus Drive, Glasgow G20 6AT, Scotland. Degrees: BA; MSc (London), 1965; MSc (Strathclyde), 1971. 1967-69 Instructor in Pol Sci, Allegheny Coll, Pennsylvania, USA; 1971-72 Research Assistant, Dept of Pol, U of Strathclyde; 1973- Lecturer in Pol, U of Strathclyde. Publs: *The International Almanac of Electoral History* (with R Rose), 1974. Fields: Comparative electoral behaviour; religion and politics; Western Europe and the Anglo-American countries.

[1207]
MADDEN A F*
Nuffield College, Oxford, England. Fellow, Nuffield Coll, U of Oxford. Fields: History of constitutions and political institutions in the Commonwealth.

[1208]
MADDICK Henry*
3 June 1915, British. Institute of Local Government Studies, University of Birmingham, Birmingham B15 2TT, England. Degrees: BA; MA (Oxon), 1952. 1948-50 Lecturer, Wadham Coll, U of Oxford; 1950 Lecturer, Senior Lecturer in Public Administration, U of Birmingham; 1964- Reader in Local Government, Professor of Local Government Studies, Director of Inst of Local Government Studies, U of Birmingham. Publs: *Democracy, Decentralization and Development*, 1963; *Panchayati Raj: Rural Local Government in India*, 1970. Fields: Local government administration and management; development through decentralization; community involvement; health services and local government.

[1209]
MADELEY John Talbot Stanley
23 January 1944, British. 61 Romilly Crescent, Canton, Cardiff, Wales. Degrees: BA. 1973-75 Research Assistant, Dept of Pol, U of Strathclyde; 1975-77 Tutorial Fellow, Dept of Pol, U Coll, Cardiff; 1977- Lecturer in Government, LSE. Publs: "Scandinavian Christian Democracy. Throwback or Portent?", *EJPR*, 1977; "Patterns of Subordination and Strategies of Separation: Norway and Scotland Compared", *Journal of the Conflict Research Society*, 1977; plus articles on elections in Scandinavia. Fields: Government and politics of Scandinavia; religion and politics.

[1210]
MADELIN Henry
26 April 1936, French. 15 rue Raymond Marcheron, 92170 Vanves, France. Degrees: Dipl (IEP), 1956; DES d'écon pol, (Paris), 1957; troisième cycle de sci pol, (IEP) Paris, 1970; Dr de recherches, 1971. Doctoral thesis: "Pétrole et politique en Méditerranée occidentale". Teacher, Coll Libermann, Cameroon; Professeur de Sci Pol, Inst d'Etudes Sociales, Inst Catholique de Paris; Maître de conférences, IEP, Paris; Rédacteur Pol, *Projet*. Publs: *Politique et foi* (co-author), 1972; *Pétrole et politique en Méditerranée occidentale*, 1973; *Les chrétiens entrent en politique*, 1975; *Chrétiens et marxistes dans la société française*, 1977. Fields: Ideology and practice in trade unions; evolution of PCF.

[1211]
MADGWICK Peter James
15 August 1925, British. 60 Danycoed, Aberystwyth, Dyfed, Wales. Degrees: BA; MA (Oxon), 1950. Lecturer, Dept of Extra-mural Studies, U of Nottingham; Reader in Pol Sci, U Coll of Wales. Publs: *American City Politics*, 1970; *Introduction to British*

Politics, 1976; *The Politics of Rural Wales*, 1973. Fields: Political behaviour; political culture; cultural conflict; elections; local government; politics in Wales; American politics.

[1212]
MADSEN Ole Nørgaard
12 June 1943, Danish. Gudrunsvej 68, 7TH, 8220 Brabrand, Denmark. Degrees: Cand sci pol. Inst of Pol, U of Aarhus. Publs: *Lokalpolitik og Lokalforvaltning i Udvalgte Fremmede Lande* (with P Meyer and S Winter), 1973; *Borger og Kommune*, 1976; *Planlaegningsorganisation* (with K H Bentzon), 1976; *En Sporgeskemaundersøgelse af Danske Kommunalpolitikeres Arbedsvilkar* (with P Meyer *et al*); *Offentlig Forvaltning i Danmark*, 1977. Fields: Public administration, especially local government and planning organizations.

[1213]
MADSEN Per Henrik Kongshøj
25 May 1949, Danish. Fuglegårdsvej 35, DK-2820 Gentofte, Denmark. Degrees: Cand pol, 1973. 1973- Assistant Professor, Associate Professor, Inst for Pol Studies, U of Copenhagen. Publs: *Alternative Undgangspunkter for Empirisk analyse al den Funktionelle Indkomstfordeling*, 1975; "Post-keynesiansk Fordelingsteori" (with F K Hansen), *Tidsskrift for Politisk Økonomi*, 1975; "Den Funktionelle Fordeling i Danmark i Efterkrigstiden", *Nordisk Tidskrift för Politisk Ekonomi* (with C Koch), 1976; "Krisen i Industrien", (with K Vangsjaer), in *Krise i Danmark* (I Grünbaum *et al* (eds)), 1977; "Trade Unions, the State and Political Business Cycles" (with P Dencik), *Nordisk Tidsskrift för Politisk Økonomi*, 1977; "Økonomi og Politik i den Politiske Økonomi", in *Økonomi og Politik* (with P Dencik), 1977; *Arbejdsløshed, Betalingsbalance og Økonomisk Politik* (with H Brink *et al*), 1976.

[1214]
MAES Rudolf Yvo L
16 July 1938, Belgian. Reeboklaan 25, 1980 Tervuren, Belgium. Degrees: Dr in Law; Dr in Pol and Soc Sci. Doctoral thesis: "De overheidsbemoeiing op het gebied van de elektriciteitsvoor in Belgie" (The Interference of Public Authorities in the Domain of Electricity Supply in Belgium). Director, Interuniversity Center for Public Law; Head, Study Service of the Belgian Association of Local Authorities; Professor, U of Leuven. Publs: "De bekrachtiging door de Wetgevendfe Kamers van de koninklijke besluiten betreffende de samenvoeging van de gemeenten en de wijziging van hun grenzen", *Rechtskundig Weekblad*, 1975-1976; "Le précédent de la Belgique", *Vers la réforme des collectivités locales*, 1977; "De samenvoeging van de gemeenten en de gemeentelijke bestuurskracht", *Res Publica*, 1976; "De samenvoeging van de gemeenten. Studie van het besluitvormingsproces", *Res Publica*, 1977; "Van klein-naar grootschalig bestuur", in *Gemeentebeleid na de fusies*, 1977. Fields: Administrative science; regional and local government.

[1215]
MAHIEU Yvon*
29 July 1938, Belgian. Avenue des Myrtes 31, 1080 Brussels, Belgium. Degrees: Dipl (Ecole Royale Militaire); Lic en sci commerciales et consulaires. Officier à l'Ecole Militaire — Chaire de Droit. Publs: *Options pour la Démocratie Parlementaire Belge*, 1970; *Enquête sur les attitudes des parlementaires à propos de la gestion de l'Etat*, 1970. Fields: Financial administration of the state; the principle of multi-year programming and the reform of the *Cour des Comptes*.

[1216]
MAHNCKE Dieter Martin
24 April 1941, German. Starweg 4a, 2070 Ahrensburg, FR Germany. Degrees: BA; MA; PhD (John Hopkins U), 1964; Habilitation (Bonn), 1968. Doctoral thesis: "Nuclear Participation: The Federal Republic of Germany and Nuclear Weapons, 1954 - 1966".
Research Associate, German Society for Foreign Affairs, Bonn; Lecturer in Pol Sci, U of Mainz; Lecturer in Pol Sci, U of Bonn; Professor of Pol Sci, Hochschule der Bundeswehr, München; Professor of Pol Sci, Hochschule der Bundeswehr, Hamburg.
Publs: *Nukleare Mitwirkung — Die Bundesrepublik Deutschland in der atlantischen Allianz 1954-1970*, 1971; *Westeuropäische Verteidigungskooperation* (with K Carstens), 1972; *Berlin im geteilten Deutschland*, 1973; *Seemacht und Aussenpolitik* (with H Schwarz), 1974. Fields: European security; US-European relations; German foreign policy.

[1217]
MAIR Peter
3 March 1951, Irish. 18 Huntly Gardens, Hillhead, Glasgow G12, Scotland. Degrees: BA; MNA (National U of Ireland). Doctoral thesis: "The Language of Politics: Party Systems and Party Competition in Ireland". Assistant Lecturer in Pol Studies, National Institute for Higher Education; Lecturer in Pol, U of Strathclyde. Publs: "Proportionality, PR and STV in Ireland", *Political Studies* (with M Laver), 1974; "Labour and the Irish Party System Revisited", *Economic and Social Review*, 1977; "The Autonomy of the Political: the Development of the Irish Party System", *Comparative Politics*, 1978; "The Marxist Left in Britain ", in *Multi-Party Politics in the United Kingdom* (H M Drucker (ed)), 1978; "The Single Transferable Vote and the Irish General Election of 1977", *Economic and Social Review* (with M Maguire), 1978. Fields: Political parties; Irish politics; Marxist revolutionary strategy.

[1218]
MAJONE Giandomenico
27 March 1932, Italian. 1365 York Avenue, New York, NY 10021, USA. Degrees: Laurea in Pol Sci (Padua); MA in Public Administration (U of Washington); PhD in Statistics (Berkeley). Doctoral thesis: "Consistency of Bayes Estimates". 1964-75 U of Rome; 1968-69 Visiting Professor, U of British Columbia; 1975-77 Research Scholar, International Inst for Applied Systems Analysis; 1977- Research Scholar, Russell Sage Foundation, New York. Publs: "The Feasibility of Social Policies", *Policy Sciences*, 1975; "On the Notion of Political Feasibility", *European Journal of Political Research*, 1975; "Standard Setting and the Theory of Institutional Choice", *Policy and Politics*, 1976; "Choice Among Policy Instruments for Pollution Control", *Policy Analysis*, 1976; "Pitfalls of Analysis and the Analysis of Pitfalls", *Urban Analysis*, 1977; "Technology Assessment in a Dialectic Key", *Public Administration Review* (forthcoming); "Technology Assessment and Policy Analysis", *Policy Sciences*, 1977; "The ABC's of Constraints Analysis", *Policy Analysis*, 1978. Fields: Methodology of policy analysis; technology assessment; problems of evidence and inference in policy disputes.

[1219]
MANDOLINI Maria*
10 May 1947, Italian. Department of Sociology and Political Sciences, University of Calabria, Via Severini 30, Cosenza, Italy. Degrees: Laurea in Econ and Commercial Sci (Urbino), 1972. Collaboratrice didattica, Inst of Historical and Soc Studies, U of Urbino; Borsista, Dept of Soc and Pol, U of Calabria. Fields: Electoral behaviour in Italy, 1919-21.

[1220]
MANNHEIMER Renato
27 July 1947, Italian. Via Olona 5, 20123 Milan, Italy. Degrees: Laurea. Doctoral thesis: "Social Integration of Immigrants in Northern Italy". Associate Professor of Soc Methodology, U of Naples and U of Salerno. Publs: *Gli Abitanti del Degrado Edilizio*, 1977; *Il Comportamento Elettorale a Milano*, 1977; *Mutamento Sociale e Comportamento Elettorale*, 1978. Fields: Electoral behaviour; political sociology.

[1221]
MANNIN Michael Leonard
8 July 1945, British. 1 Sunningdale Road, Wallasey, Merseyside, England. Degrees: BSc; MA (Kent). Senior Lecturer in Pol, Liverpool Polytechnic. Fields: Western European politics, particularly Italian politics; British local government and politics.

[1222]
MANNING Adrian F
10 July 1929, Dutch. Bosweg 27, Berg en Dal, The Netherlands. Degrees: D Litt. Professor of Contemporary History, U of Nijmegen; President, National Inst of War Documentation, Amsterdam; Catholic Documentation Centre, Historical Research Council, Nijmegen. Publs: *De confessionelen*, 1968; *Documents on Dutch Foreign Policy 1940-45* (ed), 1977; "Preliminaries of 1954 Episcopal Mandate", 1971; *Restoration of the Relations between the Netherlands and the Vatican 1940-44*, 1971; "The position of the Dutch Government in London up to 1942", *Journal of Contemporary History*, 1978. Fields: Dutch 20th century foreign policy; rise of fascism in diplomatic reports and contemporary press 1919-22; Catholicism versus socialism; Dutch catholics and political structures in the Netherlands, 1945-present.

[1223]
MANNING David John
8 April 1938, British. 9 Leazes Place, Durham City, England. Degrees: BSc; PhD (London), 1964. Doctoral thesis: "The Moral and Political Philosophy of Jeremy Bentham". Lecturer in Pol Theory, Polytechnic of Central London; 1973 Visiting Professor of Pol, U of Texas at Austin; 1976 Guest Professor, U of Tübingen; Senior Lecturer in Pol, U of Durham. Publs: *The Mind of Jeremy Bentham*, 1968. *Liberalism*, 1976. Fields: Ideological argument; political obligation; methodological aspects of the study of political life; the relationship between political and commercial activity.

[1224]
MANNING Maurice Anthony
14 June 1943, Irish. 137 Foxrock Park, Foxrock, Co Dublin, S Ireland. Degrees: BA; MA (Dublin), 1966. 1966- Lecturer in Pol, U Coll, Dublin. Publs: *The Blueshirts*, 1971; *Irish Political Parties: An Introduction*, 1972. Fields: The career of W T Cosgrave (President, Irish Free State Executive Council 1922-32); European parliament.

[1225]
MANOR James Gilmore
21 April 1945, American. 12 Westgate Road, Leicester, England. Degrees: BA; D Phil (Sussex), 1975. Doctoral thesis; "Political Change in an Indian State: Mysore 1910-1955". 1972-75 Research Fellowship, Inst of Commonwealth Studies, London; 1967-69 Teaching Posts at Chinese U of Hong Kong; 1973-75 School of Oriental and African Studies, London; 1975-76 U of Yale; 1976- Lecturer, Dept of Pol, U of Leicester. Publs: *Political Change in an Indian State*, 1978; articles in *The Making of Politicians* (W H Morris-Jones (ed)), 1976; *Congress and the Raj* (Da Low (ed)), 1978; *Aspects of Social Change in India* (M N Srinivas (ed)), 1976; *Society and Politics in*

Princely India (R B Jeffrey (ed)), 1978; articles in *Modern Asian Studies, Asian Survey, South Asia, Indian Economic and Social History Review.* Fields: Politics of developing nations, especially South Asia and East Africa; party organization; personality and politics.

[1226]
MANTZ Dirk
7 April 1918, Dutch. Grote Spie 319, Breda, The Netherlands. Degrees: MA (Free U Amsterdam), 1967. Teaching Pol Sci, Royal Military Academy. Publs: *Overheid en Krijgsmacht*, 1972; various articles. Fields: Functioning of authoritarian and democratic political systems; underdeveloped political systems.

[1227]
MANUEL Ramirez
6 June 1940, Spanish. Department of Derecha Politico, Facultad de Derecho, Zaragoza, Spain. Degrees: Dr (Granada). Doctoral thesis; "Los grupos de presión en la Segunda República Española". Professor Adjunta, U de Granada; Catedratico, U de Santiago de Compostela; Visiting Scholar, U of Columbia; Catedratico Director, Dept Derecho Politico, U de Zaragoza. Publs: *Los grupos de presión en la Segunda República Española*, 1969; *Nuevas perspectivas de la Ciencia Politica*, 1971; *Supuestos actuales de la Ciencia Politica*, 1972; *Estudios sobre la Segunda República*, 1975; *Las Reformas de la Segunda República*, 1977; *Aproximaciòn a la España actual (1939-1975)*, 1977. Fields: Political modernization in Spain 1900-1977; political parties in Spain, 1931-1936; recent trends in political science.

[1228]
MARCIC René*
13 March 1919, Austrian. Franziskanergasse 2, 5020 Salzburg, Austria. Degrees: Dr of Law (Vienna), 1942. Chief Ed, *Salzburger Nachrichten*; Professor of Legal Philosophy, Austrian Constitutional Law, Theory of State and Pol Sci, U of Salzburg. Publs: *Martin Heidegger und die Existenzialphilosophie*, 1949; *Vom Gesetzerstaat zum Richterstaat*, 1957; *Verfassung und Verfassungsgericht*, 1963; *Mensch, Recht, Kosmos — Drei Gedankenwege ins Dasein*, 1965; *Die Zukunft der Koalition*, 1966; *Das Buch und sein Verwalter*, 1966; *Verfassungsgerichtsbarkeit und Reine Rechtslehre*, 1966; *Der Staatsmann in der Demokratie*, 1966. Fields: Theory of press and journalism; philosophy, especially problems of legal philosophy; semantics; government; theories of democracy; legal sociology.

[1229]
MARCOU Lilly
9 July 1939, French. 23 rue Vergniaud, 75013 Paris, France. Degrees: Lic ès lettres; Dr. Doctoral thesis: "Contribution à l'histoire du Kominform". Assistant de recherche. Publs: *L'Union Soviétique, guide de recherche*, 1972; *Le Kominform, communisme de guerre froide*, 1977; plus various articles in *RFSP, Le Monde Diplomatique, Projet.* Fields: History of the international Communist movement.

[1230]
MARIN Bernard
6 August 1948, Austrian. 1130 Vienna, Schweizertalstrasse 5, Austria. Degrees: Mag rer Soc (Vienna), 1971; Dipl (Vienna), 1974; Dr rer Soc (Vienna), 1975. Doctoral thesis: "Political Organization of Social Science Research Work — A Case-Study". 1972-73 Instructor, Dept of Soc, U of Vienna; 1974-75 Research Consultant, Inst for Advanced Studies, Inst for Societal Pol, Inst for Conflict Research; Lecturer, Adult College for Pol Education, Mattersburg; 1975-76 Instructor, Dept of Soc, U of Vienna; 1976

Research Consultant, Inst for Contemporary History, U of Linz; 1977- Lecturer, U of Innsbruck; 1975- Assistant Professor, Inst for Conflict Research, Vienna. Publs: *Zur Politischen Organisation sozialwissenschaftlicher Forschungsarbeit*, 1978; *Antisemitismus oder Antisemiten? Zum nachfaschistischen Antisemitismus in Österreich, Der Nahost-Konflikt* (with J Bunzl and F J Hacker (eds)), 1978; *Wachstumskrisen in Österreich-eine Modellsimulation* (co-author), 1978. Fields: Political sociology and psychology; crisis and conflict research; general social and political theory; methodology of the social sciences; sociology of science; organizational research; prejudice, especially anti-semitism; political violence; law and order; political propaganda; symbolic politics.

[1231]
MARINI Giuliano
1 February 1932, Italian. Via Santa Cecilia 25, 56100 Pisa, Italy. Degrees: Dr in Jurisprudence (Pisa), 1954. Doctoral thesis: "La Riforma della Società per Azioni". 1969-70 Professor in Philosophy of Law, U of Pisa; 1970- Professor in Pol Philosophy, U of Pisa. Publs: *Dilthey e la Compresione del Mondo Umano*, 1965; *Savigny e il Metodo della Scienza Giuridica*, 1966; *L'Opera di Gustav Hugo nella Crisi del Giusnaturalismo tedesco*, 1969; *Jacob Grimm*, 1972; *Dilthey Filosofo della Musica*, 1973; *Aspetti Sistematici nella Società Civile Hegeliana*, 1976; *Friedrich Carl Von Savigny, Libertà Soggettiva e Libertà Oggettiva*, 1978; *nella 'Filosofia del Diritto' Hegeliana*, 1978. Fields: German historicism; Hegelian political philosophy.

[1232]
MARKL Karl Peter
4 October 1942, German. Göttschied D70, D-6580 Idar-Oberstein, FR Germany. Degrees: Dipl; Dipl (IEP Paris); M Litt (Cantab); D Phil (Oxon). Doctoral thesis: "The Identification of Policies in Pluralist Theories of Democracy". Fellow, Centre for Contemporary European Studies, U of Sussex; Supervisor of European Seminar, Cambridge; Visiting Professor in Pol Philosophy, U of Stanford, California; German Kennedy Memorial Fellow, U of Harvard; Director, Research Group for the Structural Analysis of Unemployment and Misemployment in the District of Birkenfeld (Rhein Pfalz, Germany). Fields: Communication studies; European questions; political philosophy; international relations.

[1233]
MARRADI Alberto
23 March 1941, Italian. ISVI, Via Beato Bernardo 6, Catania, Italy. Degrees: Laurea (Florence), 1965; Doctor in Pol and Soc Sci. Doctoral thesis: "A History of Power-checking Institutions in France, from the Revolution to the Gaullist Regime". 1968-69 Senior Researcher, Agnelli Foundation, Turin; 1969-71 Researcher, Centro Studi Politica Comparata, Florence; 1971-74 Assistente di Ruolo, Dept of Pol Sci, U of Florence; 1974-75 Professore Incaricato, U of Siena; 1975- Professore Incaricato, Methodology of Soc Research, U of Catania and Director, Data Archive, Dept of Soc Sci. Publs: *Valori, Classi Sociali, Scelte Politiche* (with Tullio-Altan), 1975; "Measuring Risk in Collective Decisions", *Quality and Quantity*, 1975; "Italy's Referendum on Divorce: Survey and Ecological Evidence Analyzed", *European Journal of Political Research*, 1976; various articles in *Rivista Italiana di Scienza Politica*. Fields: Philosophy of the social sciences; methodology of social research.

[1234]
MARS Theodor Friedrich*
21 September 1941, Dutch. School of Social Sciences, The University, Falmer, Brighton BN1 9QN, Sussex, England. Degrees: BA; MSc (London). 1967-69 Research Assistant, Inst of Development Studies and Lecturer in Pol, U of Sussex. Fields: Administration and politics; the politics of South Africa and the study of macro-level aspects of political systems; methodological problems, including the philosophy of social science, social ontology, and the idea of theory in political science.

[1235]
MARSH Michael Anthony
22 November 1947, British. Political Science Department, Trinity College, Dublin 2, Republic of Ireland. Degrees: BA; MA (Essex). Doctoral thesis: "Social Democratic Parties in Western Europe: An Assessment of some Explanations for Variations in Radicalism". Research Assistant, U of Essex; Research Assistant, U of Strathclyde; Lecturer in Pol Sci, Trinity Coll, Dublin. Publs: "European Social Democratic Party Leaders and the Working Class: Some Linkage Implications of Trends in Recruiting", in *Political Parties and Linkage: A Comparative Perspective* (K Lawson (ed)), 1978. Fields: European Social Democratic parties; European political development; recruitment in Ireland.

[1236]
MARSHALL Arthur Hedley
6 July 1904, British. 39 Armorial Road, Coventry, England. Degrees: BSc; PhD (London), 1936. 1944-64 City Treasurer, Coventry; 1964-Associate Director, Inst of Local Government Studies, U of Birmingham. Publs: *Local Government and the Arts*; *Local Authorities: Internal Financial Control*, 1936; *Consolidated Loan Funds of Local Authorities* (with J M Drummond), 1936; *Report of Local Government in the Sudan*, 1949, and on *British Guyana*, 1955; *Financial Administration in Local Government*, 1960; *Local Government Administration Abroad*, 1967; *New Revenues for Local Government*, 1971. Fields: Comparative studies in local government training; finance, and internal organization.

[1237]
MARSHALL Geoffrey
22 April 1929, British. The Queen's College, Oxford, England. Degrees: BA; MA (Manchester), 1952; PhD (Glasgow), 1954; MA (Oxon), 1957. Doctoral thesis: "Parliamentary Sovereignty in the British Commonwealth". Assistant Lecturer, U of Glasgow; Research Fellow, Nuffield Coll, U of Oxford; Fellow and Praelector in Pol, The Queen's Coll, U of Oxford; U Lecturer in Government, U of Oxford. Publs: *Parliamentary Sovereignty and the Commonwealth*, 1957; *Some Problems of the Constitution* (with G C Moodie), 1959; *Police and Government*, 1965; *Politics and Civil Liberties in Europe* (co-author), 1967; *Constitutional Theory*, 1971. Fields: British government and administration; British and American constitutional law; jurisprudence and political theory; police studies; civil liberties.

[1238]
MARTIKAINEN Tuomo Tapani*
7 April 1939, Finnish. Institute of Political Science, University of Helsinki, Hallituskatu 11-13, Helsinki 10, Finland. Degrees: Lic (Helsinki), 1968. Doctoral thesis: "Political Activity: A Study on the Political Socialization of the Finnish Youth". Teaching and Research, Dept of Pol Sci, U of Helsinki; Acting Associate Professor, Dept of Pol Sci, U of Helsinki. Publs: *Political Activity: The Basic Dimensions of the Structure and the*

Explanatory Factors, 1967; *The Behavioural Study of Politics*, 1968; *Voting in the 1968 Communal Elections in Finland*, 1969. Fields: Political socialization; political youth organizations in Finland; political inequality.

[1239]
MARTIN Laurence Woodward
30 July 1928, American. King's College, Strand, London WC2R 2LS, England. Degrees: BA; MA (Cambridge), 1945; PhD (Yale), 1955. Doctoral thesis: "British Liberalism and American War Aims 1918". Instructor, U of Yale; Assistant Professor MIT, Cambridge, USA; Associate Professor, John Hopkins U; Professor, U of Wales; Research Associate, Washington Centre of Foreign Policy Research; Professor of War Studies, King's Coll, U of London; 1978- Vice-Chancellor, U of Newcastle-upon-Tyne. Publs: *The Anglo-American Tradition in Foreign Affairs* (with A Wolfers), 1956; *Peace Without Victory*, 1958; *Neutralism and Non Alignment*, 1962; *The Sea in Modern Strategy*, 1967; *America and the World* (co-author), 1970; *Ballistic Missile Defence and the Alliance*, 1969; *Aims and Strategy*, 1973.

[1240]
MARTIN Roderick
18 October 1940, British. 62 Lonsdale Road, Oxford, England. Degrees: MA, 1966; D Phil, 1965. Doctoral thesis: "The National Minority Movement: A Study in the Organization of Trade Union Militancy in the Inter-War Period". 1966-69 Lecturer in Soc, Senior Research Fellow, Jesus Coll, U of Oxford; 1964-66 Assistant Lecturer, Lecturer, Dept of History, U of York; 1966- Lecturer in Soc, U of Oxford and Official Fellow in Pol and Soc, Trinity Coll, Oxford. Publs: *The Sociology of Power*, 1977; *Redundancy and Paternalist Capitalism*, 1974; *Communism and the British Trade Unions, 1924-33*, 1969. Fields: Industrial sociology and the relation between industry and politics at trade union and management level.

[1241]
MARTINEZ Cuadrado Miguel
5 March 1935, Spanish. C Modesto Lafuente 68, Madrid 3, Spain. Degrees: Dr en Derecho, 1967; Lic (Madrid), 1958. Doctoral thesis:. "Elections y Partidos Politicos de España 1868-1931". 1959-63 Research Assistant, Lecturer and Associate Professor, Facultad Ciencias Pol, U de Madrid; Professor, Derecho Pol, Facultad de Ciencias Pol y Soc, U Complutense de Madrid and Professor of the Europa Coll, Bruges. Publs: *Elecciones y Partidos politicos de España 1868-1931*, 1969; *Premio Taurus de Rensayo 1967*, *Cambio Social y Modernizacion Politica: Anuario Politico Español 1969*, 1970; *Anuario Politico Español 1970*, 1971; "La Burguesia Conservadora", in *Historia de España Alfaguara*, 1973, 1975, 1976. Fields: International relations; economic integration and political cooperation in Europe, Latin America, Arab countries; government; public law; political sociology.

[1242]
MARTINOTTI Guido A
18 January 1938, Italian. Caravaggio, Milan, Italy. Degrees: Dr (Milan), 1960; Libero Docente in Soc, 1969. Doctoral thesis: "Sociological Interpretations of Fascism". 1961-69 Assistente, Facoltà di Sci Pol, U degli Studi di Milano; 1967-69 Incaricato di Soc, Facoltà di Architettura, Politecnico di Milano; 1969-75 Incaricato di Soc Pol, Facoltà di Sci Pol, U degli Studi di Milano; 1972-73 Incaricato di Soc Generale, Facoltà di Lettere, U degli Studi di Torino. Publs: *Metropoli e Sottocomunità* (with Balbo (eds)), 1966; *Città e Analisi Sociologica* (ed), 1967; *Gli Studenti Universitari: Profilo Sociologico*, 1969; *Education in a Changing World* (with Kloskowska (eds)), 1977; *Stato Crisi Urbana e Enti Locali*, 1978. Fields: Political behaviour; education; urban politics.

[1243]
MARTIN URIZ Victoria
15 February 1947, Spanish. Av America no 16, Madrid 2, Spain. Degrees: Lic (Madrid).
Assistant Professor of Spanish Pol Law, Seminario de Derecho Pol, Facultad de Cien-
cias Pol y Soc, U Complutense de Madrid. Publs: "Las Elecciones en la Historia",
Historia, 1977; "Le Legislacion Electoral ante la Perspectiva de las Elecciones
Españolas de 15 de Junio de 1877", *Cuadernos Economicos de Informòcion Comercial
Español*, 1977. Fields: Political law; political sociology; electoral sociology.

[1244]
MARTINUSSEN Willy M
21 July 1938, Norwegian. Frydenbergun 20, 7000 Trondheim, Norway. Degrees:
Magister artium (Oslo), 1965. 1965-66 Research Assistant, 1967-70 Research Fellow, Inst for Social Research, Oslo; 1970-72 Fellow, U of Oslo; 1973-76 Research Director, Inst
for Social Research, Oslo; 1977- Professor of Soc, U of Trondheim. Publs: *Hjemmet
som Arbeidsplass* (co-author), 1967; *Den Norske Velger* (co-author), 1971; *Velgere og
Politisk Frontlinjer* (co-author), 1972; *The Distant Democracy*, 1977; *Det Norske Samfunn* (contributor), 1976; *Scandinavia at the Polls* (contributor), 1977. Fields: General
sociology; political ideology; political inequality; social welfare and social class.

[1245]
MASNATA Francois
18 June 1934, Swiss. Institut de Science Politique, 5 rue de l'Université, 1005 Lausanne,
Switzerland. Degrees: Lic en droit, Lic en sci pol; Dr (IEP). Doctoral thesis: "Le parti
socialiste et la tradition démocratique en Suisse". Attaché de recherches, FNSP, Paris;
Maître de conférence, IEP, Paris; Professeur, Université de Lausanne. Publs: *Le parti
socialiste et la tradition démocratique en Suisse*, 1964; *Pouvoir blanc, révolte noire*,
1968; *Pouvoir, société et politique aux Etats-Unis* (with C Masnata-Rubattel), 1970;
Autopsie d'une Amérique, 1973. Fields: Distribution of power in capitalist society.

[1246]
MASQUELIN Jean F
5 July 1908, Belgian. 69 Avenue Louis Lepentre, 1060 Brussels, Belgium. Degrees: Dr
en droit. Avocat, Cour d'Appel, Bruxelles; Juge au Tribunal de lème Instance,
Charleroi; Conseiller d'Etat; Président du Conseil d'Etat. Publs: *Les Codes Belges*.
Fields: Public and international law.

[1247]
MASSART-PIERARD Francoise*
17 July 1943, Belgian. 7 rue de la Barre, Chaumont-Gistoux (Wavre), Belgium. Degrees:
Lic en sci pol et soc (Catholic U of Louvain), 1966. Doctoral thesis: "La dynamique de
structuration régionale dans la CEE (pour une doctrine de la région en Europe)." Assistant, Centre d'Etudes Européennes et Dept de Sci Pol, U Catholique de Louvain.
Publs: Articles in *Revue Générale, Revue des Amis de l'UCL*. Fields: European
regionalization; 'Government' in the year 2000.

[1248]
MASTELLONE Salvo
27 September 1920, Italian. 5 Via San Marcellino, Florence 50126, Italy. Degrees:
Laurea in History (Naples), 1942. 1949-59 Teacher, Italian School, Paris; 1960-66 Professor of Modern History, U of Perugia; 1966- Professor of Pol Thought, U of Perugia;
1968- Professor of Pol Thought, U of Florence. Publs: *Victor Cousin e il Risorgimento
Italiano*, 1955; *La Politica Estera del Guizot*, 1957; *Mazzini e la Giovine Italia*, 1960; *La

Reggenza di Maria de'Medici, 1962; *Pensiero Politico e Vita Culturale a Napoli nella Seconda Metà del Seicento*, 1965; *Francesco d'Adrea, Politico e Giurista, 1648-98*, 1969; *Sotria Ideologica d'Europa da Sieyès a Marx*, 1974.

[1249]
MASTERSON Michael Patrick
Degrees: BA. Assistant Lecturer, Queen's U, Belfast; Lecturer, U of St Andrews; Lecturer, U of Dundee. Publs: Articles in *British Journal of Political Science, Studies on Voltaire and the Eighteenth Century, Local Government Chronicle, Community Council News*. Fields: Political thought; local politics, particularly community councils in Scotland; French politics.

[1250]
MASTIAS Jean
1 July 1939, French. 24 rue du Chant de l'Alouette, 75013 Paris, France. Degrees: Dr en droit; Dipl (IEP Paris); Lic ès lettres. Doctoral thesis: "La réforme du Sénat de la Vème République". Maître assistant, U de Paris I. Publs: *La réforme du Sénat de la Vème République*, 1973. Fields: Parliament; communications; methodology in the social sciences; law relations; political power.

[1251]
MATHIOT André
26 February 1909, French. 31 Quai de Bourbon, Paris IVème, France. Degrees: Dr (Paris), 1934; Agrégé des Facultés de Droit, 1945. Doctoral thesis: "Les accidents causés par les travaux publics". 1937-38 Chargé de cours, Faculté de Droit, U de Grenoble; 1938-39 Chargé de cours, Faculté de Droit, U de Poitiers; 1945-57 Professeur, Faculté de Droit, U de Grenoble; 1948-58 Directeur, IEP, U de Grenoble; Chargé de cours, Inst des Hautes Etudes Internationales, Paris; 1962-67 Membre, Conseil Supérieur de la Magistrature; 1952-57 Chargé de cours, IEP, Paris; 1955- Membre du Conseil d'Administration de l'ENA and Professeur, U de Paris. Publs: *Les accidents causés par les travaux publics*, 1934; *Les territoires non autonomes et l'application de la Charte de Nations Unies*, 1951; *Le régime politique britannique*, 1955; *The British Political System*, 1958. Fields: Administrative law; constitutional law and politics in France and the US; comparative political institutions.

[1252]
MATIAS Hoikka Paavo
12 February 1935, Finnish. Tuohimaki 3B, 02130 Espoo 13, Finland. Doctoral thesis: "The Cultural Administration of the Finnish Communes". Docent of Pol Sci, U of Helsinki; Acting Professor of Community Pol, U of Tampere. Fields: Public administration; local politics.

[1253]
MATTHIAS Erich
4 August 1921, German. Fliederweg 3, 6149 Rimbach über Heppenheim, FR Germany. Degrees: Dr phil (Göttingen), 1951. Doctoral thesis: "Sozialdemokratie und Nation. Ein Beitrag zur Ideengeschichte der sozialdemokratischen Emigration in der Prager Zeit des Parteivorstandes 1933-38". 1961-65 Lehrstuhl für Wiss Pol, U of Marburg; Lehrstuhl für Zeitgeschichte und Pol Wiss, U of Mannheim. Publs: *Die deutsche Sozialdemokratie und der Osten 1914-45*, 1954; *Der Interfraktionelle Ausschuss 1917/18*, 1959; *Das Ende der Parteien 1933* (with R Morsey), 1960; *Die Regierung des Prinzen Max von Baden* (with R Morsey), 1962; *Zwischen Räten und Geheimräten. Die deutsche Revolutionsregierung 1918/19*, 1970; *German Democracy and the Triumph of Hitler* (co-ed), 1971. Fields: Government; political parties; contemporary history; political biography.

[1254]
MATTINA Liborio
16 September 1949, Italian. Via Michele, Rapisardi 14, 95131, Catania, Italy. Degrees: Degree in Philosophy (Catania). Doctoral thesis: "La Critica di Marx alla Filosofia Hegeliana del Diritto Pubblico". Researcher at ISVI, Catania; Tutor, Lecturer, Faculty of Pol Sci, U of Catania. Publs: *Democrazia Cristiana e Potere nel Mezzogiorno* (with M Caciagli *et al*); *Il Sistema Democristiano a Catania*, 1978. Fields: Political development in Southern Italy; comparative analysis of social revolutions.

[1255]
MATZ Ulrich
6 January 1937, German. Gördelerstrasse 6, D-5042 Erfstadt, FR Germany. Degrees: Dr jur. Doctoral thesis: "Rechtsgefühl und objektive Werte — ein Beitrag zur Kritik des wertethischen Naturrechts". Professor für Pol Wissenschaft und Direktor des Forschungsinstituts für Pol Wissenschaft und Europäische Fragen, U of Köln. Publs: *Grundprobleme der Demokratie* (ed), 1973; *Rechtsgefühl und objektive Werte — ein Beitrag zur Kritik des Wertethischen Naturrechts*, 1966; "Staat", in *Handbuch philosophischer Grundbegriffe*, 1974; *Politik und Gewalt. Zur Theorie des demokratischen Verfassungsstaates und der Revolution*, 1975; "Emanzipations postulat und Demokratiemodell des Grundgesetzes", *Civitas*, 1973; *Verteidigung der Politik gegen die politische Theologie*, 1973; "Das Gewaltproblem im Neomarxismus", in *Die Gewalt in Politik, Religion und Gesellschaft* (E J M Kroker (ed)), 1976; *Regierbarkeit. Studien zu ihrer Problematisierung* (with W Hennis and P Graf Kielmansegg (eds)), 1977. Fields: Political theory.

[1256]
MAURER Herbert
20 September 1922, Austrian. Hagnerstrasse 3, A-4020 Linz-Donau, Austria. Degrees: Dr phil (Vienna), 1948; Mag phil. Doctoral thesis: "Die Grenzen Oberösterreichs" (The Boundaries of Upper Austria). Publs: *Atlas of Upper Austria* (ed), 1958-1969; Author of 20 maps on demography, economy, traffic; *The Development of Schools in Upper Austria since 1945*, 1972; *Elections in Upper Austria 1945-1967*, 1968. Fields: Demography; elections; social geography; cartography; educational statistics.

[1257]
MAUS Ingeborg
12 October 1937, German. Anne Frankstrasse 8, D-6200 Wiesbaden, FR Germany. Degrees: PhD. Doctoral thesis: "Die Lehre vom Pouvoir Constituant. Eine politologische Untersuchung zur bürgerlichen Rechts und Verfassungstheorie im organisierten Kapitalismus unter besonderer Berücksichtigung der Theorie Carl Schmitts". 1966-70 Wiss Assistent, Inst für Pol, Frankfurt; 1971-77 Lehrbeauftragerin am Fachbereich Gesellschaftswissenschaften, Frankfurt; 1977- Dozentin, Fachbereich Gesellschaftswissenschaften, Frankfurt. Publs: "Zur 'Zäsur' von 1933 in der Theorie Carl Schmitts", in *Kritische Justiz*, 1969; "Aspekte des Rechtspositivismus in der entwickelten Industriegesellschaft", in *Konkretionen politischer Theorie und Praxis*, 1972; "Die Basis als Überbau oder 'Realistische' Rechtstheorie", in *Probleme der Marxistischen Rechtstheorie* (H Rottlethner (ed)), 1975; *Bürgerliche Rechtstheorie und Faschismus. Zur Sozialen Funktion und Aktuellen Wirkung der Theorie Carl Schmitts*, 1976; "La Relaction actual entre Ideologia y Realidad Social: El Ejemplo de la Teoria del Derecho en la Republica Federal Alemana", in *Derecho, Razon Practica e Ideologia — Anales de la Catedra 'Francisco Suarez'*, 1978. Fields: Theory of constitutions; sociology of law; fascism; conservatism; history of political theory.

[1258]
MAWHOOD Philip North*
20 September 1924, British. Institute of Local Government Studies, University of Birmingham, PO Box 363, Birmingham B15 2TT, England. Degrees: MA (Cambridge), 1951; D Phil (Sussex), 1971. Doctoral thesis: "Decentralized Government in Tropical Africa: A Comparison of the Cases of Cameroon and Tanganyika". 1949-64 Administrative Officer, District Commissioner, Head of Division, Ministry of Local Government, Tanzania Government; 1964-67 UNESCO Adviser, African Training and Research Centre in Administration for Development, Tangier, Morocco; Lecturer, Member of Development Administration Group, U of Birmingham. Publs: *The Development of Urban Local Government in Tanganyika, 1959-60*, 1961; *Local Government in Tanganyika*, 1964; *The Creation of Municipalities in the New Hebrides: Municipal Finance*, 1972; "Decentralization for Development: A Lost Cause?", in *Local Politics, Democracy and Development* (Wiatr and Cazzola (eds)). Fields: Comparative local government in Europe and the Third World; formal and informal measures of local autonomy; structures of supervision and support from the centre; institution-building at the local level; development administration, especially in tropical Africa; national political cultures and inherited structures of administration; communication as a constraint to development; the allocation of public resources by regional and local bodies.

[1259]
MAY Roy Alfred
31 May 1938, British. 44 Northbrook Road, Solihull, Warwickshire, England. Degrees: BSc; MSc, 1969. Principal Lecturer in Pol, Lanchester Polytechnic. Fields: Politics in West Africa, with specific reference to Chad and peasant consciousness.

[1260]
MAYER-TASCH Peter Cornelius
13 March 1938, German. Am Seeberg 11, 8919 Schondorf/Ammersee, FR Germany. Degrees: Dr jur. Doctoral thesis: "Thomas Hobbes und das Widerstandsrecht". Professor, U of Mainz; Professor of Pol Sci and Theory of Law, U of Munich; Managing Director, Geschwister Scholl Inst für Pol Wissenschaft. Publs: *Thomas Hobbes und das Widerstandsrecht*, 1965; *Korporativismus und Autoritarismus*, 1971; *Guerillakrieg und Völkerrecht*, 1972; *Hobbes und Rousseau*, 1976; *Kulturlandschaft in Gefahr*, 1976; *Die Bürgerinitiativbewegung*, 1977; *Die Verfassungen Europas*, 1975; *Energiepolitik ohne Basis* (with C Amery and Meyer-Abich), 1978.

[1261]
MAYNTZ Renate
28 April 1929, German. c/o Universität zu Köln, FR Germany. Degrees: BA; PhD (Berlin), 1953; Habilitation, 1957; Dr phil hc (Uppsala), 1977. 1958-59 Fellow, Rockefeller Foundation; 1959-60 Visiting Assistant Professor, Columbia U; 1965 Professor of Soc, Free U of Berlin. 1971- Professor of Soc, Hochschule für Verwaltungswissenschaften, Speyer; Professor of Soc, Universität zu Köln. Publs: *Formalisierte Modelle in der Soziologie* (ed), 1967; *Bürokratische Organisation* (ed), 1968; *Theodor Geiger: On Social Order and Mass Society* (ed), 1969; *Einführung in die Methoden der empirischen Soziologie* (with K Kolm and P Hübner), 1969; *Soziologen im Studium* (ed), 1970; *Planungsorganisation - die Diskussion um die Reform von Regierung und Verwaltung* (with F W Scharpf), 1973; *Personal im öffentlichen Dienst-Eintritt und Karrieren* (with N Luhmann), 1973; *Policy-Making in the German Federal Bureaucracy* (with F W Scharpf), 1975. Fields: Organizational analysis; decision-making theory; sociology of administration; public administration.

[1262]
McALLISTER Ian
2 December 1950, British. 125 Dowanhill Street, Glasgow G12, Scotland. Degrees: BA; MSc (Strathclyde); PhD (Strathclyde). Doctoral thesis: "The Ballot not the Bullet: The Northern Ireland Social Democratic and Labour Party". 1976-77 Research Fellow, Inst of Irish Studies, Queen's U, Belfast; 1977- Research Fellow, Centre for the Study of Public Policy, U of Strathclyde. Publs: "Political Opposition in Northern Ireland: The National Democratic Party", *Economic and Social Review*, 1975; *The 1975 Northern Ireland Convention Election*, 1975; "Social Influences on Voters and Non-Voters: A Note on the Two Northern Ireland Elections", *Political Studies*, 1976; *The Northern Ireland Social Democratic and Labour Party*, 1977; "The Legitimacy of Opposition: The Collapse of the 1974 Northern Ireland Executive", in *Eire-Ireland*, 1977; "Bi-Confessionalism in a Confessional Party System" (with B Wilson), *Economic and Social Review*, 1978. Fields: Northern Ireland politics; political parties in Scotland and Wales; comparative nationalism in the UK.

[1263]
McAULEY Mary
25 September 1938, British. Department of Government, University of Essex, Wivenhoe Park, Colchester CO4 3SQ, England. Degrees: BA; D Phil (Oxon), 1968. Doctoral thesis: "The Settlement of Labour Disputes in the USSR 1957-65". Assistant ed, *Soviet Studies*, U of Glasgow; 1965-66 Lecturer in Pol, U of York; Lecturer, Senior Lecturer in Government, U of Essex. Publs: *Labour Disputes in Soviet Russia 1957-65*; *Politics and the Soviet Union*. Fields: Labour relations in the Soviet Union and Eastern Europe; contemporary Soviet politics; comparative politics.

[1264]
McAUSLAN John Patrick William
19 January 1937, British. 2 Lillington Road, Leamington Spa CX32 5YR, England. Degrees: BA; BCL (Oxon). 1961-66 Lecturer in Law, U Coll, Dar es Salaam, Tanzania; 1966-68 Lecturer in Law, LSE; 1968- Senior Lecturer, Reader, Professor of Law, U of Warwick. Publs: *Public Law and Political Change in Kenya* (with Y P Ghai), 1970; *Land, Law and Planning*, 1975. Fields: Planning and housing in the UK; urbanization in the Third World.

[1265]
McCARTHY Michael Anthony
16 February 1953, British. 111 Denison Street, Beeston, Nottingham NG9 1DQ, England. Degrees: BSc; MA (Keele). Part-time Lecturer in Pol, North Staffordshire Polytechnic; Lecturer in Pol, Research Associate, Trent Polytechnic. Publs: "Organizing the Independent Centre", *Political Quarterly*, 1978. Fields: Pressure group politics; the politics of poverty; tripartism and corporatism; democratic theory/participation; environmental politics; bureaucracy/political advisers.

[1266]
McCARTHY William Edward John (Lord)
30 July 1925, British. 4 William Orchard Close, Old Headington, Oxford. Degrees: MA; D Phil. Doctoral thesis: "The Closed Shop in British Unions". 1959-63 Research Fellow, Nuffield Coll, U of Oxford; 1965-68 Research Director, Royal Commission on Trade Unions and Employers' Associations; 1968-69 Fellow, Oxford Management Centre; Fellow, Nuffield Coll, U of Oxford. Publs: *The Closed Shop in Britain*, 1964; *Employers' Associations*, 1967; *Shop Stewards*, 1967; *Disputes Procedures in Britain* (with A Marsh), 1968; *Trade Unions*, 1970; *Coming to Terms with Trade Unions*, 1973. Fields: Industrial relations and labour economics.

[1267]
McCAULEY Martin
18 October 1934, British. 10 Greenway, Totteridge, London N20 8ED, England. Degrees: BA; PhD, 1973. Doctoral thesis: "Krushchev and the Virgin Lands 1953-65: Some Political and Economic Aspects". Lecturer in Russian and Soviet Institutions, U of London. Publs: *The Russian Revolution and the Soviet State 1917-1921*, 1975; *Khrushchev and the Development of Soviet Agriculture*; *The Virgin Land Programme 1953-1964*, 1976; *Communist Power in Europe 1944-1949* (ed), 1977; "Kazakhstan and The Virgin Lands Programme 1953-64", *Mizan*, 1970; "Liberal Democrats in the Soviet Zone of Germany 1945-47", *Journal of Contemporary History*, 1977. Fields: The USSR since 1917; the Communist party of the Soviet Union; the politics of economic reform; the politics of Soviet agriculture; the Socialist Unity party (SED); GDR-USSR relations.

[1268]
McDOUGALL Michael James*
12 December 1939, British. Department of Politics, Nottingham University, University Park, Nottingham NG7 2RD, England. Degrees: BSc (Econ). 1963-65 Lecturer in Pol Sci, U of Khartoum, Sudan; 1966- Lecturer in Pol, U of Nottingham. Publs: "Tightening up Whitehall, An Analysis of Government Machinery Changes", *Nottingham Council of Social Service Bulletins*, 1971. Fields: Political attitudes to discretionary powers of ministers.

[1269]
McGWIRE Michael Kane*
9 December 1924, British. Hayes, Durlston, Swanage, Dorset, England. Degrees: BSc. Lecturer in Strategic Studies, U Coll of Wales. Publs: *The Soviet Navy in the Seventies*, 1972. Fields: Soviet maritime policy; the use of the world's maritime spaces.

[1270]
McKAY David Hamilton
12 January 1944, British. Department of Government, University of Essex, England. Degrees: BSc; MA (Essex), 1970; PhD (Essex), 1975. 1967-68 Lecturer in Econ, West London Coll; 1970-71 Graduate Fellow, U of Wisconsin; 1977-78 Visiting Associate Professor, U of Cornell; 1972- Lecturer, U of Essex. Publs: *Housing and Race in Industrial Society*, 1977; *Government and Urban Change* (with A Cox), 1978; plus articles on British, American and urban politics. Fields: US and British politics; urban policy; comparative public policy.

[1271]
McKENZIE Robert Trelford
11 September 1917, Canadian. London School of Economics, Houghton Street, Aldwych, London WC2, England. Degrees: BA; PhD (London); LLD (Simon Fraser). 1949- LSE; 1964- Professor of Soc (with special reference to Pol), LSE. Publs: *British Political Parties*, 1963; *Angels in Marble*; *Working Class Conservatives in Urban England*, 1968. Fields: Political parties; voting behaviour; mass media and politics; working class political attitudes; Marxism and political sociology.

[1272]
McKINLAY Robert Davison
7 June 1946, British. Rose Cottage, Westbourne Road, Lancaster, England. Degrees: B Soc Sci; B Phil; D Phil. Doctoral thesis: "Military Intervention and Performance". 1975 Visiting Assistant Professor, U of Pennsylvania; 1970- Lecturer, U of Lancaster. Publs: Various articles on performance of military regimes, aid allocation, international

interdependence, and voting. Fields: Logic of social science inquiry; comparative politics; international political economy.

[1273]
McKNIGHT Allan Douglas
14 January 1918, Australian. 55 Cowley Drive, Woodingdean, Brighton BN2 6WD, England. Degrees: B of Laws (Sydney), 1938. 1952-54 Deputy Secretary, Australian Cabinet Office; 1955-58 Permanent Secretary, Dept of the Army; 1958-64 Executive Member, Australian Atomic Energy Commission; 1964-68 Inspector-General, IAEA; 1968-72 Visiting Fellow, Science Policy Research Unit, U of Sussex; 1972-77 Lecturer, Civil Service Coll. Publs: *Atomic Safeguards*, 1971; *Scientists Abroad*, 1971; *Nuclear Non-Proliferation*, 1970; *Science Law and Pollution* (co-ed), 1973. Fields: Constitutional law, federalism and the EEC; international scientific activities; public administration with particular reference to law, science policy and administration of scientific activities.

[1274]
McLEAN Iain S
13 September 1946, British. University College, Oxford, England. Degrees: B Phil; MA (Oxon), 1972; D Phil (Oxon), 1972. Doctoral thesis: "The Labour Movement in Clydeside Politics, 1914-22". 1969-71 Research Fellow, Nuffield Coll, U of Oxford; 1971-78 Lecturer in Pol, U of Newcastle-upon-Tyne; 1978- Fellow in Pol, Lecturer, U Coll, Oxford. Publs: *Keir Hardie*, 1975; *Elections*, 1976; plus various articles in *Political Studies, Parliamentary Affairs, Political Quarterly*. Fields: Urban politics, especially Glasgow and local government; centre-periphery politics in the UK; aspects of political theory, especially Hobbes; social choice theory.

[1275]
McLELLAN David
10 February 1940, British. 13 Ivy Lane, Canterbury, Kent, England. Degrees: BA; MA (Oxon), 1968; D Phil (Oxon), 1968. Doctoral thesis: "The Social and Political Thought of the Young Hegelians and its Influence on the Genesis of Marxism". Visiting Professor, State U of New York, USA; Guest Fellow in Pol, Indian Inst of Advanced Study, Simla; Professor in Pol, U of Kent. Publs: *Marx before Marxism*, 1970; *Karl Marx: The Early Texts*, 1971; *Marx's Grundrisse*, 1971; *The Thought of Karl Marx*, 1971; *Karl Marx: His Life and Thought*, 1973; *Marx*, 1975; *Engels*, 1977; *Karl Marx: Selected Writings*, 1977. Fields: Marx; communist parties in India; Indian politics; Marxism.

[1276]
McVEY Ruth Thomas*
22 October 1930, American. 15 Ladbroke Walk, London W11, England. Degrees: BA; MA (USA), 1954; PhD (USA), 1961. Doctoral thesis: "The Comintern and the Rise of Communism in Indonesia". 1961-63 Research Associate, Southeast Asia Studies, U of Yale, USA: 1963-65 Research Associate, Center for International Studies, MIT Cambridge, USA; 1965-68 Research Associate, Visiting Professor, Southeast Asia Program, Cornell U, USA: 1968-69 Visiting Professor, Southeast Asian Pol, U of Washington, USA; 1969- Lecturer, Southeast Asian Pol, SOAS, U of London. Publs: *The Development of Indonesian Communism and its Relations with Moscow and Peking*, 1954; *The Soviet View of the Indonesian Revolution*, 1957; *The Calcutta Conference and the Southeast Asian Uprisings*, 1958; *The Communist Rebellion in Indonesia of 1926-27: Key Documents* (ed), 1961; *A Bibliography of Soviet Publications on Southeast Asia*, 1961; *The Rise of Indonesian Communism*, 1965. Fields: International communist movement; social radicalism in Southeast Asia; culture and politics.

[1277]
MECHTERSCHEIMER Alfred
13 August 1939, German. Postfach, D-8011 Vaterstetten, FR Germany. Degrees: Dipl Pol; Dr rer Pol. Doctoral thesis: "Die politischen Entscheidungsbedingungen und die Konkurrenz der militärischen und nichtmilitärischen Interessen bei dem internationalen Rüstungsprogramm MCRA". Hochschule der Bundeswehr, München. Publs: *Rüstung in der Bundesrepublik: Geschichte und Funktion des grössen westeuropäischen Rüstungsprogramms*, 1977.

[1278]
MEDARD Jean-Francois
25 November 1934, French. 161 rue du Dr Nancel Penard, 33600 Bordeaux, France. Degrees: Dr d'Etat (Bordeaux), 1966; Dipl (IEP Bordeaux), 1959; Lic, 1957. Doctoral thesis: "Communauté locale et organisation communautaire aux Etats-Unis". 1964-73 Assistant, Maître-Assistant, U de Bordeaux; 1973-77 Maître de conférences, U de Yaoundé, Cameroun; 1977 Professeur, IEP, Bordeaux. Publs: *Communauté locale et organisation communautaire aux Etats-Unis*, 1968; "Les communautés urbaines: renforcement ou déclin de l'autonomie locale?", *Revue de Droit Public et de Science Politique en France et à l'Étranger*, 1968; "Les structures politico-administratives de l'agglomération bordelaise", *Revue de Géographie des Pyrénées et du Sud Ouest*, 1971; "La recherche de cumul des mandats sous la Vème République", in *Les facteurs locaux de la vie politique nationale*, 1972; "Le rapport de clientèle des phénomènes social à l'analyse politique. L'Etat sous-développé du Cameroun", *RFSP*, 1976. Fields: Africa; Third World; dependency; clientelism.

[1279]
MEDDING Peter Y
26 August 1938, Australian. 30 Jabotinsky Street, Jerusalem, Israel. Degrees: BA; MA (Melbourne), 1962; D Phil (Harvard), 1970. Doctoral thesis: "Mapai: The Israel Labour Party: Political Organization and Government in a New Society". 1966-78 Lecturer, Senior Lecturer, Reader, Dept of Pol, Monash U; Associate Professor, Dept of Pol Sci, Hebrew U, Jerusalem. Publs: *From Assimilation to Group Survival: A Political and Sociological Study of an Australian Jewish Community*, 1968; *Mapai in Israel: Political Organization and Government in a New Society*, 1972; *Jews in Australian Society* (ed), 1973. Fields: Political sociology; political parties, with special reference to Israel; power and democracy in contemporary industrial society; ethnicity.

[1280]
MEDHURST Kenneth Noel
25 December 1938, British. 31 Mauldeth Road, Manchester M20 9NF, England. Degrees: MA (Edinburgh), 1961; PhD (Manchester), 1969. Doctoral thesis: "The Legal and Political Institutions of Spanish Local Government". Assistant Lecturer, Senior Lecturer in Government, U of Manchester. Publs: *Government in Spain*, 1973; *Allende's Chile* (ed), 1973; *The Basques and Catalans*, 1977; *The Politics of Colombian Catholicism*, 1978. Fields: Comparative politics, with special reference to the Iberian Peninsular; the politics of Latin America; religion and politics.

[1281]
MEERTS Paul Willem
5 September 1946, Dutch. Badhuisweg 211. The Hague, The Netherlands. Degrees. Drs, 1973. Sci Co-operator, Society of International Affairs. Publs: *Members of Parliament 1815-30; Members of Parliament 1914-15; Members of the Royal Court 1813-1978*. Fields: Dutch parliamentary history; Dutch political elites; international affairs.

[1282]
MEGERLE Klaus Reiner
1 February 1942, German. Echtemeyerstrasse 4, 1000 Berlin 37, FR Germany. Degrees: Dr phil. Doctoral thesis: "Deutsche Aussenpolitik 1925. Ansatz zu aktivem Revisionismus". Assistant Professor für geschichtliche Grundlagen der Pol. Publs: *Deutsche Aussenpolitik 1925. Ansatz zu aktivem Revisionismus*, 1975; "Danzig, Westpreussen und Oberschlesien. Zur Revisionspolitik der Weimarer Republik gegenüber Polen in der Locarnodiplomatie", in *Jahrbuch für die Geschichte Mittel-und Ostdeutschlands*, 1976; "Der Beitrag Württembergs zur Industrialisierung Deutschlands", in *Zeitschrift für Württenbergische Landesgeschichte*, 1976. Fields: Social and economic history of 19th and 20th century; history of the Weimar Republic; problems of German politics from World War II to the foundation of the Federal Republic.

[1283]
MEHROTRA Sri Ram*
23 June 1931, Indian. Department of Economic and Political Studies, School of Oriental and African Studies, University of London, London WC1, England. Degrees: MA (Allahabad), 1950; PhD (London), 1960. Doctoral thesis: "The Idea of Commonwealth in India, 1900-29". Lecturer, U of Sangror. 1950-58 MP, India; Lecturer in S Asian Pol, SOAS, U of London. Publs: *India and the Commonwealth 1885-1929*, 1965. Fields: History of the Indian National Congress 1885-1947.

[1284]
MEIER Kurt G
9 May 1943, German. Im Klingen 2, D-6905 Schrieheim, FR Germany. Degrees: Dipl; Dr phil. Doctoral thesis: "Interesse, Macht und Einfluss. Entwicklung eines begrifflichen Bezugsrahmens und Interpretation einer historischen Episode". Assistant in Soc, Dept of Soc Sci, U of Mannheim. Fields: Political sociology; interest groups; organizations; theories of state-society relations; institution building.

[1285]
MEIJER Hans A B
3 September 1922, Swedish. Bondegatan 3, 58263 Linköping, Sweden. Degrees: PhD. Doctoral thesis: "Swedish ad hoc Councillors". Professor in Pol Sci, U of Stockholm; Member and former President, Committee for Higher Education and Research, Council of Europe; Chairman, Bank of Sweden Tercentenary Foundation; Vice-Chancellor, U of Linköping.

[1286]
MEISSNER Boris
10 August 1915, German. 5000 Köln, Kleine Budengasse 1, FR Germany. Degrees: Dipl rer Oec; Dr jur (Hamburg). Doctoral thesis; "Die sowjetische Intervention im Baltikum und die völkerrechtliche Problematik der baltischen Frage". 1947-53, Senior Research Fellow, Forschungsstelle für Völkerrecht und ausländisches öffentliches Recht, U of Hamburg; 1953-59 Diplomatic Service, Legationsrat I Klasse; 1959-64, Professor and Director of Seminar für Pol, Gesellschaft und Recht Osteuropas, U of Kiel; 1961-71 Member of the Directorate, Bundesinstitut für ostwissenschaftliche und internationale Studien, Köln; 1964- Professor and Director of Inst für Ostrecht, U of Köln; Member of the Directorate, Ostkolleg Köln, Honorary Member, Deutsche Gesellschaft für Osteuropakunde, Berlin. Publs: *Sowjetgesellschaft im Wandel*, 1966; *Die Breshnew-Doktrin*, 1969 (English ed. 1972); *Grundfragen sowjetischer Aussenpolitik*, 1970; *Moskau-Bonn, Die Beziehungen zwischen der Sowjetunion und der Bundesrepublik Deutschland*, 1975. Fields: Law and political science; USSR; GDR; Baltic States.

[1287]
MELICH Anna
17 November 1945, Spanish. 22 Avenue Weber, 1208, Geneva, Switzerland. Degrees: Lic ès sci pol (Geneva). Doctoral thesis: "La socialisation pré-politique des enfants en Suisse". Assistante, Dept of Pol Sci, U of Geneva. Publs: Various articles on political socialization. Fields: Political socialization; political psychology; Swiss politics.

[1288]
MELICHAR Erwin
26 September 1913, Austrian. Schulerstrasse 20, A-1010 Vienna, Austria. Degrees: Dr Law (Vienna), 1936. 1937-56 Civil Servant; 1947 Lecturer, U of Vienna; 1956 Professor of Law, U of Graz; 1958 Member, Constitutional Court; 1963 Professor of Public Law, U of Vienna; 1977- President, Constitutional Court. Publs: *Gerichtsbarkeit und Verwaltung im staatlichen und kannonischen Recht*, 1948; *Das Besoldungsrecht der Bundesbediensteten*, 1953; *Reisegebührenvorschrift*, 1955; *Das Verwaltungsverfahren, Finanzverfahren und Rechtstaat*, 1962; *Die Entwicklung der Grundrechte in Österreich*, 1964; *Von der Gewalttrennung in formellen und materiellen Sinn*, 1970. Fields: Constitutional and administrative law, especially separation of powers; Austrian administration; human rights; Austrian federalism; constitutional court.

[1289]
MELLING John
17 February 1910, British. 33 Bounds Oak Way, Tunbridge Wells TN4 0TW, England. Degrees: BA; MA (Oxon), 1947. Deputy Director, Dept of Adult Education and Extra-Mural Studies, U of Leeds; Associate Professor, Dept of Pol Sci, McMaster U; Acting Dean, Faculty of Soc Sci, McMaster U; Staff Tutor, Open U. Publs: *Undergraduate Social Welfare Education* (co-author), 1964; *The Native Peoples of Canada*, 1967. Fields: Responsibility in the public administration sub-systems of democracies; the place of law in the study of public administration.

[1290]
MENDL Wolfgang Marco Louis
1 May 1926, British. 112 Langley Way, Watford WD1 3EE, Hertfordshire, England. Degrees: MA (Cambridge), 1949; PhD (London), 1966. 1950-53 History Master, Winnington School, Yorks; 1953-61 Voluntary Service Worker in US, Japan, France; Reader in War Studies, King's Coll, U of London. Publs: *Deterrence and Persuasion: French Nuclear Armament in the Context of National Policy 1949-69*, 1970; *Prophets and Reconcilers: Reflections on the Quaker Peace Testimony*, 1978; *Issues in Japan's China Policy*, 1978. Fields: Japanese foreign and security policy; civil-military relations; problems of defensive strategies and non-violent resistance; international relations.

[1291]
MENDRAS Henri
16 May 1927, French. 11 rue Cassette, 75006 Paris, France. Degrees: Dr ès lettres (Paris-Sorbonne), 1967. Doctoral thesis: "La fin des paysans". Directeur de recherche, CNRS; Professeur, IEP, Paris. Publs: *Etudes de sociologie rurale*, 1953; *Eléments de méthode sociologique* (co-author), 1953; *Les paysans et la modernisation de l'agriculture*, 1958; *Les paysans et la politique dans la France contemporaine*, 1958; *Société paysanne*, 1977. Fields: Rural sociology.

[1292]
MERLE Marcel Louis
30 August 1923, French. 23 rue du Laos, Paris XVème, France. Degrees: Dr en droit (Paris), 1948; Dipl (Ecole Libre des Sci Pol, Paris), 1946; Agrégé des Facultés de Droit, 1950. 1950-67 Professeur, Faculté de Droit, U de Bordeaux; 1957-67 Directeur, IEP, U de Bordeaux; 1967-70 Professeur, Faculté de Droit, U de Paris; Professeur, U de Paris I. Publs: *Le procès de Nuremberg et le châtiment des grands criminels de guerre*, 1949; *La vie internationale*, 1963; *Les églises chrétiennes et la décolonisation* (ed), 1967; *Pacifisme et internationalisme*, 1966; *L'anticolonialisme européen de Las Casas à Marx*, 1969; *L'Afrique noire contemporaine* (ed), 1968; *Les partis politiques en Grande-Bretagne* (with A Mabileau), 1965, 1967, 1972; *Sociologie des relations internationales* (traduction espagnole), 1974, 1976. Fields: International relations; domestic and foreign policy; British political parties; Africa; history of political ideas.

[1293]
MERVIN David
31 July 1933, British. Oakhurst, Byfield Road, Priors Marston, Rugby, Warwickshire, England. Degrees: BA; PhD (Cornell). Doctoral thesis: "The Senate Opposition to the League of Nations". Senior Lecturer, Dept of Pol, U of Warwick. Publs: Articles in *Political Studies*, *Journal of American Studies*. Fields: US politics particularly US congress; politics and race; comparative government.

[1294]
MEYER Gerd J M
8 July 1942, German. Peter-Rossegger-Strasse 8, D-7410 Reutlingen, FR Germany. Degrees: Dr phil, 1969; Habilitation, 1976. Doctoral thesis: "The Foreign Policy of the USSR towards Germany in 1952". Professor of Pol Sci, Inst für Pol, U of Tübingen. Publs: *Die sowjetische Deutschlandpolitik im Jahr 1952*, 1970; *Bürokratischer Sozialismus: Eine Analyse des sowjetischen Herrschaftssystems*, 1977; *Sozialistische Systeme. Theorie und Strukturanalyse*, 1978. Fields: Socialist systems; election research; political participation; political parties; bureaucracy.

[1295]
MEYER Poul
2 February 1916, Danish. Institute of Political Science, University of Aarhus, 800 Aarhus, Denmark. Degrees: Dr jur (Copenhagen), 1949. Doctoral thesis: "Danske Bylag" (The Organization of Danish Farmers in Villages before 1800). 1942-59 Civil Servant, Ministry of Agriculture; 1952-59 Assistant Professor, U of Copenhagen; 1959-Professor of Pol Sci, U of Aarhus. Publs: *Administrative Organizations* (German (ed)), 1962; *Systemic Aspects of Public Administration*, 1973. Fields: Public administration; government in Denmark.

[1296]
MEYER Wim
13 June 1951, Dutch. Marshallplein 99, Rÿswÿk (ZH), The Netherlands. Doctoral thesis: "Competition Policy in the Netherlands". Planning Bureau of Provincial Government of Zuid, Holland. Fields: Public finance; public administration.

[1297]
MICHALSKY Helga
18 October 1941, German. Im Moselsgrund 15, 69 Heidelberg, FR Germany. Doctoral thesis: "Bildungspolitik und Bildungsreform in Preussen. Die Bedeutung des Unterrichtswesens als Faktor sozialen und politischen Wandels beim Übergang von der ständischen zur bürgerlich-Liberalen Gesellschaft". Wiss Assistent, Dept of Pol Sci, U of Heidelberg. Fields: Social policy; society and politics of the GDR.

[1298]
MICHELAT Guy*
11 November 1933, French. 38 rue Falguière, Paris XVème, France. Degrees: Dipl de Psychologie Appliquée; Dipl de Psychologie Expérimentale; Dipl de Psychologie Sociale (Paris). Chargé d'études, Centre de Socio-analyse; Chercheur, Commissariat Général Productivité, Laboratoire Psychologie sociale et Centre d'Etudes Sociales; Attaché de recherche (Sociologie), CNRS; Chargé de recherches (Sociologie), CNRS. Publs: *Attitudes et comportements politiques à Boulogne Billancourt. Enquête par panel (1965-67)* (with F Bon), 1960; *Dimensions du nationalisme* (with J-P H Thomas), 1966. Fields: French attitudes to authority and communists; psychosociological study of the Left and the Right.

[1299]
MICKEL Wolfgang Wilhelm
6 April 1929, German. Heuchelheimer Strasse 122, 6380 Bad Homburg, FR Germany. Degrees: Dr phil; Habilitation. Professor of Pol Sci, Pädagogische Hochschule Karlsruhe. Publs: *Methodik des politischen Unterrichts*, 1974; *Konfliktfeld: Internationale Politik*, 1974; *Europäische Einiwgungspolitik*, 1974; *Europäische Bildungspolitik*, 1978. Fields: International politics; political education; European integration policy.

[1300]
MIDDENDORP Cees P
31 October 1942, Dutch. Weteringschans 88, Amsterdam, The Netherlands. Degrees: Dr. Doctoral thesis: "Progressiveness and Conservatism: The Fundamental Dimension of Ideological Controversy and their Relationship to Social Class". Research Fellow, The Netherlands Organization for the Advancement of Pure Research; Head, Steinmetz Archives. Publs: "Determinants of Premarital Sexual Permissiveness, A Secondary Analysis", *Journal of Marriage and the Family*, 1970; "Cultural Change in the Netherlands in the Late Sixties and its Relations to TV Exposure", in *Secondary Analysis of Sample Surveys: Use and Needs*, 1973; "Replication Through Reconceptualization: Progressiveness and Conservatism and the Relation Between Social Class and Premarital Sexual Permissiveness", *Sociologische Gids*, 1974; "The Structure of Social Attitudes in Three Countries: Tests of a Criteria Referent Theory", *International Journal of Psychology*, 1976; "Rejoinder", *Netherlands Journal of Sociology*, 1977; *Progressiveness and Conservatism. The Fundamental Dimensions of Ideological Controversy and their Relationship to Social Class*, 1978; "The Structure of the Progressive Conservative Controversy: I; Attitudinal Referents in the Netherlands, 1975", *Acta Politica*, 1978; The Structure of the Progressive Conservative Controversy: II; A Structural Analysis of Ideological Developments in the Netherlands, 1970-1975", *Acta Politica*, 1978. Fields: Political sociology; social psychology; political psychology; methodology; statistics.

[1301]
MIDGAARD Knut Olav*
11 February 1931, Norwegian. Institute of Political Science, PO Box 1097, Blindern, Oslo 3, Norway. Degrees: Magistergrad in the History of Ideas (Oslo), 1959. 1959-68 Research Fellow; 1968-70 Assistant Professor; 1971- Associate Professor, Inst of Pol Sci, U of Oslo. Publs: *Forskning i Fredens og Friheterns Tjeneste* (with A Naess), 1958; *Strategisk Tenkning: Neon Spillteoretiske Emner med Sorlig Tank på Internasional Politikk*, 1967; *Communication and Strategy*, 1970. Fields: Theory of debates, negotiations, and aggregation of preferences; international negotiations on the regulation of whaling; negotiations on the extension of the Common Market.

[1302]
MIDGLEY Ernest Brian Francis
16 September 1927, British. 111 Brighton Place, Aberdeen AB1 6RT, England.
Degrees: BA; M Phil (LSE), 1967. Doctoral thesis: "The Resources of Thomism for
Dealing with the Nuclear Problems of Modern Warfare". 1951-60, Assistant Principal,
Principal, Ministry of Supply; 1960-1965 Principal, Ministry of Health; 1967- Assistant
Lecturer, Lecturer, Senior Lecturer, U of Aberdeen. Publs: *The Natural Law Tradition
and the Theory of International Relations*, 1975; "Natural Law and the Renewal of the
Philosophy of International Relations", in *Yearbook of World Affairs*, 1975;
"Authority, Alienation and Revolt", *Aberdeen University Review*, 1976; "Natural
Law and Fundamental Rights", *American Journal of Jurisprudence*, 1976; "Tradi-
tionalism and Modernism in Ecological and Liberationist Ideology", *Catholic Social
Review*, 1977. Fields: Philosophy of natural law; critique of the ideology of Max
Weber; critique of ecological and liberationist ideologies.

[1303]
MIGLIO Gianfranco*
11 January 1918, Italian. Salita dei Cappuccini 23, Como, Italy. Degrees: Dr in Legge
(Catholic U of Milan), 1940; Libero Docente, Dean and Ord Professor, Faculty of Pol
Sci, Catholic U of Milan. Fields: History of political theory and institutions.

[1304]
MIGNONE Andrea
29 April 1947, Italian. Via Chiappino 35, 15010 Ponzone, Italy. Degrees: Laurea. Doctoral thesis: "Pressure Groups in American Political Sociology. Theory and Critics".
Assistant Professor of Soc. Publs: "L'Attività Politica dei Gruppi di Pressione: Note
sul Lobby", *Controcorrente*, 1972; "I Gruppi di Pressione: Note di Terminologia", in
Annali Facoltà Scienze Politiche, 1973; *Gruppi di Interesse e Gruppi di Pressione*, 1974.
Fields: Political parties and pressure groups; political systems theory; political
sociology.

[1305]
MILLAR Jean Audrey*
5 May 1940, British. Furness College, University of Lancaster, Bailrigg, Lancaster,
England. Degrees: BSc; PhD (Hamburg), 1969. Doctoral thesis: "Die Rolle der
Sachverständigen in der politischen Willensbildung und im Entscheidungsprozess".
1969-70 Lecturer in Pol, U of Lancaster; Senior Researcher, Research Group for Planning Theory, Royal Inst of Technology, Stockholm; Lecturer in Behaviour in Organizations, U of Lancaster. Publs: *Die Rolle der Sachverständigen in der politischen
Willensbildung und im Entscheidungsprozess*, 1969.

[1306]
MILLER David Leslie
8 March 1946, British. 57 Christchurch Road, Norwich, England. Degrees: BA; B Phil
(Oxon); D Phil (Oxon). Doctoral thesis: "Social Justice". 1969-76 Lecturer in Pol, U of
Lancaster; 1976 Visiting Lecturer in Pol Sci, U of Ibadan; 1976- Lecturer in Pol, U of
East Anglia. Publs: *Social Justice*, 1976. Fields: Political theory; political thought of
Hume; aspects of socialist and anarchist theory.

[1307]
MILLER William Lockley
12 August 1943, British. Department of Politics, University of Strathclyde, McCance Building, Richmond Street, Glasgow G1 1XQ, Scotland. Degrees: MA (Edinburgh). 1965; PhD (Newcastle), 1970. Doctoral thesis: "The Evaluation of Large Scale Information Retrieval Systems". 1971-72 Consultant, BBC, Scotland; 1968- Lecturer, U of Strathclyde; 1969-75 Consultant, Independent Television News. Publs: *Electoral Dynamics*, 1977; Articles in *Journal of the Royal Statistical Society, Political Studies, EJPR, BJPS, Quality & Quantity*. Fields: Party strategies and electoral behaviour in Britain; methodology of political analysis.

[1308]
MILNE Alan John Mitchell
30 April 1922, British. 59 Hallgarth Street, Durham DH1 3AY, England. Degrees: BSc; PhD (LSE), 1952. Doctoral thesis: "Coleridge and Bentham as Political Thinkers". 1956-75 Lecturer, Reader, Professor of Soc Philosophy, Queen's U, Belfast; 1975- Professor of Pol Theory and Inst, U of Durham. Publs: *The Social Philosophy of English Idealism*, 1962; *Freedom and Rights*, 1968. Fields: Political philosophy and the history of political thought.

[1309]
MINKIN Lewis
25 June 1936, British. 2 Norwood Grove, Leeds 6, England. Degrees: BA; D Phil (York), 1976. Doctoral thesis: "The Labour Party Conference and Intra Party Democracy 1956-70". 1969- Lecturer in Government, U of Manchester. Publs: *The Soviet Achievement* (co-author), 1967; "The British Labour Party and the Trade Unions: Crisis and Compact", *Industrial and Labour Relations Review*, 1974; "The Labour Party", in *Social Democratic Parties of Western Europe* (co-author), 1977; "Left-wing Trade Unions and the Tensions of British Labour Politics", in *The European Left Confronts Modontis*, 1978; "The Labour Party and the Unions", *New Society*, 1977; *The Labour Party Conference*, 1978. Fields: The British labour party and trade unions; the political behaviour of trade unions; comparative labour movements.

[1310]
MINOGUE Kenneth Robert
11 September 1930, Australian. London School of Economics, Houghton Street, London WC2, England. Degrees: BA; BSc. 1955-56 Assistant Lecturer in Public Administration, U of Exeter; 1956- Assistant Lecturer, Lecturer, Senior Lecturer, Reader, LSE. Publs: *The Liberal Mind*, 1961; *Nationalism*, 1967; *The Concept of a University*, 1973; *Contemporary Political Philosophers* (with A R de Crespigny), 1975; various articles in *Political Studies, Encounter, Times Literary Supplement*. Fields: Exploration of the rhetorical and logical structure of ideological beliefs; analytical political theory; the idea of the social contract and the history of ideas.

[1311]
MINOGUE Martin Michael
23 December 1937, British. 7 Gaddum road, Manchester M20 0SY, England. Degrees: MA. 1966-69 Lecturer in Pol Studies, U of Kent; 1971-73 Visiting Fellow and Head of Centre of Public Administration, U of Mauritius; 1973- Senior Lecturer, Dept of Administrative Studies, U of Manchester. Publs: *African Aims and Attitudes* (with J Molloy (eds)), 1974; *Documents on Contemporary British Government*, 1977; *The Consumer's Guide to Local Government* (ed), 1977. Fields: Public policy and public administration; British public policy and institutions; the politics of public bureaucratic systems; bureaucracy and change; British local government, especially policy-making and performance.

[1312]
MINTY Abdul Samad*
30 October 1939, British. 6 Radlett Park Road, Radlett, Herts, England. Degrees: BSc; MSc (London), 1969. Research Fellow, Richardson Inst for Conflict and Peace Research. Publs: *South Africa's Defence Strategy*, 1969. Fields: South Africa's defence and foreign policies.

[1313]
MIRANDA Jorge
15 April 1941, Portuguese, Rua Tenente-Coronel Ribeiro dos Reis, 14-11e, Lisboa-4, Portugal. Degrees: Master in Law. Member of the Constitutional Commission, Professor, U of Lisbon. Publs: *Contributo para una teoria da inconstitucionalidade*, 1968; *Chefe do estado*, 1970; *Notas para una introducão ao direito constitucional comparado*, 1970; *Decreto*, 1974; *A Revolucão de 25 de Abril e o direito constitucional*, 1975; *Constituicão e democracia*, 1976; *Estudes sobre a constituicão*, 1978. Fields: Constitutional problems in the rights of man in public international law; electoral systems; devolution and regional problems in Europe today.

[1314]
MITCHELL Christopher Roger
19 October 1934, British. 37 Crane Grove, London N7, England. Degrees: BSc; PhD. Doctoral thesis: "The Problem of the Northern Frontier District of Kenya". Research Associate, Centre for the Analysis of Conflict, U Coll, London; Senior Research Officer, LSE; Lecturer in International Relations, U of Southampton; Associate Lecturer in International Relations, U of Surrey; Lecturer, Senior Lecturer in International Relations, City U, London. Publs: *International Relations Theory: A Bibliography* (with A J Groom (eds)), 1978; "Civil Strife and the Involvement of External Parties", *International Studies Quarterly*, 1970; "Foreign Policy Problems and Polarized Political Communities", *British Journal of Political Science*, 1971; "Conflict Resolution and Controlled Communications", *Journal of Peace Research*, 1973; "The Systems Analysis of Conflict" (with M Noton and F R Janes), *Futures*, 1973; "Peacekeeping: The Police Function", in *Yearbook of World Affairs*, 1976. Fields: Conflict in bicommunal societies; third party activities as intermediaries; foreign intervention in civil strife; the application of systems techniques to the study of international politics.

[1315]
MITCHELL John David Bawden
28 May 1917, British. Centre of European Governmental Studies, University of Edinburgh, Old College, South Bridge, Edinburgh EH8 9YL, Scotland. Degrees: LL B (London), 1938; PhD (London), 1952; LL D (Edinburgh), 1964; Dr hc (Lille), 1965; LL D hc (Amsterdam), 1975. Doctoral thesis: "The Contracts of Public Authorities: A Comparative Study". 1947-48 Lecturer, U Coll of Wales, Aberystwyth; 1948-49 Lecturer, Law Society School; 1949-52 Lecturer LSE; 1952-54 Reader in English Law, U of London; 1954-68 Professor of Constitutional Law, U of Edinburgh; 1968- Salvesen Professor of European Inst, U of Edinburgh. Publs: *The Contracts of Public Authorities*; *Constitutional Law*, 1968; *European Law and Institutions* (with L J Brinkhorst), 1969. Fields: Constitutional law; European integration.

[1316]
MOCHMANN Jörg Ekkehard*
10 January 1944, German. Helenstrasse 3, 5 Köln 1, FR Germany. Degrees: Dipl Kaufmann (Köln), 1968-69; Dr. Wiss Angestellter, Zentralarchiv für empirische Sozialforschung, U of Köln. Publs: "Sekundäranalyse" (with H D Klingemann), in

Methoden der Sozialforschung (J van Koolwijk (ed)), 1971. Fields: Methodology; information retrieval for indicators from empirical research; content analysis; conceptualization and perception of political phenomena.

[1317]
MODEEN Tore Gunnar Werner
25 September 1929, Finnish. Riddaregatan 9 B, 00170 Helsingfors 17, Finland. Degrees: Dr jur (Helsingfors), 1962. 1955-57 Bank Lawyer; 1957-77 Assistant Professor, Associate Professor of Law; Armfelt Professor of Public and International Law, School of Pol Sci, Swedish U of Åbo; 1977- Axel Art Professor of Local Government Law and Finances, Law School, U of Helsinki. Publs: *Det Kommunala Förtroendeuppdraft*, 1962; *Det Specialreglerade Kommunala Förtroendeuppdraget*, 1963; *De Självständiga Offentligrättsliga Anstalterna*, 1965; *The International Protection of National Minorities in Europe*, 1969; *De Folkrättsliga Garantierna för Bevarandet av Ålandsöarnas Nationaella Karaktär*, 1973; *Finlandssvenskarnas Nationella Grundlagsskydd*, 1977. Fields: Protection of human rights; liability of hospitals; the law of civil servants; trade union law.

[1318]
MOERKERK Joannes*
27 December 1939, Dutch. Lindenstraat 34, Amsterdam, The Netherlands. Degrees: Drs (Amsterdam). Assistant to Professor Daudt for Pol Research; Staff Member, Young People's Advisory Centre, Amsterdam. Publs: Articles in *Acta Politica, European Transport Law, Reflex*. Fields: Hi-jacking of aircraft; social and cultural youth policy.

[1319]
MOHAN Jitendra*
28 June 1935, Indian. Department of Political Theory and Institutions, The University, Sheffield S10 2TN, England. Degrees: BA; MA (Agra), 1956. Lecturer in Pol Sci, U of Ghana; Lecturer in Pol Econ, U of McMaster, Canada; Lecturer, U of Sheffield. Publs: Articles in *Journal of Modern African Studies, The Socialist Register, International Journal, International Studies*. Fields: Strategies of de-colonization and ideologies of development in post-independence Africa.

[1320]
MOISALA U E
9 March 1923, Finnish. Kyntäjäntie 16 F 12, 00290 Helsinki 39, Finland. Degrees: Bachelor; Lic, 1972; Dr, 1975. Doctoral thesis: "Johdatus Yrityksen Työsuhdejärjestelmän Kehittämiseen. Empiriaa Hyödyntävä Tutkimus" (Introduction to the Development of the Labour Relations of a Firm). 1948- Various posts in industry; 1977-Managing Dir of Yritysjärjestelmät Oy-Firm Systems; and Docent of Pol Sci, U of Helsinki. Publs: *Telephone and Telephone Institutions in Finland 1877-1977* (co-author). Fields: Communications studies; business administration.

[1321]
MOKKEN Robert Jan
20 April 1929, Dutch. 16-18 Badhoevedorp, The Netherlands. Degrees: Drs (Amsterdam), 1961; PhD (Amsterdam), 1970. Doctoral thesis: "A Theory and Procedure of Scale Analysis". Research Associate, Dept of Mathematical Statistics, Mathematical Centre, Amsterdam; Teaching Staff and Research Associate, Inst of Mass Communications, U of Amsterdam; Lecturer, Research Methodology and Pol Sci, U of Amsterdam; 1973-74 Fellow, Netherlands Inst for Advanced Studies (NIAS); Visiting Professor of Pol Sci, Dept of Pol Sci, U of Michigan; Professor in Research Methodology

and Pol Sci, Inst of Pol Sci, U of Amsterdam. Publs: *A Theory and Procedure of Scale Analysis — with Applications in Political Research*, 1971; *Graven naarmacht* (co-author), 1975. Fields: Methodology; mathematical statistics: mathematical social analysis; structural analysis, graph and network analysis; coalition theory and theory of games; research in elections; mass communications and politics.

[1322]
MOLIN Björn Anders
8 April 1932, Swedish. Dr Forselius gatan 4, 41326 Göteborg, Sweden. Degrees: PhD (Göteborg), 1965. Doctoral thesis: "Tjänstepensionsfragan" (The Supplementary Pensions Questions: A Study in Swedish Party Politics). 1957-63 Research Assistant; 1963-65 Lecturer; 1965-70 Docent (Assistant Professor); 1966-70 Acting Head of Dept, Dept of Pol Sci, U of Göteborg; 1970- Senior Lecturer, U of Göteborg; 1971 Member of Parliament. Publs: *Tjänstepensionsfrågan*, 1965; *Sverige efter 1900* (co-author), 1967; *Offentlig förvaltnig* (co-author), 1969; *Byråkrati och Politik* (co-author), 1972. *Den nya Utmaningen*, 1977. Fields: Political parties; public administration.

[1323]
MOLITOR André Philippe Jules
4 August 1911, Belgian. 102 rue Père Eudore Devrove, 1150 Brussels, Belgium. Degrees: Dr en droit (Louvain); Dr honoris causa (Aix-Marseille). 1936-61 Belgian Civil Service; 1961-77 Chef de Cabinet du Roi des Belges; 1949- Professeur, Catholic U de Louvain. Publs: *L'enseignement et la société d'aujourd'hui*, 1957; *Les sciences sociales dans l'enseignement supérieur: administration publique, recueil de textes*, 1958; *Administration publique*, 1971; *L'administration publique de la Belgique*, 1974. Fields: The teaching of public administration; comparative political and administrative systems.

[1324]
MOLNAR Miklos
28 October 1918, Swiss. 42 rue de Vermont, 1202 Geneva, Switzerland. Degrees: PhD. Doctoral thesis: "Le déclin de la Première Internationale. La Conférence de Londres de 1871". Professor of HEI and U of Lausanne. Publs: *Le déclin de la Première Internationale*, 1963; *Victoire d'une défaite: Budapest 1956* (in English), 1968; *Marx, Engels et la politique internationale*, 1975; *A History of the Hungarian Communist Party*, 1978. Fields: Diplomatic history; international politics; international relations.

[1325]
MOLS Manfred Heinrich
27 February 1935, German. Im Rheinblick 17, 6531 Weiler, FR Germany. Degrees: PhD (Freiburg), 1966. Doctoral thesis: "Die Bedeutung der Integrationslehre Rudolf Smends für die politische Theorie". 1966-68 Assistant Professor of Pol Sci, U of Freiburg; 1968-69 Research Associate, Inst of Pol Sci, U of Stanford, USA; Visiting Professor, U Ibero-americana, Mexico; 1973- Professor of Pol Sci, Direktor, Inst für Pol der Johannes Gutenberg U, Mainz. Publs: *Allgemeine Staatslehre oder politische Theorie*, 1969; *Mexico, die institutionalisierte Revolution* (with Tobler), 1976; plus articles on Latin American development theory and political science. Fields: US-Latin American relations; Latin-American politics; political parties as factors of modernization; theory of political development.

[1326]
MOMMEN André
21 February 1945, Belgian. Fazantenkamp 291, Maarssen, The Netherlands. Degrees: Lic, 1970; Agrégé, 1972; Dr, 1976. Doctoral thesis: "Belgian Socialism: Origins, Development and Function of the Belgian Labour Party (1880-1914)". Research Fellow, Free U of Brussels; Librarian, Inst of Pol Sci, U of Amsterdam. Publs: Various articles and papers on the Belgian labour movement and adult education. Fields: Labour movements; political sociology; Marxist thought.

[1327]
MONCONDUIT Francois
9 Mai 1937, French. 20 rue des Fossés, 35000 Rennes, France. Degrees: Dr en droit. Doctoral thesis: "La commission européenne des droits de l'homme". Professeur, Faculté de Droit, Rennes. Fields: Political philosophy.

[1328]
MOND Georges Henri
12 September 1921, French. 9 allée du Col Rivière, 94260 Fresnes, France. Degrees: Master of Law (Cracow), 1948; Dr sci pol (Sorbonne), 1963; Dr in Law (Polish U Abroad, London), 1968. Doctoral thesis: "La presse en Pologne et dans les autres démocraties populaires". 1955-57 Deputy Director, Polish Press Inst, Warsaw; 1956-57 General Secretary, Polish Journalists Association; 1964- Senior Lecturer, Inst Français de Presse et de Sci de l'Information, U de Paris, 1967; Visiting Assistant Professor, U of Minnesota; Chargé de recherche, CNRS. Publs: "Les règles du jeu hors l'Occident; les pays de l'Est", in *La Politique* (J L Parodi (ed)), 1971; "Les mass média dans les pays de l'Est", in *Les communications de masse*, 1972; "Monopole ou concentration de la presse dans les pays socialistes", *Revue d'Etudes Comparatives Est-Ouest*, 1975; "The Role of Intellectuals", in *Gierek's Poland* (A Bromke and J W Strong (eds)), 1973; "Analyse de la constitution albanaise", in *Annuaire de législation française et étrangère*, 1975; "Les échos et les conséquences du XXème Congrès du PCUS en Pologne: Octobre polonais 1956", in *Le Vingtième Congrès: mythes et réalitiés de l'Europe et de l'Est*, 1977. Fields: Political institutions in socialist states; mass media; political control of the administration in socialist states.

[1329]
MONEY William John
11 October 1932, British. 48 Victoria Crescent Road, Glasgow G12 9DE, England. Degrees: BSc. Lecturer in Public Administration, U of Glasgow. Publs: *The Need to Sustain a Viable System of Local Democracy*; *Do We Need A New Model Army?*. Fields: The administrative response to change; civil-military relations; problems of liberal democracy.

[1330]
MOODIE Graeme Cochrane
27 August 1924, British. 1 The Outgang, Heslington, Yorkshire YO1 5EW, England. Degrees: MA (St Andrews), 1943; BA (Oxon), 1946; MA (Oxon), 1953. 1947-53 Lecturer, U of St Andrews; 1953-63 Lecturer, Senior Lecturer, U of Glasgow; 1962-63 Visiting Associate, Princeton U, USA; Professor of Pol, U of York. Publs: *Some Problems of the Constitution* (co-author), 1959; *The Government of Great Britain* (with G Studdert-Kennedy), 1961; *Opinions, Publics and Pressure Groups*, 1970; *Power and Authority in British Universities* (co-author), 1974. Fields: British politics; power, pressure groups; organizational politics.

[1331]
MOODIE Robert Alan
19 November 1946, British. 14 Bembridge Court, Nottingham, England. Degrees: BA. Lecturer, Trent Polytechnic. Fields: Integration in Western Europe; the institutional development of the EEC and theories of integration; French and West German politics; British politics.

[1332]
MORAZÉ Charles
17 February 1913, French. 15 Avenue Paul Doumer, 75016 Paris, France. Directeur d'Etudes, Ecole des Hautes Etudes en Sci Soc; Professeur, Ecole Polytechnique; Directeur de l'Institut d'Etude du développement écon et soc; Président de la commission nationale pour les études et les recherches inter-ethniques, et de l'Association "Développement et Progrès"; Membre du Conseil d'Administration, FNSP et de la Maison des Sci de l'Homme; Co-Directeur, *Les Annales*; Directeur, *Tiers-Monde*. Publs: *Introduction à l'histoire économique*, 1944; *La France bourgeoise*, 1946; *Les trois âges du Brésil*, 1954; *Les Français et la République*, 1956; *Les bourgeois conquérants*, 1966; *History of the Scientific and Cultural Development of Mankind, 1775-1905* (co-author), 1969; *La logique de l'histoire*, 1975; *Le Général de Gaulle et la République*, 1972. Fields: Relations between scientific development and social representation; Third World studies.

[1333]
MOREIRA Adriano José Alves*
6 September 1922, Portuguese. Rua Vieira Lusitano 29, Lisbon, Portugal. Degrees: Master of Laws (Lisbon), 1944; Master of Laws (Madrid), 1970; Dr hc (Sao Paulo); Dr hc (Bahia); Dr hc (Brasilia); Dr hc (Rio de Janeiro). 1961 Technical U of Lisbon; Dean, Inst of Soc Sci and Overseas Pol; Director, Centre of Social Research; Member, National Council of Education; Professor, Inst Superior Naval de Guerra; Inst de Liencias Sociais e Pol Ultramarina. Publs: *Problema Prisional do Ultramar*, 1954; *Political Ultramarina*, 1961; *Ideologias Politicas*, 1964; *Politica Internacional*, 1970. Fields: Internationalization of states' problems; security problems and the challenge of the future; international ideologies; world government.

[1334]
MOREN Jorolv
20 March 1925, Norwegian. Suaneveien 19C, Oslo 11, Norway. Degrees: Master (Oslo), 1954. 1955-60 Research Associate, Administrative Research Foundation, Bergen; 1960-65 Research Associate, Christian Michelsen Inst, Bergen; 1965- Senior Lecturer, Inst of Pol Sci, U of Oslo. Publs: *Interest Groups Representation in Governmental Councils and Commissions*, 1958; *Cooperation between Government and Business in Western Europe*, 1962; *Directory of Norwegian Voluntary Associations*, 1976. Fields: Government; public policy; interest groups in politics.

[1335]
MORGAN David Rhys
22 May 1937, British. Social Studies Building, The University, Liverpool L69 3BX, England. Degrees: BA; PhD (Cambridge), 1967. 1962-64 Guest Scholar, Brookings Inst, Washington; 1965- Senior Lecturer in American Pol, Dept of Pol Theory and Inst, U of Liverpool. Publs: *The Politics of Woman Suffrage in America*, 1971; *City Politics and the Press* (with W H Cox), 1973; *Suffragettes and Liberals: The Politics of Woman Suffrage in England*, 1975; *The Capital Press Corps: Journalists and the Governing of New York State*, 1978. Fields: Feminism in Britain and the USA: American politics; mass media.

[1336]
MORGAN Roger Pearce
3 March 1932, British. 35 Lansdowne Gardens, London SW8 2EL, England. Degrees: BA; MA, 1957; PhD (Cambridge), 1959. Doctoral thesis: "The German Social Democrats and the First International 1864-72". 1953-63 Lecturer in International Pol, U Coll of Wales, Aberystwyth; 1963-67 Lecturer in History and in International Relations, U of Sussex; 1968-74 Assistant Deputy Director of Studies, Royal Inst of International Affairs, plus various visiting professorships in the USA, France and Italy; 1978- Professor of European Pol, U of Loughborough; Head, Centre of Studies in Democratic Pol, PEP, London. Publs: *Britain and West Germany: Changing Societies and the Future of Foreign Policy* (co-author and co-editor with K Kaiser); *The Study of International Affairs: Essays in Honour of Kenneth Younger* (co-author and ed); *West European Politics since 1945: The Shaping of the European Community*, 1972; *High Politics, Low Politics: Towards a Foreign Policy for Western Europe*, 1973; *The United States and West Germany, 1945-73: A Study in Alliance Politics*, 1974; *The Unsettled Peace: A Study of the Cold War in Europe*, 1974. Fields: European politics, including comparative politics and the study of European integration; international relations; decision-making in Western political systems.

[1337]
MORILLAS Bent Erik*
24 August 1942, Danish. Holstedvej 62, 5200 Odense V, Denmark. Degrees: Cand mag (Copenhagen). Lecturer, U of Odense. Fields: Latin American history; mass emigration to Latin America.

[1338]
MORIN Georges Paul Joseph
19 March 1942, French. 52 rue Jean Jaurès, 38610 Gières, France. Degrees: DES (Grenoble II). Doctoral thesis: "L'autonomie des universités et le statut des personnels enseignants". Assistant Professeur, U de Grenoble II. Fields: North Africa, especially Algeria.

[1339]
MORKEL Arnd*
26 March 1928, German. Wilhelm-Lenschner-Strasse 43, D-5500 Trier, FR Germany. Degrees: Dr phil (Freiburg), 1960. Doctoral thesis: "Hofmannsthals Politisches Bewusstsein". Lehrauftrag für Pol Wiss, U of Heidelberg; Lehrstuhlvertretungen, U of Freiburg, Heidelberg, Darmstadt; Wiss Rat, U of Köln; Professor für Pol, U of Trier-Kaiserslautern. Publs: *Politik und Wissenschaft*, 1967; *Festschrift für Rolf Sternberger*, 1967-68. Fields: Interministerial cabinet committees; voting behaviour; democracy in parties.

[1340]
MORLINO Leonardo Antonio
28 June 1947, Italian. Piazza Tasso 13, 50124 Florence, Italy. Doctoral thesis: "The Liberal Right in the Giolittian Era". Teaching Assistant of Government; Teaching Assistant of Pol Sci; Assistant Professor of Pol Sci, U of Florence. Publs: Various essays on political stability in democratic regimes, development theory and Spanish democratic transition. Fields: Political change of regimes; development theory; Spanish history.

[1341]
MORRALL John Brimyard
9 January 1923, British. 23 Slades Hill, Enfield, Middlesex, England. Degrees: BA; MA (Oxon), 1948; B Litt (Oxon), 1948; PhD (Ireland), 1954. 1950-62 Lecturer in History, U Coll, Dublin; Senior Lecturer in Pol Sci, LSE. Publs: *Church and State through the Centuries* (with S Z Ehler), 1954; *Political Thought in Medieval Times*, 1971; *Gerson and the Great Schism*, 1960; *The Medieval Imprint: The Founding of Western Civilisation*, 1967. Fields: The relations of political and religious institutions; prehistory of political theory.

[1342]
MORRIS-JONES Wyndraeth Humphreys
1 August 1918, British. 95 Ridgway, London SW19, England. Degrees: BSc. 1946-55 Assistant Lecturer, Lecturer, LSE; 1955-56 Professor of Pol Theory and Inst, U of Durham; 1966- Director, Inst of Commonwealth Studies, Professor of Commonwealth Affairs, U of London. Publs: *Parliament in India*, 1957; *The Government and Politics of India*, 1971; *The Making of Politicians: Studies from Africa and Asia* (with B Dasgupta (ed)), 1976; *Patterns and Trends in Indian Politics: an Ecological Analysis of Aggregate Data on Society and Elections* (with B Dasgupta), 1976; *Decolonization and After: British and French Studies on Independence and Dependence* (with G Fischer (eds)), 1978; *Australia and Britain: Essays on a Changing Relationship* (with A F Mudden (eds)), 1978; *Politics Mainly Indian*, 1978. Fields: Comparative government, generally and with special reference to South Asia; political philosophy.

[1343]
MORRISON Alasdair Andrew Orr*
25 March 1929, British. Mousemore Park, Gloucester, England. Degrees: BA; MA (Oxon), 1960; MA, PhD (Chicago), 1965. Doctoral thesis: "Individuals and Collectives". 1964-65 Part-time Lecturer, U of Chicago; 1965- Lecturer in Pol, U of Bristol. Fields: Politics and society.

[1344]
MORSEL Henri
12 April 1934, French. 16 rue Galilée, 34800 St Martin d'Hères, France. Agrégé de l'Université. Maître-assistant, IEP, Grenoble; Maître-assistant titulaire, UER d'Histoire, U de Grenoble; Chargé de cours, IEP, Grenoble. Publs: *Histoire économique et sociale du monde* (co-author), 1977; *Pour une histoire de la statistique*, 1977; *Histoire de Grenoble*, 1976. Fields: Economic history; political economy; economic administration.

[1345]
MORTARA Vittoria*
3 June 1937, Italian. c/o Università della Calabria, Dipartimento di Organizzazione Aziendale e Amministrazione Pubblica, Via Caloprese 90, Cosenza, Italy. Degrees: Laurea Giurisprudenza (Bologna); MA (California at Berkeley); Libera Docenza, Sci dell'Amministrazione. Assistente, Sci dell'Amministrazione, U of Bologna; Incaricato, Facoltà di Sci Pol, U of Bologna; Incaricato di Sci dell'Amministrazione, e Direttore, Dipartimento di Organizzazione Aziendale e Amministrazione Pubblica, U of Calabria. Publs: *Modelli di Comportamento Amministrativo*, 1968; *L'Analisi delle Strutture Organizzative*, 1973. Fields: Theory of bureaucracy and the problem of the Italian public administration.

[1346]
MORTELMANS Michel Petrus Constant*
9 May 1940, Belgian. Jachthuislaan 13, 3202 Linden. Belgium. Degrees: Lic pol sci (Louvain), 1965. Assistant, Dept of Pol Studies, U of Louvain. Publs: *National Influences in the EEC*, 1970; *Enfeeblement of Integration in the EEC*, 1971; *The EEC with Ten Members*, 1972; *The Paris Summit Conference*, 1972. Fields: European integration; institutional problems at the political level; local authorities; environment.

[1347]
MOSELEY-WILLIAMS Richard David*
4 April 1944, British. 13 Edithna Street, Stockwell, London SW9, England. Degrees: BA; B Phil (Oxon), 1969. Lecturer in Latin American Pol, LSE, and Inst of Latin American Studies. Fields: The Argentine Peronist movement, 1946-55; contemporary Argentine politics; the left in Latin America, especially the ideology of the 'natural left'.

[1348]
MOUHIER Jean-Pierre
7 December 1942, French. 14 rue Broca, Paris Vème, France. Maître-assistant, U de Paris I; Chargé de cours, U de Paris X-Nanterre. Publs: *Pour une sociologie politique* (with J P Cot), 1973; *Les syndicats américains, conflit ou complicité* (with J P Cot), 1977; "La publicité entre en politique", *Projet*, 1977; "Les syndicats américains et la politique", *Projet*, 1977. Fields: Political culture; parties and unions.

[1349]
MOULIN Léo
25 February 1906, Belgian. 72 rue des Echevins, 1050 Bruxelles, Belgium. Degrees: Dr ès lettres (Bologna); Dr en phil et lettres (Brussels); Lic en sci pol. Professor, College of Europe, Bruges; U of Paris II; U of Namur; U of Louvain. Publs: *De Robespierre à Lénine*, 1936; *Du Traité de Versailles à l'Europe d'aujourd'hui*, 1939; *Histoire des temps modernes*, 1941; *Socialism of the West*, 1949; *Les formes du gouvernement local et provincial dans les ordres religieux*, 1956; *Le monde vivant des religieux*, 1964; *La société de demain dans l'Europe d'aujourd'hui*, 1966; *L'aventure européenne-introduction à une sociologie du développement économique de l'Occident*, 1972. Fields: Religion and politics; religious orders as political systems; legislatures; Western economic development and Western political systems.

[1350]
MOULIN Richard
29 July 1945, French. 25 rue du Roumois, 76130 Mont-St-Aignan, France. Degrees: Dr d'Etat. Doctoral thesis: "Le présidentialisme et la classification des régimes politiques". Publs: *Le présidentialisme et la classification des régimes politiques*, 1978. Fields: Political forces in Latin America; analysis of constitutional systems; classification of forms of governments.

[1351]
MOURIAUX René
17 November 1936, French. 26 rue Chateau-Landon, 75010 Paris, France. Degrees: Lic; Dipl (IEP Paris); DES (FNSP). Collaborateur technique, CNRS; Attaché de recherche, FNSP. Publs: *Les militants de la CGT et de la CFDT* (with J Capdevielle), 1968; *Les syndicats ouvriers en France* (with J Capdevielle), 1976; *L'ouvrier français en 1970* (with J Adam *et al*), 1971; *L'ouvrier conservateur* (with F Bon and J Capdevielle), 1973; *Les jeunes ouvriers* (with J Magniadas *et al*), 1974; *Les cadres français et la politique* (with G Grunberg), 1975; *Femmes à l'usine et au bureau*, 1976. "La Charte d'Amiens à 70

ans", *Etudes*, 1976; "L'année sociale 1976", in *L'année politique économique et sociale 1976*, 1977. Fields: Professional unionism in France; unionist behaviour among workers and executives.

[1352]
MOURITZEN Hans A
20 February 1952, Danish. Institute of Political Studies, University of Copenhagen, Rosenborggade 15, 1130 Copenhagen K, Denmark. Degrees: Cand mag, 1976. 1974-76 Assistant, Inst of Pol Studies, Copenhagen; 1977 External Lecturer. Fields: Philosophy of social science; systems theory in international politics; approaches to the study of Danish and Nordic foreign policy.

[1353]
MOXON-BROWNE Edward Philip
28 January 1944, British. 85 University Street, Belfast 7, Northern Ireland. Degrees: BA (St Andrews); MA (Pennsylvania). 1971-72 Lecturer in International Relations, US International U; 1973- Lecturer in Pol Sci, Queen's U, Belfast. Publs: "Special Relations Agreements", *World Today*, 1973; "The EEC After Tindemans", *World Today*, 1975; "Ireland in the EEC", *World Today*, 1976; "Northern Ireland", in *Regional Assertion and European Integration* (M Kolinsky (ed)), 1978; "Irish Political Parties and European Integration", *Administration*, 1978. Fields: European parliament and EEC institutions generally; Northern Ireland and Republic of Ireland in the context of the EEC; Northern Ireland politics.

[1354]
MOYSER George Herbert
15 March 1945, British. 13 Hilbre Road, Burnage, Manchester M19 2PU, England. Degrees: BA; MA (Essex); MA (Michigan); PhD (Michigan). Doctoral thesis: "Electoral Regionalism in Britain and Italy: A Cross-level Analysis". Lecturer in Government, U of Manchester. Publs: *The Mind of Jeremy Bentham*, 1968; *Liberalism*, 1976. Fields: Ideological argument; political obligation; methodological aspects of the study of political life; the relationship between political and commercial activity.

[1355]
MÜCK Josef*
2 February 1926, German. 355 Marburg, Am Glaskopf 34, FR Germany. Degrees: Dr phil (Halle), 1954. Teacher; Director für Weiterbildungslehrgänge. Fields: Political pedagogy; political education.

[1356]
MÜLLER Ferdinand F
25 April 1952, German. Beerentalweg 37, 21 Hamburg 90, FR Germany. Degrees: MA (Florida), 1976; PhD (Hamburg), 1978. Doctoral thesis: "Factionalism in West Germany's Social Democratic Party 1966-1976". Research Fellow, U of Florida; Research Fellow, U of Hamburg; Lehrbeauftrafter, U of Hamburg. Publs: *Empirische Politikwissenschaft: Eine Einführung* (with M Schmidt), 1978; plus various articles on factionalism within the SPD and on SPD elites. Fields: Comparative studies of West European parties and elites.

[1357]
MÜLLER Norbert*
3 March 1945, German. 4521 Kneingdorf 3b, FR Germany. Degrees: Dipl Pol; Dr. Soz Wiss Assistent (Planning and Decision Theory). Publs: *Logic and Mathematics for Social Scientists* (with W Kliemann), 1973.

[1358]
MÜHLEISEN Hans-Otto
2 December 1941, German. Bürgerwehrstrasse 1, 78 Freiburg, FR Germany. Degrees: Dr phil. Doctoral thesis: "Theoriebildung und politische Parteien". Wiss Assistent, U of Freiburg. Publs: *Theroretische Ansätze der Parteienforschung*, 1973; *Organisationstheorie und Parteienforschung*, 1973; *Demokratietheorie als Alibi*, 1975; *Umweltschutz als politischer Prozess*, 1976; *Ikonen-Aspekte der Kunstfälschung und des Betrugs*, 1977; *Die Stifterikonographie des Klosters St Peter*, 1977; *Individuum und Befreiung*, 1978. Fields: Political theory; political process.

[1359]
MÜLLER Jörg Paul
16 September 1938, Swiss. Kappelenring 42a, CH-3032 Hinterkappelen, Switzerland. Degrees: Lic jur; Dr jur; Rechtsanwalt; LL M. Doctoral thesis: "Die Grundrechte und der Persönlichkeitsschutz des Privatrechtes". Professor of Constitutional Law, International Law and Administrative Law, U of Bern. Publs: *Die Grundrechte und der Perönlichkeitsschutz des Privatrechts*, 1964; *Vertrauensschutz im Völkerrecht*, 1971; "Soziale Grundrechte in der Verfassung?", *ZSR*, 1973; *Praxis des Völkerrechts* (with L Wildhaber), 1977. Fields: Constitutional law; the individual vs the state; philosophy of the law; environmental law; political and ethical questions.

[1360]
MÜLLER Peter*
3 September 1941, German. Wilhelmshöher Allee 10, 35 Kassel, FR Germany. Degrees: Dr phil (Münster), 1968. Assistant, Inst for Kriminologie, U of Tübingen; Assistant, Soziologisches Inst, Philipps-U, Marburg; Professor of Soc, Gesamthochschule, Kassel. Publs: *Die soziale Gruppe im Prozess der Massenkommunikation*, 1970. Fields: Socialization research; social work; social and economic problems of immigrant workers.

[1361]
MÜLLER Rudolf Wolfgang*
19 October 1934, German. Nassauische Strasse 60, Berlin 31, FR Germany. Degrees: Dr phil (Tübingen), 1964. Doctoral thesis: "Rhetorische und Syntaktische Interpunktion". Studienassessor des Höheren Lehramts; Wiss Assistent, Assistenzprofessor, Free U of Berlin. Publs: *Rhetorische und Syntaktische Interpunktion*, 1964. Fields: History of social philosophy and epistemology; theory of the state in capitalist society; of social policy in Germany.

[1362]
MUGHAN Anthony
20 January 1948, British. 6 Alma Road, Penylan, Cardiff CF2 5BD, Wales. Degrees: BA; MA (Lancaster); PhD (Iowa). Doctoral thesis: "Modernization, Ethnicity and National Integration: The Changing Pattern of Ethnic Conflict in Belgium". 1976 Research Fellow, Dept of Pol, U of Strathclyde; Lecturer, Dept of Pol, U Coll Cardiff. Publs: "The Used Vote and Electoral Outcomes", *BJPS*, 1975; "On Measuring National Integration in Regionally Divided Societies", *Quality and Quantity*, 1978; "Electoral Change in Britain: The Campaign Reassessed", *BJPS*, 1978; "The Decline of Class Voting in Britain: Problems of Analysis and Interpretation, *APSR*, 1978; "Modernization and Ethnic Conflict in Belgium", *Political Studies*, 1978. Fields: Mass political behaviour; dependency theory.

[1363]
MURILLO FERROL Francisco
15 July 1918, Spanish. Departamento de Derecho Politico y Derecho International, Universidad de Granada, Spain. Degrees: Lic en Derecho (Granada), 1941; Dr en Derecho (Madrid), 1946. 1953-61 Professor Ord de Ciencia Pol, U of Valencia; 1961-Professor Ord de Ciencia Pol, U of Granada; Professor de Soc Pol, Inst U de Ciencias de la Empresa; Granada; 1972- Professor (Catedrático) of Pol Sci, U Autónoma of Madrid. Publs: *Las Classes Medias Españolas*, 1959; *Saavedra Fajardo y la Politica de Barroco*, 1957; *Estudios de Sociologia Politica*, 1963. Fields: Social structure of Andalucia; social and political structure of contemporary Spain; political modernization.

[1364]
MURMAN Yngve Axel
19 November 1936, Swedish. Fregattvägen 2, S-18353 Täby, Sweden. Degrees: PhD. Doctoral thesis: "The Struggle for Power on the Swedish Labour Market 1905-1907". Lecturer. Fields: Interest groups; educational politics.

[1365]
MURRAY David John
19 December 1935, British. The Open University, Walton Hall, Bletchley, Buckinghamshire, England. Degrees: BA; MA (Oxon); D Phil (Oxon), 1962. Doctoral thesis: "The Colonial Office and the Plantation Colonies 1801-34: A Study of Imperial Government in Evolution". Lecturer in Pol, Makerere U Coll, Uganda; Lecturer in Government, U Coll of Rhodesia and Nyasaland; Lecturer, Senior Lecturer in Public Administration, U of Ibadan; Research Director, Graduate Inst of Administration, U of Ife; Visiting Professor, American U, Cairo; Professor of Government, Open U; Professor of Public Administration, U of the South Pacific. Publs: *The West Indies and the Development of Colonial Government*, 1965; *The Progress of Nigerian Public Administration: A Report on Research* (co-author), 1968; *The Work of Nigerian Administration*, 1969; *The Governmental System in Southern Rhodesia*, 1970; *Studies in Nigerian Administration* (ed), 1970; *Understanding Society: Readings in the Social Sciences* (co-ed), 1970; *Decisions, Organizations and Society* (co-ed), 1976. Fields: Comparative administrative development, especially in developing countries.

[1366]
MUSO Tsokolo*
15 June 1937, Lesotho. Linnégatan 68, S-413 08 Göteborg, Sweden. Degrees: M soc sci (Lund), 1969; M soc sci (Lund), 1971. Probation Officer, South Africa; Director of Community Development, Lesotho; Organising Director, courses in Euro-African Relations. Fields: Lesotho political development.

[1367]
MYKLETUN Jostein I
6 December 1948, Norwegian. c/o M R D H, Box 308, 6401 Molde, Norway. Degrees: BA; MA (Minnesota), 1972; PhD (Minnesota), 1975. Doctoral thesis: "Only Through a Function: A Case Study of Norwegian Policy Elites' Attitudes Towards the United Nations". Associate Professor in Soc Sci, Møre and Romsdal District Coll, Molde, Norway. Fields: International organizations; peace and conflict research.

N

[1368]
NAILOR Peter
16 December 1928, British. 68 Lock Chase, Blackheath SE3 9HA, England. Degrees: MA (Oxon), 1955. 1952-69 Home Civil Service; 1968-77 Professor of Pol, U of Lancaster; Professor of History and Head of the Dept of History and International Affairs, Royal Naval Coll, Greenwich. Publs: "Security in Europe", in *International Security* (K J Twitchett (ed)), 1970; "Defence Policy and Foreign Policy", in *The Management of Britain's External Relations* (Boardman and Groom (eds)), 1973; "The Military Bureaucracy", in *War in the Next Decade* (Beaumont and Edmonds (eds)), 1975; "Military Strategy in International Relations", in *Approaches to International Relations* (T Taylor (ed)), 1978. Fields: British defence policy; European security; arms control.

[1369]
NARKIEWICZ Olga Anna
7 June 1927, British. 167 Marsland Road, Sale, Cheshire, England. Degrees: BA; MA (Manchester); PhD (Manchester). Doctoral thesis: "Problems of Rural and Industrial Administration in the Soviet Union 1923-27". 1964-66 Research Assistant, Dept of Government, U of Manchester; 1966- Lecturer, Senior Lecturer in Modern Languages, UMIST. Publs: *The Making of the Soviet State Apparatus*, 1970; *The Green Flag: Polish Populist Politics 1967-1970*, 1976; *Planning in Europe* (co-ed with J E S Hayward) (forthcoming). Fields: Soviet and eastern European politics and history; planning in Europe and underdeveloped countries; agrarian politics.

[1370]
NASSMACHER Karl-Heinz
20 February 1941, German. Alma-Rogge-Strasse 14, D-2900 Oldenburg, FR Germany. Degrees: Dipl Kaufmann (Köln), 1965; Dr rer Pol (Köln), 1967. Doctoral thesis: "Das Österreichische Regierungssystem: die Wahl zwischen grosser Koalition und alternierender Regierungsweise". 1967-68 Research Assistant, U of Köln; 1969-71 Lecturer and Deputy Director, Residential Coll of Friedrich-Ebert-Stiftung, Bergneustadt; 1971-72 Wiss Assistent, PH Wuppertal; 1972-75 Professor, Sozialakademie Dortmund; 1975- Professor of Pol Sci, U of Oldenburg. Publs: *Das Österreichische Regierungssystem*, 1968; *Politikwissenschaft I*, 1977; *Demokratisierung der europäischen Gemeinschaften*, 1972; *Politikwissenschaft II*, 1978; *Kommunalpolitik und Sozialdemokratie* (ed), 1977. Fields: Comparative government; political parties; local politics.

[1371]
NÄTH Marie-Luise
30 January 1944, German. Scheidterstrasse 6, 6601 Saarbrücken-Scheidter Berg, FR Germany. Degrees: Dr phil (Berlin), 1972. Doctoral thesis: "Chinas Weg in die Weltpolitik: nationale und aussenpolitische Konzeptionen Sun-Yat-Tsens, Chiang Kai-Sheks und Mao Tse Tungs". 1971-77 Assistant, Assistant Professor, Research Unit on Chinese and Asian Pol, U of Berlin; Research Fellow, Research Unit on Chinese and East Asian Pol, U of Saarlandes,Saarbrücken. Fields: International politics in Asia; Chinese and Indian foreign policy; sino-soviet relations; politics in South East Asia.

[1372]
NAUSTDALSLID Jon
20 May 1945, Norwegian. Leitevegen 23, 5800 Sogndal, Norway. Degrees: Mag art. Lecturer, Sogn og Fjordane Regional College. Fields: Regional policy and planning, particularly public development policies in marginal/peripheral areas in developed countries; public policy in relation to oil development in the North Sea.

[1373]
NEGRI Guglielmo*
1926, Italian. Camera de Deputati, Rome, Italy. Degrees: Dr in Law (Rome), 1949; Dr in Pol Sci (Rome), 1952; Libera Docenza in Istituzioni di Diritto Pubblico. Doctoral thesis: "The Marshall Plan and the Intergovernmental Agreements for Products", 1949. Assistant Professor, Law School, U of Rome; Associate Professor, Dept of Pol Sci, U of Florence; Associate Professor, Us of Rome and Padua; Chief of the Legislative Reference Service, House of Deputies, Italian Parliament. Publs: *Raccolta delle Costituzioni Italiane 1796-1946* (co-ed), 1958; *Verso la Quinta Repubblica*, 1958; *Il Leader del Partito Anglosassone*, 1958; *La Direzione della Politica Estera nelle Grandi Democrazie: Inghilterra-Stati Uniti*, 1964; *La Direzione ed il Controlle Democratico della Politica Estera in Italia*, 1967; *Il Sistema Politico degli Stati Uniti*, 1969. Fields: Judicial standards in the field of public morality; comparative party organizations in Western Europe.

[1374]
NELLI René
20 February 1906, French. 24 rue de Palais, Carcassonne, Aude, France. Degrees: Dr en philosophie, 1963. Laureat de l'Académie française; Ancien conservateur, Musée des Beaux-Arts, Carcassonne; Director, Folklore. Publs: *L'érotique des Troubadours*. 1963; *La vie quotidienne des Cathares Languedociens: Erotique et Civilisations*, 1973. Fields: Eroticism in the middle ages; medieval heresies and their political implications.

[1375]
NERE Jacques Georges Jean
8 May 1917, French. 122 rue d'Alésia, Paris XIV, France. Degrees: Lic ès lettres, Agrégé d'histoire et géographie, 1943; Dr d'Etat. Doctoral thesis: "La crise économique de 1882 et le mouvement boulangiste". Chef de la Documentation, IEP, Paris; Assistant, Faculté des Lettres, U de Caen; Chef du Service des Etudes Econ: Publs: *La guerre de sécession*, 1961; *Le Boulangisme et la Presse*, 1964; *La Troisième République, 1914-40*, 1967; *La crise de 1929*, 1968; *The Foreign Policy of France from 1914 to 1945*, 1975; *Précis d'histoire contemporaine*, 1973. Fields: History, especially of France between the world wars.

[1376]
NEUGEBAUER Gero
23 August 1941, German. Bundesallee 74, D-1000 Berlin 41, FR Germany. Degrees: Dipl Pol; Dr rer Pol. Doctoral thesis: "Partei und Staatsapparat in der DDR" (Party and State Apparatus in the GDR). 1970-75 Wiss Assistent; 1975- Wiss Mitarbeiter. Publs: *Partei und Staatsapparat in der DDR*; "Die Volkskammer der DDR", *Zeitschrift für Parlamentsfragen*, 1974; "Die militärstrategische Konzeption der NVA", in *Studiengruppe Militärpolitik: Die NVA*, 1976. Fields: Government; military; party systems in socialist countries.

[1377]
NEUHOLD Hans Peter
29 January 1942, Austrian. Hüttelbergstrasse 28, A-1140 Vienna, Austria. Degrees: Dr (Vienna), 1965; Dipl (Inst des Hautes Etudes Internationales Paris), 1967. Staff Member, Austrian Ministry of Foreign Affairs; Assistant Lecturer, Inst of International Law and International Relations, U of Vienna; Assistant Professor, U of Vienna; Research Director, Austrian Foreign Policy Association. Publs: Articles in *Internationale Konflikte — Verbotene und erlaubte Mittel ihrer Austragung*, 1977; *Die Friedenswarte, Jahrbuch des internationalen Rechts, Archiv des Völkerrechts, Internationale Entwicklung, Österreichische Zeitschrift für öffentliches Recht*. Fields: International problems of small states; contemporary security issues; conflict theory; international peace-keeping; Austria's foreign and security problems; international law and international relations.

[1378]
NEUMANN Martin Rudolf Günther
29 October 1945, German. Geibelstrasse 19, D-4100 Duisburg 1, FR Germany. Degrees: Dr phil. Doctoral thesis: "Der politische Gehalt von Groschenheften" (The Political Content of Comics and Pulp Magazines). Wiss Assistent, Gesamthochschule Duisburg. Publs: *Der politische Gehalt von Groschenheften*. Fields: Content analysis; social economic and political aspects of fascism; militarism.

[1379]
NEWTON Kenneth
15 April 1940, British. Dept of Pol Sci, The University, Dundee, England. Degrees: BA; PhD (Cambridge). Doctoral thesis: "The British Communist Party: The Sociology of a Radical Political Party". Lecturer in Pol Soc, U of Birmingham; Visiting Professor, U of Pittsburgh; Visiting Professor, U of Wisconsin, Madison; Research Fellow, Nuffield Coll, U of Oxford; Professor of Pol, U of Dundee. Publs: *Opportunities After O-Level* (with Sonya Abrams), 1960; *The Sociology of British Communism*, 1969; *Second City Politics*, 1976. Fields: Local government and politics; public policy; urban problems and politics; political sociology; political economy.

[1380]
NIBLOCK Timothy Colin*
13 October 1942, British. 5 Kewhurst Avenue, Cooden, Bexhill, Sussex, England. Degrees: BA; Certificate of Advanced European Studies (Bruges), 1966; D Phil (Sussex). Doctoral thesis: "Aid and Foreign Policy in Tanzania". U Coll, Dar es Salaam; Lecturer in International Relations, U of Khartoum, Seconded from U of Reading. Publs: *Foreign Policy in Tanzania*, 1970. Fields: African foreign policies; Middle East politics and the Sudan.

[1381]
NICOLAS Guy
2 August 1932, French. 181 Avenue Aristide Briand, 92160 Antony, France. Degrees: Dr d'Etat. Doctoral thesis: "Dynamique sociale et appréhension du monde au sein d'une société hausa". 1960-75 CNRS; Chargé de cours, U de Bordeaux; 1975 Inst National de Langues et Civilisations Orientales; 1975- Professeur, U de Paris III. Publs: "La société africaine et ses réactions à l'impact colonial", *L'Afrique Noire Contemporaine*, 1968; "Crise de l'Etat et affirmation ethnique en Afrique Noire Contemporaine", *Revue Française de Science Politique*, 1972; "Fait ethnique et usages du concept d'ethnie", *Cahiers Internationaux de Sociologie*, 1973; "Fondements magicoreligieux du pouvoir politique au sein de la principauté Hausa du Gobir", *Journal de la Société des Africanistes*, 1969; *Dynamique sociale et appréhension du monde au sein*

d'une société hausa, 1975; "L'expansion de l'influence arabe au Sud du Sahara", *L'Afrique et l'Asie moderne*, 1978. Fields: Relations between the Arab world and Africa South of the Sahara.

[1382]
NICHOLAS Herbert George
8 June 1911, British. 3 William Orchard Close, Old Headington, Oxford, England. Degrees: MA (Oxon). Fellow of Exeter Coll, U of Oxford; Fellow of Nuffield Coll, U of Oxford; Fellow of New Coll, U of Oxford; Nuffield Reader in the Comparative Study of Inst, U of Oxford; Rhodes Professor of American History and Inst, New Coll, U of Oxford. Publs: *The American Union*, 1948; *The British General Elections of 1950*, 1951; *To The Hustings*, 1956; *The United Nations as a Political Institution*, 1975; *De Tocqueville's Democratie en Amerique* (ed), 1961; *The United States and Britain*, 1975. Fields: US government and politics; United Nations.

[1383]
NICHOLSON Michael B
21 December 1933, British. 21 Fitzwarren Gardens, London N19, England. Degrees: BA; PhD (Cambridge), 1963. Doctoral thesis: "Decision-Taking Under Uncertainty in Economics". Director, Richardson Institute for Conflict and Peace Research, London; 1958-60 Assistant Lecturer in Econ, U of Manchester; 1961 Lecturer in Advanced Mathematical Econ, Boston Coll, USA; 1961-64 Assistant Professor of Econ, Graduate School of Industrial Administration, Carnegie Institute of Technology, USA; 1964-65 Visiting Research Professor, Institute of International Econ Studies, U of Stockholm; 1965-67 Senior Research Fellow in Conflict Studies, U of Lancaster; 1967-70 Research Associate, Centre for the Analysis of Conflict, U Coll, London; 1975 Visiting Professor, Dept of Govt, U of Texas at Austin, USA. Publs: *Conflict Analysis*, 1971; *Oligopoly and Conflict: A Dynamic Approach*, 1973. Fields: Scientific approach to political studies; conflict analysis related to violent or potentially violent conflicts; formal and mathematical methods of analysis in the theory of conflict processes; conceptual problems of explanation of international behaviour; international politics.

[1384]
NICHOLSON Peter Philip
21 March 1940, British. 5 Newton Villas, Mumbles, Swansea SA3 4SS, Wales. Degrees: BA. 1963- Assistant Lecturer, Lecturer, Senior Lecturer, U Coll of Swansea. Publs: "Relationship between Political Theory and Political Practice", *Political Studies*, 1973; "The Internal Morality of Law", *Ethics*, 1974; " 'Unravelling Thrasymachos' Arguments in 'The Republic' ", *Phronesis*, 1974; "Recent Studies in English of Kant's Political Philosophy", *Political Studies*, 1975; "Philosophical Idealism and International Politics", *British Journal of International Studies*, 1976; "Kant on the Duty Never to Resist the Sovereign", *Ethics*, 1976; "What is Politics: Determining the Scope of Political Science", *Il Politico*, 1977. Fields: Analytical political theory; legal philosophy; history of idealist political philosophy, especially in Britain.

[1385]
NICLAUSS Karlheinz*
19 January 1937, German, D-5480 Remagen-Oberwinter, FR Germany. Degrees: Dr phil (Bonn). Doctoral thesis: "Die Sowjetunion und Hitlers Machtergreifung". Assistent, Seminar für Pol Wiss, U of Bonn; Scholar of Deutsche Forschungsgemeinschaft. Publs: *Die Sowjetunion und Hitlers Machtergreifung*, 1966; "Internationale Beziehungen", in *Das Fischer-Lexikon* (co-ed), 1969. Fields: Soviet-German relations; the founding of the Federal Republic as 'democracy-founding'.

[1386]
NIELSEN Hans Jørgen*
16 June 1940, Danish. Solengen 7, 2990 Nivå, Denmark. Degrees: Cand sci pol (Aarhus), 1966. 1966- Assistant Professor, U of Copenhagen. Fields: Political attitudes; differences between political parties on different hierarchical levels.

[1387]
NIESS Frank
21 January 1942, German. Schiffgasse 9, D-6900 Heidelberg, FR Germany. Degrees: MA (Heidelberg). Doctoral thesis: "Der Mythos der Einen Welt. Zur Soziologie und Geschichte der amerikanischen Weltstaatsidee 1890 bis 1950". 1972-76 Wiss Assistent, Inst für Pol, U of Stuttgart. Publs: *Amerikanische Aussenpolitik*, 1977; *Cuba libre* (with A A Guha), 1977; various articles in *Das Argument, Frankfurter Hefte, Politische Vierteljahresschrift*. Fields: German post-war history; history of political and social change in Cuba; American foreign policy.

[1388]
NIEUWENHOF Francois Philip
5 October 1942, Dutch. 3e Helmerstraat 86, Amsterdam, The Netherlands. Degrees: Drs. Teachers College, U of Amsterdam and Dutch Film and Television Academy, Amsterdam. Publs: Articles on Russian/American relations; the Cold War; Latin American states in the First World War; the electoral system in Holland; the Influence of parliament on foreign politics. Fields: Film and history; Latin-American politics; Russian and East German politics; art and politics.

[1389]
NILSON Sten Sparre
3 February 1915, Norwegian. Institute of Political Science, University of Oslo, Blindern, Oslo 3, Norway. Degrees: Dr phil (Oslo). 1947-50 Pol Research, Christian Michelsen Inst; 1950-65 Public Administration; 1965- Associate Professor, Inst of Pol Sci, U of Oslo. Publs: *Histoire et sciences politiques*, 1950; *Knut Hamsun und die Politik*, 1964; *Politisk avstand ved norske folkeavstemninger*, 1972. Fields: Electoral research, especially the study of referenda.

[1390]
NISSEN Henrik Sandø
16 October 1933, Danish. Selsøvej 15, 2720 Vanløse, Copenhagen, Denmark. Degrees: Dr phil. Doctoral thesis: "Studier i Forhandlinose Politikken og Samarbejdspolitikken" (Policy of Negotiation and Cooperation). Cand Mag Research Scholarship; Lecturer in Pol Sci, U of Copenhagen. Publs: *På Dansk Friheds Grund*, 1963; *Besaettelsestidens Historie* (with Kirchhoff and Poulsen), 1964. Fields: Methodology.

[1391]
NIZARD Lucien
2 October 1931, French. 16 Place Ste Claire, 38000 Grenoble, France. Degrees: Agrégé de droit public et sci pol; Lic. Doctoral thesis: "La jurisprudence des circonstances exceptionnelles et la légalité". Directeur, Centre de recherches sur l'administration écon, Grenoble; Directeur-adjoint, IEP, Grenoble; Directeur de l'équipe associée, CNRS du CERAT; Directeur de DEA "Sociologie de l'Etat", and Directeur de la Collection "Etat et Société". Publs: *Changement social et appareil d'Etat* (with P Bellenger *et al*), 1974; *Eléments pour une nouvelle approche de l'Etat dans la France d'aujourd'hui* (with L Nizard *et al*), 1977; "A propos des représentations sociales de l'Etat d'une mythologie à l'autre", *La Pensée*, 1974; "Les stratégies du ministère des finances",

Bulletin International des Sciences Administratives, 1976; "Défense et illustration des différences, des pratiques sociales aux idéologies", *Connexions*, 1977. Fields: Sociology of the relations between state and society in Western European capitalist countries; ideology of civil servants and representatives of union and employers' associations; changes of legitimacy and their impact at the national level.

[1392]
NOACK Paul Robert Karl
28 September 1925, German, 8034 Unterpfaffenhofen, Albert-Schweitzer-Strasse 13, FR Germany. Degrees: Dr phil (Freiburg), 1952. 1953-58 Political Ed, *Frankfürter Allgemeine Zeitung*; 1958-68 Deputy Ed-In-Chief, *Münchner Merkur*; Ord Professor of Pol Sci, U of Munich. Publs: *Die Intellektuellen*, 1961; *Die deutsche Nachkriegszeit*, 1966; *Friedensforschung — ein Signal der Hoffnung?*, 1970; *Internationale Politik — eine Einführung*, 1970; *Deutsche Aussenpolitik seit 1945*, 1972; *Das Scheitern der Europäischen Verteidigungsgemeinschaft, Entscheidungsprozesse vor und nach dem 30 August 1954*, 1977. Fields: International relations, especially German and French policy; peace research.

[1393]
NOBRE-CORREIA Jos Manuel
27 July 1946, Portuguese. Avenue des Courses, 7 BTE 6, B-1050 Bruxelles, Belgium. Degrees: Lic (Free U of Brussels), 1970; Lic en sci pol (Free U of Brussels), 1973. Collaborateur Extérieur, Bureau d'Etudes de la Radio diffusion-Télévision, Belge; Assistant, U Libre de Bruxelles; Collaborateur, Centre d'Etudes des Techniques de Diffusion Collective. Publs: *Pouvoir Persuader* (co-author), 1973; plus various articles in *Res Publica, Etudes de Radio-Télévision, Annales de la Faculté de Droit de Liège, Courrier Hebdomadaire du CRISP*. Fields: The political language of the media.

[1394]
NOCERA Cosimo
23 September 1941, Swiss. Rue de Cossonay 1 bis, 1008 Prilly, Switzerland. Degrees: Lic ès sci pol (Lausanne). Professeur aux classes de formation pédagogique, Lausanne. Publs: *Le Fossé (1914) La conférence de Carl Spitteler; Notre point de vue Suisse à Zurich; L'Anschluss de mars 1938 et ses répercussions en Suisse*. Fields: Swiss history and political system.

[1395]
NOHLEN Dieter
6 November 1939, German. H-7900 Heidelberg, Wilhelmsfelderstrasse 18/1, FR Germany. Degrees: Dr phil (Heidelberg); Habilitation (Tübingen). Doctoral thesis: "Spanischer Parlamentarismus im 19 Jahrhundert — Regimen parlamentario und parlamentarische Regierung". Assistant Professor of Pol Sci, U of Heidelberg; Scientific Advisor, Inst of International Partnership, Konrad Adenauer-Foundation; Assistant Professor, Latin American Faculty for post-graduate studies in Pol Sci and Administration, Santiago de Chile; Professor of Pol Sci and Head, Centre for Latin American Studies, U of Heidelberg. Publs: *Spanischer Parlamentarismus im 19 Jahrhundert — Regimen parlamentario und parlamentarische Regierung*, 1970; *Wahlen in Deutschland. Theorie-Geschichte-Dokumente* (co-author), 1971; *Chile — Das sozialistische Experiment*, 1973; *Feuer unter der Asche — Chiles gescheiterte Revolution*, 1974; *Handbuch der Dritten Welt* (co-ed), 1974, 1976, 1978; *Wahlsysteme der Welt — Daten und Analysen — Ein Handbuch*, 1978. Fields: Comparative politics; elections and electoral systems; underdevelopment and development in the Third World; theory and politics; Latin American economic, social and political structures.

[1396]
NONNENMACHER Günther C H
2 November 1948, German. Bouterwekstrasse 10, 56 Wuppertal 11, FR Germany. Degrees: Dr phil; MA (Heidelberg). Doctoral thesis: "Theorie und Geschichte. Studien zu den politischen Ideen von James Harrington" (Theory and History. Studies on the Political Ideas of James Harrington). Wiss Assistent, GHS Wuppertal. Publs: *Theorie und Geschichte. Studien zu den politischen Ideen von James Harrington*, 1977; "Reform — Schwierigkeiten einer Theorie der Praxis", *Res Publica*, 1977; *Abschied vom Leviathan* (with G Zellentin), 1978. Fields: Political philosophy; history of ideas; political ideologies; modern political theory; problems of communism; comparative political systems.

[1397]
NOOMEN Gerrit Willem
27 September 1943, Dutch. Zandkamp 161, Hoogland (Amersfoort), The Netherlands. Degrees: Dr Soc Sci. Doctoral thesis: "Beween en Motiveren" (Assertions and Data). Staff-member, Dept of Communications, Free U of Amsterdam. Publs: *De Tÿd in vÿf Dimensies* (with G W Noomen *et al*), 1974. Fields: Public opinion; political information and participation; freedom of speech.

[1398]
NOORDZIJ Gerard Pieter
23 July 1944, Dutch. Zaanenlaan 27, Haarlem, The Netherlands. Degrees: Dr. Doctoral thesis; "Systeem en Beleid" (System and Policy). Dept of Pol Sci, Free U of Amsterdam. Publs: *Systeem en Beleid*, 1977; *Onrust langs de groeigrenzen*, 1974; Contributions to: *Kernthema's der Politicologie* (M P C M van Schendelen (ed)), 1976; *Verkenningen in de Politiek* (A Hoogerwerf (ed)), 1971. Fields: Theoretical approaches; policy analysis/development; comparative political science.

[1399]
NOPONEN Martii Noponen
7 June 1928, Finnish. Koroistentie 13 B 26, 00280 Helsinki 28, Finland. Degrees: Dr, 1966. Doctoral thesis: "Kansanedustajien Sosiaalinen Tausta Suomessa" (The Social Background of the Finnish Legislators). 1955- Lecturer in Pol Sci, U of Helsinki; 1975- Rector, Summer U of Helsinki; 1964- Ed, *History of Finnish Parliament*; 1971- Associate Professor, Dept of Pol Sci, U of Helsinki. Publs: *Politiikka Tutkimuksen Kohteena*, 1972. Fields: Parliament: its role and function, background and function of its members; political parties; political participation and elites; political philosophy.

[1400]
NORA Pierre*
17 November 1931, French. 38 Boulevard Saint Michel, Paris VIème, France. Degrees: Agrégé d'histoire, 1958. Assistant à la Sorbonne; Maître de conférences, IEP, Paris; Maître-assistant, IEP, Paris. Publs: *Les Français d'Algérie*, 1961; *Vincent Auriol, Journal du Septennat 1947*, 1970; *Vincent Auriol, mon Septennat 1947-54* (with J Ozouf), 1970. Fields: Methodological problems in contemporary history.

[1401]
NORD Hans Robert
11 October 1919, Dutch. 15 rue Conrad 1, Luxembourg, Luxembourg. Degrees: Master of Law (Leiden), 1941; Dr of Law (Leiden), 1945. Doctoral thesis: "Historical Development and Legal Significance of the Idea of Representation in Constitutional Law". Barrister; Legal Adviser; Secretary General, European Parliament. Publs: *Problems of In-*

ternational Government, International and Supra-National Co-operation, NATO; In Search of a Political Framework for a United Europe. Fields: International politics; European affairs; comparative constitutional law.

[1402]
NORD Lars
1 March 1938, Swedish. Siktargatan 7E, 753 23 Uppsala, Sweden. Degrees: Fil lic. Statsvetenskap (Uppsala), 1968; PhD. Doctoral thesis; "Non-alignment and Socialism. Yugoslav Foreign Policy in Theory and Practice". Research. Publs: *Röd Opposition, Europas Kommunistiska Partier och Nikita Chrusjtjovs Fall* (A Sparring (ed)), 1965. Fields: Non-aligned countries in the cold war, especially the compatibility of a non-aligned position to Marxism-Leninism: the case of Yugoslavia.

[1403]
NORRENBERG Daniel Henri Ghislain*
7 July 1939, Belgian. 218 Avenue Montjoie, B-1180 Brussels, Belgium. Degrees: Lic en sci pol et diplomatiques (Free U of Brussels), 1962; Lic en journalisme (Free U of Brussels), 1962; Dipl (Coll d'Europe), 1964. 1964- Civil Servant, Ministry of National Education and Culture; 1969- Member of the Cabinet of P Vermeylen, National Education. Publs: Articles in *Socialisme, Res Publica*. Fields: Belgian civil service; education; the political aspects of European integration.

[1404]
NORRIS Pippa
10 July 1953, British. 14 Clifford Road, New Barnet, Hertfordshire, England. Degrees: BA; MSc (LSE). Doctoral thesis: "John Stuart Mill as an MP (1865-68)". Lecturer, Dept of Government, Newcastle-upon-Tyne Polytechnic.

[1405]
NØRRUNG Per*
30 October 1945, Danish. Sølystgade 8, 8000 Aarhus C, Denmark. Degrees: Magisterkonferens (Copenhagen), 1969. Doctoral thesis: "Differential Fertility — An Investigation of Married Danish Women and Their Expected Number of Children". 1969-70 Teacher of Soc, Social and General Knowledge of Society, Askov Folk High School; Lecturer and Research Assistant, U of Aarhus. Publs: "Yugoslavia, Workers' Self-management and Market Economy", *Politica*, 1970. Fields: The drug problem: the Danish debate in parliament and the press.

[1406]
NORTHEDGE Frederick Samuel
16 October 1918, British. 21 Marlborough Road, Chiswick, London W4, England. Degrees: BSc; PhD; DSc. Doctoral thesis: "International Intellectual Co-operation within the League of Nations". Lecturer, Reader, Professor in International Relations, LSE. Publs: *The Troubled Giant: Britain Among the Great Powers 1916-39*, 1966; *International Disputes: The Political Aspects* (with M Donalan), 1971; *A Hundred Years of International Relations* (with M J Grieve), 1971; *The Use of Force in International Relations* (ed), 1974; *Descent from Power: British Foreign Policy 1945-73*, 1974; *East-West Relations: Detente and After*, 1974; *The International Political System*, 1976. Fields: International politics; British foreign policy; East-West relations; European international relations.

[1407]
NORTON Alan Lewis
17 November 1926, British. 3 Green Meadow Road, Birmingham B29 4DD, England. Degrees: BA; MA (Cambridge), 1958; M Soc Sci (Birmingham). 1952-60 Senior Education Officer and Senior Inspector of Education, Overseas Civil Service, W Nigeria; 1961-64 Assistant for Further Education, County Borough of Barnsley; 1965-66 Senior Research Associate, U of Birmingham; 1966- Lecturer, Senior Lecturer, Inst of Local Government Studies and Department of Local Government Studies and Administration, U of Birmingham; Publs: *Local Government Administration in England and Wales, Management of Local Government*, 1967; *Recent Reforms in the Management Arrangements of County Boroughs in England and Wales*, 1969; *Recent Reforms in the Management Structure of Local Authorities — the London Boroughs*, 1969; *Communication with Special Reference to Problems of Management*, 1970; *Setting up the New Authorities*, 1972. Fields: Local authority structure and management in Britain and in municipalities in developing countries and Mediterranean cities.

[1408]
NORTON Philip
5 March 1951, British. Department of Politics, University of Hull, Hull HU6 7RX, England. Degrees: BA; MA (Pennsylvania), 1975; PhD (Sheffield), 1977. Doctoral thesis: "Intra-Party Dissent in the House of Commons: The Conservative Party in Government 1970-74". 1975-76 Temporary Lecturer, U of Sheffield; 1977 Lecturer, Wroxton Coll, Fairleigh Dickinson U; 1977- Lecturer, U of Hull. Publs: *Conservative Dissidents*, 1978; *Dissension in the House of Commons 1945-74*, 1975; "The Organization of Parliamentary Parties", in *The House of Commons in the Twentieth Century* (S A Walkland (ed)), 1979; plus various articles in *Parliamentary Affairs, The Parliamentarian, Public Law*. Fields: British government and politics, with special reference to parliament; American government and politics.

[1409]
NOSSITER Thomas Johnson
24 December 1937, British. 38 Newlay Lane, Horsforth, Leeds LS18 4LE, England. Degrees: BA; D Phil (Oxon). Doctoral thesis: "Elections and Local Politics in County Durham and Tyneside 1832-74". 1964-72 Lecturer, Senior Lecturer in Government, LSE. Publs: *Imagination and Precision in the Social Sciences* (ed), 1972; *Influence, Opinion and Political Idioms in Reformed England*, 1975; plus various articles in *Political Studies, South Asian Review*. Fields: Communism in Kerala State, India; 19th century British political behaviour; 20th century British electoral behaviour; political sociology; Indian politics.

[1410]
NOUAILLE-DEGORCE Brigitte Suzanne Marie
21 November 1946, French. Moulin Chapelle A24, 33170 Gradignan, France. Degrees: Lic en droit, (IEP); DES; MA (U Coll Los Angeles), Dipl (FNSP). Doctoral thesis: "L'évolution de la politique française de coopération avec les Etats africains et malgaches au Sud du Sahara de 1958 à 1977". Assistant de recherche, FNSP. Publs: "Ethiopie: un nouveau rythme", *Revue Française d'Etudes Politiques Africaines*, 1975; "Soudan", *Universalia, Encyclopaedia Universalis-France*, 1976; "Somalie 1976: consolidation du pouvoir mais incertitudes économiques et internationales", *Annuaire des Pays de l'Océan Indien*, 1976; "Marien N'Gouabi", *Universalia, Encyclopaedia Universalis-France*, 1977; "T F A I 1977; la République de Djibouti", *Annuaire des Pays de l'Océan Indien*, 1977; "Somalie 1977; l'isolement", *Annuaire des Pays de l'Océan Indien*, 1977; "L'évolution de l'Ethiopie depuis la fin de l'empire", *Revue Française d'Etudes Politiques Africaines*, 1978. Fields: The political situation in Black Africa with particular reference to the Horn of Africa.

[1411]
NOUR Salua
26 April 1944, Egyptian. Hähnelstrasse 8, 1000 Berlin 41, FR Germany. Degrees: Dr rer
Pol. Doctoral thesis: "Zur Theorie der Internationalen Beziehungen; ein
methodologischer Versuch". Assistant Professor, Dept of Pol Sci, Free U of Berlin.
Publs: *Zur Analyse internationaler Abhängigkeiten* (with G Junne), 1974; "Das Erdöl
im Prozess der Industrialisierung der Förderländer", in *Erdöl für Europa* (H Eisenhans
(ed)), 1974; "Das als entwicklungsfördernder bzw — hemmender Faktor am Beispiel
Mexikos und Venezuelas", *Internationale Entwicklung*, 1974; "Technologietransfer
nach den Entwicklungsländern — Ein Vergleich zwischen westlichen und sozialistischen
Praktiken", *Internationale Entwicklung*, 1975; "Probleme und Perspektiven der
Frauemanzipation im Nahen Osten", *Internationale Entwicklung*, 1975; "Die Entwicklungshilfe: Instrument zur Aufrechterhaltung der internationalen Arbeitsteilung
oder zur Überwindung von Unterentwicklung?", in *Weltmarkt und Ent-
wicklungsländer* (K Voll (ed)), 1976; "Die Beziehungen der Sowjetunion zur Dritten
Welt: Emanzipation fördernde und Abhängigkeit verstärkende Elemente", *Weltmarkt
und Entwicklungsländer* (K Voll (ed)); "Sozio-ökonomische Strukturen und alternative
Erziehungssysteme in der Dritten Welt", in *Symposium über alternative Erziehungssysteme in der Dritten Welt*, 1978. Fields: Third World problems; Africa, Near
East, USA and USSR in world politics and economy; multinational firms in the Third
World.

[1412]
NOUSCHI André*
10 December 1922, French. Centre de la Méditerranée Moderne et Contemporaine,
Université de Nice, 117 rue de France, 06000 Nice, France. Degrees: Lic d'histoire;
Agrégé d'histoire; Dr ès lettres. Doctoral thesis: "Enquête sur le Niveau de Vie des
Populations Rurales Constantinoises de la Conquête à 1919". 1956-59 Attaché au
CNRS; 1959-64 Professor, U of Tunis; 1967-68 Director, Centre de la Méditerranée
Moderne et Contemporaine; 1964- Professor of Contemporary History, U of Nice.
Publs: *L'Algérie, passé et présent* (co-author), 1960; *La naissance du nationalisme
algérien (1919-54)*, 1962; *Initiation aux sciences historiques*, 1969; *Le commentaire de
textes et de documents historiques*, 1969; *La France de 1848 à 1914* (with A Olivesi),
1970; *Luttes pétrolières au Proche-Orient*, 1970; *La France de 1914 à 1970* (with M
Agulhon). Fields: The Mediterranean; contemporary history and its growth; social
groups; analysis of population movements in Mediterranean countries in the 19th and
20th centuries.

[1413]
NOUSIAINEN Jaakko Ilmari
20 December 1931, Finnish. Virusmäentie 96 B, 20300 Turku 30, Finland. Degrees: MA
(Helsinki), 1952; Lic pol sci (Helsinki), 1956; Dr pol sci (Helsinki), 1956. 1953-60 Ed for
Finnish News Agency; 1961-63 Assistant Professor, U of Hyväskylä; 1963- Professor of
Pol Sci, U of Turku. Publs: *Kommunismi Kuopion läänissä*, 1956; *Puolueet Puntarissa*,
1959; *Eduskunta Aloitevallan Käyttäjänä*, 1961; *The Finnish Political System*, 1971;
Valtioneuvoston Järjestysmuoto ja Sisäinen Toiminta, 1975. Fields: Finnish political
system; political institutions.

[1414]
NOVE Alexander
24 November 1915, British. 55 Hamilton Drive, Glasgow G12 8DP, Scotland. Degrees:
BSc; D Ag (Giessen). 1958-63 Reader in Russian Soc and Econ Studies, U of London;
Professor of Econ and Director, Inst of Soviet and East European Studies, U of
Glasgow. Publs: *The Soviet Economic System*, 1977; *Stalinism and After*; *Economic*

History of the USSR; *Efficiency Criteria for Nationalized Industries*; *Socialist Economics* (co-ed); *The Soviet Economy*, 1971. Fields: Soviet and socialist economics; Russian and Soviet history; the political economy of development; international, especially East-West trade; East European agriculture.

[1415]
NUISSLE Ekkehard
15 June 1946, German. Conradstrasse 23, 6905 Schriesheim, FR Germany. Degrees: Dr phil (Bremen), 1974. Doctoral thesis: "Massenmedien im System hergestellter Öffentlichkeit. Untersuchungen zu einem Aspekt bürgerlicher Herrschaft". 1966-68 Redakteur; 1970-72 Pressereferent, U of Heidelberg; 1972- Vorstandsvorsitzender, Arbeitsgruppe für empirische Bildungsforschung, Heidelberg and Lehrbeauftragter, U of Heidelberg. Publs: *Scheitert die Hochschulreform?*, 1973; *Organisationsmodelle Hochschulpressestellen*, 1973; *Wahlkampf als Ritual?*, 1974; *Massenmedien im System bürgerlicher Herrschaft*, 1975; *Soziale Defizite in der Weiterbildung*, 1976; *Auswertung des Bildungsurlaubs*, 1977; *Ein Bildungsurlaub mit Industriearbeiterinnen*, 1978. Fields: Sociology of communication; development politics and sociology; media investigation.

[1416]
NURMI Hannu Juhani
24 August 1944, Finnish. Nostoväenk 5 B 70, SF-20350 Turku 35, Finland. Degrees: PhD (Turku), 1974. Doctoral thesis; "Causality and Complexity: Some Problems of Causal Analysis in the Social Sciences". Research Assistant, National Research Council of the Social Sciences; Assistant in Pol Sci, Assistant Professor of Methodology of the Social Sciences, U of Turku. Publs: *Rationality and Public Goods*; "Ways out of the Prisoner's Dilemma", *Quality & Quantity*, 1977; "On Strategies of Cybernetic Model-building", *Kybernetes*, 1978; "Crisis in Statistical Causal Analysis", in *Political Methodology*, 1975; "Social Causality and Empirical Data-reduction Techniques", *Quality & Quantity*, 1974. Fields: Nature and emergence of social institutions; game-theory models of the bargaining process; fuzzy set theory and its application to political decision-making.

[1417]
NUTZINGER Hans G
25 May 1945, German. Poststrasse 4, D-6903 Neckargemünd, FR Germany. Degrees: Dipl, 1968; Dr rer Pol, 1973; Habilitation, 1976. Doctoral thesis: "The Place of the Firm in Socialist Economies". Assistant, U of Heidelberg; Assistant, U of Dortmund; Research Fellow, Deutsche Forschungsgemeinschaft; Chair of Economic Policy, U of Heidelberg. Publs: *Die Marxische Theorie und ihre Kritik* (with E Wolfstetter), 1974; *Die Stellung des Betriebes in der sozialistischen Wirtschaft*, 1974; *The Firm as a Social Institution*, 1976; *Concepts of Value in Linear Economic Models*. Fields: Theory of the firm; history of economic thought; Marxist economics.

[1418]
NYBERG Tore Samuel
4 January 1931, Swedish. Lahnsgade 83, DK-5000 Odense C, Denmark. Degrees; Fil dr (Lund), 1965. Assistant Professor, U of Odense. Publs: *Birgittinische Klostergrundungen des Mittelalters*, 1965. Fields: Medieval history; towns; monasticism; South-East Asia.

[1419]
NYHOLM Pekka Gideon
3 April 1926, Finnish. Bredantie 73 D, Kauniainen, Finland. Degrees: MA (Helsinki), 1951; Lic (Helsinki), 1959; Dr (Helsinki), 1961. Doctoral thesis: "The Cohesion of Party Groups in the Finnish Parliament in the Electoral Period of the years 1948-51 and the Years 1954 and 1961". 1964-66 Assistant Professor of Soc Sci, U of Jyväskylä; 1966-72 Researcher, Finnish National Research Council for Soc Sci; 1973- Assistant Professor of Soc Sci, U of Jyväskylä. Publs: *The Agrarian Group Interest in the Finnish Parliament during the Years 1930-51*, 1965; *Parliament, Government and Multidimensional Party Relations in Finland*, 1972; *A Probabilistic View of Coalition Formation*, 1977. Fields: Models of party relations; coalition theories; government as a cybernetic control system.

O

[1420]
OBERLERCHER Reinhold
17 June 1943, German. Metzer Strasse 1, D-2000 Hamburg 70, FR Germany. Degrees: Dr phil. Doctoral thesis; "Theorien über Arbeitskraft". Publs: *Deduktion des Staates*, 1975; *Dialektik in Formeln*, 1975; *System der gesellschaftlichen Bewusstseinsformen*, 1976; *Der Begriff der politischen Massenkommunikation*, 1977. Fields: General theory of politics and law.

[1421]
OBERNDÖRFER Peter Johannes
2 September 1942, Austrian. c/o Johannes Kepler Universität Linz, 4045 Linz-Auhof, Austria. Degrees: Dr Law (Vienna); Hochschuldozent (Linz). Assistant Professor, Full Professor, U of Linz. Publs: *Das Wirtschaftsrecht als Instrument der Wirtschaftspolitik* (with L Fröhler), 1969; *Gemeinderecht und Gemeindewirklichkeit*, 1971; *Stadtrechtsreform in Österreich*; *Körperschaften des öffentlichen Rechts und Interessenvertretung: Österreichisches Raumordnungsrecht*. Fields: Local government; economic policy and law; planning policy and law.

[1422]
OBRECHT Werner Arthur
10 April 1942, Swiss. Nordstrasse 2, CH-8304 Wallisellen, Switzerland. Degrees: Lic phil. Research Fellow, Lecturer, Soziologisches Inst, Zürich. Publs: "Some Methodological Notes on the Use of Factor Analysis" (with R Levy), *Bulletin des Soziologischen Institut*, 1968; "Diachronic Data for the Main Model Variables: Operationalization, Computation and Preliminary Analysis" (with R Bautz *et al*), in *A Macrosociological Theory of Societal Systems* (P Heintz (ed)), 1972; "Operationalization of the Concept of Power" (with R Levy), in *A Macrosociological Theory of Societal Systems* (P Heintz (ed)), 1972; "Structure and Structural Change of World Society" (with P Heintz), *International Review of Community Development*, 1977. Fields: Dynamics of world society; structure and dynamics of conceptual systems and images of the social realm of reality; epistemology and theory of science; social theory.

[1423]
O'DAY John Joseph*
22 October 1941, American. 6.33 Trinity College, Dublin 2, Republic of Ireland. Degrees: BA; MA (Washington), 1967; PhD (Dublin), 1973. Doctoral thesis: "Some Classical and Contemporary Theories of Rational Democratic Voting: A Critical Analysis". 1965 Graduate Assistant, American U, Washington; 1967- Deputy Lecturer, Lecturer in Pol Sci, Trinity Coll, Dublin. Fields: Classical and contemporary theories of democracy; classical utilitarian political thought, especially J Bentham.

[1424]
OFFERDAL Audun
30 April 1941, Norwegian. Sikthaugen Terrasse 53, N-5033 Fyllingsdalen, Norway. Degrees: Mag artium (Oslo), 1968. Research Associate, Inst of Pol Sci, U of Oslo; Lecturer, Inst of Soc and Pol Studies, U of Bergen. Fields: Local government; public administration; public policy analysis.

[1425]
OGLEY Roderick Clive
24 June 1929, British. 4 King Henry's Road, Lewes, Sussex, England. Degrees: BA. 1955-57 U of Manchester; 1960-61 U of Edinburgh; 1961-65 Lecturer in International Relations, U of Aberdeen; 1969-70 Nuffield Soc Sci Research Fellow; 1965- Lecturer, Reader in International Relations, U of Sussex. Publs: *The United Nations: Its Political Role 1945-65*, 1965; *The Theory and Practice of Neutrality in the Twentieth Century* (ed), 1970; *The United Nations and East-west Relations, 1945-71*, 1972; *Whose Common Heritage?*, 1975. Fields: The theory and methodology of international relations in general, and conflict in particular; game theory and experimental games; international organization.

[1426]
ÖHGREN Bo Rolf
14 May 1925, Swedish. Dammvägen 2, 752 56 Uppsala, Sweden. Degrees: MA; PhD; Docent. Doctoral thesis: "People on the Move. Social Development, Migration Patterns and Popular Movements in Eskilstuna 1870-1900". 1972-75 Secretary General, Scandinavian Historical Meeting; Research Assistant, Research Associate, Assistant Professor, Dept of History, U of Uppsala. Publs: *The Metal Engineering Workers at Oskarshamn 1890-1905*, 1973; *People on the Move*, 1974; *Crises and Crisis Politics in the Nordic Countries Between the World Wars* (ed), 1974; *From the Middle Ages to the Welfare State* (ed), 1976; *Geocode: A Computer Code System for Administrative Division with a Boundary-Correcting Analysis Program*, 1976; *Microhistory on the Macrolevel. The Swedish Engineering Worker in a National Perspective around the Turn of the Century*, 1978; *Urbanisation in Sweden 1840-1920*, 1977. Fields: Social history; political mobilization; computer mapping; urbanization; voluntary associations and political activity.

[1427]
ÖHLINGER Theo
22 June 1939, Austrian. 1130 Vienna, Grenzgasse 15, Austria. Degrees: Dr. Doctoral thesis: "Der Völkerrechtliche Vertrag im staatlichen Recht". Professor of Constitutional and Administrative Law, U of Vienna. Publs: *Der Stufenbau der Rechtsordnung*, 1975; *Institutionelle Aspekte der österreichischen Integrationspolitik*, 1975; *Der Völkerrechtliche Vertrag im staatlichen Recht*, 1973. Fields: Legal theory, general theory of law; legal sociology.

[1428]
OHLY Heinz-Peter K E C*
8 April 1945, German. Zentralarchiv für Empirische Sozialforschung, Bachemer Strasse 40, 5 Köln 41, FR Germany. Research Assistant, Inst of Soc Psychology, Köln; Research Assistant, Zentralarchiv, Köln. Fields: Development of a formal classification system for meaningful words; analysis of usefulness of words in questions as indicators for secondary analysis.

[1429]
OLDFIELD Richard Adrian Tinker
8 August 1939, British. 43 Kenwood Road, Stretford, Manchester M32 8PS, England. Degrees: BSc; PhD. Doctoral thesis: "The Growth of the Concept of Economic Planning in the Doctrine of the British Labour Party 1914-1935". Economist, Canadian National Railways, Montreal, Canada; Lecturer in Pol, U of Salford. Publs: Articles in *International Review of Social History*, *Bulletin of the Society for the Study of Labour History*. Fields: Labour history; philosophy of history.

[1430]
O'LEARY Cornelius
15 August 1927, Irish. Queen's University, Bedford, England. Degrees: MA (NUI); D Phil (Oxon). Doctoral thesis: "The Elimination of Corrupt Practices in British Elections 1868-1911". 1960 Lecturer, Queen's U, Belfast; 1966- Reader in Pol Sci, Queen's U, Belfast. Publs: *The Irish Republic and its Experiment with Proportional Representation*, 1961; *The Elimination of Corrupt Practice in British Elections 1868-1911*, 1962; *Belfast: Approach to Crisis: A Study of Belfast Politics 1613-1970*, 1973; *Irish Elections 1918-1977*, 1978. Fields: British and Irish electoral history; American politics; nationalism within the British Isles.

[1431]
OLIVESI Antoine Sébastien Charles
24 November 1924, French. 72 rue Montecristo, 13 Marseille, France. Degrees: Lic d'historie (Aix), 1945; DES (Aix), 1946; Agrégé d'histoire (Paris), 1948. 1948-50 Professeur agrégé d'histoire, Lycée de Toulon; 1950-61, Lycée Thiers, Marseille; 1961- Maître-assistant, Faculté des Lettres, U de Provence. Publs: *La commune de 1871 à Marseille et ses origines*, 1950; *La République romaine* (with A Clerici), 1968; *Géographie électorale des Bouches du Rhône sous la IVème République* (with M Roncayolo), 1961; *La France de 1848 à 1914* (with A. Nouschi), 1970; *L'atlas historique de Provence* (co-author), 1969; *Histoire de Marseille*, 1973; *Edouard Daladier, Chef de Gouvernement*, 1977. Fields: Socio-political history of contemporary France; history of the French Labour movement from 1870.

[1432]
OLSEN Johan P
14 August 1939, Norwegian. Lyngfaret 82, 5071 Loddefjord, Norway. Degrees: Mag (Oslo), 1967; D phil (Bergen), 1970. Doctoral thesis: "On the Theory of Organizational Choice". 1968-69 Fellow, Inst of Soc Research, Oslo; Visiting Scholar and Professor, U of California, Irvine; 1972-73 U of Stanford; 1969-73 Assistant Professor, U of Bergen; 1973- Professor in Public Administration and Organization Theory in Bergen. Publs: *Ambiguity and Choice in Organizations* (with J G March), 1976; "Organizational Participation in Government", in *Handbook of Organizational Design* (Nyström and Starbuck (eds)), 1978; plus articles in *Administrative Science Quarterly*, *European Journal of Political Research*, *Acta Sociologica*, *Scandinavian Political Studies*. Fields: Organization theory; public administration.

[1433]
OLSEN Ole Jess
18 November 1942, Danish. Galgebakken, Neder 6-1, 2620 Albertslund, Denmark.
Degrees: MA. 1966-1970 Research Fellow, International Peace Research Inst, Oslo, and
Inst for Peace and Conflict Research, Copenhagen; 1973 Associate Professor, Inst of
Pol Studies, U of Copenhagen. Publs: *Proceedings of the International Peace Research
Association, Third Conference* (ed), 1970; *Papers from Peace Research Society (International)* (ed), 1970; plus articles in *Økonomi og Politik; Kurasje; Economia Publica;
Häften För Kritiska Studier; Kritik of Kapitallogikken* (co-author), 1975. Fields: Public
enterprise; economic and political development in Italy and Spain.

[1434]
OLSEN Peter Nannestad*
19 August 1945, Danish. Hvedebjergvej 88, DK-8220 Braband, Denmark. Degrees:
Cand sci pol (Aarhus), 1971. Amanuensis, Inst of Pol Sci, U of Aarhus. Publs: "Party
Distances in the Danish Folketing 1945-68" (co-author), *Scandinavian Political Studies*,
1971. Fields: Legislative behaviour; party systems, development and dimensionality.

[1435]
ÖNDER Zehra
9 August 1944, Turkish. Samoa Strasse 21, 1 Berlin 65, FR Germany. Degrees: Dipl
Pol; Dr rer Pol. Doctoral thesis: "Die Türkische Aussenpolitik im Zweiten Weltkrieg"
(Turkish Foreign Policy in World War II). Lehrbeauftrager, Inst für Internationale
Beziehungen und Regionalstudien, Free U of Berlin; 1977- Research Fellow (VW-
Stiftung), Free U of Berlin. Publs: "Die Türkische Aussenpolitik im Zweiten
Weltkrieg", *Südosteuropäische Arbeiten*, 1977; "Pan-Turanismus in Geschichte und
Gegenwart", *Österreichische Osthefte*, 1977; "Kulturelle Entfremdung", in *Betrifft Erziehung*, 1977. Fields: International relations; Third World; Middle East.

[1436]
OOSTENBRINK Ben
21 May 1943, Dutch. 1e van der Helststraat 64, 1072 NZ Amsterdam, The Netherlands.
Assistant Professor, Dept of International Relations, Free U of Amsterdam. Publs: articles in *Nieuw Europa. Transaktie, Forum Europa* and *Anti-militarismus Information*;
"A West European Nuclear Force as an Undesired Side-Effect", in *Jahrbuch für
Friedens- und Konfliktforschung*, 1977. Fields: Peace research; European security;
European integration.

[1437]
OPEL Fritz*
26 August 1912, German, Johann-Klotz Strasse 21, 6 Frankfurt/Main, FR Germany.
Degrees: Dr phil (Marburg), 1956. 1956- Trade Union Secretary. Publs: *Der Deutsche
Metallarbeiterverband während des Ersten Weltkrieges und der Revolution*, 1965; *75
Jahre Industriegewerkschaft 1891-1966* (with D Schneider), 1966. Fields: History and
ideology of the Labour movement.

[1438]
OPPENHEIM Abraham Naftali
25 November 1924, British. The London School of Economics and Political Science,
Houghton Street, London WC2A 2AE, England. Degrees: PhD (London), 1956. Doctoral thesis: "A Study of Social Attitudes of Adolescents". 1952- Lecturer, Senior Lecturer, Reader in Soc Psychology, LSE. Publs: *The Function and Training of Mental*

Nurses, 1955; *Television and the Child* (co-author), 1958; *Questionnaire Design and Attitude Measurement*, 1966; *Childhood Behaviour and Mental Health* (co-author), 1971; *Civic Education in Ten Countries* (co-author), 1976; *Civic Education and Participation in Democracy: the German Case*, 1977. Fields: Peace research and conflict studies; crisis behaviour in organizations; behavioural studies of diplomats and foreign ministries; simulation of crisis and conflicts; political socialization; foreign policy decision-making; industrial conflict; values in social research; drug-taking and alcoholism studies; epidemiology.

[1439]
ORR Robert Richmond
27 July 1930, New Zealander. 12 Erskine Hill, London NW11 6HB, England. Degrees: MA; PhD (London). Doctoral thesis: "The Thought of William Chillingworth". U of Belfast; U of Western Australia; U of Monash; LSE. Publs: *Reason and Authority*, 1968. Fields: History of political thought; political theory.

[1441]
OSTERGAARD Geoffrey Nielsen
25 July 1926, British. Faculty of Commerce and Social Science, University of Birmingham, Birmingham B15 2TT, England. Degrees: BA; MA (Oxon), 1953. Doctoral thesis: "Public Ownership in Great Britain: A Study in the Development of Socialist Ideas". 1950 Research Assistant, Action Society Trust; 1952-53 Research Fellow, U of Nottingham; 1953- Assistant Lecturer, Lecturer, Senior Lecturer in Pol Sci, U of Birmingham. Publs: *Power in Co-operatives* (with A H Halsey), 1965; *The Gentle Anarchists* (with M Currell), 1971; "Democracy in India", in *Dilemmas of Democratic Politics in India* (G S Halappa (ed)), 1966; "Power in Co-operatives" (co-author), in *Studies in British Society* (J A Banks (ed)), 1969; "Indian Anarchism: the Sarvodaya Movement", in *Anarchism Today* (A Apter and J Joll (eds)), 1971. Fields: Non-violent political action.

[1440]
OSTBYE Helge
31 October 1946, Norwegian. Nordre Toppe 3, N-5088 Mjolkeraaety, Norway. Degrees: Cand pol. Research assistant, Centre for Mass Media Research, Bergen; Lecturer in Soc, Inst of Soc and Pol Studies, U of Bergen. Fields: Mass media research; sociology and politics of language; social science methodology.

[1442]
ØSTERUD Øyvind
27 April 1944, Norwegian. Erling Sksalgssonsgt 26, Oslo 2, Norway. Degrees: Mag art (Oslo), 1970; PhD (London), 1974. Doctoral thesis: "Agrarian Structure and Peasant Policies in Scandinavia". 1970-73 Research Fellow, U of Bergen; 1973- Lecturer, Senior Lecturer in Pol, U of Oslo. Publs: *Konflikt og Administrerjon*, 1970; *Samfunnsplanlegging og Politisk System*, 1972; *De Utro Tiehere*, 1974; *Agrarian Structure and Peasant Politics in Scandinavia*, 1974. Fields: Comparative politics; development studies; public policy; public planning.

[1443]
OSTROWSKY Jürgen
4 November 1945, German. Schückingstrasse 10, 3550 Marburg, FR Germany. Degrees: MA, 1972. Doctoral thesis: "The Relationship between South Africa and the FRG". 1972-73 Lecturer, U of Kassel; 1972- Wiss Angestellter, Philipps U, Marburg. Publs: *The Angolan Revolution* (with G Broenner), 1976; *South Africa* (with W Geisler), 1978. Fields: History and actual developments in Africa, especially Southern Africa; international politics in general; USA; West German foreign policy.

[1444]
O'SULLIVAN Noel Kerry
31 July 1941, British. 113 Carr Lane, Willerby, E Yorks, England. Degrees: BSc; PhD (London), 1969. Doctoral thesis: "The Problem of Political Obligation in the Writings of Green, Bosanquet, and Oakeshott". 1963-64 Prize Fellow, U of Harvard, USA; Lecturer, U of Hull. Fields: Political philosophy and the history of political thought.

[1445]
OTTMAN Horst Henning
9 March 1944, German. Bussardstrasse 24, 8025 Unterhaching, FR Germany. Degrees: MA; Dr phil. Doctoral thesis: "Individuum und Gemeinschaft bei Hegel". Wiss Assistent, Lehrstuhl Lobkowicz, GSI, U of Münich. Publs: *Das Scheitern einer Einleitung in Hegels Philosophie. Eine Analyse der Phänomenologie des Geistes*, 1973; *Individuum und Gemeinschaft bei Hegel. Vol I, Hegel im Spiegel der Interpretationen*, 1977. Fields: German idealism; analytical philosophy and ethics; theory of social sciences; practical philosophy; European politics; conservatism.

[1446]
OURLIAC Paul
19 January 1911, French. 14 rue de la Pomme, 31 Toulouse, France. Degrees: Lic ès Lettres; Lic en droit; Dr en droit; Agrégé d'histoire de droit. Professeur, Faculté de Droit, U de Toulouse; Directeur, Inst d'Etudes Pol Sociales de Toulouse; Membre, Inst de France (Académie des Inscriptions et Belles Lettres); Membre, Conseil de Perfectionnement de l'Ecole des Chartes; Membre, Commission Juridique, CNRS. Publs: On the history of French law; history of the church and canon law of the 15th century; world civilization; history of agriculture.

[1447]
OVENDALE Ritchie
28 March 1944, British. 41 Maesceinion, Waun Fawr, Aberystwyth SY23 3QQ, Wales. Degrees: BA; MA (Natal), 1965; MA (McMaster), 1966; D Phil (Oxon), 1972. Doctoral thesis: "The Influence of United States and Dominion Opinion on the Formation of British Foreign Policy, 1937-39". Lecturer, Dept of International Pol, U Coll of Wales, Aberystwyth. Publs: *'Appeasement' and the English Speaking World. Britain, the United States, the Dominions, and the Policy of 'Appeasement', 1937-1939*, 1975. Fields: The foreign policy of the British Labour government, 1945-1951; Anglo-American relations; United States foreign policy; Southern Africa; methodology.

[1448]
OVERBOSCH Henk
28 October 1948, Dutch. Lange Poten 37, The Hague, The Netherlands. Degrees: Dr, 1976. Doctoral thesis: "Political Decentralization in the City of Amsterdam and the Relation to Community Development". Employed in local government organization at The Hague. Fields: Local government; comparative politics; re-organization of the central, intermediary and local government; decentralization; political participation.

P

[1449]
PAGE Edward Charles
19 October 1953, British. 156 Fergus Drive, Glasgow G20 6AX, Scotland. Degrees: BA; MSc (Strathclyde). Temporary Lecturer in Politics, U of Strathclyde. Publs: "Michael Hechter's Internal Colonial Thesis: Some Theoretical and Methodological Problems", *European Journal of Political Research*, 1978; "Why Should Central-Local Relations in Scotland be any Different from those in England?", *Public Administration Bulletin*, 1978. Fields: Central-local relations in Britain and West Germany; centre and periphery studies.

[1450]
PAHL Raymond Edward
17 July 1935, British. Darwin College, The University, Canterbury, Kent, England. Degrees: BA; PhD (LSE), 1964. Doctoral thesis: "Urban Influences on Rural Areas within the London Metropolitan Region". 1959-65 Staff Tutor, U of Cambridge; 1965- Lecturer, Senior Lecturer, Professor in Soc, U of Kent. Publs: *Readings in Urban Sociology* (ed), 1968; *Whose City? And Other Essays on Sociology and Planning*, 1970; *Patterns of Urban Life*, 1970; *Managers and Their Wives* (with J M Pahl), 1971. Fields: Corporatism; the informal economy; forecasting future patterns of urban life.

[1451]
PALAZZOLO Vincenzo
30 January 1913, Italian. Via Randaccio 50/A, 56100 Pisa, Italy. Degrees: Dr in Law; Libera Docenza. Doctoral thesis: "La Teoria pura del Diritto di Hans Kelsen" (The Pure Theory of Law in Hans Kelsen). Provost, Camerino U and U of Pisa; Full Professor of Philosophy of Law, U of Pisa. Publs: *Considerazioni sulla Natura dell'Azione e sul Carattere dell'Esperienza Giuridica, Contributo allo Studio dei Rapporti tra Economia e Diritto, Scienza e Epistemologia Giuridica, Sapere e Libertà, Democrazia e Persona*. Fields: Legal and political philosophy; theory of government.

[1452]
PANEBIANCO Angelo
11 June 1948, Italian. Via Milano 48, 40139 Bologna, Italy. Degrees: Laurea (Bologna), 1971; Degree in International Affairs (John Hopkins U), 1971-72. 1971- Research Fellow, Dept of Pol Sci, Assistant Professor of Pol Sci, U of Bologna. Publs: *Le Crisi della Modernizzazione*, 1973; "Analisi di una Sconfitta. Il Declino del PSI", *Il Mulino*, 1976; *I Nuovi Radicali* (with M Teodori and P Ignazi), 1977. Fields: Political participation; political parties; peace and war studies.

[1453]
PANTER-BRICK Samuel Keith
29 September 1920, British. 2 Inner Park Road, London SW19, England. Degrees: BA; B Phil. 1965-67 Professor of Public Administration, Inst of Administration, Ahmadu Bello U; 1967- Senior Lecturer, LSE. Publs: *Nigerian Politics and Military Rule* (ed), 1970; *Soldiers and Oil: The Political Transformation of Nigeria* (ed), 1978. Fields: African politics.

[1454]
PAPISCA Antonio
25 May 1936, Italian. Via Lovarini 31, 43100 Padova, Italy. Degrees: Libero Docente. Professor of International Relations, U of Catania; Professor of International Relations, U of Padova. Publs: *L'Intervento delle Nazioni Unite nelle Consultazioni Populari*, 1967; *Introduzione allo Studio delle Relazioni Internazionali*, 1973; *Comunità Europea e Sviluppo Politico*, 1974; *Europa '80: dalla Comunità all'Unione Europea*, 1975; *Democrazia alla Prova. Riflessioni alla Vigila dell'Elezione Europea*, 1978. Fields: Political development of the European Community; European political parties; new international order; peace research.

[1455]
PAPPI Franz Urban
10 March 1939, German. c/o ZUMA, B 2, 1, D-68 Mannheim, FR Germany. Degrees: Dr phil (München), 1967. Doctoral thesis: "Wahl verhalten und politische Kultur". Privatdozent, U of Cologne; Wiss Angestellter, ZUMA, Mannheim. Publs: *Politischer Radikalismus* (with H D Klingemann); *Networks of Collective Action: A Perspective on Community Influence Systems* (with E O Laumann), 1976. Fields: Political sociology; social structural determinants of voting behaviour; social stratification in communities: multi-level analysis.

[1456]
PAREKH Bhikhu
4 January 1935, Indian. Department of Political Studies, The University, Hull, E Yorks, England. Degrees: BA; MA (Bombay), 1956; PhD (LSE), 1966. Doctoral thesis: "The Idea of Equality in Nineteenth Century English Political Thought". 1957-59 Lecturer, U of Baroda, India; 1962-63 Tutor, LSE; 1963-64 Lecturer, U of Glasgow; 1968-69 Visiting Professor, U of British Columbia; 1974-75 Visiting Professor, Concordia U, Montreal, 1976-77 Visiting Professor, McGill U, Montreal; 1964- Lecturer, Senior Lecturer, U of Hull. Publs: *Politics and Experience* (ed), 1968; *Dissent and Disorder* (ed), 1971; *Bentham's Political Thought* (ed), 1973; *Jeremy Bentham: Ten Critical Essays* (ed), 1973; *Knowledge and Belief in Politics* (ed), 1973; *Colour, Culture and Consciousness* (ed), 1974; *The Concept of Socialism* (ed), 1975. Fields: Bentham and utilitarian thought; Hegel and Marx; radical political thought; problems of political philosophy.

[1457]
PARKINSON Michael Henry*
11 August 1944, British. Social Studies Building, The University, Liverpool L69 3BX, England. Degrees: BA; MA (Manchester), 1967. 1970- Lecturer, Dept of Pol Theory and Institutions, U of Liverpool; 1972-73 Visiting Associate Professor, Washington U, St Louis. Publs: *The Labour Party and Secondary Education 1918-65*, 1970. Fields: Education policy; urban politics.

[1458]
PARODI Jean Luc Alexandre Marie
8 June 1937, French. 61 rue de Varenne, 75007 Paris, France. Degrees: Dipl (IEP Paris), 1960; Cert d'histoire ancienne (Sorbonne), 1961; Cert d'histoire du Moyen Age (Sorbonne), 1962. Chargé de recherche, FNSP. Publs: *Les rapports entre l'éxécutif et le législatif sous la Vème République*, 1971; *Elections présidentielles des 5 et 19 Décembre 1966* (co-author), 1970; *La politique* (ed), 1971; *Le député français* (co-author), 1973; *La Vème République et le système majoritaire*, 1973.

[1459]
PARRIS Henry Walter
20 November 1923, British. 15 Murdoch Road, Wokingham, Berkshire RG11 2DG, England. Degrees: BA: MA (Oxon); MA (Leeds); PhD (Leicester). Doctoral thesis: "Government and Railways in Nineteenth Century Britain". 1949-58 and 1961-63 Adult Education; 1958-61 Research Fellowship, U of Manchester; 1963-70 Lecturer in Pol, U of Durham; 1969-70 Visiting Professor, U of Waterloo, Canada; Director of Studies in Public Administration, Civil Service Coll; Head of Research, Directorate of Training, Training Services Agency; Visiting Professor, U of Reading. Publs: *Government and Railways in Nineteenth Century Britain*, 1965; *Specialists and Generalists* (contributor) (F F Ridley (ed)), 1968; *Constitutional Bureaucracy*, 1969; *Going Comprehensive* (co-author), 1970; *Staff Relations in the Civil Service*, 1973. Fields: Comparative government, with special reference to Western Europe; public administration.

[1460]
PARRY Cyril
20 March 1929, British. 3 Gors Goch, Menai Bridge, Gwynedd, Wales. Degrees: BSc; PhD. Doctoral thesis: "Socialism in Gwynedd: A Study of Labour and Liberal Politics 1900-1920". Lecturer, Senior Lecturer in Government, U Coll of Wales. Publs: *The Radical Tradition in Welsh Politics*, 1970. Fields: Labour history; public administration; modern British government.

[1461]
PARRY Geraint Burton
4 August 1936, British. "Parkfield", Park Road, Hale, Cheshire, England. Degrees: BSc; PhD (London). Doctoral thesis: "Enlightened Government and its Critics in Eighteenth Century Germany". 1959-60 Assistant Lecturer in Pol Theory and Government, U Coll, Swansea; 1960-74 Assistant Lecturer, Lecturer in Philosophy, Senior Lecturer in Philosophy, Senior Lecturer in Government, U of Manchester; 1964-65 Visiting Lecturer in Pol Sci, U of Wisconsin; 1972-73 Visiting Professor in Pol Studies, Queen's U, Kingston; 1974-76 Edward Caird Professor of Pol, U of Glasgow; 1977- Professor of Government, U of Manchester. Publs: *Political Elites*, 1969; *Participation in Politics* (ed), 1972; *John Locke*, 1978; *Democracy, Consent and Contract* (with J Lively and P Birnbaum (eds)), 1978; "Political Thinkers" series (general ed); plus articles on history of political ideas, political philosophy, political sociology and modern democratic theory. Fields: Political sociology, in particular, elites; political participation; modern democratic theory; history of political thought, particularly 17th and 18th centuries.

[1462]
PASINI Dino
25 August 1913, Italian. Viale Mazzini 41, Roma, Italy. Doctoral thesis: "Fundamental Rights". Professor of Political Philosophy, U of Naples. Publs: *Saggi sulla Storia in E Kant*; *Diritto, Società e Stato in Kant*; *Saggio su Jhering*; *Vita e Forma nella Realtà del Diritto*; *Riflessioni in Tema di Sovranità*; *Stato-Governo e Stato-Società*; *Diritto, Società e Stato in Vico*; *Tirannide e Paura in Platone, Senofonte e Aristotele: Problemi di Filosofia Politica*. Fields: Fundamental rights; violence and right; European Community.

[1463]
PASQUINO Gianfranco
9 April 1942, Italian. Via Ciro Menotti 5, 40126 Bologna, Italy. Degrees: Laurea; MA (Washington), 1967. 1969- Assistant Professor, Associate Professor, Professor of Pol Sci, U of Bologna; 1970-75 Assistant Professor of Latin American Pol Institutions, Associate Professor of Theory of Pol Development, U of Florence; 1971-77 Managing

ed, *Rivista Italiana di Scienza Politica*; 1977- Vice-President, Conference Group on Italian Politics; 1975- Visiting Professor of Pol Sci, Bologna Center, John Hopkins U. Publs: *Modernizzazione e Sviluppo Politico*, 1970; *Militari e Potere in America Latina*, 1974; *Dizionario di Politica* (associate ed), 1976; *Continuità e Mutamento Elettorale in Italia* (co-ed and contributor), 1977; *La Politica nell'Italia che Cambia* (co-ed and contributor), 1978. Fields: Political development and comparative politics; Italian politics; military regimes.

[1464]
PASSIGLI Stefano
8 November 1938, Italian. Via Doccia, 7-50135 Settignono, Florence, Italy. Degrees: Dr (Florence); Libero Docente. Doctoral thesis: "Lineamenti di Sviluppo della Pubblica Admministrazione in Italia". Professore Aggregato, U of Florence; Professore Incaricato, U of Padova; Visiting Associate Professor, U of Michigan; Visiting Professor, Dartmouth College; Teaching Fellow, Harvard U. Publs: *Emigrazione e Comportamento Politico*, 1968; *The Government and Politics of Contemporary Italy* (co-author), 1967; *Potere ed Elite Politische*, 1971; *L'Analisi della Politica*, 1971. Fields: Comparative administration; political elites; party systems; methodology.

[1465]
PASTEUR David
13 September 1931, British. Institute of Local Government Studies, University of Birmingham, Birmingham, B15 2TT, England. BA; M Soc Sci (Birmingham), 1968. 1955-67 Administrative Officer, Uganda Government; 1968-72 Lecturer, Faculty of Econ and Administration, U of Malaya; 1972- Lecturer, Inst of Local Government Studies, U of Birmingham. Publs: "The Process and Techniques of Planning and Programme Analysis, in *Programme Budgeting for East Africa* (K J Davey (ed)), 1971; "Management for the Absorption of Newcomers in Lusaka", *Development Administration*, 1976. Fields: Urban management systems in developing countries with particular reference to local government organizations and reform; metropolitan techniques including programme budgeting; use of case study methods for teaching management.

[1466]
PATERNITI Pietro*
6 October 1948, Italian. Via Vincenzo Bellini 29, San Gregorio di Catania, Italy. Degrees: Laurea in Giurisprudenza (Catania), 1971. 1972- Research Assistant, U of Catania. Fields: Judiciary and politics; justice and politics.

[1467]
PATERSON William Edgar
26 September 1941, British. 7 Farmer Ward Road, Kenilworth, England. Degrees: MA (St Andrews), 1964; MSc (LSE), 1965; PhD (LSE), 1973. Doctoral thesis: "The German Social Democratic Party and European Integration 1949-57: A Study of 'Opposition in Foreign Affairs". 1967-70 Lecturer in International Relations, U of Aberdeen; 1970-75 Volkswagon Lecturer in German Pol, U of Warwick; 1975- Senior Lecturer in Pol, U of Warwick. Publs: *The SPD and European Integration*, 1974; *Social Democracy in Post War Europe* (with I Campbell), 1974; *Social and Political Movements in W Europe* (with M Kolinsky (eds)), 1976; *Social Democratic Parties in W Europe* (with A Thomas (eds)), 1977; *Foreign Policy Making in W Europe* (with W Wallace (eds)), 1978; plus various articles in *Europa-Archiv, Government-Opposition, International Affairs, Parliamentary Affairs*. Fields: West German domestic and external politics; social democratic parties; European integration.

[1468]
PAWELKA Peter
12 April 1941, German. 74 Tübingen, Haüsserstrasse 142, FR Germany. Degrees: Dr phil, 1969; Habilitation (Tübingen), 1972. Doctoral thesis: "The UN and the German Problem, 1948-67". 1969-74 Wiss Assistent; 1974-76 Universitätsdozent; 1976- Professor, Inst für Pol, U of Tübingen. Publs: *Die UNO und das Deutschlandproblem*, 1971; *Wahlkampf und Parteiorganisation. Eine Regionalstudie zum Bundestagswahlkampf 1969* (co-author), 1974; *Vereinte Nationen und strukturelle Gewalt*, 1974; *Internationales System und internationale Organisation*, 1974; *Internationale Beziehungen. Eine vernachlässigter Lernbereich* (co-author and ed), 1976; *Internationale Beziehungen*, 1977; *Politische Sozialisation*, 1977. Fields: International relations; political sociology; political socialization; comparative government.

[1469]
PAYNE Clive David
22 July 1942, British. 40 Windmill Street, Brill, Aylesbury, Buckinghamshire, England. Degrees: BSc; Dipl Stats (Wales). Lecturer in Statistics, U Coll of Aberystwyth, Wales; Lecturer in Computer Applications, School of Soc Studies, U of Strathclyde; Director, Research Services Unit, Nuffield Coll, U of Oxford; Director, Computing and Research Support Unit, Faculty of Soc Studies, U of Oxford. Publs: "Analysing Census Data", in *The British General Election* (Butler and Pinto-Duschinsky (eds)); " Features of Electoral Behaviour at By-elections", in *By-elections in British Politics*, 1973; "Another State with Nature: An Ecological Regression Model of the British Two-Party Vote Ratio in 1970", *BJPS*, 1976; "Election Night Forecasting", *JRSS*, 1975; "The Use of Logistic Models in Political Science: British Elections 1964-70", *Political Methodology*, 1977. Fields: Quantitative methods in political science; electoral politics.

[1470]
PEAR Richard Hatherley
1916, British. 11 Lenton Avenue, The Park, Nottingham, England. Degrees: BSc. 1938-39 Darwin Research Fellow, Eugenics Society; 1939-41 Commonwealth Fellowship, U of Chicago; 1941-42 British Information Services, NY; 1942-47 Army Service; 1947-65 Assistant Lecturer, Lecturer, Reader in Government, LSE. 1965- Professor and Head of Dept of Pol, U of Nottingham. Publs: *How People Vote* (co-author), 1956; *American Government*, 1963; *British Essays in American History* (contributor) (H C Allen (ed)); *American Civilization* (Skard (ed)); *Specialists and Generalists* (F Ridley (ed)); *Society: A Handbook of Sociology* (Welman (ed)). Fields: American political parties; methodology of comparative government; the university study of politics.

[1471]
PECORELLA Corrado*
16 January 1930, Italian. Piaggio 50/5, 16136 Genova, Italy. Degrees: Laurea in Giurisprudenza; Lib Doc in Storia del Diritto Italiano. Direttore degli Archivi de Stato di Sondrio, Como, Piacenza; Professore Incaricato di Storia, U of Parma. Publs: *I Governi Provvisori Parmensi*, 1959; *Studi sul Settecento Giuridico*, 1964.

[1472]
PEDERSEN Finn Stendal*
10 May 1943, Danish. Skt Knudsgade 181, 5000 Odense, Denmark. Degrees: Cand phil (Aarhus), 1969. Amanuensis, Inst of History and Soc Sci, U of Odense. Fields: Agricultural development in Scandinavia 1680-1884 and state policy; left wing policy in the Danish parliament, 1840s and 1850s.

[1473]
PEDERSEN Leif
16 August 1943, Danish. Galgebakken, Sønder 2-13, 26 20 Albertslund, Denmark. Associate Professor, Inst of Pol Studies, U of Copenhagen. Publs: *Dynamic Models of Social Systems* (in Danish), 1975. Fields: Application of general systems theory; cybernetics; computer simulation within the social sciences.

[1474]
PEDERSEN Mogens N
14 December 1939, Danish. Huindsleuvej 37, 5350 Rynkeby, Denmark. Degrees: Cand sci pol (Aarhus), 1964. 1964-72 U of Aarhus; 1970-71 Research Fellow, U of Stanford; 1973- Professor of Pol Sci, U of Odense; 1978 Visiting Professor, EUI, Florence. Publs: *Political Development and Elite Transformation in Denmark*, 1976; various articles on legislative behaviour, recruitment, university legislation, etc. Fields: Comparative politics, especially parliaments, parties, systems; decision and negotiation theory; political recruitment and elite theory; university and research policy; data archives.

[1475]
PEDERSEN Ole Karup
8 February 1929, Danish. Rosenfeldt allé 3, DK-2820 Gentoffe, Denmark. Degrees: D phil (Copenhagen), 1970. Doctoral thesis: "Udenrigsminister P Munchs Opfattelse af Danmarks Stilling i International Politik". 1955-62 Archivist, Danish Record Office; 1962-63 Documentalist, Danish Foreign Ministry; 1963-70 Research Fellow, U of Copenhagen; 1970- Professor in International Pol, U of Copenhagen. Publs: *Afrikansk Nationalisme*, 1963; *De Nye Stater*, 1966; *Tendenser i International Politik*, 1967; *Udenrigsminister P Munchs Opfattelse af Danmarks Stilling i International Politik*, 1970. Fields: State building in colonial areas; small states in international politics; international conflicts; theory-building in international politics.

[1476]
PEELE Gillian Rosemary
3 January 1949, British. 3A Fyfield Road, Oxford, England. Degrees: BA; B Phil (Oxon). Doctoral thesis: "The Conservative Party with Special Reference to the Development of Dissident Groups 1929-35". 1973-75 Research Fellow, St Anthony's Coll, U of Oxford; 1975- Fellow and Tutor in Pol, U Lecturer, Lady Margaret Hall, U of Oxford. Publs: *The Politics of Reappraisal* (with C Cook (eds)). Fields: Rule of law and politics in the United States and Europe; modern British government; Conservative party history and organization.

[1477]
PEETERS Florent Philemon Julius
9 August 1909, Belgian. Princes Jos Charlotta Avenue 56, 2100 St Niklaas, Belgium. Degrees: Dr; Dr phil; Cand jur; Baccalaurens. Doctoral thesis: "Vita Platini by Porphyrios". Dept of History of Pol Philosophy and State Philosophy, U of Ghent. Publs: "Eigendomsrecht", in *Recht op Eigendom*, 1936; *Het Bruine Bolsjewisme*, 1938; *40 Maanden Oranienburg*, 1946; *Politieke Anatomie van het Totalitarisme*, 1964; *Verzamelde opstellen over het Nationaalsocialisme*, 1946; *Die Lehren des Sun Yatsers*, 1959. Fields: Marxism-Leninism; Eurocommunism; new philosophy; anarchism.

[1478]
PEETERS Marcel August
15 December 1920, Belgian. Naamse Straat 40, 3000 Leuven, Belgium. Degrees: Dr, 1970. Doctoral thesis: "Godsdienst en tolerantie in het socialistische denken — Een historische-doctrinaire Studie". 1959- Assistant, Docent, Hoogleraar, Catholic U of

Leuven. Publs: "Het probleem van de tolerantie tijdens de XIXe Eeuw", *Politica*, 1969; "Leven en Werk van Ernst Bloch, Filosoof en Theoloog van de Revolutie", *Politica*, 1976; "Ujamaa: het socialisme van Julius K Nyerere", *Politica*, 1973; "De afhankelijkheids-theorie. Enkele kritische aanmerkingen bij een neomarxistische visie op de ontwikkelingsproblematiek", *Onze Olma Mater*, 1978. Fields: Ideologies in developing countries; fascism; theories of imperialism; Eurocommunism; political theology.

[1479]
PELINKA Anton
14 October 1941, Austrian. 5 Höhenstrasse, A-6020 Innsbruck, Austria. Degrees: Dr Law (Vienna), 1964. 1966-67 Ed, *Die Furche*; 1968-71 Research Assistant, Inst for Advanced Studies, Vienna; 1971-73 Lecturer and Assistant, U of Salzburg; 1973-74 Professor of Pol Sci, U of Essen; 1974-75 Professor of Pol Sci, Pedagogical College, Berlin; 1975- Professor of Pol Sci, U of Innsbruck. Publs: *Demokratie und Verfassung in Österreich* (with M Welan), 1971; *Stand oder Klasse? Die Christliche Arbeiterbewegung Österreichs 1933*, 1972; *Dynamische Demokratie. Zur konkreten Utopie gesellschaftlicher Gleichheit*, 1974; *Politik und moderne Demokratie*, 1976; *Bürgerinitiativen und demokratischer Staat*, 1978. Fields: Comparative politics, especially parties, party systems, pressure groups, parliaments; theory of democracy; peace research.

[1480]
PENROSE Ernest Francis
26 January 1895, British. 15 rue de la Benardière, 94300 Vincennes, France. Degrees: BA; MA, 1930; PhD (Stanford), 1934. Doctoral thesis: "Is Japan Overpopulated: A Study in Population Theories and Their Applications". Nagoya Coll of Commerce; Research Associate, Food Research Institute, Stanford U; Associate Professor, U of California (Berkeley); Chef du Section Econ, Bureau Internationale du Travail, Genève; Professor of Geography and International Relations, John Hopkins U; Professor of Econ, U of Baghdad; Inst of Historical Research, U of London, Inst of Commonwealth Studies, U of London, FNSP, Paris. Publs: *Food Supply and Raw Materials in Japan*, 1930; *Population Theories and their Application, with Special Reference to Japan*, 1934; *The Industrialization of Japan and Manchuria* (contributor), 1940; *Wartime Economics* (contributor and ed), 1940; *Economic Planning for Peace*, 1953; "Negotiating on Refugees and Displaced Persons", in *Negotiating with the Russians*, 1951; *The Revolution in International Relations*, 1965; *Iraq: International Relations and National Development* (with Edith Penrose), 1978. Fields: International relations; economic and political population; political and economic history.

[1481]
PERELMAN Chaim
20 May 1912, Belgian. 32 rue de la Pêcherie, Brussels, Belgium. Degrees: Dr of Law (Free U Brussels), 1934; PhD (Free U Brussels), 1938. Doctoral thesis: "Etude sur l'oeuvre de Gottlob Frege". Dean, Faculty of Humanities and School of Education, U of Brussels; Visiting Professor, McGill U, Montreal, Pennstate, New York State, U of Buffalo and Stony Brook; Professor of Logic, Ethics and Metaphysics, U of Brussels. Publs *The Idea of Justice and the Problem of Argument*, 1963; *An Historical Introduction to Philosophical Thinking*, 1965; *Justice*, 1967; *Droit, morale et philosophie*, 1968; *The New Rhetoric — A Treatise on Argumentation*, 1969; *Le camp de l'argumentation* (ed), 1970; *Logique juridique*, 1976. Fields: Theory of justice in values; legal reasoning; theory of argumentation; reasoning and values.

[1482]
PERNTHALER Peter*
12 April 1935, Austrian. 6020 Innsbruck, Phillipine-Welser Strasse 27, Austria. Degrees: Master of Law (Innsbruck), 1952; Dr of Law (Innsbruck), 1958. 1966-68 Associate Professor, U of Agriculture, Vienna; 1968- Professor, U of Innsbruck. Publs: *The Constitutional State and its Army*, 1964; *The Constitutional Barrier of Autonomy in Austria*, 1967; *The Comprehensive National Defence*, 1970; *Quality Evaluation in Industry and the Constitutional Guarantee of Property*, 1971; *The Basic Organization in Constitutional View*, 1971. Fields: Comparative constitutional law, especially FR Germany, Switzerland, and Anglo-American countries.

[1483]
PERRIE Maureen Patricia
20 March 1946, British. Centre for Russian and East European Studies, University of Birmingham, PO Box 363, Birmingham B15 2TT, England. MA (Edinburgh), 1967; MA (Birmingham), 1971. Lecturer in History, Centre for Russian and East European Studies, U of Birmingham. Publs: "The Social Composition and Structure of the Socialist-Revolutionary Party before 1917", *Soviet Studies*, 1972; "The Russian Peasant Movement of 1905-07: Its Social Composition and Revolutionary Significance", *Past and Present*, 1972; *The Agrarian Policy of the Russian Socialist Revolutionary Party, From its Origins Through the Revolution of 1905-07*, 1976. Fields: Peasant movements in Russia, 17th-20th centuries, the ideas which guided them and their political significance.

[1484]
PERRONE Luca
14 December 1945, Italian. 6 via Ceresio, Milan, Italy. Degrees: Dr in Filosofia (Milan), 1969; MA (Berkeley), 1972. Doctoral thesis: "Dialectics and Totality in the Work of G Lukacs (1908-1923)". Professore Incaricato of Methodology of Soc Research, Faculty of Pol Sci, U Statale of Milan; Professore Incaricato of Industrial and Labour Soc, Faculty of Econ and Pol Sci, U della Calabria, Cosenza. Publs: "Marxist Class Categories and Income Inequality", *American Sociological Review*, 1977; *Metodi Quantitativi della Ricerca Sociale*, 1978; *Inflazione e Classi Sociali* (with A Martinelli), 1979. Fields: Social stratification; bureaucratic systems; inflation, with particular reference to the 'perverse effects' of social reforms.

[1485]
PERSCHEL Wolfgang
28 June 1933, German. Am Weingarten 20, D-6301 Pohlheim 1, FR Germany. Degrees: Dr jur (Bonn), 1962. Doctoral thesis: "Die Meinungsfreiheit des Schülers". 1963-71 Assistant Professor in Administrative Law, Constitutional Law and Pol Sci, U of Bonn; 1971- Professor in Pol Sci, U of Siegen. Fields: Constitutional and administrative law; constitutional jurisdiction; educational administration; political education.

[1486]
PERSSON Sune Olav
10 March 1938, Swedish. Scheelegatan 5, S-416 60 Göteborg, Sweden. Degrees: Fil lic ex. Doctoral thesis: "The Count Bernadotte Mediation on Palestine in 1948". Lecturer, Inst of Pol Sci, U of Göteborg. Publs: *Arabstaterna och Öst-väst-konflikten i Förenta Nationera*, 1966; *Palestina-konflikten*, 1974; *Problem i Modern Historia: Mellanöstern*, 1974; "Arabvärlden", in *Regionala Organisationer i Tredje Världen*, 1973. Fields: Palestine conflict.

[1487]
PERSYN Kathie
6 July 1952, Belgian. Veerstraat 160, 2252 Viersel, Belgium. Degrees: Lic. Research
Assistant, Catholic U of Leuven. Fields: Belgian foreign policy in the Middle East.

[1488]
PESONEN Pertti Antero
22 April 1930, Finnish. Institute of Political Science, University of Helsinki,
Hallituskatu 11-13, Helsinki, Finland. Degrees: MA, 1953; PhD (Helsinki), 1958.
1965-71 Professor of Pol Sci; 1966-70 Dean, U of Tampere; 1967-71 Visiting Professor,
U of Iowa; 1971-76 Professor, State U of New York at Stony Brook; 1972- Professor of
Pol Sci, U of Helsinki. Publs: *Valitsijamiesvaalien Ylioppilas Äänestäjät*, 1958; *Tiede ja
Opetus Ministeriö*, 1961; *Valtuutus Kansalta*, 1965; *An Election in Finland*, 1968; *Pro-
testivaalit, Nuorisovaalit*, 1972. Fields: Mass political behaviour; small democracies;
comparative government.

[1489]
PESTOFF Victor Alexis
24 January 1941, American. Rickebysvängen 79-201, S-16374 Spånga, Sweden.
Degrees: PhD. Doctoral thesis: "Voluntary Associations and Nordic Party Systems".
Assistant to the General Secretary of the International Federation of Plantation,
Agricultural and Allied Workers; Lecturer, Dept of Pol Sci, U of Stockholm. Publs:
Voluntary Associations and Nordic Party Systems, 1977; "Membership Participation in
Swedish Consumer Co-operatives", *Polittikki*, 1978; "Soviet Non-Governmental
Organizations: Limits of Empirical Investigations", in *Polittikki*, 1978. Fields: Political
sociology; comparative politics; trade unions and voluntary associations.

[1490]
PETERSEN Ib Damgaard
31 October 1933, Danish. Staerevej 8, 2970, Hoersholm, Denmark. Degrees: Cand
mag. Doctoral thesis: "Laws of Development of Cybernetic Systems". Archivist, Royal
Archives, Copenhagen; Associate Professor in Pol Sci, Inst of Contemporary History
and Pol Sci, Copenhagen; Lecturer in International Pol, Inst of Pol Studies, U of
Copenhagen. Publs: *Et internationalt systems sammenbrud*, 1969; *Traek af den danske
modstandsbevaegelses opståen og udvikling*, 1974; *Laws of Development of Cybernetic
Systems (II) The Case of the Sino-Indian Border Conflict 1959-64*, 1978. Fields: International studies; cybernetics and international policy; interaction and transaction
theory; decision-making theory; bargaining theory; systems theory.

[1491]
PETERSEN Jørn Henrik
5 August 1944, Danish. Hunderupvej 142, 5230 Odense M, Denmark. Degrees: PhD
(Aarhus). Doctoral thesis: "The Application of Mathematics in the Planning of Production and Distribution in the Soviet Union and Hungary" (in Danish). 1968-70 Assistant Professor, U of Aarhus; 1970- Associate Professor, Professor of Social Policy, U
of Odense. Publs: *Aspects of the Problem of Centrally Planned Economies*, 1971; *The
Theory of Social Policy*, 1972; *The Theory of Social Policy*, 1974; *Social Policy and
Welfare Economics*, 1978. Fields: The relation between economics and politics with
special reference to social policy.

[1492]
PETERSEN Nikolaj
28 January 1938, Danish. Ørbyvej 6, DK-8240 Risskov, Denmark. Degrees: Cand mag (Aarhus), 1966. 1966-67 Research Fellowship, U of Aarhus; 1967-71 Executive Secretary, Danish Institute of International Affairs; 1970- Lektor, Inst of Pol Sci, U of Aarhus. Publs: Monographs and articles on strategic theory, foreign policy attitudes, Danish foreign policy and comparative foreign policy. Fields: Foreign policy theory; alliance theory; Danish foreign policy; the Cold War.

[1493]
PETERSSON Olof
1947, Swedish. Sysslomansgatan 31A, S-752 23 Uppsala, Sweden. Degrees: PhD, 1975. Doctoral thesis: "Change in Swedish Political Behaviour". 1971-74 Research Assistant, U of Göteborg. 1974- Research Assistant, U of Uppsala. Publs: *Väljarna och Valet*, 1976; plus articles on political behaviour. Fields: Electoral behaviour; methodology; class and politics.

[1494]
PETHYBRIDGE Roger William*
28 March 1934, British. Centre of Russian and East European Studies, University College, Swansea, Wales. Degrees: MA (Oxon), 1961; Dr ès sci pol (Geneva), 1962. Administrative Officer, aide to the Assistant Director-General, WHO, Geneva; Administrator, Centre of Russian and East European Studies, Swansea. Publs: *A Key to Soviet Politics — The Crisis of the Anti-Party Group*, 1962; *Witnesses to the Russian Revolution* (ed), 1964; *The Development of the Communist Bloc* (ed), 1965; *A History of Postwar Russia*, 1966. Fields: The Russian revolution of 1917; social influences on political trends in the USSR, 1914-28; sociological surveys in Eastern Europe.

[1495]
PETRACCHI Adriana*
4 May 1935, Italian. Viale Regina Giovanna 36, 20129 Milan, Italy. Degrees: Laurea in Sci Pol (Catholic U of Milan); Libera Docente in Storia delle Istituzioni Pol. Assistente Ordinario e Professore Incaricato di Storia delle Istituzioni Pol, Catholic U of Milan; Capo dei Servizi Scientifici alla Fondazione Italiana per la Storia Amministrativa. Publs: *Le Origini dell' Ordinamento Communale e Provinciale Italiano*, 1962; *Intendenti e Prefetti*, 1970. Fields: History of the political institutions of France and Italy in the 16th-18th centuries.

[1496]
PETRIE Anthony Julian
23 December 1941, British. 64 Velwell Road, Exeter EX4 4LD, Devon, England. BA. 1968-69 Temporary Assistant Lecturer, Dept of Pol, U of Keele; 1969- Lecturer, Dept of Pol, U of Exeter. Publs: "The 1967 Election in France", *Political Studies* (co-author), 1968. Fields: Government and politics in France, especially legislative behaviour and institutions.

[1497]
PETROGNANI Roberto
13 March 1941, Italian. Via di Ripoli 273, 50126 Florence, Italy. Degrees: Laurea in Sci Pol (Florence). Doctoral thesis: "Il Linguaggio Giornalistico: un'Ipotesi di Studio sui Mezzi d'Informazione". Addetto alle Esercitazioni in Teoria e Tecnica delle Comunicazioni di Massa, presso la Facoltà di Sci Pol 'Cesare Alfieri' dell'U di Firenza; Addetto alle Esercitazioni in Sociologia della Comunicazione, presso la Facoltà di Magistero della U di Urbino; Junior Member dell'Istituto di Sci Pol della Facoltà di Sci Pol

'Cesare Alfieri' dell'U di Firenze. Publs: *Il Linguaggio Giornalistico: un'Ipotesi di Studio sui Mezzi d'Informazione*, 1969; *Cinema Industriale e Società Italiana*, 1972; *Problemi Teorici dell'Informazione*, 1972; *Il Messaggio Estetico del Pontormo*, 1975; *Communicazione e Politica*, 1976; *Per una Teoria della Comunicazione Politica*, 1978. Fields: Political communication; media; public opinion.

[1498]
PETTERSEN Per Arnt
14 August 1944, Norwegian. Brekkelia 5A, Oslo 8, Norway. Degrees: Cand pol. Research Fellow, The Norwegian Research Council for Soc Sci and Humanities; University Fellow, U of Oslo. Publs: "Elite Perception of Welfare Inequality", *Scandinavian Political Studies*, 1976; "Parliamentary Attitudes towards Labour Market Policies", *European Journal of Political Research*, 1976. Fields: Political behaviour, especially elite behaviour and public policies concerning welfare issues.

[1499]
PETTIT Philip Noel
20 December 1945, Irish. Trinity Hall, Cambridge, England. Degrees: BA; MA (National U of Ireland); MA (Cambridge); PhD (Queen's, Belfast). 1967-68 Assistant, Queen's U, Belfast; 1968-72; 1972-75 Research Fellow, Trinity Hall, U of Cambridge; 1975-77 Lecturer U Coll, Dublin; 1977- Professor of Philosophy, U of Belfast. Publs: *On the Idea of Phenomenology*, 1969; *The Concept of Structuralism*, 1975. Fields: Philosophy of the social sciences; political philosophy.

[1500]
PEUCH Jacques Marcel
29 August 1914, French. 12 Avenue de la Mer, 06360 Eze-Bord-de-Mer, France. Degrees: Agrégé de Droit. Doctoral thesis: "Chateaubriand au Congrès de Vérone". Professeur honoraire, U de St Joseph, Beyrouth; Professeur, U de Nice. Fields: Political theory; international relations.

[1501]
PFEIFENBERGER Werner
23 October 1941, Austrian. Schalk-Strasse 4, A-5020 Salzburg, Austria. Degrees: Dr jur (Vienna), 1963; Habilitation (Salzburg), 1970. Doctoral thesis: "Die Vereinten Nationen — ihre politischen Organe in Sicherheitsfragen". 1970-73 Senior Lecturer, U of Salzburg; 1972- Professor of Pol Sci, U of Münster; 1975- Maître de conférences, U de Grenoble; 1974 Visiting Professor, U of Paderborn; 1975 Visiting Professor Potschefstroom. Publs: *Die Vereinten Nationen*, 1971; *Kruistog teen Kolonialisme*, 1974; *Die UNO-Politik der Volksrepublik China*, 1978; plus various articles on legal and political issues. Fields: International relations; foreign policy; political education; United Nations.

[1502]
PFETSCH Frank R
2 September 1936, German. Sitzbuchweg 44, 69 Heidelberg, FR Germany. Doctoral thesis: "Die Entwicklung zum faschistischen Führerstaat in der politischen Philosophie von Robert Michels". Studiengruppe für Systemforschung, Heidelberg; Ministry for Scientific Research; Dept of Pol Sci, Mannheim; Dept of Pol Sci, U of Heidelberg. Publs: *Innovation und Widerstand in der Wissenschaft*, 1973; *Zur Entwicklung der Wissenschaftspolitik in Deutschland*, 1974; *Innovationsforschung als multidiszipline Aufgabe*, 1975; *Leistungssport und Gesellschaftssystem*, 1975. Fields: Science policy; foreign policy; Third World; fascism.

[1503]
PHILIP George David Edge
29 October 1951, British. 29 Stile Hall Gardens, London W4, England. Degrees: BA; D Phil (Oxon), 1975. Doctoral thesis: "Policy Making in the Peruvian Oil Industry with Special Reference to the Period 1968-73". 1975-76 Research Fellow, Inst of Latin American Studies, U of London; Lecturer in Latin American Pol, LSE. Publs: *The Rise and Fall of the Peruvian Military Radical 1968-1976*, 1978; *Oil and Politics in Ecuador 1972-1976*, 1978; "The Soldier as Radical: The Peruvian Military Government 1968-1975", *Journal of Latin American Studies*, 1976; "The Peruvian Tightrope", *World Today*, 1977; "The Limitations of Bargaining Theory: The IPL in Peru", *World Development*, 1976; "Hydrocarbons in Bolivia, Peru and Ecuador", *Bolsa Review*, 1977; "The Political Economy of Expropriation: Three Peruvian Cases", *Millenium*, 1978; "De Val Van De Radicale Militairen in Peru", *Internationale Spectator*, 1977; "The Military in Government: Some Latin American Perspectives", *Bulletin of the Society of Latin American Studies*, 1977. Fields: Latin American politics; the politics of the military; the politics of oil.

[1504]
PHILIP Kjeld Löwenstein
3 April 1912, Danish. Rungstedvej 91, DK-2960 Rungsted Kyst, Denmark. Degrees: Dr (Aarhus), 1943. 1937-49 Assistant Professor, Full Professor, U of Aarhus; 1949-51 Full Professor, U of Stockholm; 1951-57 Full Professor, U of Copenhagen; 1957-60 Minister for Commerce, Denmark; 1960-61 Minister for Finance; 1961-64 Minister for Economic Affairs; 1965 Economic Adviser to Prime Minister, Somalia; 1965-67 Chairman, Committee on East African Cooperation; 1968- Chairman, Danish Board for Cooperation with Developing Countries; 1969- Consultant, ILO, Geneva. Publs: *La Politica Financiera y la Actividad Economica*, 1949; *Staten og Fattigdommen*, 1947; *Intergovernmental Fiscal Relations*, 1954; *Skattepolitik*, 1965; *Somalia*, 1966; *Det Østafrikanske Faellesskab*, 1969; *Den Östafrikanske Gemenskapen*, 1969; *Kenya*, 1975. Fields: Financial and fiscal policy; development problems, especially in Africa.

[1505]
PHILIPPART André
23 April 1934, Belgian. 23/25 Avenue du Martin Pêcheur, Bte 84 B-1170 Bruxelles, Belgium. Degrees: Lic sci pol (Free U of Brussels), 1959. Doctoral thesis: "Le processus de décision en politique scientifique" (Decision-Making in Science Policy). 1962- Professeur, Inst Sup d'Etudes Sociales de l'Etat; 1964- Secretary-General, Belgian Inst of Pol Sci; 1967-76 Secretary-General, IPSA; 1967- Research Fellow, Inst of Soc, Free U of Brussels. Publs: *Une expérience d'enquêtes électorales* (with J Stengers), 1959; *Synthesis Report on 20 years of Activity, IPSA*, 1970; *Rapport sur les sciences sociales en Belgique*, 1971; *Ethiques, contextes politiques, critères de choix de la science*, 1977; *Evaluation et contrôle du financement de la recherche scientifique*, 1977. Fields: Political decision-making, processes and typologies; policy science with reference to Belgium and the EEC.

[1506]
PHILLIPS Derek L
22 January 1934, American. Kerkstraat 379, Amsterdam, The Netherlands. Degrees: AB (Rutgers), 1959; PhD (Yale), 1962. Doctoral thesis: "Help-seeking and Rejection of the Mentally Ill". 1962-63 Instructor, Dept of Soc, Wellesley Coll; 1963-66 Assistant Professor, Dept of Soc, Dartmouth Coll; 1966-71 Associate Professor, U of New York; 1971- Professor of Soc, U of Amsterdam. Publs: *Knowledge from What?*, 1971; *Abandoning Method*, 1973; *Wittgenstein and Scientific Knowledge*, 1977; "Epistemology and the Sociology of Knowledge", *Theory and Society*, 1974; "The Equality Debate:

What does Justice Require?'', *Theory and Society*, 1977; ''Rationality and the Appraisal of Theories'', *Amsterdams Sociologisch Tijdschrift*, 1977; ''The Social and Moral Background of Social Contracting'', *Amsterdams Sociologisch Tijdschrift*, 1978. Fields: Political philosophy; political theory; sociology and philosophy of science; social science methodology.

[1507]
PICK Otto
4 March 1925, British. 24 Burghley House, Somerset Road, London SW19, England. Degrees: BA; Dr jur (Prague). 1950-58 BBC; 1960-66 Lecturer in History and Government, U of Maryland; 1966- Reader, Professor of International Relations, U of Surrey. Publs: *Collective Security* (with J Critchley), 1974; *Learning about International Organizations* (ed), 1972; *Detente and SALT*, 1978. Fields: Foreign policy analysis; defence policy.

[1508]
PIEHL Ernst
1 November 1943, German. 17 rue de la Fontaine, F-67800 Strasbourg-Hoenheim, France. Degrees: Dipl; Dr. Doctoral thesis: ''Multinational Corporations and the International Trade Union Movement''. 1969-75 Responsible for International Studies, Research Inst of the German Trade Union Federation; 1975- Executive Director, European Youth Foundation. Publs: Two books on multinationals and the EEC; plus various articles on the European trade union movement. Fields: International organizations; trade union movements; European co-operation of the political parties and youth organizations.

[1509]
PIEROT Robert René
22 August 1934, French. 66 Avenue Charles de Gaulle, 95160 Montrouge, France. Degrees: Dr. Doctoral thesis: ''Le statut de l'instituteur public''. Enseignement de droit constitutionnel, U de Paris II. Fields: Administrative and constitutional problems of developing countries; French civil service; law and sociology.

[1510]
PIETSCH Walter*
8 January 1940, German. 62 Wiesbaden, Taunusstrasse 73, FR Germany. Degrees: Dr phil, Doctoral thesis: ''Revolution und Staat. Institutionen als Träger der Macht in Sowjetrussland 1917-22''. 1965-68 Wiss Assistent, Osteuropäische Geschichte; 1968-71 Wiss Assistent, Wiss Pol, U of Freiburg; 1971 Oberregierungsrat; Referent Oberregierungsrat in Hess, Staatskanzlei, Wiesbaden. Publs: *Revolution und Staat. Institutionen als Träger der Macht in Sowjetrussland, 1917-22*, 1968. Fields: Indicators of how interest groups plan their goals.

[1511]
PIJPERS Alfred Eduard
5 September 1947, Dutch. Kanaalstraat 162-III, Amsterdam, The Netherlands. Degrees: Dr. Europa Inst, Pol Sci Section, U of Amsterdam. Publs: ''Transnationale betrekkingen: geen verandering van internationale politiek'', *Acta Politica*, 1977. Fields: Theory of international relations; foreign policy; political development.

[1512]
PILGRAM A J M
15 February 1941, Dutch. Zaagjesbank 12, Leiden, The Netherlands. Degrees: Dr
(Amsterdam). Doctoral thesis: "Political and Economic Convergence". Policy Adviser, Dept of Culture, Recreation and Social Welfare. Fields: Planning; macroeconomic policy; welfare; economic/political order.

[1513]
PILSWORTH Michael John
1 April 1950, British. 27 Lodge Gate, Great Linford, Milton Keynes, Buckinghamshire,
England. Degrees: BA; MA. 1972-73 Research Assistant, Manchester Polytechnic;
1973-75 Research Associate, U of Manchester; 1975-78 Lecturer in Adult Education, U
of Manchester; 1978- Research Fellow, Centre for Television Research, U of Leeds:
presently seconded to the Hansard Society. Publs: *Broadcasting in the Third World*
(with E Katz, E Wedell and D Shinar), 1978. Fields: Political communication; broadcasting of parliamentary proceedings; election broadcasting.

[1514]
PIMLOTT Benjamin John
4 July 1945, British. 166 Richmond Road, London E8, England. Degrees: B Phil; MA
(Oxon). 1969-70 Temporary Lecturer, U of Newcastle-upon-Tyne; 1972 Thanks Offering to Britain Fellow of the British Academy; 1977-78 Soc Sci Fellow of the Nuffield
Foundation; 1972- Lecturer in Pol, U of Newcastle-upon-Tyne. Publs: *Labour and the
Left in the 1930s*, 1977; plus various articles in *Journal of Contemporary History*,
Parliamentary Affairs, *Government and Opposition*, *New Society*, *Political Quarterly*,
New Statesman. Fields: 20th century British political history; political parties; elections;
Portuguese politics.

[1515]
PINKNEY Robert
20 May 1937, British. 4 Shaftesbury Avenue, Whitley Bay, Tyne & Wear NE 26 3TF,
England. Degrees: BSc; PhD. Doctoral thesis: "The Politics of Military Rule in Ghana,
1966-1969". 1975- Senior Lecturer in Government, Newcastle-upon-Tyne Polytechnic.
Publs: *Ghana under Military Rule*, 1972; "The Theory and Practice of Military
Government", *Political Studies*, 1973. Fields: African politics; comparative politics;
British politics.

[1516]
PIOTET Georges
1 February 1948, Swiss. Coteau de Becmont 12, 1816 Clarens, Switzerland. Degrees: Lic
ès sci pol (Lausanne). 1969-72, 1975-76 Assistant, Inst de Sci Pol, Lausanne. Publs: *Les
élections au Grand Conseil Vaudois de 1913 à 1966* (with R Ruffieux), 1971; *Autopsie
d'une Amérique* (with F Masnata), 1973; *Violence et régression. Essai d'analyse de
presse des évènements de mai et juin 1968 en France* (with C Durussel), 1971; *La crise
fiscale en Suisse, éléments pour une analyse de l'Etat* (with C Loertscher), 1977; *Pour
une analyse de l'Etat en Suisse*, 1977; *Corporatisme en Suisse?*, 1978. Fields: Modern
theories of the State; political structure in Switzerland.

[1517]
PISIER Evelyne*
18 October 1941, French. 366 rue de Vaugirard, Paris XVème, France. Degrees: Dr in
Law (Paris), 1970. Doctoral thesis: "La notion de service public dans l'oeuvre de Léon
Duguit". Publs: *Autorité et liberté dans les écrits politiques de Bertrand de Jouvenel*,

1967. Fields: Cuban revolution; political parties in South America; law and sociology; socialism and sociology.

[1518]
PIVASSET Jean Henri*
19 January 1935, French. E 1 Loubassane, Avenue du Docteur Bertrand, 13100 Aix-en-Provence, France. Degrees: Lic en droit, 1959; DES de sci pol, 1961; DES de droit public, 1963; Dr en sci pol, 1969; Agrégé de droit public et sci pol, 1970. Doctoral thesis: "Essai sur la signification politique du Cinéma; l'exemple français, de la libération aux évènements de Mai 1968". 1962-64 Assistant, Faculté de Droit et des Sci Econ d'Alger; 1964-69 Assistant, Faculté de Droit et des Sci Econ, Aix-en-Provence; 1969-70 Chargé de cours, Faculté de Droit et de Sci Pol, Aix; 1971- Maître de conférences, Agrégé, Faculté de Droit et de Sci Pol, Aix Marseille. Publs: *L'Univers politique de Kafka*, 1965; *Essai sur la signification politique du cinéma*, 1971. Fields: Metapsychology and politics; Freudo-Marxism; the psychoanalytic interpretation of group dynamics; leadership; communications; ideology formation; revolutionary strategies in Western Europe; political parties; radical organizations.

[1519]
PIZZORNI Reginaldo*
29 October 1920, Italian. Piazza della Minerva 42, 00186 Rome, Italy. Degrees: Dr in S Teologia (Pontifical U S Tommaso d'Aquino), 1947; Dr in Filosofia con laude (Rome), 1953. 1947-58 Professore di Religione nelle Scuole Statali di Roma; 1955-70 Professore Incaricato di Etica Sociale nella Libera U Internaz degli Studi Sociali Pro Deo; 1954-Professore Ordinario nella Pontifical U S Tommaso d'Aquino di Storia delle Dottrine Politiche e Filosofia del Diritto; 1970- Professore Incaricato di Filosofia moderna nella Facoltà di Filosofia nella Pont U Nateranense. Publs: *Garrigon-Lagrange*, 1969; *Il Concetto Cristiano di Verità, Apologetica, Il Positivismo Guiridico*, 1958.

[1520]
PLANT Raymond
19 March 1945, British. 81 Manley Rd, Manchester, England. Degrees: BA; PhD. Doctoral thesis: "The Political Thought of Hegel". 1967- Assistant Lecturer, Senior Lecturer in Philosophy, U of Manchester. Publs: *Hegel*, 1973; *Community and Ideology*, 1974; *Political Philosophy and Social Welfare*, 1978; *Hegel and Political Economy*, 1977. Fields: History of political thought; contemporary political thought; political concepts; Hegel.

[1521]
PLESCHBERGER Werner
18 August 1950, Austrian. Maxglaner Hauptstrasse 57, A-5020 Salzburg, Austria. Degrees: Dr phil. Doctoral thesis: "Preliminary Remarks to the Theoretical and Empirical Critique of Current Community Research". Publs: "Community Planning and Public", *Österreichische Zeitschrift für Politikwissenschaft* (with F Osang), 1972; "Demand for a Political Science Community", *ibid*, 1973; "Kant, Popper and Socialism", *Die Zukunft*, 1976; *Determinants of Professionalization of Political Scientists in Austria* (with R Pohoryles), 1977. Fields: Professionalization of political scientists; local community research; current political ideologies; Labour movement.

[1522]
PLOWDEN William Jucius Lowthian
7 February 1935, British. 49 Stockwell Park Road, London SW9, England. Degrees: BA; D Phil (Cambridge). Doctoral thesis: "The Motor Car and Politics in Britain". 1960-65 Civil Servant, Board of Trade; 1965-71 Lecturer in Government, LSE; 1971-77

Central Policy Review Staff, Cabinet Office; 1977- Under-secretary, Dept of Industry; Honorary Professor, Dept of Pol, U of Warwick. Publs: *The Motor Car and Politics in Britain*, 1971. Fields: The policy-making process in central government; policy analysis.

[1523]
POELMANS Matthieu Johan
25 October 1944, Dutch. Irislaan 261, Oegstgeest, The Netherlands. Degrees: Dr. Social and Economic Council of the Netherlands (SER), Committee on International Social and Economic Affairs. Publs: "Politieke Partijen", in *Grote Spectrum Encyclopedie*; "Bureaucratie in de Sovjetunie, De vierde macht in het kwadraat", *Cahiers voor de politieke en sociale wetenschappen*, 1977. Fields: European integration; Soviet affairs.

[1524]
POHORYLES Ronald
5 April 1952, Austrian. 1060 Vienna, Kaunitzgasse 33/17, Austria. Degrees: Cand Phil. Doctoral thesis: "European Integration and European Workers' Movements". Inst für Angewandte Soziologie, Vienna; Gesellschaft für Werbepsychologie und Marketingforschung; Journalist. Publs: "Zur Stellung der sozialwissenschaftlichen Intelligenz in Studium und Beruf" (with E Haider), in *Österreichisches Jahrbuch für Soziologie*, 1974; "Bürgerliche Ideologie und Kapitalinteressen im herrschenden österreichischen Recht" (with J Grey), *Österreichische Zeitschrift für Politikwissenschaft*, 1975; "Zur Professionalisierungsstrategie für Politikwissenschafter" (with P W Lachnit), *Österreichische Zeitschrift für Politikwissenschaft*, 1975. Fields: International politics (EC); law and politics.

[1525]
POLIN Raymond
1910, French. 26 Boulevard St Germain, 75006 Paris, France. Degrees: Dr d'Etat, 1945. 1945-60 Professeur, U de Lille; 1960- Professeur, U de Paris-Sorbonne. 1976- Président U de Paris - Sorbonne. Publs: *Compréhension des valeurs*, 1945; *Du laid, du mal du faux*, 1948; *Politique et philosophie chez Thomas Hobbes*, 1953; *Politique morale de John Locke*, 1960; *Le bonheur considéré comme l'un des Beaux-Arts*, 1966; *Ethique et politique*, 1968; *La politique de la solitude - Essai sur la politique de Jean Jacques Rousseau*, 1971; *La liberté de notre temps*, 1977. Fields: Moral and political philosophy.

[1526]
POLLACK Benny
27 September 1941, Chilean. 4 Childwall Park Avenue, Liverpool 16, England. Degrees: BA; MA (Northeastern U, Boston), 1968. Doctoral thesis: "Structure and Organization of the Chilean Socialist Party". 1964-73 Lecturer in Pol Sci, U of Chile; 1971-72 Political Adviser, Chilean Foreign Office (and Delegate to the UN, New York); 1973-74 Research Fellow in Latin American Pol, U of Essex; 1974-75 Research Fellow in Latin American Pol, Inst of Latin American Studies, U of London; Lecturer, Dept of Pol Theory and Institutions and Centre for Latin American Studies, U of Liverpool. Publs: "Estrategias políticas divergentes mobilización convergente y sectores medios: La Izquierda y la Democracia Cristiana en Chile, 1963-1973", *Foro Internacional*, El Colegio de México, 1976; "The Chilean Socialist Party: Prolegomena to its Structure and Organization", *Journal of Latin American Studies*, 1977; "Una ideología latinoamericanista: Introducción al Partido Socialista chileon", *Nueva Sociedad*, 1977-78; "Spain: From Corporate State to Parliamentary Democracy", *Parliamentary Affairs*, 1978. Fields: Latin American politics; political sociology of Latin America; political parties; problems of dependency, military governments and political participation in Latin America.

[1527]
PONCEYRI Robert
22 July 1948, French. 3 rue Merrheim, 42100 Saint Etienne, France. Degrees: Agrégé d'histoire; Dipl; Dr. Doctoral thesis: "La Participation Electoral dans les grandes villes sous la vème République (1958-1974)". Professeur agrégé d'histoire; Chargé de cours de sci pol, Faculté de Droit, St Etienne. Publs: *La Participation électorale dans les grandes villes sous la Vème République (1958-1974)*, 1976; *Les élections en France*, 1976. Fields: Sociology; French elections during the 5th Republic.

[1528]
POPHAM George Thomas
4 January 1925, British. 2 Ley Hill Road, Sutton Coldfield, West Midlands B75 6TF England. Degrees: BSc; D Phil (Leicester). Doctoral thesis; "Socialist Revisionism and the Labour Party". Principal Lecturer, Birmingham Polytechnic; Senior Lecturer, U of Aston at Birmingham. Fields: Government and industry; political thought 1760-1850.

[1529]
PORTER Brian Ernest
5 February 1928, British. 8 Marine Terrace, Aberystwyth, Dyfed, Wales. Degrees: BSc; PhD (LSE), 1962. Doctoral thesis: "British Opinion and the Far Eastern Crisis, 1945-54". 1961-63 Lecturer in International Relations, Le Coll Americain à Tours, France; 1963-65 Lecturer in Pol Sci, U of Khartoum; 1965-71 Lecturer in International Pol, U Coll of Wales, Aberystwyth; 1967 Vice Consul, Sultanate of Muscat and Oman; Senior Lecturer in International Pol, U Coll of Wales. Publs: *Britain and the Rise of Communist China*, 1967; *The Aberystwyth Papers; International Politics 1919-69* (ed), 1972. Fields: International relations theory; nationalism; Britain and the Middle East, 1914-71.

[1530]
POST Harry H G
20 July 1947, Dutch. Adm de Ruyterweg 343[III], Amsterdam, The Netherlands. Degrees: Dr (Amsterdam). Doctoral thesis: "Pillarization Theory and Modern Marxist Theory of the State". Instructor in Pol Sci, Queen's U of Kingston, Canada; Researcher, Free U of Brussels; Wetenschappelijk Medewerker, Dept of Pol Studies, U of Amsterdam. Publs: "Classification of Rules of International Law According to Spheres of Validity", in *Netherlands Yearbook of International Law*, 1977. Fields: Political studies; pillarization; Netherlands; Belgium; systems philosophy; theory of the state; hermeneutic tendencies in philosophy.

[1531]
POSTHUMUS MEYJES Herman Christiaan*
27 August 1927, Dutch. Cartesiuslaan 15, Oegstgeestraat, The Netherlands. Degrees: Dr in Pol Sci (Amsterdam), 1957. Deputy Director, European Integration, Ministry of Foreign Affairs; Policy Planning Adviser, Ministry of Foreign Affairs; Professor of International Relations; Agricultural U, Wageningen, The Netherlands. Fields: Long-term forecasting in international relations.

[1532]
POTRATZ Wolfgang
22 May 1948, German. Boeckenkamp 9, D-4404 Telgte 2, FR Germany. Bundesministerium des Innern, Projektgruppe Regierungs-U; International Inst of Management, Wissenschaftszentrum, Berlin; Zentralinst für Raum-Planung, U of Münster. Publs: Various articles and papers on administrative reform; bureaucracy; codetermination; industrial democracy. Fields: Public administration; bureaucracy; industrial relations; methodology.

[1533]
POTTER Allen Meyers
7 March 1924, British. 2 Grove Park, Lenzie, Kirkintilloch G66 5AH, Scotland.
Degrees: BA; MA (Wesleyan U), 1948; PhD (Columbia), 1955. Doctoral thesis:
"British Party Politics". 1963-65 Professor of Pol, U of Strathclyde; 1965-67 Professor
of Government, U of Essex; 1967-70 Director, SSRC Data Bank, U of Essex; James
Bryce Professor of Pol, U of Glasgow. Publs: *American Government and Politics*,
1978; *Organized Groups in British National Politics*, 1961.

[1534].
POTTER David C
3rd November 1931, American. Faculty of Social Sciences, The Open University,
Milton Keynes, Buckinghamshire, England. Degrees: BA; MA (California), 1959; PhD
(London), 1962. Doctoral thesis: "Public Administration Aspects of Community
Development in India (with special reference to Rajasthan)". 1960-62 Research Fellow
in Public Administration in the Commonwealth, LSE; 1963-66 Assistant Professor of
Pol Sci, U of Oakland; 1966-67 Faculty Research Fellow (in India), American Inst of Indian Studies; 1967-70 Associate Professor of Pol Sci, Simon Fraser U, Vancouver;
1970- Senior Lecturer in Pol Sci, The Open U. Publs: *Government in Rural India*, 1964;
Asian Bureaucratic Systems (co-author), 1966; *Decisions, Organizations and Society*
(co-ed), 1971; *The Practice of Comparative Politics* (co-ed), 1973. Fields: Public
bureaucracies and political change in India during the period 1919-70, and more
generally in underdeveloped countries.

[1535]
POULAT Emile
13 June 1920, French. 14-18 rue de Bièvres, 75005 Paris, France. Degrees: Dr ès lettres;
Dr (Fribourg). Doctoral thesis: "Histoire, dogme et critique dans la crise moderniste".
Directeur de recherche titulaire, CNRS; Directeur du groupe de sociologie des religions,
CNRS. Publs: *Le journal d'un prêtre d'après-demain (1902-03) de l'Abbé Calippe*,
1962; *Histoire, dogme et critique dans la crise moderniste*, 1965; *Naissance des prêtres-
ouvriers*, 1965; *Intégrisme et catholicisme intégral*, 1969; *La correspondance de Rome*,
1971; *Une oeuvre clandestine d'Henri Brémond*, 1972; *Catholicisme, démocratie et
socialisme*, 1977; *Eglise contre bourgeoisie*, 1977. Fields: Sociology of religion.

[1536]
POURVOYEUR Robert A
29 September 1924, Belgian. 8 Narcissenlaan, Jezus-Eik, 1900 Overijse, Belgium.
Degrees: LL D (Louvain), 1947; M Econ (Louvain), 1948. Director, General
Secretariat, European Communities; Professor, U of Antwerp; Professor of
Economics, Hogeschool St Aloysius. Fields: European integration; international
organizations; international economics.

[1537]
PÖYHÖNEN Pentti Kalevi
28 August 1925, Finnish. Niemenmäentie 5 A 3, 00350 Helsinki 35, Finland. Degrees:
Dr. Doctoral thesis: "City Land Market Prices". 1958-59 Acting Professor of Econ,
Helsinki School of Economics; 1959- Professor of Econ, U of Helsinki. Publs: "A Tentative Model for the Volume of Trade between Countries", *Weltwirtscaftliches Archiv*,
1963; "Towards a General Theory of International Trade", *Ekonomiska Samfundets
Tidskrift*, 1963; "World Trade Structure" (with K Pulliainen), in *Econometric Society
World Congress*, 1970; *EEC and Finland's Alternatives*, 1972. Fields: Science of
science.

[1538]
PRÄTORIUS Rainer
2 March 1952, German. Wienerstrasse 9, 7000 Stuttgart 30, FR Germany. Degrees: Dr phil (Marburg). Doctoral thesis: "Folgen der Planung. Untersuchungen zur politischen Verwaltungssoziologie des Interventionsstaates". Wiss Assistent, Inst für Pol, U of Stuttgart. Publs: *Bürokratie in Kapitalismus*, 1973; *Folgen der Planung*, 1977; "Wohlfahrtszweck und Formalisierung", *Demokratie und Recht*, 1977; "Zur Reformfähigkeit bürokratischer Institutionen", in *Zur Theorie der Reform* (M Greiffenhagen (ed)), 1978. Fields: Public administration; local government; theory of political decentralization.

[1539]
PRAVDA Alexander
6 March 1947, British. 13 St Anne's Road, Caversham, Reading, England. Degrees: BA; PhD (Oxon). Doctoral thesis: "The Czechoslovak Reform Movement, January-August 1968". Lecturer, Dept of History and Pol, Huddersfield Polytechnic; Lecturer, Dept of Pol, U of Reading. Publs: *Czechoslavakia: The Party and the People* (co-ed), 1973; *Reform and Change in the Czechoslavak Political System, January-August 1968*, 1978. "Elections in Communist Party States", in *Elections without Choice* (R Rose and G Hermet (eds)), 1978. Fields: Comparative communist politics, USSR and Eastern Europe; the working class and working-class organizations in communist states; political culture and political socialization in communist states.

[1540]
PREDIERI Alberto
7 March 1921, Italian. Via dei Servi 49, 50122 Florence, Italy. Doctoral thesis: "Pianificazione e Costituzione"; "Contraddittorio e Testimonianze del Cittadino nei Procedimenti Legislativi". Professore ord di Instituzione di diritto pubblico, Facoltà di Sci Pol e Soc di Firenze. Publs: *Lineamenti della Posizione Costituzionale del Presidente del Consiglio dei Ministri*, 1951; *Contraddittorio e Testimonianza del Cittadino nei Procedimenti Legislativi*, 1964; *Il Programma Economico 1966-70*, 1967; *Urbanistica, Tutela del Paesaggio, Espropriazione*, 1969; "Gli Elaboratori Elettronici nell'Amministrazione dello Stato", *Quaderni dell'IRSTA*, 1971; *Le Società Finanziarie Regionali*, 1972; *Il Parlamento nel Sistema Politico Italiano*, 1975; *La Legge 28.1.1977 sulla Edificabilità dei Suoli*, 1977. Fields: Legislative process; economic and social planning; land use; government organization; computers in public administration.

[1541]
PREISWERK Adrian Roy
25 December 1934, Swiss. Chemin des Poses-Longues 9, 1222 Vesenaz, Switzerland. Degrees: Lic en droit (Geneva), 1959; MA (Minnesota), 1961; Dr (Geneva), 1963. Doctoral thesis: "La protection des investissements privés dans les traités bilateraux". 1963-66 Collaborateur Technique, Dept Pol Fédéral, Berne; 1967-69 Professor and Director, Inst of International Relations, U of the West Indies, Trinidad; Professor, Geneva-Africa Inst; 1974-77 President, Swiss Association of Pol Sci; Director, Inst of Development Studies and Professor, Graduate Inst of International Studies, Geneva. Publs: *La protection des investissements privés dans les traités bilateraux*, 1963; *Regionalism and the Commonwealth Caribbean*, 1969; *Documents on International Relations in the Caribbean*, 1970; *Ethnocentrisme et histoire: L'Afrique, L'Amérique indienne et l'Asie dans les manuels occidentaux* (with D Perrot), 1975; *Relations interculturelles et développement: Le savoir et le faire*, 1975. Fields: Development studies; international and intercultural relations.

[1542]
PRICE Joseph Henry
6 June 1924, British. The Old Vicarage, Cragg Vale, West Yorkshire, HX7 5TB, England. Degrees: BA; MA (Oxon), 1948. 1950-61 Lecturer, Senior Lecturer, U Coll of Ghana; 1961-66 Dean, Faculty of Econ and Soc Studies, U of Ife, Nigeria; 1966-70 Lecturer, U of Bradford; 1970-73 Lecturer, U of Manchester; 1976 Visiting Professor, U of California, San Diego; 1973- Lecturer, U of Bradford. Publs: *The Gold Coast General Election of 1951*, 1951; *Five Elections in Africa* (contributor), 1960; *Political Institutions of West Africa*, 1977; *Comparative Government*, 1970. Fields: English local government; West African politics; international relations.

[1543]
PRICE Russell John
30 March 1933, New Zealander. Department of Politics, University of Lancaster, Bailrigg, Lancaster, England. Degrees: BA; MA (Wellington), 1961. 1961-62 Junior Lecturer in Pol Sci, U of Wellington; 1964-70 Lecturer in Pol, U of Lancaster; Senior Lecturer in Pol, U of Lancaster. Publs: Various articles in *European Studies Review*, *Political Science*, *Political Studies*, *Renaissance Quarterly*. Fields: Political and moral thought, especially 16th and 17th centuries; Machiavelli; church and state in Italy.

[1544]
PROST Antoine*
29 October 1933, French. 17 Boulevard de Verdun, 45 Orléans, France. Degrees: Agrégé; Dr de recherche. Doctoral thesis: "Les effectifs de la CGT à l'époque du Front Populaire". Maître-assistant, Sorbonne; Maître de conférences, IEP, Paris; Directeur UER Lettres, Orléans. Publs: *La CGT à l'époque du Front Populaire*, 1964; *Les conseillers généraux en France, 1870-*, 1970; *Histoire de l'enseignement 1800-1967*, 1968. Fields: Political language; historical statistics, 1870- present.

[1545]
PROVOOST Guido E
7 November 1940, Belgian. Eeuwfeestlaan 35, 9720 De Pinte, Belgium. Degrees: Dr. Doctoral thesis: "The Franco-Belgian Military Agreement of 7th September 1920. Belgian Defence Policy in the Interbellum". Assistant Professor, Faculty of Law, Ghent State U; Lecturer, Faculty of Law, Ghent State U; Professor, Lille State U. Publs: *Vijfentwintig jaar Vlaamse beweging 1945-70* (with W van de Steene), 1972; *Vlaanderen en het militair-politiek beleid in België tussen de twee Wereloborlogen*, 1976/77; *Ward Hermans (A Biography)*, 1977. Fields: Belgian politics; international relations; military history.

[1546]
PRYCE Roy*
4 October 1928, British. Centre for Contemporary European Studies, University of Sussex, Falmer, Brighton BN1 9QZ, England. Degrees: BA; MA (Cambridge), 1954; PhD (Cambridge), 1954; MA (Oxon), 1955. Doctoral thesis: "Italy 1914-15: From Neutrality to Intervention". 1953-55 Research Fellow, St Anthony's Coll, U of Oxford; 1957-64 Head of London Office, European Communities' Information Service; 1965-Director, Centre for Contemporary European Studies, U of Sussex. Publs: *The Italian Local Elections 1956*, 1957; *The Political Future of the European Community*, 1962; *Europe after De Gaulle* (with J Pinder), 1969. Fields: European integration.

[1547]
PUETZ Karl Heinz
19 September 1938, German. Spanische Allee 61, 1000 W Berlin 38, FR Germany.
Degrees: MA, 1968; Dr rer Pol, 1975. Doctoral thesis: "Strukturen Amerikanischer
Aussenpolitik". Assistenzprofessor, Free U of Berlin. Publs: *Die Aussenpolitik der
USA. Eine Einführung*, 1974; *Die USA. Eine politische Landeskunde* (with H
Kleinsteuber), 1978; *Die USA und Lateinamerika* (ed), 1978. Fields: The USA; interna-
tional politics.

[1548]
PUHLE Hans-Jürgen
8 October 1940, German. Philippistrasse 10, D-4400 Münster, FR Germany. Degrees:
Dr phil (Berlin), 1965; Habilitation (Münster), 1973. Doctoral thesis: "Agrarische Interessenpolitik und preussischer Konservatismus im wilhelminischen Reich
(1893-1914)". 1965-73 Ass Professor, U of Münster; 1966-68 Co-Director of the Instituto Latinoamericano de Ciencias Sociales (ILDIS), Santiago de Chile; 1970-71 John
F Kennedy Memorial Fellow, U of Harvard; 1966-68 Visiting Professor, U of Santiago
de Chile; 1976-77 Visiting Professor, U of Cornell; Professor of Modern History and
Pol Sci, U of Münster. Publs: *Agrarische Interessenpolitik und preussischer Konservatismus im wilhelminischen Reich*, 1975; *Politik in Uruguay*, 1968; *Tradition und
Reformpolitik in Bolivien*, 1970; *Von der Agrarkrise zum Präfaschismus*, 1972;
Politische Agrarbewegungen in kapitalistischen Industriegesellschaften, 1975; *Perspectivas del Progresso* (ed), 1969; *Revolution und Reformen in Lateinamerika*, 1976; *Lateinamerika — Historische Realität und Dependencia-Theorien* (ed), 1977; plus various
articles on German, West European, United States and Latin American problems of
19th and 20th centuries. Fields: Social and political developments in the Western World
in the 19th and 20th centuries; comparative government and administration; pressure
group politics; regionalism in Western Europe; Mediterranean and Latin American
development policies and problems; political theory; state functions in advanced industrial societies.

[1549]
PULZER Peter George Julius
29 May 1929, British. Christ Church College, Oxford OX1 1DP, England. Degrees:
BA; BSc; PhD (Cambridge), 1960. Doctoral thesis: "The Origins of Political Anti-
Semitism in Germany and Austria, 1867-1914". 1957-62 Lecturer in Pol, Magdalen Coll
and Christ Church Coll, U of Oxford; Tutor in Pol. Publs: *The Rise of Political Anti-
Semitism in Germany and Austria*, 1966; *Political Representation and Elections in Bri-
tain*, 1971; "Austria", in *European Political Parties* (J Pinder and S Henig (eds)), 1970;
"Germany, 1871-1949", in *Germany: A Companion to German Studies* (J M S Pasley
(ed)), 1971; "Der judische Beitrag zur Politik", in *Juden im Wilhelminischen
Deutschland* (W E Mosse and A Paucker (eds)), 1976. Fields: The role and appeals of
political parties and the functioning of the electoral system in the UK, Germany and
Austria.

[1550]
PUNNETT Robert Malcolm
1 May 1936, British. 'Am Bruach', Fore Road, Kippen, Stirling FK8 3DT, Scotland.
Degrees: BA; MA (Sheffield), 1961; PhD (Strathcylde), 1972. Doctoral thesis:
"Government in Opposition: the Role of the Leader of the Opposition, the Shadow
Cabinet and Opposition Spokesmen in British Politics". 1963-64 Assistant Lecturer in
Pol, U of Sheffield; 1964-74 Lecturer in Pol, U of Strathclyde; 1967-68 Visiting Assis-
tant Professor, U of Carleton; 1976-77 Visiting Professor, McMaster U, Canada;
1974-Senior Lecturer in Pol, U of Strathclyde. Publs: *British Government and Politics*,

1976; *Front Bench Opposition*, 1973; *The Prime Minister in Canadian Government and Politics*, 1977. Fields: Government and politics in Britain, Canada, Australia and other 'Anglo-American' democracies; federalism.

[1551]
PUNTILA Lauri Aadolf
24 August 1907, Finnish. Pohjolankatu 64, 00600 Helsinki 60, Finland. Degrees: PhD (Helsinki), 1944. Doctoral thesis: "Swedish Question in Finland". Professor of Pol History, Dean, Faculty of Soc Sci, U of Helsinki; Chairman, Finnish Cultural Foundation; Member, Finnish Parliament; President, Executive Board, Yrjö Jahnsson's Foundation. Publs: *Swedish Question in Finland*, 1944; *The Formation of Public Opinion in Finland in 1860s*, 1947; *Bismarck's French Policy*, 1952; *Finland's Political History in 1809-1955, 1963; Speeches and Discourses 1948-1964*, 1965; *Finland's Political History in 1809-1966*, 1971; *Letters from the Front 1944*, 1972; *Speeches and Discourses 1962-1975*, 1977. Fields: Development of political life in Finland, especially constitutional questions.

[1552]
PURNELL Robert
15 August 1923, British. Grosvenor, Dinas Terrace, Aberystwyth, Cardiganshire, Wales. Degrees: BSc; 1949-56 Archivist; 1956-57 Teacher Training; 1957-61 Technical Coll Lecturer; 1961-64 Lecturer, LSE; 1964- Lecturer, Senior Lecturer, Dept of International Pol, U Coll of Wales. Publs: *Triad* (poems), 1954; *British and French Foreign Policy* (with J Baylis), 1972; *The Society of States: An Introduction to International Politics*, 1973; plus various articles and contributions to *Dictionary of World History, Theoretical Approaches to International Politics, The International Yearbook of Foreign Policy Analysis*. Fields: Soviet foreign policy from 1918; ancient Greek city-state relations; 20th century British foreign policy; the phenomenon and role of small states in the modern world.

[1553]
PUUMALAINEN Asko Juhani
10 October 1935, Finnish. Merikorttitie 12 A 15, 00960 Helsinki 96, Finland. Degrees: Dr (Helsinki). Doctoral thesis: "The Complementing Role of State-owned Industry in Finnish Industrial Structure". Docent in Pol Sci, U of Helsinki. Fields: Business administration; economic and political effects of technological change.

Q

[1554]
QUERMONNE Jean-Louis
3 November 1927, French. 22 rue Pierre Bonnard, 92260 Fontenay aux Roses, France. Degrees: Lic ès lettres; Lic en droit, 1949; Dipl (IEP Paris), 1950; Dr en droit; Agrégé droit public et sci pol, 1952. Doctoral thesis: "L'évolution de la hiérarchie des textes en droit public français". 1952-56 Professeur agrégé, Faculté de Droit, Alger; 1958-69 Directeur, IEP, Grenoble II; 1957-77 Professeur, Faculté de Droit, U de Grenoble II; 1975 Professeur, IEP, Paris and Vice-Président, FNSP. Publs: Various articles on Algeria, public administration, constitutional and political life in France. Fields: Public administration; the state and political institutions of the 5th Republic; problems of higher education and research.

R

[1555]
RAAB Charles David
23 December 1939, American. Department of Politics, University of Edinburgh. Degrees: BA; MA (Yale), 1961. Lecturer, Dept of Pol, U of Edinburgh. Publs: "Planning and Rediscovery of Land", *The Political Quarterly*, 1978; "From Town Planning to Statecraft", *The Political Quarterly*, 1977; "Administrators as Researchers — Collaboration in the Scottish Regions" (with E Cope), *Research Intelligence*, 1976; "Ideology, Modernization and Leadership", in *Theory and Ideology in African Society*, 1972; "Suggestions for a Cybernetic Approach to Sociological Jurisprudence", *Journal of Legal Education*, 1965. Fields: Policy-making and administration, especially in planning and education; social science and public policy; spatial aspects of public order; urban government.

[1556]
RABENEICK Manfred
5 October 1939, German. Hagelkreuz 30, 5024 Pulheim 3, FR Germany. Degrees: Dipl Volkswirt; Dr rer Pol. Doctoral thesis: "Political System of Venezuela. Voting Behaviour and Political Campaigning". Research Fellow, Konrad Adenauer Foundation. Fields: Comparative political campaign studies; political communication; field research in Latin America; voting behaviour.

[1557]
RACINE FURLAUD Nicole*
9 May 1937, French. 69 Avenue Victor Hugo, Paris 16ème, France. Degrees: Lic d'histoire (Paris), 1958; Dr de recherche (Paris), 1963. Doctoral thesis: "Les écrivains communistes en France, 1920-36". Assistante de recherche, FNSP, Paris; Chargée de recherche, FNSP. Paris. Publs: *Le Communisme en France* (co-author), 1969; *Le Parti Communiste français pendant l'entre deux guerres* (co-author), 1972. Fields: French communist party; French intellectuals and politics.

[1558]
RADTKE Guenter D*
27 April 1942, German. Laacher Weg 40-44, 4005 Meerbusch 1, FR Germany. Degrees: Dipl in Econ and Pol Sci (Cologne), 1967; PhD (Mannheim), 1972. Assistant, European Inst, U of Mannheim; Director, Dept of Voting Behaviour, Soc Sci Inst, Konrad-Adenauer-Foundation. Publs: *Non-voting in the Federal Republic of Germany*, 1972. Fields: Economic and political behaviour; democratic theory; political participation; political socialization.

[1559]
RAJEWSKY, Christiane
16 June 1934, German. Fachhochschule, Düsseldorf, FR Germany. Degrees: MA (Bonn), 1963. Professor Fachhochschule, Düsseldorf. Publs: *Jährbuch für die Internationale Politik 1964/65* and *1968/69* (co-ed), 1974; *Jahrbuch für Friedens- und Konfliktforschung* (co-ed), 1973-77. Fields: Peace research; political education; social work.

[1560]
RANGER Jean*
7 June 1936, French. 28 rue Nationale, Esches 60110 Meru, France. Degrees: Dipl (IEP), 1957; Dipl supérieur d'études et de recherches pol (FNSP), 1963. Attaché de recherche, CNRS; Maître de conférences, IEP, Paris; 1969 Consultant, Ford Founda-

tion, U Federal do Rio Grande do Sul, Brazil. Publs: "Analyse des résultats" (co-author), in *Le référendum de septembre et les élections de novembre 1958*, 1960; *Le référendum de janvier 1961* (co-author), 1962; *Le référendum d'avril 1962* (co-author), 1963; *Le Communisme en France* (co-author), 1969; *La politique* (J Parodi (ed)), 1971. Fields: Electoral behaviour in France, Italy and Brazil; French and Italian Communist parties.

[1561]
RANTALA Onni Olavi
26 February 1918, Finnish. Rykmentintie 43 as 15, 20880 Turku 88, Finland. Degrees: Dr of pol sci (Helsinki), 1956. Doctoral thesis: "The Conservative Party Community". Investigation and Election Secretary, Coalition Party; Senior Scholar of Pol Sci, Assistant Professor of Pol Sci, U of Turku. Publs: *The Conservative Party Community*, 1956; *Conservatism and its Supporters*, 1960; *The Political Regions in Finland* (Part 1), 1965. Fields: Political regions in Finland: birth, background, regional changes.

[1562]
RAPHAEL David Daiches
25 January 1916, British. Imperial College of Science and Technology, London SW7 2AZ, England. Degrees: BA; D Phil; MA (Oxon), 1940. 1940 Tutor, Oriel Coll, U of Oxford; Principal Officer, Ministry of Labour and National Service; Professor of Philosophy, U of Otago, NZ; Lecturer, Senior Lecturer in Moral Philosophy, U of Glasgow; Professor of Pol and Soc Philosophy, U of Glasgow; Professor of Philosophy, U of Reading; 1973- Academic Director of Associated Studies and Professor of Philosophy, Imperial Coll of Sci and Technology. Publs: *The Moral Sense*, 1947; *Richard Price's Review of Morals* (ed), 1948; *Theory of Moral Sentiment* (co-ed), 1976; *Hobbes: Morals and Politics*, 1977; *Moral Judgement*, 1955; *The Paradox of Tragedy*, 1960; *Political Theory and the Rights of Man*, 1967; *British Moralists, 1650-1800*, 1969; *Problems of Political Philosophy*, 1970. Fields: Social and political philosophy; moral philosophy in Britain from the 17th century; the non-economic writings of Adam Smith; philosophy of law.

[1563]
RASMUSSEN Erik
20 April 1917, Danish. Fritz Sybergsvej 12, 8270 Højbjerg, Denmark. Degrees: Dr phil(Copenhagen), 1955. Doctoral thesis: "Kurantbankens forhold til Staten 1737-73" (Relations Between the Courant Bank and the State 1737-73). 1959- Professor of Pol Sci, U of Aarhus. Publs: *Indien*, 1942; *Det Radikale Venstre 1905-55* (with R. Skovmand), 1955; *Kurantbankens forhold til Staten 1737-73*, 1955; *Statslanskrisen 1919*, 1970; *Velfaerdsstaten på vej*; *Danmarks Historie Vol 13 (1913-39)*, 1965; *Komparativ Politik*, 1969; *Ideologi og Politik*, 1969. Fields: Indian politics; politico-economic history of 18th century Denmark; party politics; responsible cabinet government; ideologies in politics.

[1564]
RASS Hans Heinrich
29 April 1936, German. Feuerbachstrasse 8, D-3300 Braunschweig, FR Germany. Degrees: Dipl Pol; Dr rer Pol. Doctoral thesis: "Britische Aussenpolitik 1929-31. Ebenen und Faktoren der Entscheidung". 1968-73 Wiss Assistent, Free U of Berlin; 1973- Akademischer Oberrat, Technische U Braunschweig. Publs: "Nord-Irland — Konflikt ohne Ende?", *Politik — kurz aktuell*, 1972; *Britische Aussenpolitik 1929-31. Ebenen und Faktoren der Entscheidung*, 1975; *Grossbritannien. Eine politische Landeskunde*, 1976; *Grossbritannien*, 1977. Fields: British politics; international relations, with special reference to Europe; international organizations; energy problems; Japanese politics.

[1565]
RASSON Gregory Thomas*
26 February 1948, British/Belgian. 52 Route de Maubeuge, 7021 Mesvin, Belgium.
Degrees: Candidate (Brussels), 1969. Vice President, Students in Pol Sci Association,
Free U of Brussels. Fields: The problems which occur during the process of grouping
two or more separate administrative communities into one.

[1566]
RASTAD Svein-Erik*
26 August 1942, Norwegian. Myrdalskogen 24, N-5095 Ulset i Åsane, Norway. Degrees:
BA. 1967-70 Research Assistant to Professor J S Coleman, Rockefeller Foundation, U
Development Program, Nairobi, Kenya; Research Assistant, Development Economics
Research and Advisory Program, Christian Michelsen Inst. Publs: Articles in *Nordisk
Forum*. Fields: University development in Africa; manpower planning and university
development; Norway's technical assistance.

[1567]
RAUSCH Heinz Volker*
8 January 1940, German. Neufeldstrasse 47, 8 München 60, FR Germany. Degrees:
Wiss Hilfskraft. Research Assistant, U of Munich, Geschwister-Scholl-Inst. Publs: *Zur
heutigen Problematik der Gewaltenteilung* (ed), 1969; *Zur Geschichte und Theorie der
Repräsentation und der Repräsentativverfassung* (ed), 1968; *Der Bundestag von innen
gesehen* (co-ed), 1969; *Parlament und Regierung in der Bundesrepublik Deutschland*,
1971; *Zum Selbstverständnis des fünften Deutschen Bundestags* (co-author), 1969.
Fields: Parliamentary attitudes towards parliamentary reform in the German
Bundestag; representation, concepts and theories; coalition government in Germany;
German state legislatures.

[1568]
REASON David Alan
14 December 1946, British. 29 St Stephen's Road, Canterbury, Kent CT2 7JD,
England. Degrees: BA, Lecturer in Interdisciplinary Studies, U of Kent at Canterbury.
Publs: *A Version of the Theory of Regression*, 1975, "The Red Queen's Estate: or,
Grounds for Interdisciplinarity", *Studies in Higher Education*, 1977; "Classification,
Time and the Organization of Production", in *Systems of Classification and the An-
throplogy of Knowledge* (D A Reason and R F Ellen (eds)), 1978. Fields: Mathematical
social science; political economy; social consciousness.

[1569]
REBELO DE SOUSA Marcelo Nuno Duarte
12 December 1948, Portuguese. R Conde Ferreiro, 21 Cascais, Portugal. Degrees: Lic
(Lisbon); MA (Lisbon). 1972-76 Faculty of Law, U of Lisbon; 1975-76 Responsible for
International Inst, High School for Soc Communication plus various posts in, and ad-
viser to, the Government; 1976- Responsible for Pol Law and Pol Sci, Faculty of Law,
U of Lisbon; Pol Analyst and Vice-Ed, *Expresso*. Publs: *Pluralism and some Modern
Theories*, 1973; *The Portuguese Semi-Presidential System of Government: Definition
and Perspectives*, 1977; *The Judicial Remedies Against Administration in Portuguese
Law*, 1972; *Political Parties and the Portuguese Constitution of 1976-78*, 1978. Fields:
Comparative systems of government; political parties; public opinion; means of social
communication and political power.

[1570]
REBUFFAT Charles André Maurice*
20 March 1919, Belgian. Avenue de Fré 4, 1180 Brussels, Belgium. Degrees: Dr en droit (Brussels), 1944. Diplomatic European Correspondent, Ed, Foreign Service, Assistant Ed, *Le Soir*; Chargé de cours on journalism, U of Brussels. Publs: articles in *Le Soir*. Fields: International and national politics.

[1571
REDDAWAY Peter Brian
18 September 1939, British. London School of Economics and Political Science, Houghton Street, Aldwych, London WC2, England. Degrees: BA; MA (Cambridge), 1965. Senior Lecturer in Pol Sci, LSE. Publs: *Lenin: The Man and the Theorist, The Leader* (co-ed and contributor), 1967; *Uncensored Russia: the Human Rights Movement in the USSR* (ed and trans), 1971; *Russia's Political Hospitals: the Abuse of Psychiatry in the Soviet Union* (with S Bloch), 1977. Fields: The mechanics of the Soviet political system; church and state; political dissent in the USSR.

[1572]
REDDER Karl Werner*
17 July 1938, Danish. Department of Sociology, Institute of Political Science, University of Aarhus, 8000 Aarhus C, Denmark. Degrees: Cand econ (Aarhus). Head, Soc Dept, Inst of Pol Sci, U of Aarhus. Publs: *Indkøbsundersøgelsen*, 1968; *Foreign Policy Attitudes of the Danish Population* (co-author), 1969; *Introduktion til Sociologisk Metode* (co-author), 1970. Fields: Political sociology; political attitudes; methodology; attitude-measurement; organizational sociology; leadership; general orientations (internationalism, neutralism, etc); socio-economic factors; personality variables.

[1573]
REEVE Andrew Warden
4 August 1951, British. 57 Greatheed Road, Leamington Spa, Warwickshire, England. Degrees: BA. Doctoral thesis: "Theories of Property in some English Legal, Economic and Social Thinkers 1600-1700". Lecturer, Dept of Pol, U of Warwick. Publs: "The Benefit of Reasonable Conduct — The Leviathan Theory of Obligation", *Political Theory* (with S Beackon). Fields: Property in law and politics; 17th century political thought; normative theory.

[1574]
REGNER Hubert B
2 August 1943, Austrian. Mascagnigasse 33, A-5020, Austria. Degrees: Dr phil. Doctoral thesis: "Der Salzburger Landtag — Versuch einer Organisationstheoretischen und politikwissenschaftlichen Analyse". Director, Europe-House of Salzburg. Publs: *Der Salzburger Landtag*. Fields: Adult education; research of political management; organizations; international politics.

[1575]
REICHEL Peter
19 September 1942, German. Flemingstrasse 9, 2000 Hamburg 60, FR Germany. Degrees: Dr phil. Doctoral thesis: "Bundestagsabgeordnete in Europäischen Versammlungen. Zur Soziologie des Europäischen Parlamentariers". Deutsche Gesellschaft für Friedens- und Konfliktforschung, Bonn; Inst für Pol Wissenschaft, U des Saarlandes; Wiss Assistent, Inst of Pol Sci, U of Hamburg. Publs: *Friedens- und Konfliktforschung. Eine Einführung* (with W D Eberwein), 1976; *Interesse und Gesellschaft* (with P Massing), 1977; "Interesse und Interessenbegriff aus

sozialwissenschaftlicher Perspektive", in *Offene Welt*, 1978; "Politische Kultur. Bildungs- und Kulturpolitik", in *Handbuch des politischen Systems der Bundesrepublik Deutschland* (K Sontheimer and H Röhring (eds)), 1978. Fields: Political theory; political system and politics of the FRG; political culture; federalism; communal politics; European Community; peace and conflict research.

[1576]
REID Alexander Livingstone
8 May 1936, British. Department of Political Science, The University, Dundee DD1 4HN, Scotland. Degrees: BL; MA (Edinburgh), 1962; MA (Yale), 1963. 1957-62 Examiner in the Estate Duty Office, Edinburgh; Lecturer, U of Dundee. Fields: Political socialization; socialist realism; the literary and scientific intelligentsia; religion; nationalism; international communism.

[1577]
REIF Karlheinz
3 June 1943, German. Stephanstrasse 5, D-6730 Neustadt 1, FR Germany. Degrees: AM (Stanford), 1966; Dipl Pol (Berlin), 1968; Dr phil (Mannheim), 1974. Doctoral thesis: "Freiheit des Lernens in der wissenschaftlichen Berufsausbildung? Eine Untersuchung von Hochschuldidaktik und Zeitbudget des eigenständigen Studierens". Collaborator and Director of several research projects in the Soc of Higher Education and Soc of Pol, U of Mannheim; Lecturer in Pol Sci, U of Mannheim; Research Fellow, FNSP; Wiss Assistent, Lehrstuhl für Pol Wissenschaft and Director, Research Group on Party Systems of the European Community, Inst für Sozialwissenschaft, U of Mannheim. Publs: Articles on the sociology, politics and didactics of higher education in Germany; on political parties, European integration, direct elections to the European parliament. Fields: Comparative politics; comparative sociology of political parties; transnational co-operation of political parties in the European community.

[1578]
REISSERT Bernd
7 February 1950, German. Waltraudstrasse 36a, D-1000 Berlin 37, FR Germany. Degrees: Diplom-Verwaltungswissenschaftler (Konstanz). Research Assistant, Dept of Pol Sci, U of Konstanz; Research Fellow, International Inst of Management, Berlin. Publs: *Politikverflechtung: Theorie und Empirie des kooperativen Föderalismus in der Bundesrepublik* (with F W Scharpf und F Schnabel), 1976; *Die finanzielle Beteiligung des Bundes an Aufgaben der Länder*, 1974; "Verein für Verwaltungsreform und Verwaltungsforschung", in *Interorganizational Policy-Making* (K Hanf and F W Scharpf (eds)), 1978. Fields: Intergovernmental/interorganizational policy-making; implementation and evaluation research; local government and local finance.

[1579]
REITER Erich
13 July 1944, Austrian. Mariahilfer Strasse 74, A-1070 Wien, Austria. Degrees: Dr rer Pol; Dr jur. Doctoral thesis: "Die föderalistische Funktion des österreichischen Bundesrates, eine Erörterung der Reformbestrebungen". Bundesministerium für Wissenschaft und Forschung. Publs: *Vorschläge zur Regelung des Parteienwesens*; *Rahmenkonzept zur strukturellen Reform der öffentlichen Verwaltung*; *Das Parlament im österreichischen Regierungssystem*; *Reform des Bundesrates durch den Bundesrat*. Fields: Science of science.

[1580]
REITERER Albert F
25 October 1948, Austrian. Parkgasse 1/25, A-1030 Vienna, Austria. Degrees: Dr phil. Doctoral thesis: "Sprachstrukturen im Prozess der Massenkommunikation: Eine Untersuchung zur Funktion der Schichtsprachen in der Publizistik mit einer empirischen Vorstudie an der Wiener Tagespresse". Researcher, Publishing. Publs: *A C-B-A of the Surburban Colony in Vienna*, 1974; *Ökonomische Probleme von Stadterneuerung und Stadterweiterung*, 1974; *The Economic Position of the Slovene Minority in Austria*, 1977; plus various articles on economic and political arguments. Fields: Theory and analysis of political parties; minorities; history of political and economic theory.

[1581]
REMOND René
30 September 1918, French. 172 Avenue du Maine, 75014 Paris, France. Degrees: Lic; Dr ès lettres. Assistant d'histoire contemporaine, Sorbonne; Attaché de recherche, CNRS; Directeur d'études et recherches, FSNP; Professeur d'histoire contemporaine, Président, U de Paris X-Nanterre. Publs: *Les catholiques, le communisme et les crises, 1929-39*, 1960; *Forces religieuses et attitudes politiques en France depuis 1945 - Histoire du catholicisme* (J Latreille (ed)), 1965; *Léon Blum, chef du gouvernement*, 1967; *Atlas historique de la France contemporaine*, 1967; *La vie politique en France 1789-1848* and 1848-79, 1969; *Introduction à l'histoire de notre temps*, 1974; *L'anticléricalisme en France depuis 1815*, 1976; *Vivre notre histoire*, 1976. Fields: French political life in the 19th and 20th centuries; the Left in France since the 19th century.

[1582]
REMY Dominique
2 May 1949, French. 15 rue Germain Pilon, 75018 Paris, France. Degrees: Dipl (IEP Paris); DES (Paris); MA (Princeton). Doctoral thesis: "Functions of Small Parties in Multiparty Parliamentary Systems: One case". Researcher, Centre d'études des parlements, Paris I; Assistant, Dept of Pol Sci, U of Paris I. Publs: "L'information parlementaire: mythes et réalités", *Bulletin Parlementaire*. "Les parlements aujourd'hui- Evolution des secondes chambres", *Les Cahiers Français*, 1976; *Political Coalitions. The Case of France 1945-1958*, 1978. Fields: Political parties; political socialization; political philosophy; legislative behaviour; history.

[1583]
RENDEL Margherita Nancy
22 November 1928, British. 71 Clifton Hill, London NW8 0JN, England. Degrees: BA; MA (Cantab), 1955; PhD (London), 1967; Barrister-at-Law, 1976. Doctoral thesis: "The Administrative Functions of the French Conseil d'Etat". 1958-60 Pol and Econ Planning; 1960-61 Lecturer, U of Exeter; 1961- Research Lecturer in Human Rights and Education, Inst of Education, U of London. Publs: *Advisory Committees in British Government*, 1960; *The Administrative Functions of the French Conseil d'Etat*, 1970; *Equality for Women*, 1972; "Written Evidence to the House of Lords Select Committee on the Anti-Discrimination Bill, Session 1972-73"; *Women's Studies in the UK*, 1977; "The Contribution of Labour Women to the Winning of the Franchise", in *Women in the Labour Movement*, 1977. Fields: Control of the executive and of arbitrary power; participation of women in politics; sex roles in society; measures against discrimination.

[1584]
RERUP Lorenz Christian
15 April 1928, Danish. Roskilde Universitetscenter, PO 260, DK-4000 Roskilde, Denmark. Degrees: Mag art (Copenhagen), 1963. 1963-66 Lecturer, Danish Library in S Slesvig; 1966-72 Lecturer, U of Aarhus; Professor, U of Roskilde; 1968-74 Member, Danish Soc Sci Research Council; 1969-75 Chief Ed, *Excerpta Historica Nordica*. Publs: *Marcus Rubins Brevveksling* (ed), 1963; *Hermann Clausen: Aufbau der Demokratie in der Stadt Schleswig*, 1966; *Aage Friis Samlinger vedr Systemskiftet i 1901*, 1970. Fields: The South Slesvig question after 1945; Danish politics in the 19th century; historiography; methodological problems in history; use of history in forecasting.

[1585]
RESS Georg Rudolf Gerhard*
21 January 1935, German. Baden-Badener-Strasse 3, D-69 Heidelberg, FR Germany. Degrees: Assessor (jur), Ministry of Justice, Berlin, 1964; Referendar (jur) (Berlin), 1959; Dr rer Pol (Vienna), 1963. 1959-64 Law Practice, Berlin; 1964-66 Assistant Professor of Pol Sci, Inst of Advanced Studies, Vienna; 1965-67 Lecturer, Diplomatic Academy, Vienna; 1966-68 Research Fellow, Max-Planck-Inst, Heidelberg; 1968- Research, Max-Planck-Inst and Assistant Professor, U of Heidelberg. Publs: *Wahlen und Parteien in Österreich* (co-author), 1966/68; *Die Entscheidungsbefugnis in der Verwaltungsgerichtsbarkeit*, 1968; *Constitutional and International Law Problems of the Recent Past-Political Decisions of the Federal Republic of Germany* (co-author), 1971. Fields: International organizations; human rights; UN General Assembly; election process and elements of direct democracy in European countries.

[1586]
REUTER Lutz-Rainer
17 December 1943, German. Parkallee 50, D-2070 Ahrensburg, FR Germany. Degrees: Dr jur, 1972. Doctoral thesis: "Das Recht auf chancengleiche Bildung". 1971-74 Wiss Assistent für pol und öffentliches Recht, U of Siegen; 1974-77 Akademischer Rat für pol und öffentliches recht, U of Siegen; Professor für Pol, Schwerpunkt Bildungspolitik und Bildungsrecht, Hochschule der Bundeswehr Hamburg. Publs: *Das Recht auf chancengleiche Bildung*, 1975; *Rechtsunterricht als Teil der Gesellschaftslehre*, 1975; "Partizipation als Prinzip demokratischer Schulverfassung", *Aus Politik und Zeitgeschichte, Beilage zur Wochenzeitung Das Parlament*, 1975; "Kommunalpolitik im Parteienvergleich", *Aus Politik und Zeitgeschichte*, 1976; "Bildungs- und Beschäftigungs-system", *Aus Politik und Zeitgeschichte*, 1978; *Normative Grundlagen zum politischen Unterricht, Dokumentation — Analyse — Kritik*, 1978; "Legitimation durch Verfassung", in *Zur Legitimationsproblematik bildungspolitischer Entscheidungen*, 1976; Fields: Socio-political systems of the two Germanies; educational, cultural and scientific systems; theory of constitution and human rights; local policies; developing countries.

[1587]
REUTER-HENDRICHS Irena
4 August 1943, German. Goethestrasse 23, D-5010 Berheim, FR Germany. Degrees: Dipl; Dr rer Pol. Doctoral thesis: "Yugoslav Foreign Policy 1948-1968". Assistant, U of Hamburg; Assistant, Dept of Pol Sci and European Questions, U of Cologne. Publs: *Jugoslawische Aussenpolitik 1948-1968*, 1976; "Deutsche Ostpolitik", "Der Warschauer Pakt", and "Der Europa Rat", in *Handbuch der Deutschen Aussenpolitik* (H P Schwarz (ed)), 1976; "Sowjetische Jugoslawienpolitik, 1975/76", in *Berichte des Bundesinstituts für ostwissenschaftliche Studien*, 1977. Fields: Yugoslav foreign policy; Yugoslav political and economic system; foreign policy of socialist countries; East-West relations.

[1588]
REY Jean-Noël
23 December 1949, Swiss. 12, Haselholzweg, 3098 Berne, Switzerland. Degrees: Dr. Doctoral thesis: "Contribution à l'étude du syndicalisme en Suisse".Dept de Sci Pol, U de Genève.

[1589]
REYCHLER Luc E H G
30 December 1933, Belgian. Celestynenlaan 37/12, Heverlee 3030, Belgium. Degrees: PhD (Harvard). Doctoral thesis: "Patterns of Diplomatic Thinking: A Cross-National Study of Structural and Social-Psychological Determinants". Visiting Professor, International Relations, U of Leuven. Publs: *Patterns of Diplomatic Thinking: A Cross-National Study of Structural and Social-Psychological Determinants*, 1978; "The Effectiveness of a Pacifist Strategy in Conflict Resolution: An Experimental Study", *Journal of Conflict Resolution*, 1979; "International Politiekterrorisme en Wereld Veiligheid", *Politica*, 1978. Fields: Strategy and means of power in international politics; theories of international relations; European integration and the problem of legitimacy; institutions and politics of the United States.

[1590]
REYNAUD Jean Daniel
17 March 1926, French. 9 Square de Port Royal, 75008 Paris, France. Degrees: Agrégé, 1949. 1958-59 Maître de conférences, Faculté des Lettres, U de Lyon; 1957 Visiting Professor, U of Chile; 1963 U of Columbia; 1969 UCLA; 1954- Professeur, IEP; 1959- Professeur de Sociologie du Travail et des Relations Professionnelles, Conservatoire Nat des Arts et Métiers. Publs: *Conflit du travail et changement social* (co-author), 1978; *Tendances et volontés de la société française* (ed), 1955; *Industrial sociology* (with J R Treanton), 1962; *Current Sociology*, 1964; *Huachipato et Lota* (co-author), 1966; *Les ouvriers et le progrès technique* (co-author), 1966. Fields: Industrial relations systems.

[1591]
REYNERI Emilio*
8 May 1943, Italian. Facoltà di Scienze Politiche, via Reclusorio del Lume, Università di Catania, 44 Catania, Italy. Degrees: Degree in Econ (Bocconi, Milan), 1967. Tutor, Scuola di Formazione in Sociologia, Milan; Researcher, ILSES, Milan; Professor of Industrial Soc, Faculty of Pol Sci, U of Catania. Publs: *Lotte operaie e organizzazione del lavoro* (co-author), 1971. Fields: Trade unions; labour market in developed and underdeveloped areas; organization of industrial work; political behaviour of the working class in underdeveloped areas.

[1592]
REYNOLDS Philip Alan
15 May 1920, British. Department of Politics, University of Lancaster, Bailrigg, Lancaster, England. Degrees: BA; MA (Oxon), 1950. 1946-50 Assistant Lecturer, Lecturer in International History; LSE; 1950-64 Wilson Professor of International Pol, U Coll of Wales, Aberystwyth; 1953 Visiting Professor, U of Toronto; 1958 Visiting Professor, U of New Delhi; 1964- Professor of Pol, U of Lancaster. Publs: *War in the Twentieth Century*, 1951; *Die Britische Aussenpolitik zwischen den beiden Weltkriegen*, 1952; *British Foreign Policy in the Interwar Years*, 1954; *An Introduction to International Relations*, 1971; *The Historian as Diplomat* (with F Hughes), 1976. Fields: International theory, especially the relevance and value of general systems theory and systems analysis in the study of international relations.

[1593]
RHODES Roderick
15 August 1944, British. Department of Government, University of Essex, Wivenhoe Park, Colchester, Essex, England. Degrees: BSc. 1967-70 Research Student, St Catherine's Coll, U of Oxford; Lecturer in Public Administration, Department of Local Government and Administration, U of Birmingham; Visiting Fellow in European Local Government, Centre for Contemporary European Studies, U of Sussex; Lecturer, Dept of Pol, U of Strathclyde; Lecturer, Dept of Govt, U of Essex. Publs: *Perspectives on Organizations*, 1972; *Studies in European Local Government* (ed and contributor), 1973. Fields: European local government; local administration and politics.

[1594]
RIBO Rafael
10 May 1945, Spanish. Faculty of Economics, University of Barcelona, Diagonal, Barcelona, Spain. Degrees: MA (New York); Dr Econ and Pol Sci (Barcelona). Doctoral thesis: "The Concept of Political Culture in the Work of Gabriel Almond". Professor, Catholic Inst of Soc Studies, Barcelona; Assistant Professor, Faculty of Econ, U of Barcelona. Publs: *Sobre el Fet Nacional*; *Amalto al Centralismo*; *Marxismo, Catecismo y Cuestión Nacional*; *Class Struggle and the National Question* (ed and contributor); *Aproximaciö Metodològica al Fet Nacional*. Fields: Federalism and autonomy; communist parties; Marxism and the national question.

[1595]
RICCAMBONI Gianni
23 July 1944, Italian. Via S G di Verdara 58, Padova, Italy. Degrees: Laurea (Padova), 1970. Lecturer in Pol Sci, Facoltà di Sci Pol, U of Padova. Publs: Various articles on local politics. Fields: Non-ruling communist parties.

[1596]
RICHARDS Peter Godfrey
20 August 1923, British. Red Lodge, Hadrian Way, Chilworth, Southampton SO1 7HZ, England. Degrees: BSc; PhD (Southampton), 1955. Doctoral thesis:. "Delegation by County Councils to County Districts". 1946 Lecturer, Senior Lecturer, Reader in Pol, U of Southampton; Professor of British Government, U of Southampton; 1969 Council of the Hansard Society for Parliamentary Government; 1970-73 Chairman, Study of Parliament Group. Publs: *Parliament and Foreign Affairs*, 1967; *The New Local Government System*, 1969; *Parliament and Conscience*, 1970; *The Backbenchers*, 1972; *The Reformed Local Government System*, 1973; *The Local Government Act, 1972: Problems of Implementation*, 1975; *The History of Local Government in the Twentieth Century*, 1978. Fields: British local government; British parliament.

[1597]
RICHARDSON Jeremy Paul
15 June 1942, British. 17 Camborne Crescent, Westlands, Newcastle Upon Lyme, Staffordshire, England. Degrees: BA; MA (Manchester), 1965; PhD (Manchester), 1970. Doctoral thesis: "The Formation of Transport Policy in Britain 1950-56". 1964-66 Research Student, Dept of Government, U of Manchester; 1966- Lecturer, Senior Lecturer in Pol, U of Keele. Publs: *The Policy-Making Process*, 1969; *Campaigning for the Environment*, 1974; *Pressure Groups in Britain*, 1974; plus articles in *Public Administration*, *Political Studies*, *Political Quarterly*, *Parliamentary Affairs*. Fields: British pressure groups; environmental politics; policy analysis.

[1598]
RICKNELL Lars
9 November 1923, Swedish. Mariehemsvägen 5g, S-902 36 Umeå, Sweden. Degrees: PhD. Doctoral thesis: "Political Regions". Publs: Books on Swedish local and regional government, Swedish Parliament. Fields: Political behaviour; regionalism.

[1599]
RIDDER Helmut Karl Johannes
18 July 1919, German. Krofdorfer Strasse 43, 6301 Biebertal 1, FR Germany. Degrees: Dr (Münster), 1950 Lecturer, U of Münster; 1952-59 Lecturer, Professor, U of Frankfurt; 1959-65 Professor, U of Bonn; 1965- Professor of Public Law and Pol Sci, U of Giessen. Publs: *Die soziale Ordnung des Grundgesetzes*, 1975. Fields: Comparative government; civil liberties; judicial functions; mass media.

[1600]
RIDLEY Frederick Ferdinand
11 August 1928, British. Roxby Building, The University, Liverpool L69 3BX, England. Degrees: BSc; PhD (LSE), 1954. 1953-54 Research Fellow, CNRS, Paris; 1954-58 Assistant Lecturer, U of Manchester; 1959-65 Lecturer, U of Liverpool; 1969 Visiting Professor, Graduate School of Public Affairs, U of Pittsburgh; 1965-1975 Professor and Head of Dept of Pol Theory and Inst, U of Liverpool; 1975 Visiting Professor, Coll of Europe, Bruges; 1970- Ed, *Political Studies*; 1976- Ed, *Parliamentary Affairs*. Publs: *Public Administration in France* (with J Blondel), 1969; *Specialists and Generalists: A Comparative Study of Professional Civil Servants* (ed and contributor), 1968; *Revolutionary Syndicalism in France*, 1970; *The Study of Government*, 1975; *Studies in Politics* (ed), 1975. Fields: French and German politics; public administration in Western Europe.

[1601]
RIEDMÜLLER Barbara Eniedenike
5 September 1945, German. Agnesstrasse 62, 8000 München 40, FR Germany. Degrees: Magister. Doctoral thesis: "Evolution und Krise. Ein Beitrag zu einer Theorie der sozialen Krise". 1972-74 Hochschuldidaktik/Planung, U of München; Lehrtätigkeit, Bayer Beamten Fachhochschule; Forschung im Bereich Gesundheits/Sozial politiks. Publs: *Marktnationalität oder Systemplanung*, 1976; "A Crisis of Legitimation — Habermas' Theory of Crisis", *International Journal of Politics*, 1977; "Psychosoziale Versorgung und Systemsozialer Sicherheit", in *Die gesellschaftliche Organisierung psychischen Leidens* (H Keupp et al (eds)), 1978. Fields: Social and health politics, especially in the field of psycho-social care.

[1602]
RIFFLET Raymond Felix Emmanuel*
21 December 1919, Belgian. 60 rue Dautzenberg, Bruxelles 1050, Belgium. Degrees: Lic (Brussels), 1941; Agrégé de l'enseignement (Brussels), 1941; Candidature complémentaire en droit (Free U of Brussels), 1939. Professeur, Athénée de Schaerbeek (Bruxelles); Chargé de recherches, Inst de Soc, Free U of Brussels; Directeur de recherches, Chargé de cours, Ryksuniversitair-centrum, U of Anvers, U of Strasbourg, U of Nice, Inst des Hautes Etudes Internationales, Collège d'Europe; Inst d'Etudes Européennes, Brussels; Directeur de recherches, Inst de Soc, Free U of Brussels; Directeur, Centre National d'Etude des Problèmes de Soc et d'Econ Européenne; Chargé de cours, U d'Amiens, Coll d'Europe, Bruges, Inst des Hautes Etudes Internationales, U de Nice; Conseiller-principal aux Communautés Européennes. Publs: Books on problems of sociology and of the European economy; nationalism in Germany and Belgium; East-West relations; the Belgian business elite and Europe; the Belgian socialists and Europe. Fields: Political sociology; European integration.

[1603]
RIGAUD Jacques
2 February 1932, French. 15 Quai Paul Doumer, 92400 Courbevoie, France. Degrees:
Lic en droit, Dipl (IEP Paris); ENA. 1954- Membre du Conseil d'Etat; 1969-70
Directeur du Cabinet, Ministre de l'Agriculture; 1971-73 Ministère des Affaires
Culturelles; 1958- Maître de conférences, Professeur, IEP, Paris; Sous-Directeur
Général, UNESCO. Publs: *Débat sur la France de demain*, 1961; *La culture pour vivre*,
1975; *Les institutions administratives françaises*; "The need for a comprehensive
cultural policy", in *Great Ideas Today*, 1977. Fields: Public law; administrative science
and sociology of international institutions; cultural development; sociology of culture.

[1604]
RIGLET Marc
22 November 1943, French. 108 Boulevard du Montparnasse, 75014 Paris, France.
Degrees: Lic en droit (Paris); Dipl (IEP Paris). Doctoral thesis: "Le parti communiste
et l'école". Attaché de direction aux Presses de la FNSP; Maître de conférences, IEP,
Paris. Publs: Various articles in *Maghreb, Project, Etudes, Revue Française de Science
Politique*. Fields: French Communist party; French labour movement; the international
communist movement.

[1605]
RIKLIN Alois
9 October 1935, Swiss. Forschungsstelle für Politikwissenschaft, Dufourstrasse 45, 9000
St Gallen, Switzerland. Degrees: Dr jur (Freiburg), 1964. Ordentlicher Professor für
Pol Saint Gall Graduate School of Econ, Business and Public Administration; Leiter
der Forschungsstelle für Pol. Publs: *Selbstzeugnisse des SED — Regimes*, 1963; *Das
Berlinproblem. Historische-politische und völkerrechtliche Darstellung des
Viermächtestatus*, 1964; *Weltrevolution oder Koexistenz?*, 1969; *Die Europäische Ge-
meinschaft im System der Staatenverbindungen*, 1972; *Grundlegung der
schweizerischen Aussenpolitik*, 1975; *Die Schweiz und die Europäischen Gemeinschaften*, 1975; *Handbuch der schweizerischen Aussenpolitik* (co-ed), 1975. Fields;
International relations; comparative politics; political thought.

[1606]
RILEY Stephen Peter
8 April 1949, British. The Boathouse Cottage, Barlaston, Stoke-on-Trent, Staffordshire
ST12 2DJ, England. Degrees: BSc; MA (Cantab), 1975. Lecturer in Pol, North Staffordshire Polytechnic. Fields: The politics of development; West African politics; comparative politics.

[1607]
RINGELING Arthur Bernard
21 September 1942, Dutch. Lankforst 3126, Nijmegen, The Netherlands. Degrees: Dr.
Doctoral thesis: "Discretionary Behaviour". Assistant in Public Administration,
Catholic U of Nijmegen. Publs:. "Discretion of Officials", *Bestuurswetenschappen*,
1974; "Political Decision-Making", in *Kernthema's van de Politicologie* (M van
Schendelen (ed)), 1976; "The Council and Local Decision-Making", *Bedrijfskunde*,
1976; "Policy and Legislation", *Beleid en Maatschappij*, 1977. Fields: Public administration, in particular problems in the areas between political science and law, between political science and organizational theory and local government.

[1608]
RINGNALDA Gerben
15 July 1930, Dutch. Laan van Poot 230, The Hague, The Netherlands. Degrees: Drs; Deputy Director, International Organization, Ministry for Foreign Affairs. Publs: "East and West in Israel", *Cartoms voor Letterkunde*, 1962; "Cabinet Formation in the Netherlands", *Acta Politica*, 1965/66; "Cabinet Formation", in *Verkenningen in de politiek* (A Hoogerwerf (ed)). Fields: Political party systems; theory of international relations; foreign policy and the decision-making process.

[1609]
RITTBERGER Volker
4 May 1941, German. Institut für Politikwissenschaft, Universität Tübingen, Brunnenstrasse 30, D-7400 Tübingen, FR Germany. Degrees: LL M (Freiburg), 1965; MA (Stanford), 1968; PhD (Stanford), 1972. 1966-67 Research Associate, Lecturer in Pol Sci, U of Freiburg i Br; 1971-73 Senior Researcher, Peace Research Institute, Frankfurt; 1973- Professor of Pol Sci, U of Tübingen. Publs: *Konflikt-Eskalation-Krise* (co-author), 1972; *Evolution and International Organization*, 1973; *Die Ostpolitik der Bundesrepublik* (co-ed), 1974; *Abrüstungspolitik und Grundgesetz* (co-author), 1976. Fields: International relations; comparative politics; international organizations and integration; peace and conflict research.

[1610]
RITTER Klaus
18 September 1918, German. 8026 Ebenhausen/Isartal, FR Germany. Degrees: Dr jur. 1951. Doctoral thesis: "Zwischen Naturrecht und Rechtspositivismus — Erkenntnistheoretische Auseinandersetzung mit den neueren Versuchen zur Wiederherstellung einer Rechtsmetaphysik". Director, Forschungsinstitut für Internationale Pol und Sicherheit der Stiftung Wissenschaft und Pol, Ebenhausen bei München. Fields: International relations.

[1611]
ROBERT Jacques
29 September 1928, French. 14 Villa St Georges, 92160 Antony, France. Degrees: Agrégé de droit public. Doctoral thesis: "Les violations de la liberté individuelle commises sur l'administration et le problème des responsabilités". 1956-60 Professeur, Faculté de Droit d'Alger; 1960-62 U de Rabat; 1962-65 U de Grenoble; 1968- U de Paris II; 1965-68 Directeur de la Maison Française de Tokyo; Maître de conférences, ENA. Publs: *Le Japon, 1969; La monarchie marocaine*, 1963; *Libertés publiques*, 1978; *Introduction à l'Esprit des Lois*, 1972; *La liberté religieuse et le régime des cultes*, 1978. Fields: Public freedoms; constitutional law; law and defence.

[1612]
ROBERTS Alwyn*
28 August 1933, British. Department of Social Theory and Institutions, University College of North Wales, Bangor, Wales. LL B (Wales), 1953; BA, 1956; BA, 1958; MA (Cambridge), 1962. 1959-60 Tutor, Westminster Coll, Cambridge; 1960-67 Aijal Coll, U of Assam, India; 1967-70 U Coll, Swansea. 1970- Lecturer, U Coll of North Wales.

[1613]
ROBERTS Geoffrey Keith
15 July 1936, British. Corner Stones, Coppice Avenue, Disley, Cheshire, England. Degrees: BSc; PhD (London). Doctoral thesis: "The Development of a Railway Interest and its Relation to Parliament, 1830-68". 1967-72 Lecturer in Pol, U of Loughborough; 1972- Reader in European Studies, Dept of European Studies, UMIST, Manchester.

Publs: *Parties and Pressure Groups in Britain*, 1970; *A Dictionary of Political Analysis*, 1971; *What is Comparative Politics?*, 1972; *West German Politics*, 1972. Fields: West German politics, especially the FDP; policy analysis; comparative political analysis.

[1614]
ROBERTSON David*
British. Department of Government, University of Essex, Wivenhoe Park, Colchester CO4 3SQ, England. Degrees: BA. Lecturer in Government, U of Essex. Fields: Conservative ideology from a semi-structuralist viewpoint; an analysis of free votes in the House of Commons, 1966-70; theory of political development.

[1615]
ROBIN Roger
16 August 1924, French. 140 Avenue Victor Hugo, 75016 Paris, France. Degrees: DES; Dipl (IEP); Lic ès lettres. Doctoral thesis: "Contribution à l'étude de la censure". Directeur de Séminaires Vie Pol, IEP, Paris. Publs: *Le citoyen*; *Cité, marché et famille*. Fields: Culture and politics; political goals and freedom; political development.

[1616]
ROBINS Lynton James
15 May 1943, British. 15 The Coppice, Narborough, Leicester LE9 6FB, England. BSc; PhD (Southampton), 1974. Doctoral thesis: "The Labour Party and the European Economic Community, 1961-1971". 1974-75 Lecturer in Education, Saint Luke's Coll, U of Exeter; 1975-76 Lecturer in Soc, Worcester Coll of Higher Education; 1976- Lecturer in Pol, Leicester Polytechnic. Publs: "Consensus and Cleavage in Labour's Perception of the World: A Method for Investigating Attitude Structure and Group Similarity", *British Journal of International Studies* (with A Brier), 1977. Fields: Political socialization and political education.

[1617]
ROBINSON Ann
28 January 1937, British. Northridge House, Usk Road, Shirenewton, Gwent, Wales. Degrees: BA; MA (Oxon), 1959; MA (McGill), 1969; PhD (McGill), 1972. Doctoral thesis: "Select Committees and the Functions of Parliament". 1962-65 Part-time Lecturer, St Aidans Coll, Durham; 1969-71 McConnell Fellow, U of McGill; 1970-72 Lecturer in Pol, U of Bristol; 1972-75 Lecturer in Pol, U of Bath; 1975- Lecturer in Pol, U of Cardiff. Publs: "Public Spending", in *The Banker* (with C T Standford), 1975; "The House of Commons and Public Expenditure", in *The Commons in the 70s* (M Ryle and S A Walkland (eds)), 1977; *Parliament and Public Spending: The Expenditure Committee of the House of Commons 1970-1976*, 1978. Fields: Public expenditure and taxation; the European Community.

[1618]
ROBINSON Francis Christopher Rowland
23 November 1944, British. 13 Grove Road, Windsor, Berkshire, England. Degrees: MA; PhD. Doctoral thesis; "The Politics of U P Muslims, 1906-1922". 1969-73 Prize Fellow, Trinity Coll, U of Cambridge; 1973- Lecturer in History, Royal Holloway Coll, U of London. Publs: *Separatism Among Indian Muslims: The Politics of the United Provinces' Muslims 1860-1923*, 1974; "Nation Formation: The Brass Thesis and Muslim Separatism", *Journal of Commonwealth and Comparative Politics*, 1977; "Consultation and Control", *Modern Asian Studies*, 1971; "Municipal Government and Muslim Separatism", *Locality, Province and Nation: Essays on Indian Politics 1870-1940*, (A Seal *et al* (eds)), 1973; "The Rise of the Professional Politician in Muslim

Politics 1911-1923'', in *Leadership in South Asia* (B N Pandey (ed)), 1977. Fields: Nation-formation in South Asia; Islam and political mobilization; Islam and the modern state.

[1619]
ROBINSON Kenneth Ernest
9 March 1914, British. The Old Rectory, Westcote, Oxfordshire OX7 6SF. Degrees: BA; MA (Oxon), 1948; LL D (Chinese U of Hong Kong), 1969; D Litt (U of Hong Kong), 1972; D U (Open U), 1978. 1948-57 Assistant Secretary, UK Colonial Office, Fellow of Nuffield Coll, U of Oxford; 1957-65 Director, Inst of Commonwealth Studies and Professor of Commonwealth Affairs, U of London; 1965-72 Vice Chancellor, U of Hong Kong; 1972-74 Hallsworth Research Fellow, U of Manchester. Publs: *The Dilemmas of Trusteeship*, 1965. Fields: History of British and French imperialism; administrative history; history of the UK colonial Office.

[1620]
ROBSON William Alexander
14 July 1895, British. 48 Lancaster Road, London N6 4TA, England. Degrees: BSc; PhD LLM (London); Honorary Degrees: Durham, Manchester, Birmingham, Lille, Grenoble, Paris and Algiers. Doctoral thesis: "The Relation of Wealth to Welfare". Professor of Public Administration, U of London; Reader in Administrative Law. Chairman, Greater London Group, LSE; Lecturer and Honorary Fellow, LSE. Publs: *Justice and Administrative Law*; *The Development of Local Government*; *The Government and Misgovernment of London*; *Nationalized Industry and Public Ownership*; *Local Government in Crisis*; *Great Cities of the World: Their Government, Politics and Planning*; *Civilization and the Growth of Law*; *Problems of Nationalized Industries*; *Welfare State and Welfare Society*. Fields: Problems of great cities; public enterprise at home and abroad; theory and practice; the welfare state; the control of public administration.

[1621]
RODES GRACIA Jesus M
25 April 1945, Spanish. Llancà, 43, 8é 1ª, Barcelona 15, Spain. Degrees: Lic Ciencias Pol; Dipl Estudios Soc (CSIC). Doctoral thesis: "Movimento obrario y nacionalismo durante la II Republica. Una aproximación estasiologica: la Unió Socialista de Catalunya". 1970-72 Professor Ayudante, U of Barcelona; 1972- Professor Adjunto, Dept of Pol Sci, U Autonoma de Barcelona. Publs: *Manifiesto Comunista*, 1976; *Les Dretes i la Generalitat*, 1977; "Socialdemocracia catalana i questió nacional (1910-1934)", *Recerques*, 1978. Fields: Political parties; nationalism.

[1622]
RODRIGUEZ Federico
6 October 1918, Spanish. Avenue Alfonso XIII, 182, Madrid, 16, Spain. Degrees: Dr in Law; Dr in Pol Sci. Doctoral thesis: "Liberty in the Theory of Modern Popes". Full Professor of Social Policy, U Complutense, Madrid. Publs: *Doctrina Pontificia — Documentos Sociales*, 1964; *Curso de Doctrina Social catolica, Propiedad*, 1967; *Codigo Social de Malinas*, 1956. Fields: Social theory of property.

[1623]
ROESSLER Gerda
20 February 1938, German. Reichshofer Strasse 19, D-6800 Mannheim-71, FR Germany. Degrees: Dr phil; Habilitation. Doctoral thesis: "Zur Problematik der Struktur des Nordwestnormannischen Vokalismus". Publs: *Zur Problematik der Struktur des Nordwestnormannischen Vokalismus*, 1970; *Konnotation Untersuchungen zum Pro-*

blem der Mit- und Nebenbedeutung, 1977; *Sprache und Frieden. Versuch eines Beitrags der Linguistik im Vorfeld der Friedensforschung*, 1977; *Zum Stand eines Forschungsprojekts*, 1977. Fields: Dialect geography; semantics; European research; structural linguistics.

[1624]
ROHE Karl Ludwig
25 November 1934, German. Kohlenstrasse 28, 43 Essen, FR Germany. Degrees: Dr phil. Doctoral thesis: "Das Reichsbanner Schwarz Rot Gold". Ord Professor of Pol Sci, U of Essen. Publs: *Das Reichsbanner. Untersuchungen zut Geschichte und Struktur politischer Kampfverbände*, 1964; "Ursachen und Bedingungen des britischen Imperialismus von 1914", in *Moderner Imperialismus* (W Mommsen (ed)), 1973; *Politik. Begriffe und Wirklichkeiten*, 1978; "Kontinuität und Wandel der politischen Gesellschaft im Ruhrgebiet", in *Politik und Gesellschaft im Ruhrgebiet* (K Rohe and H Kühr (eds)), 1978. Fields: History of ideas, political theory; regional politics and policy; Great Britain: political systems and political ideas.

[1625]
ROIG Charles José
2 February 1932, French. 9A rue du 18 Aôut, 74240 Gaillard, France. Degrees: Lic en droit; Dipl études pol (Alger); Dr (Paris), 1858. Doctoral thesis: "Les circonstances exceptionnelles dans la jurisprudence administrative et la doctrine". 1960-65 Public administration and industry; 1965-71 Teacher, IEP, Grenoble; Maître de recherche, CNRS; 1971- Professor, U of Geneva. Publs: "Les circonstances exceptionnelles dans la jurisprudence administrative et la doctrine - Evolution du Parlement en 1959", in *Etudes sur le Parlement de la Vème République*, 1965; "Administration locale et changements sociaux", in *Administration traditionnelle et planification régionale*, 1964; "Tranches opératoires et politiques d'action régionale", in *La planification comme processus de décision*, 1965; *Regional Planning in France*, 1967; *La socialisation politique des enfants* (with F Billon-Grand), 1968; *Symboles et société: une introduction à la politique des symboles d'après l'oeuvre de Kenneth Burke*, 1977; *Idéologie comme grammaire: Lénine et les léninismes* (ed), 1978. Fields: Political socialization; analysis of systems applied to politics; public administration; political theory in relation to the theory of symbols; recurring problems of methodology.

[1626]
ROKKAN Stein
4 July 1921, Norwegian. Sudmannsvei 34, N-5000 Bergen, Norway. Degrees: Mag art (Oslo); Fil dr (Uppsala); Dr pol (Helsinki). 1951-60 Director of Research, Inst for Soc Research, Oslo; 1958-68 Director of Research, the Christian Michelsen Inst, Bergen; 1963-73 Recurring Visiting Professor, U of Yale; 1959-60, 1967, 1970 Fellow, Center for Advanced Study, Stanford; Professor of Soc, U of Bergen and Director, Norwegian Soc Sci Data Services. Publs: *Comparative Survey Analysis* (co-author), 1969; *International Guide to Electoral Statistics* (ed), 1969; *Quantitative Ecological Analysis* (co-ed), 1969; *Citizens, Elections, Parties*, 1970; *Imagination and Precision in the Social Sciences* (co-ed), 1972; *Building States and Nations* (co-ed), 1973-74; *Locational Analysis of Power and Conflict* (co-ed), 1974; *The Praxis of Sociology* (co-ed), 1976. Fields: Mass politics; political development; state formation; nation-building; centre-periphery relations; periphery protest movements; historical political sociology; data archiving; computer cartography.

[1627]
RÖLING Bernard Victor Aloysius
26 December 1906, Dutch. Groenesteinlaan 22, Groningen, The Netherlands. Degrees: Dr of Law (Utrecht), 1933. Doctoral thesis: "The Law concerning Habitual Criminals". Judge in the Courts of Middelburg and Utrecht; 1946-48 Judge in the International Military Tribunal for the Far East, Tokyo; Professor of Criminal Law; Professor of International Law; Director of the Polemological Inst, U of Groningen. Publs: *The Criminological Significance of Shakespeare's Macbeth*, 1973; *International Law in an Expanded World*, 1960; *On War and Peace*, 1968; *The Science of War and Peace*, 1973; *The Significance of Strategic Arms Limitation Talks*, 1970; *International Law and the Maintenance of Peace*, 1973; *Völkerrecht und Friedenswissenschaft*, 1974; *Poverty and War Problems*, 1975; *The Law of War and Dubious Weapons* (with Olga Suković), 1976; *The Weapon Problem*, 1977 (all in Dutch). Fields: Peace research; the international structure; international law and technology; the law of war; peace policy; arms control and disarmament; the method of change; the effects of unorthodox means of communication.

[1628]
RONDOT Pierre Louis Marie
2 July 1904, French. 16 rue Auguste Payant, 69007 Lyon, France. Degrees: Lic en droit; Dr en droit public; Dipl (Ecole Langues Orientales). Doctoral thesis: "Les institutions politiques du Liban". Directeur, Centre des Hautes Etudes sur l'Afrique et l'Asie Moderne, Paris; Professeur, ENA, Paris, IEP, Paris, Lyon et Strasbourg; Publs: *Les institutions politiques du Liban*, 1947; *Destin du Proche Orient*, 1959; *Islam et les Musulmans d'aujourd'hui*, 1961; *L'Islam*, 1967. Fields: Middle East; political evolution; Maghreb; Islam in the modern world; problems of minorities in Asia, the Middle East and Africa.

[1629]
RONGERE Pierrette*
4 October 1938, French. 24 rue des Plâtriers, 69 Lyon 9ème France. Degrees: Dr (Paris), 1963; Dr en droit (Paris), 1966. Doctoral thesis: "Le procédé de l'acte-type", 1966. 1962-66 Assistante, U de Lyon; 1967 Maître de conférences agrégée, Professeur, U de Lyon II. Publs: "L'apport de Henri de Man au socialisme contemporain", in *Socialisme et ethique*, 1966; *Le procédé de l'acte-type*, 1968; *Méthodes des sciences sociales*, 1971. Fields: Methods of social science; political parties and trade unions; history and events of the workers' movement.

[1630]
ROOTES Christopher Alan
12 January 1948, British. 9 Worthgate Place, Castle Row, Canterbury, Kent CT1 2QX, England. Degrees: BA; B Phil (Oxon), 1973. Doctoral thesis: "The Social-scientific Explanation of Student Radicalism: A Review and Critique of Some Recent Literature". 1975 Lecturer, School of Soc, U of New South Wales, Australia; Lecturer in Soc, U of Kent. Publs: "Demonstrations and Public Opinions", *Politics*, 1978; "The Rationality of Student Radicalism", *Australian and New Zealand Journal of Sociology*, 1978. Fields: Social and political theory; political sociology, in particular, ideology; knowledge of legitimation in advanced capitalist societies; student movements; the relationship between social theory and social practice.

[1631]
ROPPEL Ulrich
5 May 1948, German. 78 Freiburg, Sundgauallee 4/21, FR Germany. Degrees: Dr rer
Pol, 1978. Doctoral thesis: "Ökonomische Theorie der Bürokratie. Beiträge zu einer
Theorie des Angebotsverhaltens staatlicher Bürokratien". Wiss Assistent, Inst für
Allgemeine Wirtschaftsforschung, Abteilung Sozialpolitik, Freiburg. Publs:
Verteilungstheorie, 1974; *Wohlfahrtsökonomik*, 1975-76. Fields: Economic theory of
politics; bureaucracy; politics of population.

[1632]
ROSCHAR Frans Marius
7 February 1945, Dutch. Johannes Verhaulstsraat 84, Amsterdam, The Netherlands.
Degrees: Drs. Fellow, Nederlands Instituut voor Vredesvraagstukken. Publs: *Iran,
Development Towards an Independent Foreign Policy*; *Foreign Policy in Dutch Public
Opinion*; "Carter's Course"; "Enigma Carter"; "Expectations on War"; "The Dutch
Neutron Bomb Discussion"; "A Structural Model of the Dutch Foreign Policy Elite".
Fields: American foreign policy; proliferation of nuclear weapons.

[1633]
ROSE Hannan David Raphael
12 March 1944, British. Rutherford College, The University, Canterbury, Kent,
England. Degrees: BA. 1966-68 Research Student, Nuffield Coll, U of Oxford; 1968-69
U Fellowship, Dept of Soc Relations, U of Harvard; 1969-70 Temporary Lecturer in
Pol, U of Leicester; 1970- Lecturer in Interdisciplinary Studies, U of Kent; Publs: "The
Works of the Voluntary Liaison Committee', in *The Prevention of Racial Discrimination in Britain* (S Abbott (ed)). Fields: Politics of immigration in Britain and the
development of a European policy towards migrant workers in the context of the EEC
policy for the free movement of labour; effectiveness of British parliamentary institutions and the potential impact of EEC institutions on them.

[1634]
ROSE Richard
9 April 1933, British. Department of Politics, University of Strathclyde, McCance
Building, 16 Richmond Street, Glasgow G1 1XG. Scotland. Degrees: BA; D Phil (Oxon), 1960. 1954-55 Pol Public Relations, Mississippi Valley; 1953-57 Reporter, *St Louis
Post Dispatch*; 1961-66 Lecturer, U of Manchester; 1964, 1966, 1970 Election Cor-
respondent, *The Times*; 1967, 1968, 1973 President, Scottish Pol Studies Association;
Psephologist, Independent Television News; 1966- Professor of Pol, U of Strathclyde;
1970 Secretary, Committee on Pol Soc, IPSA/ISA; 1974 Guggenheim Fellowship,
Woodrow Wilson International Centre, Washington; 1976 Visiting Scholar, Brookings
Inst; 1976 Director, Centre for the Study of Public Policy, Strathclyde; 1977-78 Visiting
Professor, European U Inst, Florence. Publs: *Politics in England*, 1964; *Influencing
Voters*, 1967; *People in Politics*, 1970; *Governing without Consensus: An Irish Perspec-
tive*, 1971; *European Politics* (with M Dogan), 1971; *The Problems of Party Govern-
ment*, 1974; *Northern Ireland: A Time of Choice*, 1976; *What is Governing? Purpose
and Policy in Washington*, 1978. Fields: Political parties; policy analysis; British and
Irish studies.

[1635]
ROSE Saul
27 May 1922, British. New College, Oxford, England. Degrees: MA (Oxon), 1948; D
Phil (Oxon), 1951. Doctoral thesis: "Constitutional Government in Japan, 1918-32".
Lecturer in International Relations, U of Aberdeen; International Secretary, British
Labour Party; Fellow, St Anthony's Coll, U of Oxford; Fellow and Bursar, New Coll,

U of Oxford. Publs: *Socialism in Southern Asia*, 1959; *Britain and South-East Asia*, 1962; *Politics in Southern Asia* (ed), 1963. Fields: Government and politics of South and South-East Asia.

[1636]
ROSEN Edgar Robert
18 June 1911, American. Jasperalle 7, 33 Braunschweig, FR Germany. Degrees: Dr phil (Leipzig), 1933. 1948-65 Professor of History and Government, U of Missouri; Ord Prof für Wissenschaft von der Pol, Technical U Carolo Wilhelmina, Braunschweig; 1976- Professeur em. Publs: *Berlin — Brennpunkt Deutschen Schicksals*, 1960; *Faschismus — Nationalsozialismus*, 1964; *Deutschland und die USA 1918-1933*, 1968. Fields: Italian history since Risorgimento and during the 20th century; Italian politics.

[1637]
ROSEN Frederick
13 September 1938. Department of Government, London School of Economics and Political Science, Houghton Street, London WC2A 2AE. Degrees: BA; MA (Syracuse), 1963; PhD (LSE), 1965. Doctoral thesis: "Progress and Democracy: William Godwin's Contribution to Political Philosophy". 1968-70 Lecturer, City U; 1970-71 Associate Research Fellow, U Coll, London; 1971- Lecturer in Government, LSE. Publs: "Piety and Justice: Plato's *Euthyphro*", *Philosophy*, 1968; "Population as Political Theory: Godwin's *Of Population* and the Malthusian Controversy", *Journal of the History of Ideas*, 1970; "Basic Needs and Justice", *Mind*, 1977; "The Political Context of Aristotle's Categories of Justice", *Phronesis*, 1975; "Obligation and Friendship in Plato's *Crito*, *Political Theory*, 1973; "Labour and Liberty: Simone Weil and the Human Condition", in *Theoria to Theory* (D Emmet (ed)), 1973. Fields: Political philosophy; history of political thought; Plato; Aristotle; Bentham and utilitarianism.

[1638]
ROSENTHAL Uriel
19 July 1945, Dutch. Erasmus University, Rotterdam, The Netherlands. Degrees: BA; MA; PhD. Doctoral thesis: "Rewards, Punishments and Political Stability". Lecturer, U of Amsterdam; Lecturer, Erasmus U, Rotterdam. Publs: *Political Order*, 1978; *Public Administration* (co-author) (in Dutch), 1977; *Crisis and Continuity* (co-author) (in Dutch), 1977; *Ministers, Bureaucrats and Parliamentarians* (co-author) (in Dutch), 1975; plus various articles in *Acta Politica*, *Beleid en Maatschappij*, *Bestuurswetenschappen*, *Res Publica*; *Netherlands' Journal of Sociology*. Fields: Political stability/succession; public policy-making and the politics of public administration; crisis theory and decision-making; political succession.

[1639]
ROSSI-LANDI Guy
14 July 1943, French. 21 rue Ernest Deloison, 92200 Neuilly/Seine, France. Degrees: Dr (Paris), 1970. Doctoral thesis: "La vie politique en France pendant la drôle de guerre". 1966-68 Assistant, Assoc Française de Sci Pol; 1969-71 Attaché, FNSP; Maître de conférences, IEP, U de Paris II. Publs: *Les journalistes politiques*, 1969; *La drôle de guerre*, 1970; *Les hommes politiques*, 1973. Fields: Politics in France since 1919; 20th century political thought.

[1640]
ROTA Silvia
28 May 1929, Italian. Via delle Rosine 4, 10123 Torino, Italy. Degrees: Laurea (Torino); Libera Docenza in Storia delle Dottrine Politiche; Cattedra di Storia delle Dottrine Pol; Professore di Storia delle Dottrine Pol, U di Bari e di Pisa; Professore di Storia delle

Dottrine Pol, Facoltà di Sci Pol, U di Torino. Publs: *La Fortuna di Rousseau in Italia*, 1961; *Proudhon e Rousseau*, 1965; *G Ferrari*. *L'Evoluzione del suo Pensiero (1838-1860)*, 1969; "Il Socialismo 'Utopistico' ", *Storia delle Idee Politiche, Economiche e Sociali*, 1972; *G Ferrari, Scritti Politici*, 1973; "Scopo e Limiti della Condotta Politica in Camus", *Annali Facneta di Scienze Politiche*, 1973; *Notizie de Nessun Luogo*, 1978. Fields: History of political doctrines from the 19th century to the present day; history of socialist theory of the 20th century; history of the Liberal doctrine.

[1641]
ROTH Reinhold
29 May 1941, German. Contrescarpe 110, 2800 Bremen 1, FR Germany. Degrees: Dr; Dipl Pol. Doctoral thesis; "Aussenpolitische Innovation und politische Herrschaftssicherung. Eine Analyse von Struktur und Systemfunktion des aussenpolitischen Entscheidungsprozesses am Beispiel der sozialliberalen Koalition 1969 bis 1973". U of Hamburg; Hochschule für Wirtschaft, Bremen. Publs: *Aussenpolitische Innovation und politische Herrschaftssicherung*, 1976; *Parteiensystem und Aussenpolitik*, 1973; *Parteien-Jahrbuch 1976* (with H Kaack (eds)), 1978; *Parteien und internationale Politik*, 1977; *Die Parteien und die Aussenpolitik* (with H Kaack), 1975; *Die aussenpolitische Führungselite der Bundesrepublik Deutschland* (with H Kaack), 1972; *Östpolitik als Mittel der Deutschlandpolitik*, 1969. Fields: Party systems; foreign policy.

[1642]
ROTT Hans Christian
10 November 1944, Dutch. Pieter de Hooghstraat 92^1, 1071 EK Amsterdam, The Netherlands. Degrees: Drs. Research Fellow, Inst for the Socio-Econ Studies of Developing Regions; Instructor and Research Fellow, Econ Inst, Faculty of Pol Sci, U of Amsterdam. Fields: Development planning; macro economics.

[1643]
ROTTER Manfred J Paul
5 February 1939, Austrian. Wolf Huber Strasse 11, A-4020 Linz, Austria. Degrees: Dr jur (Vienna), 1963. 1964-66 Assistant, U of Vienna; 1968- Assistant and Lecturer in Public Law, International Law, International Relations, U of Vienna. Publs: *Die dauernde Neutralität*, 1978; plus various articles in *Österreichische Zeitschrift für öffentliches Recht, Österreichische Zeitschrift für Politikwissenschaft*. Fields: Small states diplomacy; international security; Austria's foreign relations; human rights; international law and international systems.

[1644]
ROUVIER Jean Gaston Simon
25 May 1927, French. 7 rue Berthollet, 75005 Paris, France. Degrees: Dr en sci pol, 1961; Agrégé de droit, 1963. Doctoral thesis: "Du pouvoir dans la République romaine". 1959-64 Professeur, Ecole Nat d'Administration, Paris; 1963-65 Professeur agrégé, Faculté de Droit, Nancy; 1965-68 Professeur titulaire de chaire, Faculté de Droit, Lille; 1968- Professeur, U de Paris II; 1973- Conseiller Spécial, Commission des Communautés européennes. Publs: *La république romaine et la démocratie*, 1961; *Du pouvoir dans la République Romaine*, 1963; *Les grandes idées politiques des origines à J J Rousseau*, 1973; *Les grandes idées politiques de J J Rousseau à nos jours*, 1978. Fields: History of political ideas.

[1645]
ROVAN Joseph*
15 July 1918, French. 4 rue des Capucins, 92 190 Meudon, France. Degrees: DES (Paris), 1939. Associate Professor, U of Paris VIII (Vincennes). Publs: *Allemagne*, 1955; *Histoire du catholicisme politique en Allemagne*, 1956; *Une idée neuve, la démocratie*, 1961; *L'Europe*, 1966. Fields: German history and politics; European politics; politics of culture and education.

[1646]
ROVENTI Sandro
29 November 1947, Italian. Via Bocconi 24, 20136 Milano, Italy. Doctoral thesis: "Political Capabilities in USA and USSR". Assistant Professor in Pol Sci, U of Milan. Publs: *Bibliography of the Italian Political System*. Fields: Italian political system.

[1647]
ROWE Eric Alfred
8 June 1926, British. 2 The Hat Factory, Fritchley, Derbyshire, England. Degrees: BA; B Litt (Oxon), 1959. 1956-58 Research Student, Nuffield Coll; U of Oxford; 1958-59 Assistant Lecturer, U of Liverpool; 1959- Lecturer, Senior Lecturer, U of Nottingham. Publs: *Modern Politics*; *Towards Fairer Voting*. Fields: Political parties and elections.

[1648]
RUBEL Maximilien
10 October 1905, French. 76 rue des Plantes, 75014 Paris, France. Degrees: MA Law (Rumania), 1928; M Phil (Cernauti-Rumania), (Rumania), 1930; Lic ès lettres (Sorbonne), 1934; Dr ès lettres (Sorbonne), 1954. 1947- Maître de recherches, CNRS. Publs: *Marx devant le Bonapartisme*, 1960; *Karl Marx-Oeuvres, économie*, 1963; *Marx Chronik-Daten zu Leben und Werk*, 1968; *Marx/Engels: Die russische Kommüne. Kritik eines Mythos*, 1971; *Marx Chronik*, 1975; *Marx critique du marxisme*, 1975; *Stalin*, 1975; *Marx without Myth — A Chronology of his Life and Work* (with M Manale), 1976. Fields: The Paris Commune in 1871 in the light of historical experience 1871-1971; philosophy 1838-47; Bonapartism; Marxist studies.

[1649]
RUBIO LLORENTE Francisco
25 February 1930, Spanish. Arandiga 28, Madrid 23, Spain. Degrees: Dr in Law. Doctoral thesis; "Anthropological Basis of Marxist Theory (Marx's Concept of Man)". Professor, Central U of Venezuela; Professor, U Complutense de Madrid. Publs: *Philosophy and Economics in Karl Marx. Karl Marx's Early Writings*, 1968; *The Constitutional Court of Italy*, 1970; *The Concept of Equality in the Doctrine of the Supreme Court of the USA*, 1969; *Constitution and Education*, 1977. Fields: Constitutional law.

[1650]
RUDEBECK Lars E A
10 October 1936, Swedish. Sköldungagatan, 31, 753 35 Uppsala, Sweden. Degrees: PhD (Uppsala), 1967. Doctoral thesis: "Party and People. A Study of Political Change in Tunisia". Lecturer in Pol Sci, Research Assistant, Associate Research Professor, Swedish Council for Soc Sci Research; Lecturer and Researcher, Dept of Pol Sci and the Working Group for the Study of Development Strategies (AKUT), U of Uppsala. Publs: *Party and People. A Study of Political Change in Tunisia*, 1969; *Utveckling och Politik*, 1970; *Guinea-Bissau. A Study of Political Mobilization*, 1974; *Guinea-Bissau. Folket, Partiet och Staten*, 1977. Fields: Development theory; relationship between types of development strategies in the Third World and the social basis of state power in terms of political support; international dependence; capacity for development.

[1651]
RUDELLE Odile
6 December 1936, French. 120 Avenue Félix Faure, 75015 Paris, France. Degrees: Dipl (IEP Paris); DES. Doctoral thesis: "Aux origines de l'instabilité constitutionnelle de la IIème République-la République absolue 1870-1889". CNRS. Publs: *Michel Debré, sénateur.* Fields: Political institutions; political ideas.

[1652]
RUDZIO Wolfgang
29 March 1935, German. Quellenweg 68, 2900 Oldenburg, FR Germany. Degrees: Dr phil (Frankfurt), 1967. Doctoral thesis: "Die Neuordnung des Kommunalwesens in der Britischen Zone". 1966-72 Wiss Assistent, U of Frankfurt; 1966-73 Professor, U of Frankfurt; 1973- Professor, U of Oldenburg. Publs: *Die Neuordnung des Kommunalwesens in der Britischen Zone,* 1968; *Entscheidungszentrum Koalitionsausschuss,* 1971; *Die organisierte Demokratie,* 1977; *Zwischen Marxistischer Politökonomie und Erfahrung,* 1977. Fields: Germanic studies; political parties and pressure groups; politcal thought; socialism.

[1653]
RUEFF Jacques
23 August 1896, French. 51 rue de Varenne, 75007 Paris, France. Membre de l'Académie Française; Membre de l'Académie des Sci Morales et Pol Chancelier de l'Inst de France.

[1654]
RUF Werner Klaus*
15 October 1937, German. Bürklinstrasse 15, D-763 Lahr, FR Germany. Degrees: Dr phil (Freiburg), 1967. Doctoral thesis: "Bourguibism and the Foreign Policy of Independent Tunisia". 1964 Director, Bureau of Freiburg for Contacts with Developing Countries; 1965 Research Assistant, Arnold-Bergsträsser-Inst for Socio-political Research, Freiburg; Lecturer in Pol Sci, U of Freiburg; 1968-69 Senior Fellow, New York U Center for International Studies; 1967- Head, Near East and North African Dept, Arnold-Bergsträsser-Inst; Lecturer in Pol Sci, U of Freiburg; 1970- Research Project on the Influence of Images and Ideologies on Interstate Relations in the Maghreb. Publs: *Habib Burgiba und die Idee der nordafrikanischen Einigung,* 1964; *Frankreichs Entwicklungshilfe — Politik auf lange Sicht?* (co-author), 1967; *Der Burgibismus und die Aussenpolitik des unabhängigen Tunesien,* 1969; *Group Images and Interstate Relations — On the contribution of Cybernetics to the Analysis of International Relations,* 1972. Fields: Systems analysis; interdependence between national systems and the international system; mass media research.

[1655]
RUFFIEUX Roland
9 November 1921, Swiss. Chemin des Kybourg 3, CH-1700 Fribourg, Switzerland. Degrees: Lic ès lettres (Fribourg), 1946; Dr ès lettres (Fribourg), 1953; Dipl (IEP Paris), 1954. Doctoral thesis; "Idéologie et nécessité - Essai sur le régime radical fribourgeois 1847-1956". 1947-52 Professeur, Lycée de Sion; 1962-65 Directeur, Bibliothèque Nationale Suisse; Professeur ord d'histoire contemporaine, U de Fribourg; Professeur ord de Sci Pol et Directeur de l'Inst de Sci Pol, U de Lausanne. Publs: *L'idéologie et nécéssité. Essai sur le régime radical fribourgeois,* 1957; *Le mouvement chrétien-social en Suisse Romande, 1891-1949,* 1969; *La démocratie référendaire en Suisse dans l'entredeux-guerres, analyse de décisions,* 1970; "La Suisse", in *Guide international de statistiques électorales - Elections nationales en Europe Occidentale* (S Rokkan and J Meyriat (eds)), 1969; *Les élections au Grand Conseil vaudois de 1913-66,* 1971; *Ver-*

waltung im Umbruch (with Germann and Bischofsberger), 1971; "Idéologie et nécéssité - Essai sur le régime radical fribourgeois", in *La Suisse d'entre deux guerres*, 1974. Fields: Swiss politics, especially federalism; referenda; cantonal and local government; foreign policy; political development; cross-national comparisons of legislatures and executives.

[1656]
RUIN Olaf Kristian
8 November 1927, Swedish. 29 Bergstigen, 182 74 Stocksund, Sweden. Degrees: PhD (Lund), 1960. 1960-66 Docent, U of Stockholm; 1966-67 Associate Professor, U of Lund; 1967-76 Associate Professor, U of Stockholm; 1976- Professor of Pol Sci, U of Stockholm; 1969-70 Ed, *Scandinavian Political Studies*; 1971-72 Visiting Professor, U of Michigan; 1973-76 President, Swedish Pol Sci Association; 1978- Deputy Chancellor of the Swedish Universities. Publs: *Kooperativa förbundet 1899-1929*, 1960; *Studentrekrytering och Studentekonomi*, 1963; *Mellan Samlingsregering och Tvåpartisystem. Den Svenska Regeringsdiskussionen 1945-60*, 1968. Fields: Interest organizations; executives; educational policies.

[1657]
RUIZ DE AZUA ANTON Miguel Angel
18 March 1945, Spanish. Villanueva 37, Madrid 1, Spain. Degrees: Lic (Madrid); Lic (Louvain). Assistant Professor of Spanish Public Law; Professor Encargado de Curso de Comportamiento Pol, Partidos Grupos de Presión, Seminario de Derecho Pol, Facultad de Ciencias Pol y Soc, U Complutense de Madrid. Publs: "Las Elecciones Franquistas", *Historia*, 1976; "Clase Dirigente en 1970", in *Anuario Politico Español 1970* (M Cuadrado (ed)), 1971. Fields: Public law; political sociology; electoral sociology.

[1658]
RULOFF Dieter*
13 September 1947, German. Burgstrasse 17, CH-8280 Kreuzlingen, Switzerland. Degrees: MA (Konstanz), 1971. Assistant, Historisches Seminar, U of Zürich. Fields: General systems theory; applications of system dynamics to the study of international relations; arms race; Richardson Paradigm; democratic theory.

[1659]
RUMI Geiogio*
15 March 1938, Italian. Via de Amicis, 47 Milan, Italy. Degrees: Dr in Pol Sci; Libero Docente di Storia Contemporanea. Professore Incaricato, U of Milan; Professor of History, U of Milan. Publs: *Delle Origini della Politica estera Fascista*, 1968. Fields: The Italian ruling class.

[1660]
RUNZE Dieter Hans
23 December 1937, German. Sülzburgstrasse 207, 5000 Köln 41, FR Germany. Degrees: Dr phil. Doctoral thesis: "Zur negativen Dialektik des deutschen Protestantismus nach 1918: Heinz Dietrich Wendlands Theologie der Gesellschaft". 1969-71 Jugendbildungsreferent, Landesjugendring Bremen; 1972-77 Assistanzprofessor, Otto-Suhr-Inst, Free U of Berlin; Fachhochschullehrer, Fachhochschule Niederrhein, Mönchengladbach. Publs: "Zur Kritik der politischen Soziologie" (with W D Narr), in *Theorie der Gesellschaft oder Sozialtechnologie*, 1974; "Burgfrieden? Zur Politik innerer Unsicherheit und der Genese ihrer Feindbilder", in *Wir Bürger als Sicherheitsrisiko* (W D Narr (ed)), 1977. Fields: Ideology, youth and wealth as subjects of politics; minorities; key concepts of political science and political sociology.

[1661]
RUSH Michael David
29 October 1937, British. Department of Politics, University of Exeter, Amory
Building, Rennes Drive, Exeter EX4 4RJ, England. Degrees: BA; PhD (Sheffield),
1966. Doctoral thesis: "The Selection of Parliamentary Candidates in the Conservative
and Labour Parties". 1967-68 Visiting Lecturer, Dept of Pol Sci, U of Western Ontario, Canada; 1964- Lecturer in Pol, U of Exeter. Publs: *The Selection of Parliamentary Candidates*, 1969; *The Member of Parliament and his Information* (co-author),
1970; *An Introduction to Political Sociology* (co-author), 1971; *The House of Commons: Services and Facilities* (co-ed and contributor), 1974; *Parliament and the Public*,
1976. Fields: Parties and electoral behaviour; political sociology; Canadian politics;
British parliament.

[1662]
RUSSELL-SMITH Enid Mary (Dame)
3 March 1903, British. 3 Pimlico, Durham, England. Degrees: BA; MA (Cambridge).
1925 Assistant Principal; 1963 Retired as Deputy Secretary, Ministry of Health; 1963-70
Principal, St Aidan's Coll, U of Durham; Honorary Lecturer, Dept of Pol (Public Administration), U of Durham. Publs: *Modern Bureaucracy: the Home Civil Service*,
1974. Fields: Public administration.

[1663]
RUUSALA Raili Orvokki
10 July 1930, Finnish. Kelohongantie 14, D-21 Tapiola, Finland. Degrees: Dr soc sci.
Doctoral thesis: "Social Democratic Party Organization". Teacher, Väinö Voionmaan
Opisto; Research Worker, Ministry of Justice; Research Worker, Finnish Broadcasting
Corporation; Assistant Professor, Lecturer in Pol Sci, U of Tampere. Publs: Various
on women's organizations in Finland, and on audience research. Fields: Political
organizations; political parties.

[1664]
RYAN Alan James
9 May 1940, British. Haymakers, Stanton St John, Oxford OX9 1HD, England.
Degrees: MA (Oxon). 1963-66 Lecturer in Moral and Pol Philosophy, U of Keele;
1966-69 Lecturer in Government, U of Essex; 1967-68 Visiting Professor, City U, New
York; 1972 U of Texas at Austin; 1977 U of California at Santa Cruz; 1974-75 Visiting
Fellow, Australian National U; 1969- Reader in Pol, U of Oxford, and Fellow and
Tutor in Pol, New Coll, U of Oxford. Publs: *The Philosophy of John Stuart Mill*, 1970;
The Philosophy of the Social Sciences, 1970; *Social Explanation* (ed), 1973; *J S Mill*,
1975. Fields: The political theory of property; the politics of Bertrand Russell; the life
and ideas of Godwin.

[1665]
RYAN Michael Charles
18 September 1941, Irish. 33 St Mildreds Road, Lee, London SE12, England. Degrees:
BA; MA (Sheffield). Lecturer in Pol, Thames Polytechnic. Publs: *The Acceptable
Pressure Group*, 1978. Fields: Pressure groups and the policy process; the European
Communities.

S

[1666]
SABINE John Arthur*
7 November 1934, British. 83 Heathfield, Swansea, South Wales. Degrees: BSc; MA (Manchester), 1961. 1968-69 Visiting Assistant Professor, Queen's U, Canada; Lecturer, Dept of Pol Theory and Government, U Coll, Swansea. Fields: Making of defence policy; influence of science on the character of military in Britain over last century; civil/military relations in Britain.

[1667]
SACHER Wilhelm
6 July 1917, Austrian. Langothstrasse 4, A-4020 Linz, Austria. Degrees: Dr theologiae (Innsbruck), 1948; Dr jur (Vienna), 1959. 1948-65 Official, School Administration, Linz; 1966- Dozent für Pol, U of Salzburg; Lehrbeauftragter, Pädagogische Akademie and Berufspädagogische Akademie, Linz. Publs: *Staat und Politik*, 1964; *Die Eigenständigkeit der Politikwissenschaft als Staatsführungslehre*, 1965; *Politik, Wirklichkeit und Gestaltung der staatlich verfassten Gesellschaft*, 1977. Fields: Political education of teachers; policy-science; world affairs, especially world government.

[1668]
SADOUN Marc
22 February 1944, French. 3 rue Galliéni, 94490 Ormesson, France. Degrees: DES droit public; DES sci pol. Doctoral thesis; "Le parti socialiste français (1938-44)". Assistant, U de Paris I. Publs: "La réforme de l'enseignement secondaire en France depuis 1945", *Revue Française de Science Politique*, 1976; "Les facteurs de la conversion au socialisme", *Revue Française de Science Politique*, 1978. Fields: Contemporary history; political parties and institutions, parliament; political socialization.

[1669]
SAELEN Kjell Arnstein*
30 May 1941. Norwegian. Institute of Sociology, University of Bergen, Christiesgate 19, 5000 Bergen, Norway. Degrees: Cand mag, 1970. 1966- Assistant to Professor Rokkan, Research Projects; Research Assistant, Norwegian Research Council. Publs: "Rekrutteringen til Storting og statrad i Norge 1914-1965" (with T Hjellum), *Nordisk Honf for Statsvitenskap*, 1966. Fields: Political elites; nation-building.

[1670]
SAETER Martin*
17 February 1931, Norwegian. Department of Political Science, University of Oslo, Box 1097, Blindern, Oslo 3, Norway. Degrees: Dr phil (Oslo), 1972. Doctoral thesis: "Det Politisk Europa. Europeisk integrasion: teori, ide og praksis" (The Political Europe. European Integration: Theory, Idea and Practice). 1964-70 Research Fellow, Norwegian Inst of International Affairs; 1970- Associate Professor, Dept of Pol Sci, U of Oslo. Publs: *Okkupation — Integration — Gleichberechtigung. Eine Analyse der deutschen Frage*, 1967; *Det politiske Europa. Europeisk integrasjon: teori, ide og praksis*, 1971; *Det europeiske fellesskap: Institusjoner og politikk*, 1971. Fields: European integration and integration theory; German foreign policy 1966-present; all European co-operation trends.

[1671]
SAETREN Harald
27 August 1945, Norwegian. Naustvegen 19, 5088 Mjoelkeraaen, Norway. Degrees: Cand pol (Bergen). Doctoral thesis: "Recruitment to the Study of Medicine in Norway: Simulation of some Effects of Decision-making Processes and Rules of Acceptance". Assistant Professor in Organization Theory, Norwegian School of Economic & Business Administration. Publs: "Organisasjonssamfunnet og den Segmenterte Stat", in *Kirke og Kultur*, 1975. Fields: Organization and administration theory; public policy studies and decision-making theories; implementation processes in complex organizations and public policy.

[1672]
SAHLIN E Michael I
9 January 1945, Swedish. Körvelgatan 35A, 754 48 Uppsala, Sweden. Degrees: BA; PhD. Doctoral thesis: "Neo-Authoritarianism and the Problem of Legitimacy: A General Study and a Nigerian Example". Fields: Study of actions and attitudes of some organizational actors *vis à vis* the main political and developmental issues within the present military framework in Nigeria.

[1673]
SAHNER Heinz*
23 October 1938, German. Bachemerstrasse 40, 5 Köln 41, FR Germany. Degrees: Dipl Volkswirt (Cologne), 1969. Assistant, Inst for Comparative Social Research, U of Cologne. Publs: *Politische Tradition, Sozialstruktur und Parteiensystem in Schleswig-Holstein. Ein Beitrag zur Replikation von Rudolf Heberles Landbevölkerung und Nationalsozialismus*, 1971; *Inferenzstatistik*, 1971. Fields: Voting behaviour; political sociology; methods.

[1674]
SAINSBURY Keith Arthur Frank
22 June 1924, British. 4 Upper Warren Avenue, Reading, Berkshire, England. Degrees: MA; B Phil (Oxon). 1951-55 Lecturer in History and Pol Sci, U of Adelaide, South Australia; 1955 Temporary Lecturer and Tutor, New Coll, U of Oxford; Senior Lecturer in Pol, U of Reading. Publs: *The North African Landings, 1942: A Strategic Decision*, 1976; *British Foreign Secretaries since 1945*, 1977; *International History, 1939-1970: A Select Bibliography*, 1973; "The Second Wartime Alliance", in *Troubled Neighbours*, 1972; "Harold Macmillan", *British Prime Ministers of the Twentieth Century*, 1978; "The Government of South Australia", in *The Government of the Australian States*, 1959. Fields: Diplomatic and military history of the second world war; Anglo-American relations 1939-present day; British foreign policy 1939-present day; Anglo-French relations 1939-45 and 1968-78.

[1675]
SAINT Paul Dominique
2 April 1940, French. La Louettière, 41700 Cour Cheverny, Contres, France. Degrees: MA; Dipl. Doctoral thesis: "Pour une définition subjective de la qualité de la vie". Directeur d'etudes, SOFRES, Paris and Centre d'Etudes sur la Recherche et l'Innovation, Paris. Publs: *Vers une évolution du cadre de vie*, 1976. Fields: Quality of life and environment; pre-electoral studies and opinion polls; sociology of economics.

[1676]
SAKWA George
1 January 1943, British. 5 Pool Corner, Tockington, Bristol BS12, England. Degrees: BA; M Phil (London), 1968; PhD (London), 1974. Doctoral thesis; "The Role of Parliament in a Communist Political System: the Polish Sejm 1952-1972". 1966- Lecturer in Pol, U of Bristol. Publs: Articles in *Historical Journal*, *Slavonic Review*, *Polish Review*, *European Review*, *Socialist Commentary*, *British Journal of Political Science*. Fields: Comparative communist politics; Polish politics; European communism.

[1677]
SALMON Trevor Charles
7 September 1948, British. c/o Department of Economics, St Andrews University, Scotland. Degrees: MA; M Litt. 1973-78 Assistant Lecturer, Lecturer in Pol, NIHE, Limerick, Eire; 1978- Lecturer in Pol, U of St Andrews. Publs: "Optimism and Omission in Strategic Theory", *RAF Quarterly*, 1974; "Rationality and Politics: The Case of Strategic Theory", *British Journal of International Studies*; "Policy Making Coordination in Ireland on European Community Issues", *Journal of Common Market Studies* (with B Burns). Fields: Irish defence policy in the European context; policy-making in foreign policy area.

[1678]
SALTER Brian George
10 October 1946, British. 78 Newmarket Road, Brighton, East Sussex, England. Degrees: BA; MA; D Phil. Doctoral thesis: "Latent Political Discontent in an Educational Context". Research Fellow, Middlesex Polytechnic; Research Fellow, U of Kent; Research Fellow, Education Area, U of Sussex. Publs: "Explanations of Student Unrest: An Exercise in Devaluation", *British Journal of Sociology*, 1973; "Student Militants and Counter-Culture", in *Universities Quarterly*, 1974; "Residence and the UGC: Policy or Promise?" *Higher Education Review*, 1976; *Education and the Political Order* (with T Tapper), 1978. Fields: Interpreting the relationship between education and politics from a political science viewpoint; the transition from school to working life; educational ideology and public policy.

[1679]
SAMPSON Ronald Victor
12 November 1918, British. Beechcroft, Hinton Charterhouse, Bath, Avon, England. Degrees: MA; D Phil (Oxon), 1951. Doctoral thesis: "The Conception of History and Progress in some Writers of the European Enlightenment". Part-time Lecturer, U of Bristol. Publs: *Progress in the Age of Reason*, 1956; *Equality and Power*, 1965; *Tolstoy: The Discovery of Peace*, 1973. Fields: Political theory, 19th century.

[1680]
SANCHEZ AGESTA Luis*
24 June 1914, Spanish. Ministro Ibañez, Martin 5, Residencia de profesores, Madrid 15, Spain. Degrees: Lic en Derecho, 1932; Catedratico, 1942; Academico de numero de la Real Academia de Legislación y Jurisprudencia, Madrid; Academico correspondiente de la Real Academia de Liencias Morales y Politicas; Dr in Law (Madrid), 1940; Professor, U of Oviedo, Granada, Madrid; Visiting Professor, State U of New York; Professor, U Complutense and Autonoma of Madrid; Rector, Autonoma U. Publs: *Concepto historico de la nación*. *Revista de Legislación y Jurisprudencia*, 1941; *El Pensamiento politico del Despotismo ilustrado*, 1954; *Los Orígenes del Concepto del Estado*, 1960; *Principios cristianos del Ordenpolitíco*, 1964; *Historia del Constitucionalismo Español*, 1965; *Derecho Constitucional comparado*, 1968; *Principios de Teoría Política*, 1970; *España al Encuentro de Europa*, 1971. Fields: Constitutional law; political theory.

[1681]
SANDE Terje
3 October 1947, Norwegian. Olderkjerret 93, 5087 Hordvik, Norway. Degrees: Cand pol. Research Associate, Inst of Soc, U of Bergen; Consultant, Norwegian Soc Sci Data Service. Fields: Public policy; methodology.

[1682]
SANDERSON John Bryan
18 April 1937, British. 5 Albany Drive, Rutherglen, Glasgow, G73 3QN, Scotland. Degrees: BA; MA; PhD. Doctoral thesis: "But the People's Creatures: Political Thought in the First Phase of the English Revolution, 1642-49". 1961-63 Assistant Lecturer in Government, U of Manchester; 1963- Lecturer in Pol, U of Strathclyde. Publs: *An Interpretation of the Political Ideas of Marx and Engles*, 1969; articles in *Political Studies, Western Political Quarterly*. Fields: History of political ideas, especially in the 17th century.

[1683]
SANDMANN-BREMME Maria-Gabriele*
8 January 1920, German. 1 Berlin 33, Bachstelzenweg 7, FR Germany. Degrees: Dipl Dolmetscher (Heidelberg), 1948; Dr phil (Marburg), 1956. Doctoral thesis: "Die politische Rolle der Frau in Deutschland". 1952-56 Research Assistant, UNESCO, Inst for Soc Sci, Cologne; 1957-61 Research Member, Kommission für vordringliche sozialpolitische Fragen bei der Deutschen Forschungsgemeinschaft; 1961-62 Assistant, Forschung-institut für Pol Wiss und Europäische Fragen, U of Cologne; 1965-67 Lecturer, Deutsches Inst für Entwicklungspolitik, Berlin; Independent Pol Research, Lecturer, Political Adviser. Publs: *The Political Participation of Women*, 1953; *La Participation des femmes à la vie politique*, 1954; *Die politische Rolle der Frau in Deutschland*, 1956; *Freiheit und Soziale Sicherheit*, 1961; "Die Frau in der Politik", in *Frauen in Partei und Parlament* (ed), 1969. Fields: Electoral behaviour and analysis of socio-demographic aspects; political institutions; political parties and parliament; sociology of developing countries.

[1684]
SÄNKIAHO Risto Heikki
12 March 1941, Finnish. Torpankuja 5, Jyväskyla, Finland. Degrees: MA (Helsinki), 1964; PhD (Helsinki), 1968. Doctoral thesis: "Political Areas of Uusimaa-province". Acting Assistant Professor, U of Helsinki; System Programmer, Computer Centre, U of Helsinki; Acting Professor, U of Tampere; Assistant Professor, U of Jyväskyla; Professor of Methodology, U of Tampere. Publs: Articles in *Scandinavian Political Studies*. Fields: Political planning; sociology of sport; China; evaluation of public policy; voting behaviour.

[1685]
SANNESS John Christian Muthe
27 May 1913, Norwegian. Bygdø Allé 3, Oslo, Norway. Degrees: Dr phil (Oslo). 1942-45 Foreign Office; 1945-46 Norwegian Trade Union Federation; 1946-50, 1956-60 Foreign Ed, *Arbeiderbladet*, Oslo; 1961- Director, Norwegian Inst of International Affairs; 1965- Professor of History, U of Oslo. Publs: *Stalin og ui,* 1953; contributor to *Aschehoug's World History*, 1954-56; *Patrioter, Intelligens og Skandinaver*, 1960. Fields: Developments in communist states; East/West relations in Europe.

[1686]

SARAN Rene

15 June 1921, British. 22 King's Gardens, London NW6 4PU, England. Degrees: BA; PhD (London), 1968. Doctoral thesis: "Secondary Education Policy and Administration since 1944". 1953-57 Resident Tutor, Hillcroft Coll; 1957-63 Visiting Part-time Tutor, Hillcroft Coll; 1963-66 Associate lecturer, Brunel U; 1966- Principal Lecturer in Pol, City of London Polytechnic. Publs: *Policy-making in Secondary Education: A Case Study*, 1973; *The Control of Education in Britain: The Politics of Educational Policy-making: Pressures on Central and Local Government*, 1979. Fields: Social and political thought; public policy, especially the politics of education.

[1687]

SARIS Willem Egbert

8 July 1943, Dutch. Blauwburgwal 20^l, Amsterdam, The Netherlands. Degrees: Dr (Utrecht). Doctoral thesis: "The Use of Linear Structural Equation Models in Non-Experimental Research". Lecturer in Statistics, Free U of Amsterdam. Publs: Articles in Dutch on linear structural equation models and decision-making processes in the Dutch government; "Detection of Specification Errors", *Sociological Methodology*, 1978. Fields: The use of mathematics and statistics in the social sciences; decision-making processes.

[1688]

SÄRLVIK Bo Hilding*

10 February 1928, Swedish. Department of Government, University of Essex, Wivenhoe Park, Colchester CO4 3SQ, Essex, England. Degrees: Lic (Göteborg); Dr phil (Göteborg). Research and Teaching Posts, U of Göteborg; 1965-73 Lecturer, U of Göteborg; 1973- Professor of Government, U of Essex. Publs: *Opinionsbildningen vid Folkomröstningen 1957*, 1959. Fields: Content analysis of political propaganda; political behaviour; the "representational process".

[1689]

SARTORI Giovanni

13 May 1924, Italian. 66 Virginia Lane, Atherton, California, USA. Degrees: PhD. 1950-56 Assistant Professor of History of Modern Philosophy, U of Florence; 1956-76 Associate Professor, Professor of Pol Sci, U of Florence; 1964-65 Visiting Professor of Government, Harvard U; 1966-67 and 1968-69 Visiting Professor of Pol Sci, Yale U; 1971-72 Fellow, Center for Advanced Study in the Behavioural Sciences, Stanford; Director, Inst of Pol Sci, U of Florence; 1976- Professor Pol Sci, Stanford U. Publs: *Democrazia e Definizioni*, 1976; A Teoria de Representaçao no Estado Representativo *Moderno*, 1962; *Democratic Theory*, 1978; *Il Parlamento Italiano 1946-63* (ed and co-author), 1963; *Stato e Politica nel Pensiero di B Croce*, 1966; *Antologia di Scienza Politica* (ed), 1970; *Correnti Frazioni e Fazioni nei Partiti Italiani* (ed and co-author), 1973; *Parties and Party Systems: A Framework for Analysis*, 1976; *Rivista Italiana di Scienza Politica* (ed).

[1690]

SATHYAMURTHY Tennalur Vengaraiyengar

29 December 1929, Indian. Dept of Politics, U of York, Heslington, York YO1 5DD, England. Degrees: BSc; MSc (Banaras Hindu U), 1949; PhD (Illinois), 1962. Doctoral thesis: "Contrasting Conceptions of UNESCO". Lecturer in Chemistry, U of Rangoon; Archaeological Chemist, Government Museum, Madras; Research Fellow, Indian Association for the Cultivation of Science; Research Associate in Radiation Chemistry, U of Notre Dame; Lecturer in Government, U of Indiana; Lecturer in Pol Sci, U of Singapore; Senior Research Fellow in Pol Sci, East Africa Inst of Soc

Research; Senior Lecturer in Pol Sci, U of Makerere; Special Consultant to Director-General, UNESCO; Visiting Associate Professor in Pol Sci, Northwestern U; Lecturer in International Relations, U of Strathclyde; Lecturer in Pol, U of York; Visiting Professor of International Relations and Pol Sci, Baring Fellow, Inst de Estudios Internacionales, U of Chile; Senior Lecturer in Pol, U of York; 1976-77 Guest Fellow, Center of Development Studies, Trevandrum, India. Publs: *Politics of International Cooperation: Contrasting Conception of UNESCO*, 1964; *The Modern History of Uganda*. Fields: Inter-disciplinary study of politics; political anthropology; conflict and international relations; peace studies; analysis of the state with special reference to South Asian countries.

[1691]
SATTLER Martin J
2 August 1942, German. Isestrasse 65, 2000 Hamburg 13, FR Germany. Degrees: Dr jur. Doctoral thesis: "Der deutsch-französische Zusammenarbeitsvertrag". 1973-76 Assistant, Pol Wiss, Gesamthochschule Duisburg; Wiss Mitarbeiter, Politikwissenschaft, Bundeshochschule Hamburg. Publs: *Staat und Recht* (ed), 1972; *Der deutsch-französische Zusammenarbeitsvertrag*, 1975; "Vom theoretischen Elend der kommunalpolitischen Praxis", in *Ein Konzern hält die Luft an* (M Naumann (ed)), 1976; *Rechtsradikalismus in der Bundesrepublik Deutschland. Die "Alte", die "Neue" Rechte und der Neonazismus* (with H Höffken), 1978. Fields: Political philosophy; local government; comparative government in Europe.

[1692]
SATTLER Rolf Joachim
16 February 1915, German. Heidbrink 16, 31 Celle, FR Germany. Degrees: PhD (Leipzig), 1943. Doctoral thesis: "Die Reichsreformpläne Erzherzog Franz Ferdinands und des Belvederekreises". 1950-53 Dozent für Geschichte, Pädagogische Hochschule, Celle; 1950- Mitarbeiter Internationales Schulbuchinstitut, Braunschweig; 1961-64 Dozent für Geschichte, Pädagogische Hochschule, Wuppertal; Professor für Pol Wiss, Pädagogische Hochschule, Saarbrücken. Publs: *Die französische Revolution in europäischen Schulbüchern*, 1959; *Europa-Geschichte und Aktualität eines Begriffes*, 1971. Fields: Modern history; Austria, South Eastern Europe; history of European ideas.

[1693]
SAUERBERG Steen
15 June 1942, Danish., Lysagervej 11, 2920 Charlottenlund, Denmark. Degrees: Cand pol (Copenhagen), 1970. 1964-66 Media Research Manager, Advertising Agency; 1966-70 Consultant in Media Research; Amanuensis, Senior Lecturer, Inst for Samtidshistorie og Statskundskab, U of Copenhagen. Publs: *En Vurdering af Nyere Teorier for den Enkelte Virksomheds Fastsaettelse af den Optimale Reklameindsats,*. 1969; "Lytter og Seerundersøgelser — på vej mod en Forskningspolitik for DR" (R Skovmand (ed)), 1975; "Kommunikation til Vaelgerne — og mellem Vaelgerne" (with O Borre et al), *Vaelgere i 70'erne*, 1976; "The Uncivic Culture: Communication and the Political System in Denmark 1973-1975", *Scandinavian Political Studies*, 1976; "The Political Role of Mass Communication in Scandinavia" (with N Thomson), in *Scandinavia at the Polls* (K H Cerny (ed)), 1977. Fields: Communication research, with special emphasis on mass communication; voting behaviour; communications and politics.

[1694]
SAUNDERS Sheila Rose*
10 May 1938, British. Flat 1, 20 Kelso Road, Leeds 2, Yorkshire, England. Degrees: BSc (Econ); MSc (Econ) (LSE), 1966. 1964-67 Lecturer, Senior Lecturer in Government and Pol Thought, City of London Coll; 1967- Lecturer in Pol, U of Leeds. Fields: Methodology of comparative politics; socialism and communism, with particular reference to Russia.

[1695]
SCARAMOZZINO Pasquale
1929, Italian. Facoltà di Scienze Politiche Università di Pavia, Pavia, Italy. Degrees: Laurea in Pol Sci (Pavia), 1952; Libero Docente in Social Statistics (Pavia). Associate Professor of Demography, U of Pavia; Managing Ed, *Il Politico*; Advisory Board, ABC Pol Sci. Publs: *La Popolazione Universitaria di Pavia. Indagine di Statistica Sociale*, 1970; *Il Voto di Preferenza in Italia. Prime Linee*, 1971; *Gli Studi Poltici e Sociali in Italia e il Problema degli Sbocchi Professionali* (ed), 1974; *Gli Sbocchi Professionali dei Laureati in Scienza Politiche* (ed), 1976; *Indice Venticinquennale della Rivista 'Il Politico'*, *1950-1974* (ed), 1977. Fields: Electoral statistics and policy; population policy; university statistics and policy.

[1696]
SCASE Richard
10 August 1942, British. 12 St Stephens Hill, Canterbury, Kent, England. Degrees: BA; MA (Leicester); PhD (Kent). Doctoral thesis: "Social Democracy in Sweden: A Comparative Analysis"; Senior Lecturer in Soc, U of Kent. Publs: *Social Democracy in Capitalist Society*, 1977; *Readings in the Swedish Class Structure* (ed), 1976; *Industrial Society: Class Cleavage and Control*, 1977. Fields: Comparative study of contemporary class structures.

[1697]
SCHABERT Tilo Karl
3 November 1942, German. Am Sticker 10, 4320 Hattingen — Blankenstein, FR Germany. Degrees: Dr phil, 1968. Doctoral thesis: "Natur und Revolution. Untersuchungen zum politischen Denken im Frankreich des 18 Jahrhunderts". Lecturer, U of Munich; Research Fellow, Hoover Inst, Stanford U; Lecturer, Dept of Pol Sci, Stanford U; Visiting Fellow, Humanities Research Centre, The Australian National U; Privatdozent, U of Bochum. Publs: *Natur und Revolution*, 1969; *Der Mensch als Schöpfer der Welt* (ed), 1971; *Aufbruch zur Moderne* (ed), 1974; *Gewalt und Humanität*, 1978. Fields: Political theory; comparative politics; French studies; American and Australian politics.

[1698]
SCHADEE Hans Mari Adam*
16 August 1945, Dutch. Department of Political Theory and Institutions, University of Liverpool, PO Box 147, Liverpool L69 3BX. Degrees: Drs Soc (Leiden), 1973. Lecturer in Comparative Pol, U of Liverpool. Fields: Political development; politics in India; applications of formal methods; comparative electoral behaviour.

[1699]
SCHAFFER Benjamin Bernard
20 September 1925, British. 119 Surrenden Road, Brighton BN1 6WB, Sussex, England. Degrees: BSc; PhD (London), 1956. Doctoral thesis: "Non-ministerial organization in central government 1832-1919". 1951-56 Staff Tutor, U of Southampton; 1956-65 Senior Lecturer and Reader, U of Queensland; 1965- Reader in Pol, U of

Sussex; Professorial Fellow, Development Administration, Inst of Development Studies, U of Sussex; 1967 Visiting Professor, U of Cornell; 1974-76 General Consultant, Royal Commission of Australian Government Administration. Publs: *The Administrative Factor*, 1973; *Easiness of Access*, 1972; *Official Providers*, 1977; *Rural Institutions, Public Services and Employment* (with Harvey, Jacobs and Lamb), 1978; *Underdeveloped Europe* (with Seers *et al*), 1978; *Improving Access to Public Services*, 1976; *Development Research on African Administration* (contributor) (with Adedeji and Hyden), 1974; *Development Planning in Small Countries* (contributor) (with Selwyn), 1975. Fields: Development studies; institutionalization of administrative training, a comparative study in developing areas; CODEX, a collective decision-making game; queuing, an approach to client/organization service and access relationships; corruption, including CORTEX; basic needs and poverty focussed planning.

[1700]•
SCHARPF Fritz Wilhelm
2 December 1935, German. Sachtlebenstrasse 11, D-1000 Berlin 37, FR Germany. Degrees: LLM (Yale), 1961; Dr jur (Freiburg), 1964. Doctoral thesis: "Die political-question - Doktrin in der Rechtsprechung des amerikanischen Supreme Court". 1954-66 Assistant Professor of Law, Yale Law School; 1968-73 Professor of Pol Sci, U of Konstanz; Director, International Inst of Management, Wissenschaftszentrum, Berlin. Publs: *Grenzen der richterlichen Verantwortung*, 1965; *Die politischen Kosten des Rechtsstaats*, 1970; *Demokratietheorie zwischen Utopie und Anpassung*, 1970; *Planung als politischer Prozess*, 1973; *Policy-Making in the German Federal Bureaucracy* (with R Mayntz), 1975; *Politikverflechtung: Theorie und Empirie des kooperativen Föderalismus in der Bundesrepublik* (with B Reissert and F Schnabel), 1976. Fields: Empirical studies of policy formation and policy implementation.

[1701]
SCHARPF Sophia*
6 October 1936, German. 7751 Litzelstetten, Espenweg 13, FR Germany. Degrees: BA; MA (Yale), 1957; PhD (Yale), 1962. Doctoral thesis: "Taiwan in China's Foreign Relations 1836-75". 1957-62 Research Assistant, Dept of Pol Sci, U of Yale Graduate School; 1957-59 Fellow, Ford Foundation Foreign Area Program (Asia); Research Associate, Arnold-Bergsträsser-Inst für Kultur-Forschung, Freiburg; Lecturer, Dept of Pol Sci, U of Freiburg. Publs: *Taiwan in China's Foreign Relations 1836-75*, 1965; *Ch'ing-tai Ch'ou-pan I-wu Shih-mo* (co-ed), 1961; *Soviet Plot in China* (ed), 1965. Fields: Politics and international relations of China; politics and international relations of Japan.

[1702]
SCHATZ Heribert
10 July 1936, German. Am Domblick 1, 5300 Bonn 2, FR Germany. Degrees: Dr rer Pol (Mannheim), 1966. Doctoral thesis: "Der parlamentarische Entscheidungsprozess. Bedingungen der verteidigungspolitischen Willensbildung im Deutschen Bundestag" (The Parliamentary Decision-making Process). Wiss Rat and Professor, Ruhr U Bochum; Professor of Pol Sci, German Interior Policy, U of Duisburg. Publs: *Der parlamentarische Entscheidungsprozess*, 1970; "Auf der Suche nach neuen Problemlösungsstrategien: die Entwicklung der politischen Planung auf Bundesebene", in *Planungsorganisation* (R Mayntz and F W Scharpf (eds)), 1973; *Politische Planung im Reierungssystem der Bundesrepublik Deutschland*, 1974; "Staatsbürokratie im Wandel", in *Politische Vierteljahresschrift*, 1975; "The Development of Political Planning in the Federal Republic of Germany", in *German Political Studies* (K V Beyme (ed)), 1976. Fields: German politics; bureaucracy/administrative behaviour in consumer policy and mass media policy.

[1703]
SCHEER Hermann*
29 April 1944, German. Neue Strasse 57, 7 Stuttgart 1, FR Germany. Degrees: Dipl (Free U of Berlin), 1971. Assistant Professor, U of Stuttgart. Publs: "Abrüstungsdiplomatie im internationalen System", in *Internationale Beziehungen als System* (K M Gantzel (ed)), 1973; "Innerorganisatorische und Innerparteilische Demokratie", in *Demokratisierung in Staat und Gesellschaft* (M Greiffenhagen (ed)), 1973. Fields: International organizations; arms control; history of socialism; policy science; community power research; planning and politics.

[1704]
SCHELLHORN Kai M
30 May 1945, German. Obergasse 26, 8911 Unterfinning, FR Germany. Degrees: Dr phil (München), 1970. Doctoral thesis: "Decision-making Processes in the Organization of American States". 1968-71 Wiss Mitarbeiter, Inst für Pol Wiss, U of München; 1971- Wiss Assistent, Seminar für Internationale Pol, U of München. Publs: *Die Analyse multistaatlicher Politik*, 1972; *Krisen — Entscheidung. Der geheime amerikanische aussenpolitische Entscheidungsprozess zur Bombardierung Nordvietnams 1964/1965*, 1974; *Politik zwischen Staaten. Ein Studienbuch in Frage und Antwort* (co-author), 1975; *Vietnam ohne Amerika; Die Strategie Hanois*, 1975; *Die aussenpolitische Entscheidungsanalyse. Eine Methodik zur Untersuchung einzelstaatlicher Aussenpolitik am Beispiel der Entwicklung und Erprobung eines Arbeitsmodells am Fall der US-amerikanischen Entscheidung zur Deskalation im Vietnamkrieg 1967/1968*, 1978; *Fidel Castro ante portas*, 1978. Fields: Theory and methodology of international politics; techniques of foreign policy decision-making analysis; conflict and peace research; international crisis studies; American and German foreign policy making.

[1705]
SCHEMEIL Yves
17 February 1947, French. Degrees: Dr. Doctoral thesis: "Sociologie du système politique libanais". 1975-77 Chercheur, FNSP; 1972-75 Chargé de cours, Dept de Sci Pol et Administratives, U St Joseph, Beyrouth; 1975- IEP, Grenoble. Publs: "Les élites politiques au Proche Orient: quelques exemples d'analyses comparatives", *Revue Française de Science Politique*, 1978. Fields: Middle East; epistemology; class and ethnic cleavages; comparative analysis.

[1706]
SCHENK Hans Georg
6 April 1912, British. 4 Capel Close, Summertown, Oxford, England. Degrees: Dr jur (Prague); MA (Oxon). Doctoral thesis: "The Aftermath of the Napoleonic Wars: The Conceit of Europe: An Experiment". 1935-38 Assistant am Staatswissenschaftlichen, Inst der Deutschen, U of Prague; Senior Lecturer in European Econ and Soc History, U of Oxford and Fellow, Wolfson Coll, U of Oxford. Publs: *The Aftermath of the Napoleonic Wars*, 1947; *The Mind of the European Romantics: An essay in Cultural History*, 1966. Fields: European cultural history, mainly since 1700, especially the decline of the religious outlook in life.

[1707]
SCHENNINK Ben Herman Casper*
1 January 1943, Dutch. Nijmegen, Malvert 6567, The Netherlands. Degrees: Dr (Nijmegen), 1971. Doctoral thesis: "Opinion and Attitude Research; Some Problems Concerning Interpretation and Explanation". Research Assistant, Centre for Peace Research, U of Nijmegen. Publs: *Attitudes of Clergymen, Contact Persons or IKV and Arnhemmers on the Peace Week 1969* (co-author), 1970; *Action and Effectiveness —*

the Effectiveness of the Actions of Four Action-Groups in the Peace Week 1970 (co-author), 1971. Fields: Problems of interpretation and explanation in social research, especially analysis procedures; the effects of pressure groups on the opinions and attitudes of various parts of Dutch society; problems of military service, the attitude to it and alternatives suggested.

[1708]
SCHESSWENOTER Rudolf
13 August 1939, Austrian. Degrees: Dr Legal Science; Dr Pol Sci; Dr phil; Dr rer Pol. Doctoral thesis: "Die Bühne als politisches Forum in Theorie und Praxis bei George Bernard Shaw und Bertolt Brecht". 1971-74 Assistant in Pol Sci, U of Heidelberg; 1974- Docent, U of Kassel. Publs: *Modelle zur Radikaldemokratie*, 1970; *Theorie der Subkultur*, 1978; "Subkultur und stätische Kulturpolitik", in *Plädoyer für eine neue Kulturpolitik* (Revermann *et al*), 1974; "Subkultur und Subvention", in *Perspektiven stätische Kulturpolitik* (with H Hoffmann), 1975; "Produktionseinheit Föhrenwald", *Kursbuch*, 1976; "Notate zur befreiten Technik aus futurologischer Sicht", *Kursbuch*, 1978; *Materialien zur alternativen Ökonomie* I and II, 1974-77. Fields: Political psychology; subculture research; deviance research; political culture; anti-psychiatry; future studies; political impact of ecology; social inventions and innovations; utopia research and social creation; studies of political and social institutions; political impact and functions of the media, arts, theatre.

[1709]
SCHEUCH Erwin K
9 June 1928, German. Tannenweg 2, 5032 Efferen, FR Germany. Degrees: Dipl Volkswirt (Cologne), 1953; Dr rer Pol (Cologne), 1956; Habilitation, 1961. Doctoral thesis: "The Application of Sampling Theory on Human Population"; 1961 Instructor in Soc, U of Cologne; 1962-64 Lecturer in Soc Relations, Harvard U; 1964-65 Guest Professor, U of Berlin; 1973-74 Guest Professor, Inst of Advanced Study, Princeton; 1975 U of Pennsylvania; 1976 U of Auckland; Professor of Soc, U of Cologne, Co-Director, Inst of Applied Social Research and Director, Zentralarchiv für empirische Sozialforschung, U of Cologne. Publs: "Soziologie der Macht", in *Macht oder ökonomisches Gesetz*, 1973; "Abschied von den Eliten", in *Das 19te Jahrzehnt*, 1969; *Kulturintelligenz als Machtfaktor*, 1974; *Wird die Bundesrepublik unregierbar?*, 1976; *Grundbegriffe der Soziologie* (with T H Kutsch), 1975; *Cross-National Comparative Survey Research* (with A Szalai *et al* (eds)), 1977; *Soziologie der Freizeit und Konsum* (with G Scherhorn), 1977; "Forschungstechniken als Teil der Soziologie", *Bestandaufnahme der Soziologie*, 1976. Fields: Research techniques; political sociology; mass communication; cross-cultural comparisons; sociology of leisure.

[1710]
SCHIERA Pierangelo*
15 August 1941, Italian. Via Lanzone 11, Milano, Italy. Degrees: Dr in Giurisprudenza (Catholic U of Milan), 1963. Assistente ordinario, Catholic U of Milan; Professore incaricato di storia pol moderna, U of Trento; Professore incaricato di storia delle dottrine pol, U of Bologna. Publs: *Dell Arte di Governo alle Nieuse Dello Treto de Converstinus e l'Assolutismo Tedesco*, 1968. Fields: Ideology; systems theory; the modern welfare state.

[1711]
SCHILLER Bernt
22 February 1934, Swedish. Kirsbeaerhaven 10, 4000 Roskilde, Denmark. Degrees: PhD (Gothenburg), 1967. Doctoral thesis; "The General Strike in Sweden in 1909". Docent, U of Gothenburg; Thord-Gray Visiting Professor, U of Massachusetts; Professor of

History, U of Roskilde. Publs: *Statistics for Historians* (with B Odén) (in Swedish), 1970; "Shortage and Plenty. Research Problems in Contemporary History", *Scandinavian Journal of History*, 1976; "Industrial Democracy in Scandinavia", in *The Annals of the American Academy of Political and Social Science*, 1977; "Interest Group Focus on Market Expansion Alternatives and governmental Policies", *Journal of Voluntary Action Research* (with B Andersson), 1976. Fields: Scandinavian social history; industrial democracy; interest organizations and international relations; methodology of contemporary history.

[1712]
SCHIMANKE Dieter
30 July 1944, German. Memelerstrasse, D-5309 Meckenheim, FR Germany. Degrees: Dr rer Pol. Doctoral thesis: "Verwaltungsreform Baden-Würtemberg. Verwaltungsinnovation als politisch-administrativer Prozess" (Reform of Administration in Baden-Würtemberg. A Case-Study of Innovation in Public Administration as a Politico-Administrative Process). Civil Servant; Research Associate, Post-Graduate School of Administrative Sci, Speyer. Publs: Various articles on reform of public administration, public planning, civil service, local communities, theory of public administration. Fields: Public administration.

[1713]
SCHIMMELPFENNIG Adam Hermann
10 April 1928, German. Dr Kurt Schumacherring 4, 6114 Gross-Umstadt, FR Germany. Degrees: Dipl Sozialwirt. 1965-68 Referent, Central Administration of the German Union of Salaried Employees, Hamburg; 1968- Hochschullehrer für Pol, Fachhochschule der Deutschen Bundespost, Dieburg/Hessen. Publs: *Der Wirtschaftsausschuss*, 1966; *Personalratsarbeit — Psychologisch-Soziologische Probleme in der Praxis*, 1975; "Zur Theorie des Konservatismus", in *Evangelische Verantwortung*, 1972. Fields: Pluralism problems; social policy; parties in the GDR and DDR; bureaucracy problems; authority problems.

[1714]
SCHISSLER Jakob
15 October 1940, German. Robert Roch Strasse 3, 8072 Ottobrunn, FR Germany. Degrees: PhD. Doctoral thesis: "Gewalt und Gesellschaftliche Entwicklung. Die Kontroverse über die Gewalt zwischen Sozialdemokratie und Bolschewismus". 1972-77 Wiss Assistent, U of Osnabrück; 1977- Wiss Mitarbeiter, Hochschule der Bundeswehr, München. Publs: "Das Konsensproblem in der Didaktik politischer Bildung", in *Materialien zur Politischen Bildung*, 1977; "Zur gegenwärtigen Politischen Kultur der Bundesrepublik Deutschland", *Zeitschrift für Politik*, 1977; "Politische Sozialisation" (with H H Knütter and P Gutjahr (eds)), in *Die realistische Wende in der Politischen Bildung*, 1978. Fields: Political culture; belief-systems and value-systems.

[1715]
SCHLETH Uwe
12 November 1934, German. Im Klingen 2, 6905 Schriescheim-Altenbach, FR Germany. Degrees: Dipl Volkswirt (Cologne), 1962; Dr phil (Mannheim), 1967. Doctoral thesis: "Parteifinanzierung — Ein Beitrag zur Theorie politischer Parteien". 1960-65 Research Assistant, Inst für Pol Wiss, U of Cologne; 1966-71 Assistant, Study Director, Lehrstuhl für Pol Wiss, Inst für Sozialwissenschaften, U of Mannheim; 1971-72 Visiting Professor of Pol Sci/Soc, U of Texas at Austin; 1973-74 Visiting Professor of Pol Sci, New York State U at Stony Brook; 1975-76 Lehrstuhlvertretung, Hochschule der Bundeswehr München; 1976- Professor für Pol Soziologie, Free U of Berlin; Professor für Soziologie, Inst für Soziologie, U of Heidelberg. Publs: "Once again: Does it Pay to

Study Social Background in Elite Analysis?'', in *Sozialwissenschaftliches Jahrbuch für Politik* (R Wildenmann *et al* (eds)), 1971; "Causal Models of West German Voting Behaviour", in *Sozialwissenschaftliches Jahrbuch für Politik* (R Wildenmann *et al* (eds)), 1971; *Parteifinanzen — Eine Studie über Kosten und Finanzierung der Parteientätigkeit, deren Problematik und die Gesichtspunkte einer Reform*, 1972; *Sozialwissenschaftliches Jahrbuch für Politik*. Fields: Political sociology; voting and voting behaviour; structure, function and ideology of elites; elite-mass-relations; methodology; problems of measurement.

[1716]
SCHMID Günther
14 March 1942, German. Hugo-Vogel-Strasse 23-25, D-1000 Berlin, 39, FR Germany. Degrees: Dipl Pol (Free U of Berlin), 1969; Dr phil (Free U of Berlin), 1973. Doctoral thesis: "Funktionsanalyse und politische Theorie. Funktionalismustheorie, politische-ökonomische Faktorenanalyse und Elemente einer genetisch-funktionalen System-theorie". 1970-74, Wiss Assistent; 1974- Research Fellow, Wissenschaftszentrum Berlin, Internationales Institut für Management und Verwaltung. Publs: *Funktionsanalyse und politische Theorie*, 1974; *Bürokratie und Politik* (with H Treiber), 1975; *Planung im entwickelten Kapitalismus* (with U Degen and R Werner), 1975; *Steuerungssysteme des Arbeitsmarktes — Vergleich von Frankreich, Grossbritannien, Schweden, DDR und Sowjetunion mit der Bundesrepublik Deutschland*, 1975. Fields: Labour market policy; political planning and public administration; causal modelling and dimensional approaches in cross-section analysis; policy impact studies.

[1717]
SCHMIDT Detlef Hendrik
28 January 1944, Belgian. Hotenauerstrasse 39 B, D-2300 Kiel, FR Germany. Degrees: PhD. Doctoral thesis: "Die Beteiligung der nationalitäten an der politischen Elite in Belgien 1944-1970". 1971 Research Fellow, Sozialwissenschaftliches Forschungsinst, Konrad Adenauer Stiftung; 1972 Assistant Professor, Inst for Pol Sci, Christian-Albrechts U, Kiel; 1974 Associate Professor, Dept of Pol Sci, Pennsylvania State U 1975- Assistant Professor, Inst of Pol Sci, Christian-Albrechts U, Kiel. Publs: "Röntgenfoto van een politieke Elite", *De Maand, Tijdschrift voor politieke vernieuwing*, 1971; "Nationalität und politische Elite in Belgien", in *Führung in der Politik* (W Bernhardt (ed)), 1972; "Politik in Schleswig-Holstein. Eine politische Bibliographie 1945-1972", in *Veröffentlichungen des Seminars für Wissenschaft und Geschichte der Politik*, 1974; "Das Wahlergebnis 1972 in den USA" (with P Nissen), in *Das Labile Gleichgewicht* (W Kaltefleiter and E Keynes (eds)), 1973. Fields: Comparative politics, in particular nation-building and ethnicity; empirical political theory.

[1718]
SCHMIDT Manfred G
25 July 1948, German. Schwabstrasse 8, D-7400 Tübingen, FR Germany. Degrees: Dr der Sozialwissenschaften. Doctoral thesis: "Staatsapparat und Rüstungspolitik in der Bundesrepublik Deutschland (1966-1973)". Wiss Assistent für Politikwissenschaft, U of Tübingen. Publs: *Staatsapparat und Rüstungspolitik in der Bundesrepublik Deutschland*, 1975; "Staatliche Ausgabenpolitik und Akkumulationsentwicklung im Rüstungssektor der Bundesrepublik", in *Gesellschaft Beiträge zur Marxischen Theorie*, 1975; "The Politics of Domestic Reforms in West Germany 1969-1976" (with F Müller), in *Politics and Society*, 1978; *Empirische Politikwissenschaft*, 1978. Fields: Party control and public policies in democratic capitalist nations; politometrics.

[1719]
SCHMIDT Otto
9 February 1942, Dutch. Eerste Helmersstraat 16B, 1054 DG Amsterdam, The Netherlands. Degrees: Dr. Inst for Pol Sci, U of Amsterdam. Fields: Methodology; aggregate data analysis; fascism.

[1720]
SCHMIDT Peter*
29 September 1942, German. Carl-Petersen-Strasse 100, 2 Hamburg 26, FR Germany. Degrees: Dipl Soziologe, 1969. Research Assistant, U of Mannheim. Fields: Causal modelling; policy guidelines; simulation.

[1721]
SCHMIDTCHEN Gerhard
17 May 1925, German. Ländischstrasse 74, CH-8706 Feldmeilen, Switzerland. Degrees: Dr phil; Dipl rer Pol. Doctoral thesis: "Die befragte Nation". Inst for Soc Research, U of Frankfurt; Ord Professor, U of Zürich. Publs: *Die befragte Nation*, 1959; *Zwischen Kirche und Gesellschaft*, 1972; *Priester in Deutschland*, 1973; *Gottesdienst in einer rationalen Welt*, 1973; *Umfrage unter Priesteramtskandidaten*, 1975; *Protestanten und Katholiken*, 1973; *Aussenpolitik und Oeffentlichkeit in der direkten Demokratie* (with K W Deutsch), 1977. Fields: Social psychology; communication and motivation; political behaviour; sociology of religion; connections between religious and political orientations.

[1722]
SCHMIEG Günter*
10 November 1945, German. Benquestrasse 32, 2800 Bremen, FR Germany. Degrees: Dipl Pol (Free U of Berlin), 1969; Dr rer Pol (Bremen), 1972. Publs: *Politische Planung in Theorie und Praxis* (co-ed), 1971. Fields: Marxist theory of the state; theory and practice of political planning in capitalist societies; fiscal analysis of the state; class analysis of state workers; civil servants.

[1723]
SCHMITT Eberhard
4 February 1939, German. Hans-Wölfel-Strasse 4, 8600 Bamberg, FR Germany. Degrees: Dr (Munich), 1968. Doctoral thesis: "Repräsentation und Revolution. Eine Untersuchung zur Genesis der kontinentalen Theorie und Praxis parlamentarischer Repräsentation aus der Herrschaftspraxis des Ancien Régime in Frankreich, 1760-89". 1968-72 Wiss Assistent, Historisches Seminar, U of Mainz; 1972-76 Ord Professor für Neuere Geschichte, U of Bochum; 1976- Ord Professor für Neuere Geschichte, U of Bamberg. Publs: *Repräsentation und Revolution*, 1969; *Antoine Barnave: Theorie der Französischen Revolution*, 1972; *Die Französische Revolution Anlässe und langfristige Ursachen*, 1973; *Sieyès: Politische Schriften 1788-90*, 1975; *Die Französische Revolution*, 1976; *Einführung in die Geschichte der Französischen Revolution*, 1976. Fields: Theory of political representation; history of representative and parliamentary institutions; French Revolution; European expansion 1415-1815.

[1724]
SCHMITT Karl Martin
4 June 1944, German. Kartaeuserstrasse 138, 78 Freiburg, FR Germany. Degrees: Dr phil. Doctoral thesis: "Political Education in the German Democratic Republic". Assistant Professor, Dept of Pol Sci, U of Freiburg. Fields: Political socialization; sociology of education; Eastern Europe.

[1725]
SCHMOLZ Franz Martin
16 December 1927, German. Mönschsberg 2a, A-5020 Salzburg, Austria. Degrees. Dr (Salzburg), 1962. Doctoral thesis:. "Das Naturgesetz und seine dynamische Kraft". 1959 Assistant, Inst of Pol Sci, U of Münich; Director, Inst of Pol Sci, Internationales Forschungszentrum, Salzburg; Ord Professor, Director, Inst of Pol Philosophy and Pol Theory, U of Salzburg; Dean, Faculty of Theology, U of Salzburg. Publs: *Zerstörung und Rekonstruktion der Politischen Ethik*, 1963; *Das Naturrecht in der Politischen Theorie*, 1963; *Der Mensch in der Politischen Institution*, 1964; *Chance und Dilemma der Politischen Ethik*, 1966; *Zur Reform der Österreichischen Innenpolitik*, 1955-65, 1966-68; *Christ zwischen Kirche und Politik*, 1969; *Christlicher Friedensbegriff und europäische Friedensordnung*, 1977. Fields: Political theory; history of political ideas; theological and philosophical aspects of peace research and futurology; church and atheism in our modern secular world.

[1726]
SCHNABEL Fritz
4 April 1947, German. Rothenburgstrasse 38, 1 Berlin 41, FR Germany. Research Fellow, International Inst of Management, Berlin. Publs: *Politikverflechtung* (with F W Scharpf and B Reissert). Fields: Intergovernmental relations; economic theory of federalism; organization theory.

[1727]
SCHNAPPER Bernard
14 May 1927, French. 41 rue d'Assas, 75006 Paris, France. Professor, U of Paris 1. Publs: *Les rentes au XVIème siècle: histoire d'un instrument de crédit*, 1957; *La politique et le commerce français dans le golfe de Guinée de 1838 à 1871*, 1961; *Le remplacement militaire en France: quelques aspects politiques, économiques et sociaux du recrutement au XIXème siècle*, 1968; *Histoire des faits économiques jusqu'à la fin du XVIIIème siècle*, 1968; *Les peines arbitraires du XIIIème au XVIIIème siècle, doctrines savantes et usages français*, 1974. Fields: Law and society in the 19th century; history of penal law.

[1728]
SCHNAPPER Dominique
9 November 1934, French. 75 Boulevard Saint Michel, 75005 Paris, France. Degrees: Dr en soc; Dipl. Doctoral thesis; "Les 100 familles de Bologne. Traditions dans la société industrielle". Maître-assistant, L'Ecole des Mants Etudes en Sci Soc; Maître de conférences, IEP, Paris. Publs: *L'Italie rouge et noire*, 1971; *Morphologie de la haute administration Française*, 1972; "Sociologie de l'Italie", in *Que sais-je?*, 1974; "Centralisme et Fédéralisme Culturels, les émigrés italiens en France et aux Etats Unis", *Annales*, 1975. Fields: Italy and the Italians; cultural traditions; French administration.

[1729]
SCHNEIDER Eberhard
29 August 1941, German. Im Würzgarten 9, D-5020 Frechen-Hücheln, FR Germany. Degrees: Dr phil; Lic phil. Doctoral thesis: "Einheit und Gegensatz in der Sowjetphilosophie. Über das Hauptgesetz der materialistischen Dialektik". 1966-70 Inst for the Study of the USSR, Munich; 1971-76 International Inst for Pol and Econ, "Haus Rissen", Hamburg; 1974-76 Lecturer, U of Hamburg; 1976- Federal Inst for Eastern and International Affairs, Cologne. Publs: *Die DDR, Geschichte, Politik, Wirtschaft, Gesellschaft*, 1977; *SED-Programm und Statut 1976*, 1977; *Einheit und Gegensatz in der Sowjetphilosophie*, 1978; *Die neue Verfassung der USSR*, 1978; "Soviet Vietnam Policy 1975-76", *German Foreign Affairs*, 1977; "Das Menschenrechtsverständnis der

DDR und der USSR", *Politik und Kultur*, 1977. Fields: Foreign policy; party and government structure in USSR and GDR; world communism; South-East Asian affairs.

[1730]
SCHNEIDER Franz
12 January 1932, German. Berchemstrasse 96, 8 München 21, FR Germany. Degrees: Dr phil; Dr jur. Professor, U of Munich. Publs: *Presse- und Meinungsfreiheit nach dem Grundgesetz*, 1966; *Pressefreiheit und politische Öffentlichkeit*, 1966; *Politik und Kommunikation-Drei Versuche*, 1968; *Die grosse Koalition-Zum Erfolg verurteilt?*, 1968; *Die grosse Koalition-Ende oder Neubeginn?*, 1969. Fields: Political communication.

[1731]
SCHNEIDER Herbert
5 October 1929, German. Gertberg 29, 6934 Neckargerach, FR Germany. Degrees: Dr phil (Tübingen); Dr (Geneva). Doctoral thesis; "Britische Wirtschafts - und Sozialverbände und europäische Integration". Research Assistant, Nuffield Coll, U of Oxford; Hauptgeschäftsführer, Arbeitsgemeinschaft der Bürger im Staat; Direktor, Landeszentrale für Pol Bildung, Baden-Würtemberg; Professor, Pädagogische Hochschule, Heidelberg. Publs: *Die Interessenverbände 1965*, 1975; *Grossbritanniens Weg nach Europa*, 1968; *Motive und Methoden der Europäischen Integration*, 1970; *Zur Aussenpolitik der Bundesrepublik Deutschland*, 1977; *Das Konsensproblem in der politischen Bildung*, 1977. Fields: International politics; parliamentary affairs; local politics; civic education; European integration.

[1732]
SCHOEPS Julius H
1 June 1942, German. Niederdonkerstrasse 76, 4005 Meerbusch 1, FR Germany. Degrees: Dr phil (Erlangen), 1969; Habilitation, 1973. Doctoral thesis; "Von Olmütz nach Dresden. 1850-51. Ein Beitrag zur Geschichte der Reformen am deutschen Bund". Professor, U of Duisburg. Publs: *Die rebellischen Studenten*, 1968; *Von Olmütz nach Dresden 1850-51*, 1972; *Formeln deutscher Politik*, 1969; *Geschichte in der Gegenwart*. *Festschrift für Kurt Kluxen*, 1972; *Zionismus*, 1973; *Schulbuch als Politicum*, 1974; *Friedrich Albert Lange*, 1975; *Theodor Herzl*, 1975. Fields: Modern German and European history; political theory; history of the German Jewry and the Zionist movement.

[1733]
SCHOLLAERT Willy Julien Sylva
10 January 1941, Belgian. Stationsstraat 9, B-1560 Tollembeek, Belgium. 1960-66 School Administration; 1966-67 Private Secretary to Minister of the Economy; 1967-69 Treasurer, World Federation of Radical and Liberal Youth; 1970- Member of the City Council of Galmaarden; 1964-77 Member, National Youth Council; Member, Youth Protection Committee, Brussels; 1970-75 Member, National Commission 'Army Youth'. Publs: *De Jeugd en de Maatschappij*, 1963; *De Film en de Jeugdorganisaties*, 1964. Fields: Youth problems; European integration.

[1734]
SCHOLTEN Gerard Herman
20 October 1928, Dutch. 't Kerkestuk 75, Reeuwijk, The Netherlands. Degrees: Dr in Soc Sci (Amsterdam), 1968; Drs (Amsterdam), 1957. Doctoral thesis: "De Sociaal-Economische Raad en de ministeriële verantwoordelijkheid" (The Social-Economic Council and the Responsibility of Ministers). 1957-71 Staff Member, Inst of Pol Sci, U of Amsterdam; Professor of Public Administration and Pol Sci, Erasmus U, Rotterdam. Publs: *De Sociaal-Economische Raad en de ministeriële verantwoordelijkheid*,

1968; *Politiek en Bestuur*, 1972; *Ministers, Ambtenaren en Parlementariërs in Nederland* (with U Rosenthal and M P C M van Schendelen), 1975; *Crisis en Continuiteit* (with U Rosenthal), 1977; *Openbaar Bestuur* (with U Rosenthal and M P C M van Schendelen), 1977; articles in *Acta Politica, Beleid en Maatschappij*. Fields: Politics and administration; pressure groups; public decision-making in crisis situations.

[1735]
SCHÖNBORN Mathias
29 June 1943, German. Andreastrasse 17, 8 München 19, FR Germany. Degrees: MA. Doctoral thesis: "Die Entwicklung Tanzanias zum Einparteienstaat". 1975-76 Research Associate, International Inst for Strategic Studies, London; Research Fellow, Sozialwissenschaftliches Inst der Bundeswehr. Publs: *Die Entwicklung Tanzanias zum Einparteienstaat*, 1973; "Tanzania Bibliographie", in *Tanzania: Beiträge und Dokumente zur exemplarischen Analyse eines Entwicklungslandes* (F Ansprenger *et al* (eds)), 1976; *Politisches Lexikon Schwarzafrika* (with J Werobèl and R Hofmeier (eds)), 1978. Fields: African politics, particularly East Africa; African party systems; concepts of African socialism; military alliances in theory and reality; Western security policies; civil-military relations.

[1736]
SCHÖPFLIN George A
24 November 1939, British. 90 Speed House, Barbican, London EC2, England. Degrees: MA; LL B. 1963-67 Research Assistant, Royal Inst of International Affairs; 1967-76 Research Officer, Central Research Unit, BBC External Services; 1973-74 Hayter Fellow, School of Slavonic and East European Studies, LSE; 1976- Lecturer in East European Pol, LSE and the School of Slavonic and East European Studies, U of London. Publs: *The Soviet Union and Eastern Europe: A Handbook* (ed), 1970; "The Ideology of Croation Nationalism", *Survey*, 1973; "The Ideology of Rumanian Nationalism", *Survey*, 1974; "Hungary: An Uneasy Stability", in *Political Culture and Political Change in Communist States* (A Brown and J Gray (eds)), 1977; "Hungary", in *Communist Power in Europe 1944-1949* (M McCauley (ed)), 1977. Fields: East European politics, particularly Hungary; nationalist ideologies in Eastern Europe.

[1737]
SCHOU Tove Lise
16 October 1926, Danish. Institute of Political Studies, University of Copenhagen, Rosenborggade 15, 1130 Copenhagen, Denmark. Degrees: Cand phil, 1972. Adjunkt, Inst of Pol Studies, U of Copenhagen. Publs: *En Undersøgelse af ydre Faktorers Påvirkning af Danmarks Markedspolitik*, 1972. Fields: Foreign policy decision-making; European integration.

[1738]
SCHUETT-WETSCHKY Eberhard Hermann
24 October 1937, German. Magdalenenstrasse 36, D-2000 Hamburg 13, FR Germany. Degrees: PhD (Hamburg). Doctoral thesis: "Wahlsystemdiskussion und parlamentarische Demokratie". Assistant Professor, Fachbereich Wirtschafts- und Organisationswissenschaften, Hochschule der Bundeswehr, Hamburg. Publs: *Wahlsystemdiskussion und parlamentarische Demokratie*, 1973; "Wahlsystemfrage zwischen Recht und Politik", *Zeitschrift für Politik*, 1976. Fields: Comparative government; parties; electoral systems; methodology of the social sciences.

[1739]
SCHULZ Eberhard Karl Gustav
17 August 1926, German. Forschungsinstitut der Deutschen Gesellschaft für Auswärtige Politik, Adenauerallee 133, 53 Bonn, FR Germany. 1951-61 Civil Service; 1961-64 Econ Ed, *Kölner Stadt-Anzeiger*; 1965 Department Leader, Westdeutscher Rundfunk; 1966- Deputy Director, Forschungsinst der Deutschen Gesellschaft für Auswärtige Pol, Bonn. Publs: *An Ulbricht führt kein Weg mehr vorbei*, 1967; "Die politische, ideologische und psychologische Bedeutung der DDR", und "Die militärische Bedeutung der DDR", in *Braucht der Osten die DDR?* (co-author), 1968; "Die sowjetische Deutschlandpolitik", in *Handbuch der Sowjetunion*; *Moskau und die europäische Integration*, 1975; *Die Ostbeziehungen der europäischen Gemeinschaft* (ed), 1977. Fields: Political and economic development in communist countries; German Östpolitik; integration in Eastern and Western Europe; co-operation between the two European systems.

[1740]
SCHULZ Gerhard
24 August 1924, German. Bei der Ochsenweide 16, 74 Tübingen, FR Germany. Degrees: Dr phil (Free U of Berlin), 1952; Habilitation (Free U of Berlin), 1960. Doctoral thesis: "Die deutsche Sozialdemokratie und die auswärtigen Beziehungen vor 1914". 1952-58 Research Fellow and Lecturer, Free U of Berlin; 1959-62 Head of Dept of History, Inst of Pol Sci, Free U of Berlin; 1962- Professor of Modern History, U of Tübingen. Publs: *Parteien in der Bundesrepublik* (co-author), 1955; *Die nationalsozialistische Machtergreifung* (co-author), 1974; *Zwischen Demokratie und Diktatur*, 1963; *Revolutionen und Friedensschlüsse*, 1976; *Die deutschen Ostgebiete*, 1967; *Das Zeitalter der Gesellschaft*, 1969; *Faschismus — Nationalsozialismus*, 1974; *Aufstieg des Nationalsozialismus*, 1975; *Deutsche Geschichte seit dem Ersten Weltkrieg*, 1976; *Geschichte heute* (ed), 1973. Fields: Fascism and totalitarianism; problems of democracy in current history; problems of the human mind and cultural bias.

[1741]
SCHULTZE Rainer Olaf
6 October 1945, German. Quinckestrasse 21, 6900 Heidelberg, FR Germany. Degrees: Dr phil (Heidelberg), 1975. Doctoral thesis: "Politik und Gesellschaft in Kanada". Research Fellow, Inst of Pol Sci, U of Heidelberg; Assistant Professor, Inst of Pol Sci, Ruhr-University, Bochum. Publs: *Politik und Gesellschaft in Kanada*, 1977; *Wahlen in Deutschland* (with B Vogel and D Nohlen), 1971; plus various articles in journals and handbooks, including *Handbuch der Dritten Welt* (D Nohlen and F Nuscheler (eds)), 1974; *Wahlsystem der Welt* (D Nohlen (ed)), 1978. Fields: Political sociology; political parties; interest groups; political participation; elections in liberal-pluralist societies; political and social aspects of regionalism; nationalism and federalism in fragmented and poly-ethnic societies.

[1742]
SCHUMANN Hans-Gerd
30 May 1927, German. Institut für Politikwissenschaft der Technischen Hochschule Darmstadt, Schloss, 61 Darmstadt, FR Germany. Degrees: Dr phil (Marburg), 1960. 1948-49 Lektor in Verlag Dr Hans von Chamier, Essen; 1956- Wiss Assistent, Akad Rat, Inst für Pol Wiss, U of Marburg; 1971-73 Dean, Faculty of Soc and Historical Sci, Technische Hochschule, Darmstadt; Ord Professor, Lehrstuhl für Pol Wiss, THD; Member, Board of Directors, Institut für Politikwissenschaft, THD; Member, Board of Directors, Institut dür Theologie und Sozialethik, THD. Publs: *Nationalsozialismus und Gewerkschaftsbewegung*, 1958; *Edmund Burke's Anschauungen vom Gleichgewicht in Staat und Staatensystem*, 1964; *Die politiscken Parteien in*

Deutschland nach 1945, 1967; *Gesellschaft, Recht und Politik* (ed), 1968; *Ladendorf's Historisches Schlagwörterbuch* (ed), 1968; *Konservatismus* (ed), 1974; *Die Rolle der Opposition in der Bundesrepublik Deutschland.* Fields: Civic and political culture studies; history of political theory from Locke to the present; the political and social system of the Federal Republic of Germany; trade unions; political semantics.

[1743]
SCHUON Karl Theodor
10 December 1940, German. Heinrich-Heine-Strasse 20B, 3550 Marburg, FR Germany. Degrees: Dr phil (Marburg), 1971. Doctoral thesis: "Wissenschaft und Politik im Spätkapitalismus". 1971-72 Wiss Assistent, Phillips U of Marburg; 1970-72 Lehrbeauftragter für Pol Theorie, Phillips U of Marburg; Dozent für Pol Wiss, Phillips U of Marburg. Publs: *Wissenschaft, Politik und wissenschaftliche Politik,* 1972; *Bürgerliche Gesellschaftstheorie der Gegenwart. Einführung und Kritik,* 1975; *Geschichte der Bundesrepublik in Dokumenten und Materialien,* 1976; *Abendroth-Forum,* 1977. Fields: Methodology and theory of political science; political sociology; theory and methodology of neo-positivism and Marxism; party theory.

[1744]
SCHÜTZ Hans-Joachim*
10 May 1948, Austrian. Finkenstrasse 22, A-5023 Salzburg, Austria. Degrees: Dr jur (Salzburg), 1970. Assistant Lecturer, U of Salzburg; Freelance Research Assistant. Publs: Articles in *Politische Studien, Materialen zur Friedenserziehung,* 1973. Fields: European security; international law; peace research; nationalism.

[1745]
SCHWAN Alexander
17 February 1931, German. Teutonenstrasse 6, D-1000 Berlin 38, FR Germany. Degrees: Dr phil; Habilitation. Doctoral thesis: "Der Ort der Gegenwart in der Eschatologie des Seins". 1959-65 Assistant Professor of Pol Sci, U of Freiburg/Br; 1966- Professor of History of Pol Theories, Free U of Berlin. Publs: *Politische Philosophie im Denken Heideggers,* 1965; *Reform als Alternative* (ed), 1969; *Sozialdemokratie und Marxismus* (with G Schwan), 1974; *Denken im Schatten des Nihilismus* (ed), 1975; *Wahrheit-Pluralität-Freiheit,* 1976; *Geschichtstheologische Konstitution und Destruktion der Politik,* 1976; *Sozialismus in Theorie und Praxis* (ed), 1978; *Grundwerke der Demokratie,* 1978.

[1746]
SCHWAN Gesine Marianne
22 May 1943, German. Teutonenstrasse 6, 1000 Berlin 38, FR Germany. Degrees: Habilitation. Doctoral thesis: "Leszek Kolakowski: Eine Philosophie der Freiheit nach Marx". Professor of Pol Theory, Free U of Berlin. Publs: *Leszek Kolakowski: Eine Philosophie der Freiheit nach Marx,* 1971; *Die Gesellschaftskritik von Karl Marx. Politökonomische und Philosophische Voraussetzungen,* 1974; *Sozialdemokratie und Marxismus zum Spanungsverhältnis von Godesberger Programm und Marxistischer Theorie* (with A Schwan), 1974.

[1747]
SCHWARTZ Hans-Peter
13 May 1934, German. D-5300 Bonn 2, Welfenstrasse 10, FR Germany. Degrees: Dr phil (Freiburg/Breisgau). Doctoral thesis: "Politik und Zeitkritik Ernst Jüngers". Professor für Pol Wiss, U of Köln. Publs: *Der konservative Anarchist. Politik und Zeitkritik Ernst Jüngers,* 1962; *Vom Reich zur Bundesrepublik,* 1966; *Die zweite Republik. 25 Jahre Bundesrepublik Deutschland eine Bilanz* (with R Löwenthal (eds)),

1974; *Seemacht und Aussenpolitik* (with D Mahncke (eds)), 1974; *Handbuch der deutschen Aussenpolitik* (ed), 1975; *Zwischenbilanz der KSZE*, 1977; *Amerika und Westeuropa, Gegenwarts-und Zukunftsprobleme* (with K Kaiser (eds)), 1977.

[1748]
SCHWARZ Jürgen
9 January 1939, German. Angerstrasse 9, 8190 Wolfratschausen, FR Germany. Degrees: Dr phil. Doctoral thesis: "Die deutsche Studentenschaft in der Zeit von 1918 bis 1923 und ihre Stellung zur Politik". Tutor, U of Freiburg; Secretary for Pol Education, National German Catholic Youth Association; Senior Research Fellow, Stiftung Wissenschaft und Pol, Munich; John F Kennedy Memorial Fellow, Harvard U; Senior Research Fellow/Head of Research, Dept of International Pol of Western Europe and North America, Stiftung Wissenschaft und Pol, Munich; Professor of International Pol, U of Hamburg; Ord Professor für Pol/Internationale Pol, Hochschule der Bundeswehr, München. Publs: *Studenten in der Weimarer Republik*, 1972; *Die Europapolitik Frankreichs unter Georges Pompidou als Problem der westeuropäischen Gemeinschaftsbildung*, 1973; *Vom Atlantik bis zum Ural. Die Aussenpolitik Frankreichs unter Charles de Gaulle und Georges Pompidou*, 1978; "Militärstrategische Konzepte" (with H Hansen), in *Westeuropäische Verteidigungskooperation* (K Carstens and D Mahncke (eds)), 1972; "Entwicklungsprobleme der Europäischen Gemeinschaft", in *Handbuch der deutschen Aussenpolitik* (H P Schwarz (ed)), 1975; "Frankreichs Militärstrategie von 1958-1976", in *Sicherheitspolitik* (K D Schwarz (ed)), 1976; "The European Strategic Situation: The Organisation of National Security in the North Atlantic Alliance", in *National Security* (M H Louw (ed)), 1978; "Nationalstaat versus internationale Föderation: Divergenzen und Konvergenzen in der französischen und deutschen Europapolitik", in *Deutschland-Frankreich-Europa* (R Picht (ed)), 1978. Fields: Western European integration; theory of the international system; integration theory; alliance theory; foreign policy; decision-making processes; France, Federal Republic of Germany, USA, Third World.

[1749]
SCHWARZ Urs
25 February 1905, Swiss. Zürichbergstrasse 46, CH-8044 Zürich, Switzerland. Degrees: Dr jur (Zürich), 1928; Legum Magister (Harvard), 1931. Doctoral thesis; "Die parlamentarische Immunität der Mitglieder der Schweizerischen Bundesversammlung". 1935-65 *Neue Zürcher Zeitung*; 1942-65 Foreign Ed, 1951-65 Founder and Ed, *Swiss Review of World Affairs*; 1968-76 Associate Professor, Inst U des Hautes Etudes Internationales. Publs: *Strategie Gestern Heute Morgen*, 1965; *American Strategy: A New Perspective*, 1966; *Press Law for our Times*, 1966; *Die Angst in der Politik*, 1967; *Strategic Terminology* (with L Hadik), 1967; *Confrontation and Intervention in the Modern World*, 1970; *Abkehr von der Gewalt*, 1971; *Zürcher Kunstsammler*, 1976. Fields: Institutionalization of strategic studies; problems of arms control; transatlantic relationships.

[1750]
SCHWARTZENBERG Roger-Gérard
17 April 1943, French. 7 rue Jean Goujon, 75008 Paris, France. Degrees: Dipl (IEP Paris), 1965; Dr en droit, 1967; Agrégé de droit public et sci pol, 1968. Doctoral thesis: "L'autorité de chose décidée". Professeur, U de Paris II; Professeur, IEP de Paris. Publs: *La campagne présidentielle de 1965*, 1967; *La guerre de succession ou les élections présidentielles de 1969*, 1969; *L'autorité de chose décidée*, 1969; *Sociologie politique*, 1977; *L'Etat spectacle*, 1977. Fields: Political sociology; political institutions and constitutional law.

[1751]
SCHWARZMANTEL John Joseph
30 September 1947, British. 34A Ash Grove, Leeds LS6 1AY, England. Degrees: BA: B Phil (Oxon). Lecturer in Pol, U of Leeds. Fields: Nationalism; modern political doctrines; the Third International.

[1752]
SCHWEIGLER Gebhard L
16 October 1943, German. In der Held 29, 5307 Wachtberg-Niederbachem, FR Germany. Degrees: BA, 1967; MA (California), 1968; PhD (Harvard), 1972. Doctoral thesis: "National Consciousness in Divided Germany". Research Associate, Research Inst of the German Society for Foreign Affairs, Bonn. Publs: *Nationalbewusstsein in der BRD und der DDR*, 1973; *National Consciousness in Divided Germany*, 1975; *Politikwissenschaft und Aussenpolitik in den USA*, 1977. Fields: International relations; comparative foreign policy; German politics; American politics; American politics.

[1753]
SCHWEISSGUTH Etienne
5 October 1943, French. 7 Avenue Ile de France, 91380 Chilly-Mazarin, France. Attaché de recherche, CNRS. Fields: Military sociology; political sociology.

[1754]
SCHWEITZER Carl-Christoph
3 October 1924, German. 53 Bonn-Ippendorf, Röttgener Strasse 186, FR Germany. Degrees BA (Oxon); Dr phil. Doctoral thesis: "Die Kritik der Linksliberalen an der Bismarckschen Aussenpolitik". 1963-69 Professor of Pol Sci, Berlin; 1967-68 Visiting Professor, Duke U, USA: 1977 Visiting Professor of European Studies, St Anthony's Coll, U of Oxford; 1969- Professor of Pol Sci, Pädagogische Hochschule Bonn and Professor hc, U of Cologne. Publs: *Chaos oder Ordnung- Einführung in die Probleme der Internationalen Politik*, 1975; *Krisenherd Nahost* (co-ed and author), 1972; *Das deutsch-polnische Konfliktverhältnis* (with Feger (eds)), 1974; *Die deutsche Nation von Bismarck bis Honecker*, 1976; *Die nationalen Parlamente in der EG in Bonn und Westminster*, 1977. Fields: International relations; European integration; peace and conflict research.

[1755]
SEDGWICK Peter Harold
9 March 1934, British. 2 Norwood Grove, Leeds 6, England. Degrees: BA; MA (Oxon). 1960-63 Psychologist, Child Guidance Centre, Liverpool; 1963-65 Tutor/Organizer, HM Psychiatric Prison, Grendon; 1965-67 Visiting Tutor, Ruskin College, Oxford; Research Psychologist, Rivermead Rehabilitation Unit, Oxford; 1968-74 Lecturer in Pol, U of York; 1970-71 Visiting Lecturer in Soc, Queen's Coll, SUNY; 1974- Lecturer in Pol, U of Leeds. Publs: *Victor Serge, Memoirs of a Revolutionary* (ed and trans), 1978; *Victor Serge, Year One of the Russian Revolution* (ed and trans), 1972; *Psycho Politics*, 1978. Fields: The construction of politically loaded idea-systems and their comparison with history and reality.

[1756]
SEELOW Frank
12 July 1943, German. Holsteinische Strasse 52, D-1000 Berlin 31, FR Germany. Degrees: Dipl Pol, 1969; Dr rer Pol, 1975. Doctoral thesis: "Money and Monetary Policy in Underdeveloped Capitalism of Africa, with special reference to the Genesis of

the Monteary System in Former British West Africa". Lecturer, Assistant Professor, Dept of Pol Sci, Free U of Berlin. Publs: *Weltmarkt und Weltwährungskrise*, 1971; *Weltmarktstruktur und Unterentwicklung*, 1973; *Unterentwickelte Länder und Weltwährungssystem*, 1975; *Leitfaden zur politischen Ökonomie des Geldes*, 1974; *Geld und Geldpolitik im unterentwickelten Kapitalismus Afrikas*, 1977; *Inflation in Entwicklungsländern*, 1977; *Regionale Wirtschaftsintegration von Entwicklungsländern — Möglichkeit zur Überwindung von Unterentwicklung?*, 1976; *UNCTAD VI und die Forderungen der Entwicklungsländer nach einer neuen Weltwirtschaftsordnung*, 1976. Fields: Political economy of developing countries, especially Africa; world economy; regional integration and co-operation; money and monetary policy.

[1757]
SEIBT Peter*
22 February 1929, German. Hartlaubstrasse 25, 28 Bremen, FR Germany. Degrees: Dr phil (Tübingen), 1970. Doctoral thesis: "Amerikanische Chinapolitik 1941-50". 1962-64 Wiss Assistent and Lecturer; 1967- Wiss Assistent mit Lehrauftrag, Inst für Pol Wiss, U of Tübingen. Publs: *Engagement und Indifferenz, Die Amerikanische Chinapolitik, 1941-50*, 1970. Fields: American China policy since 1950; the teaching of international relations in secondary and tertiary education; instruments of foreign policy of Western industrialized nations.

[1758]
SEIDELMANN Reimund Henning
14 September 1944, German. Am Glaskopf 32, 355 Marburg, FR Germany. Degrees: Habilitation. Doctoral thesis: "Simulation in internationaler und auswärtiger Politik". 1970-75 Wiss Mitarbeiter, U of Marburg und U of Frankfurt. 1975- Dozent, Internationale Pol, U of Giessen. Publs: *Simulation in internationaler und auswärtiger Politik*, 1973; *Sicherheit und Entspannung in Europa*, 1977. Fields: Theory and methods of international relations; conflict theory; security policy.

[1759]
SEILER Daniel-Louis
1 January 1944, Belgian. 570 rue Georges VI, St Louis-de-Terre, Montreal. Degrees: Dr en sci pol et soc. Doctoral thesis; "Le comportement politique du monde catholique wallon". Assistant, U of Namur; Assistant lecturer, U Coll, Dublin; Professor, U of Quebec at Montréal. Publs: *Idéologies et citoyens*, 1970; *Le déclin du cléricalisme*, 1975; *Les partis politiques en Europe*, 1978; plus various articles in *Res Publica, Canadian Journal of Political Science, Journal of European Integration*. Fields: Comparative electoral behaviour; political parties and political cleavages; factor analysis.

[1760]
SEIP Jens Arup
11 October 1905, Norwegian. Gamle Drammensvei 144, 1310 Blommenholm, Norway. Degrees: Dr phil (Oslo), 1945. 1936-41 Assistant Professor, U of Oslo; 1941-46 Archivist, Public Records Office, Oslo; 1946-75 Professor of History and History of Pol Ideas, U of Oslo. Publs: *Lagmann og Lagting i Senmiddelalderen*, 1934; *Saettargjerden i Tunsberg og Kirkens Jurisdiksjon*, 1942; *Et Regime foran Undergangen*, 1965; *Fra Embedsmannsstat til Ettpartistat og Andre Essays*, 1963; *Tanke og Handling i Norsk Historie. Artikler og Avhandlinger*, 1968; *Ole Jacob Broch og Hans Samtid*, 1971; *Utsikt over Norges Historie* I, 1974. Fields: Political ideas and argumentation, especially 18th to 20th centuries; political parties, especially their early development and as instruments of political control.

[1761]
SEITTER Walter
12 December 1941, Austrian. Venstrasse 10, D-519 Stolberg, FR Germany. Degrees: Dr
phil. Doctoral thesis: "Franz Grillparzers Philosophie". Wiss Assistent, Pädagogische
Hochschule, Aachen; Lehrbeauftragter, Rheinisch-Westfälische Technische
Hochschule, Aachen. Publs: Various articles on social philosophy and epistemology.
Fields: Politics of policy; history of administration; history of statistics; political styles;
political technology; structuralism and epistemology.

[1762]
SEIWERT Bärbel Rita
10 September 1951, German. Mozartstrasse 133, 3000 Hannover 1, FR Germany.
Degrees: MA. Fields: Methodology of comparative research; party politics; African
sociéties; development policy.

[1763]
SELF Peter John Otter
7 June 1919, British. 16 Vernon Terrace, Brighton BN1 3JG, England. Degrees: BA;
MA (Oxon); Hon Member RPI, 1977. 1947- LSE; Twice Visiting Professor, U of Cornell, USA; 1969-70 Director of Studies, Centre for Administrative Studies, Professor of
Public Administration, U of London. Publs: *Cities in Flood: The Problems of Urban
Growth*, 1961; *The State and the Farmer* (with H Storing), 1971; *Metropolitan Planning*, 1971; *Administrative Theories and Politics*, 1972; *Econocrats and the Policy Process*, 1976. Fields: Policy process; critical analysis of notions of administrative efficiency; decentralization of government and bureaucracy.

[1764]
SELIGER Martin Menachem
5 September 1914, Israeli. 14 Hatibonim Street, Jerusalem, Israel. Degrees: MA; PhD.
Doctoral thesis: "The Conception of History of the French Historians of the Restoration (1815-1830) in their Treatment of French History". Professor of Pol Sci, the
Hebrew U of Jerusalem.

[1765]
SEMIDEI Manuela Odile*
5 April 1935, French. 5 rue Erlangen, paris XVIème, France. Degrees: Dipl (IEP Paris),
1956; Lic, 1956; DES (Sorbonne), 1959; MS Pol Sci (Wisconsin), 1958. Doctoral thesis:
"La Grande Bretagne dans l'opinion française pendant les années de guerre (1940-44)".
1960-63 Assistante de recherche, Centre d'Etude des Relations Internationales, FNSP;
1963-68 Attachée de recherche au CNRS, CERI; Chargée de recherche, CNRS, CERI,
FNSP. Publs: "Les Eglises britanniques et la décolonisation: Les églises américaines et
la décolonisation", in *Les églises chrétiennes et la décolonisation* (M Merle (ed)), 1965;
Les Etats-Unis et la révolution Cubaine, 1959-64, 1968. Fields: US foreign policy; problems of development in the Caribbean; internal and external factors of dependence
and underdevelopment; Black Power and the case of the Commonwealth Caribbean;
radical dissent in the US; the upsurge of populist trends in American political life.

[1766]
SEMMLER Willi
29 September 1942, German. Pariserstrasse 53, 1 Berlin 15, FR Germany. Degrees: Dr
rer Pol. Doctoral thesis: "Zur multisektoralen Theorie der Kapitalreproduktion —
Bemerkungen zu neueren Ansatzen sowie Überlegungen zum Verhältnis von privaten
und staatlichen Sektor". Publs: *Zur Theorie der Reproduktion und Akkumulation*,

1977; *Vom Wirtschaftwunder zur Wirtschaftskrise-Ökonomie und Politik in der BRD nach dem Zweiten Weltkrieg* (co-author), 1978. Fields: Crisis and conjunction theory; political economic government theory.

[1767]
SENGHAAS Dieter
27 August 1940, German. Georg-Speyer-Strasse 9, 6 Frankfurt 90, FR Germany. Degrees: PhD (Frankfurt). Doctoral thesis: "Kritik der Abschreckung" (Deterrence and Peace: a Critique). 1968-70 Research Fellow, Centre for International Affairs, Harvard U; Professor of Pol Sci, U of Frankfurt; Forschungsgruppenleiter, Hessische Stiftung Friedens- und Konfliktsforschung, Frankfurt. Publs: *Aggressivität und kollektive Gewalt*, 1971; *Abschreckung und Frieden*, 1972; *Rüstung und Militarismus*, 1972; *Aufrüstung durch Rüstungskontrolle*, 1972; *Gewalt-Konflikt-Frieden*, 1974; *Weltwirtschaftsordnung und Entwicklungspolitik*, 1977. Fields: Methodology; international relations; peace and conflict research; imperialism; international stratification and dependency analyses.

[1768]
SENGHAAS-KNOBLOCH Eva
25 November 1942, German, Georg-Speyer-Strasse 9, 6 Frankfurt 90, FR Germany. Degrees: Dipl (Free U of Berlin), 1967. Teaching and Research Assistant, Kirchliche Hochschule, Berlin; Researcher, Harvard U; Independent Researcher. Publs: *Die Theologin im Beruf*, 1969; *Frieden durch Integration und Assoziation*, 1969. Fields: The role of international organizations in international political economy; labour; women.

[1769]
SERRA Enrico
26 September 1914, Italian. Via Asinio Pollione 20, Roma 00153, Italy. Regular Professor of Storia de Trattati e delle Relazioni Internazionali, U of Bologna; Head of Dept Storico e Documentazione, Italian Foreign Office. Publs: *L'Occupazione Bellica Germanica*, 1941; *L'Aggressione Internazionale*, 1946; *Camille Barrère e l'Intesa italofrancese*, 1950; "Un problema europeo: la destinazione della Ruhr", in *La Comunità Internazionale*, 1951; *L'Intesa mediterranea del 1902*, 1957; *I Partiti politici in Gran Bretagna*, 1959; *La Questione tunisina da Crispi a Rudini e il 'colpo di timone' alla politica estera dell'Italia*, 1967; *Istituzioni di Storia dei Trattati e Politica Internazionale*, 1970; *Nitti e la Russia*, 1975; *Introduzione alla Storia dei Trattati e alla Diplomazia*, 1975. Fields: Italian diplomatic history, 1896-1908; the policy of the British admiralty towards the Mediterranean, 1896-1902.

[1770]
SERTORIO Guido F*
17 July 1936, Italian. Via de Sonnaz 14, Turin, Italy. Degrees: Dr in Law (Turin), 1960; Dr in Pol Sci (Turin), 1963. 1961-70 Assistant Professor, U of Turin; Professor of Anthropology, Faculty of Pol Sci, U of Turin. Publs: *L'Applicazione del Diritto Consultudinario*, 1966; *Strutture Sociale Politica Ordinamento Fondiario Yoruba*, 1967; *Culture Politiche*, 1970. Fields: Political anthropology.

[1771]
SETON-WATSON Christopher Ivan William
6 August 1918, British. Oriel College, Oxford, England. Degrees: BA; MA (Oxon), 1946. Fellow and Tutor in Pol, Oriel Coll, U of Oxford; Lecturer in Pol, U of Oxford. Publs: *Italy from Liberalism to Fascism 1870-1925*, 1967; *R W Seton-Watson and the Making of the New Europe 1906-1930*, 1978. Fields: Contemporary western European history and politics, especially Italy; international relations.

[1772]
SETON-WATSON George Hugh Nicholas
15 February 1916, British. 8 Burghley Road, London SW19. Degrees: BA; MA (Oxon), 1946; D Litt (Oxon). 1946-51 Fellow and Praelector in Pol, U Coll, U of Oxford; Professor, Dept of Russian History, School of Slavonic and East European Studies, U of London. Publs: *The East European Revolution*, 1950; *The Pattern of Communist Revolutions*, 1953; *Neither War Nor Peace*, 1960; *Nations and States*, 1977; *The Imperialist Revolutionaries*, 1978. Fields: Nationalism, fascism, communism as movements rather than doctrines; intelligentsias and elites as social groups and political factors; greater power interrelations.

[1773]
SEYD Patrick
26 August 1940, British. 11 Taptonville Road, Sheffield S10 5BQ, England. Degrees: BSc; M Phil. Lecturer, Dept of Pol Theory and Inst, U of Sheffield. Publs: "The British Labour Party" (with L Minkin), in *Social Democratic Parties in Western Europe*, (W E Paterson and A Thomas (eds)), 1977; "Factionalism within the Labour Party: The Socialist League 1932-37", in *Essays in Labour History* (A Briggs and J Saville (eds)), 1977; "Factionalism within the Conservative Party: The Monday Club", *Government and Opposition*, 1972. Fields: Factionalism in British political parties; political attitudes and behaviour of British miners.

[1774]
SEYMOUR-URE Colin
11 November 1938, British. Rutherford College, The University, Canterbury, Kent, England. Degrees: MA (Carleton), 1962; D Phil (Oxon), 1968. Doctoral thesis: "The Press and Parliamentary Privilege in Britain, 1900-67". 1964 Temporary Assistant Lecturer, U College of Rhodesia and Nyasaland; 1965- Lecturer, Senior Lecturer, Reader in Pol, U of Kent. Publs: *The Press, Politics and the Public*, 1968; *The Political Impact of Mass Media*, 1974; *Studies in the Press* (co-author), 1977. Fields: Political communication; mass media; US Presidency; British central government.

[1775]
SFEZ Lucien Clement Paul*
27 April 1937, French. Université de Paris-IX, Place Maréchal de Lattre de Tassigny, Paris XVIème, France. Degrees: Agrégé des Facultés de Droit; Dr en droit public. 1962-64 Assistant, Faculté de Droit, U de Paris; 1964-66 Chargé de cours, Faculté de Droit, U de Strasbourg; 1968- Professeur titulaire de Sci Pol, U de Paris-IX; Directeur, Centre d'Etudes et de Recherche sur la Décision Administrative et Pol. Publs: *Problèmes de la reforme de l'Etat en France*, 1968; *Essai sur la contribution du Doyen Hauriou au droit administratif francais*, 1966; *L'administration perspective*, 1970; *Institutions politiques et droit constitutionnel* (with A Haurion), 1972; *Critique de la décision*, 1973. Fields: Decision-making; systems analysis.

[1776]
SHARPE Laurence James
26 July 1930, British. Nuffield College, Oxford, England. Degrees: BSc; MA (Oxon), 1965. 1957-58 English Speaking Union Fellowship in Pol, U of Indiana; 1958-62 Research Director, Greater London Group, LSE; 1962-65 Lecturer in Government, LSE; 1966-69 Director of Intelligence, Assistant Commissioner, Royal Commission of Local Government in England; 1970-71 Visiting Professor, Queen's U, Ontario; 1965-Fellow, Nuffield Coll, U of Oxford; U Lecturer in Public Administration; Ed, *Political Studies*. Publs: *A Metropolis Votes*, 1963; *Research and Local Government*, 1965; *Why Local Democracy?*, 1965; *Voting in Cities* (ed), 1967. Fields: Voting at-

titudes and political behaviour in Greater London, 1964-70; theories of decentralization; American democratic theory; local government policy outputs.

[1777]
SHEERMAN Barry John*
17 August 1940, British. Ceen Goleu Cottage, Cae Mansel, Gowerton, Glamorgan, Wales. Degrees: BSc (Econ); MSc (LSE), 1966. 1966-67 Lecturer in Pol Theory and Government; 1967- Secretary of American Studies, U Coll, Swansea. Publs: Articles in *Anglo-Welsh Review, Journal of American Studies*. Fields: American social movements and American social and political thought.

[1778]
SHEFFER Gabriel
1939, Israeli. 18 Ha'arazim Street, Moza Illit, Israel. Degrees: D Phil (Oxon). Doctoral thesis: "British Policy and Policy-Making Toward Palestine 1929-39". Dept of Pol Sci, U of Haifa, Israel; Visiting Professor, U of Cornell. Dept of Pol Sci, Hebrew U of Jerusalem. Publs: *Dynamics of a Conflict* (ed), 1975; *Planning in Israeli Politics* (co-author), 1978. Fields: Public policy-making, especially in small modern states; connections between foreign policies and internal politics; various aspects of the Arab-Israeli conflict.

[1779]
SHELL Donald Roderick
25 February 1945, British. 27 Kersteman Road, Redland, Bristol BS6 7BX, England. Degrees: BSc; MA (Essex), 1966. Lecturer in Pol, U of Bristol. Publs: Articles on aspects of British politics. Fields: British politics.

[1780]
SHELL Kurt Leo
17 November 1920, American. Brentanostrasse 8, 6 Frankfurt/Main, FR Germany. Degrees: BSc; MA (Columbia), 1949; PhD (Columbia), 1955. Doctoral thesis: "The Transformation of Austrian Socialism". 1950-56 Instructor, Columbia U; 1956-61 Assistant Professor, Harpur Coll, SUNY, Binghamton; 1961-64 Research Association, Inst für Pol Wiss, Free U of Berlin; 1963-66 Associate Professor, SUNY, Binghamton; 1966-67 Full Professor, SUNY, Binghamton; Professor, Fachbereich Gesellschaftswissenschaften, U of Frankfurt. Publs: *The Transformation of Austrian Socialism*, 1962; *Bedrohung und Bewahrung: Führung und Bevölkerung in der Berlin Krise*, 1965; *The Democratic Political Process: A Cross-National Reader* (ed), 1969; *Erich Fromm's Escape from Freedom: A Critical Commentary*, 1967; *Das Politische System der USA*, 1975. Fields: Analysis of the ideologies of the 'New Left'; comparative investigation of the conditions permitting or preventing 'participatory democracy', particularly for 'industrial democracy'; Yugoslav workers' control; the limitations on responsible democratic decision-making through private economic power; the linkage of normative democratic theory and empirical data.

[1781]
SHLAIM Avi
31 October 1945, Israeli. Barnaby Thatch, Hermitage, Nr Newbury, Berkshire, England. Degrees: BA; MSc (LSE). Lecturer in Pol, U of Reading. Publs: *The EEC and the Mediterranean Countries* (with G N Yannopoulos (eds)), 1976; "International Organizations", in *World Politics Yearbook* (ed), 1976; *British Foreign Secretaries since 1945* (with P Jones and K Sainsbury), 1977. Fields: British foreign policy; European integration; the Arab-Israeli conflict.

[1782]
SIDENIUS Niels Chr
4 May 1948, Danish. Steen Billes Gade 63, 8200 Aarhus N, Denmark. Assistant Professor, Inst for Pol Sci, U of Aarhus. Publs: *The Communist International 1928-1935: An Analysis and Critique of the Communist International's Policy, particularly concerning Nazism and the Development in Germany*, 1976; *The Communist International 1919-1943*, 1976. Fields: The world Communist movement; nazism and fascism in the 1920s and 30s; Danish policy during economic and political crises; Danish energy policy; Israel's economic policy since 1967; industrialization, industrial policy, and industrial interest groups in Denmark since 1930.

[1783]
SIDJANSKI Dusan
23 October 1926, Swiss. 28 Avenue Krieg, 1208 Geneva, Switzerland. Degrees: Lic ès sci pol (Lausanne), 1949; Dr ès sci pol (Lausanne), 1954; Habilitation. Doctoral thesis: "Du fédéralisme national au fédéralisme international". 1950-53 Ancien collaborateur, Professeur-adjoint au Séminaire de Droit Public et de Sci Pol, Central U of Venezuela; 1953-54 Stage au Bureau International pour la protection de la propriété intellectuelle; 1956-57 Chargé de recherches, CIME; 1957-62 Chargé de recherches, Centre Européen de la Culture; Professeur ordinaire de sci pol, U de Genève and Graduate Inst of European Studies; Directeur, Dépt de Sci Pol, U de Genève. Publs: *L'Europe des affaires* (with J Meynaud), 1968; *Verso Europa Unita* (with J Meynaud), 1968; *Les groupes de pression et la coopération européenne* (with J Meynaud), 1968; *Les groupes de pression dans la communauté européenne* (with J Meynaud), 1971; *Le rôle des institutions dans l'intégration régionale entre pays en voie de développement*, 1973; *Les Suisses et la politique* (with C Roig *et al*), 1975; *Auditions publiques dans la communauté européenne*, 1976; *Structures du pouvoir dans la CE: la politique des excédents de lait en poudre*, 1977. Fields: Comparative study of regional integration; quantitative analysis of pressure groups; Swiss political behaviour.

[1784]
SIGG Oswald
18 March 1944, Swiss. Kapellenstrasse 10, CH-3011 Berne, Switzerland. Degrees: Dr rer Pol. Doctoral thesis: "Die eidgenössischen Volksinitiativen 1892-1939". Journalism; Functionary, Swiss Federal Chancellery. Publ: *Die eidgenössischen Volksinitiativen 1892-1939*, 1978. Fields: Political system of Switzerland; direct democracies: initiatives, referendums, petitions; history of socialist parties.

[1785]
SIGNITZER Benno
25 June 1948, Austrian. Ziegelstadelstrasse 31, A-5026 Salzburg, Austria. Degrees: Dr jur (Salzburg); MA (Bowling Green State); PhD (Bowling Green State). Doctoral thesis: "The Ordering of Direct Broadcasting from Satellites: The International Legislative Process with the United Nations Committee on the Peaceful Uses of Outer Space". 1973-74 Graduate Assistant, Bowling Green State U, Ohio; 1975-76 University Assistant, Dept of International Law and International Relations, U of Graz; 1976- Research Assistant and Lecturer, Dept of Mass Communications, U of Salzburg. Publs: *Regulation of Direct Broadcasting from Satellites: The UN Involvement*, 1976; *Massenmedien in Österreich*, 1977; *International Communication. A Select Bibliography 1975-1977*, 1978. Fields: Regulation and policy in international communications; national media/communications policies; survey descriptions of national mass media systems.

[1786]
SILKIN Arthur
20 October 1916, British. Cuzco, 33 Woodnook Road, London SW16 6TZ, England. Degrees: BA. 1971-76 Lecturer in Public Administration, Civil Service Coll; 1976- Part-time Lecturer in Public Administration, South-west Coll, London. Publs: Articles in *Public Administration* and *Political Quarterly*. Fields: Government and politics.

[1787]
SIMMONDS John Christopher
20 June 1942, British. 29 Thornton Way, Girton, Cambridge, England. Degrees: BA; MA; PhD. Doctoral thesis: "The French Communist Party 1944-68: A Bureaucratic Organization". Senior Lecturer in European History, Cambridge Coll of Arts and Technology. Fields: The French Communist party; the politics of the resistance.

[1788]
SIMON Gerhard
1937, German. Lindenbornstrasse 22, 5 Köln 30, FR Germany. Degrees: Dr phil. Doctoral thesis: "K P Pobedonoscev und die Kirchenpolitik des Heiligen Sinod 1880-1905". Fellow, Bundesinst für Östwissenschaftliche und Internationale Studien, Köln. Publs: *K P Pobedonoscev und die Kirchenpolitik des Heiligen Sinod 1880-1905*, 1969; *Church, State and Opposition in the USSR*, 1974. Fields: History of Russia; the USSR and Eastern Europe; methodological problems of historical research.

[1789®
SIMON Michel
5 July 1927, French. CES, rue de l'Espérance, 59800 Lille, France. Degrees: Agrégé de philosophie; Dr ès lettres et sci humaines. Doctoral thesis: "Travaux (Contributions à une sociologie du comportement politique)". Professeur de philosophie; Assistant de soc, Sorbonne; Attaché de recherche, CNRS; Chargé de maîtrise de conférences, U des Sci de Lille I. Publs: *Lénine, la philosophie et la culture* (with G Besse and J Milhau), 1971; *Classe, religion et comportement politique* (with G Michelat), 1977. Fields: Relationships between political behaviour, religious behaviour and social position with respect to future socio-economic and cultural changes.

[1790]
SIMONS Marie Dominique*
22 January 1944, Belgian. 210 Mechelse Vest, 3000 Louvain, Belgium. Degrees: Lic (Catholic U of Louvain), 1968. Doctoral thesis: "Agressivité et théorie de l'action". Assistant, Dept of Pol Sci, Catholic U of Louvain. Publs: "L'Agressivité", *Revue Nouvelle*, 1971. Fields: Conflict and peace research; methodology of political science, especially within the framework of philosophy; psycho-sociology as applied to political science; problems of attitudes.

[1791]
SIMS Nicholas Alan
1945, British. Department of International Relations, London School of Economics and Political Science, Houghton Street, London WC2A 2AE, England. Degrees: BSc 1967. 1978- Assistant Lecturer, Lecturer in International Relations, LSE. Publs: *Approaches to Disarmament: An Introductory Analysis*, 1973; *The Search for Security: A Christian Appraisal* (contributor), 1973; plus various articles in *Politique Etrangère*, *Transnational Perspective*, *International Relations*, *Survival*. Fields: Disarmament and arms limitation, and the diplomatic pursuit of these in the UN and the Geneva conference since 1968, in particular the diplomacy of biological and chemical disarmament; disarmament policy process in Britain; United Nations and commonwealth systems of international organization.

[1792]
SINKKONEN Sirkka Ester
26 April 1935, Finnish. Haapaniemenk 42 B13, 70100 Kuopio 10, Finland. Degrees: PhD. Doctoral thesis: "Marital Happiness in Modern and Traditional Marriage: A Conceptual Analysis and an Empirical Study". Associate Professor, Inst of Pol Sci, U of Helsinki; Professor in Planning, U of Kuopio; Senior Researcher, Finnish Academy of Science, U of Kuopio and Docent of Pol Sci, U of Helsinki. Publs: *From Legalism to Information Technology and Politicization: The Development of Public Administration in Finland* (with H Heiskanen); *Redistribution via Local Government: Central Government Policies and their Constraints*; *The Need for Information within a Health Care System*; various publications in Finnish on administration of health care and other aspects of health services. Fields: Administration of health care; health and educational policies; public administration; democracy in political and administrative processes and systems.

[1793]
SIOTIS Jean
15 March 1931, Greek. 1249 Dardagny, Geneva, Switzerland. Degrees: BA; Lic ès sci pol (Geneva), 1954; PhD (Geneva), 1958; Dr ès sci pol. 1958-59 Legal Assistant, International Commission of Jurists; 1958-66 Instructor, Assistant Professor, Associate Professor, Graduate Institute of International Studies; 1961- Consultant, Carnegie Endowment for International Peace. Publs: *Le droit de la guerre et les conflits armés d'un caractère non-international*, 1958; *Essai sur le secrétariat international*, 1962; "The United Nations Economic Commission for Europe in the Emerging European System", in *International Conciliation*, 1967; "Social Science and the Study of International Relations", in *The Year Book of World Affairs*, 1970; "An Institutional Scenario for Europe", in *Europe 1980: The Future of Intra-European Relations*, 1972; "The European Economic Community and its Emerging Mediterranean Policy", in *The External Relations of the European Community* (F A M Alting von Geusau), 1974; "L'Europe communautaire et la Méditerranée: politique globale ou recherche d'un rôle?", in *Annales d'études internationales*, 1975; "Théorie des relations internationales et étude de la décision dans les systèmes institutionnalisés", in *Théories des relations internationales* (P Braillard (ed)), 1977. Fields: International organizations; theory of international relations; European institutions; humanitarian law and human rights; East-West relations.

[1794]
SIUNE Karen
27 July 1942, Danish. Gyden 13, Mejlby, 8530 Hjortshøj, Sweden. Degrees: Mag soc sci, 1969. Associate Professor, Inst of Pol Sci, U of Åarhus. Publs: *Structure and Content of the 1971 Election Campaign in Danish Radio and Television*, 1974; "Setting the Agenda for a Danish Election" (co-author), *Journal of Communication*, 1975; "Communication, Mass Political Behaviour, and Mass Society" (co-author), in *Sage Annual Reviews of Communication Research*, 1975. Fields: Mass communication.

[1795]
SIVINI Giordano*
24 September 1936, Italian. Universita della Calabria, Dipartimento di Sociologia e di Scienza Politica, Cosenza, Italy. Degrees: Laurea (Trieste), 1965. Doctoral thesis: "Libera Docenza in Sociologia dei Fenomeni Pol". Ricercatore, Inst Carlo Cattaneo, Bologna; Professor of Soc, U of Urbino; Director, Dept of Soc and Pol Sci, U of Calabria. Publs: *Il Comportamento Elettorale, Bibliografia Internazionale di Studi et Ricerche Sociologiche*, 1967; *Ceti Sociali e Origini Etniche*, 1970; *Partiti e Partecipazione Politica in Italia* (ed), 1972; *Sociologia de Partiti Politici* (ed), 1972. Fields: Social movements; political subcultures; electoral behaviour; labour market.

[1796]
SIWEK-POUYDESSEAU Jeanne
20 September 1936, French. 23 rue Saint-Amand, 75015 Paris, France. Degrees: Dipl (Bordeaux), 1959; Lic en droit public (Paris), 1961; Dr de 3ème cycle, 1962; Dr en sci pol (Paris), 1966. 1962 Stagiaire de recherche, Chargé de recherches, CNRS. Publs: *Administration Publique* (with B Gournay and J F Kesler), 1967; *Le corps préfectoral sous la III et la IV République*, 1969; *Le personnel de direction des ministères*, 1969. Fields: The change of French administration since 1945; participation in administration; trade unions.

[1797]
SJÖBLOM Bengt Gunnar Olof
28 Octobef 1933, Swedish. Möl) Möllevångsväg 31, 222 40 Lund, Sweden. Degrees: Fil dr (Lund). 1957-58 Amanuensis, Dept of Govt, U of Lund; 1959-60 Extra Universitetslektor; 1964-66 Bitr Lärare; 1966-68 Forskarassistent; 1968-72 Docent, Dept of Govt, U of Lund; 1972- Professor of Pol Sci, U of Copenhagen. Publs: *Party Strategies in a Multiparty System*, 1968; "The Cumulation Problem in Political Science", *EJPR*, 1977; plus articles in *Scandinavian Political Studies*, and *Statsvetenskaplig Tidskrift*. Fields: Political theory; party research; study of value systems.

[1798]
SKINNER Quentin Robert Duthie
26 November 1940, British. 41 Marlowe Road, Cambridge CB3 9JW, England. Degrees: BA; MA (Cambridge). Lecturer, U of Cambridge; 1976-79 Member, School of Soc Sci, Inst for Advanced Study, U of Princeton; 1978- Professor of Pol Sci, U of Cambridge. Publs: *The Foundations of Modern Political Thought*, 1978. Fields: Political philosophy; the history of political philosophy.

[1799]
SKOVSGAARD Carl-Johan
9 August 1946, Danish. Solskraenten 54, DK-8410 Rønde, Denmark. Degrees: Cand sci pol, 1975. 1975-76 Administrative Research Leader of the Aarhus based EEC project on Urban Policies in Member States of the European Communities; Assistant Professor in Public Administration, Inst of Pol Sci, U of Aarhus. Publs: *Urban Policies in Member States of the European Communities*, 1976; *Danish Report for the EEC Urban Policies Project*, 1976; *Studier i Dansk Kommunalpolitik* (C J Skovsgaard et al (ed)), 1977. Fields: Local government output studies; regional policies; urban policies.

[1800]
SLAMA Alain-Gérard
25 February 1942, French. 13 rue Tronchet, 75008 Paris, France. Degrees: Agrégé de lettres; Dipl (IEP Paris). Maître de conférences, IEP, Paris. Publs: "Un grand quotidien libéral sous Vichy", *Revue Française de Science Politique*, 1972; "Histoire et psychanalyse", *Contrepoint*, 1977. Fields: History of ideas; Vichy ideology.

[1801]
SLOMP Hans
3 July 1945, Dutch. Groesbeekseweg 114, Nijmegen, The Netherlands. Degrees: Dr. Doctoral thesis: "A Comparison of Soviet and Chinese Agricultural Collectivization" (in Dutch). Wetenschappelijk Ambtenaar, Inst voor Pol, U of Nijmegen. Publs: Various publications on Soviet politics, Chinese politics, comparative politics. Fields: Comparative politics, especially East-West comparison; political participation in Eastern and Western Europe.

[1802]
SMELLIE Kingsley Bryce
22 November 1897, British. 24 Parkside Gardens, London SW19 5E4, England. Degrees: BA. Lecturer, Reader, Professor of Pol Sci, LSE. Publs: *A Hundred Years of English Government*; *Reason in Politics*; *A History of Local Government*. Fields: Political philosophy.

[1803]
SMITH Alexander L M
28 March 1921, British. Rockcliffe, Kilcreggan, Dunbartonshire, Scotland. Degrees: MA. 1950 Senior Lecturer in Government, Scottish Coll of Commerce, Glasgow; Reader in Pol, U of Strathclyde. Fields: Policy process, underlying criteria for establishing governmental priorities and the techniques of assessing results; political and administrative devolution, especially the relationships between different tiers of government.

[1804]
SMITH Brian Clive
23 January 1938, British. 67 Warminster Road, Bath, England. Degrees: BA, 1959; MA (McMaster), 1962; PhD (Exeter), 1970. Doctoral thesis: "The Role of the District Officer in the Political Development of Northern Nigeria". 1962-63 Research Officer, Acton Society Trust; 1963-65 Lecturer in Pol, U of Exeter; 1965-66 Lecturer in Public Administration, Ahmadu Bello U, Nigeria; 1966-70 Lecturer in Pol, U of Exeter; 1970-72 Lecturer in Public Administration, Civil Service Coll, London; 1972- Senior Lecturer in Public Administration, U of Bath. Publs: *Regionalism in England*, 1964-65; *Field Administration*, 1967; *Advising Ministers*, 1969; *Administering Britain* (with J Stanyer), 1976; *Policy Making in British Government*, 1976. Fields: Public administration and public policy making; decentralization and development.

[1805]
SMITH Gordon
16 September, British. 145 Hemingford Road, London N1, England. Degrees: BSc; PhD. Doctoral thesis: "Party System and Party Structure in Western Germany". Lecturer, Senior Lecturer in Government, LSE. Publs: *Politics in Western Europe*, 1976. Fields: West German politics; West European party systems.

[1806]
SMITH Peter Melville*
30 June 1943, British. Flat 19, Boston Court, Selhurst Road, South Norwood, London SE25, England. Degrees: BA. 1969-70 Temporary Lecturer in Pol, U of Reading; Industrial Relations Officer, Commission on Industrial Relations. Fields: Economic functions of government; political and economic aspects of State intervention; economic planning, especially prices and incomes; public administration; industrial relations.

[1807]
SMITH Trevor A
14 June 1937, British. 1A Prestwood Close, Harrow, Middlesex HA3 8JY, England. Degrees: BSc. 1959-60 Assistant Lecturer, U of Exeter; 1960-62 Researcher, Action Society Trust; 1962-67 Lecturer, U of Hull; 1967-76 Lecturer, Senior Lecturer, Queen Mary Coll. Publs: *Town Councillors (with A M Rees), 1964; Town and County Hall*, 1966; *Anti-Politics*, 1972; *Direct Action and Democratic Politics* (joint ed), 1972; *The Politics of the Corporate Economy*, 1978. Fields: The politics of economic regulation; constitutionalism; sub-national politics.

[1808]
SMOKER Paul Lionel
23 September 1938, British. Casterton Grange, Casterton, Kirkby Lonsdale, Cumbria, England. Degrees: MSc; PhD. Visiting Assistant Professor, Northwestern U, USA; Fellow in Conflict Research, Reader in Peace and Conflict Research, U of Lancaster.

[1809]
SMOUTS Marie-Claude
17 May 1941, French. 4 bis rue André Chénier, 92130 Issy les Moulineaux, France. Degrees: Lic en droit; Dipl (IEP); Dr. Doctoral thesis: "Le rôle du secrétaire général des Nations-Unies dans les conflits internationaux". Professeur, Dept de Sci Pol, U de Montréal; Chargée de recherche, CNRS; Maître de conférences, IEP, Paris. Publs: *Le secrétaire général des Nations-Unies*, 1971; *La politique extérieure française et l'ONU*, 1978. Fields: International organization; international law; French foreign policy.

[1810]
SNELLEN Ignatius Theodorus Maria
16 January 1933, Dutch. St Nicasiusstraat 31, Heeze, The Netherlands. Degrees: Degree in Law (Amsterdam), 1958; Drs (Amsterdam), 1960; Dr (Amsterdam), 1975. Doctoral thesis: "Benáderingen in strategieformulering". Political Analyst, N V Philips Gloeilampenfabrieken. Publs: Articles in *International Affairs*, *Acta Politica*, *Intermediair*, *Mens en Onderneming*. Fields: Fundamentals of strategy formation.

[1811]
SNOY ET D'OPPUERS (Baron) Jean Charles
7 February 1907, Belgian. Château de Bois Seigneur Isaac, 1421 Opham, Belgium. Degrees: Dr en droit; Dr en philosophie; Dr en sci pol et diplomatiques. Doctoral thesis: "La commission des douanes et la politique commerciale des Etats Unis". Permanent Secretary for Econ Affairs; Member of the House; Minister of Finance; Burgomaster of Opham; Président de l'Inst Royale des Relations Internationales. Publs: Articles in *Revue Générale Belge*, *Revue Catholique des Idées et des Faits*, *Libre Belgique*, *Bénélux*. Fields: European integration; liberation of trade; monetary policy.

[1812]
SOEIRO DE BRITO Joaquim Baptista Viegas
9 December 1921, Portuguese. Av Viconde Valmor, 9-3° Esq, Lisboa 1, Portugal. Member of the Hydrographic Mission of Mozambique; Director, Operations Research Centre, Portuguese Navy; Lecturer in Energy and Operation Research, Naval War Coll; President of the Atomic Energy Board; Secretary of State for Energy; Lecturer, National Defence Inst, Lisbon. Publs: *Study of the Raydist System*, 1954; *Study of the Tellulometer System*, 1958; *Metric Characteristics of Some Coordinated Systems*, 1977. Fields: Political theory; problems of defence; political and economic aspects of energy.

[1813]
SOLA Giorgio
26 July 1946, Italian. Via Palestro 12/4, Italy. Doctoral thesis: "La Teoria della Classe Politica in Mosca, Pareto e Michels". Professore Incaricato Stabilizzato di Soc Presso la Facoltà di Sci Pol, U di Genova. Publs: *Per un'analisi della Teoria della Classe Politica nelle Opere di Gaetano Mosca*, 1970; *Organizzazione, Partito, Classe Politica e Legge Ferrea dell'Oligarchia in Roberto Michels*, 1975. Fields: History of political science; the classic texts of elitist thought; elitism and pluralism; ruling class and political organization; social classes and party organization.

[1814]
SONTHEIMER Kurt
31 July 1928, German. Geschwister-Scholl-Institut für Politische Wissenschaft der Universität München, Ludwigstrasse 10, 8 München, FR Germany. Degrees: MA (Kansas), 1952; Dr phil (Erlangen). 1962-69 Professor of Pol Sci, Free U of Berlin; 1969-Professor, U of Munich. Publs: *Thomas Mann und die Deutschen*, 1961; *Antidemokratisches Denken in der Weimarer Republik*, 1962; *Israel-Politik, Gesellschaft, Wirtschaft* (ed), 1968; *Handbuch des deutschen Parlamentarismus* (with H H Röhring (eds)), 1970; *Grundzüge des politischen Systems der Bundesrepublik Deutschland*, 1976; *Das Regierungssystem Grossbritanniens*, 1973; *Das Elend unserer Intellektuellen*, 1976; *Handbuch des politischen Systems der Bundesrepublik Deutschland* (with H H Röhring (eds)), 1977. Fields: Analysis of ideological and constitutional trends in the Federal Republic of Germany; methodological problems of political science.

[1815]
SØRENSEN Carsten Lehmann
17 March 1945, Danish. Tingstedet 5, 8220 Brabrand, Denmark. Degrees: Cand sci pol. Assistant Professor, Inst of Pol Sci, U of Aarhus. Publs: "Danish Elite Attitudes Towards European Integration", *Co-operation and Conflict*, 1976; "Denmark joins Europe", *Journal of Common Market Studies*, 1975; *Danmark 06 EF 1 1970 Erne*, 1978. Fields: Danish foreign policy; Nordic and European politics, especially European integration; international organization.

[1816]
SORLIN Pierre*
19 August 1933, French. 13 rue Pierre Nicole, Paris Vème, France. Degrees: Dr (Paris). Professeur, U of Paris VIII. Publs: *Lénine, Trotski, Staline*, 1961; *La société soviétique*, 1964; *Waldeck-Rousseau*, 1967; *La Croix et les juifs*, 1967; *L'antisémitisme allemand*, 1969. Fields: Society and political life in France and the Soviet Union; history and sociology of culture, especially of the cinema.

[1817]
SOUCHON-ZAHN Marie Francoise
13 November 1943, French. 15 Avenue Foch, 94160 St Mandé, France. Degrees: Dr en sci administrative; Dipl études et recherches (FNSP). Doctoral thesis: "La maire, élu local dans une société en changement". Attachée de recherche, Chargée de recherches, CNRS; Publs: *La compagnie nationale d'aménagement du Bas- Rhône Languedoc*, 1968; *Le maire, élu local dans une société en changement*, 1968; "La campagne référendaire", in *La réforme régionale et le référendum du 27 Avril 1969*, 1970; "Les réseaux de relations dans le système politico-administratif: la cas des maires élus pour la première fois en mars 1971", *Bulletin de l'Institut International d'Administration Publique*, 1974; "La région Rhône-Alpes et la mise en place des institutions de la loi de juillet 1972", *Bulletin de l'Institut International d'Administration Publique*, 1975. Fields: Change in local society; regionalization and country planning; relationship between administration and politics.

[1818]
SPALLA Flavio
5 September 1950, Italian. Via Oglio 8, 27100 Pavia, Italy. Degrees: Degree in Pol Sci. Temporary Assistant, Professor of Pol Sci, Teaching and Research Assistant, U of Pavia. Publs: "Il Corriere Della Sera e l'Unità di Fronte all'Integrazione Europea", *Il Politico*, 1977. Fields: Content analysis; political communication and political attitudes.

[1819]
SPANO Piero
25 June 1949, Italian. Via Teramo, 1 Catania, Italy. Doctoral thesis: "Attualità del Problema Teorico e Politico dei 'Ceti Medi' in Italia". Resercher, ISVI, U of Catania. Publs: *Ceti Medi e Capitalismo. La Terziarizzazione Degradata in Italia*, 1977. Fields: Social class; problems of the state.

[1820]
SPENCER Kenneth Maurice
7 April 1942, British. 241 Wake Green Road, Moseley, Brimingham B13 9UZ, England. Degrees: BA; MA (Liverpool), 1968. 1965-67 Research Assistant, School of Architecture, U of Liverpool; 1967-69 Research Associate, Senior Research Associate, Centre for Urban and Regional Studies, U of Birmingham. Lecturer, INLOGOV, U of Birmingham. Publs: *Aspects of Administration in a Large Local Authority* (with B N Downie *et al*), "Royal Commission on Local Government in England", 1968; *Socially Deprived Families in Britain* (with R Holman *et al*), 1970; *Local Government: Approaches to Urban Deprivation* (with J D Stewart and B A Webster), 1976; *Area Management: Objectives and Structures* (with C Horn *et al*), 1977. Fields: Local government administration; urban deprivation and inner city areas; housing policy; decision making.

[1821]
SPIEKER Manfred
4 April 1943, German. An der Baumschule 2, 5042 Erftstadt, FR Germany. Degrees: Dipl Pol (Free U of Berlin), 1968; Dr phil (München), 1973. Doctoral thesis: "Das Verhältnis von Christentum und Sozialismus im marxistischen Revisionismus". 1967-68 Hilfassistent, Otto-Suhr-Inst, Berlin; 1970-72 Ed, *Synode*; Secretary, Sachkommission VI Erziehung, Bildung, Information der Gemeinsamen Synode der Bistumer in der BRD; Wiss Assistent, Geschwister Scholl-Inst, U of Munich; Wiss Assistent, Forschungsinst für Pol Wissenschaft und Europäische Fragen, U of Cologne. Publs: *Neo-Marxismus und Christentum. Zur Problematik des Dialogs 2*, 1976; *Los herejes de Marx Dialogo marxismo-cristianismo*, 1977; "Rechtsstaat contra Sozialstaat? Einwände gegen die emanzipative Sozialstaatsdeutung", *Zeitschrift für Politik*, 1974; "Christentum und Marxismus", *Politica*, 1977; "Mensch und Gesellschaft im Sozialismus", *Politische Studien*, 1975; "Religiöser Sozialismus und Marxismus", in *Irrwege des religiösen Sozialismus*, 1977; "Grundwerte in der Bundesrepublik. Probleme ihrer Begründung, Geltung und Stabilisierung", *Civitas*, 1977; "Demokratie oder Diktatur? Zur Ideologie des Eurokommunismus", *Politische Vierteljahresschrift*, 1978. Fields: Political anthropology; state philosophy; Marxism and eurocommunism; constitution of the Democratic Republic of Germany; problems of state and the political system of the Federal Republic of Germany.

[1822]
SPIERS Maurice
18 March 1933, British. Browfield, Spring Gardens Lane, Keighley, Yorkshire, England. Degrees: BA; MA (Manchester). Principal, Civil Service; Lecturer in Pol, U of Bradford. Publs: *Techniques and Public Administration*, 1972. Fields: Public administration, theory and history; relationship between structuralism and Marxism.

[1823]
SPRINZAK Ehud Z
21 August 1940, Israeli. 5 Alroi St, Jerusalem, Israel. Degrees: BA; MA (Jerusalem); PhD (Yale). Doctoral thesis: "Democracy and Illegitimacy — A Study of the American and the French Student Protest Movements and Some Theoretical Implications". Lec-

turer, Senior Lecturer, Hebrew U of Jerusalem. Publs: Essays on Max Weber, Karl Marx, the New Left in USA and France, delegitimization in a democracy and extreme politics in Israel. Fields: Extreme politics and ideologies; ideology, history and their relationship with political science; the political character of the Jewish nation.

[1824]
STACEY Frank Arthur*
26 July 1923, British. Department of Politics, University College, Swansea, Wales. Degrees: MA (Cambridge), 1948; B Phil (Oxon), 1950. 1951-53 Assistant Lecturer in Pol; 1953-67 Lecturer, U Coll of Swansea; Senior Lecturer in Government, U Coll of Swansea. Publs: *The Government of Modern Britain*, 1968; *The British Ombudsman*, 1971; *The British General Election of 1951* (contributor) (D E Butler (ed)). Fields: Methods for the redress of grievances by the citizen against the State, with special reference to the parliamentary commissioner for administration in Britain, tribunals and other complaints procedures in the British Health Service; the procedure and organization of parliament; pressure groups; protection of individual rights in Britain.

[1825]
STACHOWIAK Herbert
28 May 1921, German. Taubenweg 11, D-4790 Paderborn, FR Germany. Degrees: Dr phil. Doctoral thesis: "Geschichte des axiomatischen Denkens". H O Prof, U of Paderborn, Nordrhein-Westfalen. Publs: *Denken und Erkennen im kybernetischen Modell*, 1969; *Rationalismus im Ursprung*, 1971; *Allgemeine Modelltheorie*, 1973; "Worte, Ziele und Methoden der Bildungsplanung", *Technologie und Zukunftssicherung*, 1977. Fields: General model theory; pragmatic logic; value theory and ethics; planning theory.

[1826]
STADLER Karl Rudolph
8 October 1913, British/Austrian. Wolfauerstrasse 90, A-4045 Linz, Austria. Degrees: BA; MA (London), 1952; PhD (Nottingham), 1970. Doctoral thesis: "Austrian Resistance to German Rule and the Development of Austrian National Aspirations, 1938-45". 1946-68 Lecturer, Senior Lecturer in Modern History and International Relations, Dept of Adult Education and Dept of History, U of Nottingham; 1968- Professor of Modern and Contemporary History, U of Linz. Publs: *The Birth of the Austrian Republic, 1918-21*, 1965; *Österreich 1938-1945 im Spiegel der NS-Akten*, 1965; *European Fascism* (S J Woolf (ed)), 1968; *Hypothek auf die Zukunft*, 1968; *Dr Karl Renner*, 1970; *Austria (Nations of the Modern World)*, 1971; *Opfer verlorener Zeiten*, 1974; *Richard Bernaschek, Odyssee eines Rebellen* (with I Kykal), 1976. Fields: Political theory; history of modern political movements; fascism; Labour movement; international relations and institutions.

[1827]
STAHEL Albert Alexander
3 March 1943, Swiss. Werdtweg 1, CH-3007 Berne, Switzerland. Degrees: MA (Zürich); PhD (Zürich). Doctoral thesis: "Die Anwendung der numerischen Mathematik und der Simulationstechnik bei der Darstellung des Ablaufs einer internationalen Krise". 1970-72 Researcher, U of Zürich and the Swiss Federal Inst of Technology; 1972-73 Researcher, U of Lancaster; 1973- Head, Research Dept, Federal Office of Defence. Publs: *Die Anwendung der numerischen Mathematik und der Simulationstechnik bei der Darstellung des Ablaufs einer internationalen Krise*, 1973; "Kriegsfolgen und Kriegsverhütung, Kritische Ueberlegungen zur Weizsäcker-Studie", *Kleine Studien zur Politischen Wissenschaft*, 1974; "Titos Strategie der allumfassenden Verteidigung", *Neue Zürcher Zeitung*, 1974; "Entwicklung und Planung der schwedischen

Luftwaffe", *Neue Zürcher Zeitung*, 1975; "Abschreckung oder Dissuasion", *Orientierung*, 1975; "Die schwedische Sicherheitspolitik", *Schweizer Soldat*, 1976; "Dissuasion ist nicht Abschreckung", *Schweizer Soldat*, 1976; "Variablen zur Ermittlung der Verteidigungsfähigkeit bzw unfähigkeit eines Landes", in *Schweizerisches Jahrbuch für Politische Wissenschaft*, 1977. Fields: Strategy; security politics; operations research.

[1828]
STÅLVANT Carl-Einar William*
9 March 1945, Swedish. Professorsslingan 5, 10405 Stockholm, Sweden. Degrees: Fil kand (Stockholm), 1968. 1968-69 Amanuensis; 1970-71 Administrative Assistant, Dept of Pol Sci, U of Stockholm. Publs: *Vietnamgrupperna*, 1970; "Sweden and East Europe", in *Co-operation in Europe* (J Galtung (ed)), 1970. Fields: Inter-European co-operation, especially the question of an enlarged Common Market and the relations of the Nordic countries with the EEC.

[1829]
STAMMEN Theo
11 July 1933, German. Leharstrasse 7, 8000 München 60, FR Germany. Degrees: Dr phil (Freiburg), 1961; Habilitation (Münich), 1969. Doctoral thesis: "Goethes Politische Anschaungen". 1963-69 Wiss Assistent, Geschwister Scholl Inst für Pol Wiss, U of München; 1969-70 Privatdozent, Wiss Rat und Professor daselbst; 1970-73 Ord Professor, Pädagogische Hochschule Rheinland, Abt Aachen; 1973- Ord Professor für Pol Wissenschaft, U of Augsburg. Publs: *Strukturwandel der Regierung* (ed), 1967; *Demokratie in Deutschland*, 1975; *Aspekte und Probleme der Kommunalpolitik* (with H Rausche (ed)), 1974; *DDR — das politische, wirtschaftliche und soziale System* (with H Rausch), 1974; *Einführung in die Politikwissenschaft* (with D Berg-Schlosser and H Maier), 1974; *Programme der politischen Parteien in der Bundesrepublik* (with R Kunz and H Maier), 1975; *Das politische System der Bundesrepublik Deutschland im Grundriss*, 1975; *Grundbegriffe der politikwissenschaftlichen Fachsprache* (with P Noack (eds)), 1976. Fields: German government; comparative politics; history of political ideas; contemporary political theory.

[1830]
STAMMER Otto Albert
3 October 1900, German. Markobrunnerstrasse 24^{III}, FR Germany. Degrees: PhD (Leipzig), 1924; Habilitation, 1949. Doctoral thesis: "Ideologie und Geschichte". 1949 Privatdozent, Free U of Berlin; 1951-55 Extraord Professor, Free U of Berlin; 1954 Visiting Professor, Columbia U; 1954-69 Director, Inst of Pol Sci, Free U of Berlin; 1955-59 Professor of Soc and Pol Sci, Free U of Berlin and Co-director, Inst of Soc, Free U of Berlin; 1958-59 Dean of the Faculty of Econ and Soc Sci, Free U of Berlin; 1959-63 President, German Sociological Association; 1960- Member, Committee on Political Sociology, International Sociological Association; 1969 Professor Emeritus. Publs: *Gesellschaft und Politik*, 1955; *Politische Soziologie*, 1955; *Politische Soziologie und Demokratieforschung*, 1965; *Verbände und Gesetzgebung*, 1965; *Max Weber und die Soziologie heute*, 1965; *Parteiensystem, Partienorganisationen und die neuen politischen Bewegungen*, 1968; *Hermann Heller, Gesammelte Schriften* (ed), 1971; *Politische Soziologie* (with P Weingart), 1972. Fields: Political sociology; democracy and dictatorship; social structure and unions; history of socialism.

[1831]
STANCER John David
22 January 1940, British. Shaw's Farmhouse, 36 Main Street, Keyworth, Nottingham, England. Degrees: BSc; MSc (LSE); PhD (LSE). Doctoral thesis: "A study of Backbench Members of Parliament with particular reference to Select Committee Ac-

tivity Between 1945 and 1965''. Lecturer, Senior Lecturer in Pol and Public Administration, South Bank Polytechnic; Part-time Lecturer, Central London (Regent Street), Polytechnic; Principal Lecturer in Pol and Public Administration, North Staffordshire Polytechnic; Head, Dept of Econ and Public Administration, Trent Polytechnic. Publs: *Select Committee on Public Accounts*, 1978; *Public Administration*, 1978. Fields: Select committees of the British House of Commons; public administration; British government and politics.

[1832]
STANSFIELD David Eric
1 August 1942, British. Institute of Latin American Studies, The University, Glasgow W2, Scotland. Degrees: BA; MSc (LSE). 1965-69 Lecturer in Pol, U of Lancaster; 1967-68 Ford Fellow, U of New Mexico; Lecturer in Latin American Pol, U of Glasgow. Publs: "Cuban Foreign Policy", in *External Relations of Small States* (R Barston (ed)), 1972. Fields: Patterns of elite politics in Mexico; relations between metropolitan and local political groups in Mexico; post-revolutionary Cuban politics; political change in modern Latin America.

[1833]
STANYER Jeffrey
5 November 1936, British. 1 Thornton Hill, Exeter EX4 4NJ, England. Degrees: BA; B Phil (Oxon), 1960. 1960-62 Research Fellow in Local Government, Exeter U; 1962- Senior Lecturer in Pol, Exeter U. Publs: *County Government in England and Wales*, 1967; *Administering Britain* (with B C Smith), 1976; *Understanding Local Government*, 1976; *Voting in Cities* (contributor) (L J Sharpe (ed)), 1967; *Local Government in England and Wales, 1958-69* (H V Wiseman (ed)), 1970; *The Role of Commissions in Policy-Making* (R A Chapman (ed)), 1973; *Essays on the Study of Urban Politics* (K Young (ed)), 1975; articles in *Public Administration, Political Studies, Social and Economic Administration, Policy and Politics, The Advancement of Science*. Fields: Decentralization, including local government; field administration; regionalism and devolution; local political behaviour; the methodology of the social sciences; administrative theory, including the history of administrative thought and the analysis of organizational behaviour; contemporary political theory.

[1834]
STANZEL Josef Gregor
14 January 1931, German. Hubertusstrasse 11, D-5060 Bergisch-Gladbach 2, FR Germany. Degrees: Dr jur (Utrecht). Doctoral thesis: "Schulaufsicht im Reformwerk des Johann Ignaz von Felbiger. Eine schulrechtsgeschichtliche und vergleichende Studie zur Volksschulreform sowie zur Entwicklung der gesetzlichen Grundlagen des Schulaufsichtsrechts im aufgeklärten Absolutismus Preussens und Österreichs''. 1974 Wiss Assistent, Akademischer Rat. Publs: "Zur Geschichte der Hauptschule. Frühe Ausprägungen vor allem in der ersten Hälfte des 18 Jahrhunderts", in *Wissenschaft in Hochschule und Schule* (H Hömig and J Tymister (eds)), 1972; "Erziehung zur Toleranz als Verfassungsauftrag", in *Dimensionen von Toleranz* (J Stanzel (ed)), 1974; *Die Schulaufsicht im Reformwerk des Johann Ignaz von Felbiger (1724-1788). Schule, Kirche und Staat in Recht und Praxis des aufgeklärten Absolutismus*, 1976; *Politik und Recht* (with G W Wittkämper and J G Stanzel), 1976; "Die Breslauer Bistumsgüter in der Tschechoslowakei", *Archiv für Kirchengeschichte von Böhmen-Mähren-Schlesien*, 1978. Fields: Comparative government/comparative politics; legal politics; political education; history of political ideas; history of constitutions.

[1835]
STAROPOLI André
14 October 1940, French. 44 La Quintinie, 75015 Paris, France. Degrees: Dipl (IEP Paris); Agrégé de lettres. Chef du Service de l'Information et des Relations Extérieures, Délégation Générale à la Recherche Scientifique et Technique; Sous-Directeur, Recherche et programmes, Ministère de l'Agriculture. Publs: *La technologie incontrôlée*, 1975. Fields: Technology assessment; science policy; management of public science; innovation.

[1836]
STASSEN Jacques Marcel Francois-Joseph*
15 October 1911, Belgian. 51 rue Louvrey, Liège, Belgium. Degrees: Dr en droit (Liège), 1933; Lic (Liège), 1935. Avocat près la Cour d'Appel, Liège; Professeur, Inst Supérieur des Hautes Etudes Commerciales et Consulaires, Liège; Professeur, Centre de Formation Sociale de Liège; Juge suppléant; Maître de conférence, U de Liège; Professeur ordinaire, Faculté de Droit, U de Liège; Chaire de droit administratif et de sci administrative; Directeur Général, Inst International des Sci Administratives. Publs: *Eléments de droit public et administratif*, 1965. Fields: Relations between the European communities and Europe; public enterprise; problems of administrative science and control.

[1837]
STEEDS David
23 September 1935, British. Cartrefle, Ponterwyd, Aberystwyth, Dyfed, Wales. Degrees: BA. 1961-63 Assistant Lecturer in Modern History, U of Glasgow; 1963-72 Lecturer in Far Eastern Studies, Senior Lecturer, Dept of International Pol, U Coll of Wales, Aberystwyth. Publs: *China, Japan and Nineteenth Century Britain* (with I Nish), 1977. Fields: History of the Chinese Communist party; history of the Kuomintang in China; the Sino-Japanese war, 1937-1945; British policy in the Far East in the 19th and 20th centuries.

[1838]
STEEL David Robert
29 May 1948, British. 21 Bettys Mead, Exeter EX4 8LN, England. Degrees: MA (Oxon); D Phil (Oxon). Doctoral thesis: "The British Transport Commission: A Study in the Managerial Autonomy of a Public Corporation". Lecturer in Pol, U of Exeter. Publs: "Administrative Developments in 1973 and 1974: A Survey", *Public Administration* (with J Stanyer), 1975; "Education for Management in the British Health Service", in *Program Notes*, 1976; "Administrative Developments in 1975 and 1976: A Survey" (with J Stanyer), *Public Administration*, 1977; "Nationalization and Public Ownership", in *Trends in British Politics* (C P Cook and J A Ramsden (eds)); *The Role of Higher Education in Britain in the Education and Training of Administrative Public Servants* (with F F Ridley), 1978. Fields: Public administration with special reference to public enterprise; British politics.

[1839]
STEIN Gerd
14 December 1941, German. Schildberg 43, D-4300 Essen 11, FR Germany. Degrees: Dr Paed; Dipl Pädagoge. Doctoral thesis: "Schulbuchwissen, Politik und Pädogogik. Untersuchungen zu einer praxisbezogenen und theoriegeleiteten Schulbuchforschung". 1964-70 Volksschullehrer; 1970-72 Assistent im Fach Erziehungswissenschaft, Pädagogische Hochschule, Dortmund; 1972- Akademischer Rat, Fach Politikwissenschaft, Gesamthochschule, Duisburg; Direktor, Inst für Schulbuchforschung eV. Publs: *Plädoyer für eine Politische Pädagogik*, 1973;

Politikwissenschaft als Erziehungswissenschaft? (co-ed), 1974; *Geschichte/Politik/ Pädagogik* (ed), 1975; *Theorie und Praxis schulischer Reformen im Spannungsfeld von Pädagogik und Politik* (ed), 1975; *Schulbuchkritik als Schulkritik*, 1976; *Zur Legitimationsproblematik bildungspolitischer Entscheidungen* (co-ed), 1976; *Schulbuchwissen, Politik und Pädagogik*, 1977; *Immer Ärger mit den Schulbüchern*, 1978. Fields: Course and media research; teacher formation and school reform; limits between education science and political science.

[1840]
STEINBACH Udo
30 May 1943, German. Alardusstrasse 12, 2000 Hamburg 19, FR Germany. Degrees: Dr phil. Doctoral thesis: "Dhâtal-Himma — Kulturgeschichtliche Betrachtungen zu einem arabischen Volksroman". 1971-75 Head of the Middle East Dept, Stiftung Wiss und Pol, Ebenhausen/Isar; 1975 Head of the Turkish Section, Voice of Germany, Cologne; 1976- Director, Deutsches Orient-Inst, Hamburg. Publs: Monographs and articles on the foreign policy of Turkey and Iran; Inter-Arab relations; the situation in the Gulf and the Red Sea; ideological trends in the Middle East; the relations of the Middle East with the Soviet Union and Western Europe; the Cyprus question and the problems of security in the Eastern Mediterranean. Fields: Foreign policy of Turkey and Iran; inter-Arab relations; the situation in the Gulf and the Red Sea; ideological trends in the Middle East; the relations of the Middle East with the Soviet Union and Western Europe; the Cyprus question and the problems of security in the Eastern Mediterranean.

[1841]
STEINER Hillel Isaac
7 May 1942, Canadian. 12 Gildridge Road, Manchester 16, England. Degrees; BA; MA (Carleton); PhD (Manchester). Doctoral thesis: "Political Obligation and the Concept of Scarcity". Lecturer in Pol Philosophy, U of Manchester. Publs: *The Natural Right to Equal Freedom*, 1974; *The Concept of Justice*, 1974; "Individual Liberty", in *Proceedings Aristotelian Society*, 1974-75; "The Natural Right to the Means of Production", *Philosophical Quarterly*, 1977; *Nozick on Appropriation*, 1978; "The Structure of a Set of Compossible Rights", *Journal of Philosophy*, 1977; "Can a Social Contract be Signed by an Invisible Hand?", in *Democracy, Consensus and Social Contract* (Birnbaum, Lively and Parry (eds)), 1978. Fields: Political, moral, and legal philosophy; economic theory; decision and rational choice theory; philosophy of social science.

[1842]
STEINERT Marlis G
German. 12 Avenue Adrien Jeandin, 1226 Thonex, Geneva, Switzerland. Degrees: Dr (Saar). Doctoral thesis; "Michel Chevalier. L'évolution de sa pensée économique, sociale et politique". 1955-57 Research Assistant, Carnegie Endowment, European Centre for the Study of "Le Conflit Sarrois"; 1958-59 Assistant, FNSP, Paris; 1961-62 Research Assistant, Carnegie Endowment; 1962-69 Collaboration with Jacques Freymond, Director, Graduate Inst of International Studies; 1969- Assistant Professor, Professor, Graduate Inst of International Studies, Geneva. Publs: *Die 23 Tage der Regierung Dönitz*, 1967; *Capitulation 1945*, 1969; *The Final Collapse of Nazi Germanay*, 1969; *Hitlers Krieg und die Deutschen*, 1970; *L'Allemagne national-socialiste*, 1973; *Les origines de la Seconde Guerre Mondiale*, 1974; *Le Japon face au monde contemporain*, 1975; *Hitler's War and the Germans*, 1977. Fields: International relations; public opinion; contemporary history.

[1843]
STEINKEMPER Bärbel
12 April 1947, German. Görreshof 39, D-5305 Alfter b Bonn, FR Germany. Degrees: Dipl Volkswirt; Dr rer Pol. Doctoral thesis: "Klassische und politische Bürokraten in der Ministerialverwaltung der Bundesrepublik Deutschland" (Classical and Political Bureaucrats in the Civil Service of the FRG). U of Cologne; Research Assistant, Soc Sci Research Inst, Konrad Adenauer Foundation. Publs: *Klassische und politische Bürokraten in der Ministerialverwaltung der BRD*, 1964; "Pressure Groups im öffentlichen Dienst", in *Handwörterbuch des öffentliches Dienstes: Das Personalwesen* (with W Kaltefleiter), 1977; "Beziehungen und Wechselwirkungen zwischen Koalitionen in den Ländern und im Bund", 1976; *Westdeutsche Führungsschicht. Eine sozialwissenschaftliche Untersuchung der Inhaber von Führungspositionen* (with U Lange-Hoffmann *et al*), 1973. Fields: Political institutions, especially their functioning and their interdependence; elites, especially political elites; socialization; recruitment; communication; interaction.

[1844]
STENELO Lars-Göran
20 September 1939, Swedish. Blåtungau 3, S-22375 Lund, Sweden. Degrees: PhD. Doctoral thesis: "Mediation in International Negotiations". Docent, Dept of Pol Sci, U of Lund. Publs: *Mediation in International Negotiations*, 1972. Fields: International politics.

[1845]
STENSTADVOLD Halvor*
6 April 1944, Norwegian. Snaroyvn 72a, 1330 Oslo Lufthavn, Norway. Degrees: Mag art (Oslo), 1971. 1971- Research Assistant, Inst of Pol Sci, U of Oslo. Publs: *Det Norske Studentersamfund — en Debattanalytisk Studie*, 1971. Fields: Political communication and politics; evaluation of people and their efforts as requisites for manpower decisions in private businesses.

[1846]
STENZEL Konrad
12 April 1948, German. Amsterdamerstrasse 19, B-5300 Bonn, FR Germany. Degrees: MA (Konstanz). Co-ordinator, Group for Overseas Projects, Friedrich-Ebert-Stiftung, Bonn. Publs: "Die Entstehung des republikanischen Venezuela, oder: die Grenzen des kapitalistischen, Fortschritts", in *Lateinamerika: Historische Realität und Dependencia Theorien* (H J Puhle (ed)), 1977; "The Capitalist State and Underdevelopment in Latin America: The Case of Venezuela" (with W Hein), *Capitalistie*, 1973. Fields: Latin American studies; studies in popular movements.

[1847]
STERNBERGER Dolf
28 July 1907, German. 61 Darmstadt, Park Rosenhöhe 8, FR Germany. Degrees: Dr phil, 1950. 1955 Honorarprofessor; 1960 Persönlicher Ord; 1962 Ord Professor; 1972 Emeritus Professor, U of Heidelberg. Publs: *Die grosse Wahlreform*, 1964; *Kriterien*, 1965; *Ich wünschte ein Bürger zu sein*, 1967; *Nicht alle Staatsgewalt geht vom Volke aus*, 1971; *Heinrich Heine und die Absdraftung der Sünde*, 1972; *Gerechtigkeit für das neunzehnte Jahrhundert*, 1975; *Machiavelli's — Principles und der Begriff des Politischen*, 1977; *Über den Tod*, 1977. Fields: Theory of legitimacy and typology of legitimacies in historical comparison; theory of political representation, including history of doctrines; general political theory.

[1848]
STEWART John David
19 March 1929, British. 15 Selly Wick Road, Birmingham B29 9UZ, England. Degrees: BA; D Phil (Oxon), 1956. Doctoral thesis: "The Role of Pressure Groups in Relation to the House of Commons". 1954-66 National Coal Board; 1966- Inst of Local Government Studies; 1974-76 Member of Layfield Committee on Local Government Finance; 1971-74 Member of DES Library Advisory Council; Adviser to the Greater London Council Inquiry into London Government; Director, Inst of Local Government Studies, U of Birmingham. Publs: *British Pressure Groups*, 1958; *Management in Local Government: A Viewpoint*, 1971; *The Responsive Local Authority*, 1974; *Corporate Planning in English Local Government: An Analysis of Readings* (with R Greenwood), 1974; *Management in an Era of Restraint and Central and Local Government Relationships*, 1977. Fields: Politics and management in the local authority; central-local relations; local government finance; corporate planning.

[1849]
STINNES Manfred Herbert*
31 August 1944, German. HSFK, Eschersheimer Landstrasse 14, 6 Frankfurt am Main 1, FR Germany. Degrees: MA (Minnesota), 1971. 1969-72 Teaching Assistant, Teaching Associate, U of Minnesota; 1972-73 Visiting Instructor, U of Montana; Research Fellow, Hessen Foundation for Peace and Conflict Research, Frankfurt. Publs: Articles in *Gewaltfreie Aktion*. Fields: Political philosophy; political theory; comparative politics; peace research; socialist thought.

[1850]
STJERNQUIST Nils Nilsson
29 August 1917, Swedish. 3 Spolegatan, 222 20 Lund, Sweden. Degrees: PhD (Lund), 1946. 1947 Assistant Professor of Pol Sci, U of Lund; 1951 Professor, Head of the Dept of Pol Sci, U of Lund. Publs: *Ständerna, statsregleringen och förvaltningen: Striden om makten över utgifterna 1809-44*, 1950; *Tillkomsten av 1866 års grundlag*, 1955; *Riksdagens arbete och arbetsformer*, 1966; "Sweden: Stability or Deadlock?", in *Political Oppositions in Western Democracies* (R A Dahl (ed)), 1966; *Vår nya författning* (with E Holmber), 1977. Fields: Swedish Government and politics; public administration.

[1851]
STOETZEL Jean Antoine
23 April 1910, French. 20 rue d'Aumale, 75009 Paris, France. Degrees: Dr, 1943. Doctoral thesis: "L'étude expérimentale des opinions", 1943. 1937-38 Lecturer, Columbia U; 1938-43 Teacher of Phil, Amiens, Clermont-Ferrand, Evreux, Paris; 1945-55 Professor of Soc, U of Bordeaux; 1955-78 Professor of Soc Psychology, Sorbonne; 1955-68 Director, Inst of Soc Sci for Labor; Director, Center for Soc Research; Professor, Sorbonne. Publs: *Théorie des opinions*, 1943; *L'étude expérimentale des opinions*, 1943; *Jeunesse sans chrysanthèmes ni sabre*, 1954; *La psychologie sociale*, 1963; *Les revenus et les coûts des besoins de la vie*, 1976. Fields: Public opinion.

[1852]
STOKMAN Frans N
Dutch. Doorrid 6, Haren (Gr), The Netherlands. Degrees: Dr (Amsterdam), 1977. Doctoral thesis: "Roll Calls and Sponsorship: A Methodological Analysis of Third World Group Formation". Assistant Professor, Inst for Pol Sci, U of Amsterdam; Professor of Research Methodology, Sociological Inst, State U of Groningen. Publs: Articles in *Acta Politica; Graven naar Macht op zoek naar de Kern van de Nederlandse Economie* (co-author), 1975; "Power and Influence as Political Phenomena" (with R J Mokken),

in *Power and Political Theory: Some European Perspectives* (B Barry (ed)). Fields: Research methodology; representation studies; legislative roll-call analysis and analysis of legislative bodies in general; decision-making in international organizations; links and influence structure between elites.

[1853]
STOPPINO Mario
3 February 1935, Italian. Via Scarpa 12, Pavia, Italy. Degrees: Degree in Law (Pavia). Doctoral thesis; "Recenti Sviluppi della Teoria della Classe Politica di Gaetano Mosca". Assistant Professor of Government, Associate Professor, Professor of Pol Sci, U of Pavia. Publs: *Potere Politico e Stato*, 1968; *I Metodi di Ricerca del Potere nella Comunità Locale*, 1971; *Le Forme del Potere*, 1974; "H D Lasswell: la Formazione e l'Opera" in *Potere, Politica e Personalità* (H D Lasswell), 1975; "Autorità", "Autoritarismo", "Dittatura", "Forza", "Ideologia", "Potere", "Totalitarismo", "Violenza", in *Dizionario di Politica*, 1976. Fields: Power and political theory; political participation in local and national politics; ethics and political action.

[1854]
STOUTHARD Philippe Cornelis
19 November 1924, Dutch. Willem Elsschothof 4, 5044 LJ Tilburg, The Netherlands. Degrees: Dr Soc Sci. Doctoral thesis; "Models of Data: a Methodological Investigation". Professor of Statistics and Research Methods, Depts of Soc and Psychology, Catholic U of Tilburg.

[1855]
STRAND Torodd
1 July 1941, Norwegian. Fossasen 21, 5095 Ulset, Norway. Degrees: Mag art (Oslo), 1967; MA (Syracuse), 1969; PhD, 1976. Doctoral thesis: "Geographic Policies — a Comparative Study of Norway and Sweden". Research Fellow, Norwegian Research Council for Soc Sci and the Humanities; Research Fellow, U of Bergen; Lecturer, Public Administration and Organization, U of Bergen. Publs: "Expertise, Innovation and Influence", *Scandinavian Political Studies*, 1969. Fields: Impacts of, and conditions for, introduction of spatial dimensions into political systems; administrative adaptation to spatial concerns; consequences of regional distribution of values.

[1856]
STRÖM Lars-Inge*
21 May 1942, Swedish. Ferlinsgatan 19A, 85428 Uppsala, Sweden. Degrees: Fil mag, 1968. Inst of Pol Sci, U of Uppsala. Fields: Ideology of international sport (IOC) and its confrontation with the political environment.

[1857]
STRÖMBERG Lars Olof Einar
8 June 1937, Swedish. Västra Hästskobacken 5B, 443 00 Lerum, Sweden. Degrees: Fil lic (Göteborg), 1967; PhD (Göteborg), 1974. Doctoral thesis: "Väljare och Valda" (Electors and the Elected). 1962-66 Administrative Assistant, Inst of Pol Sci, U of Göteborg; 1967-72 Research Assistant, Local Government Research Group, U of Göteborg; 1972- Assistant Professor, Inst of Pol Sci, U of Göteborg; 1976- Professor of Public Administration, Aalberg U Centre. Publs: *Offentlig Förvaltning* (co-author), 1969; *Medborgarna Informeras* (co-author), 1971; *Byråkrati och Politik* (co-author), 1972. Fields: Local representative government and public administration.

[1858]
STUDDERT-KENNEDY William Gerald
21 February 1933, British. Department of Politics, University of York, Heslington, York YO1 5DD, England. Degrees: BA; MA (California at Berkeley). 1958-62 BBC Current Affairs Television Producer; 1962-64 Commonwealth Fellow; 1964-66 Teaching Assistant, U of California at Berkeley; Lecturer, Department of Pol, U of York; Senior Lecturer, Faculty of Commerce and Soc Sci, U of Birmingham. Publs: *Opinions, Publics and Pressure Groups* (with G C Moodie), 1970; *Evidence and Explanation in Social Science*, 1975. Fields: The theoretical implications of cross-disciplinary work.

[1859]
STÜTZER Wolfgang
21 October 1946, German. Konrad-Adenauer-Strasse 27, D-5308 Rheinbach-Flerzheim, FR Germany. Degrees: Dipl Pol (Free U of Berlin), 1971. 1971-73 Political Adviser, Free Democratic Party Headquarters, Bonn; 1975-77 Partner in a political consultancy office, Bonn; 1977- Lecturer in Pol Sci, Theodor-Heuss-Academy. Publs: Various articles on grassroots-movements, constitutional problems and terrorism. Fields: Grassroots-movements; constitutional problems; terrorism.

[1860]
STUHLPFARRER Karl
23 September 1941, Austrian. Heinestrasse 27/15, A-1020 Vienna, Austria. Degrees: Dr phil. Doctoral thesis: "Die Operationszonen 'Alpenvorland' und 'Adriatisches Küstenland', 1943-1945". Lektor, Oberassistent, Inst für Zeitgeschichte, U of Wien. Publs: *Die Operationszonen "Alpenvorland" und "Adriatisches Küstenland" 1943-1945*, 1969; *Aktive Neutralität, Österreichische Aussenpolitik nach 1945*, 1975; *Österreich und seine Slowenen* (with H Haas), 1977. Fields: European contemporary history, especially Austrian and Italian; fascism and neofascism; minority problems.

[1861]
SUBILEAU Francoise
10 May 1942, French. 55 rue de la Procession, 75015 Paris, France. Degrees: Lic ès lettres; Dipl (Paris). Attachée de recherche, FNSP, Paris. Fields: Sociology; military sociology; political attitudes; militarism.

[1862]
SUCHA Marian
24 October 1949, Dutch. Prof de Langen Wendelsstraat 17, RL-6524 Nijmegen, The Netherlands. Degrees: Dipl Pol (Hamburg). Doctoral thesis: "Consequences of Détente for the Trade-Union Movement — Case Studies on Coexistence Policy". Research Assistant, U of Nijmegen. Publs: "Die Schranken einer Koordinierung von Tarifpolitik und Streiks in der EWG/EG", in *Konflikte in der Arbeitswelt, Jahrbuch für Friedens- und Konfliktforschung*, 1977; *Macht ohne Grenzen — Grenzlose Ohnmacht — Transnationale Konzerne und Interessenvertretung der Lohnabhängigen* (with K P Tudyka and T Etty), 1978. Fields: International trade unions; détente and East-West economic relations.

[1863]
SUGANAMI Hidemi
13 January 1948, Japanese. Department of International Relations, University of Keele, Staffordshire ST5 5BG, England. Degrees: BA; MSc. Lecturer, U of Keele. Publs: "'Peace Through Law' Approach in International Relations", in *Approaches and Theory of International Relations* (ed), 1978; "A Note on the Origin of the Word 'In-

ternational' ", *British Journal of International Studies*, 1978; "Why Ought Treaties to be Kept?", in *Year Book of World Affairs*, 1979. Fields: Philosophical aspects of international relations.

[1864]
SULEVO Kari Peter Kristian
11 September 1945, Finnish. Klaavuntie 16 E 38, 00910 Helsinki 91, Finland. Degrees: Dr pol sci (Helsinki), 1973. Doctoral thesis: "Finnish Political Parties and Nordic Cooperation". Docent of Pol Sci, U of Helsinki. Fields: Political communication; political change.

[1865]
SULLIVAN Terence Joseph
17 November 1946, British. 92 Norbiton Avenue, Kingston-upon-Thames, England. Degrees: BSc; MSc (LSE), 1973. Senior Lecturer in Pol, Kingston Polytechnic, Surrey. Fields: Political philosophy; history of ideas; philosophy of science; 19th and 20th century libertarian thought.

[1866]
SUMMERS Laura Jean
American. Flat 3, The County College, Bailrigg, Lancaster LA1 4YD, England. Degrees: BA; MA (Cornell); PhD (Cornell). Doctoral thesis: "The Politics of Political Decay: The Sihanouk Regime in Cambodia". Lecturer in Pol, U of Lancaster. Publs: "Non-family Agents of Political Socialization: A Reassessment of Converse and Dupeux" (with D R Cameron), *Canadian Journal of Political Science*, 1972. "Behind Khmer Smiles: Prospero's Adventures in Cambodia", *Journal of the Siam Society*, 1973; "Consolidating the Cambodian Revolution", *Current History*, 1975; *Cambodia's Economy and Industrial Development* (trans and introduction), 1977. Fields: Government and politics in Southeast Asia; political development of Europe and the Third World; international relations of Asia; comparative European politics.

[1867]
SUNDBERG Per
2 September 1924, Swedish. G Norrtäljevägen 64B, 18010 Eneryberg, Sweden. Degrees: Fil dr (Stockholm), 1961. Doctoral thesis: "The Ministries Bildt and Akerhielm: Premonition of Swedish Parliamentarism". 1961-62 Lecturer, Dept of Pol Sci, U of Stockholm; 1963- Director, Inst for English-speaking Students; Dean, International Graduate School, U of Stockholm. Fields: Swedish government; mass communications; European colonialism.

[1868]
SUSILUOTO Eero Ilmari
15 October 1947, Finnish. Tunturikatu 3 as 2, 00100 Helsinki 10, Finland. Degrees: Pol lic. Doctoral thesis: "Guidance of Society: On the Development of Systems Thinking in the Soviet Union". Research Fellow, Academy of Finland. Publs: "Scientific Communication in the Study of Socialist Countries", *Politikka*, 1972; *On the Development of the Soviet Science of Administration* (in Finnish), 1973; *Administration and Political System in the Socialist Society* (in Finnish), 1973; *Socialism and Human Needs* (in Finnish), 1974; "Russian and Soviet Studies in Finland", *Slavic Studies*, 1974; *Cybernetics and Ideology*, 1977; "Socialism and Systems Thinking", *Politikka*, 1978. Fields: History of systems theory; social scientific applications of systems theory; Soviet studies.

[1869]
SUTTON Paul Kenneth
25 October 1945, British. 23 Salisbury Street, Hull, North Humberside, England. Degrees: BSc; M Litt, 1972. Doctoral thesis: "Political Development in Trinidad and Tobago 1962-72". Lecturer in Pol, U of Hull. Publs: "Patterns of Foreign Policy Among the Independent States of Central America and the Caribbean 1948-64: A Quantitative Approach", *Social and Economic Studies*, 1977. Fields: Caribbean government and politics; socialism and development in the Third World.

[1870]
SUYKERBUYK Pieter A G M
30 April 1937, Dutch. Jan Willem Passtraat 105, Nijmegen, The Netherlands. Degrees: Dr (Nijmegen), 1970. Doctoral thesis; "Sociological Analysis and its Validity". Teaching Assistant, Inst of Pol Sci, U of Nijmegen. Publs: *Sociological Analysis and its Validity*, 1970. Fields: Political attitudes and behaviour.

[1871]
SVAASAND Lars Gerhard*
21 July 1947, Norwegian. Institute of Sociology, University of Bergen, Christiesgate 17, N-5014 Bergen, Norway. Degrees: Cand pol (Bergen), 1972. 1971-72 Data Secretary, Norwegian Soc Sci Data Service; Research Assistant, Inst of Soc, U of Bergen. Fields: Growth of party systems in Europe; local party organizations; nation-building and the developing of mass politics in Iceland and Finland; the electoral base of Communist parties in Western Europe.

[1872]
SVENSSON Palle
4 February 1944, Danish. Tulshøjvej 23, DK-8270 Højbjerg, Denmark. Degrees: Cand sci pol. Lecturer, U of Aarhus. Publs: "Support for the Danish Social Democratic Party 1924-39", *Scandinavian Political Studies*, 1974. Fields: Democratic theory; political socialization; political parties; comparative government.

[1873]
SWAISLAND Henry Charles
19 August 1919, British. 88 Rednal Road, Birmingham B38 8DU, England. Degrees: B Com; D Phil (Oxon), 1968. Doctoral thesis: "The Aborigines Protection Society and British Southern and West Africa". 1949-63 Provincial Administration, Eastern Nigeria; 1969-70, 1973-75 Professor of Public Administration, U of Mauritius; Senior Lecturer, U of Birmingham. Publs: *Report on the Eastern Nwga District Council, Nigeria*, 1955; *Great Cities of the World* (contributor) (W A Robson (ed)), 1972. Fields: Organization theory; local government; African political administration.

[1874]
SZAJKOWSKI Bodgan
22 June 1942, Australian. 13 Millbrook Close, Dinas Powis, South Glamorgan, Wales. Degrees: MA (Warsaw); Dipl Soc Sci (Birmingham). 1969-73 Research Scholar, King's Coll, U of Cambridge; 1973-75 Lecturer in Comparative Communism, The Australian National U, Canberra; 1975-76 Lecturer in Pol, U Coll, Dublin; 1976-Lecturer in Comparative Communism, Dept of Pol, U Coll, Cardiff. Publs: "A Contribution to Political History of Romania", *International Journal of Romanian Studies*, 1974; "A Growing Relationship? EEC and Eastern Europe", *Community Report*, 1976; "Europa en COMECON", *Europese Gemeenschap*, 1976; *Marxist Governments: A World Survey*, 1979. Fields: Comparative communism; international communist movement; EEC — COMECON relations.

[1875]
SZMULA Volker
5 October 1941, German. Fechtelerstrasse 22, 479 Paderborn, FR Germany. Degrees: Dr phil (Heidelberg), 1970. Doctoral thesis: "Die Arbeit des Geschäfts-ordnungsausschusses — Aufgabe und Bedeutung eines Bundestagesausschusses" (The Work of the Rules Committee in the German Bundestag). 1968-69 Tutor, Inst of Pol Sci, U of Heidelberg; 1972- Assistant Professor, Associate Professor, Gesamt-hochschule, Paderborn. Publs: *Die Arbeit des Geschäftsordnungsausschusses*, 1970; "Zum Selbstverständnis des Deutschen Bundestages", *Aus Politik und Zeitgeschichte*, 1974; "Partizipationsausweitung in sozialen Entscheidungsprozessen", *Aus Politik und Zeitgeschichte*, 1976; "Ältestenrat; Bürokratie; Geschäftsordnungen; Ministerverantwörtlichkeit; Verwaltung/Verwaltungsstruktur", in *Handbuch des politischen Systems der Bundesrepublik Deutschland* (Rohring/Sontheimer (eds)), 1977. Fields: German parliamentarism, political theory.

T

[1876]
TALOS Emmerich
29 July 1944, Austrian. A-1150 Vienna, Geyschlägergasse 11/18, Austria. Degrees: Dr. Assistant, Inst für Politikwissenschaft, U of Wien. Publs: "Sozialpartnerschaft", *Österreichische Zeitschrift für Politikwissenschaft*, 1974; "Zu den Anfängen der Sozialpolitik", *Österreichische Zeitschrift für Politikwissenschaft*, 1976; "Sozialpolitik-Sozialstaat-Wohlfahrstaat", *Zeitgeschichte*, 1977; "Krise des Sozialstaates?" (with D Bichlbauer and P Scheer), *Österreichische Zeitschrift für Politikwissenschaft*, 1977. Fields: Social policy; welfare state.

[1877]
TAMES Richard Lawrence
30 January 1946, British. 7 Pye Corner, Castle Hedingham, Essex, England. Degrees: BA; MSc (London), 1974. Secretary, Hansard Society for Parliamentary Government; Assistant Organizer of Extramural Studies, SOAS, U of London. Fields: Political education and pre-university curriculum development.

[1878]
TAMMELO Ilmar
25 February 1917, Austrian/Australian. A-5221 Lochen 38, Austria. Degrees: Mag jur , 1943; Dr jur (Marburg), 1944; Habilitation (Heidelberg), 1947; MA (Melbourne), 1951; Master of Laws (Sydney), 1964. Doctoral thesis: "Kritische Untersuchungen zur nor-mativistischen Unterscheidung des Privat- und des öffentlichen Rechts", 1944; 1947-48 Privatdozent in General Theory of Law and in Legal Philosophy, Heidelberg; 1952-54 Research Assistant; 1954-57 Research Fellow; 1958-64 Senior Lecturer; 1964-73 Reader in International Law and Jurisprudence, U of Sydney; Professor in Legal Philosophy, Methodology of Legal Sciences and General Theory of the State, U of Salzburg. Publs: *Untersuchungen zum Wesen der Rechtsnorm*, 1948; *Treaty Interpretation and Practical Reason*, 1967; *Outlines of Modern Legal Logic*, 1969; *Principles and Methods of Legal Logic* (in Japanese), 1971; *Survival and Surpassing*, 1971; *Rechtslogik und materiale Gerechtigkeit*, 1971; *Grundzüge und Grundverfahren der Rechtslogik*, 1977; *Theorie der Gerechtigkeit*, 1977. Fields: Legal philosophy and theory; political philosophy and theory; philosophy and theory of international law; interlinguistics.

[1879]
TANDON Yashpal*
1939, Ugandan. 13 Culver Grove, Stanmore, Middlesex, England. Degrees: BSc; PhD (LSE), 1968. Doctoral thesis: "United Nations Peacekeeping: A Study in Diplomatic Anthropology". 1964- Lecturer, Senior Lecturer, Reader in Pol Sci, Makerere U, Kampala; 1965-68 Executive Director, Makerere Inst for Soc Research; Visiting Lecturer, LSE. Publs: *Readings in African International Relations*, 1972; *International Technical Assistance Administration in East Africa* (ed), 1973. Fields: African international relations; East African Community; African unity; foreign policy of African states; futurology.

[1880]
TAPPER Edward Robert
25 July 1940, British. 38 Roundhill Crescent, Brighton, England. Degrees: BA; MA (Oregon), 1964; PhD (Manchester), 1968. Doctoral thesis: "The Political Socialization of Secondary School Adolescents". 1963 Teaching Assistant, U of Oregon; 1970 Research Associate, U of Oregon; 1966-68 Research Fellow, Enfield Coll of Technology; 1976-77 Associate Professor,California State U, Sacramento; Lecturer, U of Sussex. Publs: *Young People and Society*, 1971; *Political Education and Stability*, 1976; *Education and the Political Order*, 1978. Fields: Political education; policymaking process; the social control of knowledge.

[1881]
TARSCHYS Daniel
21 July 1943, Swedish. Stenbacksstigen 7, 18162 Lidingö, Sweden. Degrees: JK (Stockholm), 1965; Fil dr (Stockholm), 1972; PhD (Princeton), 1972. Doctoral thesis: "Beyond the State: The Future Policy in Classical and Soviet Marxism". Research Associate, U of Stockholm; Member of Swedish Parliament. Publs: *Den Nygamla Vänstern* (with C Tham), 1967; *Den Kommunistiska Framtiden*, 1974; *Petita* (with M Eduards), 1975; *The Soviet Political Agenda*, 1978. Fields: Political theory; comparative politics; Soviet studies; public administration; public expenditures.

[1882]
TAUSCH Arno
11 February 1951, Austrian. Kaiserjägerstrasse 17/26, A-6020 Innsbruck, Austria. Degrees: Dr phil. Doctoral thesis: "Die Grenzen der Wachstumstheorie" (The Limits to Growth Theory). Vienna Inst for Development; Assistant, Soc and Econ Sci Faculty, U of Innsbruck. Publs: *The Limits to Growth-Theory*, 1976; *Poverty and Dependence. Politics and Economics in Dependent Capitalism*, 1978; "The Political Economy of World Wide Exploitation", in *Arbeitsgemeinschaft Politische Bildung*, 1978. Fields: Theory of income distribution; poverty in Austria; dependence in the Third World; methodology of the social sciences.

[1883]
TAVERNIER Yves*
20 October 1937, French. 18 Avenue Emile Zola, 91 Ste Geneviève des Bois, France. Degrees: DES (Paris), 3ème cycle; Chargé de recherches, FNSP. Publs: *Le Syndicalisme paysan*, 1969; *Les paysans français et l'Europe* (with H Delorme), 1969; *Terre, paysans et politique* (with H Mendras), 1969-70. Fields: Agricultural politics of the Fifth Republic.

[1884]
TAYLOR Charles Lewis
8 November 1935, American. Graefentalerstrasse 4, 1000 Berlin 46, FR Germany. Degrees: BA; MA (Yale), 1959; PhD (Yale), 1963. Doctoral thesis: "The Emergence of British Working Class Politics". 1962-1966 Coll of William and Mary; 1966-1970 Yale U; 1970-1976 Virginia Polytechnic Inst and State U; Inst for the Study of Comparative Politics, Wissenschaftszentrum — Berlin. Publs: *World Handbook of Political and Social Indicators*, 1972; *Aggregate Data Analysis: Cross National Political and Social Indicators*, 1968; *Are Political Values Really Changing?*, 1977. Fields: Cross national aggregate data; election studies in Germany and Britain.

[1885]
TAYLOR Ian Hamilton
18 October 1948, British. Department of Politics, University of Exeter, Exeter, England. Degrees: BA; MSc (LSE); PhD (LSE). Doctoral thesis; "War and the Development of Labour's Domestic Programme, 1939-45". 1972-73 Lecturer, Bristol Polytechnic; 1977-78 Lecturer, U of Exeter; 1978- Lecturer, U of Aston. Fields: Politics and government of the UK and USA; federalism/regionalism; ideologies and movements.

[1886]
TAYLOR Michael John
22 September 1942, British. Pound Farm, Dedham, Colchester, Essex, England. Degrees: PhD (Essex), 1976. 1967-68 Research Associate, Dept of Pol Sci, U of Yale; 1968-70 Lecturer, Dept of Government, U of Essex; 1970-71 Visiting Lecturer, Dept of Pol Sci, U of Yale; 1970 and 1971 Guest Professor, Inst of Advanced Studies, Vienna; 1973-74 Fellow, Netherlands Inst for Advanced Study; 1971- Senior Lecturer, Dept of Government, U of Essex. Publs: *An Analysis of Political Cleavages* (with D Rae), 1970; *Anarchy and Cooperation*, 1976. Fields: Political theory, including theories of anarchy; the state and collective action.

[1887]
TAYLOR Paul Graham
24 January 1939, British. London School of Economics and Political Science, Houghton Street, Aldwych, London WC2, England. Degrees: BA; MSc (Aberystwyth), 1968. 1964-66 Assistant Lecturer, U of Liverpool; 1964-66 Lecturer, U of Hull; 1966- Lecturer, LSE. Publs: *International Co-operation Today: The Universal and the European Pattern*, 1971; *Functionalism, Theory and Practice* (with A J R Groom (eds)), 1975; *International Organizations: A Conceptual Approach* (with A J R Groom), 1977. Fields: Integration theory, particularly functionalism; philosophical aspects of international relations; West European integration; international organization.

[1888]
TAYLOR Richard
16 January 1946, British. Department of Politics, University College, Singleton Park, Swansea, Wales. Degrees: MA (Cantab), 1967; PhD (London), 1977. Doctoral thesis: "The Politics of the Soviet Cinema, 1917-1929". Lecturer in Pol, U Coll of Swansea. Publs: "A Medium for the Masses: Agitation in the Soviet Civil War", *Soviet Studies*, 1971; "The Soviet Cinema 1960-1970: A Bibliography", in *ABSEES Information Bulletin*, 1972; "From October to *October*: The Soviet Political System and its Films", in *Politics and Film* (M J Clark (ed)), 1978; *Film Propaganda*, 1978; *Marxism and the Russian Labour Movement: Key Documents* (with N Harding), 1978. Fields: Propaganda.

[1889]
TAYLOR Trevor
20 August 1946, British. 17 The Avenue, Stone, Staffordshire, England. Degrees: BSc; MA (Lehigh); PhD (London). Doctoral thesis: "Arms Supplies in US Policy towards the Middle East 1950-68". 1971-72 Maghreb Ed, *The Middle East Economic Digest*; 1972- Lecturer, Senior Lecturer, Principal Lecturer in International Relations, North Staffordshire Polytechnic. Publs: *Theories and Approaches in International Relations* (ed and contributor), 1978; "International Studies in Polytechnics", in *Case Studies in Interdisciplinarity*, 1975; "Force in the Relations Between the Great Powers and the Third World", in *The Use of Force in International Relations* (F S Northedge (ed)), 1974; "President Nixon's Arms Supply Policies", in *The Year Book of World Affairs*, 1972; "The Control of the Arms Trade", *International Relations*, 1971; "Economic Survey", articles on Algeria, Libya and Morocco, in *The Middle East and North Africa*, 1972, 1973, 1974. Fields: Arms transfers; NATO rationalization; standardization; international relations theory.

[1890]
TEIGLAND Gunnar
7 November 1929, Norwegian. N Skansemyren 8a, 5000 Bergen, Norway. Degrees: Magistergrad — Statsvitenskap (Oslo), 1956. Journalist, Associated Press, Oslo; Journalist, *Dagen*, Bergen; 1961-68 Leader, Humanistic Seminar, Christian Michelsens Inst, Bergen; Research Fellow, Inst of Soc, U of Bergen; Lecturer, Bergen Pedagogiske Högskole. Publs: "The Decision-Making Process" (contributor), in *Economic Policy in our Time* (E S Kirchen *et al* (eds)), 1964; "Embedsmakt mot Folkevilje", *Syn og Segn*, 1973. Fields: The popular movements in Norwegian democracy.

[1891]
TEMPESTINI Attilio
7 August 1947, Italian. Via Magenta 51, 10128 Turin, Italy. Degrees: Degree in Law (Bari), 1969. Inst of Pol Sci, U of Turin. Publs: "La Ricorrente Presenza degli Eccellenti Staffieri", *Critica Sociale*, 1974; "Le Elezioni sono un Test Ambiguo", *Critica Sociale*, 1977; "Un Decennale in Sordina", *Critica Sociale*, 1977; "Partiti 'Antisistema' e Partiti 'di Sinistra' ", *Rassegna Italiana di Sociologia*, 1975; "Il Problema dei Partiti in Ostrogorski", *Quaderni di Sociologia*, 1976; *Il Terzaforzista Recidivo*, 1975. Fields: Italian parties; political parties.

[1892]
TERRENOIRE Jean-Paul
24 September 1937, French. 25 rue de la Fosse-Rouge, 94370 Sucy en Brie, France. Degrees: Dr (Paris). Doctoral thesis: "Structure économique et pratiques religieuses. Analyse statistique d'un millier de cantons ruraux français et essai d'interpretation théorique". Assistant de recherche, Centre de Recherches Econ et Soc Appliquées, Paris; Professeur adjoint, Dept de Soc, Faculté des Sci Soc, U d'Ottawa; Chargé de Recherche au Groupe de Soc des Religions, CNRS. Publs: *Atlas de la pratique culturelle des catholiques en France* (with F A Isambert), 1978. Fields: Economic structure; electoral behaviour and religious practice; quantitative ecological analysis: ideological proceedings and methods; the role of the modern state; sociological analysis of the techniques and instruments of mass mobilization; secular and religious rituals; historic study of the transferences of acquisition.

[1893]
TERVASNÄKI Vilho Olavi
11 July 1915, Finnish. P Hesperiankatu 37 A 19, SF-00260 Helsinki, Finland. Doctoral thesis: "Eduskuntaryhmät ja Maanpuolustus Valtiopäivillä 1917-1939" (The Finnish Parliamentary Groups and National Defence in the Diet 1917-1939). 1951-66 Officer and Chief of Information Service, General Staff; 1966-67 Chief of Staff of Military Area; 1967-69 Chief of Defence Academy; 1970-75 Chief of Inst of Military Science; 1972- Lecturer, Technical U of Lappeenranta; 1976- Lecturer, U of Helsinki. Publs: *Puolustusministeriön Historia I-II*, 1973; *The Defence Administration in War and Peace 1938-1978* (with M V Terä), 1978; *Talvisodan Historia* (with A Juutilainen *et al*), 1977. Fields: Military administration; operations and security politics.

[1894]
TESAURO Paulo
11 October 1934, Italian. Via San Filippo 20/F, Naples, Italy. Degrees: Laurea (Naples). Doctoral thesis: "La Radio e la Televisione nell'Ordinamento Costituzionale Italiano". Assistant Professor, U of Naples; Full Professor, U of Cagliari and Bari; Full Professor of Constitutional Law, U of Naples; Attorney at Law. Publs: *L'Ordinamento del Civil Service negli Stati Uniti*. Fields: Public law.

[1895]
TEXIER Jean C
29 January 1949, French. 40 Boulevard Garibaldi, 75015 Paris, France. 1970-74 Deputy Editor, Combat; 1975-76 Special Advisor of the President, EDS International; Ed, *La Bibliothèque des Médias*; Lecturer, Ecole Supérieure de Commerce de Paris. Publs: *La presse quotidienne française*, 1974; *La publicité de A à Z*, 1975. Fields: Mass communication.

[1896]
THAYSEN Uwe
9 September 1940, German. Behrkampsweg 20k, 2000 Hamburg 54, FR Germany. Degrees: Dr. Doctoral thesis: "Der Konflikt Erzberger contra Helfferich". U of Hamburg; Professor, Gesamthochschule, Nordortniedermachsen. Publs: *Parlamentsreform*; *Parlamentarisches Regierungssystem*; *Politische Planung in Parteien und Fraktionen*; *Bürgerinitiativen und Kommunalverfassung*. Fields: Parliamentary questions.

[1897]
THIEME Hans Werner Hermann
13 October 1923, German. 2000 Hamburg 63, Am Karpfenteich 58, FR Germany. Degrees: Dr jur. 1956-62 Professor, U of Saarlandes; 1962- Professor, Geschäftsführender Direktor des Seminars für Verwaltungslehre, U of Hamburg. Publs: *Verwaltungslehre*, 1977; *Föderalismus im Wandel*, 1970; *Mängel im Verhältnis von Bürger und Staat*, 1970; *Kommentar zum Allgemeinen Teil des Sozialgesetzbuchs*, 1977. Fields: Public administration; problems of higher education.

[1898]
THIENEL Ingrid Anna Johanna
24 February 1938, German. 1 Berlin 33, Schorlemer Allee 19, FR Germany. Degrees: PhD (Berlin). Assistant Professor, Free U of Berlin. Publs: *Städtewachstum im Industrialisierungsprozess des 19 Jahrhunderts. Das Berliner Beispiel*, 1973. Fields: Industrialization and urbanization; political socialization.

[1899]
THOENIG Jean Claude
18 December 1940, French. Les Hugons, F-33336 Quinsac, France. Degrees: Dr Sociology. Professeur de Soc, Federal Inst of Technology, Switzerland; Senior Research Fellow, Centre de Soc des Organisations, Paris; Directeur de recherche, Centre d'Etude et de Recherche sur la Vie Locale IEP, Bordeaux. Fields: Public policy making; transportation; local government; organizational and political factors in government.

[1900]
THOMAS Alastair Hugh
18 July 1941, British. 28 Kingswood Avenue, Leicester LE3 0UN, England. Degrees: BSc. Senior Lecturer in Government, Leicester Polytechnic. Publs: *Parliamentary Parties in Denmark 1945-1972*, 1973; "Danish Social Democracy and the European Community", *Journal of Common Market Studies*, 1975; "Social Democracy in Denmark", in *Social Democratic Parties in Western Europe* (E Paterson and H Thomas (eds)), 1977; "The Formation of Cabinets in Denmark 1945-1977", in *Cabinet Coalitions in Western Democracies* (E C Browne and J Dreijmanis (eds)), 1978. Fields: Comparative government and politics with special reference to smaller European democracies, especially Denmark, and to political parties and legislative behaviour.

[1901]
THOMAS Neil Martin*
23 November 1942, British. Institute of Local Government Studies, University of Birmingham, Box 363, Birmingham B15 2TT, England. Degrees: BSc. 1965- Research Assistant, Assistant Lecturer, Dept of Soc Administration, U of Birmingham; Lecturer, Inst of Local Government Studies, U of Birmingham. Publs: *Business Studies — A Guide to First Degree Courses in UK Universities and Colleges*, 1969. Fields: The reorganization of personal social services in Britain; social planning; community development; social deprivation.

[1902]
THOMASSEN Jacques
23 September 1945, Dutch. Albert Sommerstraat 5, Hengelo, The Netherlands. Degrees: Dr. Doctoral thesis: "Kiezers en Gekozenen in een Representatieve Demokratie". Catholic U of Tilburg; Professor in Pol Sci,Dept of Public Administration, U of Technology, Twente. Publs: *Kiezers en Gekozenen in een Representatieve Demokratie*, 1976; "Party Identification as a Cross-National Concept", in *Party Identification and Beyond* (I Budge *et al* (eds)), 1976; "Issue — Consensus in a Multiparty System: Voters and Leaders in the Netherlands" (with G Irwin), *Acta Politica*, 1975. Fields: Voting behaviour; representation; Dutch politics.

[1903]
THOMSEN Kirsten
3 March 1937, Danish. Sneppevaenget 203, 2980 Kokkedal, Denmark. Degrees: Mag sci soc. Lektor, Inst for Samfundsfag, U of Copenhagen.

[1904]
THOMSEN Neils
21 April 1930, Danish. Christiansholms Parallelvej 1, 2930 Klampenborg, Denmark. Degrees: PhD, 1972. Doctoral thesis: "Newspaper Competition in Denmark 1870-1970. Politics journalism and economics in the rise and fall of a competitive party press system" (in Danish). 1962-65 Lecturer, Danish School of Journalism; 1965-71 Lecturer, U of Copenhagen; 1971-73 Lecturer in Pol Sci, U of Copenhagen; 1973- Professor of

Modern History, U of Copenhagen. Publs: *Partipressen*, 1965; *Scandinavian Political Studies* (contributor), 1968; *Scandinavia at the Polls* (contributor), 1977. Fields: Communications; public opinion; political parties.

[1905]
THORNDIKE Anthony Edward
28 October 1941, British. 17 Burton Manor Road, Stafford, England. BSc, 1964; MSc (London), 1966. Head of International Relations and Dept of Pol, North Staffordshire Polytechnic. Publs: "The Revolutionary Approach; The Marxist Perspective", in *Approaches and Theory in International Relations* (T Taylor (ed)), 1978; *Associated Statehood and the Eastern Caribbean*. Fields: *International relations; Marxism;* Caribbean studies.

[1906]
THORNHILL William
20 March 1920, British. Department of Political Theory and Institutions, The University, Sheffield S10 2TN, England. Degrees: BSc; MSc (London), 1948. 1938-46 Local Government Officer, Nottingham County Council; 1946-48 Civics Research Fellow, Natal U Coll, Durban; 1948- Lecturer, Senior Lecturer in Pol Theory and Inst, U of Sheffield. Publs: *Central Control of Local Government*, 1954; *The Nationalized Industries: An Introduction*, 1968; *The Growth and Reform of English Local Government*, 1971; *The Case for Regional Reform*, 1972; *The Modernization of British Government*, 1975; "Government and Administration Series" (consulting ed); *Centre Forward* (ed). Fields: The structure, organization, management and control of local authorities and nationalized industries; the structure and management of the central administration, including the Cabinet and the Civil Service.

[1907]
THOVERON Gabriel Louis Edmond
19 August 1931, French. 27 rue des Hellènes, 1050 Bruxelles, Belgium. Degrees: Dr. Doctoral thesis: "Radio et télévision dans la vie quotidienne". Président, Section de Journalisme et Communication, U de Bruxelles; Directeur, Centre d'Etudes des Techniques de Diffusion Collective. Publs: *Radio et télévision dans la vie quotidienne*, 1971; *La télévision fait-elle les élections* (with J G Blumler and R Cayrol); various articles in *Res Publica*, *Etudes de Radio et Télévision*. Fields: Mass media; electoral campaigns.

[1908]
THRÄNHARDT Dietrich Joachim
31 May 1941, German. Am Linnenkamp 2, D-44 Münster, FR Germany. Degrees: Lic rer Soc (Konstanz); Habilitation (Münster). Doctoral thesis: "Parteien und Wahlen in Bayern 1948-1953. Historisch-soziologische Untersuchungen zur Entstehung und zur Restauration eines Parteiensystems". Wiss Assistent, Dozent PH Westfalen-Lippe, Abteilung Münster. Publs: *Die Bundesrepublik Deutschland. Verfassung und politisches System*, 1974; *Funktionalreform — Probleme und Alternativen* (ed), 1977; *Schule heute. Eine Einführung in die Erziehungswissenschaften* (ed), 1977; plus various articles on the problems of foreign workers, local administration, political education and church politics. Fields: Foreign workers; local administration and politics; educational policy-making.

[1909]
TIJMSTRA Rommert Sybren
25 April 1948, Dutch. Meidoornstraat 1, Bussum, The Netherlands. Degrees: Kand Pol Wetenschappen (Amsterdam); Drs Pol Wetenschappen (Amsterdam). Research Staff, Dutch Ministry of Defence; Assistant to the President of Nijenrode, The Netherlands

School of Business. Publs: "Incorporating Ethics in Business Decision-Making", in *Trends in Business Ethics. Implications for Decision-Making* (C van Dam and L M Stallaer (eds)), 1978; *Gedrag van Bondgenoten in de Verenigde Naties*, 1975; *De Dominicaanse Republiek en haar Afhankelijkheid van de Verenigde Staten* (with J de Bock and T van Kleef), 1974; *United States Decision Not to Intervene Militarily in Laos 1960-1961*, 1973; *De Cubaanse Rakettencrisis — Oktober 1962*, 1972. Fields: International relations; multinationals; international public law.

[1910]
TILL Geoffrey
14 January 1945, British. 2 Burleigh Close, Crawley Down, Sussex, England. Degrees: BA; MA (London), 1968; PhD (London), 1976. Doctoral thesis: "The Impact of Airpower on the Royal Navy 1918-1930". 1968-72 Lecturer in History, Britannia R N Coll, Dartmouth; 1972- Senior Lecturer, Dept of History and International Affairs, R N Coll, Greenwich; Visiting Lecturer in International Relations, Dept of Systems Sci, The City U. Publs: "The Admiralty and Airpower", in *The Royal Navy and Technical Change* (B Ranft (ed)), 1977; "The Safeguard Debate: Image and Reality", *RUSI Journal*, 1974. Fields: Modern naval history; strategic studies.

[1911]
TIMONEN Pertti Aaree Sulevi
2 January 1943, Finnish. Karbunkatu 8 A 1, 33530 Tampere 53, Finland. Degrees: M soc sci (Tampere), 1967; Lic (Tampere), 1972; Dr soc sci (Tampere), 1976. Doctoral thesis: "Kansanedustajaehdokkaan Alueellisen Kannatuspohjan Määräytyminen" (Analysis of Regional Support for Parliamentary Candidates). 1968-74 Assistant in Pol Sci, U of Tampere; 1974-76 Research Assistant of the Finnish Academy; 1976- Assistant in Pol Sci, U of Tampere. Publs: *Kansanedustajaehdokkaan Alueellisen Kannatuspohjan Määräytyminen*, 1976; plus articles in *Politiikka*. Fields: Elections; parties; political behaviour; primaries.

[1912]
TINKER Hugh Russell
20 July 1921, British. Montbegon, Hornby, Lancaster, England. Degrees: BA; Dipl in Public Administration (London), 1948; MA (Cambridge), 1950; PhD, 1951. 1948-58 Lecturer in History, SOAS, U of London; 1958-63 Reader, U of London; 1963-69 Professor of Government and Pol, U of London; Director, Inst of Race Relations; 1977-Professor of Pol, U of Lancaster. Publs: *Ballot Box and Bayonet, People and Government in Emergent Asian Countries*, 1969; *Reorientation, Studies on Asia in Transition*, 1965; *South Asia, A Short History*, 1965; *Experiment with Freedom, India and Pakistan 1947*, 1967; *A New System of Slavery: The Export of Indian Labour Overseas 1830-1920*, 1974; *Separate and Unequal: India and the Indian in the British Empire 1920-50*, 1976; *The Banyan Tree: Overseas Emigrants from India, Pakistan and Bangladesh*, 1977; *Race, Conflict and the International Order*, 1977. Fields: Race problems in the Third World, especially relations of Indian communities overseas with local communities.

[1913]
TIVEY Leonard James
3 June 1926, British. 726 Shirley Road, Birmingham B28 9LF, England. Degrees: BSc. 1953-60 Research Officer, Pol and Economic Planning; Senior Lecturer in Pol Sci, U of Birmingham. Publs: co-author of PEP reports on *Industrial Trade Associations*; 1957; *Advisory Committees in British Government*, 1960; *Nationalization in British Industry*, 1973; *The Nationalized Industries since 1960* (ed), 1973; *The Politics of the Firm*, 1978. Fields: Political aspects of business enterprise; the consumer movement; political theory in relation to the economy.

[1914]
TJADEN Karl Hermann*
18 June 1935, German. Schwanallee 4, D-355 Marburg, FR Germany. Degrees: Dipl Soziologe (Frankfurt), 1961; Dr phil (Marburg), 1963; Habilitation (Marburg), 1969. Doctoral thesis: "Struktur und Funktion der 'KPD-Opposition', Eine organisationssoziologische Untersuchung zur 'Rechtsopposition' im deutschen Kommunismus zur Zeit der Weimarer Republik". 1969 Vertretung Professor Soziologie, U of Giessen, Vertretung Professor Soziologie, Director, Soziologisches Inst, U of Marburg; 1970-Professor of Sociology, U of Marburg. Publs: *Struktur und Funktion der 'KPD-Opposition'. Rechtsopposition im deutschen Kommunismus zur Zeit der Weimarer Republik*, 1970; *Soziales System und sozialer Wandel*, 1972; *Grundriss eines Bezugsrahmens der Analyse sozialer Mobilität*, 1969; *Soziale Systeme* (co-author), 1971; *Klassenverhältnisse im Spätkapitalismus* (co-author), 1973. Fields: Social structure of capitalism; functions of the state; social and political problems of urban development in contemporary capitalism; historico-materialist theory of social systems.

[1915]
TOGEBY Lise
6 June 1942, Danish. Korshøjen 53, 8240 Risskov, Denmark. Degrees: Cand sci pol (Aarhus). Lecturer, Inst of Pol Sci, U of Aarhus. Publs: *Var de Så Røde*, 1968; *Den Vopslidelige Laerebog* (with Jarlov), 1978; *Underuddannelse og Underbeskaetigelse*, 1975. Fields: Political socialization; political participation; unemployment; sociology of education; educational politics.

[1916]
TOHARIA José Juan
28 October 1942, Spanish. Eurogar B, Las Rozas, Madrid, Spain. Degrees: PhD (Yale), 1974; LL D (Madrid), 1971. Doctoral thesis: "The Spanish Judiciary: A Sociological Study. Justice in a Civil Law Country Undergoing Social Change under an Authoritarian Regime", 1974; Profesor Agregado de Soc, U Autonoma de Madrid. Publs: *Cambio Social y Vide Jurídica en España*, 1974; *El Juez Español: Un Análisis Sociológica*, 1975. Fields: Political sociology: ideologies, political parties, electoral behaviour; sociology of the judiciary; sociology of law.

[1917]
TOINET Marie-France
11 January 1942, French. 21 rue du Vieux Colombier, 75006 Paris, France. Degrees: Dipl (IEP Paris); Dr de recherche. Doctoral thesis: "Georges Boris, un socialiste humaniste". Chargée de recherche, FNSP. Publs: *Georges Boris, un socialiste humaniste*; *Le congrès des Etats-Unis*; various articles in *Revue Française de Science Politique, Etudes, Projet, Revue de Défense Nationale, France-Forum, Politique Aujourd'hui, La NEF*. Fields: American and comparative politics, especially legislative behaviour and defence policy.

[1918]
TOMASISCH Heinz Ludwig
17 May 1945, Austrian. Nattergasse 1-3/33, A-1170 Wien, Austria. Teacher, Mitarbeiter, Europahaus, Vienna. Fields: Foreign policy; small states; pedagogy and politics.

[1919]
TOONEN Theo A J
12 April 1952, Dutch. Homberg 1207, Wijchen, The Netherlands. Degrees: MA. Assistant Professor in Pol Sci and Public Administration, Erasmus U of Rotterdam. Fields: Planning; policy-implementation; public order; public choice/modern political economy.

[1920]
TORDOFF William
23 October 1925, British. Department of Government, University of Manchester, Manchester 13, England. Degrees: BA; MA (Cambridge), 1955; PhD (London), 1961. Doctoral thesis: "A Political History of Ashanti, 1888-1935". 1950-62 U of Ghana; 1962- U of Manchester; 1963-64 Senior Lecturer in Public Administration, U Coll, Dar-es-Salaam; 1966-68 Professor of Pol Sci, U of Zambia; Professor of Government, U of Manchester. Publs: *Ashanti Under the Prempehs*, 1965; *Government and Politics in Tanzania*, 1976; *Politics in Zambia* (ed), 1974. Fields: Zambian politics and administration; a comparative study of administration in new Commonwealth States; the EEC and Association.

[1921]
TÖRNUDD Klaus Mattias
26 December 1931, Finnish. Måanskensgatan 5 A, SF-02210 Esbo 21, Finland. Degrees: Pol mag (Helsinki), 1956; Pol lic (Helsinki), 1959; Pol dr (Helsinki), 1961. Doctoral thesis: "Soviet Attitudes Towards Non-military Regional Cooperation". 1967-71 Professor of International Pol, U of Tampere; 1971- Director of Pol Affairs, Ministry for Foreign Affairs of Finland, and (Part-time) Reader in Pol Sci, U of Helsinki. Publs: *Suomi ja Yhdistyneet Kansakunnat*, 1968; *The Electoral System of Finland*, 1968. Fields: Contemporary international politics and Finnish politics; human rights.

[1922]
TORRANCE John Robert
26 October 1933, British. 17 Linkside Avenue, Oxford, England. Degrees: BA; MA. Research Fellow, Nuffield College, Oxford; 1974 Visiting Lecturer, U of Auckland; Lecturer in Soc and Pol Theory, U of Oxford, Tutor in Pol, Hertford College, Oxford. Publs: "The Emergence of Sociology in Austria 1885-1935", *European Journal of Sociology*, 1975; "Social Class and Bureaucratic Innovation", *Past and Present*, 1978; *Estrangement, Alienation and Exploitation*, 1977. Fields: History and comparative sociology of bureaucracy; history of social and political theory; history of social sciences in Germany and Austria; Marxist theory.

[1923]
TOURNON Jean
15 February 1935, French. BP 17, 38040 Grenoble, France. Degrees: Dipl (IEP Paris), 1957; DES (Paris), 1965; Dr ès sci pol. Doctoral thesis: "Sociologie de l'action culturelle". 1959-62 Teaching Assistant, U of California, Berkeley; 1962-65 Chargé d'enseignement, U de Montréal; 1965-71 Assistant, U de Grenoble; 1971- Chargé de recherches, FNSP, CERAT-IEP, Grenoble. Publs: "Perceptions et demandes sociales en matière d'environnement", in *Socio-Economie de l'Environnement*, 1973; "Travail, espace et groupes sociaux", in *Annuaire de l'Aménagement du Territoire*, 1976; "Les avatars de l'opposition", in *Dialectique Gouvernement-Opposition,* 1977; *Cours d'introduction à la science politique*, 1977. Fields: Group theory; representation.

[1924]
TOUSCOZ Jean
16 June 1935, French. 4 rue Charles Péguy 06034 Nice, France. Degrees: Dr en droit; Agrégé en droit. Doctoral thesis: "Le principe d'effectivité dans l'ordre international". 1965 Maître de conférences, U de Dijon; 1966- Maître de conférences agrégé, Professeur, U de Nice; Président, U de Nice. Publs: *Le principe d'effectivité dans l'ordre international*, 1964; *La politique scientifique de l'Italie*; *La coopération scientifique internationale*, 1973; *Les cadres juridiques de la coopération scientifique internationale en Europe*, 1970; "La coopération internationale entre pays francophones", *Etudes Internationales*, 1974; *L'évaluation de la coopération Nord-Sud*, 1976; *La coopération scientifique et technique entre les Etats membres de l'UDEAC* (co-ed), 1977; *Transfert de technologie, firmes multinationales et nouvel ordre international* (ed). Fields: International public law, development law, international policy and relations; international institutions and organizations; miltinationals.

[1925]
TRAVERS David Thomas
15 March 1942, British. Rosedene, 4 Eden Park, Lancaster, England. Degrees: BA. 1964-75 Tutor, LSE; 1965-68 Assistant Lecturer, Dept of Pol, U of Lancaster; 1969 Visiting Assistant Professor, U of Waterloo, Ontario; 1971 Visiting Scholar, Inst of War and Peace Studies, U of Columbia, New York; 1968- Lecturer, U of Lancaster. Fields: Britain and the UN; Secretary-General U-Thant and his contribution to international peace and security; United States foreign policy since 1945, especially during the Truman years.

[1926]
TREVES Giuseppino*
8 January 1909, Italian. Largo Millefonti 39/1, 10126 Torino, Italy. Degrees: Dr of Law (Turin), 1930. Professor of Administrative Law, U of Trieste, U of Pavia; Professor of Public Law, U of Turin; Professor, International Faculty for the Teaching of Comparative Law, Strasbourg. Publs: *La Presunzione di Legittimità degli Atti Amminsitrativi*, 1936; *Il Commonwealth Britannico*, 1950; *Le Imprese Pubbliche*, 1950; *Government Organization for Economic Development*, 1963; *L'Organizzazione Amministrativa*, 1967; *Principi di Diritto Pubblico*, 1971. Fields: Comparative public law; administrative organization; public enterprise; judicial control of legislation and administration; constitutional practices; jurisprudence.

[1927]
TROITZSCH Klaus Gerhard
28 November 1946, German. Furchenacker 7 B, 2000 Hamburg 54, FR Germany. Degrees: Dipl (Hamburg). Assistant Secretary, Liberal Party Group, Land Hamburg; 1974-77 Whip of the Liberal Party Group, Parliament of Hamburg; 1974- Member of the Parliament of Hamburg. Publs: *Sozialstruktur und Wahlerverhalten: Möglichkeit und Grenzen ökologischer Wahlanalyse, dargestellt aus Beispiel der Wahlen in Hamburg von 1949 bis 1974*, 1976. Fields: Voting behaviour; parliament; party systems; mathematical methods.

[1928]
TROMMER Aage
9 November 1930, Danish. DK-5260 Odense SV, Denmark. Degrees: Dr phil, 1971. Doctoral thesis: "Jernbanesabotagen i Danmark under den anden Verdenskrig". Lecturer, U of Odense; 1974- Rector, U of Odense. Publs: *Folkestrejken i Esbjer August 1943*, 1966; *Jernbanesabotagen i Danmark under den anden Verdenskrig*, 1971; *Modstandsarbejde i Naerbillede det Illegale Arbejde i Syd og Sønderjylland under den*

Tyske Besaettelse af Danmark, 1973; *Myte og Sandhed i Besaetielseshestorien*, 1974; *Hiters Udenregspolitik, Realiteter contra Visioner*, 1976. Fields: Danish and European history 1933-45.

[1929]
TROPER Michel
9 April 1938, French. 19 rue d'Hautpoul, 76 Rouen, France. Degrees: Dr en droit. Doctoral thesis: "La séparation des pouvoirs et l'histoire constitutionnelle française". Faculté de Droit, Paris; Professeur, U de Rouen. Publs: *La séparation des pouvoirs et l'histoire constitutionnelle française*, 1974; *Réinventer le parlement*, 1978. Fields: Philosophy of law; political philosophy; sociology of law; government.

[1930]
TSOUKALIS Loukas
26 April 1950, Greek. St Catherine's College, Oxford, England. Degrees: BA; Dipl in European Studies (Coll of Europe); MA; D Phil (Oxon). Doctoral thesis: "National Policies and Interests in European Monetary Integration". 1975-76 Research Fellow, St Anthony's Coll, U of Oxford; 1976- Charles E Merrill Research Fellow in European Studies, St Catherine's Coll, U of Oxford. Publs: *The Politics and Economics of European Monetary Integration*. 1977; *Greece and the European Community* (ed), 1978; plus various articles in *Journal of Common Market Studies, International Affairs, Europa Archiv*. Fields: European integration; international political economy; Greece.

[1931]
TUDESQ André Jean
21 June 1927, French. 98 rue de Brach, 33 Bordeaux, France. Degrees: Agrégé d'histoire; Dr ès lettres. Doctoral thesis: "Les grands notables en France 1840-1849; étude historique d'une psychologie sociale". Assistant d'histoire contemporaine, Sorbonne; Maître de conférences, Faculté des Lettres, U de Bordeaux; Professor of Contemporary History, Directeur, Centre d'Etudes de Presse, U de Bordeaux III; Professeur, IEP, Bordeaux. Publs: *Les conseillers généraux au temps de Guizot*, 1967; *L'élection présidentielle de Louis-Napoléon Bonaparte*, 1965; *La démocratie en France depuis 1815*, 1971; *La France des notables* (co-author), 1973; *L'histoire générale de la presse française* (co-author), 1969; *L'histoire de la France* (G Duby (ed)); *Histoire de Bordeaux*, 1969; *Romantisme et politique*, 1969; *Annuaire de la Presse*, 1974. Fields: Local power in France; the press; broadcasting.

[1932]
TUDOR Henry
19 January 1937, British. 53 New Road, Oakenshaw, Nr Crook, Co Durham, England. Degrees: BA. Assistant Ed, *Transatlantic Review*; Research Assistant, LSE; Temporary Part-time Lecturer, School of Slavonic and East European Studies; Senior Lecturer in Pol, U of Durham. Publs: *Political Myth*, 1971. Fields: Political myths; the problems of practical reasoning; 16th century French political thought.

[1933]
TUDYKA Kurt Paul
14 April 1935, German. Berg En Dal, Oude Kleesebaan 130, The Netherlands. Degrees: Dipl rer Pol; Dr rer Pol. Doctoral thesis; "System und Politik der Mindestreserve". Assoc Professor, U of Erlangen-Nürberg; Prof in Pol Sci, U of Nijmegen. Publs: *Internationale Politik*, 1971; *Kritische Politikwissenschaft*, 1974; *Multinationale Konzerne und Gewerkschaftstrategie* (ed), 1974; *Marktplatz Europa*, 1975. Fields: Inter- and intrarelations of the European Community; international labour unions; international economic relations.

[1934]
TUNC André Robert
3 May 1917, French. 112 rue de Vaugirard, 75006 Paris, France. Degrees: Agrégé de droit; Dr en droit. 1943-47, 1950-58 Professeur de droit, U de Grenoble; 1947-50 Counsellor, International Monetary Fund; 1947-58 Counsellor, Commission Economique pour l'Europe; 1958- Professeur, Faculté de Droit, U de Paris I. Publs: *Le contrat de garde*, 1941; *Le particulier service de l'ordre public*, 1942; *Le système constitutionnel des Etats-Unis d'Amérique*, 1953-54; *Le droit des Etats-Unis d'Amérique*, 1974; *Dans un monde qui souffre*, 1968; *Le droit anglais des sociétés anonymes*, 1971. Fields: American constitutional law; comparative law; corporation law.

[1935]
TUNSTALL Jeremy C
14 October 1934, British. 5 College Cross, Islington, London N1 1PT, England. Degrees: MA (Cambridge). 1961-64 Research Officer, LSE; 1964-69 Fellow, U of Essex; 1969-74 Senior Lecturer; Open U; 1974- Professor of Soc, City U; 1974-77 Consultant to Royal Commission on the Press. Publs: *The Advertising Man*, 1964; *Old and Alone*, 1966; *The Westminster Lobby Correspondents*, 1970; *Journalists at Work*, 1971; *The Media are American*, 1977; *Media Sociology* (ed), 1970; *Sociological Perspectives* (with K Thompson (eds)), 1972; *The Open University Opens* (ed), 1974. Fields: Mass communications; policy making; comparative studies of national systems; communications/occupations; journalism education.

[1936]
TUOMI Helena
8 August 1943, Finnish. Kohmankaari 1 A 1, Tampere 31, Finland. Degrees: Master (Helsinki), 1968. 1972-73 Acting Research Assistant, Tampere Peace Research Inst; 1974- Assistant in International Pol, U of Tampere. Publs: *Dominanssi Kansainvälisessä Järjesteimässä*, 1972; *Suomi ja Kolmas Maailma* (co-author), 1976; "On Food Imports and Neocolonialism", in *Political Economy of Food* (V Harle (ed)), 1978. Fields: The developing countries in the international system; the structure of international food trade; Finland and the developing countries; peace research.

[1937]
TUPMAN William Arthur
10 April 1948, British. 2 Redgate Cottages, Plymtree, Cullompton, Devonshire, England. Degrees: BA. Lecturer, Dept of Pol, U of Exeter. Publs: *Purges and Government Expansion: A Comparison of the Soviet Great Purge, the Chinese Cultural Revolution and the American Loyalty Security Programme*. Fields: Urban guerillas; political violence; Soviet studies; comparative work in general.

[1938]
TWADDLE Michael John
28 March 1939, British. 79 Davencourt Road, London SE22, England. Degrees: BA; MA (Cambridge), 1965; PhD (London), 1967. Doctoral thesis: "Politics in Bukedi (Uganda), 1900-1939". 1967-70 Lecturer in History, Makerere U, Uganda; 1970-72 School of Oriental and African Studies, U of London; 1972- Lecturer in African Pol and History, Inst of Commonwealth Studies, U of London; Ed, *African Affairs*, 1974. Publs: Articles in academic journals and symposia on African politics. Fields: African politics.

U

[1939]
UCAKAR Karl
7 June 1947, Austrian. Fraungrubergasse 4/5/4, A-1120 Wien, Austria. Degrees: Dr jur. Assistant, Inst für Politikwissenschaft, U of Wien. Publs: "Die Entwicklung des Verbändewesens in Österreich", in *Das politische System Österreichs* (H Fischer), 1974; "Kommunale Selbstverwaltung und konstitutioneller Rechtsstaat" (with M Welan), in *Forschungen und Beiträge zur Wiener Stadtgeschichte*, 1978. Fields: Voting rights; communal history.

[1940]
UGEUX William Paul
20 February 1909, Belgian. 1 rue Dereune, Box 27, B-1330 Rixensart, Belgium. Degrees: Dr en droit; Dipl en philosophie. Doctoral thesis: "Les Relations Publiques". Professeur, Faculté de Sci Econ, U de Louvain. Publs: *Les relations publiques*, 1972; *Le groupe G*, 1978. Fields: Political information; the media; public opinion; public relations.

[1941]
ULERI Pier Vincenzo
25 May 1950, Italian. Borgo Santa Groce 5, 50122 Florence, Italy. Degrees: Dipl di Laurea. Doctoral thesis: "Opinione Pubblica e Integrazione Europea — Un' Analisi Empirica". Researcher, Centro Studi di Sci Pol, Florence. Publs: *Partecipazione e Istituti di Democrazia Diretta*, 1978. Fields: Empirical analysis of attitudes with special reference to the problem of European political integration.

[1942]
ULRAM Peter A
31 March 1951, Austrian. Franzensbrückenstrasse 22/12, A-1020 Wien, Austria. Degrees: Dr phil (Vienna); Dipl (Inst for Advanced Studies). Doctoral thesis: "Öffentliche Planung in Wien: Modelle der Partizipation an Planungsprozessen" (Public Planning in Vienna; Models of Participation in Planning Processes). Researcher, U of Vienna; Bundesleitung des ÖAAB, Dept of Research and Sci. Publs: "Planungspartizipation als öffentlichkeitsarbeit der Verwaltung: zur Wiener Stadtentwicklungsplanung", *Österreichische Zeitschrift für Politikwissenschaft*, 1977; *Zwischen Bürokratie und Bürger: Sozialistische Kommunalpolitik in Wien, Bologna und Stockholm*, 1978; plus various articles on participation and city-planning. Fields: Public planning; local government and participation; comparative politics and political culture.

[1943]
UNDERDAL Arild
13 August 1946, Norwegian. Grusveien 42, Oslo 11, Norway. Degrees: Mag art. 1973-76 Research Assistant, Inst of Pol Sci; 1977 Visiting Research Fellow, CFIA, Harvard U; 1977 Visiting Research Fellow, Inst for Marine Studies, U of Washington; Research Fellow (NAVF), Inst of Pol Sci, U of Oslo, and Research Associate, Fr Nansen Foundation, Lysaker. Publs: *The Negotiations on Norwegian Membership of the EEC* (in Norwegian), 1972; "Multinational Negotiation Parties; The Case of the EEC", *Cooperation and Conflict*, 1973; "An Approach to the Politics of International Regulations", *Cooperation and Conflict*, 1976; "Multiparty Conferences" (with K Midgaard), in *Negotiations: Social-Psychological Perspectives* (D Druckman (ed)),

1977. Fields: International negotiations and bargaining; international regulations of resource exploitation, particularly marine fisheries; foreign policy decision-making.

[1944]
UPPENDAHL Herbert
9 February 1944, German. Im Eichengrund 27, 442 Coesfeld, FR Germany. Degrees: PhD (Freiburg). Doctoral thesis: "Parlamentarismus im politischen Roman". Lecturer in Pol, Pädagogische Hochschule, Westfalen-Lippe. Publs: *Parlamentarismus im politischen Roman*, 1976; *Die Karikatur im politischen Unterricht*, 1978; plus articles on educational policy, political theory, political education and local government. Fields: Educational policy; local government; politics and literature.

[1945]
URBANI Giuliano
9 June 1937, Italian. Via Artisti 29, Turin, Italy. Professor of Pol Sci and Director of the Centre for Comparative Pol Research, Bocconi U, Milan. Publs: *Politica e Universitari*, 1966; *Antologia di Scienza Politica* (co-ed), 1970; *L'analisi del Sistema Politico*, 1972; *La Politica Comparata*, 1973; *Planning, Politics and Public Policy: The British, French and Italian Experience* (co-ed); *Sindacati e Politica nella Società Post-industriale* (ed). Fields: Political aspects of planning; methodology of comparative politics; political culture; Italian politics.

[1946]
URIO Paolo*
27 May 1940, Italian. 4B, rue des Délices, 1203 Geneva, Switzerland. Degrees: Lic ès sci pol (Geneva), 1965; Dr ès sci écon et soc (Geneva), 1971. Doctoral thesis: "Processus de décision et contrôle démocratique en Suisse: Etude de cas dans le domaine de la défense nationale". 1964-69 Assistant, Inst d'Etudes Européenes, Geneva; 1965-69 Assistant, Fonds National Suisse pour la Recherche Scientifique; 1966-69 Assistant, U of Geneva; 1969-71 Chef de travaux, Dept de Pol Sci, U of Geneva; 1970- Executive Secretary, Swiss Pol Sci Asssociation; Assistant Professor, Dept de Pol Sci, U of Geneva. Publs: *Processus de décision et contrôle démocratique en Suisse: Etude de cas dans le domaine de la défense nationale*, 1971. Fields: Public administration; decision-making theory and case studies; methodology.

[1947]
URWIN Derek William
27 October 1939, British. Medhaugsflaten 56, 5070 Mathopen, Norway. Degrees: BA; MA (Manchester), 1963; PhD (Strathclyde), 1973. Doctoral thesis; "The Politics of Agrarian Defence: Some Aspects of the Historical Development of Agrarian Political Movements in Europe From the End of Feudalism to the Twentieth Century". 1963-72 Lecturer, U of Strathclyde; 1969-70 Ford Foundation Visiting Research Fellow, Yale U; 1973 Visiting Professor, McGill U; 1974- Professor in Comparative Pol, U of Bergen. Publs: *Scottish Political Behaviour*, 1966; *Western Europe Since 1945*, 1972. Fields: Social structure and voting behaviour; political parties and strains in regimes in European political systems; the regional and territorial bases of European political systems.

[1948]
UTHOFF Hayo
1937, German, Klosterstrasse 58-60, 5000 Köln 41, FR Germany. Degrees: Dr rer Pol, 1972. Doctoral thesis: "Rollenkonforme Verbrechen unter einem totalitären System". Wiss Assistent. Publs: *Rollenkonforme Verbrechen unter einem totalitären System*, 1975. Fields: Empirical political theory; methodology; comparative politics; public administration.

[1949]
UTZ Arthur Fridolin
15 April 1908, Swiss. Place Georges Python 1, CH-1700 Fribourg, Switzerland.
Degrees: Dr theol. 1937-46 Professor, Albertus-Magnus-Akademie, Walberberg/Bonn;
1946- Professor of Ethics and Soc Philosophy, U of Fribourg; Direktor, International
Inst of Soc and Pol Sci; President, Inst für Gesellschaftswissenschaften,
Walberberg/Bonn; President of the International Foundation Humanum. Publs: *Recht
und Gerechtigkeit*, 1953; *Sozialethik*, 1960-63; *Ethique Sociale*, 1960-67; *Etica Social*,
1964-65; *Bibliography of Social Ethics*, 1960-77; *Maximum moderner Mittelstands-
politik*, 1968; *Grundsätze der Sozialpolitik*, 1969; *Ethik und Politik*, 1970. Fields: Bases
of political problems.

V

[1950]
VACANTE Concetta
25 March 1947, Italian. 95-100 Catania, Via Torino 61, Italy. Degrees: Laurea. Doctoral thesis: "The German Military Occupation in Sudtirol, 1943-1945". Researcher, U
of Catania. Publs: *Trent Anni del Potere Democristiano. Un'analisi*, 1978; "Il Sistema
Bancario Italiano el le sue Relazioni con il Potere Politico", 1978. Fields: Analysis of
political structures in capitalist societies.

[1951]
VÄTH Werner
9 September 1945, German. Im Bündt 7, D-7753 Allensbach 2, FR Germany. Degrees:
Dipl Pol, 1969; Dr rer Soc, 1976. Doctoral thesis: "Agglomerationsprozess und zen-
tralstaatliche Raumordnungspolitik" (Agglomeration Process and Federal Regional
Policy). Assistent, Fachbereich Pol Wiss, U of Konstanz; Lehrstuhlvertreter, Free U of
Berlin. Publs: "Arbeitnehmerorientierte Regionalpolitik", *Neue Gesellschaft*, 1976;
Raumordnung und Regional Entwicklung, 1978; "Arbeitslosigkeit und soziale
Diesintegration", *Politische Vierteljahresschrift*, 1978; "Raumordungspolitik: Pro-
gramm und Vollzug", in *Politikverflechtung* (J J Hesse (ed)), 1978. Fields: Environ-
ment; regional politics; communication politics; unemployment; government theory.

[1952]
VALE Vivian
10 June 1920, British. The Warden's Lodge, South Stoneham House, Swaythling,
Southampton SO9 4WL, England. Degrees: MA (Cantab). 1948 Lecturer in Pol Theory
and Inst, U of Durham; 1952-53 Harkness Fellow, Harvard U and U of Wisconsin; 1967
Visiting Professor, U of South Carolina and California; 1974 Visiting Professor, U of
Cornell, New York; 1975- Lecturer in Pol, U of Southampton. Publs: *Labour in
American Politics*, 1971; *American Political Institutions in the 1970s* (with M Beloff),
1974. Fields: 19th and 20th century American history and politics; Anglo-American
relations.

[1953]
VALEN Henry Halfdan
20 May 1924, Norwegian. Halvdan Svartesgate 38, Oslo 2, Norway. Degrees: Mag pol
sci (Oslo), 1954; Dr (Oslo), 1966. 1954-60 Member, Inst for Soc Research, Oslo; 1960-67
Research Director, U of Oslo; 1967-69 Associate Professor in Pol Sci; 1970- Professor
in Pol Sci, U of Oslo. Publs: "The Mobilization of the Periphery", in *Approaches to
the Study of Political Participation* (S Rokkan (ed)), 1962; *Political Parties in Norway*

(with D Katz), 1964; "Regional Contrasts in Norwegian Politics" (co-author), in *Cleavages, Ideologies and Party Systems* (E Allardt and Y Littunen (eds)), 1964; *Velgerne og Politiske Frontlinjer* (with W Martinussen), 1971. Fields: Generations in politics; preconditions for generational shifts, and consequences of change; cleavage structure and political development; analysis of voters and political leaders.

[1954]
VALKENBURGH Paul
20 May 1928, Dutch. Houtwallen 29, Vries (Dr), The Netherlands. Degrees: D Phil, 1964. Doctoral thesis; "People in the Cold War (A Study of Political Attitudes in Relation to the East-West Conflict)". Member Research Staff, Soc Inst, Groningen State U; Lecturer in Methodology of Soc Research; Professor of Pol Sci, U of Groningen. Publs: *People in the Cold War*, 1964; *An Introduction to Political Science*, 1967; *A Discussion on War and Peace*, 1968; *Anatomy of Conflict — A Model Theoretical Approach*, 1969; *Diagnostic Analysis of Social Crisis Situations*, 1973; *Conflict and Conflict Management*, 1974; *Simulation in Social Research*, 1976 (all in Dutch). Fields: Methodology of political research; conflict analysis; conflict-theory; military strategy, especially air force and naval strategy; models of political systems.

[1955]
VALLÈS Josep M
7 July 1940, Spanish. Casa Escoles Pies 38, Barcelona (17), Spain. Degrees: Graduate in Law (Barcelona), 1962; Dr in Law ("Autonoma" de Barcelona), 1973. Doctoral thesis: "La política religiosa en los primeros años de la Restauración y la Constitución de 1876" (The Religious Policy in the First Years of the Restoration and the Constitution of 1876). 1967-71 Assistant Professor, Dept of Pol Law, U of Barcelona; 1972-Associate Professor, Dept of Pol Sci, U Autonoma de Barcelona. Publs: *Les eleccions municipals de 16 d'octubre de 1973 a Barcelona* (ed), 1975; *Las elecciones. Introducción a los sistemas electorales* (with F Carreras), 1977; plus articles and papers on constitutional law, electoral sociology. Fields: Comparative government; electoral law and electoral behaviour.

[1956]
VALLINDER Torbjörn
30 November 1925, Swedish. Department of Political Science, University of Lund, S-200 05 Lund 5, Sweden. Degrees: PhD (Lund), 1962. Doctoral thesis: "I Kamp för Demokratin. Rösträttsrörelsen i Sverige 1886-1900" (In the Front Line of Democracy. The Universal Suffrage Movement in Sweden 1886-1900). 1962-69 Docent, U of Lund; 1969- Senior Lecturer in Pol Sci, U of Lund; 1970- Ed, *Statsvetenskaplig Tidskrift*. Publs: *I Kamp för Demokratin. Rösträttsrörelsen i Sverige 1886-1900*, 1962; *Press och Politik*, 1971. Fields: Mass media, especially the press and political life; the jury system in press cases.

[1957]
VANACLOCHA BELLVER Francisco J
18 November 1950, Spanish. Lope de Rueda 33, Madrid 9, Spain. Degrees: Lic (Madrid). Assistant Professor of Spanish Pol Law, Electoral Soc, Seminario de Derecho Pol, Facultad de Ciencias Pol/Soc, U Complutense de Madrid.

[1958]
VANAS Norbert
18 June 1948, Austrian. Alszeile 17/8, 1170 Vienna, Austria. Degrees: Mag rer Soc. Doctoral thesis: "Die Erweiterung der betrieblichen Mitwirkungsrechte der Arbeitnehmer in der Bundesrepublik Deutschland und Österreich". Klubsekretär

Parlamentsklub, Österreichische Volkspartei. Publs: *Thesen zur Gesundheitspolitik*, 1975; *Zur Krankheit unseres Gesundheitssystems*, 1976; *Das 1. Jahr der XIV. Gesetzgebungsperiode*, 1976; *Zielsystem für das Österreichische Gesundheitswesen*, 1978. Fields: Public health and social policy; parliamentary studies; education.

[1959]
VAN BENTHEM VAN DEN BERGH Godfried
27 January 1923, Dutch. Delistraat 57, The Hague, The Netherlands. Degrees: Drs (Leiden). 1960-64 Lecturer, Inst of European Studies, U of Leiden; 1966-67 Lecturer, Inst of European Studies, U of Leiden; 1964-65 Visiting Scholar, Center for International Affairs, U of Harvard; 1965-66 Research Associate, Inst of International Studies, U of California, Berkeley; 1974-75 Fellow, Netherlands Inst for Advanced Studies; 1967- Senior Lecturer, Inst of Social Studies, The Hague. Publs: *The Association of African States with the EEC*, 1962 (in Dutch); *The Ideology of the West*, 1969 (in Dutch); *Coercion and Liberation*, 1972 (in Dutch); "The Interconnections between Processes of State and Class Formation", *Acta Politica*, 1976; "Is a Marxist Theory of the State Possible?", in *Human Figurations, Essays for Norbert Elias*, 1977. Fields: International relations and development problems; state and nation formation; nationalism; development theory.

[1960]
VAN BRAAM Aris
1 June 1923, Dutch. Kalverringdijk 19, Zaandam, The Netherlands. Degrees: Dr (Amsterdam). Doctoral thesis; "Ambtenaren en Bureaucratie in Nederland" (Civil Servants and Bureaucracy in the Netherlands). 1946-49 Director, Sociographic Research Office; 1949-65 Head of Division, Central Bureau of Statistics, The Hague; 1966-72 Professor of Sociology and Public Administration, U of Rotterdam; 1973- Professor of Public Admin, U of Leiden. Publs: in the fields of sociography, sociology, economic history, political science and public administration. Fields: Public administration; bureaucracy; growth of administration.

[1961]
VAN CUILENBURG Jan Jacob
22 April 1946, Dutch. Het Hoogt 47, Amsterdam, The Netherlands. Degrees: PhD. Doctoral thesis: "Lezer, Krant en Politiek" (Readers, Newspapers and Politics). Lecturer in Pol Sci and Mass Communication, Free U of Amsterdam. Publs: Various reports on mass communications and articles on income inequality. Fields: Philosophy of science; mass media; political behaviour; inequality.

[1962]
VAN DE COPPELLO Kappeyne Nicolaas Johannes
21 January 1902, Dutch. Oud-over 59, Loenen aan de Vecht, The Netherlands. Degrees: Dr. Doctoral thesis: "Representative System 1926". Barrister, Court of Appeal, Amsterdam; President of the European Centre of Discussions. Publs: *Op de Tweesprong*, 1938. Fields: Human rights; constitutional law.

[1963]
VAN DEN BERG J Th J
2 April 1941, Dutch. Waalstraat 2, Alphen aan den Rijn, The Netherlands. Degrees: LB (Leiden). Assistant Ed, *Limburgs Dagblad*; 1971- Lecturer in Parliamentary History, U of Leiden. Publs: *Crisis in de Nederlandse Politiek* (with H A A Molleman), 1974; *Parlement en Politiek* (with J J Vis), 1977; plus various articles and fortnightly column in *NRC-Handelsblad*. Fields: Dutch political history; political culture; comparative government.

[1964]
VAN DEN BERGH Johannes Theodorus Joseph*
4 April 1941, Dutch. Heerlen, Peter Schinkstraat 570, The Netherlands. Degrees: LL B (Leiden), 1968. 1968-70 Desk Ed, *Limburgs Dagblad*; 1970- Pol Research, U of Leiden. Fields: Problems of comparative politics; historical dimensions of today's political phenomena and problems; history and significance of political ideologies.

[1965]
VAN DEN BOS CZN W
24 May 1940, Dutch. Helena Reitbergstraat 4, 2806 KP Gouda, The Netherlands. Degrees: Dr (Free U of Amsterdam). Doctoral thesis: "The Influence of the Town Clerk in Small Municipalities" (in Dutch). Scientific Co-operator, Pol Sci Inst, Dutch Christian-Democrats. Publs: "Public Authority, Public Transport and Open Regulation", in *Anti-Revolutionaire Staatkunde*, 1977; *Model of the Municipal and Regional Programme 1978-1982* (ed), 1977; *Municipality and Provinces 1974* (ed), 1977; *Landed Property and Landed Management* (ed), 1975; "Programmatical Harmony, Basis for the Formation of the Board of Mayor and Aldermen", in *Anti-Revolutionaire Staatkunde*, 1973. Fields: Public administration; law.

[1966]
VAN DEN DOEL Hans
4 April 1937, Dutch. Mauricialaan 7, Overveen, The Netherlands. Degrees: MA (Free U of Amsterdam), 1964; PhD (Rotterdam), 1971. Doctoral thesis: "Konvergentie en Evolutie — De konvergentie-theorie van Tinbergen en de evolutie van Economische Ordes in Oost en West". 1964 Junior Lecturer in Econ, Municipal U of Amsterdam; 1967 MP; 1973 Professor in Pol Sci, U of Nijmegen; 1975- Professor in Welfare Econ, Municipal U of Amsterdam. Publs: "Konvergenz von Verwaltungsstrukturen in Ost und West", in *Ökonomsiche Aspekte der friedlichen Koexistenz* (H Jaroslawska), 1974; *Demokratie en Welvaartstheorie*, 1975; "Carry Out the Revolution and Increase Production! The Evolution of the Chinese Economic Order to an Optimum", *De Economist*, 1977; *Democracy and Welfare Economics*, 1978. Fields: New political economy; public choice; economic policy; policy analysis; economic power.

[1967]
VAN DEN DUNGEN Peter W
12 June 1948, Dutch. 2 North Park Terrace, Bradford 9, England. Degrees: Lic (Antwerp); MA (John Hopkins); PhD (London). Doctoral thesis: "Industrial Society at the End of War — the History of an Idea". Lecturer in Peace Studies, U of Bradford. Fields: History and theory of pacifism; peace movements; disarmament; peace research.

[1968]
VAN DEN EEDEN Pieter
8 August 1941, Dutch. Lisstraat 15, 1121 AP Landsmeer, The Netherlands. Degrees: Drs. Lecturer, Catholic U of Nijmegen; Lecturer in Methodology of the Soc Sci, Free U of Amsterdam. Publs: "Niveau's van Analyse in Sociaal Onderzoek", *Geografisch Tijdschrift (Nieuwe Reeks)*, 1978; *Toepassingen van de Contextuele Methode in Verkiezingsonderzoek*, 1977. Fields: Multi-level research.

[1969]
VAN DEN HOVE Didier Henri*
15 October 1936, Belgian. 125 Avenue des Cerisiers, 1200 Bruxelles, Belgium. Degrees: PhD (Louvain), 1969. Doctoral thesis: "Etude de deux modes d'influence sociale dans la résolution d'un conflit d'intérêt. Médiation et observation". 1963-68 Assistant

chargé de recherche, Centre de Perfectionnement dans la Direction des Entreprises, U de Louvain; 1966-68 Special International Student and Research Assistant at Purdue U, Indiana, USA; Chargé de cours associé, U de Louvain; Responsable du Groupe de Recherche 'Psychologie' du CREFOR; Secrétaire, Inst des Sci Econ Appliquées, UCL. Publs: *L'éluctable métamorphose. Essai sur la démarche pédagogique* (co-author), 1971. Fields: Psycho-sociology of relations of groups and organizations; social conflict and its resolution; international relations.

[1970]
VAN DEN TEMPEL Catharina Paulina
18 September 1944, Dutch, Groenburgwal 49, Amsterdam, The Netherlands. Degrees: Drs (Amsterdam). Teaching and Research Assistant, Dept of International Relations, U of Amsterdam. Publs: "Suriname in de Internationale Politiek", 1975; "Dutch Opinions on Foreign Policy: A Function of Attention or of Social Position?", 1974; "Galtung's Index of Social Position going Dutch" (with A van Staden), 1975; contributions to national election surveys (with others), 1972-73, 1977; "Development Aid and the Causes of Poverty", 1977. Fields: Development aid and underdevelopment; foreign policy opinion studies.

[1971]
VAN DER BURG Frans Hendrik*
9 August 1930, Dutch. Burgemeester Suysstraat 3A, Tilburg, The Netherlands. Degrees: MA (Leiden), 1952; Dr in Law (Utrecht), 1961. Doctoral thesis: "Preventieve Justitie en Plaatselijke Politie" (Preventive Justice and Local Police. On the Relation Between Local Government and the Judiciary in the Field of the Police). Civil Servant, Ministry of the Interior and Ministry of Labour and Health; Professor of Constitutional Administrative Law, Catholic School of Econ, Tilburg. Publs: *Toezeggingen en pseudowetgeving in het administratieve recht*, 1969; *De overwinning van het staatsrecht*, 1970; *Overheid en onderdaan in de representatieve demokratie*, 1970. Fields: Legislation and decision-making on environmental problems.

[1972]
VAN DER EIJK Cornelis
6 July 1948, Dutch. Galileiplantsoen 36, 1098 NA Amsterdam, The Netherlands. Degrees: Dr (Amsterdam), 1971. Doctoral thesis: "On the Study of Political Beliefs". Associate Professor in Pol Sci and Research Methodology, U of Amsterdam. Fields: Political behaviour; methodology.

[1973]
VAN DER HEK Arie
12 September 1938, Dutch. Burg Martenssingel 65A, Gouda, The Netherlands. Degrees: Dr. Doctoral thesis: "Block Voting and Group Formation in the UN General Assembly". Scientific Collaborator, Int Secretary of the PvdA; Civil Servant, Foreign Affairs and Econ Affairs; MP. Publs: Articles on foreign affairs, development co-operation and trade co-operation. Fields: Foreign affairs; development co-operation; trade co-operation; political analysis of economic problems.

[1974]
VAN DER MEY Leonardus Marinus
3 July 1944, Dutch. Hugo de Grootstraat 7, Leiden, The Netherlands. Degrees: Drs (Leiden), 1970; MA (New York), 1971. 1969-1970 Student/Assistant, Dept of Pol Sci, U of Leiden; 1970-71 Junior Fellow, Center for International Studies, U of New York; Freelance Journalist. Lecturer in International Relations, Dept of Pol Sci, U of Leiden. Publs: Articles in *Acta Politica, Internationale Spectator* and *Transaktie*. Fields: International relations; peace research; Asian politics.

[1975]
VAN DER MAESEN Constance Eugenie
Dutch. Institute for Political Science, Herengracht 530, Amsterdam, The Netherlands. Degrees: PhD. Doctoral thesis: "Participation and Democracy". Medewerker, U of Amsterdam. Fields: Political socialization; participation.

[1976]
VAN DER PIJL Kees
15 June 1947, Dutch. Amstelveenseweg 116, Amsterdam, The Netherlands. Degrees: MA (Leiden). Staff Member, Vakgroep Internationale Betrekkingen, U of Amsterdam. Publs: *Een Amerikaans Plan voor Europa. Achtergronden van het ontstaan van de EEG*, 1978. Fields: Imperialism; Marxism; European integration.

[1977]
VAN DER SPRENKEL Sybille*
14 February 1919, British. Department of Social Studies, The University, Leeds LS2 9JT, England. Degrees: BA; BSc; MSc (Econ), 1956. 1952-53 Research Assistant, U of London; 1956-63 Research Assistant, Australian National U; 1962-64 Lecturer in Soc, International U, Tokyo; Lecturer in Soc, specializing in Chinese Social Structure, U of Leeds. Publs: *Legal Institution in Manchu China*, 1962; "Law in the Changing Society", in *Modern China's Search for a Political Forum* (Gray (ed)); "Secret Societies and the Law", in *Chinese Secret Societies* (J Chesneaux (ed)), 1970. Fields: Transformation of Chinese society; economic planning and co-ordination; education and changes in morality; China as a developing society — the uniqueness of the model.

[1978]
VAN DER TAK Theo
21 February 1948, Dutch. Kon Wilhelminalaan 22, Leidschendam, The Netherlands. Degrees: MA (Leiden). Dept of Public Administration, Graduate School of Business, Delft. Publs: *Kabinetsformatie 1977* (with R B Andeweg and K Dittrich), 1978; "Vertrouwen in de Tweede Kamer", in *De Nederlandfse Kiezer 1977*, 1977; "Nederlandse Topambtenaren en Anonimiteit", in *Bestuurswetenschappen*, 1977. Fields: Public administration; mass political behaviour; elite attitudes and behaviour.

[1979]
VAN DER VEEN Robert Jan
23 October 1943, Dutch. Waterlooplein 25, Amsterdam 1011 NX, The Netherlands. Degrees: Dr (Amsterdam). Doctoral thesis: "Collective keuze en sociale welvaartsfunktie" (Collective Choice and the Social Welfare Function). Assistant Professor, Econ Seminarium, Faculty of Soc Sci, U of Amsterdam. Publs; "De Rechtvaardigheidstheorie van John Rawls I, II" (with P B Lehning), *Acta Politica*, 1976, 1977; "Rationaliteit en Moraal: Het Prisoners' Dilemma" (with O Schmidt), *Acta Politica*, 1976; "On Marx's Theory of Unemployment" (with D Furth and A Heertje), *Oxford Economic Papers*, 1978. Fields: Political philosophy; political economy.

[1980]
VAN EERDEN Leonardus A
11 April 1949, Dutch. Hoffmannlaan 483, 5011 WK Tilburg, The Netherlands. Degrees: Dr. Doctoral thesis: "A Political Economic Analysis of the International Monetary Crisis". Assistant, Sub-Faculty of Pol Sci, U of Amsterdam. Fields: Monetary research; internationalization of finance capital.

[1981]
VAN ENGELDORP GASTELAARS Frits
27 May 1946, Dutch. Zwethkade 22, Delft, The Netherlands. Degrees: MA (Leiden).
Student Assistant, U of Nürnberg; Student Assistant, Common Market, Dept of Soc
Affairs; Assistant Professor of Soc, Interfaculty for Graduate Studies in Management,
Delft. Fields: Stereotypes and concept building in the social sciences; urbanization and
industrialization; functioning of business schools in Dutch society; GDR.

[1982]
VAN GINKEL Anton*
7 April 1933, Dutch. 102 Waalsdorperweg, The Hague, The Netherlands. Degrees: Drs
(Free U Amsterdam), 1967. Foreign News Ed, *Trouw*, Amsterdam; Municipal Ex-
ecutive Officer; positions in various local government administrations in Holland;
Research Officer, International Union of Local Authorities Secretariat, The Hague.
Publs: Articles in *Intermediair; Studies in Comparative Local Government*. Fields:
Theoretical problems of forecasting in the social sciences in Western countries; attitude
typologies; the study of processes of change and continuity in culture and society.

[1983]
VAN GUNSTEREN Herman
1940, Dutch. Willem de Zwijgerlaan 1, Oegstgeest, The Netherlands. Degrees: MA
(Leiden); PhD (Leiden). Doctoral thesis: "The Quest for Control". Research
Associate, U of California; Research Fellow, Russell-Sage Foundation, New York; Professor of Pol Theory, U of Leiden. Publs: *The Quest for Control*, 1976; *Politieke
Theorieën* (with G Lock), 1977. Fields: Planning; decision theory; cybernetics; citizenship.

[1984]
VANHANEN Tatu
17 April 1929, Finnish. Vanha Lahnuksentie, 02970 Espoo 97, Finland. Degrees: Lic
(Tampere), 1963; Dr (Tampere), 1968. Doctoral thesis: "Puolueet ja Pluralismi.
Tutkimus Poliittisen ja Sosiaalisen Pluralism in Riippuvuuksista Kymmenessä Kan-
sainyhteisön Jäsenmaassa" (Parties and Pluralism — a study of the Correlation bet-
ween Political and Social Pluralism in Ten Member Countries of the Commonwealth).
1958-61 Ed, *Kyntäjä*; 1962-69 Chief, Press Agency of the Agrarian Party (1965- Centre
Party); 1966-69 Chief, Research and Information Dept, Centre Party; 1969-72 Acting
Assistant Professor in Soc Sci, U of Jyväskylä; 1972-74 Junior Researcher, Academy of
Finland; 1974- Assistant Professor in Pol Sci, U of Tampere. Publs: *Dependence of
Power on Resources: A Comparative Study of 114 States in the 1960s*, 1971; *Political
and Social Structures: Part 1: American Countries 1850-1973*, 1975; *Political and Social
Structures: European Countries 1850-1974*, 1977; *Political and Social Structures: Asian
and Australasian Countries 1850-1975*, 1977. Fields: Comparative study of political
systems and social structures.

[1985]
VAN HASSEL Hugo M O
1 June 1932, Belgian. Kortrijksestraat 166, B-3200 Kessel-Lo, Belgium. Degrees: Dr soc
sci (Leuven), 1974. Doctoral thesis: 'Ministerial Cabinets: A Sociological Explanation'.
1961-62 Faculty Associate, School of Business, U of Indiana; 1959- Director of Public
Management Training Centre, Catholic U of Leuven; 1965- Secretary-General, Flemish
Chapter, Belgian Inst of Pol Sci; Associate Professor, Faculty of Soc Sci, Catholic U of
Leuven. Publs: *Sociografische aspekten van de Belgische Senaat*, 1959; *De Coordinatie
van het Overheidsbeleid in een evoluerende maatschappij* (co-author), 1966; *La gestion
de nos communes* (with Depré), 1969; *Het ministerieel cabinet. Peilen naar een*

sociologische duiding, 1974; "Belgian Public Servants and Political Decision-Making", in *The Mandarins of Western Europe: The Political Role of Top Civil Servants* (M Dogan (ed)), 1975; "Regiering en ambtenarij t.a.v. de beleidsbeheersing in België"; *Acta Politica*, 1975; "Beleidssteun voor ministers: enige internationale vergelijkingspunten", *Acta Politica*, 1975; "De madataris en de verruiming der gemeentelijke schalen", in *Gemeentebeleid na de fusies, een multimediaal projet*, 1976. Fields: Management and change mechanisms in public organizations; role and power structures of public policy-making units: government, cabinets, agencies.

[1986]
VAN MAARSEVEEN Henc T J F
20 December 1926, Dutch. Nieuwe Haven 274, Gouda, The Netherlands. Degrees: Master of Law (Utrecht), 1952. Barrister; Legal Adviser, Home Office; Head, Dept of Constitutional Affairs, Home Office Netherlands; Professor in Constitutional and Administrative Law, Erasmus U of Rotterdam. Publs: *Pardon*; *Direct Action as Birth of New Law; The Phenomenon Constitution*; *The Culture State*; *Political Law* (all in Dutch); *Human Rights as a Means of Development*; *A Computer Analysis of the Constitutions of the World*. Fields: Theory of written constitutions, comparative and general; constitutional developments in Black Africa; political law.

[1987]
VAN MIERLO Johannes Gijsbertus Andreas
10 August 1953, Dutch. Pr Mauritslaan 13, Voorschoten, The Netherlands. Degrees: MA. Research Associate for Public Econ, Inst for Fiscal Studies, U of Rotterdam. Publs: *Theorie en methodologie van uitgaven- en batenverdeling*. Fields: Welfare economics and public choice; social and economic policy; income distribution; social indicators and the measurement of welfare; economic systems.

[1988]
VAN POELJE Silvio Otto*
6 February 1912, Dutch. Van Kijfhoeklaan 22, The Hague, The Netherlands. Degrees: LL D (Leiden), 1937. Doctoral thesis: "Administrative Law and Administrative Jurisdiction in England". Civil Servant, Ministry of Housing and Physical Planning; Co-director, Netherlands Union of Municipalities; Part-time Professor of Planning and Building Law, Technological U of Delft; Professor of Constitutional and Administrative Law, Faculty of Soc, Sci, U of Amsterdam; Director, Netherlands Inst of Public Administration. Fields: The problems of municipal boundaries, amalgamation, intermunicipal co-operation, the forming of new regional districts.

[1989]
VAN PUTTEN Jan
8 November 1935, Dutch. Burg vd Voort v Zijplaan 55, 3571 VT Utrecht, The Netherlands. Degrees: Dr. Doctoral thesis: "Zoveel kerken, zoveel zinnen". Ed, *Haagsche Courant*; Lecturer in Pol Sci, Free U of Amsterdam. Publs: *Demokratie in Nederland*, 1975; *Ontevredenheid over Politiek*, 1971; *Vrijheid en Welzijn*, 1977; plus various articles in *Acta Politica, Socialisme en Democratie, VU-Magazine*. Fields: Dutch politics; political theory; political thought.

[1990]
VAN RIEL Harm
18 February 1907, Dutch. Van Alkemadelaan 350, The Hague, The Netherlands. Member of Senate; Chairman of the Liberal Faction in the First Chamber; Member of Provincial Government. Publs: *Goorsprake van Drenthe*. Fields: Political science and legal history; liberalism in the 19th century; Adolf Hitler.

[1991]
VAN RULLER Henk
1 October 1937, Dutch. Prinses Mariannelaan 193, Voorburg, The Netherlands. Degrees: Dr Soc Sci (Free U of Amsterdam). Doctoral thesis: "Agglomeratie-problemen in Nederland". Lecturer, Free U of Amsterdam; Research Officer, National Inst of Public Administration, Lusaka, Zambia; Advisor on Co-ordination-Problems, Ministry of International Affairs, The Netherlands. Publs: *Agglomeratie-problemen in Nederland*, 1972; plus various reports on rural development in Zambia and articles on Dutch local government. Fields: Local government administration and finance; development administration; urban government; intergovernmental relations.

[1992]
VAN SCHENDELEN Marius P C M
12 July 1944, Dutch. Floris Versterlaan 5, 3055 BM Rotterdam, The Netherlands. Degrees: PhD. Doctoral thesis: "Parliamentary Information, Decision-making and Representation". Associate Professor, Faculty of Law and Soc Faculty, Erasmus U, Rotterdam. Publs: *Parliamentary Information, Decision-making and Representation*, 1975; *Delegation of Authority*, 1976; *Key Themes of Political Science*, 1976; *Process of Legislation* (co-author), 1976; *Ministers, Civil Servants and Parliamentarians* (co-author), 1975; *Handbook of Public Administration* (co-author), 1977 (all in Dutch); plus articles in *Zeitschrift für Parlamentsfragen*; *Legislative Studies Quarterly, Acta Politica*. Fields: Political science and public administration; political analysis of law.

[1993]
VAN SCHUUR Wijbrandt H
21 August 1946, Dutch. Holsteinslaan 20, Haren (Gn), The Netherlands. Degrees: Drs (Amsterdam), 1975. Assistant Professor, Dept of Statistics and Measurement Theory, Faculty of Soc Sci, U of Groningen. Publs: Articles in *Acta Politica* and *Methoden en Data Nieuwsbrief*. Fields: Mass political behaviour; political elites; political parties; pressure groups; methodology; mathematical politics.

[1994]
VAN STADEN Alfred
9 March 1942, Dutch. Tollenaersingel 39, Leiderdorp, The Netherlands. Degrees: BA; MA (Amsterdam). Doctoral thesis: "The Netherlands and the Atlantic Alliance 1960-71" (in Dutch). Lecturer in International Relations, U of Amsterdam; Senior Lecturer in International Relations and Professor of Diplomatic History, U of Leiden. Publs: *Parlement, partijen en buitenlandse politiek* (contributor), 1977; *Elite en Buitenlandse Politiek in Nederland* (contributor), 1978; *Foreign Policy Making in Western Europe* (contributor), (W Paterson (ed)), 1978. Fields: Comparative approaches to foreign policy analysis; strategic studies; disarmament and arms control; historical development of the foreign policy of the Netherlands.

[1995]
VATIKIOTIS P J
5 February 1928, American. 4 The Squirrels, Nower Hill, Pinner, Middlesez HA5 3BD, England. Degrees: BA; PhD. Doctoral thesis: "The Syncretic Origins of the Fatimid Movement: A Reconstruction of their Theory of the State". 1969 Visiting Professor of Pol Sci, UCLA; 1973-74 Visiting Professor and Visiting Senior Fellow of the Council on the Humanities, U of Princeton; Professor of Pol, U of London. Publs: *The Egyptian Army in Politics*, 1975; *Politics and the Military in Jordan*, 1967; *The Modern History of Egypt*, 1976; *Conflict in the Middle East*, 1971; *Greece: A Political Essay*, 1975;

Nasser and his Generation: A Political Portrait, 1978; *Egypt since the Revolution* (ed), 1968; *Revolution in the Middle East* (ed), 1972. Fields: Civil-military relations; political leadership; political thought; political history.

[1996]
VAUGHAN Michalina Ewa Francisca
4 June 1932, British. Prizet House, Helsington, Nr Kendal, Cumbria, England. Degrees: Dr d'Etat (Paris); Dipl pol (Paris); Doctoral thesis: "Stanisias Leszczynski, Philosophie Politique, Souverain Nominal et Administrateur Bienfaisant en Lorraine, 1737-66". 1956-58 Programme Assistant, Dept of Soc Sci, UNESCO; Assistant Lecturer, Lecturer, Senior Lecturer, Professor, Head of Dept, U of Lancaster. Publs: *A Glossary of economics*, 1965; "The Grandes Ecoles", in *Governing Elites* (R Wilkinson (ed)), 1969; "Education, Secularization, Desecularization and Resecularization" (with M Archer), in *A Sociological Yearbook of Religion in Britain* (D Martin and M Hill (eds)), 1970; "The Legal Philosophy of Petrazycki" (with G Langrod), in *Polish Law Throughout the Ages* (W J Wagner (ed)), 1970; *Social Conflict and Educational Change in England and France 1789-1848* (with M S Archer), 1971; "Gaullism", in *Social and Political Movements in Western Europe* (M Kolinsky and W E Patterson (eds)), 1976; "Poland", in *Contemporary Europe: Class, Status and Power* (M S Archer and S Gines (eds)), 1971. Fields: French and English educational institutions; social stratification in Poland; Eastern European sociological theories; social history; theories of social change, comparative social institutions.

[1997]
VÄYRYNEN Raimo Veikko Antero
17 April 1977, Finnish. Haukisenkatu 3 I 5, SF-33820 Tampere 82, Finland. Degrees: MA (Tampere), 1968; Lic (Tampere), 1970; Dr (Tampere), 1973. Doctoral thesis: "Militarization, Conflict Behaviour and Interaction: Three Ways of Analyzing the Cold War, 1973". 1969-70 Lecturer in Pol Sci; 1970-72 Senior Research Fellow, Tampere Peace Research Inst; 1972-75 Ed, *Politiikka*; 1972- Director, Tampere Peace Research Inst; 1973 Docent, International Relations, U of Tampere; 1975- Secretary-General, International Peace Research Association. Publs: *Conflicts in Finnish-Soviet Relations*, 1972; *EEC ja Ulkopolitiikka*, 1973; *Suomen Ulkopolitiikka* (with H Hakovirta), 1975; articles in *Cooperation and Conflict*, *Journal of Peace Research*, *Instant Research on Peace and Violence*, *Co-existence*, *Scandinavian Political Studies*, *Politikka*, *Mediterranean Studies*, *International Social Science Journal*, and *European Journal of Political Science*. Fields: Finnish foreign and security policy; arms race/disarmament problems; political economy of international relations; theory of international relations and peace research.

[1998]
VAZIRI Charokh
19 August 1942, Iranian. Avenue Tribunal Fédéral 2, 1005 Lausanne, Switzerland. Degrees: Lic en econ pol. Doctoral thesis: "Du Ghanat à l'oléoduc-essai sur le pétrole et le pouvoir en Iran". Assistant, Ecole des Sci Soc et Pol, U de Lausanne. Fields: Powers in the Third-World countries; imperialism.

[1999]
VEDEL Georges
5 July 1905, French. 201 Boulevard St Germain, 75007 Paris, France. Degrees: Dr en droit, 1934; Agrégé, 1936. Doctoral thesis: "Essai sur la notion de cause en droit administratif français". Professeur, U de Paris II. Publs: *Traité de droit constitutionnel*; *Droit administratif*; *La dépolitisation*; *Les démocraties marxistes*. Fields: Institutions and political life.

[2000]
VEDUNG Evert Oskar
9 April 1938, Swedish. Sehlstedtsgatan 9, S-754 41 Uppsala, Sweden. Degrees: PhD (Uppsala), 1971. Doctoral thesis: "Unionsdebatten 1905: En Jämförelse méllan Argumenteringen i Sverige och Norge" (The Dissolution of the Union in 1905: A Comparison between Swedish and Norwegian Arguments). 1969- Assistant Professor, Dept of Pol Sci, U of Uppsala. Publs: *Det Rationella Politiska Samtalet: Hur Politiska Budskap Tolkas, Ordnas och Prövas*, 1977; *The Comparative Method and its Neighbours*, 1976; *The Comparative Method and John Stuart Mill's Canons of Induction*, 1977; *The Study of Contents and Functions of Political Ideas*, 1975. Fields: Comparative method; methods of policy analysis; theory of argumentation; rational choice theory; decision-making analysis; energy policy; political instruments and controls.

[2001]
VEEN Hans-Joachim
29 August 1944, German. Drachenfelsstrasse 20, D-5202 Westerhausen/b Hennef, FR Germany. Degrees: MA; PhD. Doctoral thesis: "Opposition in the German Bundestag. Its Functions, Institutional Conditions and the Behaviour of the CDU/CSU Faction in the 6th German Bundestag 1969-1972". 1974 Assistant, Seminar of Pol Sci, U of Freiburg; 1977 Director, Dept of Government and Soc Policy, Social Sci Research Inst, Konrad Adenauer Foundation; 1978- Deputy Director, Soc Sci Research Inst, Konrad Adenauer Foundation. Publs: "Government between Subordination and Political Leadership", *Aus Politik und Zeitgeschichte*, 1972; *The CDU/CSU Opposition in the Legislative Decision-making Process*, 1973; *Opposition in the German Bundestag*, 1976; *Parties and the Liberty of Parliamentarians* (co-ed and co-author), 1976; *Socialism, Communism and the Integration of Western Europe*, 1978.

[2002]
VENTURINI Giancarlo
22 January 1911, Italian. Viale Solferino 18, Parma, Italy. 1940- Lecturer, Professor in International Law, U of Parma. Publs: *Il Proterrorato Internazionale*, 1939; *Il Riconoscimento nel Dititto Internazionale*, 1945; *Diritto internazionale Privato*, 1956. Fields: Law; history.

[2003]
VERDOODT Albert
9 August 1925, Belgian. Voie du Roman Pays, 15/301, B-1348 Louvain-la-Neuve, Belgium. Degrees: Dr Pol and Soc Sci. Doctoral thesis: "Naissance et signification de la déclaration universelle des Droits de l'Homme". Professor, U of Laval (Québec), U of Bujumbura; Associate Professor, Catholic U of Louvain. Publs: *La protection des droits de l'homme dans les Etats plurilingues*, 1973; *The Multinational Society*, 1975; *Les problèmes des groupes linguistiques en Belgique*, 1977; *Linguistic Tensions in Canadian and Belgian Labor Unions*, 1977. Fields: Relations between linguistic groups.

[2004]
VEREKER Charles Henry
29 March 1913, British. Finches, Stanton-St-John, Oxford, England. Degrees: MA (Oxon), 1942; D Phil (Oxon), 1951. Doctoral thesis: "Optimism and Freedom in the Eighteenth Century". Civil Service, wartime appointment; Ministry of Information and Admiralty; Tutor in Pol Studies, U of Oxford; Senior Researcher, Lecturer in Soc Sci, U of Liverpool; Professor of Pol Theory and Inst, U of Durham and Consultant Professor in Soc and Pol Sci, U Coll, Buckingham. Publs: *The Development of Political Theory*, 1964; *Urban Redevelopment and Social Change* (co-author), 1961; *Eighteenth Century*

VERHOEF 419

Optimism, 1967; *Learning and Thinking*, 1968. Fields: 18th century studies; the problems of conflicts of 'allegiance', particularly between political, cultural and religious allegiances.

[2005]
VERHOEF, Jan
16 January 1943, Dutch, Distelveld 12, Waddinxveen, The Netherlands. Degrees: Drs. 1967-69 Assistant, Dept of Pol Sci, U of Leiden; 1970 Research Fellow, Inst for Soc Research, U of Michigan; Instructor/Lecturer, U of Leiden. Fields: Party development and the electoral system in the Netherlands, 1888-1917; Dutch parliament; data archiving.

[2006]
VERHOEF Ronald
2 August 1944, Dutch. Notenhof 16, Schagen, The Netherlands. Degrees: Drs. Dept of Pol Sci, Free U of Amsterdam. Publs: "Voorwaarden en Alternatieven inzake Zeehavenbestuur in Nederland: een Ideaal-Typische Benadering", in *Advies inzake Bestuur en Beheer der Zeehavengebieden*, 1974; "De Beleidskeuze inzake Zeehavenbestuur in Nederland (with G M Christis), in *Advies inzake Bestuur en Beheer der Zeehavengebieden*, 1974; "Current Trends in Local Power and Authority in the Netherlands" (with A Reinders), in *Polish Round Table Yearbook*, 1976-1977. Fields: Local government; policy-making in public agencies; methodology of the science of administration.

[2007]
VERHOOG Jacob Frederik
31 July 1944, Dutch. Hoornbloem 6, Castricum, The Netherlands. Degrees: Drs. Dept of Pol Sci, U of Amsterdam. Fields: Income distribution policy; normative and empirical political theory; futurology.

[2008]
VESA Unto Juhani
4 December 1944, Finnish. Valimaank 1-5 D50, 33500 Tampere 50, Finland. Degrees: VTM Pol Sci (Helsinki), 1967. 1967-1973 Assistant in International Pol, Inst of Pol Sci, U of Tampere; 1973- Research Fellow, Tampere Peace Research Inst. Publs: *Sodat kriisit ja rauhantutkimus* (ed), 1971; *Asevarustelu ja aseidenriisunta* (co-author), 1972; *The Nordic System: Structure and Change, 1920-1970* (co-author), 1973; *Etykista Eteenpain* (ed and co-author), 1976; *International Detente and Disarmament* (co-author), 1977. Fields: Armament and disarmament, particularly Chinese disarmament; United Nations.

[2009]
VESTUTI Guido
15 February 1931, Italian. Via Bellini 14, 22100 Como, Italy. Degrees: Dr in Law (Pavia); Dr in Philosophy (Genova); Dr in Law (Fribourg), 1972. Doctoral thesis: "Rinunzia e transazione nel diritto del lavoro: La Politica di Trotsky". Professor di Storia del Pensiero Sociologico, U Cattolicà del Sacro Cuore di Milano. Publs: *La Rivoluzione Permanente- Un o Studio sulla Politica di Trotsky*, 1960; *Il Partito Politico - Una Introduzione Critica*, 1962; *Schumpeter Teorico dell'Economia*, 1968. Fields: The right to strike in Italy and Switzerland; the political problems deriving from the analysis of economic theories.

[2010]
VIALLE Pierre
26 February 1944, French. 24 rue Vaubécour, 69002 Lyon, France. Degrees: MCJ (New York); IEP (Lyon); Dr d'Etat. Doctoral thesis: "La cour suprême et la représentation politique aux Etats-Unis". Maître de conférences agrégé, U de Jean Moulin, Lyon III. Publs: "Vision idéale et connaissance du réel chez Tocqueville", in *Annales de la Faculté de Droit de Lyon*, 1975; "Le privilège de l'éxécutif et l'arrêt de la cour suprême relatif à l'affaire du Watergate", *RIDC*, 1976. Fields: Comparative politics.

[2011]
VIET Jean*
1920, French. 22 rue Violet, Paris 15, France. Degrees: Dr. Doctoral thesis: "Les méthodes structuralistes en sciences sociales" (Structuralist Methods in Social Sciences). Maître de conférences, IEP, U de Paris; Chargé de conférence, Ecole Pratique des Hautes Etudes; Secrétaire général adjoint du Comité international pour l'information et la documentation des sciences sociales; Consultant, UNESCO, UNCTAD, OCDE, Conseil de l'Europe; Directeur du Service d'Echange d'Informations Scientifiques, Maison des Sciences de l'Homme. Publs: *Les méthodes structuralistes dans des sciences sociales*, 1965; *Démographie. Tendances actuelles et organisation de la recherche, 1955-65* (with L Tabah), 1966; *Input-output. Essai de présentation documentaire du système de W Léontief*, 1966; *Comparative survey analysis* (co-author), 1969; *La psychologie sociale. Une discipline en mouvement* (co-author), 1970; *Thesaurus for information processing in sociology/Thesaurus pour le traitement de l'information en sociologie*, 1972. Fields: Social science information storage and retrieval.

[2012]
VIGOR Peter Hast
25 July 1918, British. The Royal Military Academy, Sandhurst, Camberley, Surrey, England. Degrees: BA; MA (Cantab), 1953. Senior Lecturer in Soviet Studies, RMA Sandhurst; Head of Soviet Studies Centre, Ministry of Defence. Publs: *A Guide to Marxism and Its Effects on Soviet Development*, 1966; *Books on Communism: A Select Bibliography*, 1971; *The Soviet View of War, Peace and Neutrality*, 1975. Fields: Soviet foreign policy; Soviet military thinking; the effects of ideology on Soviet military strategy.

[2013]
VILE Maurice John
23 July 1927, British. Little Cob, Garlinge Green, Petham, Canterbury, Kent, England. Degrees: BSc (London), 1951; PhD (London), 1954; MA (Oxon), 1962. Doctoral thesis: "Federalism in the United States and Australia". 1954-62 Lecturer, U of Exeter; 1962-65 Fellow, Nuffield Coll, U of Oxford; 1965-68 Reader in Pol and Government; 1968- Professor of Pol Sci, U of Kent and Pro-Vice-Chancellor, U of Kent. Publs: *The Structure of American Federalism*, 1961; *Constitutionalism and the Separation of Powers*; 1967; *Politics in the USA*, 1976; *The Presidency, American Historical Documents*, 1974. Fields: Federalism; government and politics of the USA; European integration; constitutional theory.

[2014]
VILLERS Robert Louis Marie
8 May 1912, French. 13 rue du Mal Galliéni, 78 Versailles, France. Degrees: Dr en droit (Paris); Agrégé, 1943. Professeur, Faculté de Droit, Caen; Professeur, Faculté de Droit, U de Paris II. Publs: *L'organisation du parlement de Paris et des conseils supérieurs d'après la réforme de Maupeou (1771-74)*, 1937; *Droit romain - Les obligations*, 1953;

Droit romain et ancien droit français (with A Giffard), 1970; *Rome et le droit privé*, 1977. Fields: Irish issues; comparative history of European institutions.

[2015]
VILLEY Michel
6 April 1914, French. 104 rue d'Assas, 75006 Paris, France. Degrees: Dr en droit; Dipl de hautes études. Professor, Us of Saigon, Paris, Strasbourg; Professor, U of Paris II. Publs: *La croisade*, 1942; *Recherches sur la littérature didactique de droit romain*, 1944; *Leçons d'histoire de la philosophie de droit*, 1962; *Seize essais de la philosophie de droit*, 1968; *Critique de la pensée juridique moderne*, 1976; *Philosophie de droit*, 1977; *La formation de la pensée juridique moderne*, 1968. Fields: Philosophy of law and political philosophy.

[2016]
VILMAR Fritz
28 July 1929, German. Kurfürstenstrasse 83, 1 Berlin 30, FR Germany. Degrees: Dr phil. Doctoral thesis: "Strategies of Democratization". Referent, Educational Dept, Metal Workers Union of Germany; Professor of Pol Sci, Free U of Berlin. Publs: *Armament and Disarmament in Late Capitalism*, 1973; *Socialist Peace Policy for Europe*, 1973; *Co-Determination at Workplace*, 1971; *Strategies of Democratization*, 1973; *Industrial Democracy*; 1978, *Humanization of Work* (with K D Sattler), 1978. Fields: Theory of democratic socialism; theory of industrial democracy.

[2017]
VINCENT Gérard Etienne
29 July 1922, French. 14 rue Bachamont, 75002 Paris, France. Degrees: Agrégé d'histoire. Professeur, IEP, Paris. Publs: *Les professeurs du second degré*, 1967; *Les lycéens*, 1971; *Le peuple lycéen*, 1974; *Aujourd'hui*, 1975; *Les Français 1945-1975. Chronologie et structures d'une société*, 1975; *Jeux français*, 1978. Fields: Study of the background of an 'event' in French contemporary society.

[2018]
VINCENT Raymond John
28 February 1943, British. 11 Woodland Avenue, Wolstanton, Newcastle-under-Lyme, Staffordshire, England. Degrees: BA; MA (Wales); PhD (ANU). Doctoral thesis: "The Principle of Non-intervention and International Order". 1973-74 Research Associate, International Inst for Strategic Studies, London; 1972-73 Research Fellow, Centre of International Studies, U of Princeton; 1974-76 Research Fellow, Australian National U; 1976- Lecturer in International Relations, U of Keele. Publs: *Non-intervention and International Order*, 1974; *Military Power and Political Influence: The Soviet Union and Western Europe*, 1975. Fields: Theory of world politics; international organization; strategic studies.

[2019]
VIOT Pierre*
9 April 1925, French. 38 Avenue Emile Zola, Paris XVème, France. Degrees: Ancien élève (Ecole Nationale d'Administration), 1950-52. 1956- Professeur, IEP, Paris; 1958- Conseilles référendaire à la Cour des Comptes; 1961-68 Chef de service, Commissariat général au Plan. Fields: Planning and use of the country.

[2020]
VIRALLY Michel André
6 January 1922, French. 73 Avenue de Mategnin, 1217 Meyrin, Switzerland. Degrees: Dr en droit (Paris), 1948; Doctoral thesis: "L'administration internationale de l'Allemagne 1945-47". 1945-51 Deputy Legal Adviser, French High Commission, Germany; 1952-61 U of Strasbourg; 1964 Legal Adviser, UN Mediator, Cyprus; 1961-75 Professor, U of Geneva; 1975- Professor of Law, Econ and Soc Sci, U of Paris and Graduate Inst of Int Studies, Geneva. Publs: *L'administration internationale de l'Allemagne, 1945-47*, 1948; *La pensée juridique*, 1959; *L'ONU d'hier à demain*, 1961; *Les résolutions dans la formation du droit international du développement* (ed), 1971; *Les Nations Unies face à un monde en mutation* (ed), 1971; *L'organisation internationale*, 1972. Fields: The study of international organizations, especially the UN system; the international law of development.

[2021]
VIRÓS M Rosa
10 December 1935, Spanish. Reina Elisenda 10, Barcelona 34, Spain. Degrees: Dr in Law. Doctoral thesis: "El Comportamiento Electoral de los Municipios de la Circonscripción de Girona Durante la II Republica: Una Approximación a su Base Económica y Social". Professor of Constitutional Law, Catholic Inst of Soc Sci, U of Barcelona; Assistant Professor of Pol Sci, U of Barcelona. Publs: *Las Elecciones Legislativas de 15 Junio de 1977 en las Circonscripciònes electorales de Catalunuya*. Fields: Electoral behaviour; political socialization of children.

[2022]
VIVER Carles
1 November 1949, Spanish. Calle de la Budallera no 6, Barcelona 17, Spain. Degrees: Dr in Law (Barcelona), 1977. Doctoral thesis: "El Personal Politico de Franco 1936-45: Contribución Empírica a Una Teoria del Régimen Franquista". Assistant Professor of Theory of the State, U of Barcelona; Director, Dept of Pol Sci, Inst Católic d'Estudis Soc de Barcelona. Publs: *El Personal Politico de Franco 1930-45: Contribución Empirica a una Teoria del Régimen Franquista*, 1978; "El Personal Politic del Franquisme", *Perspectiva Social*, 1978; "Aproximació a l'Ideologia del Franquisme en l'Etapa Fondacional del Regim", 1978. Fields: Political personnel; Franco's regime and constitutional law.

[2023]
VLACHOS George
1 December 1912, Greek. 68 Argolidos Street, Athens, Greece. Doctoral thesis: "Fédéralisme et Raison d'Etat dans la Pensée Internationale de Fichte". 1951-57 Maître de recherche, CNRS; Professeur Associé, U de Paris I; 1965-67 Conseiller Spécial du Gouvernement Hellénique; 1966-67 Délégué, Conseil de l'Europe. 1967- Recteur de l'Ecole Supérieure des Sci Pol d'Athènes; Professeur de Sci Pol et d'Histoire des Idées Pol. Publs: *Essai sur la politique de Hume*, 1955; *La pensée politique de Kant*, 1962; *Les sociétés politiques homériques*, 1974; *La politique de Montesquieu*, 1974; *La constitution de la Grèce*, 1954-55; *Introduction à l'histoire de la pensée politique*, 1975; *Psychologie Politique*, 1976; *Politique*, 1977-78; *Le pensée politique de la Chine classique*, 1976. Fields: Political theory; history of ideas, especially ancient Greece, and in the 17th and 18th centuries in the West.

[2024]
VLOEBERGHS Gustaaf Antoon Maria
11 December 1943, Belgian. Koning Albertlaan 100/23, B-3200 Kessel-Lo, Belgium. Degrees: Lic. Assistant, Dept of Pol Sci, Catholic U of Leuven. Publs: "Changes in

China's Leadership" (in Dutch), *Kultuurleven*, 1978. Fields: International relations; China: internal and foreign policy; less developed countries.

[2025]
VOGEL Ursula
26 August 1938, German. 29 St John Street, Oxford, England. Degrees: Dr (Free U of Berlin), 1968. Doctoral thesis: "Politische-historische Kritik an der französischen Revolution". 1967-68 Lecturer, U of Oxford; 1968-70, Wiss Assistent, Dept of Pol Sci, U of Freiburg; 1970-73 Research Fellow, Wolfson Coll, U of Oxford; 1973- Lecturer in Govt, U of Manchester. Publs: *Konservative Kritik an der bürgerlichen Revolution*, 1971. Fields: Romantic political thought and modern right-wing ideologies; relationship between aesthetic and political theory; philosophy of history.

[2026]
VOISSET Michèle*
1 December 1938, French. 3 rue Jean Bart, 75006 Paris, France. Degrees: Lic en Droit public et Sci Pol; Dipl d'études supérieures de droit public; Dipl d'études supérieures de Sci Pol; Dr en Droit; Dipl IEP (Paris); Agrégée de Droit public et de Sci Pol, 1972 (all Faculté de Droit et des Sci écon de Paris). Doctoral thesis: "L'article 16 de la Constitution du 4 octobre 1958". 1965-70 Assistante, 1970-72 Maître-assistant, Faculté de Droit et des Sci écon de Paris; Chargée de cours, Faculté de Droit et des Sci Pol de Caen; Maître de Conférences agrégé des Facultés de Droit. Publs: *L'article 16 de la Constitution du 4 octobre*, 1969. Fields; Administrative science; decision-making in plublic bodies; modernization in public administration.

[2027]
VOLTERRRA, Sara*
24 June 1934, Italian. Via Masaccio 216, Florence 50132, Italy. Degrees: Laura (Florence), 1961; Libera docenza (Florence), 1971. 1961-68 Assistente straordinaria in Constitutional and Comparative Law, U of Florence; 1968 Assistente di ruolo in Constitutional and Comparative Public Law; Associate Professor of American Public Law, U of Florence. Publs: *Sistemi Elettorali e Partiti in America*, 1963; *L'Indipendenza de Giudice Ugli Stati degli Stati Uniti d'America*, 1970. Fields: Comparative problems of federalism and the regional state; Indian constitutional law; civil liberties, especially in US and Italy; constitutional problems with regard to ecology.

[2028]
VON BEYME Klaus
3 July 1934, German. 69 Heidelberg, Sitzbuchweg 40, FR Germany. Degrees: PhD (Heidelberg), 1963; Habilitation (Heidelberg), 1967. 1970-71 Dean, Faculty of Pol Sci, U of Tübingen; 1967- Director, Inst of Pol Sci, U of Tübingen; Professor of Pol Sci, U of Tübingen. Publs: *Die parlamentarischen Regierungssysteme in Europa*, 1973; *Die politische Elite in der Bundesrepublik*, 1974; *Vom Faschismus zur Entwicklungsdiktatur*, 1971; *Die politischen Theorien der Gegenwart*, 1976; *Empirische Revolutionsforschung* (ed), 1973; *Ökonomie und Politik im Sozialismus*, 1977; *Gewerkschaften und Arbeitsbeziehungen in kapitalistischen Ländern*, 1977; *Sozialismus oder Wohlfahrtsstaat? Sozialpolitik und Sozialstruktur der Sowjetunion im Systemvergleich*, 1977. Fields: Developing countries; political theory; comparative politics; elites and pressure groups.

[2029]
VON BONSDORFF Göran Edvard
18 March 1918, Finnish. Inst of Political Science, University of Helsinki, 00100 Helsinki 10, Finland. Degrees; Dr pol sci (Helsinki), 1950. Doctoral thesis: "Självstyrelsen-tanken i Finlandssvensk Politikåaren 1917-23". 1952-68 Associate Professor of Pol Sci, U of Helsinki; 1968- Professor of Pol Sci, U of Helsinki. Publs: *Självstyrelsetanken i Finlandssvensk Politik åren 1917-23*, 1970; *De Politiska Partierna i Finland*, 1951; *Studeir Rörande den Moderna Liberalismen i de Nordiska Länderna*, 1954; *Världspolitik i Teknikens Tidsålder*, 1961; *Regionalismen i den Internationella Politiken*, 1967; *Europas val av Framtid*, 1971; *Makt och Samarbete*, 1975; *Finland i Blickpunkten*, 1976. Fields: International politics; international organizations; transformation of world society; European security.

[2030]
VON BREDOW Wilfried
2 January 1944, German. Savigny Strasse 17, 355 Marburg/Lahn, FR Germany. Degrees: Dr phil (Bonn), 1968. 1969-72 Assistent, Seminar für Pol Wiss, U of Bonn; Professor of Pol Sci, Phillips U, Marburg. Publs: *Der Primat militärischen Denkens. Die Bundeswehr und das problem der okkupierten Öffentlichkeit*, 1969; *Entscheidung des Gewissens. Kriegsdienstverweigerer heute*, 1969; *Vom Antagonismus zur Konvergenz? Studien zum Ost-West Problem*, 1972; *Die unbewältigte Bundeswehr*, 1973; *Militär-Politik*, 1974; *Film und Gesellschaft in Deutschland* (with R Zurek), 1975; *Economic and Social Aspects of Disarmament* (ed), 1975. Fields: Military sociology; peace research; international relations.

[2031]
VON EYNERN Gert
12 February 1929, German. Fischerhüttenstrasse 40A, D-1000 Berlin 37, FR Germany. Degrees: Dipl Volkswirt; Dr der Staatswissenschaften. Doctoral thesis: "Die Reichsbank". Redakteur; *Wirtschaftsverwaltungen*; Dozent, Deutschen Hochschule für Pol, Berlin; Emeritus Professor, Free U of Berlin. Publs: *Grundriss der politischen Wirtschaftslehre*, 1972; *Wörterbuch zur politischen Ökonomie* (ed), 1977. Fields: Interdependence of economy and politics.

[2032]
VON KROCKOW Christian (Graf)
1927, German. Auf dem Bui 2, D-34 Göttingen-Nikolausberg, FR Germany. Degrees: Dr phil (Göttingen), 1954. 1956-1961 Assistent, U of Göttingen; 1961-1965 Professor, Pädagogische Hochschule, Göttingen; 1965-1968 Ordinarius Professor, U of Saar-brücken; 1968-69 Ordinarius Professor, U of Frankfurt; Private Research. Publs: *Die Entscheidung*, 1958; *Soziologie des Friedens*, 1962; *Sozialwissenschaften*, 1969; *Nationalismus als deutsches Problem*, 1970; *Soziale Kontrolle und autoritäre Gewalt*, 1971; *Reform als Politisches Prinzip*, 1976; *Herrschaft und Freiheit-Politische Grund-positionen der bürgerlichen Gesellschaft*, 1977. Fields: Reform of education systems; political and social institutions in Germany; peace research; democracy.

[2033]
VON KROSIGK Friedrich
26 December 1937, German. Am Sachsenberg 7, 2057 Wentorf/Hamburg, FR Germany. Degrees: Dr phil (Munich), 1967; Habilitation (Heidelberg), 1977. Doctoral thesis: "Philosophy und Politische Aktion bei J P Sartre". Visiting Assistant Professor, U of Washington; Research Fellow, Deutsche Forschungsgemeinschaft; Research Associate, U of Lancaster; Professor of International Relations, U of Erlangen. Publs: *Philosophy und Politische Aktion bei J P Sartre*, 1968; *Multinationale Konzerne und*

die Krise der europäischen Integration, 1978; plus various articles on international relations. Fields: European integration; autonomy movements; theory and practice of nationalism.

[2034]
VON LÖWIS OF MENAR Henning
23 March 1948, German. Voigtelstrasse 23, D-5000 Köln 41, FR Germany. Degrees: Dipl Pol; PhD. Doctoral thesis: "Bilateralism and Multilateralism in Portugal's Foreign Policy 1945-1974". Assistant Professor, Research Inst for Pol Sci and European Affairs, U of Cologne. Publs: "Die Beziehungen zu Spanien und Portugal"; "Die deutschen Interessen im südlichen Afrika"; "Die Rolle des Rundfunks im Ost-West-Konflikt", all in *Handbuch der deutschen Aussenpolitik* (H P Schwarz (ed)), 1975; "Das Engagement der DDR im Portugiesischen Afrika", *Deutschland Archiv*, 1977; "Solidarität und Subversion. Die Rolle der DDR im südlichen Afrika", *Deutschland Archiv*, 1977; "Das politische und militärische Engagement der Deutschen Demokratischen Republik in Schwarzafrika 1953-1978", *Beiträge zur Konfliktforschung*, 1978. Fields: Foreign policy of the German Democratic Republic and the Federal Republic of Germany; African affairs; international broadcasting.

[2035]
VOYENNE Bernard
12 August 1920, French. 40 rue du Père Corentin, 75014 Paris, France. Degrees: Lic ès lettres. Professeur chargé des études et recherches, Centre de Formation et Perfectionnement des journalistes de Paris. Publs: *Textes choisis de P J Proudhon*, 1952; *Histoire de l'idée européenne*, 1964; *Histoire de l'idée fédéraliste*, 1973; *La presse dans la société contemporaine*, 1973; *Le droit à l'information*, 1970. Fields: Mass communication; history of political ideas.

[2036]
VUURENS Petrus Antonius*
15 December 1940, Dutch. Sportlaan 50, Amstelveen, The Netherlands. Degrees: Drs (Amsterdam), 1970; Teacher, Inst for Pol Sci. Publs: "Bibliography of Foreign-language Literature on the Netherlands of Interest to Political Scientists" (with R E van der Land), *Acta Politica*, 1970. Fields: Primitive political systems as models for international political systems.

[2037]
VYŠNÝ Michal Paul
23 April 1944, British. Department of Modern History, University of St Andrews, St Andrews, Fife, Scotland. Degrees: BA; PhD, 1972. Doctoral thesis: "A Study of Czechoslovak-Russian Relations 1900-14". Lecturer in Modern History, U of St Andrews. Publs: *Neo-Slavism and the Czechs 1898-1914*, 1977. Fields: Politics and modern history of Russia and Eastern Europe; origins of the Second World War.

W

[2038]
WADE Henry William Rawson
16 January 1918, British. Gonville and Caius College, Cambridge, England. Degrees: MA; LL D; DCL. 1946-61 Fellow of Trinity Coll, Cambridge; 1959-61 Reader in English Law, U of Cambridge; 1961-76 Fellow of St John's Coll, U of Oxford; 1961-76 Professor of English Law, U of Oxford; Master of Gonville and Caius Coll, Cambridge and Rouse Ball Professor of English Law, U of Cambridge. Publs: *Administrative Law*, 1978; *The Law of Real Property* (with Sir R Megarry), 1975; *Legal Control of Government* (with B Schwartz), 1972; *Towards Administrative Justice*, 1963. Fields: Administrative law; constitutional law; land law; European community law.

[2039]
WAHLBÄCK Martin Krister
21 November 1937, Swedish. Svarvargatan 14, Stockholm, Sweden. Degrees: PhD (Stockholm), 1965. 1965-68 Ed, *Co-operation and Conflict: Nordic Studies in International Politics*; 1964-72 Assistant Professor, Dept of Pol Sci, U of Stockholm; 1972-76 Associate Research Professor in International Pol, Swedish Council for Soc Sci Research; 1976- Head of Policy Planning Section, Ministry of Foreign Affairs. Publs: *Finlandsfrågan i Svensk Politik 1937-40*, 1964; *Från Mannerheim till Kekkonen: Huvudlinjer i Finländsk Politik 1917-67*, 1967; *Politik i Norden*, 1972. Fields: International politics, particularly foreign policy decision-making of small democracies; the concept of neutrality; the comparative study of foreign policies of the Nordic countries; Finnish and French politics.

[2040]
WAITES Neville Herbert
18 February 1939, British. 20 Repton Road, Earley, Reading, England. Degrees: BA; PhD (London). Doctoral thesis; "British Foreign Policy Towards France Regarding the German Problem from 1929 to 1934". 1965-67 Assistant Lecturer, Dept History, U of Glasgow; 1967- Lecturer in French History, Dept of French Studies, U of Reading. Publs: *Troubled Neighbours: Franco-British Relations in the Twentieth Century* (ed), 1971. Fields: French Third Republic 1871-1940; French and British foreign policies 1918-1978; Aristide Briand 1862-1932; French politics since 1945.

[2041]
WALDOCK Claud Humphrey Meredith
13 August 1904, British. 6 Lathbury Road, Oxford OX2 7AU, England. Degrees: MA; DCL. 1947-72 Chichele Professor of International Law, U of Oxford and Fellow, All Soul's Coll; 1954-61 Member, European Commission on Human Rights; 1966-74 Judge, European Court of Human Rights; 1961-73 Member, International Law Commission; 1973- Judge, International Court of Justice, The Hague. Publs: *English Law, The Law of Mortgages, International Law, The Regulation of the Use of Force*, 1952; *General Course on Public International Law*; *Law of Nations*, 1963. Fields: International law; international relations.

[2042]
WALKER Nigel David
6 August 1917, British. King's College, Cambridge, England. Degrees: MA (Oxon); PhD (Edinburgh); D Litt (Oxon); LL D (Leicester). Doctoral thesis; "The Logical Status of the Freudian Unconscious". Assistant Secretary, Scottish Office; Reader in Criminology, U of Oxford; Wolfson Professor of Criminology and Director, Inst of Criminology, U of Cambridge and Professorial Fellow, King's Coll, U of Cambridge.

Publs: *Delphi*, 1936; *A Short History of Psychotherapy*, 1957; *Morale in the Civil Service*, 1961; *Crime and Punishment in Britain*, 1965; *Crime and Insanity in England*, 1973; *Sentencing in a Rational Society*, 1969; *Crimes, Courts and Figures*, 1970; *Behaviour and Misbehaviour*, 1977. Fields: Theories of punishment; philosophy of explanation in the social sciences; definitions of mental disorder; deviance; sentencing problems.

[2043]
WALKLAND Stuart Alan
13 January 1925, British. 9 Taptonville Road, Sheffield S10 5BQ, England. Degrees: MA (St Andrews), 1951. Assistant in Pol, U of Aberdeen; Assistant Lecturer, Lecturer, Senior Lecturer, Reader in Pol, U of Sheffield. Publs: *The Legislative Process in Great Britain*, 1968; *The Commons in the Seventies* (with M Ryle (eds)), 1977; *The House of Commons in the Twentieth Century*, 1978. Fields: British central government, with emphasis on parliament.

[2044]
WALLACE Helen Sarah
25 June 1946, British. 79 Clande Road, Manchester M21 2DE, England. Degrees: BA; PhD (Manchester), 1975. Doctoral thesis: "The Domestic Policy-Making Implications of the Labour Government's Application for Membership of the EEC 1964-1970". 1968-69 Administrative Assistant, Dept of Extra-Mural Studies, U of Manchester; 1973-74 SSRC Research Fellow, Dept of Government, U of Manchester; 1974-78 Lecturer in European Studies, UMIST; 1978- Lecturer in Public Administration, Civil Service Coll. Publs: *National Government and the European Communities*, 1973; *Policy-Making in the European Communities* (with W Wallace and C Webb (eds)), 1977; *The Council of Ministers of the European Communities and the President-in-Office* (with G Edwards), 1977; plus articles in *Government and Opposition, Journal of Common Market Studies, International Affairs, World Today*. Fields: European communities; British central government; comparative West European politics; French government and administration.

[2045]
WALLACE William John Lawrence
12 March 1941, British. c/o Royal Institute of International Affairs, 10 St James's Square, London SW1, England. Degrees: BA; PhD (Cornell), 1968. Doctoral thesis: "The Liberal Revival: The Liberal Party in Britain, 1955-66". 1962-65 Teaching Assistant, Cornell U; 1965-67 Walter F Carpenter Fellow, Cornell U; Student, Nuffield Coll, U of Oxford; 1967-77 Lecturer, U of Manchester, 1977- Director of Studies, Royal Inst of International Affairs, London; Ed, *Journal of Common Market Studies*. Publs: *Foreign Policy and the Political Process*, 1972; *The Foreign Policy Process in Britain*, 1976; *A Wider European Community? Issues and Problems of Further Engagement* (with G Edwards), 1977; *Policy-Making in the European Communities* (with H Wallace and C Webb (eds)), 1977; *Foreign Policy-Making in Western Europe* (with W E Paterson (eds)), 1978. Fields: Policy-making, both national and international; interdependence and integration; comparative foreign policy; West European politics; the European communities.

[2046]
WALLER David Michael
14 February 1934, British. 28 Victoria Road, Manchester M14 6AP, England. Degrees: BA; MA (Oxon). Lecturer, U of Manchester. Publs: *The Language of Communism*, 1972. Fields: Communist politics.

[2047]
WALLES Malcolm John
4 February 1935, British. 9 Scotland Way, Horsforth, Leeds, Yorkshire, England. Degrees: BA; PhD (London), 1958. Doctoral thesis: "The St Lawrence Seaway Development: A Study in American Politics and Pressure Groups". 1954-62 Research Officer in Advertising, LSE; 1962-65 Lecturer in Pol, U of Monash, Australia; 1965 Lecturer in Pol, U of Leeds; 1970-72 Visiting Professor of Government, City U, New York; 1977-78 Visiting Professor of Pol Sci, U of Vanderbilt. Publs: *Governing Britain* (with A H Hanson), 1970. Fields: The Port of New York Authority; the Arkansas River Basin development.

[2048]
WALTERS Peter Llewellyn Henry*
6 October 1940, British. Social Studies Building, The University, Liverpool L69 3BX, England. Degrees: BA; PhD (Manchester), 1970. 1967- Lecturer, Dept of Pol Theory and Inst, U of Liverpool. Fields: British government; economic planning.

[2049]
WASSMUND Hans
8 May 1941, German. Ilsestrasse 6, 6600 Saarbrücken 3, FR Germany. Degrees: Dipl Pol (Berlin), 1966; Dr phil (Berlin), 1971. Doctoral thesis: "Die Interdependenz sowjetischer Innen- und Deutschlandpolitik von 1953-1955". Assistant, Director, Deutsche Gesellschaft für Friedens- und Konfliktforschung; Akademischer Oberrat, U of Saarland. Publs: *Kontinuität im Wandel-Bestimmungsfaktoren sowjetischer Deutschland-politik in der nach Stalin-Zeit*, 1974; "Revolutionsforschung — Ihr Stand und ihre Aspekt", *Universitas*, 1976; *Revolutionstheorien — Eine Einführung*, 1978. Fields: International relations; Soviet-American relations; comparative communist studies; revolution — modernization; German-Soviet relations; European integration.

[2050]
WATERMAN Peter
26 January 1936, British. Galileistraat 130, The Hague, The Netherlands. Degrees: BA; M Soc Sci (Birmingham). Lecturer, Ahmadu Bello U; Lecturer, Inst of Social Studies, The Hague. Publs: *African Social Studies: A Radical Reader* (with P Gutkind (eds)), 1977; "Communist Theory in the Nigerian Trade Union Movement", *Politics and Society*, 1973; "The Labour Aristocracy in Africa, Introduction to a Debate", *Development and Change*, 1975; "Conservatism amongst Nigerian Workers", in *Nigeria: Economy and Society* (G Williams (ed)), 1976. Fields: Structure, consciousness, organization and action of workers, particularly Africa, Asia and Latin America; Nigeria.

[2051]
WATSON Michael Martin
23 January 1938, British. Department of Political Science, University College of Wales, Penglais, Aberystwyth, Wales. Degrees: BA; MA (Oxon), 1969. Doctoral thesis: "Regional Development Policy and the Structures of the State, With Special Reference to France". 1962-64 *Economist* Intelligence Unit; 1964-66 Research Officer, Dept of Econ Research, U Coll of Wales; 1966- Lecturer, Dept of Pol Sci, U Coll of Wales. Publs: *Regional Development Policy and Administration in Italy*, 1970; *Planning, Politics and Public Policy* (with J E S Haywood (eds)), 1975; *Government, Business and Labour in European Capitalism* (contributor) (R T Griffiths (ed)), 1977. Fields: The political economy of regionalism and planning; questions of 'advanced' development; competing rationalities and the ecological and cultural challenges to capitalism.

[2052]
WEALE Albert Peter
30 May 1950, British. 5 Fountayne Street, Haxby Road, York YO3 7HN, England. Degrees: MA (Cantab); PhD (Cantab). Doctoral thesis; "Equality as a Rational Criterion of Social Policy". 1974-76 Sir James Knott Fellow, Dept of Pol, U of Newcastle; 1976- Lecturer, Dept of Pol, U of York. Publs: *Equality and Social Policy*; "Power Inequalities", in *Theory and Decision*, 1976; "An Anti-Egalitarian Fallacy", in *Philosophy*, 1977; "Consent", *Political Studies*, 1978; "Paternalism and Social Policy", *Journal of Social Policy*, 1978. Fields: Analytical political theory; social policy and political theory; methods and data analysis.

[2053]
WEBB Carole
29 November 1946, British. 66 Heywood Road, Prestwich, Manchester, England. Degrees: BA; MSc (LSE). 1970-72 Lecturer in Pol, Lanchester Polytechnic; 1972- Lecturer in European Studies, UMIST, U of Manchester. Publs: *Policy-Making in the European Communities* (H Wallace *et al* (eds)), 1977; "Europeans and the European Movement", in *Social and Political Movements in Western Europe* (W Paterson and M Kolinsky (eds)); "Sugar Politics in the European Communities", *Government and Opposition*, 1976. Fields: International relations theory; European integration, theoretical and policy-making aspects; West European Communist parties; European integration and foreign policy.

[2054]
WEBB Keith
25 May 1943, British. 32 Towncourt Lane, Petts Wood, Orpington, Kent, England. Degrees: BA; MSc. 1972-74 Lecturer in Pol, U of Iceland; 1974-75 Lecturer in Pol, U of Strathclyde. Research Fellow, City U, London. Publs: *The Growth of Nationalism in Scotland*, 1977; "The Myth of Classless Iceland" (with T H Broddason), *Acta Sociologica*, 1975. Fields: Nationalism; regionalism; political movements in ideology in democratic theory.

[2055]
WEBER Hermann
23 August 1928, German. Gontardstrasse 24, 6800 Mannheim 1, FR Germany. Degrees: Dr phil, 1968; Habilitation, 1970. Doctoral thesis: "Veränderungen der innerparteilichen Struktur der KPD". 1947-49 SED-Parteihochschule "Karl Marx", danach Publizist; 1970 Universitätsdozent; 1973- Professor, Lehrstuhl für Pol Wiss und Zeitgeschichte, U of Mannheim. Publs: *Demokratischer Kommunismus? Zur Theorie, Geschichte und Politik der Kommunist*, 1969; *Ansätze einer Politikwissenschaft in der DDR*, 1971; *Lenin*, 1970; *Das Prinzip links*, 1973; *Lenin-Chronik* (with G Weber), 1974; *Die SED nach Ulbricht*, 1974; *SED, Chronik einer Partei 1971-1976*, 1976; *DDR. Grundriss der Geschichte 1945-1976*, 1976. Fields: History of communism and working-class movement; problems and history of the DDR.

[2056]
WEBER-SCHÄFER Peter Sebastian
28 April 1935, German. Äskulapweg 24, D-46300 Bochum 1, FR Germany. Degrees: Dr phil (München), 1958. Doctoral thesis: "Ono no Komachi. Leben und Legende im No-Spiel". 1967 Wiss Rat, U of München; 1968- Professor of Pol Sci, Ruhr U, Bochum. Publs: *Der Edle und der Weise*, 1963; *Oikumene und Imperium*, 1968; *Das politische Denken der Griechen*, 1969; *Einführung in die antike politische Theorie*, 1976. Fields: History of political ideas; Chinese political thought; Japanese politics.

[2057]
WEBSTER Barbara Ann
25 May 1949, British. 6 Esher Drive, Coventry, West Midlands CV3 5PY, England.
Degrees: BA; MA (Sussex). Research Fellow, Inst of Local Government Studies, U of
Birmingham. Publs: "Area Analysis of Resources", (with J D Stewart), *Policy and
Politics*, 1974; *Local Government: Approaches to Urban Deprivation* (with J D Stewart
et al), 1976; *Area Management: Objectives and Structures* (with C Horn *et al*), 1977;
Tackling Urban Deprivation: The Contribution of Area-Based Management (with T
Mason *et al*), 1977. Fields: Decentralization and area management in local government;
the impact and distributional effects of local authority policy-making and administration; urban deprivation and social policy.

[2058]
WEDEBYE Jørgen Walter Bay
14 March 1930, Danish. Bakkevej 1, 3500 Vaerløse, Denmark. Degrees: Degree in
Econ and Stat Sci (Copenhagen), 1956. 1956-67 Statistician, Danish Central Statistical
Bureau; 1965- Lecturer, U of Copenhagen; 1967- Statistician, Copenhagen Municipality. Publs: *Nyere Tendenser i Dødelighenden*, 1965; *Regionale Forskelle i Dødeligheden*,
1969. Fields: Demographic problems; fertility and death rates; social problems.

[2059]
WEDGWOOD-OPPENHEIM Felix
8 October 1938, British. 140 Selly Park Road, Birmingham B29 7LH, England.
Degrees: BA; MSc (Birmingham), 1968. Hospital Administration; Lecturer in Operational Research, U of Birmingham. Publs: "Operational Research in Planning", *Town
and Country Planning*, 1970; "Planning under Uncertainty", *Local Government
Studies*, 1972; "A Process of Strategic Choice", in *Proceedings of the 31st World Con-
gress*, 1972; "The Strategic Choice Approach to Planninig", in *Urban Development
Decisions and Finance*, 1972; "Management Training at the Institute of Local Govern-
ment Studies", *Local Government Management Training*, 1972; "Planning under
Uncertainty", *Surveyor*, 1973; *LOGIMP Experiment: A Collaborative Exercise in the
Application of a New Approach to Local Planning Problems* (with J Friend), 1970;
"An Exploratory Study in Strategic Monitoring: Establishing a Regional Performance
Evaluation and Policy Review Unit for the North West" (with D Hart and B Cobley),
Progress in Planning, 1975; *Planning and Landscape Manpower Project: Methodology
Report* (with J Earwicker), 1978. Fields: Public policy-making; theory of planning; in-
formation systems for planning and monitoring; training of senior officials.

[2060]
WEDL Kurt Josef
7 July 1931, Austrian. Babenbergerstrasse 11, A-3390 Melk, Austria. Degrees: Dr rer
Pol. Doctoral thesis: "The Aim of Federalism in Programmes of German and Austrian
Political Parties". Lecturer, U of Munich; Publishing. Publs: *Der Gedanke des
Föderalismus in Programmen politischer Parteien Deutschlands und Österreichs*, 1970;
plus various articles in *Politische Studien*. Fields: Political parties.

[2061]
WEEDE Erich
4 January 1941, German. Torwiesenstrasse 1, 68 Mannheim 1, FR Germany. Degrees:
Dipl (Hamburg), 1966; PhD (Mannheim), 1970; Habilitation (Mannheim), 1975.
1969-72 Wiss Assistent, U of Mannheim; 1974 ZUMA. Publs: *Weltpolitik und
Kriegsursachen im 20 Jahrhundert*, 1975; *Hypothesen, Gleichungen und Daten*, 1977;

plus various articles in *Journal of Conflict Resolution*, *Journal of Peace Research*, *European Journal of Political Research*, *Comparative Political Studies*, *Sozialwissenschaftliches Jahrbuch für Politik*. Fields: International conflict and war; domestic conflict and praetorianism; quantitative methods.

[2062]
WEHLING Hans Georg
4 January 1938, German. Bellinostrasse 118, D-7410 Reutlingen, FR Germany. Degrees: Dr phil (Tübingen). Doctoral thesis: "Die politische Willensbildung auf dem Gebiet der Weinwirtschaft", (The New German Wine Law and the Interests of the Winegrowers and Merchants). Lecturer in Pol Sci, U of Tübingen; Ed, *Der Bürger im Staat*. Publs: *Handbuch der politischen Bildung* (ed), 1973; *Jugend zwischen Auflehnung und Anpassung* (ed), 1973; *Kommunalpolitik* (ed), 1975; *Dorfpolitik*, 1978. Fields: Local politics; community power; interest groups; the political system of the DDR.

[2063]
WEIBEL Ernest
21 February 1942, Swiss. Racherelles 18, 2036 Cormondrèche, Switzerland. Degrees: Dr (Lausanne). Doctoral thesis: "La création des régions autonomes à status spécial en Italie". Professeur de français et d'histoire, Collège Secondaire, Lausanne; 1965-68 Assistant diplômé de soc, U de Lausanne; Journaliste à la Radio Suisse romande; Adjoint scientifique, Administration Fédérale Suisse, Berne; 1973- Professeur ord de sci pol, U de Neuchâtel. Publs: "La problématique des minorités, le pluralisme suisse et le cas du Tessin", *Geschichte und politische Wissenschaft*, 1975; *Les comptes culturels de la Suisse. Objet et méthode* "Notes de recherche concernant le pluralisme grison", in *Annaire Suisse de Science Politique*, 1976. Fields: Group minorities; Italy: parties; Swiss ethnic structure and politics; political violence.

[2064]
WEIBULL Lennart
20 March 1946, Swedish. Kabelgatan 18, S-414 57 Göteborg, Sweden. Degrees: Fil kand. 1968-71 Research Assistant; 1971- Lecturer, U of Göteborg. Publs: *Socialdemokratisk press och press politik 1899-1909* (with S. Hadenius and J. O. Seveborg), 1968; "Social Democratic Press and Press Policy 1899-1909", *Scandinavian Political Studies* (with S. Hadenius and J. O. Seveborg), 1968; *Socialdemokratiskpress 1910-1920* (with S. Hadenius and J. O. Seveborg), 1970; *Press Radio TV* (with S. Hadenius), 1970, 1973, 1978; "News Reporting to the Scandinavian Countries" *Scandinavian Political Studies*, 1971; *Pressens funktioner i samhället*, 1975; "Tidskrifterna i Massmediesamhället", in *DsFi*, 1976. Fields: Mass media; political communication.

[2065]
WEILL Pierre
3 April 1936, French. SOFRES, 16-20 rue Barbès, 92129 Montrouge, France. Degrees: Dipl (IEP Paris); Lic en droit; DES. Publs: *Les familles politiques aujourd'hui en France* (co-author), 1966; *Attitude des français à l'égard du PC* (with A Lancelot), 1969; *Le choix d'un député* (co-author), 1972.

[2066]
WEINACHT Paul Ludwig*
28 May 1938, German. 8059 Wifling bei München, Nr 56, FR Germany. Degrees: Dr phil (München), 1967. Studienreferendar, Regierungs-angestellter, Wiss Assistent, Geschwister-Scholl-Inst für Pol Wiss, U of München; Habilitand im Rahmen eines Forschungsprojekts der VW-Stiftung. Publs: *Staat — Studien zur Bedeutungsgeschichte*

des Wortes von den Anfängen bis ins 19 Jahrhundert, 1968; *Humanist und Politiker —
Leo Wohleb* (with H Maier), 1969; *Bildungsplanung*, (von der Bayer (ed)), 1971;
Politiker des 20 Jahrhunderts (with H Maier and R K Hocevar), 1971. Fields: Development of government; decision-making process in education.

[2067]
WEINSTEIN William Leon
Degrees: BA; B Phil. Fellow and Tutor in Pol, Balliol Coll, Oxford. Fields: Political
theory; government/industry.

[2068]
WEINZIERL Erika*
6 June 1925, Austrian. Mönchsberg 2a, A-5020 Salzburg, Austria. Degrees: PhD, 1948.
Archivist, Vienna; 1964- Professor, U of Salzburg. Publs: *Geschichte der Benediktiner
Klosters Millstatt*, 1951; *Die österreichischen Konkordate 1855-1933*, 1960; *Österreichische Zeitgeschichte in Bildern, 1918-68*, 1968. Fields: Antisemitism; church
history; women's rights.

[2069]
WELAN Manfried*
13 June 1937, Austrian. 1060 Vienna, Gumpendorferstrasse 14, Austria. Degrees: Dr
jur (Vienna), 1961. 1961-62 Secretary, Technical U of Vienna; 1962-66 Secretary, Constitutional Court; 1967-69 Secretary, Federal Chamber of Commerce; 1969- Professor
of Law, U of Agriculture; Director, Inst of Law, U of Agriculture. Publs: *Parteien und
Verbände in Österreich*, 1970; *Parteien und Verbände in der modernen Demokratie,
1970; Der Bundeskanzler im Österreichischen Verfassungsgefüge*, 1971; *Demokratie
und Verfassung in Österreich*, 1971. Fields: Government.

[2070]
WEMEGAH Monica
18 January 1944, Swiss. 19 Avenue des Cavaliers, 1224 Genève, Switzerland. Degrees:
PhD (Genève). Doctoral thesis: "Aménagement du territoire et administration fédérale:
Etude de la coordination horizontale en matière d'aménagement du territoire". 1970-71
Professor of Econ, Ghana; 1973-77 Research/Teaching Assistant in Pol Sci, Genevea;
1977- Research Fellow/Coordinator, United Nations U, Tokyo and Consultant of the
Society for International Development, Rome. Publs: "Self-reliance: a last life-style in
the industrial countries?", in *Self-Reliance* (J Galtung, P O'Brian, R Preiswerk (eds)),
1978; *Aménagement du territoire et administration fédérale*, 1978; "Les négociations
commerciales", *Revue Tiers-Monde*, 1973; "La corruption politique dans le Tiers-Monde", *Helvetes Partenaires*, 1976. Fields: Alternative development; underdeveloped
countries.

[2071]
WENTURIS Nikolaus
21 October 1936, German. Eschenweg 3, G-7400 Tübingen, FR Germany. Degrees: Dr
phil, 1970; Habilitation, 1975. Doctoral thesis: "Der Integrationsprozess im politischen
System der Republik Zypern". Assistant Professor; Privat Dozent; Professor, U of
Tübingen. Publs: "Essentialism, Eschatology and Empiricism", *The Greek Review of
Social Research*, 1975; *Political Culture*, 1977; "Knowledge and Participation", *Syntagma*, 1977; *Die soziopolitischen und ökonomischen Strukturen Griechenlands im
Hinblick auf seinen Integration in die EG*, 1977; *Modellentwurf einer kybernetischen
Relationstheorie zwischen Mikro und Makrosystemen*, 1977; "Marxismus", in

Handwörterbuch der Wirtschaftswissenschaften (1978). Fields: Philosophy of social science; political philosophy; political theory and political cybernetics; political sociology and psychology; European Community and underdeveloped areas; comparative politics.

[2072]
WERCK Victor Albert
11 November 1919, Belgian. Rietveld 11, 2510 Morstel Antwerp, Belgium. Degrees: Dr in Law (Louvain), 1946. 1952-62 Professor of International Law and Relations, U Inst of Overseas Territories, Antwerp; Former co-editor, *World Justice;* Professor of International (War) Law, Royal Military Academy, Brussels; Professor of Peace Research, Catholic U of Leuven. Publs: Articles in *Kultuurleven, Politica, Streven, Civilisations, World Justice, Maatschappelijk Werk, Africa-Latin America-Asia*. Fields: International affairs; international law with special reference to war law; peace research; ethical problems of defence.

[2073]
WERDER Hans
25 January 1946, Swiss. Obere Halde 31, CH-5400 Baden, Switzerland. Degrees: Lic jur (Zürich); Dr rer Soc (Konstanz), 1978. Doctoral thesis: "Die Bedeutung der schweizerischen Volksinitiative in der Nachkriegszeit". Research project, "Wachstum und Umwelt"; Inst für Orts, Regional und Landesplanung, Zürich. Publs: "Bedingungen politischer Planung in der Schweiz" (with B Holz), in *Schweizerisches Jahrbuch für politische Wissenschaft*, 1971; "Das schweizerische politische System vor den Anforderungen der Zukunft", *DISP*, 1978; *Die Volksinitiative in der Nachkriegszeit*, 1978; *Planung in der schweizerischen Demokratie* (with W Linder and B Hotz), 1979. Fields: Political system of Switzerland; public policy; political planning; state economy.

[2074]
WERLE Raymund
17 July 1944, German. Schwalbenweg 60, 69 Heidelberg, FR Germany. Degrees: D Phil; Dipl Volkswirt. Doctoral thesis: "Justizorganisation und Selbstverständnis der Richter" (Judicial Organisation and Self-Conception of Judges). Research Fellow, Lehrstuhl für Pol Wiss, U of Mannheim; Research Fellow, Abteilung für Angewandte Systemanalyse, Kernforschungszentrum, Karlsruhe; Assistant Professor, Inst für Soziologie, U of Heidelberg. Publs: *Soziologische Probleme Juristischer Berufe*, 1975; plus various articles on the judiciary, sociology of law and on implementation of new technologies and employment. Fields: Courts; judicial systems; structural problems of technological change; local policy analysis.

[2075]
WERNER Victor
6 January 1913, Belgian. 24 Avenue Jean Vanhaelen, 1160 Bruxelles, Belgium. Degrees: Dr en sci pol et administrative (Bruxelles). Doctoral thesis: "Le Ministre et le Ministère de la Défense Nationale". Chef de Cabinet du Ministre de la Défense Nationale; Directeur de l'Ecole des Administrateurs Militaires; Directeur du Centre de Sociologie de la Guerre, Brussels. Publs: *Le Ministre et le Ministère de la Défense Nationale*,. 1964; *La grande Peur — la 3ème Guerre Mondiale*, 1976; "La paix par la recherche scientifique", 1970; "La Nationalisme — Facteur belligerant", 1972; "La communication sociale de la guerre", 1974. Fields: Sociology of war; defence policy.

[2076]
WESCHE Hans Eberhard
18 November 1943, German. Willmanndamm 12, 1000 Berlin 62, FR Germany.
Degrees: Dipl Soziologie; Dr rer Pol. Doctoral thesis; "Zur Methodologie der nor-
mativen Sozialwissenschaften — Tauschprinzip — Mehrheitsprinzip — Gesam-
tinteresse". Wiss Assistent, Assistenzprofessor, Fachbereich Pol Wiss, Free U of
Berlin. Publs: "Politologie als Emanzipations-Wissenschaft", *Berliner Zeitschrift für
Politologie*, 1968. Fields: Normative political theory; normative economics.

[2077]
WESTERSTÅHL Jörgen
25 January 1916, Swedish. Institute of Political Science, University of Göteborg, Box
5048, S-402 21 Göteborg, Sweden. Degrees: PhD (Stockholm), 1945. 1944-45 Assistant
Professor, 1945-52 Docent, Dept of Pol Sci, U of Stockholm; 1952- Professor of Pol
Sci, U of Göteborg; Chairman, Dept of Pol Sci, U of Göteborg. Publs: *Svensk
Fackföreningsrörelse*, 1945; *Svenska Metallindustriarbetarförbundets Historia*, 1948;
Politisk Press (with C-G Jansson), 1958; *Ett Forskningsprogram*, 1970; *Objektiv
Nyhetsförmedling*, 1972; *Demokrati och Intresserepresentation* (with M Persson), 1975.
Fields: Local government and local politics; mass media, political propaganda and
political communication.

[2078]
WESTHOLM Carl-Johan
13 August 1947, Swedish. Storgatan 7B, 753 31 Uppsala, Sweden. Degrees: Fil dr (Uppsala), 1976. Doctoral thesis: "Ratio and Universality. John Stuart Mill and the Debate
Today about Democracy" (in Swedish). Fields: Political theory; the majority principle
and the contract principle.

[2079]
WETLESEN Tone Schou
11 April 1940, Norwegian. Nils Baysvei 76, Oslo 8, Norway. Degrees: Mag art, 1967; Dr
phil, 1976. Doctoral thesis: "Rasjonalisering og Forvaltningspolitikk. En studie av Ras-
jonaliseringsdirektoratets Virksomhet 1948-72". 1969 Secretary, Organization and
Methods Division, Norwegian Government; 1970-73 Research Fellow, Norwegian
Research Council; 1969-76 Staff Member, Inst of Soc Research, Oslo; 1976- Lecturer,
Inst of Soc, U of Oslo. Publs: *Rasjonalisering og Forvaltningspolitikk. Rasjonaliser-
ingsdirektoratets Virksomhet 1948-72*, 1977; *Kvinnekunnskap* (with Storen *et al*), 1976;
"The Politics of Governmental Reorganization: the case of Norway", *Acta
Sociologica*, 1976. Fields: Social policy and women's studies; health problems in men
and women related to sex roles in society.

[2080]
WHEATON Michael Alfred*
12 September 1944, British. 20 New Village Road, Cottingham, East Yorkshire,
England. Degrees: BA. 1968-69 Assistant Lecturer in Pol, U Coll of Swansea; Lecturer
in German Pol, U of Hull. Publs: *Politics of European Integration* (with G Ionescu
(eds)), 1972. Fields: The political development of the EEC; the development of British
attitudes towards Europe; Dutch politics.

[2081]
WHITAKER Philip
5 October 1927, British. 10 Park Road, Letham, Forfar, Angus, Scotland. Degrees: MA
(Dublin); PhD (Manchester). Doctoral thesis: "The Development of the Liberal
Organization in Manchester from the 1860's to 1906". 1956 Research Assistant, U of

Manchester; 1957-63 Lecturer, Makerere Coll, Uganda; 1964- Lecturer, U of Dundee. Publs: *Political Theory and East African Problems*, 1964; "The General Election of 1956 in the Western Region of Nigeria", in *Five African Elections* (Mackenzie and Robinson (eds)), 1957. Fields: Government and politics of the USA; political problems of Third World countries; religion and society, especially in Scotland.

[2082]
WHITE Douglas Gordon
13 October 1942, British. c/o IDS, University of Sussex, Brighton, England. Degrees: BA; MA (Oxon); MA (Cornell); PhD (Stanford). Doctoral thesis: "Social Inequality and Distributive Politics in China, 1949-69". Lecturer, Dept of Pol Sci, Australian National U. Publs: The Politics of Hsia-Hsiang Youth", *The China Quarterly*, 1974; "North Korean Chu-Che: The Political Economy of Independence", *Bulletin of Concerned Asian Scholars*, 1975; *The Politics of Class and Class Origin: The Case of the Cultural Revolution*, 1976; *Teaching About China in the Secondary School* (co-author), 1974. Fields: Chinese politics and economics generally; socialist development strategies, with particular interest in China, North Korea and Vietnam; the industrialization process in socialist countries.

[2083]
WHITE Stephen Leonard
1 July 1945, Irish. Department of Politics, University of Glasgow, Glasgow G12 8RT, Scotland. Degrees: BA; MA (Dublin), 1977; PhD (Glasgow), 1973. Doctoral thesis: "Anglo-Soviet Relations 1917-24: A Study in the Politics of Diplomacy". Lecturer, Dept of Pol, and Member, Inst of Soviet and East European Studies, U of Glasgow. Publs: *The USSR: Portrait of a Super-power*, 1978; *Political Culture and Soviet Politics*, 1979; *Britain and Bolshevik Russia: A Study in the Politics of Diplomacy, 1920-24*, 1979. Fields: Soviet politics; Soviet history.

[2084]
WHITEHEAD Laurence Andrew
28 November 1944, British. 15 The Green, Bladon, Oxford, England. Degrees: MA (Oxon). Assistant Research Officer, Inst of Econ and Statistics, and Faculty Fellow, St Anthony's Coll, U of Oxford; Official Fellow in Pol and Senior Tutor, Nuffield Coll, U of Oxford. Publs: *The United States and Bolivia: A Case of Neo-colonialism*, 1969; *The Lesson of Chile*, 1970. "The State and Sectional Interests: the Bolivian Case", *European Journal of Political Research*, 1975; "Linowitz and the 'Low Profile' in Latin America", *Journal of Inter-American Studies and World Affairs*, 1975; "The Chilean Directorship", *The World Today*, 1976; "British Economic Relations with Latin America", 1977; *A History of the Bolivian Labour Movement* (G. Lora (ed)), 1978; *Inflation and Stabilization in Latin America* (co-ed), 1978. Fields: Latin American politics, particularly politics of the mining industry; politics of inflation.

[2085]
WHITELEY Paul Frederick
6 February 1946, British. Department of Politics, University of Bristol, Senate House, Bristol B58 ITH, England. Degrees: BA; MA. 1971-78 Senior Lecturer, School of Econ and Pol, Kingston Polytechnic; Senior Lecturer, U of Bristol. Publs: *Statistical Methods for Data Analysis and Causal Modelling*, 1975; "Bayesian Statistics and Political Recruitment", *BPS*, 1976; "The Political Ideology of Labour Councillors", *Policy and Politics*, 1977; "The Structure of Socialist Ideology in Britain", *Political Studies*, 1978. Fields: Positive political theory; methodology and statistics in political science; public policy analysis; empirical political theory.

[2086]
WHYTE John Henry
30 April 1928, British. Department of Political Science, Queen's University, Belfast BT7 1NN, Ireland. Degrees: BA; B Litt (Oxford), 1951; PhD (Belfast), 1970. Doctoral thesis: "Church and State in the Republic of Ireland". 1958-61 Lecturer in History, Makerere Coll, U of Uganda; 1961-66 Lecturer in Pol, U Coll, Dublin; 1966- Lecturer, Reader, Queen's U, Belfast. Publs: The *Independent Irish Party 1850-59*, 1958; *Church and State in Modern Ireland 1923-1970*, 1971. Fields: Ireland 1945-present; 20th century Ulster; political history; history of community relations; comparative church-state relations; politics of both parts of Ireland.

[2087]
WIDDER Helmut Stefan
13 January 1943, Austrian. Sombarstrasse 8, A-4045 Linz, Austria. Degrees: Dr jur (Vienna), 1966; 1966-67 Assistant Lecturer, U of Innsbruck; 1970 Associate Professor of Pol Sci, California State U of Fullerton; 1968- Assistant Professor of Pol Sci and Public Law, U of Linz. Publs: *Organisationprobleme im parlamentarischen Regierungssystem*, 1977; *Parlamentarische Strukturen im politischen System*, 1978; plus various articles in *Juristische Blätter, Zeitschrift für Parlamentsfragen, Österreichische Zeitschrift für Politikwissenschaft*. Fields: Parliamentarism; Austrian and comparative government; political theory.

[2088]
WIDMAIER Uli
22 January 1944, German. Schinkelstrasse 2, 1 Berlin 33, FR Germany. Degrees: Dipl Soc (Mannheim); Dr phil (Mannheim). Doctoral thesis: "Politische Gewaltanwendung als Problem der Organisation von Interessen". Lehrstuhl für Pol Wiss, U of Mannheim; Researcher, Wissenschaftszentrum, Berlin. Publs: *Politische Gewaltanwendung als Problem der Organisation von Interessen*, 1978. Fields: Theoretical and empirical aspects of social and political conflicts; formal and statistical models; policy analysis; political economy.

[2089]
WIEBECKE Ferdinand
1 March 1935, German. Friedrich Allee 3, D-5300 Bonn 2, FR Germany. Degrees: Dr phil. Referent der SPD-Bundestagsfraktion. Publs: "Wissenschaft und gesellschaftliche Effizienz", in *Wissenschaftspolitik und Demokratisierung* (with U Lohmar (ed)), 1973; "Die Kernenergie, eine Change?", *Aus Politik und Zeitgeschichte*, 1978. Fields: Research and technology in politics; formation politics.

[2090]
WIEGMANN Hildegard
14 February 1932, German. 2848 Vechta, Georg-Reinke Strasse 4, FR Germany. Degrees: Dipl Volkswirt; Dr rer Pol. Doctoral thesis: "Probleme der Eigentumsbildung". Ord Professor für Pol Wiss, U of Osnabrück, Abteilung Vechta. Publs: "Breitere Vermögenssteurung" (with J Hoffner), in *Jahrbuch des Institut für christliche Sozialwissenschaften der Westfälischen Wilhelms-Universität Münster,* 1961. Fields: Governmental systems of West Germany.

[2091]
WIETEN Jan
19 March 1940, Dutch. Van der Helstpark 39, 1399 GH Muiderberg, The Netherlands. Degrees: Drs. Assistant Professor, Dept of Mass Communication, U of Amsterdam, Publs: *Presidental Elections in West Berlin. A Study of the Influence of Detente on the Information in Some Dutch National Newspapers,* 1969 and 1973; *Baptists in the Soviet Union,* 1971; *Editorial Participation* (with F Kempers), 1974; *Journalists and Press Concentration* (with F Kempers), 1976. Fields: Mass communication; political communication; aftermath of World War II in politics; communication and the churches.

[2092]
WIGHTMAN Gordon
16 June 1943, British. Roxby Building, The University, Liverpool L69 3BX, England. Degrees: MA (Glasgow), 1966. 1971 Temporary Lecturer, U of Glasgow; 1972- Lecturer, Dept of Pol Theory and Inst, U of Liverpool. Publs: "Czechoslovakia: Revival and Retreat", in *Political Culture and Political Change in Communist States* (A Brown and J Gray (eds)), 1977. Fields: Soviet politics; Czechoslovak politics.

[2093]
WIHTOL Robert Fabian Ilmari
10 June 1953, Finnish. 150 Ruobertinkatn 52 C 55, 00120 Helsinki 12, Finland. Degrees: M Soc Sci. Assistant in International Pol, Inst of Pol Sci, U of Helsinki; Trainee, Commission of European Communities; Research Assistant, International Food Pol Project, Finland. Publs: *An Evaluation of the European Communities' Generalized System of Tariff Preferences,* 1977. Fields: International organizations; development problems.

[2094]
WIKLUND Claes Lennart
13 July 1942, Swedish. Lunkentusvägen 28, 161 38 Bromma, Sweden. Degrees: Fil kand, 1967. 1971-74 Research Assistant, Dept of Pol Sci, U of Stockholm; 1972- Secretary, Social and Environmental Committee, The Nordic Council. Publs: *Norden på Världsarenan* (contributor))A Landqvist (ed)), 1968; *Politik i Norden. En Jämförande Översikt* (co-author), 1972; *Nordisk Råd i 25 år* (contributor) (K Kauffeldt (ed)), 1977. Fields: Nordic and European integration; comparative politics: Nordic and West European; international relations.

[2095]
WILDENMANN Rudolf
15 January 1921, German. Lehrstuhl für Politische Wissenschaft, Universität Mannheim, 68 Mannheim, Schloss, FR Germany. Degrees: Dipl rer Pol (Heidelberg); PhD (Heidelberg); Habilitation (Cologne). Doctoral thesis: "Macht und Konsens". 1952-56 Journal Ed; 1956-59 Chairman, Federal Agency for Civic Education; 1959-66 Assistent Privatdozent, U of Cologne; 1964- Professor of Pol Sci, U of Mannheim; 1970-75 Visiting Professor, SUNY at Stony Brook. Publs: *Partei und Fraktion,* 1954; *Neue Dimensionen der Aussenpolitik,* 1961; *Macht und Konsens,* 1963; *Funktionen der Massenmedien* (with W Kaltefleiter), 1964; *Wahler, Parteien, Parlament* (with H Unkelbach and W Kaltefleiter), 1965; *Zur Soziologie der Wahl* (co-author), 1965; *Politik und Wähler* (with E Scheuch R König, F A Hermens); *Gutachten zur Frage der Subventionierung politischer Parteien,* 1968; *Sozialwissenschaftliches Jahrbuch für Politik* (ed), 1970. Fields: Comparative politics; political sociology of sub-systems, such as parties, groups, military organizations, bureaucracy; empirical theory of democracy.

[2096]
WILI Hans-Urs
30 March 1949, Swiss. Kirchackerstrasse 12, CH-3250 Lyss, Switzerland. Degrees: Lic jur (Berne). Functionary, Legal Dept, Federal Chancellery of Switzerland. Publs: "Die hängigen Partialrevisionen der Bundesverfassung. Stand 15 Januar 1976", *Zeitschrift für schweizerisches Recht,* 1975; "Die hängigen Partialrevisionen der Bundesverfassung. Stand 15 Januar 1977", *Zeitschrift für schweizerisches Recht,* 1976; "Die hängigen Partialrevisionen der schweizerischen Bundesverfassung. Stand 31 December 1977", *Zeitschrift für schweizerisches Recht,* 1977. Fields: Popular votes in all countries; political rights of citizens.

[2097]
WILKINSON Paul
9 May 1937, British. c/o Department of Politics, University College, Cardiff, PO Box 78, Cardiff CF1 1XL, Wales. Degrees: BA; MA (Wales). 1966- Assistant Lecturer, Lecturer, Senior Lecturer in Pol, U Coll, Cardiff. Publs: *Social Movement,* 1971; *Political Terrorism,* 1974; *Terrorism and the Liberal State,* 1977; plus various articles in *Contemporary Review, Political Science Quarterly, Political Studies.* Fields: Civil violence and terrorism; international terrorism; public order, laws of war; theory of social movements; defence policy and strategy.

[2098]
WILL Hans-Dieter*
19 June 1943, German. Otto-Suhr-Institut, Freie Universität, Ihnestrasse, 1 Berlin, FR Germany. Degrees: Magister Artium of Sociology. Research Assistant, Fachbereich Pol Wiss, U of Konstanz; Research Assistant, Otto-Suhr-Inst, Free U of Berlin. Publs: "Konstanzer Soziologen Kollektiv", *Berufe für Soziologen,* 1971. Fields: Public administration; a Marxist analysis of the functions of the capitalist state; welfare policy and the development of industry.

[2099]
WILLETTS Peter
22 June 1943, British. 25 Kings Way, Harrow, Middlesex HA1 1XT, England. Degrees: BA; MSc (Strathclyde), 1969; PhD (Strathclyde), 1976. Doctoral thesis: "The Principles and the Practice of Non-Alignment 1960-70". 1966-68 Research Executive, Gallup Poll; 1969-72 "Study and Serve" Lecturer, Dept of Pol Sci and Public Administration, Makerere, Uganda; 1972-73 Research Officer, Dept of Pol, U of Strathclyde; 1973- Lecturer in International Relations, Dept of Systems Sci, City U. Publs: "Cluster-Bloc Analysis and Statistical Inference", *American Political Science Review,* 1972; "Uganda's Military Government", *African Contemporary Record,* 1972; "The Politics of Uganda as a One-Party State 1969-70", *African Affairs,* 1975; *The Non-Aligned Movement: The Origins of a Third World Alliance,* 1978. Fields: International relations of the Third World; United Nations; quantitative, methods in international relations.

[2100]
WILLIAMS Gavin Peter
22 September 1943, British. 121 Southfield Road, Oxford, England. Degrees: BA; B Phil (Oxon). 1967-70, 1972-75 Lecturer in Sociology, U of Durham; 1970-72 Research Fellow in Soc Anthropology, U of Sussex; 1975- Fellow and Tutor in Pol, St Peters Coll, U of Oxford; CUF Lecturer in Pol and Soc, U of Oxford. Publs: *Sociology and*

Development (with E Kudt (eds)), 1974; *Nigeria: Economy and Society* (ed), 1976; *African Perspectives* (contributor) (C A Allen and R W Johnson (eds)); *West African States* (J Dunn (ed)); *The Political Economy of Contemporary Africa* (P C W Gutkind and I Wallerstein (eds)); *African Social Studies,* (P C W Gutkind and P Waterman (eds)). Fields: Marxist theory, especially German and Russian Marxism; political economy of underdevelopment, especially Nigeria: ideology and practice of rural development.

[2101]
WILLIAMS Geraint Lynn
13 December 1942, British. 65 Glenalmond Road, Sheffield 11, England. Degrees: BA; MA (wales), 1968. 1966-68 Temporary Lecturer, Dept of Pol, U Coll, Swansea; 1971-72 Professor, Dept of Pol, U of Calgary; 1968- Lecturer, Dept of Pol, U of Sheffield. Publs: *J S Mill on Politics and Society* (ed), 1976; "Mill's Principle of Liberty", *Political Studies,* 1976. Fields: Political philosophy; history of political thought; John Stuart Mill.

[2102]
WILLIAMS Kenneth*
16 September 1938, Welsh. Institute of Local GOvernment, University of Birmingham, Birmingham B15 2TT, England. Degrees: BSc. Head of OR Section, Edinburgh Coll of Commerce; Lecturer in Statistics and OR; Tutor in Charge of Post Graduate Courses, Inst of Local Government Studies, U of Birmingham. Publs: *Problems in Statistics,* 1968; *Linear Programming,* 1969; *Dynamic Programming,* 1970. Fields: Role of decision-making in local government, especially in Europe; role of central statistical bureaux.

[2103]
WILLIAMS Philip Maynard
17 March 1920, British. Nuffield College, Oxford OX1 1NF, England. Degrees: BA; MA (Oxon). 1946-53 Lecturer, Trinity Coll, U of Oxford; 1950-53 Fellow, Nuffield Coll, U of Oxford; 1953-58 Fellow, Jesus Coll, U of Oxford; 1956-57 Visiting Associate Professor, U of Columbia; 1968 Visiting Professor, U of Princeton; 1958- Official Fellow, Nuffield Coll, U of Oxford. Publs: *Politics in Post-War France; De Gaulle's Republic* (with M Harrison); *Politics and Society in De Gaulle's Republic* (with M Harrison); *Crisis and Compromise; The French Parliament 1958-1967; French Politicians and Elections; Wars, Plots and Scandals in Post-War France; Hugh Gaitskell and the Labour Party,* 1978. Fields: British, French and American politics.

[2104]
WILLIAMS Robert John
10 September, British. 32 Balliol Square, Durham City, England. Degrees: BA; M Phil. 1969-71 Tutor, Lecturer, Dept of Pol, U of York; 1971- Lecturer in Pol, U of Durham. Publs: "The Referendum in British Politics: A Dissenting View" (with J R Greenway), *Parliamentary Affairs,* 1975; "Politics and the Ecology of Regulations", *Public Administration,* 1976; "The Politics of American Broadcasting: Public Purposes and Private Interests", *Journal of American Studies,* 1976; "The Problem of Corruption: A Conceptual and Comparative Analysis", *PAC Bulletin,* 1976; "Politics and Regulatory Reform", *Public Administration,* 1978; "Kennedy and Congress", *Political Studies,* 1979. Fields: American government and politics; British politics and administration; African politics; socialism.

[2105]
WILPERT Bernhard
1 March 1936, German. Douglasstrasse 11, 1000 Berlin 33, FR Germany. Degrees: Dipl; Dr phil. Doctoral thesis: "Wertpsychologische Beiträge für Entwicklungsländerforschung". Head of Project Dept, German Volunteer Service, Bonn; Research Fellow, German Development Inst, Berlin; Research Fellow, Science Centre, Berlin; Professor of Psychology, Pädagogische Hochschule, Berlin. Publs: *Führung in deutschen Unternehmen,* 1977; plus various articles on development issues, participation in industry, leadership behaviour. Fields: Problems of participation; work and society.

[2106]
WILSON David Jack
6 December 1946, British. 56 Grangefields Drive, Rothley, Leicester LE7 7NB, England. Degrees: BA; B Phil (Liverpool), 1969; PhD (Warwick), 1974. Doctoral thesis: "Regional Organization in the Conservative and Labour Parties". 1969-71 Tutor, U of Warwick; 1971- Lecturer, Senior Lecturer, Leicester Polytechnic. Publs: "Party Bureaucracy in Britain: Regional and Area Organization", *British Journal of Political Science,* 1972; "Constituency Party Autonomy and Central Control", *Political Studies,* 1973; "Conservative City Machines: The End of an Era", *British Journal of Political Science* (with M Pinto-Duschinsky), 1976; *Power and Party Bureaucracy in Britain,* 1975. Fields: Party bureaucracy in Britain; the politics of elected local government.

[2107]
WILSON Graham Keith
22 August 1949, British. 3 Valley Road, Wivenhoe, Colchester, Essex, England. Degrees: BA; MA (Essex), 1971; D Phil (Oxon), 1975. Doctoral thesis: "The Politics of Subsidiary Agriculture in Britain and the United States, 1957-70". Lecturer, Dept of Government, U of Essex. Publs: *Unions and Politics: The American Experience,* 1978; "Mr Nixon's Triumph", *Parliamentary Affairs* (with P M Williams), 1973; "The American Midterm Elections", *Parliamentary Affairs* (with D H McKay), 1975; *Special Interests and Policy Making,* 1977; "Special Interests, Interest Groups and Mis-Guided Interventionism", *Politics,* 1976; "Department Secretaries: Are They Really a President's 'Natural Enemies' ", *British Journal of Political Science,* 1977; "The American Elections of 1976" (with P Williams), *Political Studies,* 1977; "The British Policy Process", in *Agriculture,* 1975; "Farmers' Organizations in Advanced Societies", in *Research in Rural Studies* (H Newby (ed)), 1977.

WILSON John Robert Swainson*
9 June 1944, British. 32 Merchiston Avenue, Edinburgh EH10 4NZ, Scotland. Degrees: BA; MA (Cambridge), 1969; PhD (Cambridge), 1969. Doctoral thesis: "The Intentionality of Emotions and Other Mental States". 1969-70 Research Fellow, Corpus Christi Coll, U of Oxford; 1970- Lecturer, U of Edinburgh. Publs: *Emotion and Object,* 1972. Fields: Political theory; Northern Ireland.

[2109]
WING Martin A
12 December 1953, British. 11 Clewer Court Road, Windsor, Berkshire SL4 5JD, England. Degrees: BA; MSc. Research Associate, Work Research Group, ASC Henley. Publs: "Committees in the European Parliament", 1978; "Role Perceptions and Clientele Relations in the European Parliament", 1978; "The Legislation of Direct Elections to the European Parliament", 1978. Fields: Parliamentary committees; legislative behaviour; comparative European politics; European parliament.

[2110]
WINKLER Günther
15 January 1929, Austrian. Reisnerstrasse 22/5/11, A-1030 Vienna, Austria. Degrees: Dr jur, 1953; Dr phil hc. Doctoral thesis: "Der Bescheid — Ein Beitrag zur Lehre vom Verwaltungsakt". 1955 Lecturer, U of Innsbruck; 1956-75 U reader, Dean of the Law Faculty, Rector, Pro-rector, U of Vienna; 1975- Professor of Pol and Administrative Sci, Austrian Constitutional and Administrative Law, Theory of Law and State, Inst für Staats- und Verwaltungsrecht, U of Vienna. Publs: *Der Bescheid,* 1956; *Die absolute Nichtigkeit von Verwaltungsakten,* 1960; *Das österreichische Konzept der Gewaltentrennung,* 1965; *Staat und Verbände,* 1966; *Wertbetrachtung im Recht und ihre Grenzen,* 1969; *Gesetzgebung und Verwaltung im Wirtschaftsrecht,* 1970; *Die Wissenschaft vom Verwaltungsrecht,* 1979. Fields: General theory of law; general theory of state.

[2111]
WINKLER Heinrich August
19 December 1938, German. Reckenbergstrasse 1, 7801 Stegen-Eschbach, FR Germany. Degrees: Dr phil (Tübingen), 1963. Doctoral thesis: "Preussischer Liberalismus und deutscher Nationalstaat". 1964-70 Assistant, Otto-Suhr Inst, Free U of Berlin; 1970-71 Wiss Rat und Professor, Otto-Suhr Inst, Free U of Berlin; Professor, Dept of Pol Sci, Free U of Berlin; 1972- Professor of Modern History, U of Freiburg. Publs: *Preussischer liberalismus und deutscher Nationalstaat,* 1964; *Mittelstand, Demokratie und Nationalsozialismus,* 1972; *Pluralismus oder Protektionismus? Verfassungspolitische Probleme des Verbandswesens im deutschen Kaiserreich,* 1972; *Die grosse Krise in Amerika: Vergleichende Studien zur politischen Sozialgeschichte 1929-1939,* 1973; *Organisierter Kapitalismus — Vorausseizungen und Anfänge,* 1974. Fields: Modern social and political history, parties and interest groups, liberalism; fascism and nazism; political theory.

[2112]
WINTER Sóren
1 September 1947, Danish. Højkolvej 36, 8210 Aarhus V, Denmark. Degrees: Chad sci pol. Doctoral thesis: "A Comparative Analysis of the Decisions of the Danish Conservative Party about the Participation or Non-participation in the Vote-Coalitions Concerning Defence, Environment and Housing in 1973". Principal, Social Welfare Administration, County of Aarhus; Assistant Professor, Inst of Pol Sci, U of Aarhus and Part-time Consultant, Social Welfare Administration, County of Aarhus. Publs: "Boger og Amtskommune" (with O N Madsen), in *Danmarks Amstråd,* 1975; "Kommunalforvaltning" (with Bruun et al), in *Fødselsdagsbrev til Professor Dr Jur Poul Meyer,* 1976; "Borger og Kommune" (with P Meyer and O N Madsen), 1976; "Udlaegningen af Saerforsorgen i Danmark", *Nordisk Administrativt Tidsskrift,* 1978. Fields: Public administration; local government; public participation in local politics; social welfare administration.

[2113]
WISEMAN John Adrian
12 June 1945, British. 69 Ferne Avenue, Jesmond, Newcastle-upon-type, England. Degrees: BA; PhD. Doctoral thesis: "The Organization of Political Conflict in Botswana 1966-1973". Lecturer in Pol Sci, Ahmadu Bello U, Nigeria; Lecturer in Pol, U of Newcastle-upon-Tyne. Publs: Various articles in *African Affairs, Journal of Modern African Studies, New Society, Journal of Southern African Studies, Savanna.* Fields: African politics, with special reference to Botswana and Nigeria; political anthropology.

[2114]
WITTKAEMPER Gerhard Wilhelm
5 April 1933, German. Hecken 5, D-5060 Berisch-Gladbach 4, FR Germany. Degrees: Dr jur (Cologne). Doctoral thesis. "Grundgesetz und Interessenverbände". 1964-69 Research Fellow, Policy Sci Consultant; 1969-71 Company Counsel, Cologne Bar; 1971-75 Ord Professor für Pol Wiss, U of Cologne; Direktor, Inst für Pol Wiss, Westfälische Wilhelms U, Münster. Publs: *Grundgesetz und Interessenverbände,* 1963; *Theorie der Interdependenz,* 1971; *Analyse und Planung,* 1972; *Politik und Recht,* 1976; *Politik und Technologie,* 1977; *Funktionale Verwaltungsreform,* 1978; *Didaktik des Politikunterrichts,* 1978. Fields: Planning; international relations; simulation; administrative science; public administration.

[2115]
WITTROCK Björn
4 November 1945, Swedish. Docentbacken 5, S-104 05 Stockholm, Sweden. Degrees: B soc sci (Stockholm), 1967; M soc sci (Stockholm), 1968; PhD (Stockholm), 1974. Doctoral thesis: "The Parties Facing the Voters" (in Swedish). 1970-74 Part-time Lecturer, U of Stockholm and Stockholm School of Soc Sci and Public Administration; 1974-Research Associate, U of Stockholm; 1976 Visiting Assistant Professor, U of Washington, St Louis. Publs: *The Parties Facing the Voters* (in Swedish), 1974; *The Uses and Abuses of Forecasting* (contributor) (T Whiston (ed)), 1978; *Politics as Rational Action* (contributor) (Lewin and Vedung (eds)), 1978; plus articles in *Statsvetenskaplig Tidskrift, Internationelle Studier, Scandinavian Political Studies, Futures, Journal of General Philosophy of Science.* Fields: Forecasting; future studies; policy planning; philosophy of social science; science policy.

[2116]
WOHLGEMUTH Ernst
22 September 1924, British. Department of Politics, University of Leicester, Leicester LE1 7RH, England. Degrees: BSc; MA (Chicago), 1953; PhD (Chicago), 1956. Doctoral thesis; "The Politics of Labour in Western Germany (The Trade Unions and Codetermination)". Senior Research Officer, PEP; Senior Information Officer, HM Treasury; Deputy Head of Economic Dept, EFTA Secretariat, Geneva; 1970-71 Visiting Professor, Dept of Pol Sci, State U of NY at Buffalo; Lecturer in Pol, U of Leicester. Publs: *Industrial Trade Associations: Activities and Organization* (co-author), 1957; *European Organizations,* 1959; *Building EFTA: a Free Trade Area in Europe,* 1966; *European Unity: A Survey of the European Organization* (contributor) (N Palmer and J Lambert (eds)), 1968. Fields: The development of common political institutions in Western Europe; European integration; comparative study of subsidies from public funds for party political activities.

[2117]
WOKLER Robert Lucien
6 December 1942, American. Degrees: BA; MSc (London); MA (Cantab); D Phil (Oxon). Doctoral thesis: "The Social Thought of Jean-Jacques Rousseau: An Historical Interpretation of His Early Writings". 1968-71 Junior Lecturer in Modern History, Magdalen Coll, U of Oxford; 1973-75 David Thomson Senior Research Fellow, Sidney Sussex Coll, U of Cambridge; 1971 Lecturer in Government, U of Manchester; 1978-79 Research Fellow Commoner, Trinity Coll, U of Cambridge. Publs: "Rousseau's Politics", *Government and Opposition,* 1973; "Rameau, Rousseau and the Essai sur l'Origine des Langues", *Studies on Voltaire and the Eighteenth Century,* 1974; "The Influence of Diderot on the Political Theory of Rousseau", *Studies on Voltaire,* 1975; "Rousseau and the Perfectability of Man", *Political Theory,* 1978;

"Perfectable Apes in Decadent Cultures: Rousseau's Anthropology Revisited", *Daedalus*, 1978; "Rousseau on Rameau and Revolution", *Studies in the Eighteenth Century*, 1978. Fields: Rousseau; social theories of the enlightenment; Saint-Simon; Utopian socialism; political theory in the context of the history of ideas; philosophy of history; contemporary political philosophy.

[2118]
WOLF Friedrich O
1 February 1943, German. Ermanstrasse, 14, D-1000 Berlin 41, FR Germany. Degrees: Dr phil (Kiel), 1969. Doctoral thesis; "Die neue Wissenschaft des Thomas Hobbes. Zu den Grundlagen der politischen Philosophie der Neuzeit". 1966-71 Wiss Assistent, Philosophisches Inst, U des Saarlandes; 1971- Assistenz-professor, Psychologisches Inst im Fachbereich 11, Free U of Berlin; 1976-77 Professor Extraordinario (Equiparado), Faculdade de Econ, U of Coimbra. Publs: *Wissenschaftskritik, und Sozialistische Praxis. Konsequenzen aus der Studentenbewegung* (with J Klüver (co-eds)), 1972; "John Stuart Mill versus Auguste Comte" in *Rehabilitierung der praktischen Philosophie* (M Riedel (ed)), 1974; "Psychologie oder kritische Psychologie?" in *Psychologie ohne Gegenstand?* (Eberlein and Pieper (eds)), 1976. Fields: Science and politics; political socialization; education and labour politics; history of the social and behavioural sciences; theory of the capitalist state.

[2119]
WOLFF Jürgen H
28 July 1940, German. In der Breite 29, D-7801 Umkirch, FR Germany. Degrees: Dipl Volkswirt; Dr phil. Doctoral thesis: "Bildungsplanung für Entwicklungsländer: Ein Modell und seine Anwendung auf den Kongo (Kinshasa)" (Educational Planning in Third World Countries). 1970-71 Expert on Manpower Organization in the Labour Ministry of Gabon; Numerous research missions in African and Latin American countries; Research Associate, Arnold Bergsträsser Inst, Freiburg. Publs: *Bildungsplanung für Entwicklungsländer: Ein Modell und seine Anwendung auf den Kongo (Kinschasa),* 1969; Planung in Entwicklungsländern. Eine Bilanz aus politik-und verwaltungswissenschaftlicher Sicht, 1977. Fields: Politics and administration of developing countries; problems of foreign aid and international economic co-operation.

[2120]
WOLFFSOHN Michael
17 May 1947, German. Hans-Böcklerstrasse 13, D-6653 Bliekskastel, FR Germany. Degrees: Dr phil. Doctoral thesis: "Industrie und Handwerk im Konflikt mit staatlicher Wirtschaftspolitik? Studien zur Politik der Arbeitsbeschaffung in Deutschland 1930-1934". Assistent, U des Saarlandes, Saarbrücken. Publs: Various articles on German economic history, politics in Israel, fascism, communism. Fields: Near East; multinational corporations; fascism.

[2121]
WOLLMANN Hellmut
12 April 1936, German. Bambergerstrasse 39, 1000 Berlin 30, FR Germany. Degrees: Dr. Doctoral thesis: "Stellung der Parlamentsminderheiten in Deutschland, England und Italien" (Parliamentary Minorities in Germany, England and Italy), 1974- Professor of Public Administration, Free U of Berlin. Publs: Various in the field of urban development and urban renewal law, urban politics, inter-governmental relations, evaluation research methodology. Fields: Urban politics; regional policies; intergovernmental relations; evaluation research.

[2122]
WOLTERS Menno
23 September 1948, Dutch. Douwencamp 12, Nijkerk, The Netherlands. Degrees; Dr (Leiden), 1972. Doctoral thesis: "Interspace Politics". 1973 Dutch Broadcasting Union "VARA"; 1974 Dept of Pol Sci, U of Iowa; 1974 Wiardi Beckmann Stichting, Amsterdam; 1974- Dept of Data Theory, U of Leiden. Publs: "Pak en Polarisatie", *De Gemeente*, 1972; "Polarisatie in de Provincie", in *De Gemeente*, 1974; *Dimensions of Dutch Parties*, 1975; *Kollegevorming en Polarisatie*, 1976; "Een Cognitieve Kaart van de Nederlandse Politieke Partijen — een Reactie", *Acta Politica*, 1977; "Polarisatie in Parlementair Stemgedrag", *Beleid en Maatschappij*, 1977; "Models of Roll-Call Behaviour", *Political Methodology*, 1977-78. Fields: Legislative behaviour; spatial/dimensional analysis; local politics; formal modelling; methodology of multivariate analysis.

[2123]
WOLTERS Rudolf
22 January 1941, German. 7815 Kirchzarten, Im Bachmättle 15, FR Germany. Degrees: Dr rer Pol. Doctoral thesis; "Strategien der Verhandlungsführung". Wiss Assistent, Inst für Sozialpolitik, Ruhr-U, Bochum; Wiss Assistent, Inst für Sozialpolitik, Ruhr-U, Bochum; Wiss Assistent, Inst für Allgemeine Wirtschaftsforschung, Abteilung Sozialpolitik, Freiburg. Publs: *Verteilungstheorie*, 1974; *Wohlfahrtsökonomik*, 1975-76. Fields: Social policy; labour market research.

[2124]
WOOD Bruce
22 April 1943, British. 104 Manchester Road, Bury, Lancashire BL9 0TH, England. Degrees: Bsc (Econ). 1964-66 Research Assistant, Greater London Group, LSE; 1966-68 Assistant Research Officer, Royal Commission on Local Government in England; 1968- Lecturer in Government, U of Manchester. Publs: *Town Government in South-East England* (co-author), 1967; contributor to *Trends in British Society* (A H Halsey (ed)), 1971; *The Scope of Local Initiative: A Study of Cheshire County Council 1961-1974* (with J M Lee); *English Local Government Reformed* (with Lord Redcliffe-Maud); *The Process of Local Government Reform 1966-1974*. Fields: Local government.

[2125]
WOODCOCK George Henry
29 October 1942, British. Eliot College, The University, Canterbury, Kent, England. Degrees: BA; D Phil (Oxon), 1968. Doctoral thesis: "Regional Government in Republican Italy". 1966-67 Lecturer in Pol, Corpus Christi Coll, U of Oxford; 1968-70 Lecturer in Government, U of Manchester; 1970- Lecturer in Pol and Government, U of Kent. Publs: Articles in Il Politico, Public Administration. Fields: Study of implementation of regional governments throughout Italy; regional government as a functioning system; political, constitutional relationships between regions and the state.

[2126]
WOODHEAD David John
1 March 1944, British. 37 Poplar Mount, Belvedere, Kent, England. Degrees: BA; MA (Manchester); PhD (Durham). Doctoral thesis: "Leadership and Decision-Making in the Tyneside Conurbation". Research Assistant, U of Durham; Senior Lecturer in Pol, Thames Polytechnic. Fields: Urban politics; politics in Czechoslovakia.

[2127]
WOODWARD Peter Robert
13 March 1944, British. 36 Betchworth Avenue, Reading, Berkshire, England. Degrees: BA; MA (Essex); PhD (Reading). Doctoral thesis: "Condominium and Sudanese Nationalism". Lecturer, U of Khartoum; Lecturer, U of Reading. Publs: *Transition in Africa: From Direct Rule to Independence* (ed); "The PSA Today", in *Studies in Politics* (F F Ridley (ed)); *The Condominium and Sudanese Nationalism*, 1978, plus articles in *Middle Eastern Affairs, African Affairs, Political Studies, Contemporary Review*. Fields: African and comparative politics.

[2128]
WORRE Torben
4 January 1940, Danish. Strandvejen 392, 3060 Espergaerde, Denmark. Degrees: Cand sci pol (Aarhus), 1966. 1965-67 Research Fellow, U of Aarhus; Lektor, Inst of Contemporary History and Pol Sci, U of Copenhagen. Publs: *Det Politiske System i Danmark,* 1974; *Vaelgerne i 70'erme* (contributor), 1976. Fields: Danish electoral behaviour; Danish general elections.

[2129]
WOTZEL Walter
10 November 1950, Austrian. 1140 Wien, Freesienweg 11, Austria. Degrees: Dr jur; Mag rer Soc. Law practice. Publs: "Austrian Models of Bureaucracy", 1975; "Anti-Parliamentarism in Austria"; "The Activities of Administration — Are They in the Interest of the Whole Population?", 1975-76; "Under-development", 1976-77; "Foreign Workers and Instruction of German", 1977; plus various papers on economic subjects. Fields: Developing countries; foreign workers; women; minority groups.

[2130]
WREDE Klaus Martin*
25 February 1931, German. Steinweg 22, 33 Braunschweig, FR Germany. Degrees: Dipl Volkswirt, 1955; Dipl Kaufmann (Munich), 1956; Dr rer Pol (Freiburg/Br), 1960. Doctoral thesis; "Wage Theory and Wage Policy of German Trade Unions 1870-1933". 1959-60 Scientific Employee, Stifterverband für die deutsche Wissenschaft, Essen; 1959-60 Assistant Professor, U of Freiburg; 1960-63 Wiss Angestellter, Deutsches Industrie Inst, Cologne; 1963-65 Stifterverband für die deutsche Wissenschaft, Essen; 1965- Akademisoher Oberrat, Technical U of Braunschweig.

[2131]
WRIGHT Frank A
4 June 1948, British. Department of Political Science, Queen's University, Belfast, N Ireland. 1971-73 Research Fellow, New Coll, U of Oxford; 1973- Lecturer, Queen's U, Belfast. Publs: "Protestant Ideology and Politics in Ulster", *European Journal of Sociology,* 1973. Fields: Irish history.

[2132]
WRIGHT Jonathan Richard Cassé
24 October 1941, British. 20 The Paddox, Banbury Road, Oxford OX2 7PN, England. Degrees: MA; D Phil (Oxon). Doctoral thesis: "The Political Attitudes of the German Protestant Church Leadership 1918-1933". Tutorial Fellow, Christ Church Coll, U of Oxford. Publs: *Above Parties: The Political Attitudes of the German Protestant Church Leadership 1918-1933,* 1974. Fields: Conservative politics in Germany 1918-1933, and in general; German politics since 1870.

[2133]
WRIGHT Maurice William
5 July 1933, British. Department of Government, University of Manchester M13 9PL, England. Degrees: BA; D Phil (Oxon), 1962. 1960-72 Research Associate, Assistant Lecturer, Lecturer, Senior Lecturer, Dept of Government, U of Manchester; 1964-66 Econ Consultant, H M Treasury; 1966-69 Research Adviser, Dept of Econ Affairs; Tutor in Public Administration, Civil Service Coll; 1972- Reader in Government, U of Manchester; 1973- Director, Graduate School. Publs: *Treasury Control of the Civil Service 1856-1874,* 1969. Fields: Government and industry; planning and control of public expenditure; bureaucracy; policy analysis.

[2134]
WRIGHT Vincent
6 August 1937, British. Nuffield College, Oxford, England. Degrees: BSc; PhD. Doctoral thesis: "The Basses-Pyreness 1848-1870". 1965-1969 Lecturer, Newcastle-upon-Tyne; 1969-1970 Senior Research Associate, St Anthony's Coll, Oxford; Lecturer, Senior Lecturer, Reader, LSE; Official Fellow, Nuffield Coll, U of Oxford. Publs: *Le Counseil d'Etat du Second Empire,* 1972; *Les Préfets du Second Empire* (with B le Clere), 1974; *The Government and Politics of France,* 1978; *West European Politics* (joint ed). Fields: Modern French history; French government, politics and administration and local government.

[2135]
WUTHE Gerhard Max
19 October 1927, German. Pädagogische Hochschule Ruhr, Emil-Figge-Strasse 4, 6 Dortmund, FR Germany. Degrees: Dipl Pol (Deutsche Hochschule für Politik, Berlin), 1955; Dr phil. 1959-63 Studienleiter, Heimvolkschochshule Bergneustadt, Friedrich F Ebert-Stiftung; 1960-64 Redaktionssekretär, Archiv für Sozialgeschichte; 1963-68 Wiss Assistent, SPD-Franktion, Landtag Nordrhein Westfalen, Düsseldorf; Ord Professor of Pol Sci, Pädagogische Hochschule Ruhr, Abteilung Dortmund. Publs: "Der junge Gewerkschafter als Staatsbürger", in *Gewerkschaften und Politische Bildung,* 1962; *Nationalsozialismus,* 1962; 1863-1963 — Hundert Jahre deutsche Sozialdemokraite (co-author), 1953; *4 Jahre Kulturpolitik in Nordrhein-Westfalen,* 1966; *Harmonie und Konflikt — Zur Struktur und Funktion sozialer Leitbilder,* 1971; *Politikwissenschaft als Erziehungswissenschaft* (co-author), 1974; *Demokratischer Gesellschaftkonsensus und Konflikt* (co-author), 1975; *Die Lehre von den politischen Systemen,* 1977. Fields: Political systems, especially Federal Republic of Germany; political culture; educational organization and policy.

[2136]
WUYTS Herman Joannes
18 November 1942, Belgian. Zegelaan 39, 3030 Heverlee-Leuven, Belgium. Degrees: Dr Soc Sci, 1975. Doctoral thesis: "The Participation of Citizens in Decision-Making of Physical Planning in Municipalities. Analysis of the Dutch Speaking Part of Belgium" (in Dutch). 1968-71 Research Assistant, Management Development Centre, U of Leuven; 1971-74 Fellow in the Doctoral Program of the Interuniversity College for Doctoral Studies in the Management Sciences, Brussels; 1974- Research Assistant, Dept of Pol Sci, Catholic U of Leuven. Publs: *Demokratie-participatie-ruimtelijke ordening. De toestand in de Vlaamse Gemeenten,* 1975; *Inspraak in opspraak. Over zin en onzin van gemeentelijke adviersraden* (with F Delmartino), 1977. Fields: Political decision making; democracy theory; local government structure; urban planning; information and participation problems.

[2137]
WYLLER Thomas C
16 September 1922, Norwegian. Nordstrandsveien 9, Oslo 11, Norway. Degrees: Phd (Oslo). Doctoral thesis: "Nyordning og Motstand" (New Order and Resistance). Professor of Pol Sci, U of Oslo. Publs: *Frigjøringspolitik*, 1963; *Landsforbund og Lønn-skamp*, 1970; *Christian Michelsen*, 1975; *Mortforestillinger* (ed), 1975-78. Fields: Interest groups; contemporary political history.

X

[2138]
XIFRA George
17 March 1926, Spanish. Barcelona (8), Corcega 329, Spain. Degrees: Dr in Law, 1947; Dr in Pol Sci (Madrid), 1949. Professor of Pol Law, Faculty of Law; Professor of Theory of the State, Faculty of Econ Sci, U of Barcelona; Director, Inst de Ciencias Soc de Barcelona; Professor, U of Barcelona; Professor, High School of Journalism, Barcelona; Director, *Revista del Instituto di Ciencias Sociales*. Publs: *Modernas Tendencias Políticas*, 1954; *Curso de Derecho Constitucional*, 1962; *Síntesis Histórica del Pensamiento Político*, 1957; *Formas y Fuerzas Políticas*, 1958; *Instituciones y Sistemas Políticos*, 1962; *Introducción a la Política*, 1965; *La Información, Análisis de una Libertad Frustrada*, 1972. Fields: Political sociology, theory and sociology of information; social communication.

Y

[2139]
YAHUDA Michael Benjamin
29 September 1940, British. 35 Colebrooke Road, London N1, England. Degrees: BA; MSc. 1966-73 Lecturer, Dept of Pol, U of Southampton; 1976 Visiting Research Fellow, Research School of Pacific Studies, Australian National U; 1973- Lecturer, Dept of International Relations, LSE. Publs: *China's Role in World Affairs*, 1978; "Chinese Foreign Policy after 1963: The Maoist Phases", *China Quarterly*, 1968; "China's Nuclear Option", *Bulletin of the Atomic Scientists*, 1969; "Kremlinology and the Chinese Strategic Debate 1965-1966", *China Quarterly*, 1972; "Chinese Conceptions of Their Role in the World", *Political Quarterly*, 1974; "Towards a New Chinese Political Order", *Round Table*, 1977; "Problems of Continuity in Chinese Foreign Policy", *Asian Affairs*, 1977. Fields: Chinese politics and foreign relations; international relations; the Asia-Pacific region.

[2140]
YOUNG Kenneth George*
3 January 1943, British. Department of Government, London School of Economics and Political Science, Houghton Street, Aldwych, London WC2, England. Degrees: BSc; MSc (LSE), 1968. 1966-68 Research Assistant, Greater London Group, LSE; 1968-69 Lecturer, Sociology Department, Goldsmith's Coll, London; Research Officer, Dept of Government, LSE. Publs: *Local Government Re-organization* (contributor) (H J Harkes (ed)), 1971; *Civil Liberties and Service Recruitment*, 1971; *The Government of*

London. Reform in Practice (contributor) (G Rhodes (ed)), 1972. Fields: Local politics and policies; patterns of cleavage in metropolitan areas; Conservative party in local government.

[2141]
YOUNG Stephen Clement
25 November 1946, British. Woodfarm, Charlestown, Hebden Bridge, West Yorkshire, England. Degrees: BA. Lecturer in Government, U of Manchester. Publs: *Intervention in the Mixed Economy: The Evolution of British Industrial Policy 1964-72* (with A V Lowe), 1974; *Planning, Politics and Public Policy* (contributor) (J E S Hayward and M Watson (eds)), 1975; *Planning in Europe* (contributor), (J E S Hayward and O Norkiewicz (eds)), 1978. Fields: Regional and industrial policy and planning; administration and politics of land-use planning in Britain; the role of the local authority in the local economy; the role of industrial and amenity groups.

[2142]
YSMAL Colette*
7 December 1936, French. 5 Villa Virginie, 75 Paris XIVème, France. Degrees: Lic (Lyon); DES (Lyon). Attachée de recherche, FNSP; Maître de conférence, IEP, Paris. Publs: *La carrière de Gaston Defferre*, 1966; *Defferre parle*, 1967; *L'élection présiden- tielle de 1965* (co-author), 1969; *Les élections législatives de mars 1967* (co-author), 1971. Fields: French political leaders; ideologies.

[2143]
YUILL Douglas MacDonald
17 July 1950, British. 36 Hawthorn Avenue, Bearsden, Glasgow, Scotland. Degrees: MA (Glasgow); M Phil (Glasgow). 1972-75 Lecturer in Applied Economics, Dept of Soc and Econ Research, U of Glasgow; 1975-78 Research Fellow, International Inst of Management, Berlin; 1978- Research Fellow, Centre for the Study of Public Policy, U of Strathclyde. Publs: "The Accuracy of pre-1971 Local Employment Data" (with K Allen), *Regional Studies,* 1977; *Small Area Employment Forecasting: Data and Pro- blems* (with K Allen), 1978; *Regional Problems and Policies in the European Communi- ty, A Bibliography* (ed), 1978; *Options in Regional Incentive Policy* (with K Allen and C Hull), 1978. Fields: European regional incentives and policy; policy design and evalua- tion.

Z

[2144]
ZAMPETTI Pierluigi
Italian. Uboldo, Varese, Italy. Degrees: Laurea in Filosofia; Laurea in Giurisprudenza. Publs: *Dallo Stato Liberale allo Stato dei Partiti*, 1965; *Democrazia e Potere dei Partiti*, 1969; *La Partecipazione Popolare al Potere*, 1976. Fields: The study of political matters in industrial society.

[2145]
ZAPF Wolfgang
25 April 1937, German. Mörikestrasse 8, D-6945 Hirschberg, FR Germany. Degrees: Dipl Soz (Frankfurt), 1961; Dr phil (Tübingen), 1963; Habilitation (Konstanz), 1967. Doctoral thesis: "Wandlungen der deutschen Elite. Ein Zirkulationsmodell deutscher Führungsgruppen, 1919-1961". 1962-66 Wiss Assistent Soziologie, Tübingen; 1966-67 Wiss Assistent Soziologie, Konstanz; 1967-68 Privatdozent Soziologie, Konstanz;

1968-72 Professor Soziologie, Frankfurt; 1972- Professor Soziologie, Mannheim. Publs: *Beiträge zur Analyse der deutschen Oberschicht*, 1965; *Theorien des sozialen Wandels* (ed), 1969; *Soziale Indikatoren* (ed), 1974-75; *Sozialberichterstattung: Möglichkeiten und Probleme*, 1976; *Sozialpolitik und Sozialberichterstattung* (with H J Krupp), 1977; *Gesellschaftspolitische Zielsysteme* (ed), 1977; *Lebensbedingungen in der Bundesrepublik* (ed), 1977; *Probleme der Modernisierungspolitik* (ed), 1977. Fields: Elite research; theories of social change and modernization; historical indicators; social indicators and social reporting; social policy.

[2146]
ZELDIN Theodore
22 August 1933, British. Tumbledown House, Tumbledown Hill, Oxford, England. Degrees: MA; D Phil (Oxon). Doctoral thesis: "The Parliamentarians of the Second Empire in France". Research Fellow, CNRS, Paris; Visiting Professor of History, U of Harvard; Fellow of St Anthony's Coll, U of Oxford. Publs: *The Political System of Napoleon III*, 1958; *Emile Ollivier and the Liberal Empire of Napoleon III*, 1963; *Conflicts in French Society* (ed), 1970; *France 1948-1945*; *Ambition, Love and Politics*, 1973; *Intellect, Taste and Anxiety*, 1977. Fields: Nationalism; political psychology; public opinion.

[2147]
ZELLENTIN Gerda
5 January 1934, German. Schillingsroter Weg 7, 5 Köln 51, FR Germany. Degrees: Dipl disc Pol (Wilhelmshaven-Rüstersiel), 1958; Dr disc Pol (Göttingen), 1961; Habilitation (Cologne), 1969. Doctoral thesis: "Der Wirtschafts-und Sozialausschuss der EWG und Euratom. Interessenrepräsentation auf übernationaler Ebene". 1959-69 Assistant, U of Cologne; 1971- Professor of Pol, Forschungsinst für Pol Wiss, U of Cologne and U of Wuppertal. Publs: *Budgetpolitik und Integration*, 1964; *Formen der Willensbildung in den Europäischen Organisationen* (ed), 1965. *Bibliographie der europäischen Integration*, 1965; *Wege nach Gesamteuropa. Dokumentation der Beziehungen zwischen West- und Osteuropa 1943-65* (co-author), 1966; *Intersystemare Beziehungen in Europa. Bedingungen der Friedenssicherung*, 1970; *Europa 1985*, 1971; *Les missions permanentes auprès des organisations internationales*, 1976; *Annäherung, Abgrenzung und friedlicher Wandel in Europa* (ed), 1976; *Grünbuch zu den Folgewirkungen der KSZE* (co-ed), 1977. Fields: Peace research; German foreign policy; futurology; international bureaucracy.

[2148]
ZIEGLER Rolf
22 July 1936, Austrian/German. Peter Jordan Strasse 145/4, A-1180 Wien, Austria. Degrees: Dipl Volkswirt; Dr rer Pol; Habilitation. Doctoral thesis: "Kommunikationsstruktur und Leistung sozialer Systeme" (Communication Structure and Performance of Social Systems); 1971-73 Professor, U of Cologne; 1973-75 Professor, U of Kiel; 1975- Professor, U of Vienna. Publs: *Kommunikationsstruktur und Leistung sozialer Systeme*, 1968; *Theorie und Modell. Der Beitrag der Formalisierung zur soziologischen Theorienbildung*, 1972; "Typologien und Klassifikationen", in *Soziologie-Sprache-Beziehung zur Praxis und anderen Wissenschaften* (G Albrecht, H Daheim and F Sack (ed)), 1973; "Zur Verwendung linearer Modelle bei der Kausalanalyse nicht-experimenteller Daten" (with H J Hummell), in *Korrelation und Kausalität*; "Soziologie der Organisation" (with R Mayntz), in *Handbuch der empirischen Sozialforschung* (R König (ed)), 1976; "Militärsoziologie", (with K Roghmann) in *Handbuch der empirischen Sozialforschung* (R König (ed)), 1969. Fields: Organizational sociology; social network analysis; social stratification and mobility; educational sociology; application of mathematical models in the social sciences; methodology.

[2149]
ZIEMER Klaus
24 June 1946, German. Kirchenbergweg 34, D-6900 Heidelberg, FR Germany. Degrees: Dr phil. Doctoral thesis: "Politische Parteien im frankophonen Afrika". Assistant Professor, Inst of Pol Sci, U of Heidelberg. Publs: "Verfassung und Politik in Senegal seit der Unabhängigkeit", *Verfassung und Recht in Übersee*, 1974; *Handbuch der Dritten Welt* (contributor) (D Nohlen and F Nuscheler (eds)), 1976-78; *Politische Parteien im frankophonen Afrika* (contributor), 1978; *Politische Organisation und Repräsentation in Afrika* (contributor) (F Nuscheler and K Ziemer (eds)), 1978. Fields: Politics and economy in Africa South of the Sahara; political systems of Eastern Europe, especially Poland; German-Polish relations in the 20th century.

[2150]
ZIMMER Marcel
19 December 1914, Belgian. Fonds Belgo-Congolais d'Amortissement et de Gestion, 30 rue Joseph II, Brussels, Belgium. Degrees: Lic en sci commerciales et consulaires (ISC), 1944; Lic en sci commerciales et financières, 1945. Belgian Civil Service; Administrateur et Directeur Général, Fonds Belgo-Congolais d'Amortissement et de Gestion; Directeur Général, Ministère des Finances; Chargé de cours, Inst du Travail, Free U of Brussels; Chargé de cours, Inst Supérieur de Commerce, Brussels; Vice Président, Inst de Médecine Tropicale, Anvers.

[2151]
ZIMMERMAN Ekkart
8 August 1946, German. Kyllburger Strasse 14, D-5000 Köln, FR Germany. Degrees: Dr (Cologne); MA (Cologne). Doctoral thesis: "The Sociology of Political Violence". 1970-74 Research Assistant, U of Cologne; 1973-74 Leverhulme Visiting Fellowship, Dept of Govt, U of Essex; 1975- Akademischer Oberrat, Dept of Soc Sci, U of Wuppertal. Publs: *Das Experiment in den Sozialwissenschaften*, 1972; "Factor Analyses of Conflicts Within and Between Nations: A Critical Evaluation", *Quality and Quantity*, 1976; *Soziologie der politischen Gewalt*, 1977; "Crises and Performance — Toward a New Synthetic Approach", *European Journal of Political Research*, 1979; "Bringing Common Sense Back In: Some Neglected Assumptions in Status Inconsistency Theory and Research", *European Journal of Sociology*, 1978; "Political Violence, Crises and Revolutions: Theories and Research", *Current Sociology*, 1978; "Protest and Turmoil", in *Handbook on Conflict and Peace Research* (E R Gurr (ed)), 1978. Fields: Political violence; crisis research; conflict research; comparative politics; historical sociology; social stratification.

[2152]
ZUANON Jean Paul
20 May 1944, French. 3 rue Dr Valois, 38400 St Martin d'Hères, France. Degrees: Dipl (IEP Grenoble). Attaché de recherche, FNSP (Grenoble). Publs: *Communauté rurale et tourisme*, 1964; *Organisations décentralisées de planification urbaine*, 1969; "Techniciens et politiques face à la planification urbaine", in *Aménagement du territoire et développement régional*, 1972; *Recherches sur la structuration de l'espace*, 1970; *Evaluation de la préoccupation environnement-cadre de vie dans l'administration française* (with F Gerbaux and J Tournon), 1975; *L'espace convoité d'une grande vallée*, 1978. Fields: Country planning, especially in rural areas; rural sociology; sociology of administration.

[2153]
ZÜLCH Ruediger
18 March 1941, German. Gangelshauserweg 14, 4322 Sprockhoevel 2, FR Germany. Degrees: Dipl Volkswirt; Dr rer Pol. Doctoral thesis: "Third Party in a Coalition System". Research Assistant, Foreign Policy Research Inst, Philadelphia; Assistant, Inst of Pol Sci, U of Cologne. Publs: *Im Wechselspiel der Koalitionen — Analyse der Bundestagswahl 1969* (co-author), 1970; *Von der FDP zur FDP — Die Dritte Kraft im Deutschen Parteiensystem?*, 1972. Fields: Parties; party systems; elections and electoral behaviour; minority governments.

INDEX

Legislatures, Executives, the Constitution

Mass Political Behavior

Methodology

Peace and Conflict Studies